More information about this series at https://link.springer.com/bookseries/558

Tiziana Margaria · Bernhard Steffen (Eds.)

Leveraging Applications of Formal Methods, Verification and Validation

Software Engineering

11th International Symposium, ISoLA 2022
Rhodes, Greece, October 22–30, 2022
Proceedings, Part II

Springer

Editors
Tiziana Margaria
University of Limerick, CSIS and Lero
Limerick, Ireland

Bernhard Steffen
TU Dortmund
Dortmund, Germany

ISSN 0302-9743 ISSN 1611-3349 (electronic)
Lecture Notes in Computer Science
ISBN 978-3-031-19755-0 ISBN 978-3-031-19756-7 (eBook)
https://doi.org/10.1007/978-3-031-19756-7

This Springer imprint is published by the registered company Springer Nature Switzerland AG
The registered company address is: Gewerbestrasse 11, 6330 Cham, Switzerland

Introduction

As General and Program Chairs we would like to welcome you to the proceedings of ISoLA 2022, the 11th International Symposium on Leveraging Applications of Formal Methods, Verification and Validation held in Rhodes (Greece) during October 22–30, 2022, and endorsed by EASST, the European Association of Software Science and Technology.

Returning to the traditional in-person event, ISoLA 2022 provided a forum for developers, users, and researchers to discuss issues related to the adoption and use of rigorous tools and methods for the specification, analysis, verification, certification, construction, testing, and maintenance of systems from the point of view of their different application domains. Thus, since 2004 the ISoLA series of events has served the purpose of bridging the gap between designers and developers of rigorous tools on one side, and users in engineering and in other disciplines on the other side. It fosters and exploits synergetic relationships among scientists, engineers, software developers, decision makers, and other critical thinkers in companies and organizations. By providing a specific, dialogue-oriented venue for the discussion of common problems, requirements, algorithms, methodologies, and practices, ISoLA aims in particular at supporting researchers in their quest to improve the practicality, reliability, flexibility, and efficiency of tools for building systems, and users in their search for adequate solutions to their problems.

The program of ISoLA 2022 consisted of a collection of special tracks devoted to the following hot and emerging topics:

1. Rigorous Engineering of Collective Adaptive Systems
(Organizers: Rocco De Nicola, Stefan Jähnichen, Martin Wirsing)
2. Programming: What is Next?
(Organizers: Klaus Havelund, Bernhard Steffen)
3. X-by-Construction meets Runtime Verification
(Organizers: Maurice H. ter Beek, Loek Cleophas, Martin Leucker, Ina Schaefer)
4. Automated Software Re-Engineering
(Organizers: Serge Demeyer, Reiner Hähnle, Heiko Mantel)
5. Digital Twin Engineering
(Organizers: John Fitzgerald, Peter Gorm Larsen, Tiziana Margaria, Jim Woodcock, Claudio Gomes)
6. SpecifyThis - Bridging gaps between program specification paradigms
(Organizers: Wolfgang Ahrendt, Marieke Huisman, Mattias Ulbrich, Paula Herber)
7. Verification and Validation of Concurrent and Distributed Heterogeneous Systems
(Organizers: Marieke Huisman, Cristina Seceleanu)
8. Formal Methods Meet Machine Learning
(Organizers: Kim Larsen, Axel Legay, Bernhard Steffen, Marielle Stoelinga)
9. Formal methods for DIStributed COmputing in future RAILway systems
(Organizers: Alessandro Fantechi, Stefania Gnesi, Anne Haxthausen)

10. Automated Verification of Embedded Control Software
(Organizers: Dilian Gurov, Paula Herber, Ina Schaefer)
11. Digital Thread in Smart Manufacturing
(Organizers: Tiziana Margaria, Dirk Pesch, Alan McGibney)

It also included the following the embedded or co-located events:

- Doctoral Symposium and Poster Session (Sven Jörges, Salim Saay, Steven Smyth)
- Industrial Day (Axel Hessenkämper, Falk Howar, Hardi Hungar, Andreas Rausch)
- DIME Days 2022 (Tiziana Margaria, Bernhard Steffen)

Altogether, the proceedings of ISoLA 2022 comprises contributions collected in four volumes:

- Part 1: Verification Principles
- Part 2: Software Engineering
- Part 3: Adaptation and Learning
- Part 4: Practice

We thank the track organizers, the members of the program committee, and their reviewers for their effort in selecting the papers to be presented, the local Organization Chair, Petros Stratis, and the EasyConferences team for their continuous precious support during the entire period preceding the events, and the Springer for being, as usual, a very reliable partner for the proceedings production. Finally, we are grateful to Christos Therapontos for his continuous support for the Web site and the program, and to Steve Bosselmann for his help with the editorial system EquinOCS.

Special thanks are due to the following organizations for their endorsement: EASST (European Association of Software Science and Technology) and Lero - The Irish Software Research Centre, along with our own institutions - TU Dortmund and the University of Limerick.

We wish you, as an ISoLA participant, lively scientific discussions at this edition, and also later, when reading the proceedings, valuable new insights that contribute to your research and its uptake.

October 2022

Bernhard Steffen
Tiziana Margaria

Organization

Program Committee Chairs

Margaria, Tiziana	University of Limerick and Lero, Ireland
Steffen, Bernhard	TU Dortmund University, Germany

Program Committee

Ahrendt, Wolfgang	Chalmers University of Technology, Sweden
Cleophas, Loek	Eindhoven University of Technology (TU/e), The Netherlands
De Nicola, Rocco	IMT School for Advanced Studies, Italy
Demeyer, Serge	Universiteit Antwerpen, Belgium
Fantechi, Alessandro	Università di Firenze, Italy
Fitzgerald, John	Newcastle University, UK
Gnesi, Stefania	ISTI-CNR, Italy
Gomes, Claudio	Aarhus University, Denmark
Gurov, Dilian	KTH Royal Institute of Technology, Sweden
Havelund, Klaus	Jet Propulsion Laboratory, USA
Haxthausen, Anne	Technical University of Denmark, Denmark
Herber, Paula	University of Münster, Germany
Hessenkämper, Axel	Schulz Systemtechnik GmbH, Germany
Howar, Falk	TU Dortmund University, Germany
Huisman, Marieke	University of Twente, The Netherlands
Hungar, Hardi	German Aerospace Center, Germany
Hähnle, Reiner	TU Darmstadt, Germany
Jähnichen, Stefan	TU Berlin, Germany
Jörges, Sven	FH Dortmund, Germany
Lamprecht, Anna-Lena	University of Potsdam, Germany
Larsen, Kim	Aalborg University, Denmark
Larsen, Peter Gorm	Aarhus University, Denmark
Legay, Axel	UCLouvain, Belgium
Leucker, Martin	University of Lübeck, Germany
Mantel, Heiko	TU Darmstadt, Germany
Margaria, Tiziana	University of Limerick and Lero, Ireland
McGibney, Alan	Munster Technological University, Ireland
Pesch, Dirk	University College Cork, Ireland
Rausch, Andreas	Clausthal University of Technology, Germany

Saay, Salim	University of Limerick, Ireland
Schaefer, Ina	Karlsruhe Institute of Technology, Germany
Seceleanu, Cristina	Mälardalen University, Sweden
Smyth, Steven	TU Dortmund University, Germany
Steffen, Bernhard	TU Dortmund University, Germany
Stoelinga, Marielle	University of Twente, The Netherlands
Ulbrich, Mattias	Karlsruhe Institute of Technology, Germany
Wirsing, Martin	LMU Munich, Germany
Woodcock, Jim	University of York, UK
ter Beek, Maurice	ISTI-CNR, Italy

Additional Reviewers

Abbas, Houssam
Adelt, Julius
Alberts, Elvin
Arbab, Farhad
Bainczyk, Alexander
Barbanera, Franco
Beckert, Bernhard
Berducci, Luigi
Beringer, Lennart
Bettini, Lorenzo
Bhattacharyya, Anirban
Blanchard, Allan
Boerger, Egon
Bogomolov, Sergiy
Bonakdarpour, Borzoo
Bortolussi, Luca
Bourr, Khalid
Brandstätter, Andreas
Breslin, John
Broy, Manfred
Bubel, Richard
Bures, Tomas
Busch, Daniel
Chaudhary, Hafiz Ahmad Awais
Chiti, Francesco
Ciancia, Vincenzo
Cok, David
Cordy, Maxime
Damiani, Ferruccio
De Donato, Lorenzo
Demrozi, Florenc
Di Stefano, Luca
Dierl, Simon
Dubslaff, Clemens
Duchêne, Fabien
Eldh, Sigrid
Ernst, Gidon
Feng, Hao
Flammini, Francesco
Freitas, Leo
Gabor, Thomas
Gerastathopoulos, Ilias
Groote, Jan Friso
Grosu, Radu
Grunske, Lars
Hallerstede, Stefan
Hansen, Simon Thrane
Hartmanns, Arnd
Hatcliff, John
Heydari Tabar, Asmae
Hnetynka, Petr
Inverso, Omar
Jakobs, Marie-Christine
John, Jobish
Johnsen, Einar Broch
Jongmans, Sung-Shik
Kamburjan, Eduard
Katsaros, Panagiotis
Kittelmann, Alexander
Knapp, Alexander
Kosmatov, Nikolai
Kretinsky, Jan

Kuruppuarachchi, Pasindu
Köhl, Maximilan
König, Christoph
Könighofer, Bettina
Lee, Edward
Lluch Lafuente, Alberto
Loreti, Michele
Madsen, Ole Lehrmann
Massink, Mieke
Mauritz, Malte
Mazzanti, Franco
Merz, Stephan
Micucci, Daniela
Monica, Stefania
Monti, Raul
Morichetta, Andrea
Nardone, Roberto
Naujokat, Stefan
Nayak, Satya Prakash
Neider, Daniel
Niehage, Mathis
Nolte, Gerrit
Ölvecky, Peter
Pace, Gordon
Perez, Guillermo
Petrov, Tatjana
Phan, Thomy
Piterman, Nir
Pugliese, Rosario
Reisig, Wolfgang
Remke, Anne
Riganelli, Oliviero
Ritz, Fabian
Rocha, Henrique
Runge, Tobias
Santen, Thomas
Scaletta, Marco
Schallau, Till
Schiffl, Jonas
Schlatte, Rudolf
Schlüter, Maximilian
Schneider, Gerardo
Schürmann, Jonas
Seisenberger, Monika
Smyth, Steven
Soudjani, Sadegh
Spellini, Stefano
Stankaitis, Paulius
Stewing, Richard
Stolz, Volker
Tapia Tarifa, Silvia Lizeth
Tegeler, Tim
Tiezzi, Francesco
Trubiani, Catia
Tschaikowski, Max
Tuosto, Emilio
Valiani, Serenella
Van Bladel, Brent
van de Pol, Jaco
Vandin, Andrea
Vittorini, Valeria
Weber, Alexandra
Weigl, Alexander
Wright, Thomas
Zambonelli, Franco

Contents – Part II

Automated Software Re-engineering

DIME Days

Programming - What is Next: The Role of Documentation

Discussing the Future Role of Documentation in the Context of Modern Software Engineering (ISoLA 2022 Track Introduction)

Klaus Havelund[1], Tim Tegeler[2(✉)], Steven Smyth[2], and Bernhard Steffen[2]

[1] Jet Propulsion Laboratory, California Institute of Technology, Pasadena, USA
klaus.havelund@jpl.nasa.gov
[2] TU Dortmund University, Dortmund, Germany
{tim.tegeler,steven.smyth,bernhard.steffen}@cs.tu-dortmund.de

Abstract. The article provides an introduction to the track *Programming - What is Next?: The Role of Documentation*, organized by Klaus Havelund and Bernhard Steffen as part of ISoLA 2022: the 11th International Symposium On Leveraging Applications of Formal Methods, Verification and Validation. Software has to run on machines, but it also has to be understood by humans. The latter requires some form of documentation of the software, which explains what it does if the human is a user of the software, and how it does it if the user is a programmer who wants to modify the software. Documentation is usually the neglected artifact. This track attempts to focus attention on documentation as a first-class citizen of the software development process.

Keywords: Documentation · Domain-specific languages · Modeling · Programming

1 Motivation and Background

In 1973, Hoare made the following statement in his famous *hints on programming language design*:

> *"The purpose of program documentation is to explain to a human reader the way in which a program works, so that it can be successfully adapted after it goes into service, either to meet the changing requirements of its users, to improve it in the light of increased knowledge, or just to remove latent errors and oversights. The view that documentation is something*

The research performed by this author was carried out at Jet Propulsion Laboratory, California Institute of Technology, under a contract with the National Aeronautics and Space Administration.

T. Margaria and B. Steffen (Eds.): ISoLA 2022, LNCS 13702, pp. 3–9, 2022.
https://doi.org/10.1007/978-3-031-19756-7_1

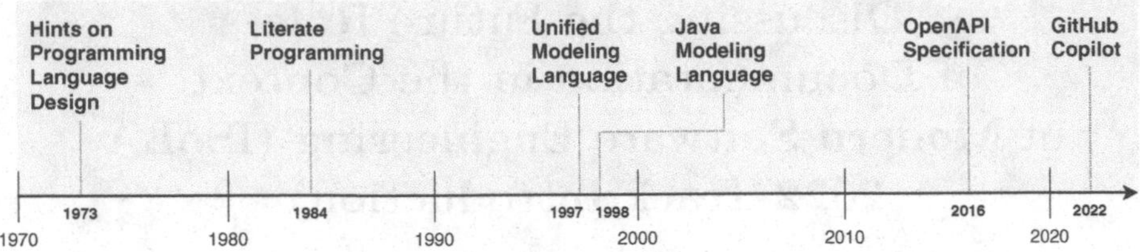

Fig. 1. Selected milestones in the historical evolution of software documentation.

> *that is added to a program after it has been commissioned seems to be wrong in principle and counterproductive in practice. Instead, documentation must be regarded as an integral part of the process of design and coding."* [10]

Despite the maturity of this statement, it is our observation that software documentation is often still considered a burden and merely realized as plain source code comments or concluded in a post-development fashion [4] as standalone documents. We believe this results from a *love-hate* relationship that we as software engineers have with software documentation. On the one hand we cherish well documented software and on the other hand we don't enjoy creating and maintaining the documentation of our own projects.

Almost 50 years after Hoare's statement, software documentation has gone beyond helping programmers to orient themselves during the programming and has many facets today. Not only gained it importance with the increasing collaboration of highly distributed teams, but it became a structured means that is more than human-readable text:

- Classic approaches such as Javadoc [11] are legitimate successors of Knuth's literate programming [14]. They were instrumental in enhancing comments by the adoption of structured tags that carry processable metadata of commented source code and the automatic generation of documentation in a browsable output format (e.g. HTML).
- JML [12,15] goes beyond Javadoc. In particular, it supports design by contract by allowing pre and post-conditions to be written as annotations.
- Standardized modeling with UML introduced graphical notations to support documentation and understanding of object-oriented software [7,17].
- Projects like the OpenAPI initiative [18] support a documentation-first approach to describe (RESTful) APIs in a human and machine readable format that allows automatic service discovery.
- Web-based documentations, e.g. [1], have evolved to software products themselves, making use of version control software and distinct build processes. This trend lead to the need for frameworks and libraries to generalise the creation of documentation, e.g. [2].
- GitHub Copilot [3] generates complete source code from comments, with the result of blurring the lines between documenting and programming.

We think this evolution (cf. Fig. 1) has the potential to overcome our prejudices against documenting and finally position documentation in the center of software development. The aim of the track is to review current pragmatics and discuss the future role of documentation in the context of modern software engineering.

2 Contributions

In this section we present the contributions of the PWN track in the order of their presentation at ISoLA in three sessions which, incrementally, consider enhanced roles of documentation from mere additions to the code, via code/documentation conglomerates to various forms of executable documentation.

2.1 Session 1: Duality Between Documentation and Code

This session addresses the duality between documentation and code. A seamless interplay of both entities is vital for the success of software projects; in particular for projects relying on the continuous collaboration of various stakeholders. The following papers lay the foundation for this track by discussing how abstraction in form of models can be used to represent software properties and reducing the need for additional documentation.

Coherent Description of Software System Properties. Broy [5] introduces his paper by discussing the term software documentation from different points of view and underscores that the development of software systems involves a wide-ranging set of challenging tasks, including the understanding of technical entities, maintaining the source code and operating the overall system. He argues that documentation is not only useful for each of these tasks but badly needed for software system development and evolution, especially in the context of DevOps-driven projects. Therefore continuously improving documentation, while verifying its consistency, is a key issue. One practical way of enriching documentation for this purpose is the use of models to abstractly describe important properties (e.g. functionality and architecture) of the considered software systems.

Models as Documents, Documents as Models. Stevens [20] reflects on similarities and differences between both terms. Documentation and models are broad concepts and overlap in software engineering. Models can serve to document certain parts of a software project and, in the context of model-driven engineering documents can be viewed as models as well. The paper approaches the questions "What counts as a model?" and "What counts as a document?".

Using Supplementary Properties to Reduce the Need for Documentation. Programming languages serve two purposes in general. Firstly to instruct computers by being executed and secondly to describe the intended computational processes to humans. However, practice has shown that source code can be difficult to understand, even for experts. Thus, source code requires to be documented by supplementary documentation using natural language, diagrams, specifications and models. Madsen and Møller-Pedersen [16] dedicate this paper to the challenge of extending the expressive power of programming languages in order to reduce the need for such supplementary documentation on the one hand, and to reduce the need for additional (documentational) languages on the other hand.

2.2 Session 2: Synergies Between Documentation and Code

We often think of documentation as text written in natural language, explaining how code works or how it is used. However, documentation can also be understood more formally. This session focuses on such more formal forms of documentation, including visualization of code, assurance arguments, and models. Visualization of code can be viewed as visual documentation. An assurance argument is a semi-formal argument about the correctness of a system, and can be viewed as a structured form of documentation. Similarly, a design model is a form of documentation. The papers in this session discuss the tight integration of these forms of documentation and code, either by concretely linking artifacts with tooling, or by providing precise semantics of the documentation that supports correct code development and generation from a model.

Pragmatics Twelve Years Later. In 2010, Fuhrmann et al. introduced *modeling pragmatics* as a term for tools that combine the best of the textual and graphical worlds. A key enabler for this combination in practice was the ability to automatically synthesize customized (graphical) views from (possibly textual) models. Now, von Hanxleden et al. [8] reflect on their proposal twelve years later with the example of the recently developed coordination language Lingua Franca and discuss the obstacles, opportunities, and the outlook for modeling pragmatics in general.

Assurance Provenance. Modern society relies heavily on high-assurance systems software for transportation, medicine, finance, defense, and other areas. However, the rigorous requirements and processes for such safety-critical systems do not mesh well with modern agile software development practices, which focuses on 'good enough' software 'fast enough'. Karsai and Balasubramanian [13] argue that current CI/CD pipelines should be extended by Continues Assurance (CA) high-assurance software systems enabling rapid re-analysis and re-evaluation. For this, integrated tooling is essential: Developers need assistance for managing and maintaining complex systems.

Formalization of the AADL Run-Time Services. Hatcliff et al. [9] note that documentation is not only needed for a specific program or model but on the meta-level for the definition of modeling languages, e.g., for the Architecture and Analysis Definition Language (AADL). AADL is a modeling language focussing on strong semantics for real-time embedded systems. The definition of modeling languages require expressive documentation in order to allow all stakeholders to reason about the modeled system. However, in case of the AADL standard, the documentation of run-time services is semi-formal. This allows divergent interpretations of the definition which renders the implementation of analysis or code generation functionality difficult. The authors show how rule-based formalization of key aspects of the AADL semantic can be documented to enable functions for realistic, interoperable, and assurable implementations.

2.3 Session 3: Executable Documentation

Executable Documentation is an umbrella term which includes all parts of a documentation that can be executed directly, create executable components (e.g., higher-level models or even running products), or components that manually or automatically generate parts of the documentation.

Test-First in Action. Smyth et al. [19] present two test-first scenarios. At first, a test-driven development approach tailored to the needs of programming beginners is illustrated. A focus is set on a test-guided, auto-didactic exploration through appropriate automatic diagram syntheses for runtime visualization for an immediate, tangible feedback. The test-based guidance can be automated, e.g., via randomized testing, or used to foster student-tutor interaction. In the second scenario, a similar test-first approach can be leveraged to improve modern web development. Instead of relying on static templates, concrete test instances are used to instantaneously visualize the final product in a WYSIWYG style. This radically reduces the time for tedious development cycles.

Runtime Verification as Documentation. In contrast to a runtime verification monitor that returns a Boolean verdict, Dams et al. [6] present three monitor examples that document system behaviour. For this, they combine runtime verification with techniques from data science. The three examples cover state reconstruction from traces, a data analysis of operations on a distributed database, and timed debugging. While the considered notion of dynamic documentation is rooted in runtime verification, such systems produce rich data, which require analysis that goes beyond Boolean verdicts. The authors argue that monitors written in a high-level programming language allow for arbitrarily complex data processing, which is often needed in industrial contexts.

From Documentation Languages to Purpose-Specific Languages. Domain-specific notation and documentation languages are usually used in the requirements and design phases. Tegeler et al. [21] illustrate how to turn these languages into fully-fledged purpose-specific modeling languages. These languages are designed to tightening the semantic gap between the *what* should be done and the *how* is it implemented, while also reducing the need for handwritten *why* specifications. The approach is illustrated within the DevOps scenario. Here, typical graphical CI/CD workflows are turned into an integrated modeling environment, called Rig. At a larger scale, Rig specifications, that are themselves executable documentations, can be regarded as means to automatically provide corresponding running systems which can be considered the 'ultimate' (executable) documentations where the understanding of all stakeholders should converge.

The PWN track closes with a panel discussion regarding the role of documentation in the context of modern software engineering.

References

1. Laravel - the PHP framework for web artisans. https://laravel.com/docs. Accessed 31 Aug 2021
2. Vuepress. https://vuepress.vuejs.org. Accessed 31 Aug 2022
3. Your AI pair programmer. https://github.com/features/copilot. Accessed 31 Aug 2022
4. Aghajani, E.: Software documentation: automation and challenges. Ph.D. thesis, Università della Svizzera italiana (2020)
5. Broy, M.: Software system documentation: coherent description of software system properties. In: Margaria, T., Steffen, B. (eds.) ISoLA 2022, LNCS, vol. 13702, pp. 10–27. Springer, Cham (2022)
6. Dams, D., Havelund, K., Kauffman, S.: Runtime verification as documentation. In: Margaria, T., Steffen, B. (eds.) ISoLA 2022, LNCS, vol. 13702, pp. 157–173. Springer, Cham (2022)
7. Fernández-Sáez, A.M., Caivano, D., Genero, M., Chaudron, M.R.: On the use of UML documentation in software maintenance: results from a survey in industry. In: 2015 ACM/IEEE 18th International Conference on Model Driven Engineering Languages and Systems (MODELS), pp. 292–301 (2015). https://doi.org/10.1109/MODELS.2015.7338260
8. von Hanxleden, R., et al.: Pragmatics twelve years later: a report on lingua franca. In: Margaria, T., Steffen, B. (eds.) ISoLA 2022, LNCS, vol. 13702, pp. 60–89. Springer, Cham (2022)
9. Hatcliff, J., Hugues, J., Stewart, D., Wrage, L.: Formalization of the AADL runtime services. In: Margaria, T., Steffen, B. (eds.) ISoLA 2022, LNCS, vol. 13702, pp. 105–134. Springer, Cham (2022)
10. Hoare, C.A.: Hints on programming language design. Tech. rep., Stanford University Stanford, Stanford, CA Department of Computer Science (1973)
11. Javadoc. https://docs.oracle.com/en/java/javase/13/javadoc/javadoc.html. Accessed 02 Sept 2022
12. JML. http://www.eecs.ucf.edu/~leavens/JML. Accessed 02 Sept 2022
13. Karsai, G., Balasubramanian, D.: Assurance provenance: the next challenge in software documentation. In: Margaria, T., Steffen, B. (eds.) ISoLA 2022, LNCS, vol. 13702, pp. 90–104. Springer, Cham (2022)
14. Knuth, D.E.: Literate programming. Comput. J. **27**(2), 97–111 (1984)
15. Leavens, G.T., Baker, A.L., Ruby, C.: Preliminary design of JML: a behavioral interface specification language for java. SIGSOFT Softw. Eng. Notes **31**(3), 1–38 (2006). https://doi.org/10.1145/1127878.1127884

16. Madsen, O.L., Møller-Pedersen, B.: Using supplementary properties to reduce the need for documentation. In: Margaria, T., Steffen, B. (eds.) ISoLA 2022, LNCS, vol. 13702, pp. 35–59. Springer, Cham (2022)
17. Object Management Group (OMG): Documents associated with Object Constraint Language (OCL), Version 2.4. https://www.omg.org/spec/UML/2.5.1/ (2017). Accessed 8 Feb 2019
18. OpenAPI Initiative: Openapi specification v3.1.0. Febraury 2021. https://spec.openapis.org/oas/latest.html. Accessed 25 Mar 2022
19. Smyth, S., et al.: Executable documentation: the real power of test-first. In: Margaria, T., Steffen, B. (eds.) ISoLA 2022, LNCS, vol. 13702, pp. 135–156. Springer, Cham (2022)
20. Stevens, P.: Models as documents, documents as models. In: Margaria, T., Steffen, B. (eds.) ISoLA 2022, LNCS, vol. 13702, pp. 28–34. Springer, Cham (2022)
21. Tegeler, T., Boßelmann, S., Schürmann, J., Smyth, S., Teumert, S., Steffen, B.: Executable documentation: from documentation languages to purpose-specific languages. In: Margaria, T., Steffen, B. (eds.) ISoLA 2022, LNCS, vol. 13702, pp. 174–192. Springer, Cham (2022)

Software System Documentation: Coherent Description of Software System Properties

Manfred Broy(✉)

Institut für Informatik, Technische Universität München, 80290 München, Germany
broy@in.tum.de

Abstract. Software systems, also those that are part of cyber-physical systems, are represented by data structures and code which are static, syntactic descriptions of complex dynamic behavior. They are complex technical entities, difficult to understand, difficult to develop, difficult to correct, to maintain, to use, to operate, to evolve, to market. For each of these tasks documentation is useful, helpful, and badly needed. In any case, when dealing with software systems, improving understanding and therefore documentation is a key issue. There is a wide range of properties of software systems that have to be described and a huge number of different documentation techniques. This defines the broad spectrum of documentation and also the wide range of documentation in use. To overcome the complexity of software systems and cyber-physical systems abstraction is a key concept. A very helpful and promising form of abstraction is by achieved by carefully selected models that can be used for documentation.

Keywords: Documentation · Modeling · Software system properties · Specification

1 Software System Documentation – for Whom and Why

Documentation of software systems is a term that covers a wide spectrum of concepts, activities, and documents in the development and usage of software systems.

Wikipedia says:
"Software documentation is written text or illustration that accompanies computer software or is embedded in the source code. The documentation either explains how the software operates or how to use it, and may mean different things to people in different roles.

Documentation is an important part of software engineering. Types of documentation include:

Requirements – Statements that identify attributes, capabilities, characteristics, or qualities of a system. This is the foundation for what will be or has been implemented.

Architecture/Design – Overview of software. Includes relations to an environment and construction principles to be used in design of software components.

Technical – Documentation of code, algorithms, interfaces, and APIs.

T. Margaria and B. Steffen (Eds.): ISoLA 2022, LNCS 13702, pp. 10–27, 2022.
https://doi.org/10.1007/978-3-031-19756-7_2

End user – Manuals for the end-user, system administrators and support staff.
Marketing – How to market the product and analysis of the market demand".

Obviously, this whole spectrum of types of documentation helps in software construction and maintenance – and there is even more. Documentation in the sense of in line documentation of code is a rather narrow understanding of the term. In any case, documentation is always for humans. It is worked out for certain groups of people that are to read and use the documentation.

Documentation addresses both the activity of working out documents as well as a set of documents providing official information or evidence or that serves as a record describing a system, a process, an activity or something else. Documentation is also understood as records in fulfillment of some regulation, for instance, in documenting that certain standards are fulfilled such es for example safety standards.

Software system documentation is a very broad term and addresses a broad spectrum. David Parnas [11] writes:

"The prime cause of the sorry "state of the art" in software development is our failure to produce good design documentation. Poor documentation is the cause of many errors and reduces efficiency in every phase of a software product's development and use. Most software developers believe that "documentation" refers to a collection of wordy, unstructured, introductory descriptions, thousands of pages that nobody wanted to write and nobody trusts. In contrast, Engineers in more traditional disciplines think of precise blueprints, circuit diagrams, and mathematical specifications of component properties."

When David L. Parnas advocated that software documentation is a key in software development he was sometimes misunderstood. One misunderstanding was brought up by people who understood software documentation as a post-mortem activity describing the result of development steps after they have been completed. They had the following view: You develop a piece of software and afterwards you work out the documentation. This is a weird idea, because one of the most difficult parts of software development is understanding software. This addresses the understanding of the data structures that are used within the software system, the understanding of the algorithms and what they are supposed to compute, finally, the understanding of the architecture of the software system as well as the interaction between its components, and last, but not least, the understanding of the functionality offered by the software system.

Investigations and our experiences in projects show that it is literally impossible to derive, for instance, the idea of the architecture of a software system simply from the code after the software was developed, if the architectural structure is not documented in some appropriate way or if the architectural structure is not carefully expressed by documentation within the code. In the end, it seems appropriated to work out documentation in development and to use documentation in development.

There is a wide spectrum of different forms and concepts of documentation. Roughly there are the following possibilities to distinguish ways of working out documentation:

- Post-mortem documentation: development steps and their results are documented afterwards.
- Joint documentation and development: development steps and documentation are worked out hand-in-hand.

- Documentation is done before development: documentation is part of the requirement specification and design – preparing and driving the development.

All these approaches are interesting and are practiced in software development. However, it is obvious that some of those bring in more overhead and some bring more advantages, some are even dictated by obligatory standards. This suggests a carefully chosen concept of documentation.

Apart from that, one of the issues here is that today more than ever software is developed and evolves over long time periods using techniques like DevOps and continuous integration, continuous deployment and continuous delivery. Then there does not exist a real "final" version of the software that has to be documented. Software and therefore its documentation change over time – and documentation may even document the changes – and have to be changed hand-in-hand. Moreover, it is quite obvious that for large software systems design is an important issue. Therefore, it is much more helpful to work out, at least, some of the documentation before going into a detailed implementation of software. This, of course, brings in real key questions: How much documentation is needed during the development and at which point this documentation should be done?

Other questions are: What are the properties that should be documented, which are properties that are relevant? How should these properties be documented? And, finally, the question: For which purpose is the documentation done – just for understanding, for helping in the implementation, for helping in the verification (See [10]), for helping in the maintenance, or as a support for the people using the software? Which methods and which tools are applied to work out, store, and to present the documentation. Documentation is a key issue, in particular, since software systems are typically rather complex and difficult to understand. It is well-known that especially in the long-term development of systems program understanding is a key. As we observed in case studies, more than half of their time developers spend in understanding and re-understanding parts of their software. If documentation is done in an appropriate way such times can be sufficiently reduced and errors or misunderstandings can be avoided.

However, coming up with the conclusion that software documentation is a key issue, there remains the question how to do the documentation. What are techniques to describe system parts? This needs, in particular, ways to document certain system aspects which is exactly what is achieved by appropriate software system models. In the following, we present an overview over the properties of software systems that are interesting for documentation, we discuss possibilities to describe those properties, we try also to be precise about the relationship between the context in which a software system is used and its properties and which of them have to be documented. Finally, we refer to a structured system model as it was developed in a project done under the sponsoring of the German ministry of research which ended up with a detailed understanding of the modeling of software systems, in particular, in relationship with physical parts as found in cyber-physical systems (see [5]).

In addition, we describe how the behavior of cyber-physical systems with respect to the physical parts can be specified and documented which then is needed for both verification and simulation.

2 Properties of Software Systems and Their Documentation

When thinking about documenting software systems, the first quite obvious question is: What is a software system or more precisely how is a software system represented? A software system is an executable application. A software system is represented by a number of data bases and software components. Each software component is – according to Szyperski [14] – a piece of code that is executable and represents the software unit. We expect that software components are available in compiled form such that they can be executed on a hardware platform including everything which is necessary like operating systems and middleware. In the end, a software system is a system that can be executed and run with everything needed to do that. Then we can collect observations about the software system that correspond to system properties.

In this light, software documentation is everything which describes and records relevant aspects of software systems. Such aspects can be very technical, close to issues of implementation such as the code and comments inside the code as well as descriptions of run-time aspects such as scheduling or of test cases. They can touch several context aspects of software such as its history, its developers, design decisions, or its future. But the documentation will also consider more abstract fields of the software system including issues such as

- description of context systems with which the system interacts (including cyber-physical system, see Sect. 4.4),
- description of the user interfaces and the functionality offered by the system (often called services or features),
- description of functionality, features and services by interfaces and interface behavior in relation to users or to physical devices in the case of cyber-physical systems,
- architectures and other levels of abstraction describing the decomposition of software systems into subsystems that interact (for architecture documentation we can, for instance, distinguish between platform-independent description of architectures and platform-dependent descriptions of architectures), and
- the wide field of what is called requirements for software systems. Such requirements may encompass a rich variety of software properties, so the description of requirements is a quite general way of software documentation where, in principle, everything that can be documented about software could also appear in a requirement document.

A further way of characterizing documentation is the question for which purpose and for which group of people a documentation is written. For instance, documentation may address different stakeholders:

- owners of software systems,
- customers, people who are supposed to buy a software system,
- operators and operating organizations, who are supposed to operate the software system,
- users, who are supposed to use the software system for their individual purposes,
- developers and implementers who are responsible for implementation of software such as requirements engineers, architects, programmers, testers, integrators and many more.

A very general form of documentation may be a description for which purpose the software is best used, how it is supposed to be successful in the market and which issues it addresses.

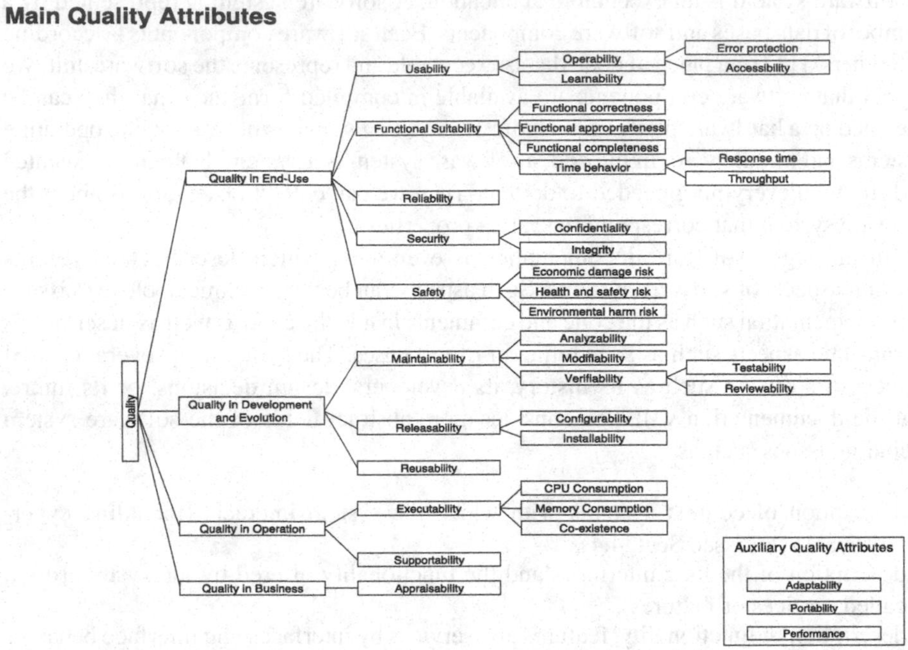

Fig. 1. Quality attributes of software systems (due to Klaus Lochmann, Stefan Wagner)

Another way to structure documentation follows the structuring of software systems. There we may distinguish

- external views (where the important properties of software are described from the viewpoint of other systems and users who want to use the services provided by the software system),
- internal views (which is interesting for people who deal with internal properties of software, for instance, how it is implemented, which algorithms are used, how it is related to operating systems or communication concepts and much more), and
- operators (who are responsible for the operation of software systems and their properties).

All these issues are also related to quality concerns which talk about specific aspects of quality of software systems. We give a description of various quality issues in Fig. 1 as they were worked out in a project in my group some years ago and which give a kind of a structured view onto quality properties.

When describing various aspects of software in documents we better carefully choose the appropriate technique of documentation:

- informal descriptions (where we use text or graphics to document and to describe parts of the documentation), or
- formalized descriptions (which typically employ ideas of models by choosing how to model the selected aspects of software systems in a formal way).

Using text in documentation, a very structured and carefully worked out text is sensible – perhaps even using well-defined standards. In any case, it has to be identified, which kind of people are going to work with the documentation. In some way, a specific well-chosen terminology as defined in a glossary should be used. In addition, when working very properly this needs a kind ontology. When ontologies are described in all their details, it is getting closer and closer to a formal model.

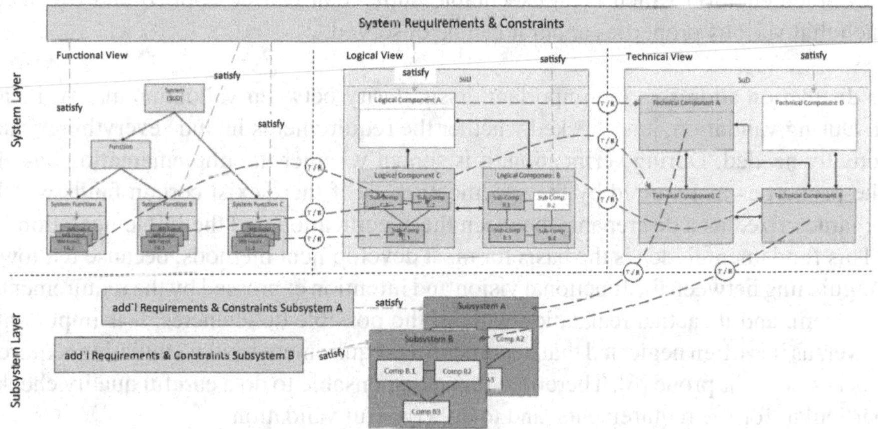

Fig. 2. Meta-model for the system modeling approach Spes (due to Wolfgang Böhm)

For graphical descriptions and diagrams, their proponents claim "a picture is worth a thousand words". Yes, but unfortunately this does not mean that all readers of a diagram share the same semantic interpretation – and therefore it may need a thousand words to explain the meaning.

Formal system models have been worked out in system modeling approaches. We show in the following Fig. 2 a meta-model for a system modeling approach as it was developed within the Spes projects [5] in Germany during the last 12 years which gives a quite comprehensive description of software systems and their development artefacts, and therefore a formalized documentation.

This approach follows a particular philosophy, not only using a syntactic approach such as SysML, where a coherent semantics is missing, but starting from a semantic model for software systems, in particular, for software interfaces. Based on this, a comprehensive model of the software system is worked out including the systems, their context, their interface behavior, and their syntactic interfaces as well as ways to represent the internal behavior by states or the decomposition of a system into architectures.

An important part of that is the functional architecture which describes the services provided by a system in a structured way. We give a few brief examples along these lines in the following section.

3 Documentation in System Development and Evolution

It is a key concept in software and system development, and in programming to distinguish between requirements specification and implementation:

- The requirement specification which describes what the intended properties of a piece of software or program are (including its functionality and its behavior, but also quality aspects, such as human machine interfaces, and many more), and
- its implementation which is an executable entity that can be applied and executed such that various properties about it can be observed.

This distinction addresses the important dissimilarity between validation and verification. During validation, it is checked whether the requirements include everything what is actually needed. During verification, it is shown whether the implementation has all of the properties as required by the specification, or if there exist certain faults which are characterized as a discrepancy between the specification and the implementation.

This fundamental idea is the basis for most development methods, because it allows distinguishing between the functional vision and intention expressed by the requirements of a system, and its actual realization with all the possible deficiencies. It is important, however, as it is often neglected that documenting requirements and formulating requirements is also error prone [6]. Therefore, it is indispensable to do a careful quality check, in particular, for the requirements, and to do a careful validation.

3.1 From Abstract Ideas to Design and Implementation

For understanding design and implementation, it is a key to understand the basic idea which is behind a piece of software. Over the years, software engineering and, in particular, computer science have developed a large list of design and implementation patterns and also algorithms such that in a number of cases for documentation it is sufficient to mention the idea by a particular key word, then for every educated engineer it is clear what is meant.

A good example would be "quick sort" [7], an algorithm which is very useful, which has a lot of quite different implementations, also implementations where it may take some time to find out that it is an implementation of "quick sort". Therefore, it is highly helpful, that for a piece of software to be implemented by "quick sort" there is a documentation, perhaps by a comment, that explains that this is "quick sort" - and perhaps also how it is implemented.

If ideas are used or combined in a way that is not standard and just what is taught in text books, it might be very helpful and necessary, first to document the abstract ideas, and then also how those ideas are realized by the design and the implementation. Such documentation makes it easier to understand and makes it easier to change a piece of software.

3.2 The Significance of Understanding

It is well known that, when dealing with software, in particular, with software development, maintenance and software evolution, for instance, in connection with DevOps, one of the big challenges is to read and understand pieces of code. This applies to requirement specifications as well as to programming and software implementation. Therefore, understanding the problem, the requirements is a sometimes painful task. The result of this process has to be documented. But often it is also necessary to understand a piece of software developed some time ago. Usually, if only code is given, some re-engineering is necessary to find out the ideas behind implementations. This is a very important step in software development. If people who change the software misunderstand the original design ideas, this may result in changes that include errors.

In projects where people implement change requests, I found out that in the worst case the implementation of change requests, that were formulated to correct certain failures, injected new failures – in the end sometimes to an extent that the number of newly introduced errors when implementing change requests was getting higher than the number of initial failures which were to be corrected that way. It is absolutely key to have an understanding of software systems which, of course, has to do with local understanding, but also global understanding. Some changes of software may just change some algorithms in a way that nothing has to be changed outside this particular part of the code, but other changes may affect other pieces of code. Here well-documented architectures can help.

Good examples are the re-design of algorithms or the re-design of certain functionalities. Here the understanding is extremely important, because what we need there is a kind of understanding the previous design and implementation decisions and the locality of the changes such that we can be sure that a certain change does not affect other parts of the system which to a large extent can be a result of a properly documented architecture.

3.3 Requirements Management

Requirements are most significant parts of the documentation of a software system. They are the basis for understanding, agreement, and for verification. As already pointed out, requirements have to be documented, and it has also to be documented how requirements are verified for the implementation. Practical examples are the documentation of test cases, and the result of test runs.

Another important issue of documentation is the documentation by tracing [4]. A trace is a relation between different documents in development with the idea that a trace connects properties in these different documents which are in a kind of a semantic relationship. A simple standard example of a trace would be a relationship between a requirement and a particular system component or program module that is responsible for the implementation of that requirement.

3.4 Documentation, Validation, and Verification

Documentation describes properties of software systems that may be properties that are to be achieved and formulated before development, or properties that are expected and have to be verified after an implementation has been finished. In both cases, it is decisive in which way those properties are described and what the techniques are to make sure that the documentation is appropriate.

Considering the issue of specifications: In many, in particular, academic publications it is over-looked that specifications are equally error prone as implementations – as some studies show [6]. Therefore, also specifications have to be justified. What is even more critical is the validation of specifications and requirements. When building software systems, a key question is whether the specified functionality and the required quality attributes do reflect actually what the users need. In many cases, this is a problem. If something goes wrong here, this is more critical than most other issues.

Of course, there is a reason why this particular question is not so much in the center exactly of scientific publications: It is much less clear what we can do to come up with an adequate software system concept and requirement specification – and how to document it. One has to keep in mind that in software development the design space is much larger, in general, than for the development of mechanical systems where the design space is limited by the law of physics. Approaches like design thinking [8] may help. At least, they give a kind of a systematic process to come up with specifications. But, nevertheless, it is to a large extent depending on the competency of the involved personnel. Therefore, we have to be much better in education and to make engineers aware that this is one of the most decisive steps in system development.

3.5 Avoiding Outdated Documentation

In many large software projects it can be observed that even in cases where the development of software starts with a kind of complete requirements documentation and specification, a large number of changes is still necessary during development. Technically, this is often implemented by a number of change requests that lead to changes in the implementation, and also often to changes in the documented requirements. But many software projects fail to do these changes according to change requests also in the requirements documentation.

As a result, in the end of the development, there is no proper valid requirements documentation any more. The original requirements documentation is outdated, not kept up-to-date. So very soon no one has a clear understanding which of the requirements are actually realized and implemented by the software an which are obsolete. An attempt to re-construct a requirement specification post-mortem turns out to be very difficult, because this means a lot of error prone and time consuming re-engineering, re-thinking, and re-understanding the development steps used so far.

In contrast, in a well-organized development, documentation is kept up-to-date. This requires that not only change requests are documented, but that the implied changes are not only applied to the code but also to the documentation. Done properly, in the spirit of continuous integration, also the documentation is continuously kept up-to-date.

3.6 Artefact Modelling

An approach which goes a very consequent way into documentation is model-based development. In model-based development we describe all aspects of complex systems, in particular, also cyber-physical systems at a number of different levels of abstraction including functionality, logical sub-system architectures, and technical architectures.

Within the Spes projects this approach was carefully worked out in all its details. The result is the idea of an artefact model [9]. This model contains the information which has been worked out during the development and the maintenance of the system which is relevant. Therefore, we need a very carefully worked out artefact structure which describes not only the artefacts, but also the rationale and the relationships including traces and arguments for correctness. Then principles can be implemented such as "single point of truth" which states that certain data should be defined at one place and then referred to instead of copying them in many places with the danger that when changing these data the change is not consistently carried out.

3.7 Rationale

An important part of documentation is not just describing requirements or explaining how a system is realized or how parts of a system are realized, but also why this particular choice of requirements or realization has been made. Understanding not only means to understand what has been done, but also to understand why it has been done. If this is not properly explained, the result might be that it is difficult to understand the motivation, the reasons for certain implementation or design decisions, or certain specifications, when changes of the system are requested.

Therefore, we need documented rationales. Of course, rationales always have to be carefully written with respect to what are the targets of the rationales, and who is supposed to read and understand the rationales, and who will have advantages by them.

3.8 Abstraction, Modularity, Encapsulation, and Information Hiding

One of the key ideas of software development is modularity, encapsulation and information hiding. This is an approach which supports many of the steps that have been mentioned before. Modularity means that we have a clear idea of structuring and a model of components. We understand which properties of the components are local encapsulated (and do not have to be considered, if we want to understand the role of the components within a larger architecture), and which parts and properties of components are relevant for the architecture and the interaction with the other components within the architecture. This should be done by a notion of an interface, where the interface has to be not only the syntactic properties of a software component, but where the interface has to include much more: The interface behavior which describes that by the interactions between the different components a certain behavior and specification is realized. An extensive theory of this approach can be found in the work on FOCUS [1].

Such an approach, of course, needs an idea of encapsulation which describes how we can protect and encapsulate the details of a component implementation from what is relevant for its interface behavior. This leads immediately to information hiding [12], the idea that to understand the role of a component we do not have to understand how a component is realized by the algorithms and data structures, but only how the behavior of the component is relevant and how it influences the behavior of the whole system at the level of architecture.

3.9 Documentation in DevOps

Today, system are often developed and evolve over longer time periods. Then the role of documentation gets even more important.

3.9.1 DevOps and Continuous Documentation

In recent years agile software and system developed was advocated depending on particular context conditions of software development. This can be a very helpful and successful development technique. In particular, techniques of continuous integration, continuous deployment, and continuous delivery have been advocated and successfully practiced.

This approach neglects that – when doing so – it is also important to keep documentation up-to-date. Therefore, the approach can be easily be extended to *continuous documentation*, which is highly important and helpful. If documentation is not updated, if it is out-of-date, or, at least, if some parts are outdated, developers do not longer look at the documentation, because it is not guaranteed that is still valid. They rather study the code to re-discover and to re-understand the ideas in the code, but they might not completely understand why certain implementation decisions have been made. Then they run into the danger, on one hand to spend a long time to understand what is going on, and on the other hand to change certain parts of the implantation not being aware that these are changes which destroy some of the principles and correctness arguments of the original design.

3.9.2 DevOps and System Owner

Finally, it is key to have responsible people, who we call system owners in the following, in a long-term development where software or software intensive systems are developed over long time periods – in contrast to the product owners of approaches like Scrum (see [13]) who are responsible for a software system and its development. This means that the system owner has to do all the major decisions in system development and so they are responsible for the market success, for the usability, for the achieved user experience, and for the quality profile to be implemented last not least for the appropriate functionality implemented.

However, such system owners cannot know all the details, ideas and decisions just in their head, they have to document that and have to develop and document a kind of a road map, how the system should be developed over time, and what the reasons and rationales are as justifications for decisions in system development.

In fact, today such system owners cannot be found and are badly missing in many development projects although they are would be urgently needed. This means that we have to define these roles more carefully, integrated such roles into development process models beyond the role of a product owner in Scrum, and to educate software engineers to be prepared to take over this role.

4 Documentation via Modelling

In this section, we shortly illustrate, how models can be used in documentation.

4.1 Specification of Functionality

The functionality of systems can formally be described by a relation on streams. We use here a very basic version of streams. Given a set Data, a stream of data is defined as follows ($\mathbb{N}$ denotes the natural numbers including 0, $\mathbb{N}_+ = \mathbb{N}\backslash\{0\}$)

$$\text{Stream Data} = (\mathbb{N}_+ \rightarrow \text{Data}_+)$$

where $\text{Data}_+ = \text{Data} \cup \{\varepsilon\}$ where ε stands for *no message*.

The functional behavior of a system MIX is documented by a specification written as a template:

MIX

in x, z: Stream Data
out y: Stream Data

∀ d ∈ Data: d#x+d#z = d#y

where d#x denotes the number of copies of d in stream x. The system can also be presented graphically by a data flow node as shown in Fig. 3.

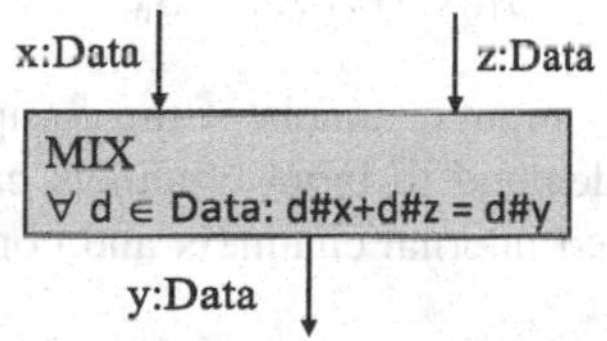

Fig. 3. System or service MIX as a data flow node

In the specification x, y, and z are channels that denote data streams. We write MIX(x, z, y) for the logical assertion ∀ d ∈ Data: d#x + d#z = d#y that specifies the behavior of the data flow node MIX by an *interface assertion.*

4.2 Architecture Documentation

In a number of investigations of projects we have reviewed over the years, it became obvious that it is nearly impossible to reconstruct a well-defined abstract architecture, if we just have access to the code without an architecture documentation. After the code was produced, it is literally impossible to reconstruct the architecture, if a proper architecture documentation is no longer available, or no longer valid. In fact, there is a whole subfield of software engineering of research dedicated to this topic. However, it is certainly much more appropriate to document architectures carefully while designing them.

A typical example would be, if in an architecture there are certain rules which subsystem might interact with another subsystem – as it is typical, for instance, for layered architectures. If there is an implementation of an interaction between two subsystems it is quite unclear whether this is following the architectural principles, or whether it is a failure with respect to the architectural constraints.

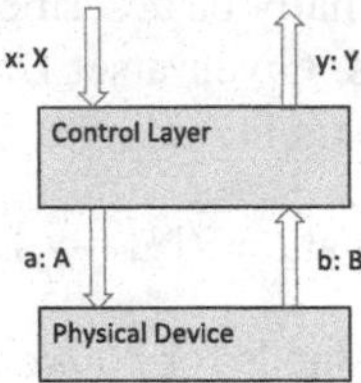

Fig. 4. Architecture of a control layer composed with a physical device

Formally, a specification of an architecture consisting of a set $K = \{C_1, C_2, \ldots, C_n\}$ of components C_k with specifications S_k in terms of interface assertions is composed into a specification of the architecture which is formed by the composition of the components

$$C_1 \times C_2 \times \ldots \times C_n$$

defined by (for details see [3])

$$S_1 \wedge S_2 \wedge \ldots \wedge S_n$$

Here we assume that the sets of input channels of the components are disjoint and that all output channels that are identical to input channels carry the same type of messages. These channels are called internal channels and connect the components in the architecture.

The specification of the composition of the Control Layer specified by CL with the Physical Layer specified by PD (see Fig. 4) is given by

$$CL(x,\ b,\ y,\ a) \wedge PD(a,\ b)$$

If we want to hide the channels a and b we specify the system by

$$\exists\, a,\ b\!: CL(x,\ b,\ y,\ a) \wedge PD(a,\ b)$$

This way we get a documentation of an architecture by a specification.

4.3 Correctness of Documentations

There is a similarity between documentation and logical assertions about systems and programs. A documentation can be valid or not. Thus, we may speak about the correctness of documentation. This way we run into the challenge to make sure that documentation is correct. This brings in the challenge of *documentation verification.*

4.4 Documenting Physical Systems

A challenging approach is the development of cyber-physical systems which means that we develop systems where parts are digital and parts are physical. In the end, we have software and hardware, on one hand, digital hardware and computing devices as well as communication devices. On the other hand, we have physical systems that are concrete mechanical machines and mechanical devices which are usually controlled by the software.

Here it is important to understand that the functionality of those systems is a result of the interaction of the software with the physical devices. One way to achieve this is to work it out with all its technical details. Therefore, one has to study the complexity of the technicalities of software and hardware, often called software/hardware co-design, and of the details of the physical devices. Such an approach is very difficult to explain and to document. Therefore, it might be more interesting to come up with a more abstract level of documentation and description. This means that we can understand systems by describing the functionality of the software controllers, and, in addition, by describing the functional properties of the physical devices – also at a digital level. This means that we introduce a kind of a state machine representation for such systems. To make it a bit easier to understand we give a short simple example in the following.

We demonstrate this approach by a simple example, a power window in a car. It is modelled by a state machine with input and output. The state space is used to model the state of the window. A state consists of two attributes:

mode: {stopped, goin_up, goin_down, alarm}
p: [0:100]

Here p stands for position and represents the position of the window. The position $p = 100$ holds if the window is closed, $p = 0$ holds if the window is open. The mode indicates the actual movement of the window, the position indicates how far the window is closed. The state mode = goin_up, position = 50 models the state of the window moving up in a situation where it is half closed.

The control input to the system and its output are given by the following two sets defined as follows:

Input = {open, close, stop}
Output = {open, closed, stopped, alarm, mov_up, mov_down}

The state transition function is defined as follows (here we write for any set M the set $M_+ = M \cup \{\varepsilon\}$ where ε stands for *no message*):

$$\Delta\text{: State} \times \text{Input}_+ \rightarrow \wp(\text{State} \times \text{Output}_+)$$

It is defined by a table that represents a formula that specifies the state transition function. The attributes of the next state are represented by mode′ and p′.

Table 1. State transitions

mode	p	input	mode′	p′	output
≠alarm		stop	stopped	=p	stopped
stopped		ε	stopped	=p	stopped
goin_down | stopped		close	goin_up	=p	mov_up
goin_up | stopped		open	goin_down	=p	mov_down
goin_up	=100	ε | close	stopped	=100	closed
goin_up	<100	ε | close	goin_up	>p	mov_up
goin_up			alarm	=p	alarm
goin_down	=0	ε | open	stopped	=0	open
goin_down	>0	ε | open	goin_down	<p	mov_down
alarm	>0		alarm	<p	alarm
alarm	=0		stopped	=0	open

The Table 1 defines the state transition relation by a disjunctive formula. Every line in the table defines an assertion. For instance, the following line

goin_up	=100	ε | close	stopped	=100	closed

represents the conjunctive formula:

$$\text{mode} = \text{goin\_up} \wedge \text{p} = 100 \wedge (\text{input} = \varepsilon \vee \text{input} = \text{close})$$
$$\wedge\, \text{mode}' = \text{stopped} \wedge \text{p}' = 100 \wedge \text{output} = \text{closed}$$

These conjunctive formulas represented by the lines of the table are connected by disjunction to deduce the formula that specifies the state transition from data.

Note that the state machine is highly nondeterministic since when moving up or down the speed is not fixed – it may jump an arbitrary distance.

In fact, it is straightforward to abstract the behavior of this state machine into an interface assertion between an input and an output stream. This way the state is abstracted away – we no longer have the information how the input and output streams are related to certain states of the physical system.

The specification of a relation represented by the function

$$\varphi\text{: State} \rightarrow ((\text{Stream Input} \times \text{Stream Output}) \rightarrow \text{IB})$$

that describes the specification of the behavior of the physical device is derived from the state transition function as follows

$$\varphi(\sigma)(\langle e\rangle\hat{\ }a, \langle r\rangle\hat{\ }b) = \exists\, \sigma' \in \text{State}: (\sigma', r) \in \Delta(\sigma, e) \wedge \varphi(\sigma')(a,\ b)$$

This example shows that we can model physical systems by state machines with input and output. Actually, it means that these state machines have input that at a technical level corresponds to signals to actuators, and that the physical systems produce output which – viewed from the software systems – are signals and messages that are generated by the sensors of the systems. As a result, we have a view onto a physical device as a system that produces given a stream of actuator messages streams of sensor signals. By the states of the state machines we can model the reaction of the physical devices at the physical level such that we can see what the effects of those input and output streams are.

In addition, we may introduce a model for a software system which controls the physical device, in our example the automatic window and form an architecture (see Fig. 6). We can prove properties both, about the automatic window, and about the system that consists of the controller which may get input from some user interfaces and controls the power window. To do so we may enrich the model by showing the stream of states. We define the function

$$\phi\text{: State} \rightarrow ((\text{Stream Input} \times \text{Stream Output} \times \text{Stream State}) \rightarrow \text{IB})$$

that describes the specification of the behavior of the physical device. It is derived from the state transition function as follows

$$\phi(\sigma)(\langle e\rangle\text{\^{}}a, \langle r\rangle\text{\^{}}b, \langle\sigma'\rangle\text{\^{}}s) = ((\sigma', r) \in \Delta(\sigma, e) \wedge \phi(\sigma')(a, b, s))$$

This way we get a stream of states that shows the modes and the positions of the physical system, in our example the automatic window, depending on the input stream a (Fig. 5).

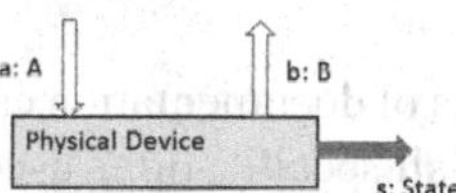

Fig. 5. Physical device, showing the stream of states

We may compose the physical device modelled by $\varphi(\sigma)(a, b)$ with initial state σ with the control layer described by CL and get the specification

$$CL(x, b, y, a) \wedge \varphi(\sigma)(a, b)$$

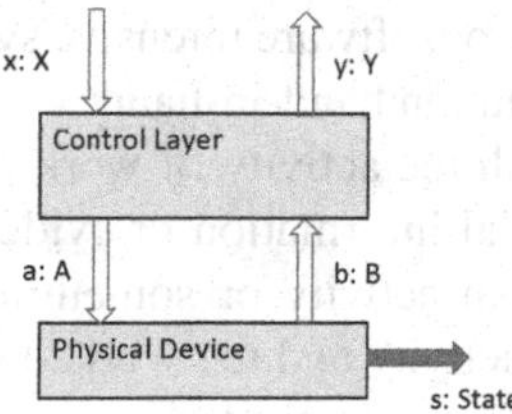

Fig. 6. Architecture of a control layer composed with a physical device and showing the stream of states

We get the interface assertion for the system in Fig. 6 where the behavior of the physical device is captured by the relation $\phi(\sigma_0)(a, b, s)$ where σ_0 is the initial state of the physical device as follows

$$\exists a, b: CL(x, b, y, a) \wedge \phi(\sigma_0)(a, b, s)$$

This way we specify the dependency between input x and the states of the physical device. We end up with a model based documentation of physical subsystems as they are part of cyber-physical systems.

4.5 Integrated Documentation – Semantic Coherence

What is demonstrated by our examples is the semantic coherence and how the different styles documentation fit together. We have used the following styles of specifications:

- the functionality is described by a specification template describing the syntactic interface and the system behavior by an interface assertion (see Sect. 4.1)
- the functionality can also be described by graphical means (see Fig. 3)
- the architecture can both be described by a composition operator on interface assertions as well as by graphical means (see Fig. 4)
- the behavior of a physical system can be described by a state machine with input and output (also software system can be specified that way)
- state machines with input and output can be transformed schematically into interface assertions.

This underlines how different styles of documentation can be used side-by-side and how they fit together. In our examples, all specifications used for documentation are logical in the end and can be used as a direct basis of verification.

5 Conclusion

As outlined, documentation is a very broad topic, at least, if we understand documentation in a very broad sense. Documentation includes the description of all properties of software systems that are relevant in software system development and usage.

Thus, talking about documentation requires talking about general system properties (see [2]) and ways to represent them. This is in the center of software and systems engineering. Developing software or software intensive systems therefore always means to develop code and its documentation hand-in-hand.

Documentation addresses both the activity of working out documents as well as a set of documents providing official information or evidence or that serves as a record describing a system, a process, an activity or something else. It is a term that indicates already the purpose of the activity and the worked out record – providing official information or evidence that serves as a record.

This indicates that the idea of modeling is at a different level. Modeling means abstraction by using concrete mostly predefined techniques and methods of description. Of course, documentation can be provided by giving models – and models can be documented. Nevertheless, these are notions at different levels: documentation indicates the purpose, the why, modelling indicates the technique of the description, the how. Models can be used in documentation, however, modelling may support further goals such es exploration, specification, or verification. And of course, there is documentation without modelling. As we stated in the introduction, documentation is to be consumed by humans. This does not necessarily apply to models. Models can be used to generate code, for instance, or in simulation and may other ways. Documentation has the connotation of official records of description.

References

1. Broy, M., Stølen, K.: Specification and Development of Interactive Systems: Focus on Streams, Interfaces, and Refinement. Springer, Berlin (2001). https://doi.org/10.1007/978-1-4613-0091-5
2. Broy, M.: Software and system modeling: structured multi-view modeling, specification, design and implementation. In: Hinchey, M., Coyle, L. (eds.) Conquering Complexity, pp. 309–372. Springer, London (2012). https://doi.org/10.1007/978-1-4471-2297-5_14
3. Broy, M.: A logical basis for component-oriented software and systems engineering. Comput. J. **53**(10), 1758–1782 (2010)
4. Broy, M.: A logical approach to systems engineering artifacts: semantic relationships and dependencies beyond traceability—from requirements to functional and architectural views. Softw. Syst. Model. **17**(2), 365–393 (2017). https://doi.org/10.1007/s10270-017-0619-4
5. Pohl, K., Broy, M., Daembkes, H., Hönninger, H.: Advanced model-based engineering of embedded systems. In: Pohl, K., Broy, M., Daembkes, H., Hönninger, H. (eds.) Advanced Model-Based Engineering of Embedded Systems, pp. 3–9. Springer, Cham (2016). https://doi.org/10.1007/978-3-319-48003-9_1
6. Ciupa, I., Pretschner, A., Oriol, M., Leitner, A., Meyer, B.: On the number and nature of faults found by random testing. Softw. Test. Verif. Reliab. **21**, 3–28 (2011)
7. Hoare, C.A.R.: Quicksort. Comput. J. **5**(1), 10–15 (1962)
8. Lockwood, Th.: Design Thinking: Integrating Innovation, Customer Experience and Brand Value. Allworth, New York (2010)
9. Méndez, F.D., et al.: Artefacts in software engineering: a fundamental positioning. Softw. Syst. Model. **18**(5), 2777–2786 (2019)
10. Parnas, D., Lawford, M.: The role of inspection in software quality assurance. IEEE Trans. Softw. Eng. **29**, 674–676 (2003)
11. Parnas, D.L.: Precise documentation: the key to better software. In: Nanz, S. (ed.) The Future of Software Engineering, pp. 125–148. Springer, Heidelberg (2011). https://doi.org/10.1007/978-3-642-15187-3_8
12. Parnas, D.L.: The secret history of information hiding. In: Broy, M., Denert, E. (eds.) Software Pioneers, pp. 398–409. Springer, Heidelberg (2002). https://doi.org/10.1007/978-3-642-59412-0_25
13. Schwaber, K., Beedle, M.: Agile Software Development with Scrum. Prentice Hall (2002)
14. Szyperski, C.: Component Software: Beyond Object-Oriented Programming, 2nd edn. Addison-Wesley Professional (2000)

Models as Documents, Documents as Models

Perdita Stevens(✉)

Laboratory for Foundations of Computer Science School of Informatics, University of Edinburgh, Edinburgh, UK
Perdita.Stevens@ed.ac.uk
http://homepages.inf.ed.ac.uk/perdita

Abstract. In software engineering, documentation and models are both broad concepts which attract varying approaches and attitudes. Moreover, as the title indicates, they overlap: in some circumstances, an artefact thought of as a model can serve to document a software project, while in others, an artefact thought of as a document can be manipulated by model-driven engineering tools just like any other kind of model. In this short paper we briefly explore these issues and provide pointers to some of the relevant literature.

Keywords: Documentation · Programming · Modelling

1 Introduction

What most software developers today think of as a "document" in software development, and what they think of as a "model", bear little resemblance to one another. The canonical document in today's practice is word-processed; it has a narrative structure, being intended to be read, at least initially, from beginning to end; and its intended consumers are humans, not machines. The canonical model is developed in a drawing tool or a specialised modelling tool, or perhaps is sketched on a whiteboard; it is graphical, making essential use of a two-dimensional canvas, and its elements are often capable of being apprehended in many orders; and depending on its form, its intended consumers may be tools, as well as humans.

Unfortunately, in writing that opening paragraph, I have already made steam start to curl out of the ears of some readers, whose ideas of "document", "model", or both, are different from the ideas I am intending to invoke. A reviewer asked for precise definitions of the terms: while on the surface the request is reasonable, I fear that it would be sterile to attempt to meet it. When we ask ourselves what documents and models are, and – crucially – what they are for, we find that there is a great overlap between the two concepts; indeed, both the positions "every document is a model" and "every model is a document" will turn out to be arguable.

T. Margaria and B. Steffen (Eds.): ISoLA 2022, LNCS 13702, pp. 28–34, 2022.
https://doi.org/10.1007/978-3-031-19756-7_3

This short paper, intended to accompany an expository talk, does not purport to present original research. Instead, we explore the similarities and differences between the connotations of the terms "document" and "model", and draw attention to some of the work that has already been done making use of the connections between the two concepts. Further pointers and comments would be very welcome.

2 The Purposes of Software Modelling

Modelling has been used within the process of software development, since the earliest days, as a means of controlling the information overload that otherwise prevents human software developers from effectively making decisions about how to build the software (see [17] for one interesting early example). Indeed some of the models that have been most commonly used with software pre-date the idea of computer software: flow charts, for example.

The key point about a model is that it presents all of, and ideally only, the information that is necessary for some particular purpose. Although this has arguably been the case since the earliest days of graphical modelling, it has become more important as the increasing scale of software development has made separation of concerns essential: key decisions must be taken safely, without requiring the decision-maker to understand everything about the software. (We will return to the implications of this for automation momentarily.) The purpose might be the support of any software engineering process, including requirements management, architecture, detailed design, verification, etc. For example, a flow chart (or activity graph) might show how one important process is to be carried out by the software, but abstract away from how the software is structured. On the other hand an architecture diagram might show the high level packages into which a large software system is split, without giving any information about the behaviour to be coded in each package.

When software developers talk about "models", we should usually understand a *graphical* representation of some aspect of a software system, perhaps placed within its environment. Latterly, especially with the formalisation and codification of techniques such as metamodelling for defining and manipulating models, it has become clear that it does not matter very much whether a model is graphical or textual: this is a matter of concrete syntax, and it is often useful to separate concrete syntax conceptually from abstract syntax and from semantics. This observation is a key part of what makes "model" and "document" overlap.

Models were originally used in software development for informal communication purposes between humans. The idea that they could be formal was relatively late to arrive: in 1976, Chen felt the need to emphasise that a graphical representation of an entity-relationship model could be isomorphic to a symbolic one [4]. This conception of graphical models as essentially informal is natural given many other human relationships with pictures: originally, and often still today, a model is seen as an informal aid to understanding of what the corresponding formal artefact, the code which is actually used to instruct the computer, should do. However, there are advantages to making a graphical notation precise, and indeed, once it is normal for a software development to involve separated representations of different concerns, and for there to be nobody who can understand every detail simultaneously, it becomes almost essential to have tool support for the tasks of relating models to one another and to the code. Once the code is materially affected by *precisely* what is in the model – and it no longer matters what the human who drew the model hand-waved while drawing it – the model has become, in a certain sense, a formal artefact. Thus we reach modern conceptions of model-driven development, in which models are related by model transformations and code is (in part or in whole) generated from models, and related approaches such as language-driven engineering [15].

3 The Purposes of Software Documentation

Documentation, broadly conceived, serves a number of processes within software development [1]. We will limit scope to documents that relate somewhat directly to the software – they describe or constrain its usage, structure, functionality, or development.

For us, then, a document in some sense *specifies* the software or part of its structure or function. Typically it records the result of some software engineering process, more than supporting the doing of that process – even if its purpose is then to support a downstream process. It may support:

- communication within the software project, e.g. clarifying the API of a component to both implementers and users of the component
- verification, validation and testing, e.g. when what software actually does is compared with what a document says it should do
- maintenance, e.g. by explaining to a future human developer what decisions have been taken by the original developers and why
- use of the software, e.g. by explaining to a human reader how to interact with the software to achieve some aim
- litigation, e.g. demonstrating that the software developers have not delivered what they were contractually obliged to deliver.

4 What Counts as a Model?

We have already mentioned that models may be formal or informal, graphical or textual. The reader may reasonably wonder what would *not* count as a model and indeed the author has often proclaimed "everything's a model!". For our purposes today, a model is an artefact which records all, and preferably only, the information necessary for some decision-making purpose relating to a software development.

As is by now apparent, in this paper "model" typically indicates a prescriptive model of the kind used in model-based or model-driven development, rather than a descriptive, mathematical model. The distinction between prescriptive and descriptive models can become blurred – after all, if a prescriptive model is correctly followed, so that it prescribes something about a resulting system, we expect that same model now describes something about that system, i.e., can now be regarded as a descriptive model. However, the primary purpose of models within model-driven development is prescriptive: descriptions don't drive things!

5 What Counts as a Document?

The prototypical "document" in software development is written using a word processor, e.g. Microsoft Word. The term "documentation" has broader connotations, and might include, for example, the in-program "Help" text a user can access. For purposes of this paper, key characteristics are:

- a document is intended to be read by humans, typically by a predicted class of humans with predictable background knowledge, e.g., developers, users;
- a document is relatively long-lived, typically having a lifetime that is commensurate with that of the software to which it relates; we would normally consider the minutes of a design meeting to be too ephemeral to count as documentation, for example.

Within these bounds, there are possibilities other than the prototypical Word document, differing especially in how long-lived human-readable text is structured and perhaps entwined with other software artefacts such as code. For example, comments within the code might well be considered to be documentation, especially if, as with JavaDoc, they are structured for extraction. By considering JML text embedded within programs, and indeed "self-documenting code", where code is considered to be so clearly written that it does not require comments or other form of documentation, we see the blurred edges of this concept: a key point is that not all humans are the same and so "human-readable" often has to be qualified with which humans are the intended readers.

6 Models as Documents

Martin Fowler's seminal classification of the uses of UML as sketch, as blueprint, and as programming language [10] gives a suitable setting in which to discuss when models can be seen as documents. Within this setting, it is the second mode, models as blueprints, which is most convincing.

When models are used purely informally, as sketches, for example on a whiteboard, they will fail our second criterion for documents. Being produced to support a particular discussion, they will be ephemeral.

On the other hand, when a modelling language like UML is used as a programming language – by which Fowler meant, when the model becomes fully detailed *and* is used as input to tools – the model may fail our first criterion. The model is to be read by a tool, and there is a danger that in order to make it amenable to being read by a tool its readability by humans is reduced. We say "may" because the premise of model-driven engineering is that this is not the inevitable result of using models that can be processed by tools. It is important to note, here, that Fowler was writing not about all modelling languages but specifically about UML, in a context where UML2.0 was emerging.

The middle use, models as blueprints, gives "a way to express software designs in such a way that the designs can be handed off to a separate group to write the code, much as blueprints are used in building bridges" [9]. The model documents the intended design, and the document is then read by the human programmer. The models thus produced might, indeed, be printed in the specification documents alongside explanatory text (this was a standard part of the ISO9000 process of the organisation the author worked for in the early 1990s). The problem is that one may end up with what John Daniels memorably called "the Great Corporate Data Modeling Fiasco" [6] – a model which contains so many details that it is readable, and maintainable, by nobody and nothing. The lesson here is that some models need to be more than documents: only rather simple software engineering artefacts can sensibly be long-lived, if they are only readable by humans and not by tools.

7 Documents as Models

The idea that documents can usefully have structure which can then be exploited to use the document effectively is an old one. In the W3 standard, DOM stands for "document object model" although use of this standard is usually within the context of a program or model, rather than anything normally thought of as a document. Files following the DOM format are not easy for humans to read (or write); in that sense they are not really documents in the sense we have laid out. Readers may also think of the standard DTD, "document type definition", which preceded XML schema as a way to specify how an XML document should be structured. This, similarly, uses "document" in a broad sense, more usually applied to artefacts we would think of as models than to documentation.

Already a decade ago, Erisson, Wingkvist and Löwe were concerned about the variable quality of traditional technical documentation, which they found frequently to involve many clones (or near-clones) of text passages, leading to maintenance difficulties and error-prone-ness. Their paper [8] exploits metamodelling techniques to propose a software infrastructure for assessing and improving the quality of technical documentation.

Other work in this vein, which starts with a document, and produces from it a descriptive model for purposes of analysis or remediation, starts to stray out of our declared scope, but is nonetheless interesting. Before leaving behind this field we mention work on the modelling of contracts [3] and on privacy conditions of websites [7,16]. However, to pursue this avenue would take us too far afield, into natural language processing.

Returning to central documentation of software, we should consider the OpenAPI standard (also known as Swagger). OpenAPI descriptions document application programmer's interfaces of components in standardised, plain text which, it is claimed, can be easily read and written by human developers using any text editor. A key part of how OpenAPI is marketed is that an API description in this format can also be used as input to a tool.

The team contrast "code first" and "design first" approaches and advocate the latter: that is, the idea is that the OpenAPI document should be developed first, before the code that implements the API. There is a small academic literature amplifying this; David Sferruzza is prominent among researchers who have investigated using OpenAPI descriptions as sources from which to generate web services [13,14].

A problem is that OpenAPI API descriptions often fail to follow the format properly (e.g. as analysed by Ralphson [12]) or include content that is inadvisable from a security point of view [5]. It might be argued that any editing that a human is allowed to do, they will do: because the files are designed to be readable, and writable, by unassisted humans, such errors creeping in is unsurprising. The same could be said about ordinary programs, which are typically built in a text editor; but the compiler or interpreter normally catches such problems, and programmers are used to this. The lesson here is that blurring the line between human- and machine-readable text increases the risk of failing to achieve either.

An alternative approach is to make more central use of artificial intelligence to bridge the gap between a specification that is natural for a human to write, and an implementation; a recently famous example is GitHub Copilot[1], but the problems of naively adopting this technology have been well rehearsed [2,11].

8 Conclusions

In this short paper we have suggested that there are overlapping intentions and purposes of documents and of models, which have more in common with one another than either does with programs.

What implications does this have for the future of programming? Most importantly, researchers and practitioners concerned with either models or documents should pay heed to advances that concern the other class of artefacts. There is, for example, scope for model-driven engineering to pay more attention specifically to documents, and to how documents interrelate with "other models".

Acknowledgements. I thank the anonymous reviewers for insightful comments, questions and pointers to relevant literature.

References

1. Aghajani, E., et al.: Software documentation: the practitioners' perspective. In: Rothermel, G., Bae, D.-H. (eds.) ICSE 2020: 42nd International Conference on Software Engineering, Seoul, South Korea, June 27 - July 19 2020, pp. 590–601. ACM (2020)

[1] https://copilot.github.com/.

2. Anderson, T., Quach, K.: GitHub copilot auto-coder snags emerge, from seemingly spilled secrets to bad code, but some love it. https://www.theregister.com/2021/07/06/github_copilot_autocoder_caught_spilling/ (2021)
3. Camilleri, J.J., Schneider, G.: Modelling and analysis of normative documents. J. Log. Algebraic Methods Program. **91**, 33–59 (2017)
4. Chen, P.P.: The entity-relationship model - toward a unified view of data. ACM Trans. Database Syst. **1**(1), 9–36 (1976)
5. Cybersprint: Swagger API: discovery of API data and security flaws. https://www.cybersprint.com/blog/swagger-api-discovery-of-api-data-and-security-flaws (2020)
6. Daniels, J.: Modeling with a sense of purpose. IEEE Softw. **19**(1), 8–10 (2002)
7. de Jong, M., et al.: Terms of service; didn't read. https://tosdr.org/ (2011)
8. Ericsson, M., Wingkvist, A., Löwe, W.: The design and implementation of a software infrastructure for IQ assessment. Int. J. Inf. Qual. **3**(1), 49–70 (2012)
9. Fowler, M.: UmlAsBlueprint. https://martinfowler.com/bliki/UmlAsBlueprint.html (2003)
10. Fowler, M.: UmlMode. https://martinfowler.com/bliki/UmlMode.html (2003)
11. Howard, J.: Is github copilot a blessing, or a curse? https://www.fast.ai/2021/07/19/copilot/ (2021)
12. Ralphson, M.: What we learned from 200,000 OpenAPI files. https://blog.postman.com/what-we-learned-from-200000-openapi-files/ (2021)
13. Sferruzza, D.: Plateforme extensible de modélisation et de construction d'applications web correctes et évolutives, avec hypothèse de variabilité. (Towards an extensible framework for modelling and implementing correct and evolutive web applications, under variability hypothesis), Ph. D thesis, University of Nantes, France (2018)
14. Sferruzza, D.: Top-down model-driven engineering of web services from extended OpenAPI models. In: Huchard, M., Kästner, C., Fraser, G. (eds.) Proceedings of the 33rd ACM/IEEE International Conference on Automated Software Engineering, ASE 2018, Montpellier, France, 3–7 September 2018, pp. 940–943. ACM (2018)
15. Steffen, B., Gossen, F., Naujokat, S., Margaria, T.: Language-driven engineering: from general-purpose to purpose-specific languages. In: Steffen, B., Woeginger, G. (eds.) Computing and Software Science. LNCS, vol. 10000, pp. 311–344. Springer, Cham (2019). https://doi.org/10.1007/978-3-319-91908-9_17
16. Wilson, S., et al.: The creation and analysis of a website privacy policy corpus. In: Proceedings of the 54th Annual Meeting of the Association for Computational Linguistics, ACL 2016, 7–12 August 2016, Berlin, Germany, vol. 1: Long Papers. The Association for Computer Linguistics (2016)
17. Zurcher, F.W., Randell, B.: Iterative multi-level modelling. a methodology for computer system design. In: Morrel, A.J.H., (ed.) Information Processing, Proceedings of IFIP Congress 1968, Edinburgh, UK, 5–10 August 1968, vol. 2 - Hardware, Applications, pp. 867–871 (1968)

Using Supplementary Properties to Reduce the Need for Documentation

Ole Lehrmann Madsen[1(✉)] and Birger Møller-Pedersen[2]

[1] Department of Computer Science, Aarhus University, Aarhus C, Denmark
olm@cs.au.dk
[2] Department of Informatics, University of Oslo, Oslo, Norway
birger@ifi.uio.no

Abstract. The purpose of programming languages is to instruct computers and to communicate descriptions of computational processes among people. However, a program has to be supplemented by additional documentation using natural language, diagrams, specifications, models, etc. that also serve the purpose of supporting design and validation. A number of languages have been developed for this purpose, with the cost of having to maintain several descriptions. In this paper, we describe how to include supplementary properties in a programming language to reduce the need for additional languages and to reduce the need for additional documentation. Supplementary properties may restrict access to global variables, enforce restrictions on subclasses, specify required interfaces of modules, etc.

Keywords: Modeling · Programming · Languages · Documentation

From the Algol 60 report:
Was sich überhaupt sagen läßt, läßt sich klar sagen;
und wovon man nicht reden kann, darüber muß man schweigen.
Ludwig Wittgenstein

1 Introduction

Most programming languages serve two purposes: (1) being languages for instructing a computer, (2) being languages for communicating descriptions of computational processes. As early as in 1963 (and in the work that led to Algol 60) the Algol Report [1] recognized that the language definition should include a Publication Language meant for the purpose of communication as expressed by the quote of Wittgenstein.

For SIMULA [2] this was manifested in SIMULA being a language for modeling as well as for programming. This was further pursued in Beta [3], with the mantra "To program is to understand" – a program should reflect the concepts and phenomena of the application domain and thereby contribute to a better understanding of the domain. This is why we advocate a unified language for modeling and programming [4] – we think that *Programming is modeling*, and in the rest of this paper the term programming also covers modeling.

T. Margaria and B. Steffen (Eds.): ISoLA 2022, LNCS 13702, pp. 35–59, 2022.
https://doi.org/10.1007/978-3-031-19756-7_4

Programming languages have limited expressive power. In most cases the code has to be supplemented by documentation in the form of comments and additional documents using descriptions in natural language, formal and informal diagrams, formal specifications, etc. Documentation takes over when the programming language falls short. In the ideal programming language, you can express all relevant properties of the program in an understandable way and there will thus be no need for additional documentation. A problem with documentation in general is that there is no immediate benefit for programmers to make documentation and keeping it up to date.

Formal and informal models are among others useful for improving the understandability of a program. Modeling is an approach for designing a system by focusing on identifying relevant phenomena and concepts from a given application domain and representing these as classes, objects, process descriptions, and functionality descriptions. Models among others serve the purpose of focusing on the essential properties of a given system, and it is often used for communication. Object-oriented modeling is an example of a technique for defining models and formal specifications based on mathematics is another example. Models whether it be object-oriented models or formal specifications also serve a purpose as documentation of a given system, but compared to natural language descriptions, such models are structured and (semi-) formal.

Object-oriented programming and modeling implied a major step in the expressiveness of imperative languages with respect to representing phenomena and concepts from the application domain. In addition, object-oriented models reduced the need for additional documentation. Formal specifications make it possible to prove properties of a program and this also reduce the need for additional documentation.

JML [5, 6] is an example of a tool that support formal specifications and the form of an extended version of design by contract as in Eiffel [7].

As for natural language documentation, models and formal specifications must be kept up to date to be useful, but often when the program evolves, the models are left behind and become obsolete. JavaDoc [8], and other similar tools add structured comments to Java programs and use them for producing documentation. It is of course useful to be able write documentation as part of the program, but since it is in the form of comments, it requires an effort to keep it up to date.

In the Scandinavian approach to object-orientation, with SIMULA and Beta, the intention has been to use the same language for both modeling and programming, with programs as the primary artifacts. This is in contrast to current state of art where different languages are used for modeling and programming. UML [9] may typically be used for modeling whereas programming languages like C++ [10], Java [11], C# [12], and Python [13] are used for implementation. The benefit of a unified language is that the model is always up to date, see [3, 4, 14, 15].

Recently Broy et al. [15] have argued that that modern programming languages exemplified by Scala [16] can express the same as traditional specification languages like VDM++ [17, 18] except for the parts of VDM++ that are not executable. So also for specification there is no need for separate languages.

There are of course aspects/properties of a given system/application that may not be expressed even in a unified modeling and programming language but require a different kind of modeling language such as Petri Nets. If there is a quest for a separate modeling language, such a language should be able to describe other properties than those that can be described in a programming language, and tools must ensure that the different descriptions are consistent.

The current available abstraction mechanisms in programming languages are limited with respect to describing intensional properties of phenomena and concepts of a given application domain. We describe these limitations in Sect. 2.

The *challenge* we consider in this paper is therefore to extend the expressive power of programming languages for describing intensional properties, and thereby reduce the need for documentation. In Sect. 3, we show how to use *supplementary properties* to describe intensional properties. Supplementary properties may be associated with a class or method and describe properties in the form of constraints for the class (and method) and possible subclasses (and submethods). Supplementary properties may be checked by the compiler and thus provide an immediate benefit for the programmer. The details of supplementary properties are provided in Sect. 4.

As an example, supplementary properties may be used to restrict access to global variables, enforce restrictions on the interface in a subclass of a given class, and e.g. be used to define safe concurrency abstractions. Supplementary properties may also be used to define provided and required interfaces of modules as in architecture description languages.

As we discuss in Sect. 6, supplementary properties extend the expressive power of the language, but there may still be a need for additional mechanisms.

Supplementary properties are a further development of subpattern restrictions as presented in [19] and have been implemented in qBeta, which is an object-oriented language derived from Beta. Supplementary properties may, however, be added to any class-based language.

2 The Limitations of Abstraction Mechanisms

In the development of our understanding of complex phenomena, the most powerful tool available to the human intellect is abstraction.
– Tony Hoare: Notes on Data Structuring [20].

As mentioned in the introduction, we consider programming to be modeling, and the program must reflect phenomena and concepts from the application domain. The more directly these are reflected in the program the easier it is to understand and the less need there is for additional documentation.

Objects, properties of objects and action sequences carried out by active objects (concurrent objects), and execution of methods represent phenomena from the application domain. Abstraction mechanisms like class, type, function, method, etc. are used to represent concepts from the application domain, see Chapter 18 in [3].

The expressiveness of abstraction mechanisms of a given language sets the limits for the kind of (intensional) properties that can be described and thus represented in a program. In this section, we discuss limitations of a number of abstractions mechanisms describing properties of phenomena and concepts that otherwise must be described in additional documentation.

2.1 Classification and the Class Mechanism

A class may model/represent a concept from a given application domain [3]. The *extension* of a concept is the set of phenomena covered by the concept – the instances (objects) of a given class may thus be considered a model/representation of the extension of the concept.

The *intension* of a concept is the set of properties characterizing phenomena belonging to the concept – the attributes and structure of a given class may thus be considered a representation of the intension of the concept being modeled.

All object-oriented languages have limited mechanisms for describing the intension, and part of the intension is often implicit in the sense that a class/method is supposed to be used in a specific way that is 'just' formulated informally in the documentation – protocols, etc.

In the original version of SIMULA, you may define the properties of a class of objects in terms of the data-items (simple values and references to object) and (virtual and non-virtual) methods of the objects, arguments to classes and methods, etc. Properties such as relations between objects, behavioral properties, and other intensional properties may only be expressed to a limited extent.

Subclass substitutability was the intention behind SIMULA, later followed up by Liskov et al. [21]. It is an example of an intensional property that cannot be enforced by a SIMULA compiler – or by a compiler for any object-oriented language.

The power of the class/subclass mechanism is that a given superclass describes properties (in terms of data-items and methods) that are imposed for all its subclasses – instances of a subclass have all the attributes described in the superclass.

Since the advent of the class/subclass mechanism in SIMULA a number of new language mechanisms have been proposed to describe the intension of a given class.

In the ground-breaking paper by Hoare [22] the notion of abstract data types including invariants and pre- and post-conditions were proposed and the SIMULA class mechanism was used for defining such abstract data types. In order to protect the representation of an abstract data type, Palme [23] proposed to extend SIMULA with the protection mechanisms public, private and protected - and these have later been adopted by mainstream languages such as C++, Java, and C#.

2.2 Limitations in Describing Concurrent Processes

In concurrent programming it is well known that data structures shared by two or more concurrent processes easily leads to race conditions and other problems. Many programming languages include abstraction mechanisms that prevent concurrent processes from accessing the same data without synchronization – these include Concurrent Pascal [24], CSP [25], and Actor-based languages like Erlang [26].

This is not the case for mainstream object-oriented languages. As pointed out by Brinch Hansen [27], a language like Java is inherently insecure with respect to race-conditions, and as stated in [19], this is the case for most other object-oriented languages like C++, C#, and Beta.

We agree with Brinch Hansen that for a concurrent programming language, the most important security measure is to check that processes access disjoint sets of variables only and do not interfere with each other in time-dependent ways. Safety in the sense of Brinch Hansen is an example of an intensional property that is not supported by modern mainstream object-oriented languages such as C++, Java and C#. The synchronized mechanism in Java supports monitor-like behavior, but due to aliasing two or more tasks may access the same objects. In addition, a programmer may forget to annotate a method as synchronized.

In Beta, it is possible to define concurrency abstractions such as monitor, but they have the same deficiencies with respect to safety as Java, C++ and C#. In the design of Beta, there was a tradeoff between the generality and flexibility of the basic abstraction mechanisms and safety; flexibility and generality were preferred at the expense of being able to define safe concurrency abstractions. Thus, all concurrency abstractions defined in Beta are inherently unsafe. In [19], Madsen addressed this problem using subclass restrictions.

2.3 Mechanisms for Describing Architecture of Systems

An important part of documentation is the documentation of the *architecture* of a system. Architecture Description Languages (ADLs) e.g. AADL [28], have been defined for this purpose, but also for analysis of how architecture has implications for certain (non-functional) properties of systems. There are many different kinds of ADLs. Clements et al. [29] have categorized the mechanisms of ADLs in three views:

- Module: how code and other kinds of descriptions are organized, with mechanisms for *composition*, *generalization* and *specialization*, modules *using* other modules, and *layering* of modules.
- Component connector: computational entities and how they communicate, with mechanisms for interfaces (*provided/required*) and connectors. A component *provides* properties to other components, while other components *require* which properties are needed from other components.
- Allocation: work assignment, deployment, organization of modules in files.

The fact that there has been a need for separate languages for describing architecture shows a limitation of the expressive power of programming languages. In a unified language for modeling and programming it should also be possible to describe the architecture, by language mechanisms similar to those proposed for ADLs.

We are primarily looking for architecture-specific extensions of programming languages; we are therefore not considering e.g. work assignment, and we are not looking for mechanisms already supported by languages.

Most object-oriented languages have support for composition, generalization and specialization by means of mechanisms for describing objects and classes/subclasses, and they have objects as the components. Packages (with import or similar) in some respect support the use of modules and the organization of modules in file systems.

Provided interfaces on components correspond to interfaces or just public properties of objects in object-oriented languages; however, few languages have support for required properties and for special connectors between objects beyond references between objects. The actual modules being required are only implicitly defined in the statement parts of the methods of a given class in the form of invocation of methods in external objects.

2.4 Representative/Non-representative Aspects/Parts of Programs

In our approach, a program execution is a model [4, 30, 31]. A model has elements that represent phenomena from the application domain; a program execution being a library system will e.g. have objects That represent phenomena like books, loans, persons, etc. A program therefore contains elements that describe model elements that represent these phenomena; and it contains elements (classes) that similarly describe model elements that represent the corresponding domain concepts.

Programs will, however, also contain elements that do *not* represent elements of the domain. In a program that describe a library system there will be elements that implement an efficient storing of book objects using databases and/or hash tables that ensures fast search for books. Databases and hash tables are examples of technical domains and the program elements implementing these domains also consists of a representative part (often the API) and non-representative part.

The various domains, including the application domain and the technical domains must be kept separate from each other just as a distinction between the representative and non-representative part of each domain is necessary. This put requirements on the abstraction and modularization mechanisms of the programming language and the associated tools. It is especially important that the representative part of the application domain model can be identified/showed.

3 The Essentials of Supplementary Properties

In Sect. 2, we discussed the limitations of language mechanisms for describing intensional properties of objects and classes of objects. This section describes a further development of the notion of subclass restrictions as proposed by Madsen in [19] for describing intensional properties.

SIMULA introduced a mechanism for defining subclasses of a given (super-)class and the notion of qualified reference variable. Any instance of a subclass also belongs to the superclass, and a reference qualified by a class may refer instances of all subclasses of the class. Instances of a subclass may thus replace instances of the superclass and a subclass is supposed to be behavioral compatible with the superclass.

As mentioned in Sect. 2.1, subclass substitutability cannot be enforced by a compiler. The rationale behind supplementary properties is to be able to describe properties of a class that can be enforced on the class and/or its subclasses, however, this does not support full subclass substitutability.

A class description extended with supplementary properties that add additional properties and/or restrictions to the class and/or its subclasses may often replace documentation. With subclass restrictions, the programmer defines restrictions that make the class function as a wrapper for all of its subclasses, and thus avoid annotations of its subclasses.

3.1 Accessing Global Variables

As an example, consider block-structure (nested classes and methods). Block-structure is a powerful mechanism for grouping related classes and methods. Methods may in general access global variables in the enclosing scope. These include variables in the class containing the method. In the case of general block-structure, it also includes variables defined in outer scopes. Similarly, inner classes may access variable in the enclosing scopes. This is in general a convenient feature.

Unrestricted access to global variables is especially a problem in the case of concurrent processes – two or more concurrent processes should not access the same global variables. But also in the sequential case, it might a problem with unrestricted access to global variables.

Using the `%globals` property it is possible to restrict the type of variables that may be accessed by an object. A simple example is the definition of a function method that prohibits access to global variables:

```
function:
    %globals
    inner(function)
```

The `%globals` property defines the globals that may be accessed by the method. Since none are listed in the `%globals` above, no globals can be accessed in `function` and submethods of `function`. A submethod of `function` may be defined as follows:

```
sqrt: function
   ...
```

The `%globals` restriction is imposed on `sqrt`, which means that no globals may be accessed in `sqrt`. It is, however, possible to access methods and classes that are also restricted by `%globals` with an empty argument list. A submethod thus behave like a function in the sense that its return value only depends on its input arguments.

As another example, consider a Producer process, which we want to prevent accessing global variables other than references to objects of class Monitor (class Monitor is described in Sect. 3.2 below) and references to immutable objects:

```
Producer: obj Process
    %globals Monitor, immutable
    ...
    Buffer.put(exp)
    ...
```

In this example, the Buffer object is a subobject of Monitor, declared as follows:

```
Buffer: obj Monitor
    put: ...
    get: ...
```

so the Producer object is allowed to access the Buffer object.

The Producer has Process as a superclass, and if we associate the %globals property with class Process:

```
class Process:
    %globals Monitor, immutable
    ...
    inner(Process)
    ...
```

then the restriction is imposed on all subclasses of Process, e.g. Producer:

```
Producer: obj Process
    ...
    Buffer.put(exp)
    ...
```

Producer inherits the %globals restriction imposed on class Process.

The examples above are written in a language qBeta derived from Beta. The Producer and Buffer are examples of singular objects that are not instances of classes. The statements in class Process are combined with the statements in Producer using **inner** as in Beta. We provide details of qBeta, including singular objects and **inner** in Sect. 4.

3.2 Enforcing Interface Restrictions

A more elaborate example is the definition of class `Monitor` as shown below. As mentioned in Sect. 2, Java and Beta are not safe with respect to race conditions.

```
class Monitor:
    S: obj Semaphore
    entry:
        S.wait
        inner(entry)
        S.signal
    inner(Monitor)
```

```
Buffer: obj Monitor
    L: ref List
    put: entry
        in v: var integer
        ...
        L.put(V)
    get: entry
        out v: var integer
        ...
        v := L.get
    L := List(integer)
```

The methods `put` and `get` of the `Buffer` inherits from `entry`, based on inheritance for methods as in Beta [3, 32] – `entry` is thus a supermethod for `put` and `get`. This guarantees exclusive access to the data-items (in this case `L`) in the buffer, as `S.wait` is executed before and `S.signal` is executed after the statements of `put` and `get`. The details are explained in Sect. 4.

The method `entry` plays a similar role to synchronized in Java. However, if the Java programmer forgets to write synchronized or the Beta programmer forgets to use `entry` as a supermethod, the exclusiveness is broken.

To ensure exclusiveness, we need to be able to specify that:

- All public methods of subclasses of `Monitor` must inherit from `entry`.
- A subclass of `Monitor` (here `Buffer`) may not be able to access global variables.
- The arguments of public `entry`-methods must be variables representing *values*, references to *immutable* objects and/or references to *unique* objects.
- Variables representing values (`v` in `put` and `get`) are passed by means of *value assignment*, which means that two or more processes cannot have a reference to the same value object. The state of immutable objects cannot be changed, and unique objects have the property that there is at any time at most one reference to such an object. Further details are described in Sect. 4.

We may specify these properties using supplementary properties as shown below:

```
class Monitor:
    %globals
    %interface entry
    entry:
        %signature value, immutable, unique
        ...
    ...
```

1. The `%globals` property with an empty argument list specifies that no global variables may be accessed from within a `Monitor` object.
2. The `%interface` property specifies that all public methods of a `Monitor` and subclasses of `Monitor` must inherit from `entry`.
3. The `%signature` property of `entry` specifies that arguments of `entry`-methods must be variables representing values, references to immutable objects or references to unique objects.

With these supplementary properties, it is possible for the compiler to check that all subclasses of `Monitor` obey the specified restrictions, and thereby mutual access to data-items in `Monitor` objects is guaranteed.

In practice class `Monitor` will be defined as part of a concurrency framework for implementing concurrent processes that communicate and synchronize using monitors. The qBeta library contains a number of similar concurrency frameworks and in [19, 33] other examples may be found. The advantage of this approach is that it is possible to define a broad variety of safe concurrency abstractions that address different kinds of applications. The burden of defining the concurrency abstractions is put on the designer of the framework, but when a given concurrency framework is defined it may be used in a safe way by many users.

3.3 Provided and Required Properties

As mentioned in Sect. 2.3, the provides-clause of ADLs corresponds to the public interface of classes and singular objects. For qBeta, we have added a `%requires` property that corresponds to a required-clause.

In qBeta, a *module* is a description of a singular object in the form of a program text. Modules may thus also have a public interface corresponding to provides-clause as well as one or more requires-clauses.

A singular object generated from a module is called a *module object*. Modules are organized in a hierarchy of nested modules that follow the general mechanism of nesting in qBeta. The top-level module is a description of a singular object, but nested modules may be singular objects or instances of classes. The nested structure of modules has similarities to nested packages in Java – we return to this in Sect. 4.

In the following, we describe a simple example using modules containing producers and consumers communicating via a buffer. A class `Buffer` is defined as a subclass of `Monitor` and defined in a `BufferModule`. `Producer` and `Consumer` are defined as classes in a `ProducerModule` and `ConsumerModule`, respectively.

As mentioned above, `%public` is similar to the provided-clause of ADLs, and in general for object-oriented languages the required modules and interfaces of these are only implicitly defined by inspecting the code of the module.

In qBeta, it is possible to specify a %requires clause that specifies a list of modules that a given module depends on. The list is exclusive in the sense that only modules appearing in the list may be used.

```
BufferModule: module
   %requires MonitorSystem
   %public
   class Buffer: MonitorSystem.Monitor
      %public
      put:< entry ...
      get:< entry ...
      ...
   class BoundedBuffer: Buffer
      in size: var integer
      ...
   class VariableSizedBuffer: Buffer
      ...
   ...
   %private
   ...
```

The module BufferModule has a %requires MonitorSystem that specifies that MonitorSystem is the only module being used in the BufferModule.

Class Buffer in BufferModule is an abstract class with virtual (:<) methods put and get and used as a superclass for BoundedBuffer and Variable-LengthBuffer. The methods put and get are *extended* in BoundedBuffer and VariableSizedBuffer. In Beta and qBeta a virtual is not redefined but extended – see Sect. 4 for details.

The modules ProducerModule and ConsumerModule both have a %requires BufferModule, MonitorSystem, which means that they depend on these modules.

```
ProducerModule: module
   %requires BufferModule,MonitorSystem
   %public
   class Producer: MonitorSystem.Process
      in b: ref BufferModule.Buffer
      ...
   %private
   ...
```

The actual *'connection'* of a Buffer to a Producer and a Consumer is made via the input argument (in b:...) of class Producer and class Consumer.

As can been seen, elements in required modules are accessed by remote names like MonitorSystem.Monitor and ProducerModule.Producer.

As for modules and packages in other languages, it is possible to make declarations in a module visible without using remote names. In qBeta this may be specified using the %visible property.

```
ConsumerModule: module
   %requires BufferModule,MonitorSystem
   %public
   class Consumer: MonitorSystem.Process
      in b: ref BufferModule.Buffer
      ...
   %private
   ...
```

The above modules are used by the ProducerConsumerSystem below. A BoundedBuffer object B of length 10 is generated and passed as a parameter to a Producer object, P and a Consumer object, C. The example also illustrates the use of %visible:

```
ProducerConsumerSystem: module
   %requires BufferModule, ProducerModule, ConsumerModule
   %visible BufferModule, ProducerModule, ConsumerModule
   B: obj BoundedBuffer(10)
   P: obj Producer(B)
   C: obj Consumer(B)
   ...
```

The `%visible` property is similar to import/include-directives in other languages in the sense that it makes declarations in the listed modules available in the scope of the `%visible`. The `%visible` property in `ProducerConsumerSystem` thus makes `BoundedBuffer, Producer`, and`Consumer` visible in the module.

The `ProducerConsumerSystem` is a description of how elements from the three modules are connected and in this way corresponds to language elements in some ADLs for specifying how modules are connected. Possible `%requires` properties will become part of the external interface of a given module together with declarations marked as public and then of course also part of the documentation of the interface.

In a realistic example, each module may contain other classes and other declarations in addition to the three `Buffer` classes and similarly for the `ProducerModule` and `ConsumerModule`. In addition, the modules may contain a number of private auxiliary classes and/or other declarations. To keep the example short, such additional declarations are illustrated by dots ('…').

In the current version of `%requires`, only module names may be listed. It is currently being investigated whether or not to generalize this to be able to specify (singular) objects and classes within modules. It will then e.g., be possible to have a `%requires Buffermodule.buffer` in `ProducerModule` specifying that only class `Buffer` from `BufferModule` may be used. This might then be further restricted in class `Buffer` using a `%requires b.put` stating that only the `put` method of `Buffer` may be used and similarly for `get` in class `Consumer`. The argument against this is that the purpose of a module mechanism is to be able to describe the units of code to be provided and/or required.

4 Details of qBeta and Supplementary Properties

The mechanism of supplementary properties has been implemented in the language qBeta, which is derived from the Beta language. Beta and qBeta has just one abstraction mechanism, the *pattern*, which means that e.g., class and method have been unified. A pattern may thus define a class or a method. Patterns also play the roles of value types and patterns may also define types of active objects in the form of coroutines and/or concurrent processes. Unification means that inheritance is defined for patterns: the implication is that not only class patterns may inherit from a super class pattern, but a method (a pattern defining a method) may inherit from a supermethod [32]. Similarly, a pattern defining classes of concurrent processes may inherit from a superpattern.

4.1 Explaining qBeta

A qBeta pattern is the association of a name and an *object descriptor* (or just *descriptor*). A pattern declaration has the form given in a) below:

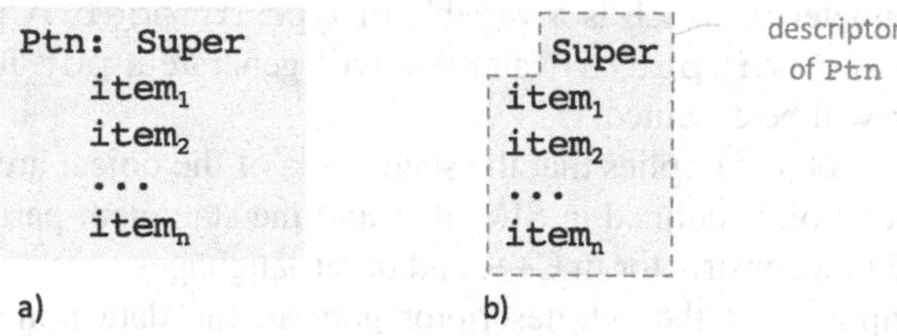

P is the name of the pattern, `Super` is the name of a possible superpattern and `Item`$_1$`, Item`$_2$`, ..., Item`$_n$ are *items.* An item may be a declaration of a data item or a pattern, an executable statement, or a supplementary property. The descriptor for `Ptn`, see b) above, consists of the name of a possible superpattern `Super` followed by (the indented) items `Item`$_1$`, Item`$_2$`, ..., Item`$_n$.

An object may be either an *instance* of a pattern, or a *singular* object. Instances of a pattern are described by the associated descriptor. A singular object is described by a descriptor.

We use a slightly extended version of the `Monitor` and `Buffer` example from Sect. 3 to illustrate qBeta. Figure 1a is the declaration of the `Monitor` (class) pattern with two properties, a data item `S` that is a *constant reference* to an object of pattern `Semaphore`, and a (method) pattern `entry`, which in turn has properties and a sequence of statements. `Monitor` has a statement (**`inner`** `(Monitor)`). `S` is generated as part of the generation of an enclosing `Monitor` object.

Figure 1b is the declaration of the *singular object* `Buffer:` its descriptor inherits the items of the descriptor of `Monitor` and adds the data item `L`, the (method) pattern items `put` and `get`, and an assignment statement. We use the term *sub-descriptor* for a descriptor that has a superpattern as is the case for the descriptor of `Buffer`.

```
Monitor:
   %globals
   %interface entry
   S: obj Semaphore
   entry:
      %signature value, immutable, unique
      S.wait
      inner(entry)
      S.signal
   inner(Monitor)
```
a)

```
Buffer: obj Monitor
   L: ref List
   put: entry
      in v: var integer
      ...
      L.put(v)
   get: entry
      out v: var integer
      ...
      v := L.get
   L := List(integer)
```
b)

Fig. 1. qBeta explained

The descriptor of a pattern may also inherit the items of the descriptor of a pattern, thereby forming hierarchies of super/sub patterns. As this applies to patterns in general, it also applies to the method patterns, as e.g., put and get of Buffer: they have descriptors that are sub-descriptors of entry from Monitor.

The L: **ref**List in Buffer declares a *variable reference*, which means that L may be assigned references to different List objects during program execution. Data items marked with **in/out** are parameters. The method pattern put in Buffer have e.g., an input parameter v, which is a variable of type integer. A producer object will typically call Buffer.put(5), and this will generate a put instance and the statements of put will be executed.

Generation of an object implies that the statements of the object are executed. This is how object generation is defined in SIMULA and the statement part of a descriptor thus plays the role of a constructor in C++, and other languages.

Inheritance implies that the sub-descriptor gets all the data items, patterns, and properties of the super-pattern. Inheritance of statements works as shown in Fig. 2.

The invocation Buffer.put(5) works as follows: As put is a sub-pattern of entry (from Monitor), execution of a put(5) on a Buffer B starts by executing S.wait from entry.

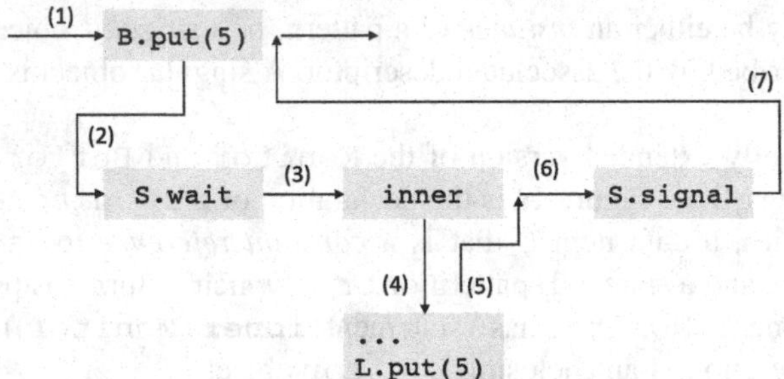

Fig. 2. Execution of B.put(5)

The execution of the special statement **inner** implies that the statements of the put sub-descriptor are executed, i.e.

```
...
L.put(5)
```

After completion of the statements of the sub-descriptor of put, execution continues with the statements after **inner**, in this case S.Signal.

The specification of Monitor in Sect. 3 includes a supplementary property that ensures that all methods of Monitor and subclasses/subdescriptor of Monitor must be submethods of entry, which ensures that execution of these methods is controlled by the associated semaphore.

In qBeta, the access properties of attributes may be described using the supplementary properties %public, %private and %protected. A given access property holds for all attribute declarations until a new access property is specified. For example, all declarations following %public until a %private and/or %protected property are part of the public interface of given class or singular object. Since modules are objects, `%private`, `%public` and `%protected` also apply to module objects as e.g., can be seen in class `Buffer`.

4.2 Supplementary Properties

A descriptor may declare one or more supplementary properties using the syntax:

```
%property A1, A2, ..., An
```

where `%property` is the name of the property and A_1, A_2, ..., A_n are arguments.

A given supplementary property imposes restrictions on the descriptor and/or sub-descriptors depending on the property. Some supplementary properties can only be imposed if they are consistent with possible supplementary properties of a given superpattern of the descriptor.

In the following sections, we describe a subset of the supplementary properties currently implemented in qBeta. In the descriptions the term THE- DESCRIPTOR refers to the descriptor that contains the property being described. Similarly, the term THE-OBJECT(S) refers to objects generated from the-descriptor. If THE- DESCRIPTOR is the descriptor of a pattern then THE- OBJECT(S) refer to any object generated from the pattern. If THE- DESCRIPTOR is used to define a singular object, THE- OBJECT refer to this singular object.

4.3 The Immutable Supplementary Property

The `%immutable` property may be used to define immutable objects. It has the form

A descriptor that has an `%immutable` property must obey the following restrictions:

1. It is not possible to change the state of objects of THE- DESCRIPTOR and objects of sub-descriptors.
2. The state of THE- OBJECT(S) of THE- DESCRIPTOR must be defined during generation of THE- OBJECT(S).
3. All data-items of THE- DESCRIPTOR are private.
4. Variables in THE- DESCRIPTOR and its sub-descriptors cannot be assigned to except during generation of THE- OBJECT(S).
5. Reference variables in THE- DESCRIPTOR can only refer to immutable objects.
6. Input arguments (**`in`**) of pattern attributes of THE- DESCRIPTOR may only be immutable. The return value (**`out`**) of a method pattern attribute is thus a function of its input arguments and the state of THE- OBJECT(S).
7. A possible superpattern of THE- DESCRIPTOR must also be restricted by `%immutable`.
8. The self-reference `this` may not be passed as an actual parameter to method calls of THE- OBJECT(S).

The pattern `Complex` is an example of how a supplementary property may be used to define immutable objects:

```
Complex:
    in re: var Float
    in im: var Float
    %immutable
    ...
```

4.4 The Globals Property

The `%globals` property has the following form

$$\%\text{globals } G_1,\ G_2,\ \ldots,\ G_n$$

where each G_i is one of: the name of a pattern, the name of a data-item, `immutable`, `unique`, and $n \geq 0$. In the following G = $[G_1, G_2, \ldots, G_n]$.

The `%globals` restriction imposes restrictions on which global data-items and global patterns that can be referred in THE- DESCRIPTOR and its sub-descriptors:

1. A global data-item `X` can only be referred if:

   a. `X` is in G.
   b. The type of `X` is a pattern in G.
   c. `X` is a sub-descriptor of a pattern in G.

2. A global pattern `P` can only be referred if:

   d. `P` is in G or a sub-descriptor of a pattern in G.
   e. `P` is restricted by `%globals` $Q_1, Q_2, \ldots, Q_m$ where G is a subset of $Q_1, Q_2, \ldots, Q_m$. I.e., `P` must be at least as restricted as THE- DESCRIPTOR.

3. There are no additional restrictions on a given G_i other than what may be defined directly for G_i.

If a descriptor is restricted by `%globals` i.e. with no arguments, then no global data-items or global patterns in enclosing objects may be referred, except for descriptors that are also restricted by `%globals` with no arguments.

4.5 The Interface Property

The `%interface` property has the form

$$\%\text{interface } P_1,\ P_2,\ \ldots,\ P_n$$

where each P_i is a pattern and n ≥0. The %interface property restricts the public interface of THE- DESCRIPTOR and sub-descriptors:

1. Any public pattern in sub-descriptors of THE- DESCRIPTOR must be a subpattern of a pattern P_i.
2. All data-items in sub-descriptors of THE- DESCRIPTOR are private.

4.6 The Signature Property

The %signature property has the form:

```
%signature S1 , S2 , . . . , Sn
```

where each s_i is a pattern name, immutable, or unique, and n ≥0. The %signature property may only be used in descriptors of patterns.

The %signature property is used to restrict the signature of pattern attributes in sub-descriptors of THE- DESCRIPTOR of the pattern: Input parameters (**in**) and return values (**out**) of sub-descriptors of pattern attributes in THE- DESCRIPTOR may only contain data-items that are typed by patterns listed in the %signature property.

The entry pattern of the Monitor class in Sect. 3.2 is an example of using the %signature property. Entry is a pattern intended to be a superpattern for methods defined in sub-descriptors of Monitor. As mentioned, patterns in qBeta may in general have parameters, and the %signature property will therefore also apply to possible class patterns declared in the-descriptor or sub-descriptors, but no example is included in this paper.

4.7 qBeta Modules

In qBeta, a module is a descriptor for a singular object. BufferModule in Sect. 3 is an example of a module. An object generated from a module is called a *module object*. Modules are organized in a hierarchy inspired by the organization of Java packages. But where packages are namespaces, qBeta modules are just descriptors of singular objects.

```
qBetaWorld: module
   qBeta: module
      ...
   LIB: module
      Containers: module
         ...
      MonitorSystem: module
         ...
      ...
   ...
   Workspace: module
      ISoLA22_example: module
         BufferModule: module
            ...
         ...
      ...
```

The module hierarchy of qBeta is basically just a (large) nested structure of descriptors. qBeta contains all basic declaration of qBeta. LIB contains all standard library modules for containers etc. Workspace is for trying out various examples, etc., and the example above is located in the ISoLA2022_example module.

The module hierarchy is mapped to a corresponding folder hierarchy and each folder has a source file containing the corresponding qBeta code. The `BufferModule` is located in a folder `BufferModule`, which is in the folder `ISoLA2022_example`, etc. The `BufferModule` folder has a file containing the source code for the `BufferModule` object.

Since modules are just nested descriptors, all modules are visible from any module at any place in the hierarchy but constrained by supplementary properties like `%public`, `%private`, and`%required`. In this paper, we use the keyword **`module`** for emphasizing that a given singular object is a module. In qBeta, **`obj`** is used since the one-to-one mapping of modules to folders and files defines which objects that are modules.

4.8 The %Visible Property

The declaration of a reference to a `List` object in the `Monitor` example in Sect. 3.2 may can be made using the path from the top of the module hierarchy:

```
L: ref LIB.Containers.Lists.List
```

As in Java, it is possible to avoid using the full path by using the `%visible` property:

```
%visible M1, M2, ..., Mn
```

where M_1, M_2, ..., M_n are *remote names* denoting declarations including modules. The declaration may then be made as follows:

```
%visible LIB.Containers.Lists
...
L: ref List
```

In general, a *remote name* has the form $R_1.R_2. „ ,.R_n$ where each R_i is a pattern name or a singular object name.

4.9 The Requires Property

The `%requires` property defines the names of modules that may be accessed in THE-DESCRIPTOR or its sub-descriptors. It has the form:

```
%requires M1, M2, ..., Mn
```

where each M_i is

1. A *module name* – in this case the module M_i and all its public attributes may be accessed.

2. A *remote name* `R.M` where `R` is a remote name and `M` is a module and

   a. the remote name has the form $R_1.R_2.,,.R_j$ where each R_i is a module name and $j > 0$.
   b. `M` and all its public attributes may be accessed.
   c. The modules and attributes of each R_i in the path do not become accessible by this `%requires` property.

In addition to possible %requires properties, the following rules apply:

1. All `%requires` properties in lexical enclosing modules are also valid for THE-DESCRIPTOR.
2. All `%requires` properties in superpatterns of THE- DESCRIPTOR are also valid for THE- DESCRIPTOR.

The main/primary use of the `%requires` property is to list modules that are needed/used by THE- DESCRIPTOR and its sub-descriptors. In most cases THE-DESCRIPTOR containing a `%requires` property is a module, but it may appear in any descriptor.

The `%requires` property may conflict with a `%globals` property in the sense that a `%globals` property my list e.g. a module not listed in a possible `%requires` property. In this case the `%requires` property overrules the `%globlas` property.

5 Related Work

As mentioned in the introduction, in the work that led to Algol 60 it was recognized that the language definition should include mechanisms meant for communication, not just for instructing a computer. In the Preliminary report: international algebraic language [34], the following objectives were agreed upon: The new language should be as close as possible to standard mathematical notation and be readable with little further explanation; it should be possible to use it for the description of computing processes in publications; the new language should be mechanically translatable into machine programs; there were three different languages: reference language, publication language and several hardware languages.

However, despite the many qualities of Algol 60, neither Algol 60 and other modeling and programming languages are well suited for describing computing processes. Even small algorithms are accompanied by an explanation in e.g., English.

Separate specification and modeling languages like VDM and UML were introduced to be used for the analysis and design of systems prior to implementation, but also to serve a purpose as documentation. ADLs are also examples of separate languages. SIMULA did this differently, by being a language for modeling and programming. This was further developed in Beta, and in qBeta, see [4].

Broy et al. [15] have argued that that modern programming languages exemplified by Scala can express the same as traditional specification languages like VDM++ except for the parts of VDM++ that are not executable.

Documentation by means of annotating programs is found in many programming languages. The most well-known are JavaDoc and JML. They both rely on just one artifact, the Java program, but they are very different, and they are both different from supplementary properties.

JavaDoc add comments in terms of (structured) text to Java programs and use them for producing API documentation as a separate document (via HTML). It has means for identifying names in the Java program in the comments, and it has HTML tags for e.g., parameters to methods, so that documentation of parameters follow the same style. Supplementary properties on the other hand are part of the language and may therefore by checked by the compiler, while JavaDoc tools check that the comments have the required to produce a proper HTML-form of the documentation.

JML goes one step further than JavaDoc, with a mechanism of Java annotations that is a further development of Design by Contract assertions in Eiffel, which in turn is based upon the work by Hoare [22] on invariants and pre/post conditions. JML has an almost separate formal specification/modeling language that is used in assertions and handled by a separate tool. The strength of JML is that it extends pre- and post-conditions and invariants from design by contract to include a number of more advanced concepts that allow for verification of Java programs. JML is, however, not an extension of Java as the specifications are just annotations. And as for qBeta, the intension of JML is behavioral inheritance, but this has to be proven for each subclass. Behavioral inheritance in qBeta is partly supported by an extended form of structural inheritance by means of inner.

The model fields in JML are just part of the JML specification of a class and not fields of the Java objects, while with our unified approach to modeling and programming, our public properties corresponds to the model fields, with the difference that they are properties of objects and not just defined as part of a specification.

Almost all mainstream object-oriented languages have a kind of assertion mechanism. While assertions are predicates on the state of program execution, our supplementary properties are predicates on the program.

Many object-oriented languages meet the challenge of restricting access to global variables (`%globals`) by special kinds of objects (e.g. concurrent processes represented by isolates in Dart [35]) that cannot access global variables and which only share immutable objects or values. Similarly, interface restrictions (`%interface`, `%signature`) are done by restricting methods to have parameters that are only value parameters or references to immutable objects.

The $4 + 1$ view model [36] is a model for documenting software architecture, with different views: Logical view (class diagrams, and state diagrams); Process view (processes and how they communicate); Development view (also known as the implementation view); Physical view (deployment); Scenarios.

The categorization of ADLs in Clements et al. [29] have three main types of views: Module, Component-connector, and Allocation, and each of these contains a number of view styles. Clements et al. point out that other views and styles than the ones in the $4 + 1$ view may be needed.

Our approach covers most of these views: qBeta supports composition, generalization and specialization for objects and patterns. Objects play the role of components and they provide %public properties. Modules are organized in file systems, and the `%requires` supplementary property describes the dependencies between modules. For the Allocation view we only support that modules are organized in file systems. Section 6 gives more details on how the different views may be supported by appropriate tools.

Java Modules [37] introduces a module level above packages. A module is a collection of packages, and a `requires` directive in a module specifies that this module depends on another module. Each module must explicitly state its dependencies. An `exports` module directive specifies one of the module's packages whose public types (and their nested public and protected types) should be accessible to code in all other modules. Java thus have anonymous classes, packages, and modules, while these mechanisms are subsumed by singular objects in qBeta.

In qBeta, an object provides its %public properties which applies to descriptors of patterns and of singular objects, including modules and the %requires property specifies which modules are required by a given module.

6 Discussion

As mentioned in the introduction, our approach to documentation is to extend the expressiveness of programming languages. Central in this work is the goal of avoiding having languages that serve different purposes when it is possible to do with a unified language. SIMULA was intended for modeling as well as programming and this was also the goal for Beta and is the goal for qBeta. In this paper, we have shown how to use supplementary properties to put restrictions on the program abstractions – restrictions that you otherwise will have to describe in comments or other additional documentation.

Subclass substitutability has been mentioned as a desired property of languages with a class/subclass mechanism. Wegner and Zdonik [38] coined this class/subclass compatibility. A virtual pattern has a descriptor like every pattern has. A redefinition of a virtual pattern is an extension, as if the 'redefined' pattern is a subpattern of the virtual pattern: Properties are inherited and statements of the two descriptors are combined by means of inner. Beta/qBeta thus supports an extended form of *structural compatibility* (as defined in [38]) between a subpattern and its superpattern. This does not guarantee behavioral compatibility, but it guarantees that statements in the superpattern are always executed and is thus a useful mechanism for describing 'action' properties in a pattern that are imposed on its subpatterns.

Since the early days of programming, diagrams and other illustrations have been used as an important part of the documentation and for communication between developers, users and customers. Diagrams can be informal drawings to illustrate e.g. a class hierarchy or formal diagrams like flow charts and UML diagrams. Programming languages usually have a textual syntax whereas modeling languages like UML have a diagrammatic syntax. The disadvantage of this is that different languages are used for modeling and programming, which easily leads to impedance mismatch [4, 31].

In the Mjølner project [39], a combined text and graphical editor, the MjølnerTool [40] was developed for Beta. Part of this was development of a graphical syntax for Beta in addition to its textual syntax. Examples are diagrams showing class hierarchies corresponding to generalization, diagrams showing nesting and diagrams showing composition hierarchies in the form of part objects. The MjølnerTool supports presentation, editing and construction of Beta programs using diagrams as well text. It is possible to alternate between editing the diagrams or editing the textual syntax. A change to the diagrams is immediately reflected in the text and vice versa. The obvious advantage of this is that the model and the program is always consistent.

For documentation purposes, class diagrams composition diagrams, nesting diagrams, etc. are thus different views on the program in accordance with the 4+1 view and the views and styles presented by Clemens et al. Being able to describe the various views as part of the program ensures that these are kept up to date and consistent and future work involves support for further views and styles.

We have a qBetaDoc, which is similar to JavaDoc for the purpose of being able to browse the interface of qBeta modules on the Web. For qBetaDoc, the view of a given module is the public interface of the module. This includes all public attributes of the module, public attributes of public patterns and singular descriptors, relevant supplementary properties, etc. In addition, comments placed at public declarations are shown. The view is thus an abstract version of the code without private attributes and statements. Compared to JavaDoc, there has been no need to introduce a special syntax for comments to be extracted for the documentation.

As mentioned, Beta and qBeta are intended for modeling as well as programming and the public interface corresponds to the model – the representative part of the program as mentioned in Sect. 2.4. Some languages, like Modula distinguish between interface modules and implementation modules to separate the 'public' part from the implementation. The Beta fragment system, see Chapter 17 of [3], makes it possible to make a more fine-grained split of the representative parts from the non-representative part, as a model may include more than just signatures of methods, e.g. part-objects.

JML adds language mechanism to Java for expressing assertions to support design by contract. As for JavaDoc these extensions might as well have been part of Java. For qBeta, we have started using supplementary properties for specifying assertions like pre-, and post-conditions and invariants. We also use them to specify constraints as in OCL/UML [41]. The exact form of how to do this is still being pursued.

A program is a description of algorithms and data structures used to generate a program execution. In modeling languages like UML, it is also possible to describe required properties of a system e.g., by means of object diagrams, sequence diagrams, etc. that describe snapshots that must be fulfilled by the system. Mechanisms for describing snapshots are rarely an integrated part of programming languages.

For qBeta it is a goal to integrate mechanisms for describing snapshots. As a step towards this, a debugger generating object diagrams and sequence diagrams has been implemented for qBeta. The snapshots generated by the debugger are thus *observed properties* of the program execution. The aim is that these diagrams may also be used for specifying requirements in the design phase as in UML and thus the same language may be used to define *required properties* as well as observed properties.

State-machines, associations, etc. are other mechanisms from UML that may be used for documentation of programs, but there has not yet been a successful integration of these in mainstream programming languages.

As mentioned in Related Work, supplementary properties are predicates over the program text. The definitions of supplementary properties are given in English, but it should be a relatively simple task to formalize these definitions.

Supplementary properties as described in this paper and in [19] have been implemented in qBeta. As mentioned, supplementary properties can be added to any object-oriented language. Future work includes, as mentioned above, to use supplementary properties for describing assertions and constraints. In addition, the aim is to formalize supplementary properties as predicates. A given supplementary property may be defined as a predicate over the program.

In summary, we think that supplementary properties is a small but useful step towards reducing the need for additional documentation and additional languages.

Acknowledgement. We would like to thank the anonymous reviewers for useful comments.

References

1. Naur, P., Revised report on the algorithmic language ALGOL 60. Commun. ACM **6** (1963)
2. Dahl, O.-J., Myhrhaug, B., Nygaard, K.: SIMULA 67 Common Base Language (Editions 1968, 1970, 1972, 1984). 1968: Norwegian Computing Center, Oslo
3. Madsen, O.L., Møller-Pedersen, B., Nygaard, K.: Object-Oriented Programming in the BETA Programming Language. Addison Wesley (1993)
4. Madsen, O.L., Møller-Pedersen, B.: A unified approach to modeling and programming. In: Petriu, D.C., Rouquette, N., Haugen, Ø. (eds.) Model Driven Engineering Languages and Systems. MODELS 2010. LNCS, vol. 6394. Springer, Berlin (2010). https://doi.org/10.1007/978-3-642-16145-2_1
5. Leavens, G.T., Cheon, Y.: JML. 2022. https://www.cs.ucf.edu/~leavens/JML/index.shtml
6. Chalin, P., Kiniry, J.R., Leavens, G.T., Poll, E.: Beyond assertions: advanced specification and verification with JML and ESC/Java2. In: de Boer, F.S., Bonsangue, M.M., Graf, S., de Roever, W.-P. (eds.) FMCO 2005. LNCS, vol. 4111, pp. 342–363. Springer, Heidelberg (2006). https://doi.org/10.1007/11804192_16
7. Meyer, B.: Eiffel: The Language. Prentice Hall, Upper Saddle River (1992)
8. Oracle. *JavaDoc* (2022). https://www.oracle.com/java/technologies/javase/javadoc-tool.html
9. OMG, *UML 2.5.1.* 2017, OMG
10. Stroustrup, B.: The C++ Programming Language. Addison-Wesley Longman Publishing Co., Inc., Boston (2000)
11. Gosling, J., Joy, B., Steele, G., Bracha, G.: The Java Language Specification, 3rd edin, Addison-Wesley, Boston (2005)
12. Hejlsberg, A., Wiltamuth, S., Golde, P.: The C# Programming Language. Addison-Wesley, Boston (2003)
13. Python_Software_Foundation Phyton (2021). https://www.python.org
14. Kristensen, B.B., Madsen, O.L., Møller-Pedersen, B.: The when, why and why not of the BETA programming language. In: HOPL III - The Third ACM SIGPLAN Conference on History of Programming Languages, San Diego (2007)
15. Broy, M., Havelund, K., Kumar, R., Steffen, B.: Towards a unified view of modeling and programming (ISoLA 2018 Track Introduction). In: Margaria, T., Steffen, B. (eds.) ISoLA 2018. LNCS, vol. 11244, pp. 3–21. Springer, Cham (2018). https://doi.org/10.1007/978-3-030-03418-4_1

16. Odersky, M., Spoon, L., Venners, B.: Programming in Scala, A Comprehensive Step-By-Step Guide. 3rd edn. Artima Incorporation, Sunnyvale (2016)
17. Bjørner, D., Jones, C.B.: The Vienna Development Method: The Meta-Language. LNCS, vol. 61. Springer, Heidelberg (1978). https://doi.org/10.1007/3-540-08766-4
18. Fitzgerald, J., Larsen, P.G., Mukherjee, P., Plat, N., Verhoef, M.: Validated Designs for Object-Oriented Systems. Springer, New York (2005)
19. Madsen, O.L.: Building safe concurrency abstractions. In: Agha, G. et al. (eds.) Concurrent Objects and Beyond Papers dedicated to Akinori Yonezawa on the Occasion of His 65th Birthday Lecture Notes in Computer Science, LNCS 8665, pp. 66–104.Springer, Heidelberg (2014). https://doi.org/10.1007/978-3-662-44471-9_4
20. Hoare, C.A.R.: Notes on data structuring. In: Structured Programming. Academic Press, London (1972)
21. Liskov, B.H., Wing, J.M.: A behavioral notion of subtyping. ACM Trans. Program. Lang. Syst. **16**(6), 1811–1841 (1994)
22. Hoare, C.A.R., *Proof of Correctness of Data Representations.* Acta Informatica, 1972. **1**
23. Palme, J., Protected program modules in Simula 67. Modern Datateknik **12** (1973)
24. Brinch-Hansen, P.: The programming language concurrent pascal. IEEE Trans. Softw. Eng. **SE-1**(2) (1975)
25. Milner, R., Milner, R.: A Calculus of Communicating Systems. Springer Verlag, Heidelberg (1980). https://doi.org/10.1007/3-540-10235-3
26. Armstrong, J.: Programming Erlang - Software for a Concurent World (2013)
27. Hansen, P.B.: Java's insecure parallelism. SIGPLAN Notices **34**(4), 38–45 (1999)
28. Feiler, P.H., Gluch, D.P., Hudak, J.J.: The Architecture Analysis & Design Language (AADL): An Introduction (2006). https://resources.sei.cmu.edu/asset_files/TechnicalNote/2006_004_001_14678.pdf
29. Clements, P., Bachmann, F., Bass, L., Garlan. D.: A practical method for documenting software architectures (2008). https://www.researchgate.net/publication/228977397_A_practical_method_for_documenting_software_architectures
30. Madsen, O.L., Møller-Pedersen. B.: What Object-Oriented Programming May Be—and What It Does Not Have to Be. In: ECOOP'88 – European Conference on Object-Oriented Programming. Springer Verlag, Oslo: (1988)
31. Madsen, O.L., Møller-Pedersen, B.: This is not a model. In: Margaria, T., Steffen, B. (eds.) ISoLA 2018. LNCS, vol. 11244, pp. 206–224. Springer, Cham (2018). https://doi.org/10.1007/978-3-030-03418-4_13
32. Kristensen, B.B., Madsen, O.L., Møller-Pedersen, B., Nygaard, K.: Classification of actions or Inheritance also for methods. In: Bézivin, J., Hullot, J.-M., Cointe, P., Lieberman, H. (eds.) ECOOP 1987. LNCS, vol. 276, pp. 98–107. Springer, Heidelberg (1987). https://doi.org/10.1007/3-540-47891-4_10
33. Madsen, O.L.: Using coroutines for multi-core preemptive scheduling. In: Proceedings of the 11th Workshop on Programming Languages and Operating Systems, pp. 46–52. ACM (2021)
34. Perlis, A.J., Samelson, K.: Preliminary report: international algebraic language. Commun. ACM **1**(12), 8–22 (1958)
35. Dart. Concurrency in Dart (2022). https://dart.dev/guides/language/concurrency
36. Kruchten, P.: Architectural blueprints—the "4+1" view model of software architecture. IEEE Softw. **12**(6), 42–50 (1995)
37. Deitel, P., Understanding Java 9 Modules. Java Magazine September/October (2017)
38. Wegner, P., Zdonik, S.B.: Inheritance as an incremental modification mechanism or what like is and isn't like. In: Gjessing, S., Nygaard, K. (eds.) ECOOP 1988. LNCS, vol. 322, pp. 55–77. Springer, Heidelberg (1988). https://doi.org/10.1007/3-540-45910-3_4

39. Knudsen, J.L., Löfgren, M., Madsen, O.L., Magnusson, B.: Object-Oriented Environments—The Mjølner Approach. Prentice Hall, Englewood Cliffs (1994)
40. Sandvad, E.: An object-oriented CASE tool. In: Knudsen, J.L., et al. (eds.) Object-Oriented Environments—The Mjølner Approach. Prentice Hall, Englewood Cliffs (1994)
41. OMG. OCL. (2014). https://www.omg.org/spec/OCL/2.4/About-OCL/

Pragmatics Twelve Years Later: A Report on Lingua Franca

Reinhard von Hanxleden[1(✉)], Edward A. Lee[2], Hauke Fuhrmann[3], Alexander Schulz-Rosengarten[1], Sören Domrös[1], Marten Lohstroh[2], Soroush Bateni[4], and Christian Menard[5]

[1] Kiel University, Kiel, Germany
{rvh,als,sdo}@informatik.uni-kiel.de
[2] University of California, Berkeley, USA
{eal,marten}@berkeley.edu
[3] Scheidt & Bachmann, Kiel, Germany
Fuhrmann.Hauke@scheidt-bachmann-st.de
[4] University of Texas at Dallas, Richardson, USA
soroush@utdallas.edu
[5] Technical University Dresden, Dresden, Germany
christian.menard@tu-dresden.de

Abstract. In 2010, Fuhrmann et al. argued for enhancing modeler productivity by providing tooling that, put simply, combines the best of textual and graphical worlds. They referred to this as *pragmatics*, and argued that a key enabler would be the ability to automatically synthesize customized graphical views from a (possibly textual) model. The model would be the "ground truth" used, for example, for downstream code synthesis and simulation; the graphical views would typically be abstractions from the model serving various purposes, including documentation.

Twelve years later, we reflect on their proposal, and illustrate the current state with the recently developed polyglot coordination language Lingua Franca (LF). LF has been designed with pragmatics in mind since early on, and some characteristics of LF make it particularly suited for pragmatics-aware programming and modeling. However, the underlying pragmatic principles are broadly applicable, and by now a set of mature open source tools is available for putting them into practice.

Keywords: Pragmatics · Lingua Franca · Model-driven engineering · Diagram synthesis · KIELER

1 Introduction

Visual modeling, by some seen as synonymous with modeling altogether, offers the advantage of naturally providing visual diagrams that, ideally, self-document a system under development. However, practicioners often experience authoring with diagrams only as less efficient than working on textual artefacts, which

T. Margaria and B. Steffen (Eds.): ISoLA 2022, LNCS 13702, pp. 60–89, 2022.
https://doi.org/10.1007/978-3-031-19756-7_5

for example has given high momentum to textual Domain Specific Languages (DSLs). Twelve years ago, Fuhrmann et al. [8] proposed to enhance designer productivity by employing *pragmatics*, interpreted, roughly speaking, as combining the best of textual and visual modeling worlds. They argued that key enablers would be the separation of model and view, and the automatic construction of (graphical) customized views. The graphical views would not be necessary in a technical sense, for example to simulate a model, to formally analyze it, or to synthesize code. However, they would be valuable artefacts for the human modeler for various purposes, a primary purpose being the documentation of the model. As proof of feasibility, they presented the open-source KIEL Integrated Environment for Layout Eclipse Rich Client (KIELER) framework for *pragmatics-aware modeling*. At the time, von Hanxleden et al. [17] envisioned that by 2020, the use of pragmatics in software engineering tools would be widespread.

While it is hard evaluate the level of adoption of the approach, there are several projects centered around pragmatics that certainly have had a major impact. The most popularized contribution from the KIELER initiative might be the Eclipse Layout Kernel (ELK)[1] Java code library that implements sophisticated graph layout strategies and thus is a key driver for many of the pragmatics improvements in the KIELER approach. The transpiled ELK for JavaScript (ELKJS) library has, at the time of this writing, received around 1,000 stars on GitHub[2].

As an official project hosted at the Eclipse Foundation it has some visibility, leading to its adoption in quite a few downstream tools. Just recently, ELK has been adopted in the Graphical Language Server Platform (GLSP)[3] meta-framework for graphical modeling, which follows Microsoft's approach for a textual integrated development environment (IDE) with the language server protocol (LSP)[4]. It extends the LSP philosophy of having a clear separation between a backend for language and semantics and a frontend for GUI features to the domain of graphical modeling languages. Hence, the complex tasks of the backend can be reused in different frontend implementations and open up for broader technology mixes. Also other established meta-frameworks adopted ELK, such as Sirius[5], the Graphical Modeling Framework (GMF), and Graphiti[6].

More than a decade of employing pragmatics in various languages and tool kits, both in academic and industrial contexts, has also created a host of users that can reflect on their experience with pragmatics. As one practitioner from Bosch Siemens Hausgeräte GmbH put it after using KIELER for some time:

> "In our experience, over many years, my colleagues and I concluded that textual modeling is the only practical way, but that a graphical view of the models is a must-have as well. Your technology closes exactly that gap" [44].

[1] https://www.eclipse.org/elk/.
[2] https://github.com/kieler/elkjs.
[3] https://www.eclipse.org/glsp/.
[4] https://microsoft.github.io/language-server-protocol/.
[5] https://blog.obeosoft.com/a-picture-is-worth-a-thousand-words.
[6] https://www.eclipse.org/modeling/gmp/.

In this paper, we demonstrate the state of the art and the value of pragmatics-aware modeling with the recently developed Lingua Franca (LF) language serving as prime example, while also taking the opportunity to reflect on the broader developments and feedback received over time.

1.1 Contributions and Outline

We will first review the key concepts of pragmatics and its model-view separation (Sect. 2). For several reasons, including the hierarchical structure and the separation of coordination language and target language, LF lends itself particularly well to pragmatics-aware modeling, and its tool chain has incorporated that from its beginning. We elaborate on this with several practical examples in Sect. 3. An important component of pragmatics is the choice of graphical syntax, including its amenability to automatic layout; case in point, we discuss some of our design choices for LF in Sect. 4. The issues that arise from a graph drawing/diagram synthesis perspective and some ongoing work are covered further in Sect. 5. For readers interested in possibly employing modeling pragmatics in other tools/languages than presented here, Sect. 6 briefly covers the underlying technology, which is all available open-source. Feedback from users on their experience with pragmatics and an outlook on the challenges ahead is summarized in Sect. 7. Some related work is covered in Sect. 8, we wrap up in Sect. 9.

2 Pragmatics in Linguistics and Modeling

In linguistics, the study of how the meaning of languages is constructed and understood is referred to as *semiotics*. It divides into the disciplines of syntax, semantics, and pragmatics [32]. These categories can be applied both to natural as well as artificial languages (i. e., languages that are consciously devised), such as programming languages. In the context of artificial languages, *syntax* is determined by formal rules defining expressions of the language [13] and *semantics* determines the meaning of syntactic constructs [18]. "Linguistic *pragmatics* can, very roughly and rather broadly, be described as *the science of language use*" [14]. This definition can be applied verbatim to our domain of interest; programming languages, or modeling languages, as they are often referred to in the context of Model-Driven Engineering (MDE). However, before we further discuss and define pragmatics in the realm of software engineering and MDE, we first introduce some more terminology.

The main artifacts in MDE are *models*, which adhere to two main concepts. First, a model *represents* some software artifact or real world domain. Second, it *conforms* to a *metamodel* or *grammar* [19], defining its *abstract syntax*. The *concrete syntax*, on the other hand, is the concrete rendering of the abstract concepts. Concrete syntax can be textual or displayed in a structured way, such as a tree view extracted from an Extensible Markup Language (XML) representation of the abstract syntax. Graphical syntax is often used to visualize model structure; the Unified Modeling Language (UML) encompasses several graphical example languages. According to Gurr, a *visual language* is any language that is expressed to the reader's visual sense. Therefore, diagrams as well as textual programs or mathematical models, are visual languages. One special characteristic of diagrams is that they exhibit intrinsic properties, and these properties directly correspond to properties in the represented domain [13], such as containment relations of boxes.

A *graphical model* is a model that can have a graphical representation, like a UML class model. A *view* of the model is a concrete drawing of the model, sometimes also *diagram* or *notation model*, e. g., a UML class diagram. The abstract structure of the model leaving all graphical information behind is the *semantical* or *domain model*, or just *model* in short. E. g., a class model can also be serialized as an XML tree. Hence, a *model* conforms to the abstract syntax, while a *view* conforms to a concrete syntax.

A view can represent any subset of the model, which in some frameworks is used to break up complex models into multiple manageable views. Hence, there is no fixed one-to-one relationship between model and view.

In linguistics, *pragmatics* traditionally refers to how elements of a language should be used, e. g., for what purposes a certain statement is eligible, or under what circumstances a level of hierarchy should be introduced in a model. It denotes the "relation of signs to (human) interpreters" [32] and therefore Gurr calls it the "real semantics" of a language [13]. Pragmatics addresses questions concerned with avoiding ambiguities or misleading information in graphical representations, for example by improper usage of layout conventions, termed *secondary notation* by Petre and Green [11]. As Gurr states:

> "A major conclusion of this collection of studies is that the correct use of pragmatic features, such as layout in graph-based notations, is a significant contributory factor to the effectiveness of these representations."[13]

In the context of MDE, Selic [45] (somewhat implicitly) uses "pragmatics" in a rather broad sense, referring to practical aspects such as code synthesis. We here slightly extend the linguistic interpretation of pragmatics as follows:

Pragmatics concern all practical aspects of handling a model in its design process. This includes practical design activities such as editing and browsing of graphical and/or textual model representations in order to construct, analyze, and effectively represent a model's meaning. Pragmatics aim to increase modeler productivity and product quality. Pragmatics-aware tooling helps achieve a separation of model and view, in line with the well-established Model-View-Controller (MVC) paradigm [36]. A key enabler is the ability to automatically construct customized graphical views of a model.

3 Diagrams for Development of Lingua Franca Programs

LF (LF) is a recently-developed polyglot coordination language for concurrent and possibly time-sensitive applications ranging from low-level embedded code to distributed cloud and edge applications [29]. An LF program specifies the interactions between components called *reactors*. The emphasis of the framework is on ensuring deterministic interaction with explicit management of timing. The logic of each reactor is written in one of a suite of target languages (currently C, C++, Python, Rust, or TypeScript) and can integrate (possibly legacy) code in those languages. A code generator synthesizes one or more programs in the target language, which are then compiled using standard toolchains. If the application has exploitable parallelism, then it executes transparently on multiple cores. This happens without compromising determinacy because data dependencies between reactors translate into scheduling constraints at runtime. A distributed application translates into multiple programs and scripts to launch those programs on distributed machines. The communication fabric connecting components is synthesized as part of the programs.

There are a number of features of LF that make its programs particularly well suited to diagram representations:

1. The LF language expresses only the structure of programs, not their detailed logic. The latter is done in chunks of target-language code that are ignored by the LF parser.
2. The language encourages the use of hierarchy, where components contain other components. This lends itself well to the KIELER mechanisms for handling hierarchy, where hierarchical components can be expanded or collapsed to focus attention.
3. LF components (reactors) are concurrent, lending themselves naturally to being rendered as side-by-side boxes coexisting in a space.
4. The interactions between components are explicit. Each reactor has input and output ports, and a container reactor explicitly connects the ports of its contained reactors. This contrasts with most actor frameworks, such as Akka [38], where the existence and interconnections of actors is buried in the logic of target-language code.

LF's interactive diagram synthesis capability is an integral part of its IDE support. An Eclipse-based LF IDE called Epoch is available at GitHub[7]. An LSP-based Visual Studio Code Extension for LF is installable from both the Visual Studio Marketplace[8] and the Open-VSX Registry[9].

3.1 Data Dependencies

We begin with the use of automatically generated diagrams that emphasize reasoning about data dependencies in a LF program. Consider the program in Fig. 1a. The program is constructed textually and is hopefully reasonably easy to read. It defines three reactor classes, `Sense`, `Compute`, and `Actuate`, creates one

[7] https://github.com/lf-lang/lingua-franca/releases.

[8] https://marketplace.visualstudio.com/items?itemName=lf-lang.vscode-lingua-franca.

[9] https://open-vsx.org/extension/lf-lang/vscode-lingua-franca.

```
target C;
reactor Sense {
    output y:int;
    timer t(0, 1 msec);
    reaction(t) -> y {=
    //... C code to produce output.
    =}
}
reactor Compute {
    input x:int;
    output y:int;
    reaction(x) -> y {=
        // ... C code to process data.
    =}
}
```

```
reactor Actuate {
    input x:int;
    reaction(x) {=
        // ... C code to take action.
    =}
}
main reactor {
    s = new Sense();
    c = new Compute();
    a = new Actuate();

    s.y, c.y -> c.x, a.x after 1 msec;
}
```

(a) Textual LF code

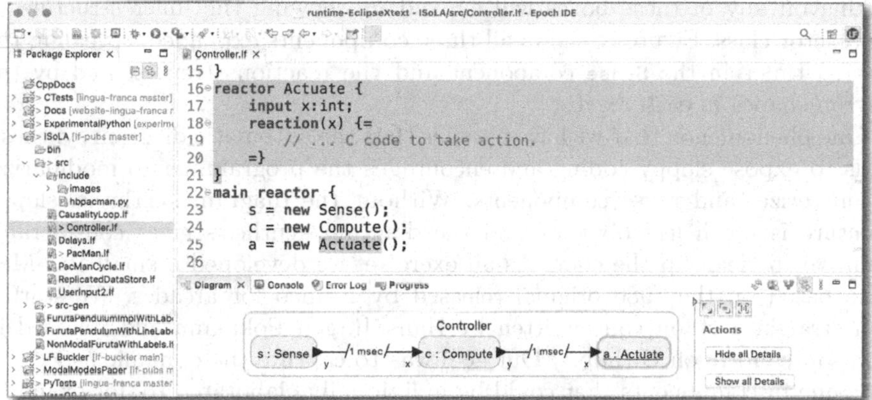

(b) An interactive rendered diagram in the Epoch IDE; selecting `Actuate` in the diagram highlights the definition and instantiation in the textual code.

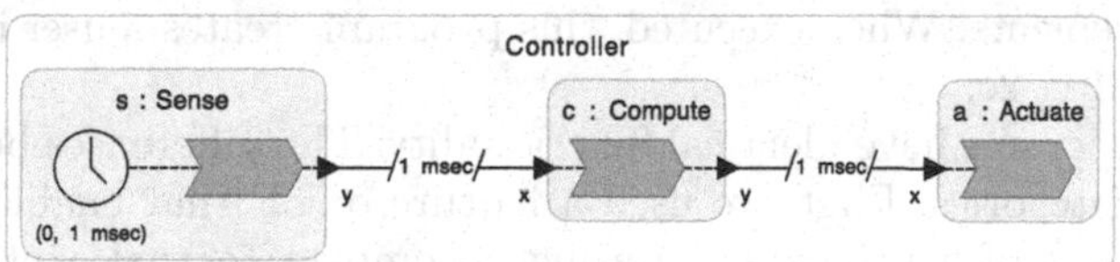

(c) Expanded diagram, exposing internals of reactors.

Fig. 1. A simple pipeline in LF.

instance of each, named `s`, `c`, and `a`, respectively, and connects their two output ports to their two input ports (with a logical delay of 1 ms) on a line that reads like this:

```
s.y, c.y -> c.x, a.x after 1 msec;
```

Although such a statement is not difficult to read, it is dramatically easier to see what is going on with the automatic diagram rendering provided through LF's IDE support. To underscore this difference, we had an interaction with a user who had built a program similar to this. This person filed a bug report saying that the logical delay introduced was 2 ms rather than the intended 1 ms. It turned out that this individual was using the command-line tools rather than one of the IDEs. Upon opening the program in Epoch, rendering the diagram reproduced in Fig. 1b, it was immediately obvious that the specified end-to-end delay was in fact 2 ms.

Figure 1b illustrates a number of features that make building and understanding LF programs much easier. For example, the diagram can be used to efficiently navigate in the textual source code. The box labeled `a : Actuate`, which represents the instance `a` of class `Actuate`, is highlighted, by a thick border, having been clicked on by the user. The corresponding instantiation and class definition are both highlighted, by non-white backgrounds, in the source code. Double clicking on any of these boxes will expand it, showing the inner structure of the reactor class. Figure 1c shows all three components expanded, revealing the internal timer in the `Sense` component and the reactions (represented by the chevron shape) in each reactor.

One phenomenon that we have noted is that the automatic diagram synthesis tends to expose sloppy coding and encourages the programmer to modularize, parameterize, and reuse components. Without the diagram synthesis, sloppy structure is much less obvious, and the diagram synthesis gives considerable incentive to clean up the code. As an exercise, we developed a small Pac-Man game based on the 1980 original released by Namco for arcades. We started with straight Python code written by Hans-Jürgen Pokmann and released in open-source form on Github.[10] Our goal was to capture the dynamic aspects of the game in components that could be individually elaborated to, for example, replace the player with an AI. Our first working version of the game rendered as the diagram in Fig. 2a. A more refined version rendered as the diagram in Fig 2b. The incomprehensibility of the first diagram was a major driving factor for the improvements. When executed, this program creates a user interface like that shown in Fig 2c.

The two programs have identical functionality. The differences between them fall into two categories. First, we used a feature of LF that enables creating a bank of instances of a reactor class using a compact textual syntax that also renders more compactly in the diagram. The textual syntax in this example is the following:

```
ghosts = new[4] Ghost(
    width = {= ghost_specs[bank_index]["width"] =},
    height = {= ghost_specs[bank_index]["height"] =},
    image = {= ghost_specs[bank_index]["image"] =},
    directions = {= ghost_specs[bank_index]["directions"] =},
    character_class = ({= pacman.Ghost =})
)
```

[10] https://github.com/hbokmann/Pacman.

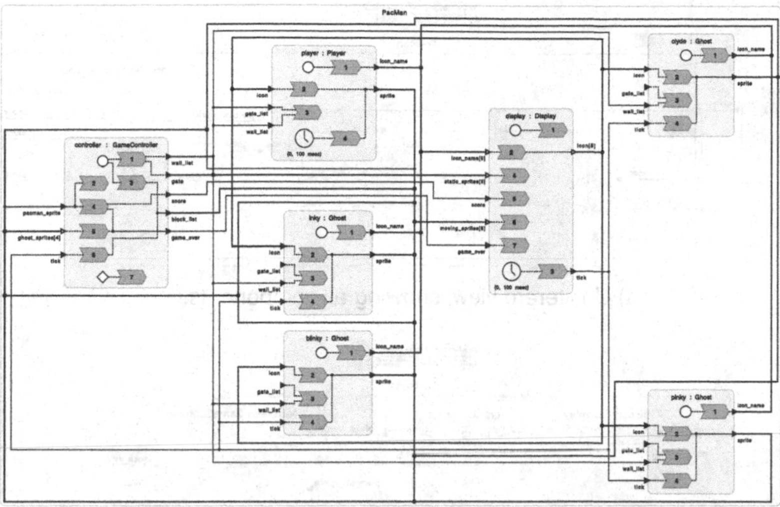

(a) First attempt, with four individual `Ghost` reactors.

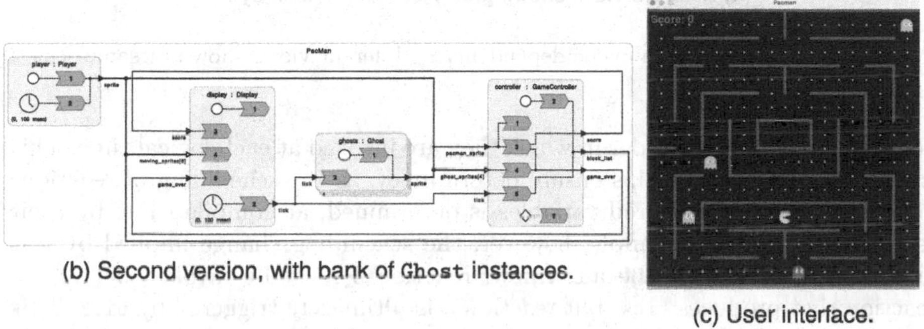

(b) Second version, with bank of `Ghost` instances.

(c) User interface.

Fig. 2. Pac-Man game, with different `Ghost` instantiation strategies shown at same scale, and UI.

This creates four instances of class `Ghost` and sets their parameters via a table lookup. This version of the program renders much more compactly, as shown at the bottom center of Fig. 2b.

The second significant change was to avoid using messages to pass around static information that does not change during runtime, such as the configuration of the walls. Such information is converted to parameters (when the information differs for distinct instances) or shared constant data structures (when the information is identical across the whole game). We believe that the automatic diagram rendering was *the* driving factor for improving the design.

The diagram also aids during debugging. Take Fig. 3a as an example. This is a small variant of the Pac-Man program that simply moves reaction 2 of the `Display` reactor, which produces the `tick` output, from position 2 to position 4. This move has semantic implications, since in LF, the order in which reactions

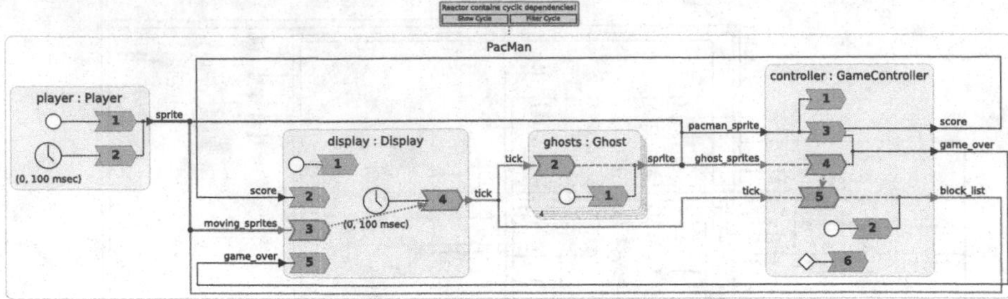

(a) Unfiltererd view, showing all components.

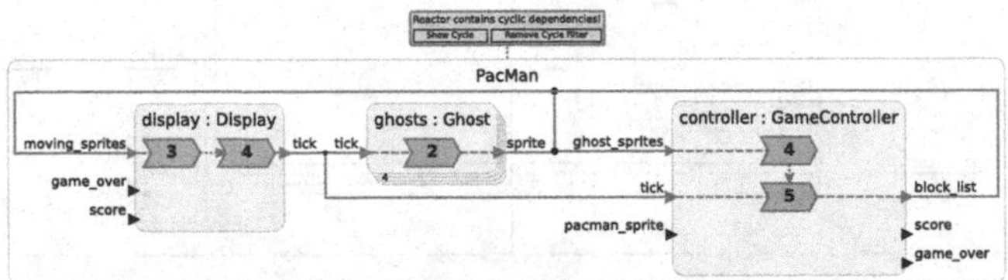

(b) Filtererd view, showing only components in cycle.

Fig. 3. Pac-Man game with cyclic dependencies, different views shown at same scale.

are declared affects the order in which they are invoked at each logical time. This is a key property that helps ensure determinacy, as the scheduling of reactions and their accesses to shared variables is determined, at compile time, by their textual order. In the example, however, the scheduling change implied by this move creates a problem because, now, reaction 3 must be invoked before the reaction that produces `tick`, but reaction 3 is ultimately triggered by `tick`. This "scheduling cycle," sometimes also referred to as "causality loop," is extremely difficult to see in the textual source code. To help identify such problems, LF diagrams highlights the offending causality loops in red, as shown in Fig. 3a. The tools also adds dashed arrows that indicate exactly where the flaw may be due to reaction ordering, in this case indicating a path from reaction 3 to 4 in the `Display` reactor.

When LF programs have feedback, such causality loops commonly arise during development and require careful reasoning to get the intended behavior. The LF tools provide a further filter that can help understand the root cause and suggest fixes. By clicking on the "Filter Cycle" button at the top, a new diagram is rendered that includes only the components that are involved in the causality loop, as shown in Fig. 3b. Simply by inspecting this diagram, it is clear that swapping the order of reactions 3 and 4 in the `Display` reactor could resolve the cyclic dependency. The ability to generate such a filtered view automatically depends on the model-view-controller architecture of the system and on its sophisticated automated layout.

3.2 Control Dependencies

So far, the diagrams emphasize the flow of data between components and the ensuing execution dependencies. Decision making, i.e., whether to perform action A or action B, is hidden in the target language code and not rendered in the diagrams. Indeed, rendering the detailed logic of the reaction bodies would likely lead to unusably cluttered diagrams.

Nevertheless, sometimes, the logic of decision making is truly essential to understanding the behavior of a program, even at a high level. Consider a program to control a Furuta pendulum [9], a classic problem often used to teach feedback control. As shown in Fig. 4, it consists of a vertical shaft driven by a motor, a fixed arm extending out at 90° from the top of the shaft, and a pendulum at the end of the arm. The goal is to rotate the shaft to impart enough energy to the pendulum that it swings up, to then catch the pendulum and balance it so that the pendulum remains above the arm. Each of these steps requires a different control behavior, which makes a controller a prime candidate for a *modal model.* It cycles through the three modes, which we will name `SwingUp`, `Catch`, and `Stabilize`.

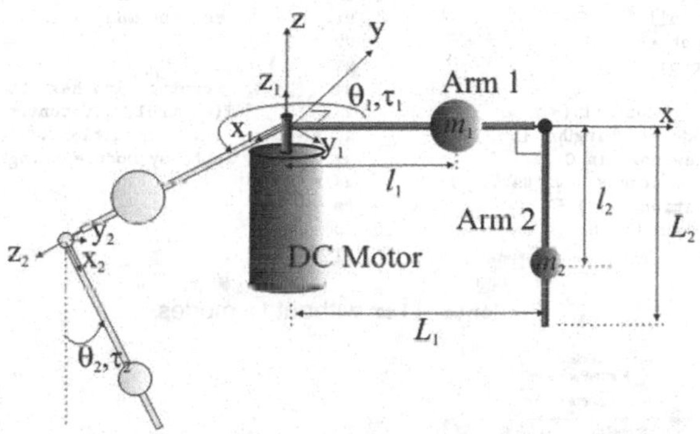

Fig. 4. Schematic of the Furuta pendulum from Wikipedia by Benjamin Cazzolato | CC BY 3.0.

Figure 5a shows an LF program for such a controller based on the design of Eker et al. [28]. This program uses a newly added feature of LF to explicitly represent modal models, programs with multiple *modes* of operation and switching logic to switch from one mode to another. The overall program consists of three connected reactors `Sensor`, `Controller`, and `Actuator`. The diagram in Fig. 5c shows these modes very clearly.

Of course, such modal behavior could easily be written directly within reactors in target-language code without using the modal models extension of LF. Such a realization, shown in Fig. 5b, in this case, is even slightly more compact. Notice that the existence of modes is now hidden in the control logic of the imperative target language, C in this case. As covered in the related work

```
reactor Controller {
  input angles:float[];
  output control:float;

  initial mode SwingUp {
    reaction(angles) -> control, Catch {=
      ... control law here in C ...
      SET(control, ... control value ... );
      if ( ... condition ... ) {
        SET_MODE(Catch);
      }
    =}
  }

  mode Catch {
    reaction(angles) -> control, Stabilize {=
      ... control law here in C ...
      SET(control, ... control value ... );
      if ( ... condition ... ) {
        SET_MODE(Stabilize);
      }
    =}
  }
  mode Stabilize {
    reaction(angles) -> control, SwingUp {=
      ... control law here in C ...
      SET(control, ... control value ... );
      if ( ... condition ... ) {
        SET_MODE(SwingUp);
      }
    =}
  }
}

import Sensor ...
import Actuator ...
main reactor {
  s = new Sensor();
  c = new Controller();
  a = new Actuator();
  s.angles -> c.angles;
  c.control -> a.control;
}
```

(a) Sketch of the `Controller` reactor code with LF modes

```
target C;
preamble {=
  typedef enum {SwingUp, Catch, Stabilize} modes;
=}
reactor Controller {
  input angles:double[];
  output control:double;
  state my_mode:modes;

  reaction(angles) -> control {=
    if (self->my_mode == SwingUp) {
      ... control law here in C ...
      SET(control, ... control value ... );
      if ( ... condition ... ) {
        self->my_mode = Catch;
      }
    } else if (self->my_mode == Catch) {
      ... control law here in C ...
      SET(control, ... control value ... );
      if ( ... condition ... ) {
        self->my_mode = Stabilize;
      }
    } else {
      ... control law here in C ...
      SET(control, ... control value ... );
      if ( ... condition ... ) {
        self->my_mode = SwingUp;
      }
    }
  =}
}
```

(b) `Controller` without LF modes

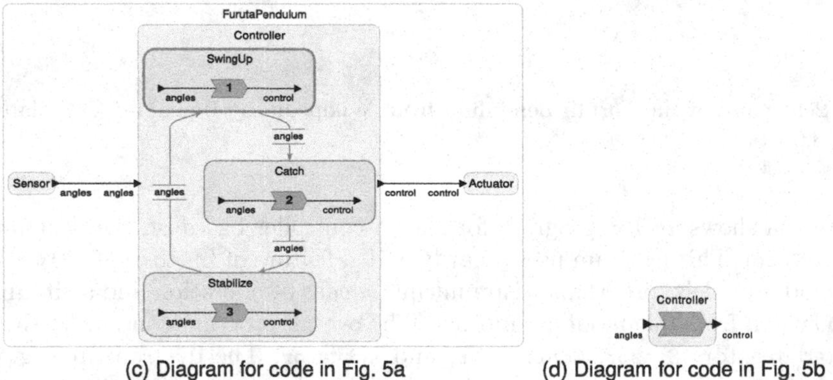

(c) Diagram for code in Fig. 5a

(d) Diagram for code in Fig. 5b

Fig. 5. Alternative LF realizations to drive the Furuta pendulum, with and without using LF-level modes.

in Sect. 8, there are several approaches for extracting state/modal structures for various programming languages. However, it is notoriously difficult for tools to discern modal structure in such code, and the rendered diagram, shown in Fig. 5d gives no hint.

4 On the Graphical Syntax in Lingua Franca

An important design decision for LF diagrams is how data flow and control flow should visually relate to each other. In LF, reactors are denoted with rounded rectangles and their data flow is visualized with rectangular edge routing. Reactions are depicted by chevrons, a choice that was made intentionally to reduce visual clutter. Because the shape of the reaction already implies a direction (left-to-right), it is unnecessary to show arrows on incoming and outgoing line segments that connect to triggers/sources (attached on the left) and effects (attached on the right).

Following established practices for state machine models, modes are also represented using rounded rectangles. As illustrated in Fig. 5c, modes are distinguished from reactor instances via a differing color scheme, and state transitions are drawn as splines. Initial states are indicated with a thicker outline. Transition labels are drawn on top of the edge, instead of the more common label placement alongside the transition, which is prone to ambiguities. LF diagrams offer various ways for a user to influence the appearance and level of detail. For example, transitions may be shown without labels, or with labels that indicate which inputs and/or actions could cause a mode transition to be taken.

Labeling itself is also subject to design considerations. Traditionally, transition labels include triggers and effects. However, this would require an analysis of target code, and the conditions that actually lead to taking a transition, as well as the effects that result from taking that transition, might become arbitrarily complex. We therefore opted to restrict the transition labels to the events that *may* trigger a reaction, omitting whatever further logic inside the host code determines whether a transition will actually be taken. This appears adequate in practice so far, but if one would want to visualize triggers further, it would for example be conceivable to let the user control what part of the program logic should be shown by some kind of code annotation mechanism. If labels are filtered out, we bundle multiple transitions between the same modes into one to further reduce diagram clutter.

After defining the basic visual syntax for data flow and control flow, the next question is how to combine these different diagram types. One option would be to fully integrate these diagrams. This would mean, for example, that a data flow edge would cross the hierarchy level of the mode to connect any content of the mode. We created several visual mockups for that. However, all variants that included some form of cross-hierarchy edges were considered confusing as soon as they exceeded a trivial size. Additionally, the interaction for collapsing modes to hide their contents and the feasibility with respect to automatic layout algorithms seemed non-trivial. In the end we opted for breaking up these outside connections on the level of each mode. This makes some connections more implicit, but leads to cleaner diagrams and simplifies the layout task. For ports, we duplicate those used in a mode and represent them by their arrow figure. The name is used to create an association to the original reactor port. In Fig. 5c one can see this in the `angles` input triggering reactions.

5 Auto-Layout of Lingua Franca Diagrams

As explained in Sect. 2, a key to pragmatics-aware modeling and programming is the ability to synthesize graphical views of a model, which is commonly also referred to as "automatic layout". As discussed further in Sect. 7, key to acceptance is a high-quality layout, which should meet a number of aesthetic criteria such as minimal edge crossings.

While the average user should not be required to have a deep understanding of the graph drawing algorithm engineering employed by an IDE, just like the average programmer should not need to know the inner workings of the compiler used, it is helpful to understand some of the basics. This in particular when one wants to tweak the layout in some ways, e. g., via the model order covered below. We consider this basic understanding also essential for tool developers who want to harness layout libraries effectively. Even though these libraries may produce reasonable results out of the box, they typically have numerous parameters that one may adjust to fine-tune the results.

A natural candidate for the synthesis of LF diagrams is the "Sugiyama" algorithm, also known as *layered algorithm* [51], which is, for example, employed in the well-known GraphViz package [5]. The LF tooling uses an extension of the Sugiyama algorithm that can handle hierarchical graphs, hyperedges, and port constraints necessary for LF [43]. That extension is provided by ELK[11], which provides automatic layout for a number of commercial and academic visual tool platforms, including, e. g., Ptolemy II [35]. All the LF diagrams shown in this paper have been generated automatically by ELK, using the tooling described further in Sect. 6. In this section, we very briefly review the basics of the underlying algorithm and point out some of the issues that arise in practice.

The Sugiyama algorithm is divided into five *phases* to break down complexity: 1) The graph is made acyclic, by reversing a set of edges. One tries to minimize the number of reversed edges, to create a clear left-to-right data-flow, which makes it easier to follow edges. 2) Nodes, which correspond to reactors, reactions, actions, and timers, are assigned to vertical *layers* such that edges only occur between layers, which can be seen in the `Display` reactor in Fig. 3a. Here, reactions 1 and 4 are in the second layer, the other nodes are in the first (leftmost) layer. 3) Edge crossings are minimized by changing the node order inside a layer and the port or edge order on a node. With that, the "topology" of the layout, consisting of the assignments of nodes to layers and node ordering within the layers, is fully defined. 4) Nodes are assigned coordinates within layers, trying to minimize edge bends. 5) Layers are assigned coordinates, edges are routed.

[11] https://www.eclipse.org/elk/.

This basic approach is unchanged since the beginnings of KIELER and the underlying ELK algorithmics. However, a current development, also spurred by the LF effort, is to give the modeler more and easier control over the layout than is traditionally the case. Specifically, the *model order*, which refers to the order in which nodes (e. g., reactors or modes) or edges (e. g., transitions) are declared in the textual LF code, should have a direct influence on the layout topology. This is not the case in standard graph drawing practice, which considers a graph to consist of an *unordered* set of nodes and an *unordered* set of edges. Thus, when computing the layout topology, if the Sugiyama algorithm has multiple solutions of the same aesthetic quality to choose from, it usually picks one of them randomly, which may not be what the modeler wants. One common way to give the modeler influence over the layout topology is to allow *layout annotations* in the textual code, and this is also possible in KIELER. However, this requires some extra effort, also in communicating and familiarizing oneself with these annotations, whereas the model order is a concept that is already inherent in the process of modeling.

For example, concerning Phase 1 of the Sugiyama algorithm, if the graph contains a cycle, then one may randomly choose any edge to be reversed. At least from a graph drawing perspective that only tries to minimize the number of reversed edges, that solution will be as good as any other that only reverses one edge. However, when considering the model order, here the order of declaration of the states, it seems desirable to break cycles such that the model order is preserved. For example, the mode transitions in the `Controller` in Fig. 5c form a cycle[12], meaning that (at least) one transition has to be rendered in the reverse direction. The model order suggests to order `SwingUp` first, and hence to reverse the edge that leads from `Stabilize` back to `SwingUp`. Thus, we say that model order should serve as "tie breaker" whenever there are several equally good solutions to choose from. For modal models, there is also the convention to place initial states first, which in Fig. 5c also happens to be `SwingUp`.

The model order also concerns the textual order of reactor instantiations. This would, e. g., in Fig. 2a suggest to place `clyde` and `pinky` in the same vertical layer as `inky`, `blinky`, and the `player`, which are currently only placed in the rightmost layer because of a random decision of the used edge reversal heuristic.

Also, the order of reactions in the same layer should be taken into account during crossing minimization, as seen in Fig. 3a. The startup and shutdown actions, which are not in the textual model, should be placed at the top and bottom of the first layer, as seen in the `Display` and `GameController` reactor. Furthermore, reactions should be ordered based on their order inside their respective vertical layers, as their numbering suggests.

Reactors are laid out left-to-right, resulting in vertical layers. Modes are laid out top-to-bottom, which turned out to result in a better aspect ratio. Therefore, horizontal layers are created, as seen the `Controller` reactor in Fig. 5c. The greedy cycle breaker reverses edges based on the difference of inputs and outputs, called the outflow. As discussed, if several modes have the same outflow,

[12] The reactions do not form a causality loop in this case, so the program is well-formed.

the model order should be taken into account. The model order of the modes can also be used as a tie-breaker during crossing minimization, as described by Domrös and von Hanxleden [4].

6 Diagram Synthesis Tooling

Providing a comprehensive modeling experience that combines textual editing and interactive diagrams with automatic layout requires sophisticated tooling. The tool has to account for model parsing and editing, diagram synthesis, diagram layout, rendering, and providing a user interface. The KIELER project [8] has been a testbed and birthplace of some key technologies in pragmatics-aware modeling. In the past, it was primarily build upon Eclipse, a versatile and extensible Java-based IDE. Recent development also allows a simultaneous support for Visual Studio Code using the LSP. A major factor in supporting both IDEs is the Xtext framework[13] [7] that enables the development of DSLs with multi-platform editor support. Based on a grammar specification, it automatically creates a parser, as well as editor support for syntax highlighting, content-assist, folding, jump-to-declaration, and reverse-reference lookup across multiple files, in the form of either Eclipse plugins or a language server. Furthermore, Xtext follows a model-based approach that uses the ecore meta-model of the Eclipse Modeling Framework (EMF) to represent the parsing result in a more abstracted format that is easier to process.

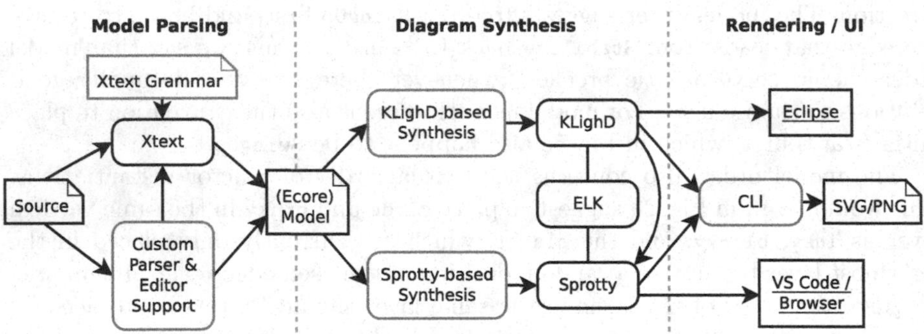

Fig. 6. Overview of the frameworks involved in and around the KIELER project. Sticker-like boxes indicate (in-memory) artifacts, rectangles are IDEs. Rounded boxes represent frameworks or modules, where red ones are language-specific. (Color figure online)

We will now take a look at how these technologies come together in the tool chain created around the KIELER project. Figure 6 gives a schematic overview of the frameworks and steps involved in turning a textual source into an interactive

[13] https://www.eclipse.org/Xtext/.

diagram. There are different paths, we start with the one used by LF. We will discuss alternatives afterwards, as they represent options to utilize this tool chain for a new project. Boxes in red indicate where a user has to provide a model-specific implementation.

Since the very start, LF was based on an Xtext grammar, so it was relatively quick and easy to integrate with the KIELER framework. As Fig. 6 illustrates, Xtext produces an ecore model. Next is a model-specific diagram synthesis that defines the graphical elements and their appearance. In case of LF, the KIELER Lightweight Diagrams (KLighD)[14] [41] framework is used. Based on the internal representation (also an ecore model), KLighD performs layout by using ELK and is able to display the diagram in Eclipse. In case of LF, the result is a custom Eclipse product, called Epoch. It is also possible to bundle the Xtext and KLighD infrastructure into a command line tool to export diagrams without an IDE. To incorporate diagrams in VS Code, KLighD utilizes the Sprotty framework[15], a more basic diagramming framework built with web technologies. The final VS Code extension for LF only needs to bundle KLighD into the language server and depends on a KLighD extension.

A project that does not rely on Xtext, Eclipse, or even Java can still utilize the given tool chain. For example the Blech language[16] [12] has a custom parser written in F# but uses the Sequentially Constructive StateCharts (SCCharts) language [16] as an exchange format with diagram support, to visualize an abstracted view of its structure [30]. In a Java-based context, even non-ecore-based model representations can be used to create KLighD diagram syntheses. For a fully web-based solution targeting only VS Code and browsers, Langium[17] could be a viable replacement for Xtext, and instead of KLighD, a Sprotty-based synthesis would be written. Sprotty is likewise capable of performing layout using ELKJS.

7 Modeling Pragmatics—Obstacles, Opportunities and Outlook

As explained, the practicality and value of modeling pragmatics has been validated now for some time. However, it is still far from standard practice, which begs the question of what is holding progress back. We believe the underlying issues are as much of psychological as of technical nature. In the following, we review some of the impediments, but also cover some (overall rather positive) user feedback beyond the LF context and reflect on what we see as the main challenges ahead.

---

[14] https://github.com/kieler/KLighD.
[15] https://github.com/eclipse/sprotty.
[16] https://www.blech-lang.org/.
[17] https://langium.org/.

7.1 A Priori User Concerns

When first presented with the concept of pragmatics-aware modeling, the reactions typically range from all-out enthusiasm to pronounced scepticism. Here are some of the more common reactions.

"I Want Full Control" As Gurr states, "people like having feedback and control" [13]. There is the fear to lose control when handing the layout problem to the machine. Of course, there is some truth in this—when using a compiler, people cannot fully control how the assembler is written anymore. In a similar vein, Taylor commented on What You See is What You Get (WYSIWYG) for typesetting and states its two-faced nature [53]:

> "Why has WYSIWYG succeeded so spectacularly, while other typesetting approaches have languished? I think WYSIWYG's main appeal is that it appears to offer its users superior cybernetics—i. e., feedback and control. To the extent that you can trust its authenticity, the screen gives immediate feedback. Acting on that feedback, the user then has immediate control. And people like having feedback and control. [...]
> It is worth remarking in this context that while WYSIWYG may have won the hearts and minds of designers through "superior cybernetics," the degree of control that such programs offer may be more illusory than real. Or perhaps it is more accurate to say that desktop publishing programs let you fiddle interactively with the details of your typography until the cows come home, but they do not let you control the default behaviors of the composition algorithms in a way that efficiently and automatically delivers the kind of quality typography that was formerly expected of trade compositors."

However, in practice, experience shows that one often is satisfied with *any* readable layout and thus does not invest efforts in making the layout sound with a freehand Drag-and-Drop (DND) editor. Therefore, in practice the issue of full control may be less relevant than it may seem at first. We also see an analogy here to the usage of auto-formatters in coding that is well-accepted by now and that helps to achieve a consistent "look" for textual code. Still, when propagating automatic layout, one should listen carefully to the potential users and try to extract what it really is that they want control of. Often this is not the individual pixel-by-pixel placement, but something more abstract, that might even be integrated into automatic layout. We see the incorporation of model order into the layout sketched in Sect. 5 as a prime example for that.

Graphical $\neq$ Informal. "I'm not a graphical person, I'm a formal person" is another, not untypical comment. However, graphical vs. textual is a question of syntax, and both diagrams and text can have arbitrarily formal or informal semantics. Therefore, the proposal here is to combine the best of both worlds and not to play text off against diagrams.

Layout Algorithms Not Good Enough. One claim of this work is that automatic layout must be so good that people are willing to replace manual placing and routing by it. However, a common opinion is that the layout algorithms today do not meet this requirement. And indeed, there have been several examples of tools that provided some auto-layout functionality that produced rather unsatisfactory results. However, there also are positive examples, also in commercial tools; e. g., LabView has employed sophisticated layout algorithms in its "clean-up" functionality [39], which seems quite satisfactory (see also a quote citing LabView further below).

Not Aware of Productivity Loss. Many decision makers seem to be unaware of the productivity losses of the usual freehand DND editing and manual static view navigation for diagrams. Practitioners of graphical modeling realize the benefits more immediately. Numbers from industry partners indicate that about 30% overhead is induced by manual layout. However, current trends towards textual DSL modeling might indicate that some people already see drawbacks with the traditional graphical modeling. Still, the consequences should not be to replace diagrams by text but to enhance the pragmatics of diagrams.

Loose the Mental Map. A spontaneous fear expressed for automatic layout is about losing the mental map that one may already have of a diagram. However, for rather stable layouters and employing them consistently from the beginning, the mental map can be kept very well. Conversely, for radical model changes the value of preserving the mental map seems overrated. Experience shows that a clean and reproducible auto layout results in more comprehensible models than a very effort-prone manual incremental layout that tries to change as little as possible. Especially when working with different people, maybe in different roles, adherence to a consistent layout style may be more important than preserving the mental map of an individual developer throughout the design process. And as discussed in Sect. 5, incorporating the model order into the layout process may help to align a modelers mental map with the automatically created layout.

7.2 Feedback After Usage and Lessons Learned

Get Used to It—Don't Want to Miss it Anymore. Even if it may be unfamiliar to work only with auto layout in the beginning, users get used to it. Finally they find it hard to go back to other tools employing manual layout again. In a survey conducted by Klauske [21] with around thirty practicioners at Daimler that used a version of Simulink enhanced with automatic layout [23], users reported massive time savings and expressed the wish for keeping that functionality. That feedback was also put forward to the tool supplier.

Interactive Layout Overrated. First, some users request ways to interactively influence the layout, either by specific means to configure the layout algorithm or by simply tagging regions as "manually laid out, don't touch!" Therefore many configuration options have been added to the KIELER Infrastructure for Meta Layout (KIML) including an interactive mode for some layout algorithms and tagging regions as manual layout. While this seems to ease initial acceptance, in the long term people often get used to full automatic layout, such that these interactive features are only rarely used any longer.

User Interface Must be Simple. Users usually have no sense about the layout approach of a specific layout algorithm or requirements of the tool. Therefore, the user interface to call layout must be simple and intuitive. Otherwise, people tend to not use it at all. One example is the first approach to the routing problem in the Ptolemy II editor Vergil. It introduced five buttons, all changing the diagram massively in different ways while users without any background usually did not understand what the differences were. Therefore, the functionality was barely adopted and required a different approach allowing a cleaner interface with only one button. While configurability is very good and important, this tells us that user interfaces have to be very clear and simple. They should always provide meaningful default configurations that lead to good results if the user is not willing to spend any efforts in understanding all customization options.

7.3 A Short Experience Report from the Railway Domain

An early adaptor in industry of SCCharts [16] and its pragmatics-aware modeling support based on KIELER is the German railway signalling manufacturer Scheidt & Bachmann System Technik GmbH (S&B). Just like LF, SCCharts are edited in a textual form and get embedded into host code (Java or C++). Engineers at S&B widely recognize the benefits of textually editing models right next to the host code, and are accustomed to using automatically generated diagrams for communication purposes. Typical communication tasks are documentation of the system architecture and detailed behavior. An important use case where the automatically synthesized, always up-to-date diagrams are particularly useful, is the onboarding of new team members working on the SCCharts models. A major advantage is that complex domain logic is abstracted such that it can be read and written and understood by domain experts who are not familiar with the host programming languages. This takes advantage of the fact that SCCharts models, like LF models, can be written and visualized before filling in host code. This allows a good division of work where domain experts can directly contribute domain logic as real technical artifacts, without a laborious and error-prone manual transition of domain knowledge into code. In fact, this practical aspect was a main driver for adopting the SCCharts tooling, and we consider this a great success.

In the early days, the generated diagrams were quite often printed on large "wallpapers" to collaboratively reason about design and find flaws in the implementation. Bugs in the models still get analyzed mainly in static diagrams rather manually. However, in practice is also desirable to inspect actual run time behavior, and although simulation of SCCharts is possible, the problems usually appear when used in the complex contexts in which they are embedded in some distributed application. Thus, the simpler the context outside of the model is, the better are the possibilities of analyzing the behavior of the whole system. That experience has prompted the development of a run-time debugging capability that seamlessly integrates SCCharts and host code [6]. However, this is still rarely used because the design problems are often too timing dependent and depend on the interaction of multiple distributed models, making them unlikely to surface in debugging sessions. Instead, when a rare unexpected behavior occurs, logged event traces of the distributed models are used to reproduce the state transitions to find the model flaw. Thus, the S&B use case might very much benefit from explicitly modeling the distribution of the system parts and the messaging between them with the LF approach.

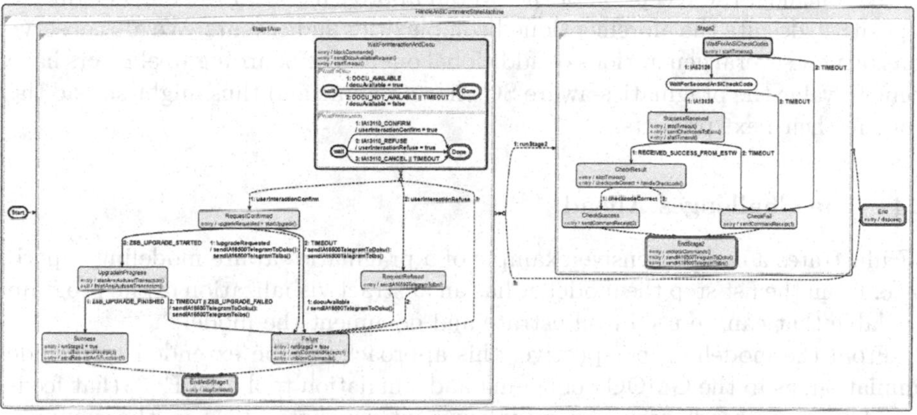

Fig. 7. A typical reactive SCChart diagram for the railway domain, illustrating label management.

Despite its limitations, the high level of abstraction of SCCharts and the possibility to view the models as diagrams has increased productivity. Especially textual editing next to automatic diagram generation, with diagrams that link elements back to the textual source, facilitates rapid changes such as refactorings and additions to models. In a classic what-you-see-is-what-you-get editing approach, these operations might be considered too costly to do, which tends to deteriorate code quality and increase technical debt on the long run. A typical, still relatively small SCChart is shown in Fig. 7. One feature that can be seen here is *label management* [42], which in this case is configured such that transition labels are shortened by introducing line breaks between triggers and actions and between actions. As most of our SCCharts tend to have even longer labels than in this example, label management—which also allows truncating labels at a freely defined width—is an essential feature to keep diagrams manageable.

One word of caution, however, about tooling in general. Fancy complex modeling environments with a shiny Graphical User Interface (GUI) are nice for the editing experience, but may be counterproductive for solving the obsolescence problem. In industry, one needs tools that last for a long period of time. We need to make sure that we are able to work on our technical source artifacts for the whole life-span of our product, i. e., at least 15–20 years in the railway domain. While it is remarkable that the Eclipse-based tooling of KIELER is in active development and use for over a decade now, the successor generation with web-based, cloud-ready tooling is already there, as outlined in Sect. 6. Hence, it seems essential in practice to create modular tooling, where the core functionality can be used even when the GUI originally developed is no longer technically supported by operating systems or hardware platforms and might be replaced by some next generation frontend. For SCChart, this prompted the development of a commandline tool for SCChart compilation and essential diagram generation, while we use any additional tooling frontend as "pragmatic sugar".

To conclude, the reception of the overall approach within the S&B engineers is positive, despite the aforementioned complexities and caveats. We also observe that by now several generations of additional on- and offboarding freelancers have come to value the pragmatics-aware SCCharts tooling and thus might spread the word in their next projects.

7.4 The Challenges Ahead

LF illustrates a comprehensive example of a pragmatics-aware modeling experience. From the fist step the modeller has an abstract visualization of the program available that can be used to illustrate and document the model[18].

From the modelling perspective, this approach can be extended to include simulation, as in the GMOC debugging and simulation tool for LF [3] that feeds live data into the diagram, or visualizing intermediate steps in the compilation, such as dependencies determined by the compiler, e. g. as available in the KIELER tool for SCCharts [49]. With the support of the LSP and Visual Studio Code, the pragmatics-aware modeling support is also available in the latest IDEs (see Sect. 6). We hope that the the pragmatic development idea will flourish in this large and vibrant ecosystem.

From the documentation perspective, pragmatics-aware diagrams can improve the effectiveness of static documentation and maybe ease classical certification processes. Ongoing work automatically synthesizes diagrams for System-Theoretic Process Analysis (STPA) [56]. The commercial EHANDBOOK tool[19] uses ELK and other technologies described in this paper to serve interactive documentation for electronic control unit (ECU) software in the form of Simulink diagrams. Web-based technologies (Sect. 6) combine the classical written documentation with embedded interactive diagrams, including dedicated views or links that navigate the reader into different locations and configurations of the model and that support collaborative browsing.

---

[18] https://www.lf-lang.org/docs/handbook/overview.

[19] http:/www.etas.com/ehandbook.

While the fundamental concepts and technologies for pragmatics-aware modeling are already realized and validated, there are still challenges ahead that need to be addressed to further improve the usability and ultimately the acceptance of this approach.

Finding the Right Abstraction Level. Having support for a pragmatics-aware modeling is one side, but creating effective views for complex models is another aspect. Here, abstraction is key. Visualizing the general coordination structure of a program, such as in LF diagrams, is probably more economic and helpful than, e. g., generating a huge control-flow diagram that displays all underlining machine instructions. Also, while we in this paper focussed on synthesizing abstract views from implementation-level textual models, system architects may want to start with abstract models as well. As mentioned earlier, the separation of high-level coordination language and low-level host code is one step in that direction.

Browsing Complex Systems. Related to the abstraction challenge, in particular large and complex models require further development of filtering and browsing techniques. We see an approach inspired by Google Maps as a promising direction to tackle this issue [15].

Configuring Automatic Layout Effectively. Layout algorithms typically provide many options to influence the way the layout works and thus the aesthetic of the final result. In our experience, achieving very good results for non-trivial diagram types requires an at least basic understanding of how the underlying graph drawing algorithm works, just like crafting high-performance software requires some basic understanding of modern compilers and computer architectures. Also, layout documentation and configuration guidance should be improved. Luckily, diagrams can aid in this, to interactively showcase options and their effects.

Lowering the Entry Barrier. Creating pragmatic concepts for new DSLs is easier than integrating it into existing design methodologies and tools. Yet, from a commercial and psychological perspective, low invasiveness is a circuital factor in the acceptance of these concepts. Hence, it is important to provide low entry barriers and allow augmenting existing languages and tools, rather than trying to replace them. For example, mode diagrams were added to Blech [30] in a way that did not impact the existing tool chain, but augmented it as an add-on. Again, the change into web-based technologies is an important step in this direction. A related challenge is to provide pragmatics capabilities in a way that one the one hand integrates well into existing tools and work flows, but on the other hand is robust against technology changes, see the obsolescence issue raised earlier. Technology-independent standards like LSP and the aforementioned more recent GLSP might help.

Establishing a Diagrammatic Modeling Mindset. In our experience, users do not normally consider the automatic diagram synthesis as an option for visualizing internal or conceptual structures of their model. Addressing this requires a change in the mindset of the tool developers, but we are convinced the effort will pay off.

8 Related Work

The Interactive Programmatic Modeling proposed by Broman [2] also advocates to combine textual modeling with automatically generated graphical views. He argues for an MVC pattern as well, albeit with different roles for model and controller than in our case, as for him the controller concerns the parameterization and the model is an execution engine. He identifies several problems with standard modeling approaches, including the *model expressiveness problem*, implying that graphical models become less intuitive when trying to capture more complex models. While we argue here that model complexity is actually an argument in favor of (automatically generated) graphical models, we concur with his point that graphical models are particularly helpful when they do not aim to capture a system in full detail, but rather provide abstractions.

The *intentional programming* paradigm proposed by Simonyi, in a sense, also advocates a separation of model and view [47]. There, a developer should start with formulating rather abstract "intantions" that successiveley get refined working on a "program tree", which can be viewed using an arbitrary and non-permanent syntax. One may argue that we here take the inverse approach, where the developer directly authors a (detailed) model, but gets assisted by a continuously updated visual, abstract documentation.

Computational notebooks, such as Jupyter[20], follow the *literate programming* paradigm proposed by Knuth that integrates documentation and source code [24]. They are increasingly popular in data science and are related to modeling pragmatics in that they also advocate a mix of representations.

The Umple framework also follows a pragmatic approach in that it also explicitly aims to provide the best of textual and diagrammatic worlds [27]. It allows both textual and graphical editing of UML models, and it can automatically synthesize class diagrams and other diagram types, using GraphViz layouts. However, these diagrams appear to be rather static, without further filtering/-navigation capabilities as we propose here.

There are several approaches for extracting, and typically also visualizing, state structures from textual sources. As mentioned in Sect. 6, the tooling for the textual Blech language [12] allows to automatically visualize an abstracted modal view [30]. Unlike in LF, modes are not explicit in the textual Blech source, but must be derived from Esterel-like await statements and overall imperative control flow. Kung et al. [26] and Sen and Mall [46] present ways to extract state machines from object-oriented languages. They analyze the behavior of classes and infer state machines describing the class behavior. Giomi [10] and Said et al. [40] describe state machine extractions based on control flow to represent the program's state space.

Less common is the automatic synthesis of actor diagrams, as proposed by Rentz et al. for legacy C/C++ code [37]. Ishio et al. [20] have investigated interprocedural dataflow for Java programs. They propose Variable Data-Flow Graphs (VDFGs) that represent interprocedural dataflow, but abstract from

[20] https://jupyter.org/.

intraprocedural control flow. There are further tools and frameworks to reverse engineer diagrams from C code. CPP2XMI is such a framework as used by Korshunova et al. [25] for extracting class, sequence, and activity diagrams, or MemBrain for analyzing method bodies as presented by Mihancea [31]. UML class models are extracted from C++ by Sutton and Maletic [52], and another framework for the analysis of object oriented code is presented by Tonella and Potrich [54]. Smyth et al. [48] implemented a generic C code miner for SCCharts. The focus was to create semantically valid models from legacy C code, whereas in modeling pragmatics, the aim typically is to synthesize graphical abstractions. However, all these tools and frameworks show the importance of reverse engineering and presenting views to programmers.

There are several pragmatics-oriented proposals that go beyond the basics presented here. Early on, Prochnow et al. proposed *dynamic focus and context* views that highlight the run-time state of a system by presenting active regions in detail and collapsing others [33], realized in the KIEL Integrated Environment for Layout (KIEL) tool, a predecessor or KIELER. KIEL also included *structure-based editing*, which combines WYSIWYG editing (without a textual source) with continuous automatic layout [34]. More recent work includes the *induced data flow* approach that synthesizes actor-oriented diagrams from SCCharts [55], and interactive compilation models that visualize intermediate transformation results, which can be helpful for users and compiler developers alike [50].

Finally, as explained, a key enabler for the pragmatics approach presented here is the large body of work produced by the graph drawing community. Conversely, pragmatics has become a significant use case that prompted advancements in graph drawing [1]. Interested readers may look at the publication lists of the ELK contributors, which include flagship venues and several dissertations. However, like writing a compiler, the authoring of a graph drawing library that works well in practice is a significant piece of engineering. Fortunately, the contributors to ELK and other projects covered in Sect. 6 not only strived for publishable algorithms, but also made good software engineering a priority. For example, one of the lessons learned over the years is that one has to strike a good balance between functionality and maintanability, and if in doubt, one should probably favor the latter.

9 Summary and Conclusions

To recapitulate, the main driver of modeling pragmatics as presented here is to enhance developer productivity by combining the best of the textual and visual modeling worlds. Traditionally, visual models 1) are manually created, often in a rather time-consuming process in particular when one wants to maintain good readability in an evolving model, 2) have a fixed level of detail, and 3) may get out-of-date with respect to an implementation model. In the pragmatic approach, visual models 1) are created automatically, 2) can be customized and apply filtering, and 3) are consistent with the model from which they are synthesized. Clearly, the capability to automatically create abstract, up-to-date visual diagrams from textual models is a boon for documentation. This encompasses documentation in a very broad sense, where it is an integral, supportive part of the design process itself. We postulate that whenever developers may need to document or communicate a model aspect that cannot be readily gleaned from looking directly at source code, a viable approach might be to automatically generate a diagram that fits on a screen. Even though automatic graph drawing is not a trivial process and a still a research topic in its own right, the primary challenge in modeling pragmatics might be less the task of computing good layouts, but rather to filter/abstract the model appropriately; i. e., once one knows *what* to visualize, the question of *how* to visualize it can be answered quite well with today's technology.

Looking back at the story of modeling pragmatics so far, the main conclusion may be that it takes some perseverence to change tools and habits, just like it probably took quite some convincing to wean programmers off their assembly writing when compilers came about. In some way, it seems a bit like a chicken-and-egg problem; the average user is not aware of its potential, and thus the average tool provider sees no sufficient demand for it. Also, for an existing language with existing, traditional tooling, the conversion barriers seem significantly higher than for a newly created language without any such legacy.

However, progress seems possible, also for existing languages and tools that already have a large user base. As exemplary point in case, consider the following (abbreviated) exchange, on a Mathworks user forum[21]. On Feb. 23, 2012, User K E inquired: "Is there an automatic way to rearrange a Simulink block diagram so that it is easy to read?" Staff Member Andreas Gooser responded March 14, 2012: "A year ago, I worked with users and developers (I called it myself Simulink Beautifier :-)) to find out if such things are possible. I found myself convinced that this is a non-trivial undertaking, if you try this in a generic way, as there are too many criteria/rules." On that, User Ben noted Nov. 14, 2012: "Mathworks should invest the energy to develop an auto-cleanup feature. Tools like these are expected for serious and relevant 21st century software. Yes, it is non-trivial, but take a look at National Instrument's LabView—they've implemented such a feature beautifully and it saves hours of aggravation especially if you are developing complex code." That thread then fell silent for eight years. However, Staff Member Anh Tran posted Jan. 31, 2020: "From MATLAB R2019b, you can improve your diagram layout and appearance by opening the FORMAT tab on the toolstrip and click on Auto Arrange. This command can realign, resize, and move blocks and straighten signal lines". We have not evaluated the quality of the layout ourselves and have not heard of user feedback yet. However, already back at the 2010 MathWorks Automotive Conference, Klauske and Dziobek of the Daimler Center for Automotive IT Innovations (DCAITI) presented a Simulink extension for doing automatic layout that received quite positive user feedback, from actual users and during the workshop presentation, which makes us hopeful [21–23].

[21] https://www.mathworks.com/matlabcentral/answers/30016-clean-up-simulink-block-diagram.

In case of LF, the situation was certainly quite different from an established commercial tool that already has a very large user base accustomed to doing things in a certain way. We used that chance to harness modern, state-of-the art tooling infrastructure, building on insights won over many years in earlier projects such as Ptolemy and SCCharts. The pragmatics-aware approach presented here, with the automatic synthesis of abstract diagrams, is part of the LF toolchain since early on. As it turned out, while that approach of continuous, automatic diagram synthesis is still anything but standard practice, it does not seem to command much attention in that is basically "just there" and taken for granted. And when somebody is unhappy with certain aspects of some specific diagram, it is usually not an actual tool user working on some LF application, but somebody from the "pragmatics team" themselves with a close eye on graphical detail, who then also sets about finding a fix for it.

Thus, to conclude, we think that it certainly has helped in the case of LF to have considered pragmatics from the start, rather than as an afterthought. Also, as explained, some properties of LF such as its separation of coordination language and target language make it particularly natural to automatically synthesize abstract diagrams, as part of the design process and for documentation purposes. However, we also believe that much of the underlying pragmatics concepts are also transferrable to other languages and contexts. We thus conclude this report with an open invitation to try out the approaches presented here, and to share experiences and direct inquiries to the authors or to one of the public message boards associated with the open-source tools presented here.

References

1. Binucci, C., et al.: 10 reasons to get interested in graph drawing. In: Steffen, B., Woeginger, G. (eds.) Computing and Software Science. LNCS, vol. 10000, pp. 85–104. Springer, Cham (2019). https://doi.org/10.1007/978-3-319-91908-9_6
2. Broman, D.: Interactive programmatic modeling. ACM Trans. Embed. Comput. Syst. **20**(4), 33:1–33:26 (2021). https://doi.org/10.1145/3431387
3. Deantoni, J., Cambeiro, J., Bateni, S., Lin, S., Lohstroh, M.: Debugging and verification tools for LINGUA FRANCA in GEMOC studio. In: 2021 Forum on specification Design Languages (FDL), pp. 1–8 (2021). https://doi.org/10.1109/FDL53530.2021.9568383
4. Domrös, S., von Hanxleden, R.: Preserving order during crossing minimization in Sugiyama layouts. In: Proceedings of the 14th International Conference on Information Visualization Theory and Applications (IVAPP 2022), Part of the 17th International Joint Conference on Computer Vision, Imaging and Computer Graphics Theory and Applications (VISIGRAPP 2022), pp. 156–163. INSTICC, SciTePress (2022). https://doi.org/10.5220/0010833800003124
5. Ellson, J., Gansner, E., Koutsofios, L., North, S.C., Woodhull, G.: Graphviz—open source graph drawing tools. In: Mutzel, P., Jünger, M., Leipert, S. (eds.) GD 2001. LNCS, vol. 2265, pp. 483–484. Springer, Heidelberg (2002). https://doi.org/10.1007/3-540-45848-4_57
6. Eumann, P.: Model-Based Debugging. Master thesis, Christian-Albrechts-Universität zu Kiel, Department of Computer Science (2020). https://rtsys.informatik.uni-kiel.de/biblio/downloads/theses/peu-mt.pdf

7. Eysholdt, M., Behrens, H.: Xtext: implement your language faster than the quick and dirty way. In: Proceedings of the ACM International Conference Companion on Object Oriented Programming Systems Languages and Applications Companion, OOPSLA 2010, Reno/Tahoe, Nevada, USA, pp. 307–309 (2010). https://doi.org/10.1145/1869542.1869625
8. Fuhrmann, H., von Hanxleden, R.: Taming graphical modeling. In: Petriu, D.C., Rouquette, N., Haugen, Ø. (eds.) MODELS 2010. LNCS, vol. 6394, pp. 196–210. Springer, Heidelberg (2010). https://doi.org/10.1007/978-3-642-16145-2_14
9. Furuta, K., Yamakita, M., Kobayashi, S.: Swing-up control of inverted pendulum using pseudo-state feedback. Proc. Inst. Mech. Eng. Part I: J. Syst. Control Eng. **206**(4), 263–269 (1992). https://doi.org/10.1243/PIME_PROC_1992_206_341_02
10. Giomi, J.: Finite state machine extraction from hardware description languages. In: Proceedings of Eighth International Application Specific Integrated Circuits Conference, pp. 353–357. IEEE (1995). https://doi.org/10.1109/ASIC.1995.580747
11. Green, T.R.G., Petre, M.: When visual programs are harder to read than textual programs. In: Human-Computer Interaction: Tasks and Organisation, Proceedings ECCE-6 (6th European Conference Cognitive Ergonomics) (1992)
12. Gretz, F., Grosch, F.J.: Blech, imperative synchronous programming! In: Proceedings of Forum on Specification Design Languages (FDL 2018), pp. 5–16 (2018). https://doi.org/10.1109/FDL.2018.8524036
13. Gurr, C.A.: Effective diagrammatic communication: syntactic, semantic and pragmatic issues. J. Vis. Lang. Comput. **10**(4), 317–342 (1999). https://doi.org/10.1006/jvlc.1999.0130
14. Haberland, H., Mey, J.L.: Editorial: linguistics and pragmatics. J. Pragmat. **1**, 1–12 (1977)
15. von Hanxleden, R., Biastoch, A., Fohrer, N., Renz, M., Vafeidis, A.: Getting the big picture in cross-domain fusion. Inform. Spektr. (2022). https://doi.org/10.1007/s00287-022-01471-2
16. von Hanxleden, R., et al.: SCCharts: sequentially constructive statecharts for safety-critical applications. In: Proceedings of ACM SIGPLAN Conference on Programming Language Design and Implementation (PLDI 2014), pp. 372–383. ACM, Edinburgh (2014). https://doi.org/10.1145/2594291.2594310
17. von Hanxleden, R., Lee, E.A., Motika, C., Fuhrmann, H.: Multi-view modeling and pragmatics in 2020—position paper on designing complex cyber-physical systems. In: Calinescu, R., Garlan, D. (eds.) Monterey Workshop 2012. LNCS, vol. 7539, pp. 209–223. Springer, Heidelberg (2012). https://doi.org/10.1007/978-3-642-34059-8_11
18. Harel, D., Rumpe, B.: Meaningful modelling: what's the semantics of "semantics"? IEEE Comput. **37**(10), 64–72 (2004). https://doi.org/10.1109/MC.2004.172
19. Hoffmann, B., Minas, M.: Defining models–meta models versus graph grammars. In: Ninth International Workshop on Graph Transformation and Visual Modeling Techniques (GT-VMT 2010). Electronic Communications of the EASST, vol. 29. Berlin, Germany (2010). https://doi.org/10.14279/tuj.eceasst.29.411
20. Ishio, T., Etsuda, S., Inoue, K.: A lightweight visualization of interprocedural dataflow paths for source code reading. In: Beyer, D., van Deursen, A., Godfrey, M.W. (eds.) IEEE 20th International Conference on Program Comprehension (ICPC), pp. 37–46. IEEE, Passau (2012). https://doi.org/10.1109/ICPC.2012.6240506
21. Klauske, L.K.: Effizientes Bearbeiten von Simulink Modellen mit Hilfe eines spezifisch angepassten Layoutalgorithmus. Ph.D. thesis, Technische Universität Berlin (2012)

22. Klauske, L.K., Dziobek, C.: Improving modeling usability: automated layout generation for simulink. In: Proceedings of the MathWorks Automotive Conference (MAC 2010) (2010)
23. Klauske, L.K., Schulze, C.D., Spönemann, M., von Hanxleden, R.: Improved layout for data flow diagrams with port constraints. In: Cox, P., Plimmer, B., Rodgers, P. (eds.) Diagrams 2012. LNCS (LNAI), vol. 7352, pp. 65–79. Springer, Heidelberg (2012). https://doi.org/10.1007/978-3-642-31223-6_11
24. Knuth, D.E.: Literate programming. Comput. J. **27**(2), 97–111 (1984). https://doi.org/10.1093/comjnl/27.2.97
25. Korshunova, E., Petković, M., van den Brand, M.G.J., Mousavi, M.R.: CPP2XMI: reverse engineering of UML class, sequence, and activity diagrams from C++ source code. In: 13th Working Conference on Reverse Engineering (WCRE 2006), pp. 297–298. IEEE Computer Society, Benevento (2006). https://doi.org/10.1109/WCRE.2006.21
26. Kung, D., Suchak, N., Gao, J.Z., Hsia, P., Toyoshima, Y., Chen, C.: On object state testing. In: Proceedings Eighteenth Annual International Computer Software and Applications Conference (COMPSAC 1994), pp. 222–227. IEEE (1994). https://doi.org/10.1109/CMPSAC.1994.342801
27. Lethbridge, T.C., et al.: Umple: model-driven development for open source and education. Sci. Comput. Program. **208**, 102665 (2021). https://doi.org/10.1016/j.scico.2021.102665
28. Liu, J., Eker, J., Janneck, J.W., Lee, E.A.: Realistic simulations of embedded control systems. IFAC Proc. Vol. **35**(1), 391–396 (2002). https://doi.org/10.3182/20020721-6-ES-1901.00553
29. Lohstroh, M., Menard, C., Bateni, S., Lee, E.A.: Toward a Lingua Franca for deterministic concurrent systems. ACM Trans. Embedd. Comput. Syst. (TECS) **20**(4), Article 36 (2021). https://doi.org/10.1145/3448128. Special Issue on FDL'19
30. Lucas, D., Schulz-Rosengarten, A., von Hanxleden, R., Gretz, F., Grosch, F.J.: Extracting mode diagrams from Blech code. In: Proceedings of Forum on Specification and Design Languages (FDL 2021). Antibes, France (2021). https://doi.org/10.1109/FDL53530.2021.9568375
31. Mihancea, P.F.: Towards a reverse engineering dataflow analysis framework for Java and C++. In: Negru, V., Jebelean, T., Petcu, D., Zaharie, D. (eds.) 2008 10th International Symposium on Symbolic and Numeric Algorithms for Scientific Computing (SYNASC), Timisoara, Romania, pp. 285–288 (2008). https://doi.org/10.1109/SYNASC.2008.7
32. Morris, C.W.: Foundations of the Theory of Signs, International Encyclopedia of Unified Science, vol. 1. The University of Chicago Press, Chicago (1938)
33. Prochnow, S., von Hanxleden, R.: Comfortable modeling of complex reactive systems. In: Proceedings of Design, Automation and Test in Europe Conference (DATE 2006), Munich, Germany (2006). https://doi.org/10.1109/DATE.2006.243970
34. Prochnow, S., von Hanxleden, R.: Statechart development beyond WYSIWYG. In: Engels, G., Opdyke, B., Schmidt, D.C., Weil, F. (eds.) MODELS 2007. LNCS, vol. 4735, pp. 635–649. Springer, Heidelberg (2007). https://doi.org/10.1007/978-3-540-75209-7_43
35. Ptolemaeus, C.: System Design, Modeling, and Simulation using Ptolemy II. Ptolemy.org, Berkeley (2014). http://ptolemy.org/books/Systems
36. Reenskaug, T.: Models – views – controllers (1979). Xerox PARC technical note

37. Rentz, N., Smyth, S., Andersen, L., von Hanxleden, R.: Extracting interactive actor-based dataflow models from legacy C code. In: Basu, A., Stapleton, G., Linker, S., Legg, C., Manalo, E., Viana, P. (eds.) Diagrams 2021. LNCS (LNAI), vol. 12909, pp. 361–377. Springer, Cham (2021). https://doi.org/10.1007/978-3-030-86062-2_37
38. Roestenburg, R., Bakker, R., Williams, R.: Akka in Action. Manning Publications Co. (2016)
39. Rüegg, U., Lakkundi, R., Prasad, A., Kodaganur, A., Schulze, C.D., von Hanxleden, R.: Incremental diagram layout for automated model migration. In: Proceedings of the ACM/IEEE 19th International Conference on Model Driven Engineering Languages and Systems (MoDELS 2016), pp. 185–195 (2016). https://doi.org/10.1145/2976767.2976805
40. Said, W., Quante, J., Koschke, R.: On state machine mining from embedded control software. In: 2018 IEEE International Conference on Software Maintenance and Evolution (ICSME), pp. 138–148. IEEE (2018). https://doi.org/10.1109/ICSME.2018.00024
41. Schneider, C., Spönemann, M., von Hanxleden, R.: Just model! - Putting automatic synthesis of node-link-diagrams into practice. In: Proceedings of the IEEE Symposium on Visual Languages and Human-Centric Computing (VL/HCC 2013), San Jose, CA, USA, pp. 75–82 (2013). https://doi.org/10.1109/VLHCC.2013.6645246
42. Schulze, C.D., Lasch, Y., von Hanxleden, R.: Label management: keeping complex diagrams usable. In: Proceedings of the IEEE Symposium on Visual Languages and Human-Centric Computing (VL/HCC 2016), pp. 3–11 (2016). https://doi.org/10.1109/VLHCC.2016.7739657
43. Schulze, C.D., Spönemann, M., von Hanxleden, R.: Drawing layered graphs with port constraints. J. Vis. Lang. Comput. Spec. Issue Diagram Aesthet. Layout **25**(2), 89–106 (2014). https://doi.org/10.1016/j.jvlc.2013.11.005
44. Seibel, A.: Personal communication (2017)
45. Selic, B.: The pragmatics of model-driven development. IEEE Softw. **20**(5), 19–25 (2003). https://doi.org/10.1109/MS.2003.1231146
46. Sen, T., Mall, R.: Extracting finite state representation of Java programs. Softw. Syst. Model. **15**(2), 497–511 (2014). https://doi.org/10.1007/s10270-014-0415-3
47. Simonyi, C.: The death of computer languages, the birth of intentional programming. Technical report MSR-TR-95-52, Microsoft Research (1995)
48. Smyth, S., Lenga, S., von Hanxleden, R.: Model extraction for legacy C programs with SCCharts. In: Proceedings of the 7th International Symposium on Leveraging Applications of Formal Methods, Verification and Validation (ISoLA 2016), Doctoral Symposium. Electronic Communications of the EASST, Corfu, Greece, vol. 74 (2016). https://doi.org/10.14279/tuj.eceasst.74.1044. With accompanying poster
49. Smyth, S., Schulz-Rosengarten, A., von Hanxleden, R.: Guidance in model-based compilations. In: Proceedings of the 8th International Symposium on Leveraging Applications of Formal Methods, Verification and Validation (ISoLA 2018), Doctoral Symposium. Electronic Communications of the EASST, Limassol, Cyprus, vol. 78 (2018). https://doi.org/10.1007/978-3-030-03418-4_15
50. Smyth, S., Schulz-Rosengarten, A., von Hanxleden, R.: Towards interactive compilation models. In: Margaria, T., Steffen, B. (eds.) ISoLA 2018. LNCS, vol. 11244, pp. 246–260. Springer, Cham (2018). https://doi.org/10.1007/978-3-030-03418-4_15

51. Sugiyama, K., Tagawa, S., Toda, M.: Methods for visual understanding of hierarchical system structures. IEEE Trans. Syst. Man Cybern. **11**(2), 109–125 (1981). https://doi.org/10.1109/TSMC.1981.4308636
52. Sutton, A., Maletic, J.I.: Mappings for accurately reverse engineering UML class models from C++. In: 12th Working Conference on Reverse Engineering (WCRE 2005), pp. 175–184. IEEE Computer Society, Pittsburgh (2005). https://doi.org/10.1109/WCRE.2005.21
53. Taylor, C.: What has WYSIWYG done to us? Seybold Rep. Publ. Syst. **26**(2), 3–12 (1996)
54. Tonella, P., Potrich, A.: Reverse Engineering of Object Oriented Code. Springer, New York (2005). https://doi.org/10.1007/b102522
55. Wechselberg, N., Schulz-Rosengarten, A., Smyth, S., von Hanxleden, R.: Augmenting state models with data flow. In: Lohstroh, M., Derler, P., Sirjani, M. (eds.) Principles of Modeling. LNCS, vol. 10760, pp. 504–523. Springer, Cham (2018). https://doi.org/10.1007/978-3-319-95246-8_28
56. Young, W., Leveson, N.G.: An integrated approach to safety and security based on systems theory. Commun. ACM **57**(2), 31–35 (2014). https://doi.org/10.1145/2556938

Assurance Provenance: The Next Challenge in Software Documentation

Gabor Karsai(✉) and Daniel Balasubramanian

Institute for Software-Integrated Systems, Vanderbilt University, Nashville, TN, USA
gabor.karsai@vanderbilt.edu

Abstract. High-assurance software is often used in safety- and mission-critical systems where loss of functionality can lead to loss of life or property. Naturally, such systems need to be certified before use and several technologies have been developed to support such efforts. The techniques build structured assurance arguments to justify the safety and performance of the system. Most frequently, software is certified as part of a larger system where that larger system changes rather infrequently. However, this contradicts the current practice of rapid software evolution, where the need for new functionality is addressed by a software upgrade. As a consequence, assurance arguments often lag behind, leading to delays in implementing new capabilities. Hence, there is a clear need for the rapid re-analysis and re-evaluation of the assurance arguments. This paper argues that assurance arguments are a special kind of software documentation that need to be tightly integrated with the implementation, and their construction and managed evolution are critical to the safety and performance of software-integrated systems.

Keywords: Software assurance · Formal methods · Traceability · Software evolution

1 Introduction

In the state-of-the-art practice of agile software development [5], the engineering of high-assurance systems software[1] (HASS) is problematic. For these systems, software is critical and software-induced failures may lead to catastrophic loss of life or property. Modern society relies heavily on such systems, considering their prevalence in transportation, medicine, finance, infrastructure, defense, and other areas. Although the overall process and documentation requirements for such systems have been defined for more than 20 years (see, e.g., the DO-178B standard [16]), their development is still expensive, requires specialized skills and does not mesh well with agile practices. Especially problematic is the rapid

[1] We use the term 'high-assurance' instead of the more conventional 'safety-critical' to emphasize that these systems are required to be certified by some independent authority before operational use.

T. Margaria and B. Steffen (Eds.): ISoLA 2022, LNCS 13702, pp. 90–104, 2022.
https://doi.org/10.1007/978-3-031-19756-7_6

assurance: the construction and maintenance of documented logical arguments for their safety and reliability. Test-driven development is a well-understood paradigm [4], and, similarly, Continuous Integration/Continuous Deployment (CI/CD) [26] is practiced widely in the industry, yet they are not folded into an overall - agile - assurance approach for HASS.

HASS requires a higher degree of assurance than more common software systems. Regression testing is necessary but not sufficient, and so are design and code reviews. Formal methods and static and dynamic code analysis offer additional advantages and new, more exhaustive verification of a software system. Although formal methods and their automation have made significant advances during the past few decades, their integration into agile development flows has not been fully realized yet. Their use is often decoupled from the practice of the highly dynamic evolution of the code base so typical today.

The current agile development paradigm ([3]) is focusing on delivering 'good enough' software 'fast enough'. We argue that HASS requires a different approach where Continuous Assurance (CA) is an integral part of the process; i.e. 'Continuous Integration/Continuous Deployment' (CI/CD) becomes CI/CA/CD. This has to be accomplished in a way that does not contradict or prevent the use of the agile approach, rather CA has to extend and enhance that process. The key ingredient for such a development paradigm is an integrated view and management of software engineering artifacts for modeling, for implementation, and for assurance. Furthermore, these artifacts will be interspersed with or directly contain human readable natural language text that corresponds to what we call documentation today.

The rest of the paper briefly reviews the assurance argumentation, proposes a paradigm for organizing the artifacts for assurance, and lays out a vision for how it can be implemented. The paper closes with a brief review of related work and plans for future work.

2 Paradigm for Assured Software

Official documents define software assurance as: 'the level of confidence that software is free from vulnerabilities, either intentionally designed into the software or accidentally inserted at any time during its lifecycle, and that the software functions in the intended manner' [10]. Here, we use a more informal but technical definition: 'Software assurance is a phase of a software development process that produces engineering artifacts for logical arguments regarding the correctness, safety, and functionality of the software produced.' By 'correctness' we mean that the software implementation is correct with respect to its specification, by 'safety' we mean that the software does not cause harm, and by 'functionality' we mean that the software provides some utility for its user. Obviously, software assurance is necessary for safety and mission critical systems, and it is typically used in a larger system context: for the certification of a system (e.g., an airliner) one needs to produce a considerable amount of supporting documentation why it is safe for public use.

Assurance documentation needs to be structured to assist reviewers. One of the most commonly used structured forms is the Goal Structuring Notation (GSN) [17] standard. From the documentation [12]:

> GSN is a graphical argument notation that can be used to document explicitly the individual elements of any argument (claims, evidence and contextual information) and the relationships that exist between these elements (i.e. how claims are supported by other claims, and ultimately by evidence) and the context that is defined for the argument. GSN is a generic argument structuring language, which can be used to document arguments in any domain.

The central notion in GSN is that of the 'assurance argument' that lays out why a specific, concrete *safety goal* is achieved by the system. Note that GSN assurance cases are constructed *after* the system has been constructed, typically independently by safety engineers. Note also that GSN, as used in the industry, is a 'system-level' tool whose subject is the entire (cyber-physical) system, not only the software. When a GSN argument is constructed, a safety claim is stated (e.g., 'The autonomous vehicle avoids collisions with stationary obstacles'), then that claim is decomposed into sub-claims (e.g., 'The perception system detects the obstacle in path of the vehicle with sufficient probability', 'The braking system operates with sufficient reliability', etc.), assumptions are stated (e.g., 'The road surface is dry'), and the context is described (e.g., 'The vehicle speed is less than X', etc.).

A GSN assurance argument explains why a safety claim is true. Figure 1 shows an example GSN argument. The argument follows a tree like arrangement, with a top-level claim (or 'Goal', e.g., **G1**) at the root, followed by sub-claims ('sub-Goals', e.g., **G2**, etc.), some (e.g., **G4**, **G5**, **G6**) of which may be combined via a strategy (e.g., **S1**). The lowest level goals (e.g., **G4**) are supported by a solution (e.g., **Sn1**) that is ultimately grounded in some 'evidence' (not shown on the diagram). Goals are interpreted in some context (e.g., **C1** and **C2** for **G1**).

The argument explains how a top-level goal is decomposed into sub-goals, which are then decomposed further, possibly with the help of some strategy, recursively until we reach a level of abstraction where a goal can be directly supported by evidence. The tree can be interpreted (or 'read') following it top-down or bottom-up, as in a logical inference network, or a proof tree. Although the GSN arguments (and the corresponding reasoning) are deliberately mixing the formal and informal [14], recent efforts aim at introducing more formal reasoning [8]. More recent work [13] describes how formal analysis of GSN can be used to identify 'assurance deficits' in a software system.

While GSN can be correctly evaluated as subjective (as far as it is limited by the imagination of safety engineers), it is beneficial in the sense that it leads to concrete artifacts that can be used in the certification process. GSN has been used in industries building safety-critical systems and is a required standard for some defense applications. However, it is typically not tightly integrated into development tools and processes. To a certain degree, it is understandable, as

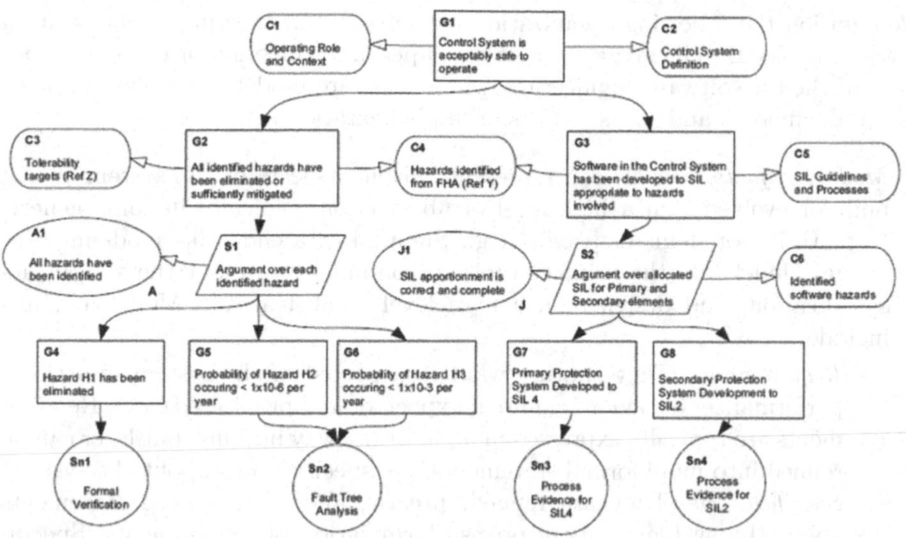

Fig. 1. Example assurance argument in GSN (Source: SCSC AWG [21])

system safety engineers who perform reviews and construct and analyze GSN arguments need to operate independently of designers, implementers, and testers, without unintended influence from the developers.

There is a valid argument for treating assurance arguments as 'documentation' for safety-critical systems. However, they are highly specialized documents: they are descriptive (of the design and implementation), but they also make statements about some (critical) properties of the software system and how those properties were established (through formal proofs, tests, etc.). In this sense, assurance arguments must exhibit *provenance*: they need to be connected to evidence about their subject (i.e., the software system) - the reviewer has to understand why the argument is valid, what parts of the specification, design, or implementation of the system it is related to, and how it is grounded in hard evidence produced by tests, proofs, automatic analysis of the code, or other means. Furthermore, whenever the design or implementation of the system changes this provenance must be re-validated. Our understanding is that today very few tools are available to support such engineering activities, while the complexity and functionality of HASS is continuously increasing. As system assurance requires significant resources, there is a clear need for a different, tool-based approach.

2.1 Artifacts and Organization

We propose an approach called Continuous Assurance-Integrated Development (CAID) that aims at addressing the issues raised above, while following (and thus maintaining the benefits of) existing development processes and practices.

We envision the following organization for software engineering artifacts in an instance of CAID. The artifacts can be grouped into three major categories, per state-of-the-art software engineering, where software models may play a role as design documents and/or as sources of implementation artifacts.

1. *Model artifacts.* Models can represent various aspects of the system (being built or evolved), on a high level of abstraction, typically in some generic (e.g., UML) or domain-specific (e.g., Simulink/Stateflow [9]) modeling language. Models are the primary tools to communicate about the system, its specification, and design - on a high level of abstraction. Model artifacts include:
   - *Requirements.* They capture what is expected of the system: functions, performance, behavior (required, expected, and prohibited), etc. Requirements are typically expressed in an informal way initially, but later can be refined into more formal statements; i.e. specifications about the system.
   - *Specifications.* They are refined, precise, and often formal statements about the system; a more precise formulation of requirements. Specifications are often used in system verification and validation, thus helping to define and develop evidence for assurance claims.
   - *Design models.* They represent design decisions about the system: its architecture, behavior, functions, interfaces, etc. Design models could serve as documentation, as sources of (generated) implementation artifacts, or both.
2. *Implementation artifacts.* These form the actual implementation that is eventually translated into binary or script-form executable(s) and configuration data, as well as the tests and the tool choices used to produce the implementation. We also include here the human-readable documentation for code (API documents) and for the human end-user who interacts with the system.
   - *Code.* The actual implementation of the system, 'production code'. Note that code often integrates documentation text [18,24] from which the actual documentation is automatically generated.
   - *Tests.* Unit and system-level tests showing the lack of flaws (though not the correctness) of the system or its components, for selected situations and scenarios.
   - *Tooling.* Set of tools used to build, test, validate, and verify the system, as well as their integration into a development environment.
   - *Documentation.* Code-level and end-user documentation of the system. Code-level documentation (e.g., an API) is generated from the (annotated) code, but end-user documentation is independently developed and maintained.
3. *Assurance artifacts.* These form the basis for the assurance process that enables the certification of the system.
   - *Arguments.* Structured assurance arguments lay out claims about the safety, correctness, performance, etc. of the system and the formal argument structure that explains why those claims are true. The claims (or

goals) are typically hierarchical, where lower-level claims support higher level claims (possibly via a reasoning strategy) and, on the lowest level, claims are supported by evidence. The argument structure represents, at a minimum, dependencies with nodes, but, in a more formal setting with well-defined semantics, can represent chains of logical inferences.

- *Evidence artifacts.* They provide the ultimate grounding of claims, in the form of reproducible - or reviewed - artifacts. These include:
    - *Proofs.* They represent a logical inference process that proves a formal statement (typically a specification) about code or a model of the code.
    - *Test results.* They capture the execution trace of tests that were executed on the system and demonstrate some relevant property of the system.
    - *Documents.* They are reviewed and vetted sources of information, typically produced by human experts.

All of the above, and possibly other artifacts, play a role in the design, development, and maintenance of a system. Note that for HASS, the assurance artifacts are critical, as they enable the certification of, and, ultimately foster trust in the system. To some degree, all artifacts can be considered as 'documentation', while some of them form the actual operational 'software system'.

2.2 Observations

Development is a *process*, enacted by many designers/developers/testers, that unfolds over time, often with concurrent activities. Development tools must be prepared to support continuous software evolution, with potentially multiple concurrent activities. Software development is unlike conventional engineering product development, in the sense that there is no single 'arrow' of development but rather multiple branches, in different state of readiness (or even correctness), with occasional synchronization points where changes are consolidated, tests executed, etc. Figure 2 shows a typical version control graph during the development of a system - each node corresponds to a specific 'state' of the code base under version control. Nodes with multiple emanating arrows represent 'forks' or 'branches' where the development proceeds along parallel alternative versions, while nodes with multiple incoming arrows denote 'merge points' where content from multiple branches are merged into a single version.

Version controlled development is essential for state-of-the-art software, as it appears to be the only pragmatic approach to manage the effective, large-scale development of complex software. Consequently, version control of all artifacts is essential - and this applies not only to source code (as today) but also to assurance artifacts, including evidence for claims, i.e. proofs, test results, etc. We envision that the collection of software engineering artifacts of a project is in constant flux, but there are stable configurations - of all relevant artifacts that represent the models + implementation + assurance of the system - in a coherent manner. In other words, while the artifacts are in an inconsistent state

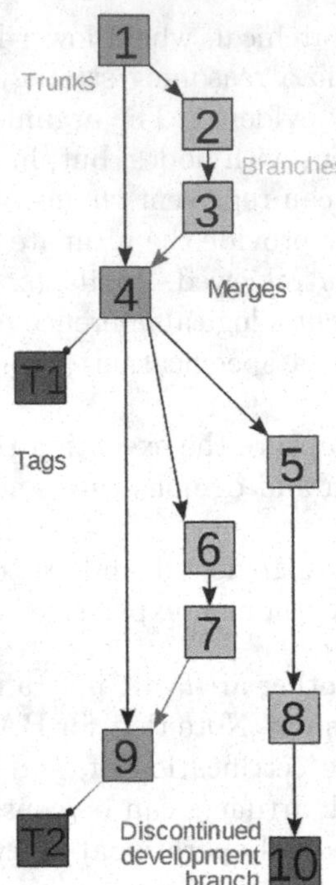

Fig. 2. Typical flow for version control (Source: Wikipedia). Each numbered node represents a state of the entire code base, nodes labeled as Tx denote tags that uniquely identify specific states.

most of the time, there are stable states that apply 'across the board' - for some specific version and subset of the artifacts.

The software engineering artifacts are *interlinked.* The DO-178* standards already require traceability (from requirements to code and back), but this should be extended to all artifacts required for the system, including specifications, design models, code, tests, tool configurations, and, most importantly everything related to assurance. Architects, developers, and reviewers should be able to navigate, for example, from requirements to design models to code to tests to test results (i.e. evidence) to assurance argument, and back to a requirement. It is understandable if such navigation is possible only for a 'stable configuration' and not for any intermediate state of the artifact database. Navigation happens via dependency links among artifacts that need to be explicitly set up during the development process. The management of such links should happen automatically, whenever a change is made to an artifact. Figure 3 shows a few example links across artifacts.

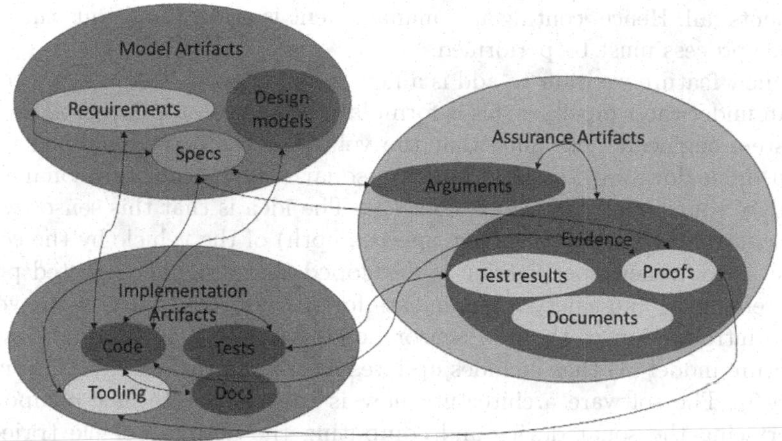

Fig. 3. Example links across artifacts

Integrated tooling is essential for managing the artifacts. To facilitate the management of artifacts, version control and dependency tracking must be integrated into an Interactive Development Environment (IDE) that provides a unified access point to models + implementation + assurance artifacts, as well allows the invocation of individual tools for building (the product), testing, analysis, assurance evaluation, etc. All interaction with the artifacts should happen via the IDE to maintain integrity and quality of the artifacts. This is beyond what typical version control systems support - they do not typically support dependency tracking (or traceability) across versions.

2.3 Use Case for CAID: Maintaining Assurance Provenance

Software development is often a highly-iterative process and developing new features often touches many artifacts, not only the code. Updating requirements, specifications, design models, the code base, and the tests need to be done in a coherent and consistent manner to be followed by the re-evaluation and/or extension of the assurance arguments. Below we present a hypothetical use case for a CAID tool environment where software for an Autonomous Underwater Vehicle (AUV) needs to be extended with a new feature. AUVs are small submarine robots [20] with various sensors, including sensors for navigation, propulsion and steering systems, and an energy source. They must operate completely autonomously underwater because communication is not possible. These vehicles are often used to inspect harbors and industrial infrastructure, like oil pipelines or underwater cables. Their control architecture follows a two-level model with a high-level, supervisory and low-level, reactive controller, see, e.g., [22]. Their safe operation is a hard requirement: the vehicle shall not cause damage to its environment or to itself and shall return to the surface even if some of its components fail. Hence, contingency management is critical and thus the safety assurance process must be performed.

The new feature we want to add is a new 'mission type': the vehicle needs to follow an underwater pipeline; this is formulated as a new, top-level requirement (1). System engineers determine that the vehicle needs to be equipped with a new sensor: a downward-looking imaging sonar (i.e. a 'side-scan sonar') that produces a 'sonar image' of the seafloor (2). The idea is that this sensor will be used to control the motion (heading, speed, depth) of the vehicle by the control software. Next, a new specification is developed that sets the expected performance, reliability, and safety requirements for the new capability of the vehicle (3). The introduction of the new sensor necessitates an update of the system architecture model (4) that includes updates to the software architecture model as well (5). The software architecture now is to incorporate new components for interfacing the sonar device and computing the desired vehicle trajectory based on the sonar image. This latter addition induces changes in the autonomy (supervisory controller) (5) that makes high-level decisions about the system's behavior. Having implemented these changes (6) new tests and verification procedures need to be developed (7) to provide evidence for the safety of the vehicle. As changes have been made to requirements (1), hardware devices (2), specifications (3), hardware (4) and software (5) architecture, the implementation (6), and the verification (7) regime, the CAID IDE will flag the affected assurance arguments (8) to indicate that they need to be re-evaluated, possibly extended (e.g., 'the vehicle maintains a safe distance from the pipeline'). Having these completed (10) the IDE marks (or 'tags') the engineering artifacts as 'stable' indicating an acceptable state for the project.

3 Related Work

There are a few example tool environments that make steps towards the overall vision described above.

The Evidential Tool Bus (ETB) [11] is a tool integration framework that allows the construction of assurance cases in a distributed manner. The framework allows the invocation of 'tool servers' (e.g., theorem provers) that maintain their own repositories for claims. Complex assurance arguments can be validated (and re-validated) by invoking tools through a Datalog interface, which uses Prolog's "backward-chaining with unification" semantics to evaluate the assurance arguments on the fly. This is clearly a powerful approach but it does not address the problem of managing versions of complex arguments that are related to various elements of a large (source) code base.

DIME [6] is an integrated toolsuite for the rigorous model-driven development of sophisticated web applications that is designed to flexibly integrate features such as high assurance and security via a family of Graphical Domain-Specific Languages (GDSL). Each GDSL is tailored towards a specific aspect of typical web applications, including persistent entities, data retrieval, business logic, the structure of the user interface, dynamic access control, and security. The tool provides an elegant and integrated environment for building web applications, but the version control, traceability, and assurance aspects of the development process are not in scope.

AutoFOCUS3/ExplicitCase [7] is a model-based development tool for embedded software systems. It provides direct support for model-based development (by supporting a subset of UML) and assurance case modeling (by supporting a variant of the Goal Structuring Notation - an industry standard for assurance cases). The tool does support linking models to assurance case, but it seems to stop there: no linking to implementation artifacts.

4 CAID: A Vision for a Next Generation Development Tool Environment

Arguably, many ingredients for a 'Continuous Assurance-Integrated Development' tool environment are available. The most relevant tools include:

- Modeling tools that provide a graphical/textual environment to construct models for requirements, specifications, and designs - either via standard languages (e.g., UML/SYSML) or domain-specific modeling languages (e.g., Simulink/Stateflow).
- Code development tools that provide for activities including: (1) construction (or generation) of implementation and test code, (2) performing static and dynamic analysis of the code, (3) verifying models (or implementation code) using formal techniques, and (4) producing documentation.
- Assurance tools for constructing and reviewing assurance and storing assurance evidence data sets. What appears missing is a tool framework that connects all these ingredients into a coherent ensemble, with semantically sound tool support for managing the versions and dependencies among the myriad artifacts produced during the software development process.

Our vision for such a framework includes the following elements, with some technical challenges listed as well:

- A (possibly distributed or decentralized) repository for all software engineering artifacts that provides fundamental services for version control and dependency tracking. The repository should follow the 'append-only' semantics of today's version control systems: nothing gets deleted, we only append to an existing database.
  Challenge: Implementing the repository such that it can handle model objects, source code files, datasets, etc., that are possibly located in different databases in a uniform, coherent, and consistent manner. Note that the simultaneous solution of version control and dependency management (combined with the need for fault tolerance) could potentially require new distributed algorithms, with formal proofs of correctness.
- An integration of the modeling tools, code development tools, and assurance tools with the repository layer. All editing operations executed by a tool must

be reflected in the repository: whenever a model (or implementation code or assurance artifact) is edited a new version is created, etc.
Challenge: finding the right level of granularity for the operations: too fine-grain changes (e.g., changing one line of code) lead to inefficient operations, too coarse-grain changes lead to loss of details of the changes.

– Automation for assisting in the development, made possible by the repository and integration. Examples include: interactive navigation across the repository of artifacts using the dependencies; generating notifications about the impending changes (e.g., changing a code fragment should trigger the automatic re-execution of a test/proof that supplies evidence for an assurance claim); setting up and automatically executing complex tools operations that automate development chores, including re-evaluating assurance arguments.
Challenge: implementing automation in a way that it matches well with existing development practices i.e. "edit, test, debug, repair, repeat" cycles.

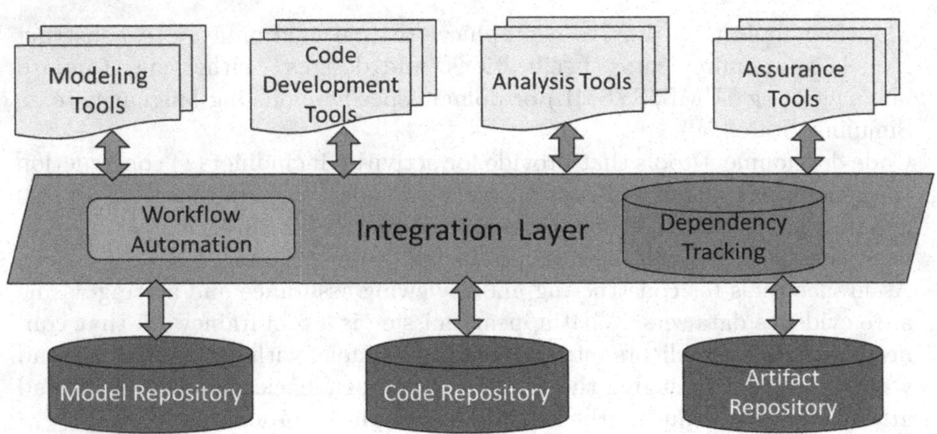

Fig. 4. Notional toolsuite architecture for CAID

Figure 4 shows a notional architecture for the framework. A required attribute of the framework is that it should be open and extensible. Every development project is different, hence different tools and resources are used, thus the framework should adaptable to any arbitrary combination of tools.

4.1 Proof of Concept Prototype for CAID

Based on previous work [1] a prototype for a CAID tool framework is being constructed. The current ALC Toolchain [15] has been designed for the development and assurance of Cyber-Physical Systems (CPS) with Learning-Enabled Components (LEC). The toolchain includes a customized WebGME [19], a meta-programmable modeling environment, as modeling tool and model repository.

For code development Microsoft's VS Code [2] IDE was integrated that operates on a Git repository. A few design-time tools for model checking have been integrated, including NNV [23], a MATLAB-based reachability tool. For assurance artifacts WebGME models are used, and assurance tools are for reviewing only. This basic tool framework is being extended with an 'Integration Layer' as shown above, that includes tooling for dependency tracking and coordinates the version control across the models and code artifacts. There is a sufficiently complex example model- and code-base for the project containing models and executable code for a small AUV, based on the BlueROV2 [25] system. The code base includes simulation models for the environment and the vehicle, as well as the code for the on-board software that runs on an embedded computing hardware platform.

4.2 A Draft Use Case: AUV Control

One potential application of an AUV is infrastructure inspection. The infrastructure can be an undersea cable carrying Internet traffic. The AUV's mission is to (1) descend to the sea floor, (2) find the cable using a side-scan (imaging) sonar, (3) trace it up to a distance determined by its battery charge (so that it can safely return to its starting point on the surface), even if some segments of the cable are covered by sand, (4) monitor is battery charge its control surfaces for degradation, and (4) safely return to the starting point, under all foreseeable scenarios. These requirements are to be stated formally and more precisely, as requirement models, to guide the development process.

The design of the AUV software stack can then proceed following a model-driven paradigm, i.e., (1) functional decomposition, (2) architecture definition, (3) function to component mapping, (4) component definition, design, implementation, (5) component testing, (6) system integration, and (7) testing. Design models and implementation artifacts (some of which are directly generated from models) are used throughout these steps.

For assurance, a set of GSN assurance arguments will then be constructed that explain why specific safety and performance claims are satisfied by the system. Such high-level claims are (recursively) decomposed into sub-claims, which, on the lowest level are supported by concrete evidence (i.e. formal verification or test results, etc.).

Engineering artifacts in the above process are to be linked together, allowing traceability. For example, the '(4) safely return' requirement can be linked to software components that (a) monitor battery health and compute the remaining useful charge, (b) continuously estimate a safe return trajectory based on the vehicle's position, and (c) control the movement of the vehicle and switch to a 'return to home' mode of operation if the battery charge reaches a critical level which is not sufficient for executing the safe return trajectory. The developer should be able to navigate from requirement to component, possibly even specific code fragments (e.g., decision points in the code) that address the requirement, and *vice versa*.

The safety argument for the 'safe return' assurance case is constructed by developing sub-claims, stating the need for (1) correct estimation of remaining useful charge in the battery, (2) correct calculation of the safe return trajectory, (3) correct reaction of the vehicle controller to critical battery charge levels under all foreseeable modes of operation, and (4) the correct integration of the above components to support the top-level function and its safety claim. Low-level claims are to be supported by formal proofs or test results, high-level claims are can be approved by human review, later possibly by automatic inference over the GSN network. Again, the developer should be able to navigate among the artifacts: claims, evidence, implementation artifacts, etc.

Whenever a change is made, for example in the implementation of the controller component, the tool will point out what requirements are assigned to that component, and what assurance claims are dependent on it, hence what evidence need to be re-generated to keep the safety argument valid.

5 Conclusions

The documentation of software intended for systems requiring strong assurances regarding safety and reliability is a challenge. Ultimately, 'documentation' shall (1) contribute to the assurance of the system, and (2) demonstrate the provenance of the assurance arguments by connecting it to design, implementation, and evidence artifacts.

We argue that the use of integrated tooling is essential: developers need assistance for maintaining and managing the complex and heterogeneous 'work products': models, implementation and assurance artifacts. Today, these artifacts are conceptually related but, in the future, they also need to be physically linked with the help of a 'tool integration' layer that also supports version control over the graph of relationships. Having identified relevant artifacts we presented the outline for a generic tool architecture that supports this vision. This vision is actively being implemented in a related project.

Acknowledgments. The work was supported by the Defense Advance Research Projects Agency (DARPA), under its Assured Autonomy program, and the Air Force Research Laboratory (AFRL). Any opinions, findings, and conclusions or recommendations expressed in this material are those of the author(s) and do not necessarily reflect the views of DARPA or AFRL.

References

1. Assurance-based learning-enabled CPS. https://assured-autonomy.isis.vanderbilt.edu/. Accessed 30 May 2022
2. Microsoft Visual Studio Code. https://code.visualstudio.com/. Accessed 30 May 2022
3. Agile Alliance: Agile practices. https://www.agilealliance.org/agile101/subway-map-to-agile-practices/. Accessed 30 May 2022

4. Astels, D.: Test Driven Development: A Practical Guide. Prentice Hall Professional Technical Reference (2003)
5. Beck, K., et al.: Manifesto for agile software development (2001)
6. Boßelmann, S., Neubauer, J., Naujokat, S., Steffen, B.: Model-driven design of secure high assurance systems: an introduction to the open platform from the user perspective. In: The 2016 International Conference on Security and Management (SAM 2016). Special Track "End-to-End Security and Cybersecurity: From the Hardware to Application, pp. 145–151 (2016)
7. Cârlan, C., Nigam, V., Voss, S., Tsalidis, A.: Explicitcase: tool-support for creating and maintaining assurance arguments integrated with system models. In: 2019 IEEE International Symposium on Software Reliability Engineering Workshops (ISSREW), pp. 330–337. IEEE (2019)
8. Cassano, V., Maibaum, T.S.E., Grigorova, S.: Towards making safety case arguments explicit, precise, and well founded. In: Ait-Ameur, Y., Nakajima, S., Méry, D. (eds.) Implicit and Explicit Semantics Integration in Proof-Based Developments of Discrete Systems, pp. 227–258. Springer, Singapore (2021). https://doi.org/10.1007/978-981-15-5054-6_11
9. Colgren, R.: Basic MATLAB®, Simulink®, and Stateflow®. American Institute of Aeronautics and Astronautics (2006)
10. Committee on National Security Systems Glossary Working Group and Others: National Information Assurance Glossary (2010)
11. Cruanes, S., Hamon, G., Owre, S., Shankar, N.: Tool integration with the evidential tool bus. In: Giacobazzi, R., Berdine, J., Mastroeni, I. (eds.) VMCAI 2013. LNCS, vol. 7737, pp. 275–294. Springer, Heidelberg (2013). https://doi.org/10.1007/978-3-642-35873-9_18
12. Group, A.C.W., et al.: Goal structuring notation community standard version 2, January 2018 (2018). http://www.goalstructuringnotation.info
13. Groza, A., Letia, I.A., Goron, A., Zaporojan, S.: A formal approach for identifying assurance deficits in unmanned aerial vehicle software. In: Selvaraj, H., Zydek, D., Chmaj, G. (eds.) Progress in Systems Engineering. AISC, vol. 366, pp. 233–239. Springer, Cham (2015). https://doi.org/10.1007/978-3-319-08422-0_35
14. Habli, I., Kelly, T.: Balancing the formal and informal in safety case arguments. In: VeriSure: Verification and Assurance Workshop, Co-located with Computer-Aided Verification (CAV) (2014)
15. Hartsell, C., et al.: Model-based design for CPS with learning-enabled components. In: Proceedings of the Workshop on Design Automation for CPS and IoT, DESTION@CPSIoTWeek 2019, Montreal, QC, Canada, pp. 1–9, April 2019. https://doi.org/10.1145/3313151.3313166
16. Johnson, L.A.: Do-178b. Software Considerations in Airborne Systems and Equipment Certification, Crosstalk Magazine (1998)
17. Kelly, T., Weaver, R.: The goal structuring notation - a safety argument notation. In: Proceedings of Dependable Systems and Networks 2004 Workshop on Assurance Cases (2004)
18. Kramer, D.: API documentation from source code comments: a case study of Javadoc. In: Proceedings of the 17th Annual International Conference on Computer Documentation, pp. 147–153 (1999)
19. Maróti, M., et al.: Next generation (meta) modeling: web-and cloud-based collaborative tool infrastructure. In: MPM@ MoDELS 1237, pp. 41–60 (2014)
20. Moore, S., Bohm, H., Jensen, V., Johnston, N.: Underwater robotics. Science, Design and Fabrication. Marine Advanced Technology Education Center (MATE), Monterrey CA, USA (2010)

21. Safety-Critical Systems Club: Goal Structuring Notation (GSN) standard, Version 2. http://scsc.uk/gsn. Accessed 30 May 2022. Standard licensed under the Creative Commons Attribution 4.0 International License
22. Stojcsics, D., Boursinos, D., Mahadevan, N., Koutsoukos, X., Karsai, G.: Fault-adaptive autonomy in systems with learning-enabled components. Sensors **21**(18), 6089 (2021)
23. Tran, H.-D., et al.: NNV: the neural network verification tool for deep neural networks and learning-enabled cyber-physical systems. In: Lahiri, S.K., Wang, C. (eds.) CAV 2020. LNCS, vol. 12224, pp. 3–17. Springer, Cham (2020). https://doi.org/10.1007/978-3-030-53288-8_1
24. Van Heesch, D.: Doxygen: source code documentation generator tool (2008). http://www.doxygen.org
25. Willners, J.S., et al.: From market-ready ROVs to low-cost AUVs. In: OCEANS 2021: San Diego-Porto, pp. 1–7. IEEE (2021)
26. Zampetti, F., Geremia, S., Bavota, G., Di Penta, M.: CI/CD pipelines evolution and restructuring: a qualitative and quantitative study. In: 2021 IEEE International Conference on Software Maintenance and Evolution (ICSME), pp. 471–482. IEEE (2021)

Formalization of the AADL Run-Time Services

John Hatcliff[1(✉)], Jerome Hugues[2], Danielle Stewart[3], and Lutz Wrage[2]

[1] Kansas State University, Manhattan, KS 66506, USA
hatcliff@ksu.edu
[2] Software Engineering Institute, Pittsburgh, USA
[3] Adventium Labs, Minneapolis, MN 55401, USA

Abstract. The Architecture and Analysis Definition Language (AADL) is an industry standard modeling language distinguished by its emphasis on strong semantics for modeling real-time embedded systems. These features have led to AADL being used in many formal-methods-oriented projects addressing critical systems. With regard to future directions in programming and systems engineering in general, questions naturally arise regarding how modeling language definitions should be documented so that the meaning of modeled systems can be made clear to all stakeholders. For example, the AADL standard describes Run-Time Services (RTS) that code generation frameworks can implement to realize AADL's standards-based semantics for thread dispatch and port-based communication. The documentation of these semantics in the AADL standard is semi-formal, allowing for divergent interpretations and thus contradictions when implementing analysis or code generation capabilities.

In this paper, we illustrate how key semantic elements of the AADL standard may be documented via a rule-based formalization of key aspects of the AADL RTS as well as additional services and support functions for realistic, interoperable, and assurable implementations. This contribution provides a basis for (a) a more rigorous semantic presentation in upcoming versions of the standard, (b) a common approach to assess compliance of AADL code generation and analysis tools, (c) a foundation for further formalization and mechanization of AADL's semantics, and (d) a more intuitive documentation of a system's AADL description via simulation and automatically generated execution scenarios.

This work is supported in part by Collins Aerospace, the U.S. Army Combat Capabilities Development Command, Aviation and Missile Center under Contract No. W911W6-20-C-2020, and the US Department of Defense under Contract No. FA8702-15-D-0002 with Carnegie Mellon University for the operation of the Software Engineering Institute, a federally funded research and development center. See the acknowledgements section for full details.

T. Margaria and B. Steffen (Eds.): ISoLA 2022, LNCS 13702, pp. 105–134, 2022.
https://doi.org/10.1007/978-3-031-19756-7_7

1 Introduction

Model-based development tools are increasingly being used for system-level development of safety critical systems. The quality of model-based development depends greatly on the modeling language and its semantics. Models developed in languages with well-defined semantics can be a more faithful abstraction of deployed systems, if the analysis correctly reflects the semantics and the system as implemented likewise reflects the semantics. Furthermore, having a rigorous semantics reduces the risk of misinterpretation when processing a model: analysis or code generation capabilities will deliver comparable results and can be composed with confidence.

AADL, the Architecture Analysis and Design Language [15], has historically been distinguished from other standardized modeling languages by having a semantics that precisely describe the architecture of safety-critical embedded systems. This definition for a focused semantics has motivated the use of AADL on multiple large scale industrial research projects, especially those that emphasize formal methods [11,20,29,33,38]. In AADL, component categories and other model elements have a comprehensive descriptions of intent and associated properties, which provides consistent definitions across models designed by different developers and supports early cross-vendor integration.

An important aspect of AADL's current standard definition is the inclusion of Run-Time Services (RTS). From an implementation view, the RTS are meant to be implemented as library functions in an AADL run-time that realize key actions of the infrastructure, including communication over ports and dispatching of threads. RTS aim to (a) hide the details of specific RTOS and communication substrates (e.g., middleware) and (b) provide AADL-aligned system implementations with canonical platform-independent actions that realize key steps in the integration and coordination of component application logic. From a semantics perspective, the RTS can be seen as basic operations in an abstract machine realizing the AADL run-time. In the current standard, RTS are presented in a highly descriptive narrative with suggestive notation for the type signature of the services, e.g., how they may be represented in code [22].

There are three main challenges with regard to RTS. First, there are no formal semantics for the services: the standard provides only an incomplete capture of run-time actions into standardized services. Second, the RTS are not sufficiently described to allow for a portable Application Programming Interface (API) to be derived. Third, AADL is highly configurable and the RTS are meant to support multiple computational models (e.g., synchronous, asynchronous, with configuration of details to support different application policies). Thus, existing formalisms cannot be used directly to support the general intent of the RTS. Previous work has formalized subsets of AADL [6] and other work has transformed AADL into formal languages for specific computational models [16,37], but to our knowledge, a formalization of the general RTS semantics of AADL has never been defined.

We believe that appropriately documenting the semantics of the AADL RTS is an important step to meeting the challenges above. While one typically thinks of documentation as it applies to a specific model or program, in our setting, documentation is needed at the meta-level, i.e., for the *definition of the modeling language*. We argue in Sect. 3 that, with the future of programming being increasingly supported by modeling and meta-programming, arriving at effective solutions for documentation at different meta-levels of the programming framework is important for grounding the next generation of programming environments. Formally specifying the semantics of a modeling language is not a new idea. Rather, our contribution is to tackle the challenges of documenting key aspects of a modeling language that is being used for rigorous industry model-driven development in a manner that can support evolution of the modeling language standard and associated ecosystem. The main benefit of the work is to begin to fill a gap that, once closed, can provide a much more solid foundation for a community that is already invested in rigorous system engineering with AADL.

The contributions of this paper are as follows.

- Formalize the primary notions of thread state and communication state within an AADL system. These notions provide the foundation of conformity assessment by specifying what portions of a executing system's state must be documented for traceability to definitions within the AADL standard and observed for conformance testing based on execution traces.
- Develop rule-based formal documentation of the AADL standard's run-time services, providing a basis for soundness of AADL analysis and verification and the ability to develop conformity assessment for AADL run-time libraries.
- Identify additional run-time services and support functions needed to fill gaps in the current AADL standard.

Combined together, our goal is to provide an initial proposal for a formal documentation of services for AADL RTS for upcoming major revisions to the AADL standard. Expansion of this formalization can serve as a specification for establishing the correctness of AADL analyses and code generation. Our formalization aims to support the *general* nature of the AADL RTS and to provide a foundation for creating *specialized* semantic definitions for particular models of computation or platforms. From an implementation view, this provides a means by which implementers that optimize communication pathways or thread management can justify executions in their context to be sound refinements of the standardized general notions.

It is important that a proposal for aspects of a standardized AADL run-time be based on significant implementation experience with multiple code generation approaches, multiple languages, and multiple target platforms. The formalization presented here is informed by significant experience with the Ocarina and HAMR code generation frameworks. These frameworks have been used on industry and military research projects, target multiple real-time embedded platforms, and support multiple programming languages including C, Ada [3], Ada/Spark2014 [9], and Slang [30]. This work is supported by a technical report [18] that provides expanded treatment of semantics rules and examples.

We start with a background description of AADL in Sect. 2, This is followed by a summary of potential stakeholders of our proposed documentation and potential impact within the AADL ecosystem. Next, we summarize important concepts of run-time services in Sect. 4. Section 5 provides the static model definitions, and Sects. 6, 7, 8 describe run-time services and semantics, and Sect. 9 illustrates these with examples. Section 10 presents related work, and Sect. 11 concludes.

2 AADL Background

SAE International standard AS5506C [22] defines the AADL core language for expressing the structure of embedded, real-time systems via definitions of components, their interfaces, and their communication.

AADL provides a precise, tool-independent, and standardized modeling vocabulary of common embedded software and hardware elements using a component-based approach. Components have a category that defines a standard interpretation. Categories include software (e.g., threads, processes), hardware (e.g., processor, bus), and system (interacting hardware and software). Each category also has a distinct set of standardized properties that can be used to configure the specific component's semantics for various aspects: timing, resources, etc.

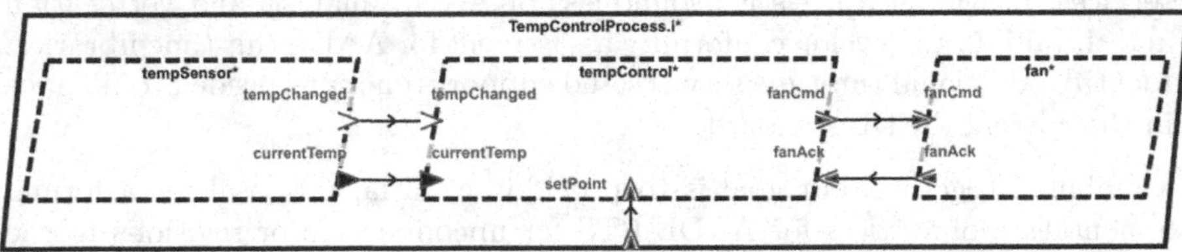

Fig. 1. Temperature control example (excerpts) – AADL graphical view

Figure 1 presents a portion of the AADL standard graphical view for a simple thermostat that maintains a temperature according to a set point structure. The `system` (not shown) contains a `process` called `tempControlProcess`. This process consists of three threads: `tempSensor`, `tempControl`, and `fan`, shown in the figure from left to right. The data passed from one thread to another is done through the use of `ports`. Each port can be classified as an *event port* (e.g., to model interrupt signals or other notification-oriented messages without payloads), a *data port* (e.g. modeling shared memory between components or distributed memory services where an update to a distributed memory cell is automatically propagated to other components that declare access to the cell), or an *event data port* (e.g., to model asynchronous messages with payloads, such as in publish-subscribe frameworks). Inputs to event and event data ports are buffered. The buffer sizes and overflow policies can be configured per port using standardizes AADL properties. Inputs to data ports are not buffered; newly arriving data overwrites the previous value.

The periodic **tempSensor** thread measures the current temperature, e.g., from memory-mapped IO, which is not shown in the diagram, and transmits the reading on its **currentTemp** data port. If it detects that the temperature has changed since the last reading, then it sends a notification to the sporadic (event driven) **tempControl** thread on its **tempChanged** event port. When the **tempControl** thread receives a **tempChanged** event, it will read the value on its **currentTemp** data port and compare with the most recent set points. If the current temperature exceeds the high set point, it sends a command to the **fan** thread to turn *on*. Similarly, if the current temperature is low, it will send an *off* fan command. In either case, **fan** acknowledges whether it was able to fulfill the command by sending user-defined data types **FanAck.Ok** or **FanAck.Error** on its **fanAck** event data port.

AADL provides a textual view to accompany the graphical view. The following listing illustrates the *component type* declaration for the **tempControl** thread for the example above. The data transmitted over ports are of specific types, and properties such as **Dispatch_Protocol** and **Period** configure the tasking semantics of the thread.

```
thread TempControl
features
 currentTemp: in data port TempSensor::Temperature.i;
 tempChanged: in event port;
 fanAck: in event data port CoolingFan::FanAck;
 setPoint: in event data port SetPoint.i;
 fanCmd: out event data port CoolingFan::FanCmd;
properties
 Dispatch_Protocol => Sporadic;
 Period => 500 ms;   -- the min sep between incoming msgs
end TempControl;
```

The next listing illustrates how architectural hierarchy is realized as an integration of subcomponents. The body of **TempControlProcess** type has no declared features because the component does not interact with its context in this simplified example. **TempControlProcess** implementation specifies subcomponents and subcomponent communications over declared connections between ports.

```
process TempControlProcess
  -- no features; no interaction with context
end TempControlProcess;

process implementation TempControlProcess.i
subcomponents
 tempSensor : thread TempSensor::TempSensor.i;
 fan : thread CoolingFan::Fan.i;
 tempControl: thread TempControl.i;
 operatorInterface: thread OperatorInterface.i;
connections
c1:port tempSensor.currentTemp -> tempControl.currentTemp;
c2:port tempSensor.tempChanged -> tempControl.tempChanged;
c3:port tempControl.fanCmd -> fan.fanCmd;
c4:port fan.fanAck -> tempControl.fanAck;
end TempControlProcess.i;
```

AADL provides many standard properties, and allows definition of new properties. Examples of standard properties configure the core semantics of AADL, e.g., thread dispatching or port-based communication. User-specified property sets enable one to define project-specific configuration parameters.

In this paper, we limit our semantics presentation to thread components since almost all of AADL's run-time services are associated with threads and port-based communication. Other categories will be treated in later work.

3 AADL Semantic Documentation Impact

In code-centric development, when there is a semantics-related question ("what's the behavior of this section of code?" or "what's the behavior of this language construct?"), the relevant code/construct can be executed and tested against expected results. While this approach may have its limitations (multiple compilers/interpreters may implement different semantics), it is generally effective in practice for the typical end user.

With a modeling language, the ability to understand semantics through experimentation seems less direct. Often modeling notations (at least the ones that we are considering for AADL) cannot be directly executed. Moreover, due to the intent to use modeling early in an incremental development process, models are often incomplete or partially developed. There is the possibility of understanding the semantics through generating code from the model or using a model simulator. However, for AADL and related modeling languages like SysML, there are currently no "reference implementations" of code generators or simulators. In addition, AADL is designed to be used with multiple languages, multiple RTOS, multiple middleware, etc. Therefore, a further challenge is to specify some portions of the semantic behavior as required or canonical, while at the same time admitting variations in behavior between platforms in a controlled way.

Accordingly, our long-term goal with this work is to provide a programming language-independent, RTOS-independent, middleware-independent formal documentation of semantic behavior. The formal description should then be refinable to describe lower-level variations of behavior and optimizations for different platforms. As refinements are developed, there must be a means to demonstrate conformity of implementations to refined semantic descriptions and of refined descriptions to the canonical (top-level) reference semantics. Since one of the objectives of AADL is to enable model analysis and verification, there is a need in the conformity assessment, tool qualification, and standardization contexts to precisely specify (a) soundness of verification and analysis tools, (b) the extent to which soundness of these tools is maintained in the presence of refinements to various platforms, (c) the specific situations (particular modeling features used, particular platform implementation strategies) in which tool soundness cannot be guaranteed. All of this complexity suggests that a mechanization of the semantic framework will be required to be able to appropriately manage the concerns and provide appropriate levels of assurance.

In this paper, our goals are to lay out some of the key concerns and provide an illustration of some of the most important aspects of the semantics. In ongoing work, we are pursuing a mechanization in Coq of the rules presented here, along with the broader coordination aspects of AADL. In some sense, a formal semantics lies at extreme end of the spectrum of documentation. Nevertheless, it seems crucial to enabling the next generation of model-based "programming" and system development.

In this section, we summarize the stakeholders for the semantic documentation presented in this paper, along with anticipated impact and connections within the AADL ecosystem.

3.1 Stakeholders

Modelers/System Engineers – The End Users of the Modeling Language: End users often have questions about the intended execution semantics of AADL-based systems. For example, questions often arise about the semantics of port-based communication (e.g., exactly when are values available to read on input ports?, do unread values in input buffers carry over from one dispatch to another?, what is the ordering of values in an input buffer in the presence of multiple senders to the associated input port?, etc.) and threading (what should the structure of the application code be within a thread? when and how does thread application get executed?). These types of questions are addressed in the standard through informal textual descriptions that are distributed throughout different sections. Our aim is to develop more rigorous formal documentation that can be presented at one place in the standard, then referenced and assessed throughout. An example-based document that illustrates traces of threads, communication, and system composition in terms of the semantics rules (e.g., as presented in Sect. 9) may also be helpful.

Analysis/Verification Tool Providers: As mentioned above, one of the key objectives of AADL is to enable *analyzeable* models. There are many different forms of AADL analysis. Some of the most mature analysis areas include scheduling and timing analysis, information flow analysis, assume/guarantee contract specification and verification, and fault modeling and hazard analysis. To provide sound results, analysis and verification tools need to have a clear and unambigous specification of the aspects of the modeling language semantics. For example, information flow analysis needs to understand precisely how information flows between components and how information is propagated from component inputs to component outputs. For this area, even basic questions such as "is there an implicit acknowledgement of successful communication from a receiving component to a sending component" affects whether or not a potential "backflow" of information should be reported by the analysis. Current versions of AADL contract languages such as AGREE [12] and BLESS [25], make different assumptions about the behavior of component inputs outputs. Providing canonical documentation (as begun in Sect. 6) of the input/output behavior of components, structure of application code and infrastructure code, and the semantics of component composition is essential for reconciling the differences between these current verification frameworks and for establishing their soundness as needed for assurance in current industrial projects. Regarding hazard analysis in AADL's Error Modeling framework [21,24], there is a need to clearly understand the nominal behavior of modeled systems to be able to clearly delineate and categorize faulty behavior.

Code Generation Tool Providers: Having clear, unambigous documentation of threading and communication behavior is essential for AADL code generation tools such as [7,17,26]. In fact, the original motivation of this work was to document the semantics of a set of APIs for AADL RTS that could be implemented in each of the code generation tools above. Work on verified compilers and code generators for modeling languages has demonstrated the feasibility of proving the correctness of realistic code generation frameworks. To ensure that model-driven development strategies, which represent an emerging approach for next generation system development, can be inserted into tool chains for certified critical systems, a clear documentation of intended semantics that can also support conformity assessment is needed. A challenging aspect for AADL is that we must eventually support, not a single semantics, but rather a family of semantics that can be configured by AADL model `property` annotations.

3.2 AADL Ecosystem Synchronization

In addition to supporting the stakeholders above, behavioral documentation is needed to establish consistency across different aspects of the AADL standard itself. For example, AADL includes a Behavior Annex (BA) that provides a state-machine-based formalism for specifying thread behaviors. The semantics of BA needs to be aligned with the semantics of AADL entry points and port-based communication as presented in Sect. 6. AADL presents a variety of timing-related properties that are utilized by latency analysis and scheduling tools. Those timing properties need to be mapped onto documented behavioral semantics so as to eventually be reflected directly in abstract communication traces of the kind presented in Sect. 9. We have already discussed above the need to align AADL's Error Modeling framework with a documented semantics. In summary, work on the AADL standard itself as well as similar work in, e.g., the SysML community, can be made much more rigorous by exploring effective strategies for documenting system modeling language semantics.

4 Concepts

In this section, we enhance the presentation in the current AADL standard by describing the overall relationship between the AADL RTS, thread component code organization, and AADL communication infrastructure. Many of AADL's thread execution concepts are based on long-established task patterns and principles for achieving analyzeable real-time systems [8]. Following these principles, at each activation of a thread, the application code of the thread will abstractly compute a function from its input port values and local variables to output port values while possibly updating its local variables. In the general case, an AADL thread may explictly call the RTS to receive new inputs at any point in

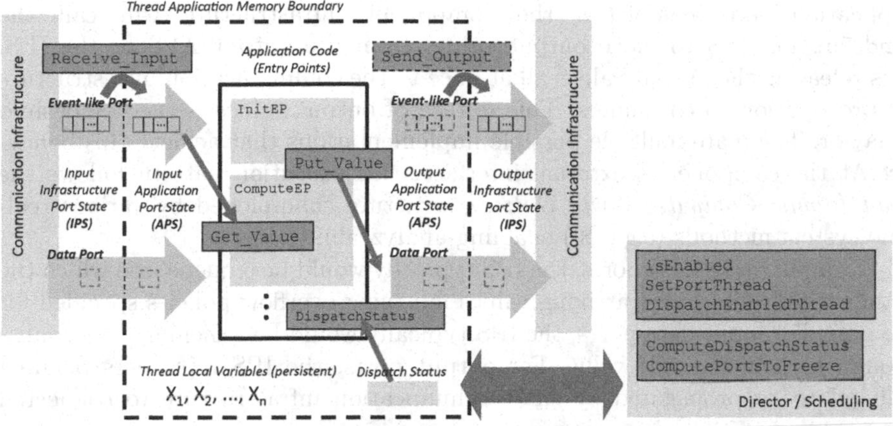

Fig. 2. Thread and port state concepts

its execution. Yet, this would break the atomicity of a dispatch execution. We explictly forbid this in our formalization as this would introduce unsoundess in many AADL analyses and contract languages [12,25]. Furthermore, this capability is barely used in practice. In AADL terminology, dispatching a thread refers to the thread becoming ready for execution from a OS scheduler perspective. The thread `Dispatch_Protocol` property selects among several strategies for determining when a thread should be dispatched. In this paper, we consider only `Periodic`, which dispatches a thread when a certain time interval is passed, and `Sporadic`, which dispatches a thread upon arrival of messages to input ports specified as *dispatch triggers*. When a thread is dispatched, information describing the reason for its dispatch is stored in the thread's state and is retrievable via the `Dispatch_Status` RTS. For example, in a sporadic component, `Dispatch_Status` returns information indicating which port triggered the dispatch. This may be used in either the component application or infrastructure code to branch to a message handler method dedicated to processing messages arriving on the particular port.

Figure 2 illustrates that a thread's state includes the state of its ports, local variables, and dispatch status. The state of each port is further decomposed into the Infrastructure Port State (IPS) and the Application Port State (APS). The IPS represents the communication infrastructure's perspective of the port. The APS represents the thread application code's perspective of the port.

The distinction between IPS and APS is used to represent AADL's notions of *port freezing* and *port variable* as presented in more detail in [14]. Typically, when a thread is dispatched, the component infrastructure uses the `Receive_Input` RTS to move one or more values from the IPS of input ports into the input APS. Then the component application code is called and the APS values then remain "frozen" as the code executes. This provides the application a consistent view of inputs even though input IPS may be concurrently updated by communication infrastructure behind the scenes. The application code writes to the output APS throughout execution. Our intended design for this is that when the application code completes, the component infrastructure will call the Send_Output RTS to move output values from the output APS to the IPS, thus releasing the output values all at once to the communication infrastructure for propagation to consumers. This release of output values is the key desired behavior. There are multiple possible implementations that achieve this behavior. At the component's external interface, this execution pattern follows the *Read Inputs; Compute; Write Outputs* structure championed by various real-time system methods (e.g., [8]) enabling analyzeability.

For input event data ports, the IPS typically would be a queue into which the middleware would insert arriving values following overflow policies specified for the port. For input data ports, the IPS typically would be a memory block large enough to hold a single value. For output ports, the IPS represents pending value(s) to be propagated by the communication infrastructure to connected consumer ports.

The AADL standard specifies a collection of RTS including `Get_Value`, `Put_Value`, etc. that application code may use to access input and output APS.[1] We view these as less important semantically because they do not determine the overall semantic model of computation but rather suggest programming language-level idioms for accessing the APS.

The AADL standard indicates that a thread's application code is organized into entry points (e.g., subprograms that are invoked from the AADL run-time). For example, the *Initialize Entry Point* (`InitEP`) is called during the system's initialization phase, the *Compute Entry Point* (`ComputeEP`) is called during the system's "normal" compute phase. Other entry points are defined for handling faults, performing mode changes, etc. We plan to address the higher-level coordination semantics for these phases in follow-on work. Multiple organizations of entry points are allowed. Here, we address a single `InitEP` and `ComputeEP` for each thread.

Overall, AADL emphasizes a specific canonical usage pattern of the RTS to achieve the Read; Compute; Write pattern described above. It also allows other usage patterns for flexibility and generality, but these may reduce the analyzeability of the system. For example, it allows the application code to call `Receive_Input` and `Send_Output` at any point and for multiple times. This "breaks" the view of the `ComputeEP` as a function from inputs to outputs. Our approach in this paper will be to define the semantics for key RTS (which hold regardless of usage pattern), and then provide a semantics for entry points that (a) adheres to the canonical usage pattern and (b) better supports formal reasoning.

[1] The AADL standard uses the term *port variable* to refer to the APS concept; "variable" suggests an application programming view of the port state. However, the port variable concept is somewhat ambigiously presented in the current standard and is intertwined with the binding to a particular programming language. For these reasons, we use a more mathematically oriented presentation of the concept in this paper and suggest that upcoming versions of the standard allow different programming language bindings to specify how they realize the concept in a particular language.

5 Static Semantics

Prior to defining the semantic rules of AADL RTS, we introduce some key definitions and notations that map AADL concepts onto mathematical notations. The AADL standard includes informal rules that specify how model elements are organized in terms of containment hierarchy, allowed relationships (e.g., connections, bindings) with other components, and modeling patterns for system configuration and deployment. The static system model specifies components, ports, and connections. The intent of this section is not to exhaustively capture all static model information, but rather the information that influences the execution semantics presented in the following sections.

The root AADL system is instantiated and compiled into an abstract syntax tree. The resulting instance model, which we call $\mathcal{M}$, is the static AADL model consisting of an organized hierarchy of components. The set of all components of $\mathcal{M}$ we refer to as $\mathcal{C}$. The static instance model defines the hierarchical structure and interconnection topology of an operational system. An AADL instance model $\mathcal{M}$ represents the runtime architecture of an actual system that consists of application software components and execution platform components. A complete system instance that represents the containment hierarchy of the actual system is created by starting at the root component and instantiating all subcomponents recursively. We assume that $\mathcal{M}$ is completely instantiated and bound.

Next we define the structure of a generic AADL component. This definition covers both component type and implementations and derives from the implementation of the instance model from the OSATE AADL editor. Model information in $\mathcal{M}$ includes component descriptors that hold static information needed to determine the semantics of AADL components.

Definition 1. *A component Comp* $\in \mathcal{C}$ *is a tuple* $(c_{id}, cat_C, \mathcal{F}, Prop, \mathcal{S})$ *s.t.*

c_{id}: the unique component id,
cat_C: the component category,
$\mathcal{F}$: the set of features,
Prop: the set of properties associated with this component, and
$\mathcal{S}$: the set of subcomponents.

Given that all component identifiers are unique at each layer of the instance model, navigation of the hierarchy is performed through top-down access of component identifiers starting from the root component r and traversing down the subcomponent hierarchy, e.g., *r.childId*.

An AADL component can have one of several categories cat_C, including software (e.g., `thread`, `process`), hardware (e.g., `processor`), and more. In this document, we focus on a subset of component categories: $cat_C \in \{thread, process, system\}$. Component properties *Prop* specify relevant characteristics of the detailed design and implementation descriptions from an external perspective (e.g., a thread component's `Dispatch_Protocol`, as illustrated in Sect. 2). These can be viewed as rules of conformance between the described components and their implementation. A detailed summary of relevant component properties addressed in this document may be found in our related tech report [18].

A *feature* describes an interface of a component through which control and data may be provided to or required from other components.

Definition 2. *A feature* $f \in \mathcal{F}$ *is a tuple* $(f_{id}, cat_F, d, type, Prop)$ *such that:*

f_{id}*: is the unique feature identifier,*
cat_F*: is the category of the feature,*
d*: is the direction of the feature, where* $d \in \{in, out\}$*,*
$type$*: is a component instance of the data type, and*
$Prop$*: is the set of properties associated with this feature.*

The AADL standard defines several kinds of features. We focus on a subset of categories: $cat_F \in \{data, event, eventdata\}$[2]. Given that we focus on ports as a relevant subset of feature categories, we use the terms *port* and *feature* interchangeably. The direction d of a feature corresponds to either `in` or `out`. A feature *type* corresponds to a data component instance. Feature properties $Prop$ are configuration parameters that specify relevant characteristics of the feature and its implementation.

We refer to the global set of unique thread component identifiers as *ThreadIds*. We use the meta-variable $t \in ThreadIds$ to range over component identifiers. Port (feature) identifiers f_{id} can also be accessed globally in $\mathcal{M}$ similar to component identifiers. We use the meta-variable $p \in PortIds$ to range over port identifiers. To access the elements of the instance model $\mathcal{M}$, a number of helper methods and predicates are defined. For more detail on these predicates, see our companion tech report [18].

6 Threads

This section formalizes the primary elements of thread component state described in Sect. 4 along with associated AADL RTS. Section 7 addresses the aggregation of thread states into system states and RTS that are used in the coordination of thread actions with platform scheduling and communication.

6.1 Value Domains and Port Queues

Because the operational steps associated with RTS and entry points are agnostic to the values in port queues and user code variables, we assume a universal unspecified domain of values. To simplify the formalization, we adopt a uniform representation for IPS and APS for event, event data, and data ports:

[2] AADL other categories of features denote either abstract features or access to resources. They do not directly participate in the semantics of a thread and are omitted in this paper.

a queue q is a bounded sequence of values, $\langle v \rangle$ denotes a queue with a single data value v, e.g., as for a data port, and $\langle \cdot \rangle$ denotes an empty queue. $\langle q' \triangleright v \rangle$ represents a queue with v being the first item to be dequeued (head) and q' being the rest of the queue. This representation is specialized for data ports and event ports. For a data port, the queue size is always one and enqueueing overwrites the previous value. For event ports, queues hold 0 or more values, and $*$ denotes the presence of an event in a queue (e.g., $\langle * \rangle$ is a queue holding a single event). The maximum size of queues for a particular event and event data port is statically configurable via an AADL port property. To support AADL's specialized semantics for attempts to insert values in event and event data ports when a queue is full (configured by the overflow policy on a port), the function $enqueue(q, v, \mathit{overflow\text{-}policy})$ can be defined in a straightforward manner to return a new queue with v enqueued if the maximum size is not exceeded, else a value (e.g., the oldest in the queue) is dropped based on the given *overflow-policy* to make space for the newly enqueued value.

6.2 Thread State

Following the concepts of Fig. 2, the state of each thread is formalized as a 6-element tuple

$$\langle I_t^i, A_t^i, A_t^o, I_t^o, V_t, D \rangle.$$

I_t^i (IPS) maps each input port identifier of the component to a queue q holding buffered messages. For data ports, q is always non-empty and has a size of one. A_t^i (APS) maps each input port identifier of the component to a queue q representing the application code's view of frozen port values during its execution. AADL has configurable policies that enable a single value or a collection of values (up to the entire queue) to be dequeued from the IPS into APS. The representation of A_t^i as a mapping to queues is general enough to handle all of these variations. A_t^o (APS) maps each output port identifier for the component to a queue q of values representing the application code's view of output port. Typically, the application code will put 0 or 1 values onto the port during each dispatched execution. I_t^o (IPS) maps each input port identifier of the component to a queue q holding output values has been been moved from A_t^o, typically at the end of a entrypoint execution, to be available to the communication infrastructure for propagation to consumers. For any of these port state structures, the notation $A_t^i[p \mapsto q]$ denotes an updated port state structure that is like the original A_t^i except that port p p now maps to the queue q.

V_t represents a thread's local state, e.g., a mapping from variables to values, that may be accessed by the application code during entrypoint execution. Since manipulation of local variables is orthogonal to the semantics of the AADL RTS, we omit a more detailed formalization. D holds information, accessible during entry point execution, that provides information about the thread's current dispatch.

We assume that the thread state for a thread t is consistent with the static model specification of t (e.g., if t has an inport port p, there is an entry in the map

I_t^i that provides a value/queue for p) and that consistency is maintained by the semantics rules. Such consistency properties are a straightforward formalization [18] and are omitted due to space constraints.

6.3 Dispatch Status RTS

Previous versions of the standard introduced a `Dispatch_Status` RTS, but left its behavior unspecified. The most recent version (a) introduces dispatch status as information held in the thread's state and (b) allows the status information to be platform independent but indicates that it should provide a basis to determine what triggered the thread's most recent dispatch. To move forward with formalizing these concepts, we introduce a basic set of status values for D to support periodic and sporadic dispatch protocols. $D \in \{\mathit{TimeTriggered(ps)}, \mathit{EventTriggered(p, ps)}, \mathit{Initializing}, \ \mathit{NotEnabled}\}$. *TimeTriggered(ps)* indicates that a thread with a periodic dispatch protocol is enabled with ports *ps* to be frozen before application code executes (see the discussion in Sect. 4), *EventTriggered(p, ps)* indicates that a thread with a sporadic dispatch protocol is enabled and that the triggering port is p with ports *ps* to be frozen, *Initializing* indicates that the thread is enabled in the *Initializing* system phase, and *NotEnabled* indicates that the thread is not enabled. Following the description in the most recent version of the standard, the `Dispatch_Status` can be formalized as a function that, when executed by a thread's application or infrastructure code returns the D information from the thread's current state. The returned D information can be used, e.g., by sporadic threads to select a message handler for the event-like port that triggered the dispatch.

6.4 Port RTS

The `Receive_Input` and `Send_Output` provide the interface to transfer messages between the IPS and APS. The following quote and accompanying interface description illustrates the level of descriptive detail for these services in the current AADL standard [1].

> A `Receive_Input` runtime service allows the source text of a thread to explicitly request port input on its incoming ports to be frozen and made accessible through the port variables. Any previous content of the port variable is overwritten, i.e., any previous queue content not processed by `Next_Value` calls is discarded. The `Receive_Input` service takes a parameter that specifies for which ports the input is frozen. Newly arriving data may be queued, but does not affect the input that thread has access to (see Sect. 9). `Receive_Input` is a non-blocking service.

Note that our introduction of I_t^i and A_t^i and IPS-APS terminology clarifies the distinction between the state of the infrastructure and the notion of port variable, respectively.

The interface for `Receive_Input` in version 2.3 of the standard is presented as follows:

$$\frac{\begin{array}{l}\mathcal{M}.isInPort[t](p)\\ \mathcal{M}.isDataPort[t](p)\\ I_t^i(p) = \langle v\rangle \qquad A_t^{i\prime} = A_t^i[p \mapsto \langle v\rangle]\end{array}}{\langle I_t^i, A_t^i, A_t^o, I_t^o, V_t, D\rangle \xrightarrow{\text{RecInP}(p)}_t \langle I_t^i, A_t^{i\prime}, A_t^o, I_t^o, V_t, D\rangle}\ ReceiveInputData$$

$$\frac{\begin{array}{l}\mathcal{M}.isInPort[t](p)\\ \mathcal{M}.isEventLikePort[t](p)\\ \mathcal{M}.DequeuePolicy[t](p) = OneItem \quad I_t^{i\prime} = I_t^i[p \mapsto q]\\ I_t^i(p) = \langle q \rhd v\rangle \qquad A_t^{i\prime} = A_t^i[p \mapsto \langle v\rangle]\end{array}}{\langle I_t^i, A_t^i, A_t^o, I_t^o, V_t, D\rangle \xrightarrow{\text{RecInP}(p)}_t \langle I_t^{i\prime}, A_t^{i\prime}, A_t^o, I_t^o, V_t, D\rangle}\ ReceiveInputEventLikeOneItem$$

$$\frac{\begin{array}{l}\mathcal{M}.isInPort[t](p)\\ \mathcal{M}.isEventLikePort[t](p)\\ \mathcal{M}.DequeuePolicy[t](p) = AllItems \quad I_t^{i\prime} = I_t^i[p \mapsto \langle\rangle]\\ \neg\, isEmpty(I_t^i(p)) \qquad A_t^{i\prime} = A_t^i[p \mapsto I_t^i(p)]\end{array}}{\langle I_t^i, A_t^i, A_t^o, I_t^o, V_t, D\rangle \xrightarrow{\text{RecInP}(p)}_t \langle I_t^{i\prime}, A_t^{i\prime}, A_t^o, I_t^o, V_t, D\rangle}\ ReceiveInputEventLikeAllItems$$

$$\frac{\begin{array}{l}\mathcal{M}.isInPort[t](p)\\ \mathcal{M}.isEventLikePort[t](p)\\ isEmpty(I_t^i(p)) \qquad A_t^{i\prime} = A_t^i[p \mapsto \langle\rangle]\end{array}}{\langle I_t^i, A_t^i, A_t^o, I_t^o, V_t, D\rangle \xrightarrow{\text{RecInP}(p)}_t \langle I_t^i, A_t^{i\prime}, A_t^o, I_t^o, V_t, D\rangle}\ ReceiveInputEventLikeEmpty$$

$$\frac{\begin{array}{l}newq = enqueue(A_t^o(p), I_t^o(p), \mathcal{M}.OverflowProtocol[t](p))\\ A_t^{o\prime} = A_t^o[p \mapsto \langle\rangle]\\ \mathcal{M}.isOutPort[t](p) \qquad I_t^{o\prime} = I_t^o[p \mapsto newq]\end{array}}{\langle I_t^i, A_t^i, A_t^o, I_t^o, V_t, D\rangle \xrightarrow{\text{SendOutP}(p)}_t \langle I_t^i, A_t^i, A_t^{o\prime}, I_t^{o\prime}, V_t, D\rangle}\ SendOutput$$

Fig. 3. *Receive Input* and *Send Output* RTS rules (excerpts)

```
subprogram Receive_Input
features
 InputPorts: in parameter <implementation-
     dependent port list>;
end Receive_Input;
```

The rules in the top portion of Fig. 3 formalize the Receive_Input RTS. The rules are stated for a single port, but extend to a list of ports (matching the informal subprogram interface from the standard) in a straight-forward way.

The rules have the following relational structure:

$$\langle I_t^i, A_t^i, A_t^o, I_t^o, V_t, D\rangle \xrightarrow{\text{RecInP}(p)}_t \langle I_t^{i\prime}, A_t^{i\prime}, A_t^o, I_t^o, V_t, D\rangle$$

The $\xrightarrow{\text{RecInP}(p)}_t$ relational symbol indicates that thread t (typically component infrastructure code) is invoking the Receive_Input service on the port with identifier p. As a side-effect of the invocation, the state $\langle I_t^i, A_t^i, A_t^o, I_t^o, V_t, D\rangle$ of thread t is transformed to a new state $\langle I_t^{i'}, A_t^{i'}, A_t^o, I_t^o, V_t, D\rangle$. The rule conclusions indicate that only the I_t^i and A_t^i portions of state are modified, e.g., by moving/copying values from the IPS into the APS. In source code, the call to the service would take the form RecInP(p) (here RecInP abbreviates the full name of the service). The other elements of the rule are implicit in the code execution context, e.g., t is the currently active thread with the associated thread states. Each of the clauses above the rule vertical bar represent antecedents to the rule (stacked, to conserve space). Clauses on the left side are typically preconditions or conditions selecting rule cases, whereas those on the right represent relationships between inputs and outputs. Each of the rules has an implicit side condition that its state elements I_t^i, etc. are compatible with the model's port declarations for t.

The rule for data ports (first rule) indicates that the single value held by a data port is copied from the infrastructure port state I_t^i to the application port state A_t^i. To conform with the AADL data port concept, the value is not removed from the infrastructure (I_t^i is not updated in the resulting state). The rule for event-like ports for a *OneItem* policy indicates that for a non-empty infrastructure port state I_t^i, a single item is dequeued and placed in the application port state. For the *AllItems* case, the entire contents of the infrastructure queue for p is moved to the application port state, leaving the infrastructure queue empty. Receive Input for p may be called when the infrastructure queue for p is empty, and this sets the application port to an empty queue.

At the bottom of Fig. 3, the rule for `Send_Output` specifies that values are moved from the APS of the port p into the IPS, subject to developer specified overflow policy for p. There is only a single rule because the action is the same regardless the type of port.

6.5 Thread Entry Points

In Fig. 4, there are two rules for each entry point category: the *AppCode* rules reflects the execution of "user's code", while the *Infrastructure* rules captures the code structure that AADL code generation tools would typically use for enforcing AADL's *Read; Compute; Write* emphasis. The distinct *AppCode* rules allow us to parameterize the semantics with the user code (thus, the use of the distinct $\Rightarrow$ symbol), i.e., our framework semantics for AADL RTS, entry point concepts, etc., is orthogonal to the application-specific semantics of the entry point user code.

The `InitEP` application code rule for a thread t formalizes the AADL standard's statements that (a) no input port values are to be read during the initialization phase (access to A_t^i is not provided to the code), (b) a thread's `InitEP` should set initial values for *all* of t's output data ports (i.e., after execution completes, all data port queues in $A_t^{o'}$ are required to have size of 1), and (c) sending initial values on event-like ports is optional. The `InitEP` infrastructure rule indicates that when the scheduling framework invokes the entry point, the infrastructure code typically provides default values for all local variables, invokes the user code, then uses the `Send_Output` to release the thread's APS to

InitEPAppCode :

$$\frac{\forall p \in \mathcal{M}.OutDataPorts(t)\ .\ size(A_t^{o\prime}(p)) = 1 \qquad \forall p \in \mathcal{M}.OutEventLikePorts(t)\ .\ size(A_t^{o\prime}(p)) \leq 1}{(A_t^o,\ V_t) \Rightarrow_t^{\text{InitEP:app-code}} (A_t^{o\prime},\ V_t{}')}$$

InitEPInfrastructure :

$$\frac{V_t^d = DefaultVarValues[t] \qquad (A_t^o,\ V_t^d) \Rightarrow_t^{\text{InitEP:app-code}} (A_t^{o\prime},\ V_t{}') \qquad ps = \mathcal{M}.OutPorts[t] \qquad \langle I_t^i, A_t^i, A_t^{o\prime}, I_t^o, V_t', D\rangle \xrightarrow{\text{SendOutPL}(ps)}_t \langle I_t^i, A_t^i, A_t^{o\prime\prime}, I_t^{o\prime}, V_t', D\rangle}{\langle I_t^i, A_t^i, A_t^o, I_t^o, V_t, D\rangle \xrightarrow{\text{InitEP}}_t \langle I_t^i, A_t^i, A_t^{o\prime\prime}, I_t^{o\prime}, V_t', D\rangle}$$

ComputeEPAppCode :

$$\frac{}{A_t^i,\ A_t^o,\ V_t,\ D \Rightarrow_t^{\text{ComputeEP:app-code}} A_t^{o\prime},\ V_t'}$$

ComputeEPInfrastructure :

$$\frac{A_t^i,\ A_t^o,\ V_t,\ D \Rightarrow_t^{\text{ComputeEP:app-code}} A_t^{o\prime},\ V_t' \qquad ps = \mathcal{M}.OutPorts[t] \qquad \langle I_t^i, A_t^i, A_t^{o\prime}, I_t^o, V_t', D\rangle \xrightarrow{\text{SendOutPL}(ps)}_t \langle I_t^i, A_t^i, A_t^{o\prime\prime}, I_t^{o\prime}, V_t', D\rangle}{\langle I_t^i, A_t^i, A_t^o, I_t^o, V_t, D\rangle \xrightarrow{\text{ComputeEP}}_t \langle I_t^i, A_t^i, A_t^{o\prime\prime}, I_t^{o\prime}, V_t', D\rangle}$$

Fig. 4. Thread entry point semantics

the communication infrastructure for propagation. As the user code executes, it may set specific initial values for local variables (as indicated by the output $V_t{}'$).

The `ComputeEP` user code rule indicates that, abstractly, the user code computes a function *from* the input APS A_t^i, local variable state, and dispatch status *to* output APS values $A_t^{o\prime}$ and (updated) local variable state. A_t^o is present among the rule inputs even though it is *not* an input for the application code. The AADL standard indicates application code is prevented from reading the values of output ports, and A_t^o is only included in the rule inputs to enable the Director to provide initial values for output ports in the *SetPortState* rule of Fig. 6 according to configurable policies. The `ComputeEP` infrastructure rule indicates that when the scheduling framework invokes the entry point, the infrastructure code will typically first invoke the user code, then use the `Send_Output` to move values from thread's output APS to IPS (receiving values for input ports is addressed in the dispatching rules of Sect. 7).

Overall, these rules enhance the AADL standard by clarifying the specific portions of thread state that entry points may read or write and indicating other semantic properties. The infrastructure rules illustrate how future versions of the standard may present code pattern options for enforcing important semantic properties of AADL.

7 Director

To support model analyzability, as well as a variety of embedded execution platforms, our formulation includes structured real-time tasks, without specifying concrete scheduling and communication implementations. This supplements the current AADL standard which underspecifies the necessary coordination between the thread and the underlying scheduling and communications. The standard uses hybrid automata to specify constraints and timing aspects on the operational life-cycle of a thread (e.g., through initialization, compute, and finalization phases, along with mode changes and error recovery). Guarded transitions in the automata correspond to checks on the thread state, interactions with the scheduler, etc. Since the focus of the automaton is on a single thread, broader aspects of the system state, including the scheduling dimension and communication substrate, are not reflected in the standard. In practice, parts of the automata semantics would be realized by a "director" that coordinates multiple types of code – including RTS used in thread infrastructure code, thread application code, and underlying platform scheduling and communication to achieve the semantics of the modeled system. A standardized description of this system-wide director concept would facilitate both interoperability and analyzability.

One of the contributions of our formalization is to fill gaps in the standard with initial definitions of the notion of the system state, and provide rules that characterize how the actions of individual threads, AADL run-time, scheduling, and communication evolve the system state (see [18] for a fuller treatment). Due to space constraints, we focus the presentation here on aspects related to the goals for state and rules above and omit timing aspects.

7.1 System State

For the subset of AADL that we are addressing, the state of an AADL system is a 4-tuple

$$\langle \mathit{Phs}, \mathit{Thrs}, \mathit{Schs}, \mathit{Comms} \rangle.$$

The *system phase* $\mathit{Phs} \in \{\mathit{Initializing}, \mathit{Computing}\}$ indicates the current system phase (initialization entry points are being executed, or compute entry points are being executed). *Thrs* maps each thread identifier t to the thread's state (as defined in Sect. 6). *Schs* maps each thread identifier t to the scheduling state of the thread (*WaitingForDispatch*, *Ready*, or *Running*). *Comms* represents the state of the communication infrastructure.

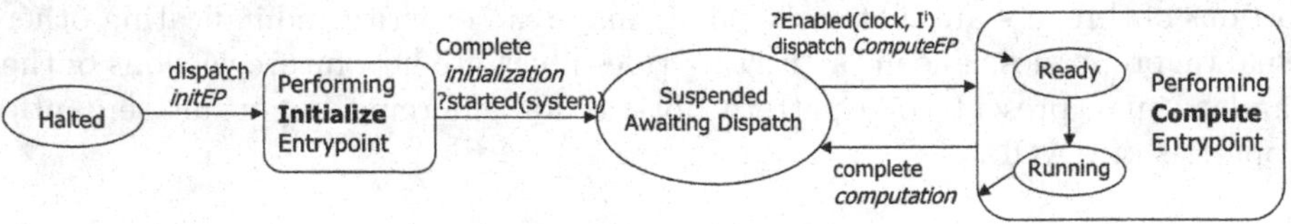

Fig. 5. Thread operational life-cycle

$$\frac{\begin{array}{l} A_t^{i\prime} = InitInAppPorts(t) \\ A_t^{o\prime} = InitOutAppPorts(t) \\ ps = PortsToFreeze(t, D) \\ \langle I_t^i, A_t^{i\prime}, A_t^{o\prime}, I_t^o, V_t, D\rangle \xrightarrow{\mathrm{RecInPL}(ps)}_t \langle I_t^{i\prime}, A_t^{i\prime\prime}, A_t^{o\prime}, I_t^o, V_t, D\rangle \end{array}}{\langle I_t^i, A_t^i, A_t^o, I_t^o, V_t, D\rangle \xrightarrow{\mathrm{SetPortState}(t)}_{\mathrm{Dir}} \langle I_t^{i\prime}, A_t^{i\prime\prime}, A_t^{o\prime}, I_t^o, V_t, D\rangle} \quad SetPortState:$$

$$\frac{\begin{array}{l} Phs(t) = Computing \\ Schs(t) = WaitingForDispatch \\ Thrs(t) = \langle I_t^i, A_t^i, A_t^o, I_t^o, V_t, D\rangle \\ ComputeDispatchStatus(\langle I_t^i, A_t^i, A_t^o, I_t^o, V_t, D\rangle) = D' \\ D' \neq NotEnabled \\ \langle I_t^i, A_t^i, A_t^o, I_t^o, V_t, D'\rangle \xrightarrow{\mathrm{SetPortState}(t)}_{\mathrm{Dir}} \langle I_t^{i\prime}, A_t^{i\prime}, A_t^{o\prime}, I_t^o, V_t, D'\rangle \\ Thrs' = Thrs[t \mapsto \langle I_t^{i\prime}, A_t^{i\prime}, A_t^{o\prime}, I_t^o, V_t, D'\rangle] \\ Schs' = Schs[t \mapsto Ready] \end{array}}{\langle Phs, Thrs, Schs, Comms\rangle \xrightarrow{\mathrm{DispatchEnabledThr}(t)}_{\mathrm{Dir}} \langle Phs, Thrs', Schs', Comms\rangle} \quad Dispatch\ Enabled:$$

Fig. 6. Director services and system actions (excerpts)

Figure 5 shows an adaption of the automata from Fig. 5 (Sect. 5.4.2) of the AADL standard [1] that is simplified to our setting by removing notions related to mode switches, error recovery, and preemption. As discussed above, we aim to clarify the intent of such figures in the standard by providing formal definitions of the transitions, introducing new standardized services and revising the automata concepts when necessary. For example, consider the dispatch transition from the thread Suspended Awaiting Dispatch state to the Performing Compute Entrypoint state. The standard's narrative indicates that the dispatch action causes the thread's input ports to be frozen and that the thread is released to the scheduling framework for the compute entry point to be scheduled and executed. The execution of the dispatch action is conditioned on the notion of *enabled*, which itself is based on a non-trivial set of conditions concerning pending messages in port queues (sporadic components) and timing constraints (periodic components).

Figure 6 proposes a formalization of a new RTS *DispatchEnabledThread* to be used by the AADL Director. This rule is enabled when the system is in the *Computing* phase and the thread's scheduling state is *WaitingForDispatch*. The appropriate thread state is retreived from the system threads, and a new proposed auxiliary service `Compute_Dispatch_Status` is used to compute this dispatch status of the thread. If the thread is enabled, its input queue contents are transferred from the IPS to APS. The thread's scheduling state is set to *Ready* to indicate to the underlying scheduling framework that the thread is available for scheduling.

$$\frac{\begin{array}{l} \mathcal{M}.isOutPort[t](p) \\ Thrs(t) = \langle I^i_t, A^i_t, A^o_t, I^o_t, V_t, D\rangle \\ I^o_t(p) = \langle q \rhd v\rangle \\ \mathcal{M}.ConnDests[t](p) = ps \\ makeMessages(p, ps, v) = M \quad I^{o\prime}_t = I^o_t[p \mapsto q] \\ Thrs' = Thrs[t \mapsto \langle I^i_t, A^i_t, A^o_t, I^{o\prime}_t, V_t, D\rangle] \\ Comms' = Comms \cup M \end{array}}{\langle Phs, Thrs, Schs, Comms\rangle \overset{\text{CommOutCP}(t,p)}{\longrightarrow} \langle Phs, Thrs', Schs, Comms'\rangle}\ CommOutput:$$

$$\frac{\begin{array}{l} (p_s, v, p) \in Comms \\ Thrs(t) = \langle I^i_t, A^i_t, A^o_t, I^o_t, V_t, D\rangle \\ newq = enqueue(v, I^i_t(p), \mathcal{M}.OverflowProtocol[t](p)) \\ I^{i\prime}_t = I^i_t[p \mapsto newq] \\ Thrs' = Thrs[t \mapsto \langle I^{i\prime}_t, A^i_t, A^o_t, I^o_t, V_t, D\rangle] \\ Comms' = Comms - (p_s, v, p) \end{array}}{\langle Phs, Thrs, Schs, Comms\rangle \overset{\text{CommInCP}(t,p)}{\longrightarrow} \langle Phs, Thrs', Schs, Comms'\rangle}\ CommInput:$$

Fig. 7. Communication substrate rules

8 Communication

The design philosophy of the AADL standard is to integrate with existing communication frameworks including local communication using shared memory, middleware for distributed message passing, and scheduled communication such as ARINC 653. The standard provides no API or semantic representation for communication actions – it only provides properties that are used to state constraints/assumptions about communication frameworks. To move toward a formalization that supports this philosophy, we introduce a small number of very general rules whose actions and orderings within system traces that can subsequently be formally constrained to reflect different communication implementations. In particular, the rules are general enough to handle through subsequent refinements both distributed communication as well as local communication where queue state representations can be optimized, e.g., using the same storage for the output IPS of sender components with the input IPS of receiving components as has been done for AADL code generation for microkernels [17]. Space constraints do not allow a full development of this concept here. Instead we expose only enough concepts to support illustration of the port RTS actions in Sect. 9.

Figure 7 presents rules reflecting actions carried out by the communication substrate (middleware). The first rule reflects the substrate's transfer of messages M from a sending thread onto the communication substrate *Comms*. The second rule reflects the substrate's delivery of a message (p_s, v, p) from a sender port p_s into the input infrastructure port state of a receiver port p.

For the first rule, when the sender port p has an output infrastructure port queue $\langle q \rhd v\rangle$ with value v at its head, the substrate will form a collection of messages M, one message for each destination port in $\mathcal{M}.ConnDests[t](p)$ =

ps as determined by static model connections. A new version of the output instructure port state with v dequeued is formed, and the newly created messages M are placed on the communication substrate.

With these general concepts, contraints applied to system traces that include these rule instances can accomodate concepts like immediate or delayed communication between input/output, order preserve delivery versus possible reorderings, and lossy vs non-lossy communication.

9 Example Traces

The section illustrates the AADL RTS rules using a simple execution scenario based on the example of Sect. 2. Steps in both the *Initializing* and *Computing* phases are shown for the `TempSensor` and `TempControl` components. These examples focus on the manipulation of thread states. See [18] for additional examples that include a broader treatment of system-level execution and communication. To validate that our rules reflect a realistic implementation of an AADL run-time, the HAMR AADL code generation framework [17] has been enhanced to emit trace states and traceability information that aligns with the rules in the previous sections. That feature generates outputs that are equivalent to the type set trace information presented in this section.

TempSensor Initialize Entry Point: Consider first the *InitEPAppCode* rule from Fig. 4 capturing the execution of the application code for the Initialize Entry Point as applied to the TempSensor component. Given the values below for the initial output application port state, which includes empty queues for both output ports and default variable values supplied from the *InitEPInfrastructure* rule context (there are no thread local variables for this component),

$$\begin{aligned} A_t^o &= [\texttt{currentTemp} \mapsto \langle\rangle, \texttt{tempChanged} \mapsto \langle\rangle] \\ V_t &= [] \end{aligned}$$

executing the application code for Initialize Entry Point is represented by the following relation, reflected in the *InitEPAppCode* rule.

$$(A_t^o,\ V_t) \Rightarrow_t^{\text{InitEP:app-code}} ([\texttt{currentTemp} \mapsto \langle 73.0\rangle, \texttt{tempChanged} \mapsto \langle\rangle],\ [])$$

This reflects the fact that the application code initializes the `currentTemp` port with the value 73.0 via the `Put_Value` run-time service, but does not put an event on the `tempChanged` port (this is not done until the Compute Entry Point where temperature values are retrieved from the sensor hardware). Making the assumption that the fan inherently knows the initial safe state is acceptable in this nominal fault-free safe state startup scenario, but would need to be discharged in other safety-critical design scenarios.

In the context of the Fig. 4 *InitEPInfrastructure* rule, which formalizes the component *infrastructure's* invocation of the application code for the Initialize Entry Point, when the above structures are placed in the context of the

TempSensor thread state, we have the following state thread elements, representing the state of the TempSensor thread after the execution of the *application code* (the tuple element values on the right side of the vertical bar reflect the instantiation of the meta-variables on the left side that are used in the *InitEPInfrastructure* rule).

$$\begin{array}{r|l} I_t^i & \langle [], \\ A_t^i & [], \\ A_t^{o\prime} & [\texttt{currentTemp} \mapsto \langle 73.0 \rangle, \texttt{tempChanged} \mapsto \langle \rangle], \\ I_t^o & [\texttt{currentTemp} \mapsto \langle \rangle, \texttt{tempChanged} \mapsto \langle \rangle], \\ V_t' & [], \\ D & \mathit{Initializing} \rangle \end{array}$$

Then, the invocation of the SendOutput RTS moves the currentTemp value to the output infrastructure port state to obtain the following thread state at the completion of the execution of the *infrastructure* for the Initialize Entry Point.

$$\begin{array}{r|l} I_t^i & \langle [], \\ A_t^i & [], \\ A_t^{o\prime\prime} & [\texttt{currentTemp} \mapsto \langle \rangle, \texttt{tempChanged} \mapsto \langle \rangle], \\ I_t^{o\prime} & [\texttt{currentTemp} \mapsto \langle 73.0 \rangle, \texttt{tempChanged} \mapsto \langle \rangle], \\ V_t' & [], \\ D & \mathit{Initializing} \rangle \end{array}$$

The presence of value 73.0 in the currentTemp port of the $I_t^{o\prime}$ output infrastructure port state represents the fact that it has been made available to the communication substrate for propagation to consumers.

TempControl Initialize Entry Point: Following a similar sequence of rules for the TempControl Initialize Entry Point yields the following thread state.

$$\begin{array}{r|l} I_t^i & [\texttt{currentTemp} \mapsto \langle \rangle, \texttt{tempChanged} \mapsto \langle \rangle, \\ & \texttt{setPoint} \mapsto \langle \rangle, \texttt{fanAck} \mapsto \langle \rangle] \\ A_t^i & [\texttt{currentTemp} \mapsto \langle \rangle, \texttt{tempChanged} \mapsto \langle \rangle, \\ & \texttt{setPoint} \mapsto \langle \rangle, \texttt{fanAck} \mapsto \langle \rangle] \\ A_t^{o\prime\prime} & [\texttt{fanCmd} \mapsto \langle \rangle] \\ I_t^{o\prime} & [\texttt{fanCmd} \mapsto \langle \rangle] \\ V_t' & [\texttt{latestTemp} \mapsto 73.0, \texttt{currentSetPoint} \mapsto (70.0, 75.0),] \\ & \ \texttt{currentFanState} \mapsto \texttt{Off} \\ D & \mathit{Initializing} \end{array}$$

The primary difference is that the TempControl thread initializes thread local variables (e.g., set points are iniitialized to low and high values (70.0, 75.0)), but does not put any initial values on its output ports (i.e., the queue for fanCmd is empty).

Before the system transitions from the *Initializing* to the *Computing* phase, the initial value placed on the TempSensor currentTemp output port is propagated to connected input port of TempControl according to the rules of Fig. 7.

Completed Initialization: Following these communication steps, the system transitions to the *Computing* phase, with the following states for the TempSensor

$$\begin{array}{r|l} I_t^i & \langle [], \\ A_t^i & [], \\ A_t^o & [\texttt{currentTemp} \mapsto \langle \rangle, \texttt{tempChanged} \mapsto \langle \rangle], \\ I_t^o & [\texttt{currentTemp} \mapsto \langle \rangle, \texttt{tempChanged} \mapsto \langle \rangle], \\ V_t & [], \\ D & \mathit{NotEnabled} \rangle \end{array}$$

and TempControl thread components.

$$
\begin{array}{l|l}
I_t^i & [\mathtt{currentTemp} \mapsto \langle 73.0 \rangle, \mathtt{tempChanged} \mapsto \langle\rangle, \\
 & \mathtt{setPoint} \mapsto \langle\rangle, \mathtt{fanAck} \mapsto \langle\rangle] \\
A_t^i & [\mathtt{currentTemp} \mapsto \langle\rangle, \mathtt{tempChanged} \mapsto \langle\rangle, \\
 & \mathtt{setPoint} \mapsto \langle\rangle, \mathtt{fanAck} \mapsto \langle\rangle] \\
A_t^o & [\mathtt{fanCmd} \mapsto \langle\rangle] \\
I_t^o & [\mathtt{fanCmd} \mapsto \langle\rangle] \\
V_t & [\mathtt{latestTemp} \mapsto 73.0, \mathtt{currentSetPoint} \mapsto (70.0, 75.0),] \\
 & \mathtt{currentFanState} \mapsto \mathtt{Off} \\
D & \mathit{NotEnabled}
\end{array}
$$

The TempSensor currentTemp out data port has been initialized and its value propagated to the infrastructure port state I_t^i for the TempControl currentTemp input data port. The thread local variables of TempControl have been initialized. Director rules (omitted due to space constraints) set the dispatch status of each thread to *NotEnabled*.

TempSensor Compute Entry Point: The TempSensor compute entry point is dispatched periodically as discussed in Sect. 2. Its entry point application code reads the current temperature from a hardware sensor (how this is modeled is not discussed in this paper), places the value on the currentTemp out data port and a notification event on tempChanged out event port. Assume the physical sensor responds with a temperature value of 78.3.

We use the TempControl component to illustrate the details of compute entry point rules, and simply note that at the end of a similar application of the rules for TempSensor, its thread state is the following.

$$
\begin{array}{r|l}
I_t^i & \langle [], \\
A_t^i & [], \\
A_t^{o\prime\prime} & [\mathtt{currentTemp} \mapsto \langle\rangle, \mathtt{tempChanged} \mapsto \langle\rangle], \\
I_t^{o\prime} & [\mathtt{currentTemp} \mapsto \langle 78.3 \rangle, \mathtt{tempChanged} \mapsto \langle * \rangle], \\
V_t^{\prime} & [], \\
D & \mathit{NotEnabled} \rangle
\end{array}
$$

Here we see that an event is queued in the tempChanged infrastructure port and the value 78.3 is held in the currentTemp infrastructure data port.

Communication: If we are following AADL's "immediate" port communication property, at this point that communication infrastructure would propagate values from the TempSensor output ports to the TempControl input ports. This results in the following TempSensor thread state below in which currentTemp and tempChanged have been communicated and no longer appear in I_t^o.

$$
\begin{array}{r|l}
I_t^i & \langle [], \\
A_t^i & [], \\
A_t^o & [\mathtt{currentTemp} \mapsto \langle 78.3 \rangle, \mathtt{tempChanged} \mapsto \langle\rangle], \\
I_t^o & [\mathtt{currentTemp} \mapsto \langle\rangle, \mathtt{tempChanged} \mapsto \langle\rangle], \\
V_t & [], \\
D & \mathit{NotEnabled} \rangle
\end{array}
$$

At the other end of the port connections, the values have been placed in the input infrastructure ports I_t^i of the TempControl thread (the previous value of

73.0 in the infrastructure `currentTemp` data port has been overwritten by the value of 78.3).

$$\begin{array}{c|l} I_t^i & [\texttt{currentTemp} \mapsto \langle 78.3 \rangle, \texttt{tempChanged} \mapsto \langle * \rangle, \\ & \texttt{setPoint} \mapsto \langle \rangle, \texttt{fanAck} \mapsto \langle \rangle] \\ A_t^i & [\texttt{currentTemp} \mapsto \langle \rangle, \texttt{tempChanged} \mapsto \langle \rangle, \\ & \texttt{setPoint} \mapsto \langle \rangle, \texttt{fanAck} \mapsto \langle \rangle] \\ A_t^o & [\texttt{fanCmd} \mapsto \langle \rangle] \\ I_t^o & [\texttt{fanCmd} \mapsto \langle \rangle] \\ V_t & [\texttt{latestTemp} \mapsto 73.0, \texttt{currentSetPoint} \mapsto (70.0, 75.0),] \\ & \texttt{currentFanState} \mapsto \texttt{Off} \\ D & \mathit{NotEnabled} \end{array}$$

TempControl Dispatch and Compute Entry Point: `TempControl` is a sporadic thread. In the current execution, its dispatch is triggered by the arrival of an event on the `tempChanged` port. Dispatching is formalized by the rules in Fig. 6.

Conditions in premises of the *Dispatch Enabled* rule ensure that the system is in the *Computing* phase and that the `TempControl` scheduling state is *WaitingForDispatch*. Then an auxiliary function is called to determine the dispatch status of the thread.

$$\begin{array}{l} \mathit{ComputeDispatchStatus}(\langle I_t^i, A_t^i, A_t^o, I_t^o, V_t, D \rangle) = \\ \quad \mathit{EventTriggered}(\texttt{tempChanged}, \{\texttt{tempChanged}, \texttt{currentTemp}\}) \end{array}$$

This indicates that thread dispatch has been triggered by the arrival of the `tempChanged` event and that, following the AADL standard's rules for port freezing, the `tempChanged` is to be frozen since it is the triggering event port and `currentTemp` is to be frozen because it is a data port (data ports are frozen by default).

Since the computed dispatch status indicates that the thread is enabled, the *SetPortState* rule prepares the port states for entry point execution. First, auxiliary functions are used to initialize the input and output application port state as follows (where t = `TempControl`):

$$\begin{array}{c|l} A_t^{i\prime} & [\texttt{currentTemp} \mapsto \langle \rangle, \texttt{tempChanged} \mapsto \langle \rangle, \ = \mathit{InitInAppPorts}(t) \\ & \texttt{setPoint} \mapsto \langle \rangle, \texttt{fanAck} \mapsto \langle \rangle] \\ A_t^{o\prime} & [\texttt{fanCmd} \mapsto \langle \rangle] = \mathit{InitOutAppPorts}(t) \end{array}$$

An auxiliary function is also used to extract the set of ports to freeze.

$$\begin{array}{c|l} ps & \{\texttt{tempChanged}, \texttt{currentTemp}\} = \\ & \quad \mathit{PortsToFreeze}(t, \mathit{EventTriggered}(\texttt{tempChanged}, \\ & \qquad \{\texttt{tempChanged}, \texttt{currentTemp}\})) \end{array}$$

Given the thread state at this point, which instantiates the metavariables in the *SetPortState* rule as follows,

$$\begin{array}{c|l} I_t^i & [\texttt{currentTemp} \mapsto \langle 78.3 \rangle, \texttt{tempChanged} \mapsto \langle * \rangle, \\ & \texttt{setPoint} \mapsto \langle \rangle, \texttt{fanAck} \mapsto \langle \rangle] \\ A_t^{i\prime} & [\texttt{currentTemp} \mapsto \langle \rangle, \texttt{tempChanged} \mapsto \langle \rangle, \\ & \texttt{setPoint} \mapsto \langle \rangle, \texttt{fanAck} \mapsto \langle \rangle] \\ A_t^{o\prime} & [\texttt{fanCmd} \mapsto \langle \rangle] \\ I_t^o & [\texttt{fanCmd} \mapsto \langle \rangle] \\ V_t & [\texttt{latestTemp} \mapsto 73.0, \texttt{currentSetPoint} \mapsto (70.0, 75.0),] \\ & \texttt{currentFanState} \mapsto \texttt{Off} \\ D & \mathit{EventTriggered}(\texttt{tempChanged}, \{\texttt{tempChanged}, \texttt{currentTemp}\}) \end{array}$$

and given the list of ports to freeze *ps* as instantiated above, applying the rule for the Receive Input RTS yields the following updated thread state (instantiating the metavariables in the *SetPortState* rule)

$$\begin{array}{r|l} I_t^{i\prime} & [\texttt{currentTemp} \mapsto \langle 78.3\rangle, \texttt{tempChanged} \mapsto \langle\rangle, \\ & \texttt{setPoint} \mapsto \langle\rangle, \texttt{fanAck} \mapsto \langle\rangle] \\ A_t^{i\prime\prime} & [\texttt{currentTemp} \mapsto \langle 78.3\rangle, \texttt{tempChanged} \mapsto \langle *\rangle, \\ & \texttt{setPoint} \mapsto \langle\rangle, \texttt{fanAck} \mapsto \langle\rangle] \\ A_t^{o\prime} & [\texttt{fanCmd} \mapsto \langle\rangle] \\ I_t^{o} & [\texttt{fanCmd} \mapsto \langle\rangle] \\ V_t & [\texttt{latestTemp} \mapsto 73.0, \texttt{currentSetPoint} \mapsto (70.0, 75.0),] \\ & \texttt{currentFanState} \mapsto \texttt{Off} \\ D & \mathit{EventTriggered}(\texttt{tempChanged}, \{\texttt{tempChanged}, \texttt{currentTemp}\}) \end{array}$$

Continuing in the *Dispatch Enabled* rule, the scheduling state of `TempControl` is set to *Ready* to indicate to the underlying OS scheduler that the thread is available for scheduling.

In the `TempControl` compute entry point, dispatch is triggered by the `tempChanged` event port, which triggers the application code to read the `currentTemp` data port, store the value in the `latestTemp` thread local variable, and compare the read value to the `currentSetPoint` values. If the current temperature is greater than the high set point, a message will be put on the `fanCmd` port to turn the fan on. If the current temperature is less than the low set point, the application code puts a message into the `fanCmd` port to turn the fan off. In both cases, the application code updates the `currentFanState` variable to reflect the new desired state of the fan. Otherwise, if the current temperature is equal to or falls between the low and high set points, no command is sent and the `currentFanState` is not changed.

Picking up from the current state of the `TempControl` thread after dispatch above, in the formalization of the representation of the execution of the user code in Fig. 4, the metavariables in the *ComputeEPAppCode* rule have the following values representing the application's view of the thread state at the beginning of the application code execution

$$\begin{array}{r|l} A_t^{i} & [\texttt{currentTemp} \mapsto \langle 78.3\rangle, \texttt{tempChanged} \mapsto \langle *\rangle, \\ & \texttt{setPoint} \mapsto \langle\rangle, \texttt{fanAck} \mapsto \langle\rangle] \\ A_t^{o} & [\texttt{fanCmd} \mapsto \langle\rangle] \\ V_t & [\texttt{latestTemp} \mapsto 73.0, \texttt{currentSetPoint} \mapsto (70.0, 75.0),] \\ & \texttt{currentFanState} \mapsto \texttt{Off} \\ D & \mathit{EventTriggered}(\texttt{tempChanged}, \{\texttt{tempChanged}, \texttt{currentTemp}\}) \end{array}$$

and at the end of execution

$$\begin{array}{r|l} A_t^{o\prime} & [\texttt{fanCmd} \mapsto \langle \texttt{On}\rangle] \\ V_t^{\prime} & [\texttt{latestTemp} \mapsto 78.3, \texttt{currentSetPoint} \mapsto (70.0, 75.0),] \\ & \texttt{currentFanState} \mapsto \texttt{On} \end{array}$$

In the context of the Fig. 4 *ComputeEPInfrastructure* rule, when the above structures are placed in the context of the complete `TempControl` thread state, we have the following, representing the state of the thread after the execution of the *application code*.

I_t^i	[currentTemp $\mapsto$ ⟨78.3⟩, tempChanged $\mapsto$ ⟨⟩, setPoint $\mapsto$ ⟨⟩, fanAck $\mapsto$ ⟨⟩]
A_t^i	[currentTemp $\mapsto$ ⟨⟩, tempChanged $\mapsto$ ⟨⟩, setPoint $\mapsto$ ⟨⟩, fanAck $\mapsto$ ⟨⟩]
$A_t^{o\prime}$	[fanCmd $\mapsto$ ⟨On⟩]
I_t^o	[fanCmd $\mapsto$ ⟨⟩]
V_t'	[latestTemp $\mapsto$ 78.3, currentSetPoint $\mapsto$ (70.0, 75.0),] currentFanState $\mapsto$ On
D	*EventTriggered*(tempChanged, {tempChanged, currentTemp})

Then, the invocation of the SendOutput RTS moves the `fanCmd` message to the output infrastructure port state to obtain the following thread state at the completion of the execution of the *infrastructure* for the Compute Entry Point.

I_t^i	[currentTemp $\mapsto$ ⟨78.3⟩, tempChanged $\mapsto$ ⟨⟩, setPoint $\mapsto$ ⟨⟩, fanAck $\mapsto$ ⟨⟩]
A_t^i	[currentTemp $\mapsto$ ⟨⟩, tempChanged $\mapsto$ ⟨⟩, setPoint $\mapsto$ ⟨⟩, fanAck $\mapsto$ ⟨⟩]
$A_t^{o\prime\prime}$	[fanCmd $\mapsto$ ⟨⟩]
$I_t^{o\prime}$	[fanCmd $\mapsto$ ⟨On⟩]
V_t'	[latestTemp $\mapsto$ 78.3, currentSetPoint $\mapsto$ (70.0, 75.0),] currentFanState $\mapsto$ On
D	*EventTriggered*(tempChanged, {tempChanged, currentTemp})

Following this, a director rule (omitted) resets the thread's dispatch status to *NotEnabled*. The message `On` is propagated to the `Fan` thread which is dispatched in manner similar to that illustrated above for the `TempControl` component.

10 Related Work

There are numerous contributions to the formal specification, analysis, and verification of AADL models and annexes. These works, whether implicitly or explicitly, propose semantics for AADL in the model of computation and communication of the verification framework considered [6]. Many contributions focus on static semantics of models [2,34] while others consider run-time behavior and use model translation to extract executable specifications from AADL models, e.g., [4,5,10,16,37]. Many related works formalize a subset of AADL (e.g., for synchronous systems only) or focus on analyzing an aspect of the system, such as schedulability [32], behavioral [6,35], or dependability analyses [13].

Closely related work has made strides towards the formalization of a AADL run-time behavior. Rolland et al. [31] formalized aspects of AADL's coordination and timing behavior through the translation of AADL models into the Temporal Logic of Actions (TLA+) [27]. Hugues et al. [19,28] provided a Ada/SPARK2014 definition of selected RTS as part of a broader implementation of the AADL run-time. In addition, SPARK2014 verification was used to demonstrate absence of run-time errors in the implementation. However, aspects of the semantics of the given services as well various notions of thread and system state are implicit in that they are expressed using Ada constructs (and thus rely on the underlying semantics and state of Ada). To complement this programming language-based approach, we aim for a language-independent specification of RTS and a more explicit exposition of notions of port state, thread state, as well as director and communication aspects.

11 Conclusion

Over the last fifteen years, AADL has been an effective vehicle within the formal methods community for developing rigorous model-based analysis and verification techniques. However, individual tools have often only treated a slice of AADL or have re-interpretered AADL's informal semantics to match the computional model supported by their particular tool. While it is impossible to provide a comprehensive semantics in a single conference paper, this work (with the accompanying technical report [18]) represents an initial step in providing a canonical and comprehensive treatment of AADL semantics by providing a formalization of the AADL RTS. Due to the central role played by the RTS, this formalization clarifies the standard's informal descriptions, provides a clearer foundation for model-level analysis and verification, and elucidates important aspects of the semantics for AADL code generation.

This lays the foundation for multiple lines of future work. First, AADL committee discussions suggest that future versions of the AADL will include formalizations that better ground the standard's descriptions. In addition to the RTS aspects, this will include more "coordination level" aspects that address AADL life-cycle and interactions of process and systems, scheduling, and distributed communication. This is important for establishing soundness arguments for analyses and contract languages such as AGREE [12] and BLESS [25]. Second, under consideration is a new approach to the AADL Code Generation annex which does not focus on syntactic conventions for representing AADL model artifacts but instead focuses on (a) disclosure and traceability to key aspects of a AADL RTS formalization including representation of port and thread state, implementation of AADL RTS, (b) testing- and formal-methods-based demonstration of conformance to key aspects of the forthcoming canonical semantics. Third, regarding refinement, our semantics was designed to support AADL's general threading (periodic and event-driven threads) and port communication (synchronous data flow as well as message-passing). For future work, we imagine developing refinements that specialize the semantics to particular computational paradigms (e.g., synchronous data flow only, or message passing only) – with the end result be simplified special case semantics with a proof of refinement to the more general case. Also of interest are refinements to particular scheduling regimes (our semantics focuses on the RTS and leaves a placeholder for scheduling actions that determine execution order of threads). We expect to continue refining the semantics at lower levels of abstraction to capture details of mapping AADL to classes of RTOS and standard architectures like ARINC 653 [36]. For AADL code generation that targets the formally verified seL4 micro-kernel [17,23], mechanizing the AADL semantics and formally verifying aspects AADL run-time can continue to expand the stack of formally verified infrastructure that can be applied to critical system development.

Finally, we are interested in considering issues of usability and utility for "formal semantics as documentation". In this paper, we presented formal specifications in conventional rule-based notation with symbols and rule style chosen somewhat arbitrarily. If this type of material is to be part of a industry standard used by people with a variety of backgrounds, we need formal descriptions to be presented using notations that are accessible and easy to understand. Furthermore, we need approaches for machine-readable versions of the semantics that can be leveraged by tools in multiple ways. Similar goals have existed for decades in the programming language semantics and formal methods communities. But now we find the need a bit more pressing, because to achieve the next innovations in critical system development, we need to effectively capture and connect semantics across multiple modeling languages and programming languages, along with many forms of accompanying tooling.

Acknowledgements. Copyright 2022 Carnegie Mellon University, Adventium Labs and Kansas State University. This material is based upon work funded and supported by the Department of Defense under Contract No. FA8702-15-D-0002 with Carnegie Mellon University for the operation of the Software Engineering Institute, a federally funded research and development center.

References

1. SAE AS5506/2. AADL annex volume 2
2. Backes, J., Cofer, D., Miller, S., Whalen, M.W.: Requirements analysis of a quad-redundant flight control system. In: Havelund, K., Holzmann, G., Joshi, R. (eds.) NFM 2015. LNCS, vol. 9058, pp. 82–96. Springer, Cham (2015). https://doi.org/10.1007/978-3-319-17524-9_7
3. Barnes, J.G.: Programming in ADA. Addison-Wesley Longman Publishing Co., Inc, London (1984)
4. Berthomieu, B., Bodeveix, J.-P., Chaudet, C., Dal Zilio, S., Filali, M., Vernadat, F.: Formal verification of AADL specifications in the topcased environment. In: Kordon, F., Kermarrec, Y. (eds.) Ada-Europe 2009. LNCS, vol. 5570, pp. 207–221. Springer, Heidelberg (2009). https://doi.org/10.1007/978-3-642-01924-1_15
5. Berthomieu, B., et al.: Formal verification of AADL models with Fiacre and Tina. In: ERTSS 2010-Embedded Real-Time Software and Systems, pp. 1–9 (2010)
6. Besnard, L., et al.: Formal semantics of behavior specifications in the architecture analysis and design language standard. In: Nakajima, S., Talpin, J.-P., Toyoshima, M., Yu, H. (eds.) Cyber-Physical System Design from an Architecture Analysis Viewpoint, pp. 53–79. Springer, Singapore (2017). https://doi.org/10.1007/978-981-10-4436-6_3

7. Borde, E., Rahmoun, S., Cadoret, F., Pautet, L., Singhoff, F., Dissaux, P.: Architecture models refinement for fine grain timing analysis of embedded systems. In: 2014 25nd IEEE International Symposium on Rapid System Prototyping, pp. 44–50 (2014)
8. Burns, A., Wellings, A.: Analysable real-time systems: programmed in Ada. CreateSpace (2016)
9. Carré, B., Garnsworthy, J.: SPARK - an annotated Ada subset for safety-critical programming. In: Proceedings of the Conference on TRI-ADA 1990, pp. 392–402 (1990)
10. Chkouri, M.Y., Robert, A., Bozga, M., Sifakis, J.: Translating AADL into BIP - application to the verification of real-time systems. In: Chaudron, M.R.V. (ed.) MODELS 2008. LNCS, vol. 5421, pp. 5–19. Springer, Heidelberg (2009). https://doi.org/10.1007/978-3-642-01648-6_2
11. Cofer, D., et al.: Cyber-assured systems engineering at scale. IEEE Secur. Priv. **01**, 2–14 (2022)
12. Cofer, D., Gacek, A., Miller, S., Whalen, M.W., LaValley, B., Sha, L.: Compositional verification of architectural models. In: Goodloe, A.E., Person, S. (eds.) NFM 2012. LNCS, vol. 7226, pp. 126–140. Springer, Heidelberg (2012). https://doi.org/10.1007/978-3-642-28891-3_13
13. Feiler, P., Rugina, A.: Dependability modeling with the architecture analysis and design language (AADL). Technical report, Software Engineering INST, Carnegie-Mellon University, Pittsburgh, PA (2007)
14. Feiler, P.H.: Efficient embedded runtime systems through port communication optimization. In: 13th IEEE International Conference on Engineering of Complex Computer Systems (ICECCS 2008), pp. 294–300 (2008)
15. Feiler, P.H., Gluch, D.P.: Model-Based Engineering with AADL: An Introduction to the SAE Architecture Analysis and Design Language. Addison-Wesley, Reading (2013)
16. Hadad, A.S.A., Ma, C., Ahmed, A.A.O.: Formal verification of AADL models by Event-B. IEEE Access **8**, 72814–72834 (2020)
17. Hatcliff, J., Belt, J., Robby, Carpenter, T.: HAMR: an AADL multi-platform code generation toolset. In: Margaria, T., Steffen, B. (eds.) ISoLA 2021. LNCS, vol. 13036, pp. 274–295. Springer, Cham (2021). https://doi.org/10.1007/978-3-030-89159-6_18
18. Hatcliff, J., Hugues, J., Stewart, D., Wrage, L.: Formalization of the AADL runtime services (extended version) (2021)
19. Hugues, J.: A correct-by-construction AADL runtime for the Ravenscar profile using SPARK2014. J. Syst. Archit., 102376 (2022). https://www.sciencedirect.com/science/article/pii/S1383762121002599
20. Hugues, J., Zalila, B., Pautet, L., Kordon, F.: Rapid prototyping of distributed real-time embedded systems using the AADL and Ocarina. In: IEEE International Workshop on Rapid System Prototyping, vol. 7 (2007)
21. SAE International: SAE AS5506/1, AADL Annex E: Error Model Annex. SAE International (2015). http://www.sae.org
22. SAE International: SAE AS5506 Rev. C Architecture Analysis and Design Language (AADL). SAE International (2017)
23. Klein, G., et al.: seL4: formal verification of an OS kernel. In: Proceedings of the ACM SIGOPS 22nd Symposium on Operating Systems Principles, pp. 207–220 (2009)

24. Larson, B., Hatcliff, J., Fowler, K., Delange, J.: Illustrating the AADL error modeling annex (v.2) using a simple safety-critical medical device. In: Proceedings of the 2013 ACM SIGAda Annual Conference on High Integrity Language Technology, HILT 2013, pp. 65–84. ACM, New York (2013)
25. Larson, B.R., Chalin, P., Hatcliff, J.: BLESS: formal specification and verification of behaviors for embedded systems with software. In: Brat, G., Rungta, N., Venet, A. (eds.) NFM 2013. LNCS, vol. 7871, pp. 276–290. Springer, Heidelberg (2013). https://doi.org/10.1007/978-3-642-38088-4_19
26. Lasnier, G., Zalila, B., Pautet, L., Hugues, J.: OCARINA: an environment for AADL models analysis and automatic code generation for high integrity applications. In: Kordon, F., Kermarrec, Y. (eds.) Ada-Europe 2009. LNCS, vol. 5570, pp. 237–250. Springer, Heidelberg (2009). https://doi.org/10.1007/978-3-642-01924-1_17
27. Merz, S.: The specification language TLA+. In: Bjørner, D., Henson, M.C. (eds.) Logics of Specification Languages, pp. 401–451. Springer, Heidelberg (2008). https://doi.org/10.1007/978-3-540-74107-7_8
28. Mkaouar, H., Zalila, B., Hugues, J., Jmaiel, M.: A formal approach to AADL model-based software engineering. Int. J. Softw. Tools Technol. Transf. **22**(2), 219–247 (2019). https://doi.org/10.1007/s10009-019-00513-7
29. Perrotin, M., Conquet, E., Delange, J., Schiele, A., Tsiodras, T.: TASTE: a real-time software engineering tool-chain overview, status, and future, pp. 26–37, January 2011
30. Robby, Hatcliff, J.: Slang: the Sireum programming language. In: Margaria, T., Steffen, B. (eds.) ISoLA 2021. LNCS, vol. 13036, pp. 253–273. Springer, Cham (2021). https://doi.org/10.1007/978-3-030-89159-6_17
31. Rolland, J.F., Bodeveix, J.P., Chemouil, D., Filali, M., Thomas, D.: Towards a formal semantics for AADL execution model. In: Embedded Real Time Software and Systems (ERTS 2008) (2008)
32. Sokolsky, O., Lee, I., Clarke, D.: Schedulability analysis of AADL models. In: Proceedings 20th IEEE International Parallel and Distributed Processing Symposium, p. 8. IEEE (2006)
33. Stewart, D., Liu, J.J., Cofer, D., Heimdahl, M., Whalen, M.W., Peterson, M.: AADL-based safety analysis using formal methods applied to aircraft digital systems. Reliab. Eng. Syst. Saf. **213**, 107649 (2021)
34. Stewart, D., Liu, J.J., Whalen, M., Cofer, D., Peterson, M.: Safety annex for architecture analysis design and analysis language. In: ERTS 2020: 10th European Conference Embedded Real Time Systems (2020)
35. Tan, Y., Zhao, Y., Ma, D., Zhang, X.: A comprehensive formalization of AADL with behavior annex. Sci. Program. **2022** (2022)
36. VanderLeest, S.H.: ARINC 653 hypervisor. In: 29th Digital Avionics Systems Conference, pp. 5-E. IEEE (2010)
37. Yang, Z., Hu, K., Ma, D., Bodeveix, J.P., Pi, L., Talpin, J.P.: From AADL to timed abstract state machines: a verified model transformation. J. Syst. Softw. **93**, 42–68 (2014)
38. Yuan, C., Wu, K., Chen, G., Mo, Y.: An automatic transformation method from AADL reliability model to CTMC. In: 2021 IEEE International Conference on Information Communication and Software Engineering (ICICSE), pp. 322–326 (2021). https://doi.org/10.1109/ICICSE52190.2021.9404135

Executable Documentation: Test-First in Action

Steven Smyth[1(✉)], Jette Petzold[2], Jonas Schürmann[1], Florian Karbus[1], Tiziana Margaria[3], Reinhard von Hanxleden[2], and Bernhard Steffen[1]

[1] Chair of Programming Systems, TU Dortmund University, Dortmund, Germany
{steven.smyth,jonas2.schuermann,florian.karbus, bernhard.steffen}@tu-dortmund.de

[2] Real-Time and Embedded Systems Group, Kiel University, Kiel, Germany
{jep,rvh}@informatik.uni-kiel.de

[3] Department of Computer Science and Information Systems, University of Limerick, Limerick, Ireland
tiziana.margaria@ul.ie

Abstract. Regarding documentation as *anything that supports understanding*, we present two test-first scenarios of executable documentation that involve and support different roles during program development through concrete data visualizations. The first is a teaching scenario. Within classical programming, different stages of executable documentation provide faceted layers of self-learning and user-centric diagnostics. Students and teachers benefit from auto-didactic exploration, appropriate diagram syntheses for runtime visualization, and automated test case generation. The latter can be created using reference implementations provided by the teacher but can also be used to foster the dialog between students and tutors. The second scenario introduces a new approach to WYSIWYG GUI editing that is able to render the runtime GUI appearance in real-time within the editor. Using scenario-based test cases, users can seamlessly experience, inspect, and test the GUI while they are editing. The paper discusses the impact of the provided tangible experiences and their role in modern IDEs.

Keywords: Documentation · Teaching · Test-driven development · Automatic layout · Verification · Web technologies

1 Introduction

Historically, documentation evolved from necessary source code descriptions about how a particular task has been solved, as e.g., in assembler code, to "optional" descriptions in form of comments on what should be solved. In the last decades, these have been enriched with annotations or HTML tags and served as source to generate API documentation, as it is done with JavaDoc [14]. Recently, in platforms such as Jupyter, source code can be embedded into elaborate reports to access databases and generate visual outputs directly inside the document [18]. However, in all these concepts there is "just one truth" that is usually not tailored to multiple individual needs of different stakeholders.

T. Margaria and B. Steffen (Eds.): ISoLA 2022, LNCS 13702, pp. 135–156, 2022.
https://doi.org/10.1007/978-3-031-19756-7_8

In our vision, anything that supports understanding is regarded as *the documentation*, which should be presented according to the individual needs of the observing stakeholder. A programmer might have requirements towards the documentation that greatly differ from a marketing salesperson. Therefore, generating reasonable parts automatically, instantaneously, and appropriately is a huge benefit. In this scenario, "reasonable" depends on the particular documentation domain, which should be supported by the IDE used by the concrete stakeholder. To include the front-line developer/programmer in this methodology and to provide a platform to talk about the project with other stakeholders, running test instances can be instrumented as Executable Documentation (ED) for immediate and tangible feedback. ED is an umbrella term which includes all parts of a documentation that can be executed directly, create executable components (e.g., higher-level models or even running products), or components that manually or automatically generate parts of the documentation. As will be demonstrated throughout the paper, different parts of the ED can be intertwined. For example, in the teaching domain, a reference solution to a student task is an ED and can generate an appropriately visualized correct result. Test instances, also EDs, can then identify and document erroneous software components.

Running concrete test instances is in line with the *test first* core principle in agile software development [3]. While we concur that it is a good practice to work against formulated expectations, some hurdles, such as low test coverage, remain. Especially for programming beginners, Test-Driven Development (TDD) comes with disadvantages: 1) expectations may be unknown, 2) skills are not advanced enough for testing, and 3) even if tests succeed, the learning effect may be low because it is not understood what is happening and how, because students focus on output correctness [13] rather than computations and execution mechanisms. However, the test-first approach can be leveraged to improve the situation.

In our first use-case, we consider a teaching scenario. Since learning should be an individual experience, there is hardly "one best approach." However, the ED methodology can provide several layers that support different intensities of (self-)learning. Students should be able to explore own ideas in a more reactive way but must be assisted as soon as simple (static) measures fail. Figure 1 shows three hierarchical layers of ED treated in this paper.

- The source code in situated in the core in Layer 0 and is itself considered as an ED. This is in line with the agile manifesto that only sees the source code as sole truth.
- Layer 1 provides additional diagnostics through concrete test cases. We distinguish between classical TDD where test cases with expected output must be invoked (manually) and commonly return a binary result[1], and Integrated Modeling Environments (IMEs), where these ED *traces* are added to the document, e.g., as comments, and are executed automatically. They provide

[1] We acknowledge that such test cases can also provide additional information. However, the interpretation of this data is commonly tightly bound to the skill set of the developer and mostly not directly supported by the IDE.

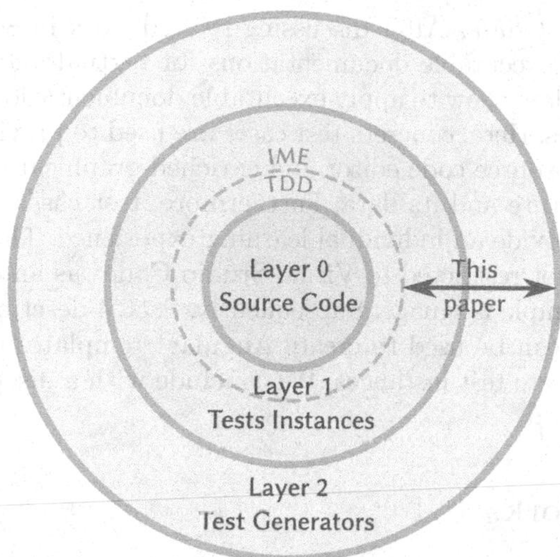

Fig. 1. Different layers of executable documentation

instant feedback, which can be visualized appropriately to increase understanding, and to check correctness if an expected result is present.

- Lastly, Layer 2 comprises generative means that support the included layers with concrete data. This is important because for students the actual expectation might not be obvious and they require individual guidance. In such a case, a test case can still be executed and compared to a generated result, e.g., provided by a sample solution.

Overall, this ED hierarchy presents a user-centric learning experience that helps students validate the <u>results</u>, explore <u>how</u> results form, and <u>what</u> is expected in the first place. Analogously, teachers can inspect the progress of their students using the same framework, communicate specific (counter-)examples, and provide reference solutions from which individual data for the students can be generated. A dialog between student and teacher can happen on each layer.

In the second scenario we discuss the design of a WYSIWYG editor for web application UIs. Similarly to the teaching example, ED provides developers with immediate, accurate and thorough feedback about the appearance and behavior of the GUI through a leveraged test-first approach. This relieves developers from the additional need to mentally map the textual web templates that describe the GUI under development to the actual rendered visualization, as it is common in web development. Early and accurate visual feedback on concrete data reduces the tedious cycle of repeated compilation and manual testing that is usually needed to evaluate the result.

Tegeler et al. present a third scenario [38] that is not included in this contribution but can been seen as a part of the ED series. The scenario illustrates the impact of ED in the DevOps context where graphical notations for CI/CD workflows are turned into a fully fledged IME.

Contributions and Outline. After discussing related work in Sect. 2, we present different aspects of executable documentations for textual and visual programming. Section 3 explains how to apply executable documentations to textual programming languages. Here, concrete test cases are used to provide instantaneous feedback inside the source code editor and enriched graphical representations of the programs structure and its data. Furthermore, test cases can be generated automatically to provide an individual learning experience. The concept is illustrated within but not restricted to Visual Studio Code[2] as an example IDE and TypeScript[3] as example language. Subsequently, Sect. 4 describes how graphical WYSIWYG editors can be used to create Angular[4] templates and explore their behavior with concrete test instances. We conclude with a discussion and future work in Sect. 5.

2 Related Work

For the longest time, direct documentation inside the source code merely served as description of what the particular piece of code should do. There is usually a short description of the behavior and an explanation of the parameters and expected return result of, e.g., a function. In the last two decades these descriptions were usually processed to create an overall documentation for APIs, such as JavaDoc [14], subsequent to the actual programming work. In the execution documentation approach, parts of this documentation can be created instantly and automatically. It also serves as immediate validation instead of being a pure descriptive documentation.

Within a document of the Jupyter project[5] [18], textual descriptions can be interleaved with source code that can be executed on-the-fly. The results of these programs can be inserted into the document, for example, in form of detailed diagrams. This produces a high degree of tangible documentation when it comes to report creation which we also envision. In the best case for programming, anything that supports understanding becomes the documentation and is reasonably available for the developer.

Many IDEs, such as Visual Studio[6], Visual Studio Code, or Eclipse[7], support post visualizations for source code, such as class or sequence diagrams, natively or through installable components. Especially, open-source communities usually provide a whole range of tools to support various different kinds of visualization, such as EMF[8] in Eclipse, which interestingly supported visual class diagrams in its earlier versions, but not later on. However, tools such as KlassViz[9] [31]

[2] https://code.visualstudio.com.
[3] https://www.typescriptlang.org.
[4] https://angular.io.
[5] https://jupyter.org.
[6] https://visualstudio.microsoft.com.
[7] https://www.eclipse.org.
[8] https://www.eclipse.org/modeling/emf.
[9] https://github.com/kieler/klassviz.

quickly filled the gap. Additionally, many intermediate or final results in textual form can be post-processed into appealing images using layout engines, such as Graphviz [15] or ELK [30]. Giving immediate feedback while working on the code strengthens understandability and potentially avoids frustration. Eventually, one can observe what is happening and must not deduce effects from the potential erroneous results.

Noone and Mooney [27] give an extensive overview over visual programming languages and discuss their benefits in teaching. Most visual languages, e.g., Scratch [23] or Alice [10], target specific age groups and, if learned early, they can be very helpful for students later on, even if this programming style is not something that will be pursued for a long period. At some point in time (at least considering general-purpose programming languages), students usually have to switch to textual programming, because most visual learning languages lack capabilities to create more complex programs [27]. Executable documentations also want to support within textual programming the higher retention of knowledge and interest that is usually provided by visual languages.

The evaluation of concrete test cases within the documentation is a form of TDD. One of the pre-dominant, iterative TDD approaches nowadays was presented by Beck [4] but still struggles in some areas in the industry [9] and teaching, even though the "test-first" approach is important in teaching to foster comprehension and analytical skills [12]. Desai et al. give a summary about TDD in academia and argue that classical TDD and test-driven learning can help students to acquire design skills and confidence [11]. However, they concur with Edwards [13] that there are several hurdles that may manifest as roadblocks. Mainly, 1) students may not be ready to write tests, 2) they need frequent, concrete feedback, and 3) they must appreciate any practices that are required alongside programming. Executable documentations aim at lowering the bar for students and help them to achieve faster a more reflective view w.r.t. software development.

Tools like PlantUML[10] immediately generate diagrams according to their diagram DSLs via Graphviz. More generically, Python Preview[11] gives information of the current Python program graphically and displays connections between AST entities while editing. Especially Python Preview reaches degrees of interactivity w.r.t. information available in the Abstract Syntax Tree, such as static initialization and call hierarchies, because the developer can see changes immediately. Analogously, the Python doctest module[12] combines the documentation within source code comments with TDD. It allows the specification of interactive read evaluate-print loop (REPL) sessions within the source code comments, containing Python statements and the text output that is expected from the REPL. To check the correctness of these REPL traces, the doctest definitions are automatically extracted from the source code and evaluated. Going one step further, executable documentations visualize concrete reactions to specific traces/instances, which

[10] https://marketplace.visualstudio.com/items?itemName=jebbs.plantuml.

[11] https://github.com/dongli0x00/python-preview.

[12] https://docs.python.org/3/library/doctest.html.

can be even more helpful w.r.t. understanding if combined with automatic layout techniques. The KIELER modeling tools provide an immediate automatic visualization by generating graphical statecharts automatically from the textual SCCharts language [17,32] and for other model types, such as sequence diagrams [29].

DIME [6] is an integrated development environment for the model-driven development of web applications. As such, it includes a DSL for the specification of web GUIs, accompanied by a graphical editor. Although users edit the GUI graphically, the editor has no WYSIWYG capabilities, as it works on a separate graph-based representation to describe the GUI template. Furthermore, the DIME GUI language consists of a restricted subset of UI components and layouts and does not cover the whole set of HTML elements. Custom UI components have to be written manually and packaged as GUI plugins, outside the IDE. In contrast, our approach for a GUI WYSIWYG editor allows the usage of low-level HTML just as well as high-level component libraries, providing the same level of support and usability for expert and non-expert users alike.

Many low-code platforms, such as Flutter Flow[13] or Bubble.io[14], employ WYSIWYG *template* editors but struggle to accurately visualize how the GUI looks when the developed application is executed. The same is true for the WYSIWYG editor in Android Studio, which in addition only provides generic placeholder content for lists without showing their actual content.

Xcode/SwiftUI[15] continuously compiles and executes the GUI under development, providing immediate and accurate feedback to the developer. However, they heavily rely on the general-purpose programming language Swift for the definition of the GUI as well as for state management in the preview system making it unsuitable for non-expert users. In standardizing the state management and evaluation of the UI specification, we can achieve a superior integration into the IDE and simplify the usage of our tool.

Storybook[16] uses state-based evaluation similar our approach to present UI scenarios and showcases. Thus, it is able to render accurate UI previews for different application states, but it lacks any form of WYSIWYG editing.

3 Executable Documentation in Textual Programming

The goal of ED inside textual programming is to provide the developer with instant, relevant information about the concrete behavior of the program. Especially for beginners, it is important to provide a framework that can be used without the need to know anything about a (complicated) test infrastructure. Therefore, concrete test data should be integrated easily and their results should be displayed automatically without the need of any further actions.

[13] https://flutterflow.io.
[14] https://bubble.io.
[15] https://developer.apple.com/xcode/swiftui.
[16] https://storybook.js.org.

```
1  // isPalin("aaaa") == true
2  // isPalin("abaa") == true
3  function isPalin(s: string): boolean {
4      if (s.length < 2) {
5          return true;
6      } else if (s[0] == s[s.length - 1]) {
7          return isPalin(s.substring(1, s.length - 1));
8      } else {
9          return false;
10     }
11 }
```

(a) Succeeded and failed test feedback

```
1  // isPalin("aaaa") == true
2  // isPalin("abaa") != true
3  function isPalin(s: string): boolean {
4      if (s.length < 2) {
5          return true;
6      } else if (s[0] == s[s.length - 1]) {
7          return isPalin(s.substring(1, s.length - 1));
8      } else {
9          return false;
10     }
11 }
```

(b) Corrected expected test result

Fig. 2. Instantaneous test feedback (Color figure online)

While a programmer is writing the function shown in Sect. 3.1, the expected outcomes are indicated, similarly to common TDD practice but automatically and instantaneously. The feedback that can be given back to the developer ranges from simple expression evaluation to extensive data visualizations, which also provide valuable information about the runtime even if no expected outcome is specified. Two possibilities of enriched visualizations are discussed in Sect. 3.2. Particular further benefits for teaching are explored in Sect. 3.3. Similarly to modifying the source code of the function, the documentation can be amended if additional information must be verified and preserved. This enables student-teacher interaction through ED. Moreover, the executable documentation can be extended by further information, e.g., additional aid from the tutor through extensions, see Sect. 3.4, or individually generated concrete test data, which will be discussed in Sect. 3.5.

3.1 Test-Driven Executable Documentation

Figure 2 shows two examples of immediate feedback to the developer of expected results within the textual source code editor. The source code shows a function that checks if a string variable contains a palindrome. It is preceded by two lines of comment that document two expected results for different concrete parameters. These test cases are executed automatically and follow the *test first* character from agile software development. In contrast to more complex test frameworks, they can be extended or changed at any time without any additional knowledge.

Figure 2a shows one successful and one failed test case. The second case fails because it specified an expected result of `true`. However, as the function works properly, it detects that `abaa` is not a palindrome. The mistake in the documentation is fixed in Fig. 2b in Line 2, which now expects the correct result: Both passed tests are displayed in green. Analogously, if the function would not return the correct result, potentially both test cases would fail. To clearly indicate that the comment lines are test cases and to separate them from other comments, the color schemes of successful and failed test cases can be adjusted if desired.

3.2 Instantaneous Views

The test cases in the previous section provide immediate textual feedback without any further knowledge about TDD. While this is a plus in granting easy access to TDD to students via ED, the available data can be leveraged to facilitate understanding. Therefore, the acquired information about the executed tests can be instantaneously transformed into appropriate additional views, which is considered an extension to the ED in the sense of IMEs. While for experienced developers it may suffice to see how data is transformed during runtime to find oversights, beginners might struggle to comprehend all the relationships, because they are still developing their analytical skills especially w.r.t. more complex data structures. This section will exemplify how to augment the presentation to facilitate understanding. The first example shows how to provide more context in presenting a general program flow chart of the concrete execution. The second example shows relationships between elements in linked lists; a common task for first term students.

Concrete Flowcharts. While the textual feedback within the program code hints to (functional) issues, beginners may struggle to comprehend what is actually happening inside their code during execution. Therefore, the documentation can be enriched by control-flow information similar to the nodes known from program flowcharts [26]. For beginners it is especially important to display branching, loops, and subroutine calls.

Figure 3a shows the program flowchart of the isPalin function from Fig. 2. Both test cases are depicted. The red background indicates a failed test case. The graph is enriched with further information: First, the concrete condition is shown inside the *conditional node*. In both cases a==a, and the *true branch* of the if statement is taken. Here, the recursive call to the next isPalin instance is highlighted with a special *call node*. The recursion is further illustrated by an indentation to the right, which can be turned off if desired. Inside the next isPalin call, the test string has been shortened. This time, the conditions evaluate differently depending on the test case. In the b==a case, the functions exits with false and gives back control to the caller, indicated by the left indent. The caller then exits, too. In the other case, the recursive path is continued until the string is empty and true is returned through the stack. The indentations indicate a recursive depth of two for the second test case.

Linked Lists. Working with linked data structures, such as linked lists, is common in beginners programming classes. The concept and often recursive solutions make this a relatively hard problem for beginners. However, iterative alternatives are equally challenging.

Commonly, when students are struggling with such kind of problems in practice classes, the tutor explains the link concept via pen and paper, often several times per class. At least, the visualization of this process can be automatized. Then, at best, the students recognize the relationships by themselves interactively, or the teacher can use the diagram to explore the thinking process

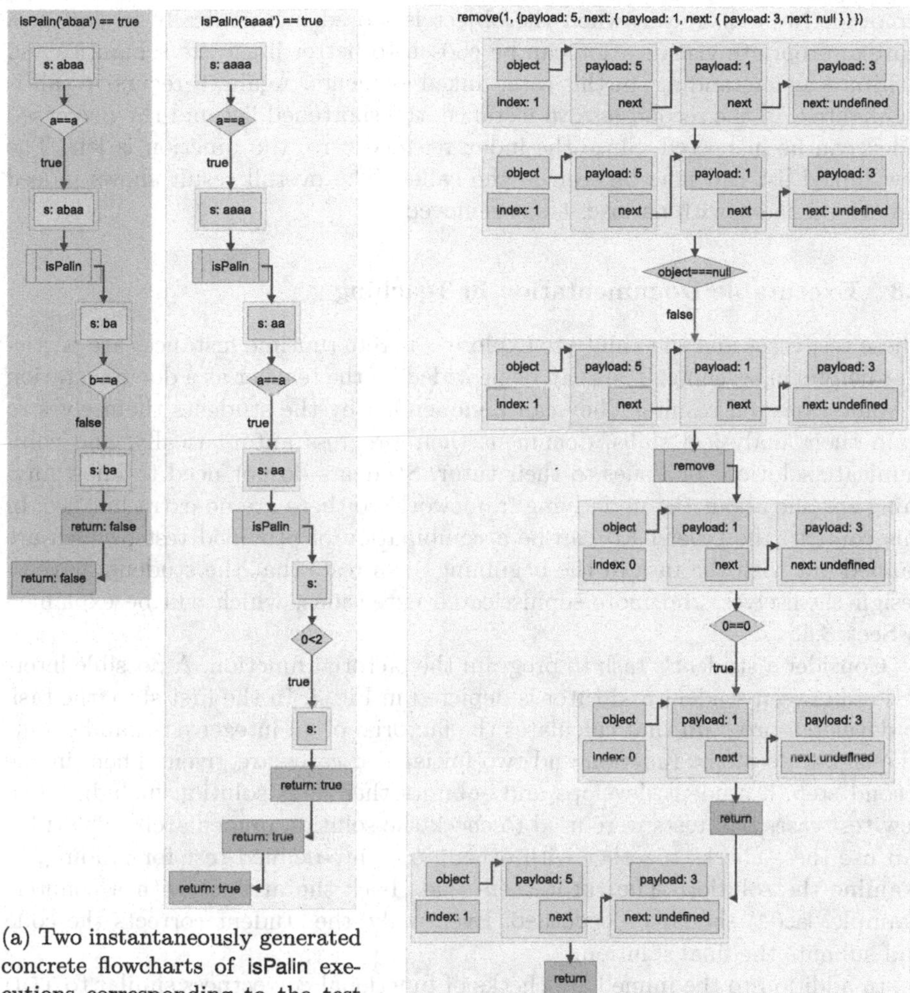

(a) Two instantaneously generated concrete flowcharts of isPalin executions corresponding to the test cases. The red background (left) indicates a failed test instance: Since b≠a the recursive call returns false instead of the expected true.

(b) Instantaneous concrete flowchart displaying a remove operation on a linked list. When the index reaches 0 the first linked element is not returned to the caller.

Fig. 3. Instantaneous visual feedback (Color figure online)

together. Consider Fig. 3b, which shows a flowgraph similar to the one before for a test call remove(1, {payload: 5, next: { payload: 1, next: {payload: 3, next: null}}}). The function should remove the element with the index 1 from a exemplarily linked list structure in JSON that stores the values 5, 1, and 3. Even though the test case did not specify an expected result because the student may yet be unsure about the final result, the flow of data can be easily inspected immediately. It shows the linked list object together with the index of the item that should be removed. Note that even when the object is stored hierarchically in JSON, a more appropriate visualization can be chosen to better illustrate semantics and facilitate understanding; in this case, linked elements. Again, a recursive call is highlighted. In the second remove instance, the shortened list and the decreased index can be inspected. Since the index reached zero, the function is left. The new linked list can now be seen in the caller. The overall result shows indeed that the element with payload: 1 was removed.

3.3 Executable Documentation in Teaching

These test cases and the ability to explore concrete runtime instances are particular helpful in teaching. Tests can be provided by the teacher as a documentation of some expected results. They can be amended by the students themselves to train their analytical skills, document their progress automatically, and communicate solutions or issues to their tutor. Students do not need to know anything specific about the underlying framework, so there are no extra hurdles. In this context, the Layer 1 ED can be a combination of provided tests, which are handed out with the task in the beginning, own tests that the students have to design themselves, and more sophisticated extensions, which will be explained in Sect. 3.4.

Consider a student's task to program the factorial function. A possible interaction between student and tutor is depicted in Fig. 4. In the first step, the task to develop a program that calculates the factorial of an integer n is handed out. The signature of the function and two initial test cases are given. Then, in the second step, a student develops and submits their first solution including two new test cases. All tests were used to check the solution immediately. The tutor can use these checks together with others, e.g., pre-defined test for grading, to examine the solution. The tutor then sends back the artifact with a counter-example: fac(-1) should be undefined. Eventually, the student corrects the code and submits the final solution.

In addition to the immediate checks of functional correctness similar to TDD and their exploration for the students, the tutor can see, test, and react to the ideas brought by the students. Moreover, the tutor can use the same system to add new information for the students, e.g., via counter-examples, or use the same system to grade the solution with a pre-defined list of checks for all submissions. Students can then see which cases they might have missed. Note that this interaction can also be automated. However, supervisors should be careful with automated (instant) grading to avoid a focus on output correctness [13].

The example shows that besides being able to provide instant feedback automatically, ED can also be used to communicate solutions and train analytical skills, especially concerning corner cases. The individual progress for each task can be easily documented this way within the same source code/document.

```
/*
Task 1: Factorial

Write a function fac with the given signature
that calculates and returns the factorial of n.
*/

// fac(3) == 6
// fac(5) == 120



function fac(n: number): number | undefined {






}
```

(a) Task hand-out

```
/*
Task 1: Factorial

Write a function fac with the given signature
that calculates and returns the factorial of n.
*/

// fac(3) == 6
// fac(5) == 120
// fac(10) == 3_628_800
// fac(0) == 1

function fac(n: number): number | undefined {

    var result: number = 1;
    for (var i = 1; i <= n; i++) {
        result *= i;
    }
    return result;
}
```

(b) First student solution

```
/*
Task 1: Factorial

Write a function fac with the given signature
that calculates and returns the factorial of n.
*/

// fac(3) == 6
// fac(5) == 120
// fac(10) == 3_628_800
// fac(0) == 1
// fac(-1) == undefined
function fac(n: number): number | undefined {

    var result: number = 1;
    for (var i = 1; i <= n; i++) {
        result *= i;
    }
    return result;
}
```

(c) Supervisor feedback

```
/*
Task 1: Factorial

Write a function fac with the given signature
that calculates and returns the factorial of n.
*/

// fac(3) == 6
// fac(5) == 120
// fac(10) == 3_628_800
// fac(0) == 1
// fac(-1) == undefined
function fac(n: number): number | undefined {
    if (n < 0) { return undefined; }
    var result: number = 1;
    for (var i = 1; i <= n; i++) {
        result *= i;
    }
    return result;
}
```

(d) Second student solution

Fig. 4. Example of layered student-tutor interactions

3.4 Executable Documentation Extensions

Tutors can provide additional functionality and automatic feedback through extensions. Writing extensions might exceed the capabilities of beginners since it requires additional knowledge about the framework, but it strengthens immediate feedback if it is provided by the supervisor and it is not part of the task. The IME can even take over some of the teacher's guidance through this feature.

Consider Fig. 5, which depicts a variation of one task of the infamous *datalab*[17] [8]. The datalab contains several subtasks that challenge students to solve specific calculations but restrict the kind and number of operators that they are allowed to use. Figure 5a shows a variation the subtask bitOr handed-out to the students, who should implement a *bitwise or* function that only allows an overall maximum of eight operators from a specific set, namely *bitwise negate*, *bitwise*

[17] http://csapp.cs.cmu.edu/3e/labs.html.

```
1 /*
2  * bitOr - x|y using only ~ and &
3  *   Example: bitOr(6, 5) == 7
4  *   Legal ops: + ~ &
5  *   Max ops: 8
6  *   Rating: 1
7  */
8
9 // CONTEST.ts: Ops {operators: ["+","~","&"], max: 8}
10 // bitOr(1, 2) == 3
11 function bitOr(x: number, y: number): number {
12
13     return 0;
14 }
```

(a) Subtask's bitOr hand-out

```
1 /*
2  * bitOr - x|y using only ~ and &
3  *   Example: bitOr(6, 5) == 7
4  *   Legal ops: + ~ &
5  *   Max ops: 8
6  *   Rating: 1
7  */
8
9 // CONTEST.ts: Ops {operators: ["+", "~", "&"], max: 8}
10 // bitOr(1, 2) == 3
11 // bitOr(6, 5) == 7
12 // bitOr(x, y) == bitOrReference(y, x)
13 function bitOr(x: number, y: number): number {
14     let z: number = x + y;
15     return z;
16 }
```

(b) Subtask's bitOr first solution

```
1 /*
2  * bitOr - x|y using only ~ and &
3  *   Example: bitOr(6, 5) == 7
4  *   Legal ops: + ~ &
5  *   Max ops: 8
6  *   Rating: 1
7  */
8
9 // CONTEST.ts: Ops {operators: ["+","~","&"], max: 8}
10 // bitOr(1, 2) == 3
11 // bitOr(6, 5) == 7
12 // bitOr(x, y) == bitOrReference(y, x)
13 function bitOr(x: number, y: number): number {
14     let z: number = x | y;
15     return z;
16 }
```

(c) Violating contest rules for testing

```
1 /*
2  * bitOr - x|y using only ~ and &
3  *   Example: bitOr(6, 5) == 7
4  *   Legal ops: + ~ &
5  *   Max ops: 8
6  *   Rating: 1
7  */
8
9 // CONTEST.ts: Ops {operators: ["+", "~", "&"], max: 8}
10 // bitOr(1, 2) == 3
11 // bitOr(6, 5) == 7
12 // bitOr(x, y) == bitOrReference(y, x)
13 function bitOr(x: number, y: number): number {
14     let z: number = ~(~x & ~y);
15     return z;
16 }
```

(d) Subtask's bitOr with De Morgan's rules

Fig. 5. Evolution of the bitOr task solution

and, and the *arithmetical addition*. The hand-out contains the description of the subtask (Lines 1–7), the function body including signature (Lines 11–14), and two given test cases (Lines 9–10). The first test case is an extension to the built-in test-driven straightforward evaluations, and it is provided by the tutor. It is invoked by specifying a source file, the name of a class for the reactive framework and an object with auxiliary data for configuration. This is by design not intended to be programmed by beginners because it would require additional knowledge about the test system. However, tutors can use such extensions to provide additional functionality and, hence, customized immediate feedback. Here, the call to CONTEST.ts provides a check of the operators for the datalab task and also additional reference functions that can be parameterized and used in further test cases (cf. bitOrReference(x, y) in Fig. 5b). The second comment actually provides the functional test bitOr(1, 2) == 3.

A possible but generally wrong solution to the task is depicted in Fig. 5b. The student solved the problem by using the addition. This will work for the provided test case. However, already the example test from the task's description will fail with this solution, as shown in the figure in Line 11. Furthermore, the previously mentioned reference implementation provided by the tutor can also be used within the tests, as shown in Line 12.

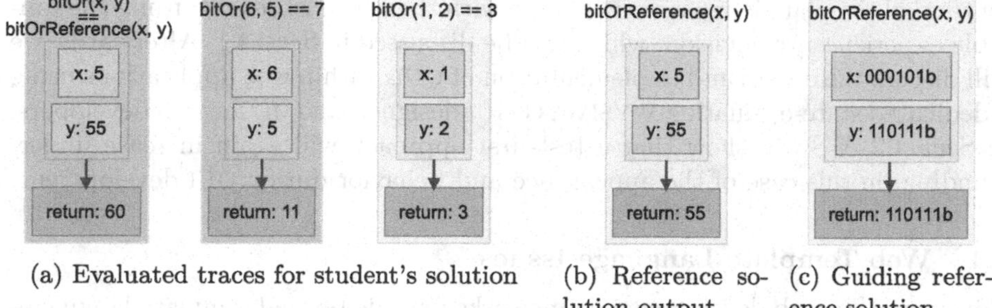

(a) Evaluated traces for student's solution (b) Reference solution output (c) Guiding reference solution

Fig. 6. Generated individual counter-example from reference solution

Replacing the *addition* in the first try with the *binary or* operator in the task's function will set all functional tests to green because the *bitwise or* is calculated correctly, as can be seen in Fig. 5c. However, the contest extension now indicates an error since the rules of the contest are violated: The *bitwise or* operator is not allowed. Eventually in Fig. 5d, all tests, including the test verifying the contest's rules, succeed by using De Morgan's rules to solve the task.

3.5 Individual Test Case Generation

The student might be unsure about concrete expected results for a given task, which makes it difficult to come up with helpful test cases themselves and requires further guidance. Reference solutions, as the one shown in the previous section, can be used as input for Layer 2 of the ED. Note that it is in the supervisor's responsibility to actually provide meaningful values for x and y, i.e., values that have no (or at least a low) probability to indicate a false positive. However, different strategies, such as an exhaustive search or fuzz testing, are imaginable.

Figure 6a depicts the evaluated traces for the student's solution for the example from Fig. 5b. In addition to the static test cases that are depicted, the reference solution provided by the teacher identifies the case {x:5; y:55} as erroneous and provides the student with an individual counter-example. The program the student provided returned a value of 60, whereas the reference solution's result is 55, as depicted in Fig. 6b. Of course, individual counter-examples can be added to the list of tests, e.g., for documentation reasons.

To go one step further, reference solutions can be empowered to provide additional guidance through use-case-specific views, as illustrated in Fig. 6c. By representing the data in a more appropriate way for the example's task, the expectation becomes more obvious.

4 Executable Documentation in Visual Programming

Similarly to the classical programming domain, understanding and alignment can be improved in web development. Web development nowadays is dominated by textual template languages that come with their own issues regarding the tangible experience we envision, which will be discussed in Sect. 4.1. Afterwards, we will discuss the design and implementation of GUIs within web applications using a dedicated state-evaluating WYSIWYG GUI designer, an IME for web developers, in Sect. 4.2. We will show that a test-first approach will again increase understanding, in this case of the appearance and behavior during GUI development.

4.1 Web Template Language Issues

Contemporary web development frameworks provide textual template languages to declaratively specify the GUI, e.g., React JSX[18] or Angular Templates[19]. While these languages significantly ease the development of GUIs compared to classical approaches, they still can be improved w.r.t. understanding and providing immediate feedback of the actual visual appearance of the GUI. As these languages introduce a separate representation for GUI descriptions, users are required to learn a new textual language and mentally translate between their vision of the GUI and the textual description. This is challenging for non-expert users and even for experts this incurs a mental overhead. Evaluating how the GUI actually looks and behaves requires a compilation step and tedious manual testing to reach certain concrete scenarios within the web application. Yet, visual examination of the layout and testing, e.g., different screen sizes, is an important aspect of GUI development and frequently required.

WYSIWYG editors overcome this necessity for a compilation step by rendering the GUI directly in the editor, giving the developer immediate feedback how it actually looks like. The term WYSIWYG is sometimes used ambiguously to include side-by-side live previews of textual definitions, e.g., writing LaTeX with a live PDF preview in tools like Overleaf[20]. In the context of executable documentation however, WYSIWYG only includes editors where the user directly sees and manipulates the artifact they are creating without introducing a separate textual or graphical language for specification.

Building WYSIWYG editors for static websites is pretty straightforward as they are basically rich text documents that can be easily previewed and manipulated. However, creating such editors for the GUIs of dynamic web applications is more challenging, because they include conditions, loops, and data bindings that are evaluated at runtime based on the current state of the application. This implies an arbitrary number of possible ways the GUI can be rendered, so a single preview is probably insufficient to visualize its appearance in every case. To avoid this problem, it is possible to build a WYSIWYG editor for the template of the GUI, which is basically a tree expression consisting of control structures and UI elements. Figure 7 exemplarily shows Flutter Flow, a state-of-the-art WYSIWYG template editor. In such a template editor, the developer can see the static parts of the actual GUI but not the actual appearance of the final GUI. As conditions are not evaluated, content from all the different branches is included in

[18] https://reactjs.org/docs/introducing-jsx.html.
[19] https://angular.io/guide/template-syntax.
[20] https://www.overleaf.com.

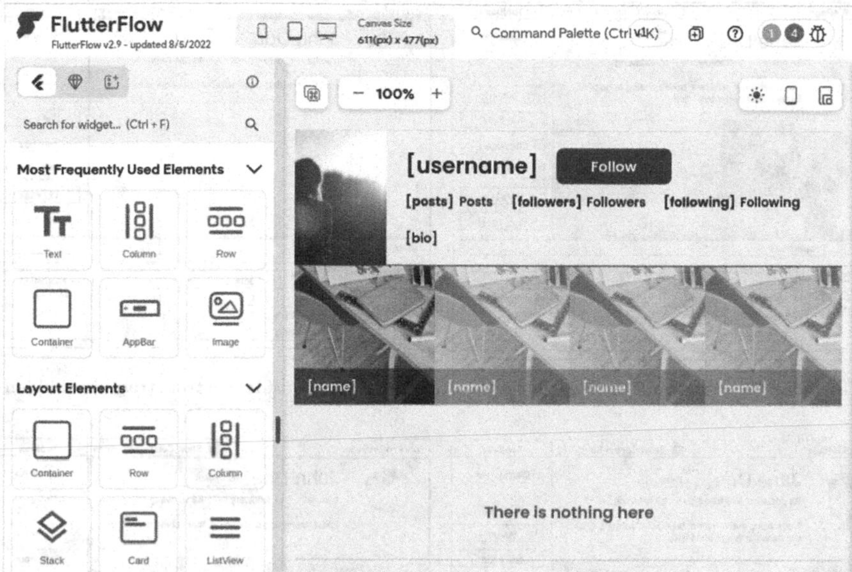

Fig. 7. Flutter Flow, a state-of-the-art WYSIWYG template editor

the preview, including all UI elements. E.g., the figure shows the grid of images and the default text "There is nothing here" at the same time, although only ever one of both will be displayed at runtime. Moreover, since loops are not evaluated, items in lists cannot be properly rendered. In the grid view of Fig. 7, Flutter Flow simply shows several identical but slightly grayed out copies of the first image. Additionally, bindings to runtime data are not fulfilled, showing only placeholders where data will appear at runtime. However, especially when testing the layout, it is important to see how the GUI reacts to short or long texts, and small or large images. Overall, WYSIWYG template editors fail to provide a tangible experience during the development of GUIs and still require frequent compilation and manual testing to actually experience the GUI behavior.

4.2 State-Evaluating WYSIWYG GUI Designer

A state-evaluating WYSIWYG GUI editor relies on user-defined test scenarios to render the GUI in different states right within the editor itself. Developers provide data for different scenarios, which is then used by the editor to evaluate and render the GUI preview. They can switch between them to explore and compare the appearance and behavior of different states as they are editing the GUI. For each condition in the GUI, only the appropriate branch is rendered and in loops the UI elements are repeated according to the lists provided in the data instance. During editing, the current state is considered as well and rendered appropriately. Changes

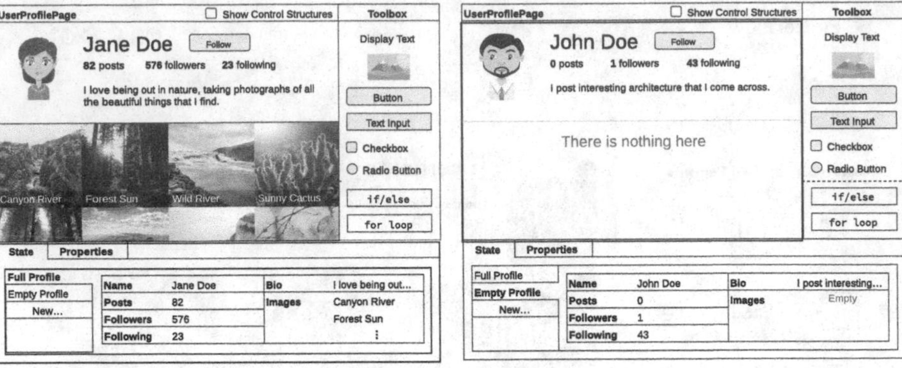

(a) Full profile, control structures hidden (b) Empty profile, control structures hidden

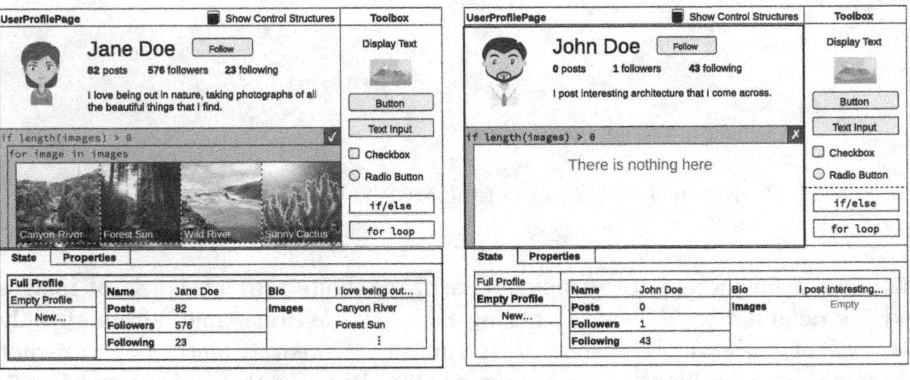

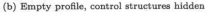

(c) Full profile, control structures visible (d) Empty profile, control structures visible

Fig. 8. State-Evaluating WYSIWYG GUI designer

within condition blocks only affect the currently active branch and changes in loop elements naturally affect all other elements of the loop.

Figure 8 illustrates the concept of such an editor. The GUI under development is shown in the main area with a toolbox on the right and the state management at the bottom. New elements can be added from the toolbox to the GUI via drag and drop. In the state panel, different data instances can be selected to be evaluated in the GUI preview. The properties panel (currently hidden) is used to configure UI elements and to define the behavior of control structures and data bindings. Figure 8a shows a decently filled profile with several images. The profile image, username, stats, and bio are rendered via data bindings and a loop is used to render the list of images into a grid. In contrast, Fig. 8b shows the profile of a different data instance, where the user has not yet made any postings. We can see that in this case an *if condition* is used to render the notice "There is nothing here." Figure 8a and Fig. 8b show the GUI exactly as it will appear at runtime, giving non-experts a clear understanding. However, experts may wish to zoom into how all the conditions and loops were actually evaluated. So akin to the instantaneous views introduced for textual programming in Sect. 3.2, our editor supports the rendering of control structures and their evaluation as shown in Fig. 8c and Fig. 8d. In this approach we follow a test-first strategy, where we develop scenario-based test cases from the very beginning alongside the GUI itself. This enables accurate previews of the runtime appearance and provides the developer continuously with valuable feedback.

5 Conclusion

IDEs are tools for documentation and communication. Depending on the concrete roles, different parts of the documentation may be considered more or less important, but every part serves understanding. From this, specific parts can be extracted or generated to guide on an on-demand basis.

We explained two instances of *executable documentations* to help developers, and especially beginners, to better analyze their programs and potential mistakes. This facilitates understanding in an reactive way and reinforces analytical skills. We explained how a layered reactive programming approach can strengthen student-tutor interaction and showed further extensions on how executable documentations can be employed in teaching. Teachers can provide reference solutions from which customized test cases can be generated. Even if only a few people foster their analytical skills through self-observation, we consider this a win.

With our state-based evaluation approach to WYSIWYG GUI editing we are able to let developers accurately experience all facets of their UI within the editor in real-time. This ability eases and accelerates GUI development. It relieves the developer from mental translations between specification and artifact and avoids tedious cycles of compilation and manual testing. Yet, the approach does not only improve the immediate development experience: In modeling the state of different scenarios, developers implicitly create a large amount of examples that document all the features and corner cases of the application.

That direct execution supports understanding, especially for technically weaker individuals who may not be able to imagine what happens behind the code or model, has been clear for a while, and in fact we were asked already in 1994 to include a "red line tracing" feature in our IN-METAFrame tool for Service Definition of what was back then the Intelligent Network Services by Siemens [34,36]. This feature was especially useful for non-programmers, typically sales people and their customers, to understand and explain the workflows implementing the services. Due to its success, it was then included in the METAFrame [33,35] and ABC/jABC environments [37] but with a green line tracing depicting on the process model the execution path along the ongoing (interpreted) execution.

Similarly, in education the visual and self-documenting character of processes and workflows is a precious support to business logic comprehension and to (programming language) syntax-independent representation of "what is happening

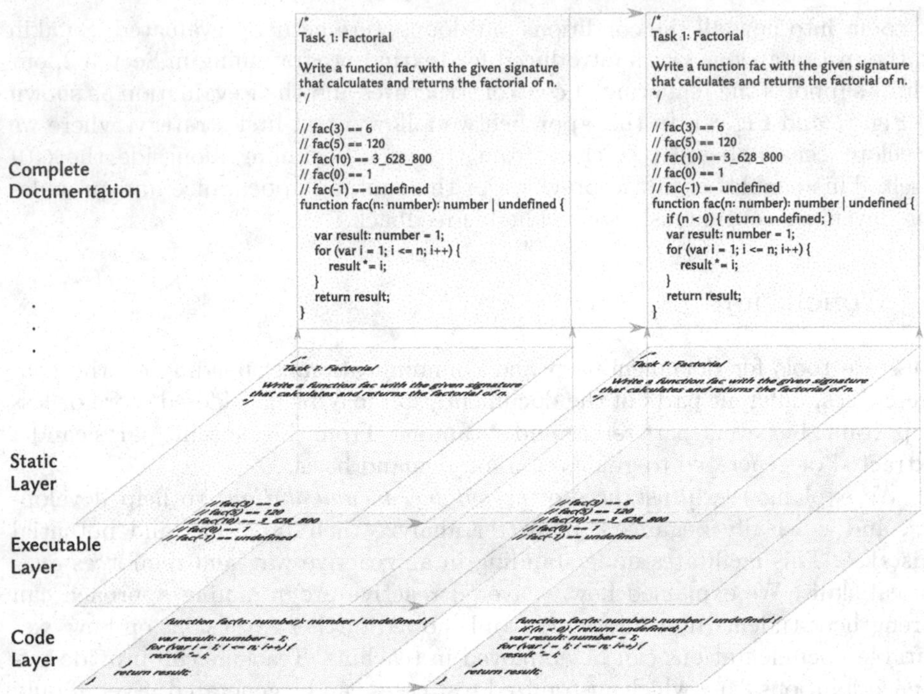

Fig. 9. A vision: two-dimensional layered programming paradigm showing different example document layers on the vertical axis and the document chronological revisions on the horizontal axis.

when ...” The indirection of code w.r.t. the execution is a central hurdle to comprehension, especially given that programming is traditionally not taught with a direct depiction of execution. Tools like DIME [6] and Pyrus [39] on the contrary adopt a user-facing dataflow (Pyrus) and control flow + data flow (DIME) approach that has been greatly useful for young and mature learners. We have leveraged this successfully in the past from short two days Introduction to CS courses to girls [20,25], to first year CS students [16], in Software engineering classes [5,21] to non-CS users like biologists [19,22], or historians [7,28]. In all these cases, an essential benefit of the XMDD approach was the explicitation of the “logic” and its stepwise layout with clearer illustration of various kinds of dependencies [24].

In the future, we intend to investigate further presentations of potentially enriched feedback to give more guidance to developers for both visual and textual programming. What kind of feedback and visualizations are most helpful for beginners is an open question. The methodologies presented in this paper integrate quite seamlessly into current state-of-the-art IDEs. However, there is no dedicated support for the layered programming paradigm as presented in Sect. 3. Tighter tool integration could facilitate student-tutor interaction. We envision more tool support for a generic kind of textual *layered programming*, so that the developer can toggle the visibility of different layers easily similarly to layers in common graphics tools. Different layers could be ordered chronologically as before or defined for specialized categories. Figure 9 exemplarily illustrates both directions of a layered programming approach with specialized layers of the student-teacher interaction from Sect. 3.3. The vertical axis shows layers for static documentation, executable documentation, the source code, and a combined view that comprises all layers below. Chronological evolution of the artifact is displayed on the horizontal axis. Here, as before, after interaction with the tutor, the solution is fixed on the code layer, which automatically updates the test layer and eventually the overall documentation. Moreover, we want to investigate further individual and potentially auto-generated feedback for students embedded in such a user-centric IME.

Regarding the state-evaluated view on the GUI, an additional template editor is also valuable to get a general overview of everything that exists in a GUI. It is not illustrated in this paper because such template editors already exist, but it is still part of our envisioned approach. To further increase the usefulness of this editing environment an execution mode could be added. This would instrument the web application build with additional state management logic, so that users could launch the actual application starting in a specific state or record the current state of the running application as a new data instance. To generate new scenarios, automata learning approaches, such as ALEX [1,2], look promising. They capture the processes within a web application as state transition diagrams allowing the user to discover previously undisclosed or newly created states.

References

1. Bainczyk, A., Schieweck, A., Isberner, M., Margaria, T., Neubauer, J., Steffen, B.: ALEX: mixed-mode learning of web applications at ease. In: Margaria, T., Steffen, B. (eds.) ISoLA 2016. LNCS, vol. 9953, pp. 655–671. Springer, Cham (2016). https://doi.org/10.1007/978-3-319-47169-3_51
2. Bainczyk, A., Schieweck, A., Steffen, B., Howar, F.: Model-based testing without models: the TodoMVC case study. In: Katoen, J.-P., Langerak, R., Rensink, A. (eds.) ModelEd, TestEd, TrustEd. LNCS, vol. 10500, pp. 125–144. Springer, Cham (2017). https://doi.org/10.1007/978-3-319-68270-9_7
3. Beck, K.: Aim, fire [test-first coding]. IEEE Softw. **18**(5), 87–89 (2001)
4. Beck, K.: Test-Driven Development: By Example. Addison-Wesley Professional (2003)
5. Bordihn, H., Lamprecht, A.L., Margaria, T.: Foundations of semantics and model checking in a software engineering course. In: FMSEE&T@ FM, pp. 19–26 (2015)
6. Boßelmann, S., et al.: DIME: a programming-less modeling environment for web applications. In: Margaria, T., Steffen, B. (eds.) ISoLA 2016. LNCS, vol. 9953, pp. 809–832. Springer, Cham (2016). https://doi.org/10.1007/978-3-319-47169-3_60
7. Breathnach, C., Murphy, R., Margaria, T.: Transcribathons as practice-based learning for historians and computer scientists. In: 2021 IEEE 45th Annual Computers, Software, and Applications Conference (COMPSAC), pp. 1131–1136 (2021)
8. Bryant, R.E., David Richard, O.: Computer Systems: A Programmer's Perspective, vol. 2. Prentice Hall, Upper Saddle River (2003)

9. Causevic, A., Sundmark, D., Punnekkat, S.: Factors limiting industrial adoption of test driven development: a systematic review. In: 2011 Fourth IEEE International Conference on Software Testing, Verification and Validation, pp. 337–346. IEEE (2011)
10. Cooper, S.: The design of Alice. ACM Trans. Comput. Educ. (TOCE) **10**(4), 1–16 (2010)
11. Desai, C., Janzen, D., Savage, K.: A survey of evidence for test-driven development in academia. ACM SIGCSE Bull. **40**(2), 97–101 (2008)
12. Edwards, S.H.: Rethinking computer science education from a test-first perspective. In: Companion of the 18th Annual ACM SIGPLAN Conference on Object-Oriented Programming, Systems, Languages, and Applications, pp. 148–155 (2003)
13. Edwards, S.H.: Using software testing to move students from trial-and-error to reflection-in-action. In: Proceedings of the 35th SIGCSE Technical Symposium on Computer Science Education, pp. 26–30 (2004)
14. Friendly, L.: The design of distributed hyperlinked programming documentation. In: Fraïssé, S., Garzotto, F., Isakowitz, T., Nanard, J., Nanard, M. (eds.) Hypermedia Design. WORKSHOPS COMP., pp. 151–173. Springer, London (1996). https://doi.org/10.1007/978-1-4471-3082-6_17
15. Gansner, E.R., Koutsofios, E., North, S.C., Vo, K.P.: A technique for drawing directed graphs. Softw. Eng. **19**(3), 214–230 (1993)
16. Gossen, F., Kühn, D., Margaria, T., Lamprecht, A.L.: Computational thinking: learning by doing with the Cinco adventure game tool. In: 2018 IEEE 42nd Annual Computer Software and Applications Conference (COMPSAC), vol. 01, pp. 990–999 (2018)
17. von Hanxleden, R., et al.: SCCharts: sequentially constructive statecharts for safety-critical applications. In: Proceedings of the ACM SIGPLAN Conference on Programming Language Design and Implementation (PLDI 2014), Edinburgh, UK, pp. 372–383. ACM, June 2014
18. Kluyver, T., et al.: Jupyter notebooks–a publishing format for reproducible computational workflows. In: Loizides, F., Scmidt, B. (eds.) Positioning and Power in Academic Publishing: Players, Agents and Agendas, pp. 87–90. IOS Press (2016)
19. Lamprecht, A.L., Margaria, T.: Scientific workflows with XMDD: a way to use process modeling in computational science education. Procedia Comput. Sci. **51**, 1927–1936 (2015)
20. Lamprecht, A.L., Margaria, T., McInerney, C.: A summer computing camp using ChainReaction and jABC. In: 2016 IEEE 40th Annual Computer Software and Applications Conference (COMPSAC), vol. 2, pp. 275–280 (2016)
21. Lamprecht, A.L., Margaria, T., Neubauer, J.: On the use of XMDD in software development education. In: 2015 IEEE 39th Annual Computer Software and Applications Conference, vol. 2, pp. 835–844 (2015)
22. Lamprecht, A.L., Tiziána, M.: Process Design for Natural Scientists. Springer, Heidelberg (2014). https://doi.org/10.1007/978-3-662-45006-2
23. Maloney, J., Resnick, M., Rusk, N., Silverman, B., Eastmond, E.: The scratch programming language and environment. ACM Trans. Comput. Educ. (TOCE) **10**(4), 1–15 (2010)
24. Margaria, T., Steffen, B.: eXtreme model-driven development (XMDD) technologies as a hands-on approach to software development without coding. In: Tatnall, A. (ed.) Encyclopedia of Education and Information Technologies, pp. 1–19. Springer, Cham (2020). https://doi.org/10.1007/978-3-319-60013-0_208-1

25. McInerney, C., Lamprecht, A.-L., Margaria, T.: Computing camps for girls – a first-time experience at the university of limerick. In: Tatnall, A., Webb, M. (eds.) WCCE 2017. IAICT, vol. 515, pp. 494–505. Springer, Cham (2017). https://doi.org/10.1007/978-3-319-74310-3_50
26. Myler, H.R.: Fundamentals of Engineering Programming with C and Fortran. Cambridge University Press, Cambridge (1998)
27. Noone, M., Mooney, A.: Visual and textual programming languages: a systematic review of the literature. J. Comput. Educ. **5**(2), 149–174 (2018). https://doi.org/10.1007/s40692-018-0101-5
28. Schieweck, A., Murphy, R., Khan, R., Breathnach, C., Margaria, T.: Evolution of the historian data entry application: supporting transcribathons in the digital humanities through MDD. In: 2022 IEEE 46th Annual Computers, Software, and Applications Conference (COMPSAC), pp. 177–186 (2022)
29. Schulze, C.D., Hoops, G., von Hanxleden, R.: Automatic layout and label management for UML sequence diagrams. In: Proceedings of the IEEE Symposium on Visual Languages and Human-Centric Computing (VL/HCC 2018) (2018)
30. Schulze, C.D., Spönemann, M., von Hanxleden, R.: Drawing layered graphs with port constraints. J. Vis. Lang. Comput. Spec. Issue Diagram Aesthetics Layout **25**(2), 89–106 (2014)
31. Schulze, C.D., Spönemann, M., Schneider, C., von Hanxleden, R.: Two applications for transient views in software development environments (showpiece). In: Proceedings of the IEEE Symposium on Visual Languages and Human-Centric Computing (VL/HCC 2014), Melbourne, Australia, July 2014
32. Smyth, S., Schulz-Rosengarten, A., von Hanxleden, R.: Guidance in model-based compilations. In: Proceedings of the 8th International Symposium on Leveraging Applications of Formal Methods, Verification and Validation (ISoLA 2018), Doctoral Symposium. Electronic Communications of the EASST, Limassol, Cyprus, vol. 78, November 2018
33. Steffen, B., Margaria, T.: METAFrame in practice: design of intelligent network services. In: Olderog, E.-R., Steffen, B. (eds.) Correct System Design. LNCS, vol. 1710, pp. 390–415. Springer, Heidelberg (1999). https://doi.org/10.1007/3-540-48092-7_17
34. Steffen, B., Margaria, T., Braun, V., Kalt, N.: Hierarchical service definition. Ann. Rev. Commun. ACM **51**, 847–856 (1997)
35. Steffen, B., Margaria, T., Claßen, A., Braun, V.: The METAFrame'95 environment. In: Alur, R., Henzinger, T.A. (eds.) CAV 1996. LNCS, vol. 1102, pp. 450–453. Springer, Heidelberg (1996). https://doi.org/10.1007/3-540-61474-5_100
36. Steffen, B., Margaria, T., Claßen, A., Braun, V., Reitenspieß, M.: An environment for the creation of intelligent network services. In: Intelligent Networks: IN/AIN Technologies, Operations, Services and Applications - A Comprehensive Report, pp. 287–300. IEC: International Engineering Consortium (1996)
37. Steffen, B., Margaria, T., Nagel, R., Jörges, S., Kubczak, C.: Model-driven development with the jABC. In: Bin, E., Ziv, A., Ur, S. (eds.) HVC 2006. LNCS, vol. 4383, pp. 92–108. Springer, Heidelberg (2007). https://doi.org/10.1007/978-3-540-70889-6_7

38. Tegeler, T., Boßelmann, S., Schürmann, J., Smyth, S., Teumert, S., Steffen, B.: Executable documentation: From documentation languages to purpose-specific languages. In: Margaria, T., Steffen, B. (eds.) ISoLA 2022, LNCS, vol. 13702, pp. 174–192. Springer, Cham (2022)
39. Zweihoff, P., Steffen, B.: Pyrus: an online modeling environment for no-code data-analytics service composition. In: Margaria, T., Steffen, B. (eds.) ISoLA 2021. LNCS, vol. 13036, pp. 18–40. Springer, Cham (2021). https://doi.org/10.1007/978-3-030-89159-6_2

Runtime Verification as Documentation

Dennis Dams[1], Klaus Havelund[2(✉)], and Sean Kauffman[3]

[1] ESI (TNO), Eindhoven, The Netherlands
dennis.dams@tno.nl

[2] Jet Propulsion Laboratory, California Institute of Technology, Pasadena, USA
klaus.havelund@jpl.nasa.gov

[3] Aalborg University, Aalborg, Denmark
seank@cs.aau.dk

Abstract. In runtime verification, a monitor is used to return a Boolean verdict on the behavior of a system. We present several examples of the use of monitors to instead *document* system behavior. In doing so, we demonstrate how runtime verification can be combined with techniques from data science to provide novel forms of program analysis.

1 Introduction

The phrase "show me the code"[1] is well known amongst programmers, and reflects the need, and even desire, to read code in order to understand how it works. However, code can be arbitrarily complex and hard to comprehend, even for the most experienced. Program documentation, after all, remains the best way to convey information between humans about how a program works. Unfortunately, many software products are created without proper documentation. We can distinguish between at least three kinds of users of documentation: the programmer who wants to modify the code, the programmer who wants to use the code (e.g. a user of Python's `matplotlib` library), and finally the person that just wants to use the code as an application (e.g. a user of www.github.com).

When we think of documentation, we usually think of what we shall refer to as *static documentation*. Static documentation is ideally written once and does not change unless improved or modified due to changes in the software. Static documentation includes, but is not limited to, comments in the code. From comments in a special format, API documentation can be generated, as e.g. with JavaDoc [25], meant for programmers using the code as a library. Static documentation can also take the form of user guides or requirements documents. Documentation can be graphical as well as text-based. For example, sequence diagrams [38] are commonly used in requirements documents to illustrate the typical (happy-flow) behavior of an application. Graphical documentation can

[1] The full quote, "Talk is cheap. Show me the code.", is attributed to Linus Torvalds.

The research performed by this author was carried out at Jet Propulsion Laboratory, California Institute of Technology, under a contract with the National Aeronautics and Space Administration.

T. Margaria and B. Steffen (Eds.): ISoLA 2022, LNCS 13702, pp. 157–173, 2022.
https://doi.org/10.1007/978-3-031-19756-7_9

even be generated automatically from the code, as shown in [39]. Formalized specifications of the code can also function as documentation. This includes tests (unit or integration). That is, every pair of (input, expected output) provides a concrete, easy-to-understand example of how the code is supposed to behave. Formal specifications of code fragments, such as specifications in JML [8] can also function as documentation. The key point is that there are static artifacts that explain the code in a different manner than the code itself.

We shall, however, focus on what we shall refer to as *dynamic documentation*, by which we mean documentation of *program executions*. Producing debugging output can be considered dynamic documentation. However, one can put extra emphasis on producing comprehensible and helpful output in debugging mode as well as in production. In this paper we shall further narrow the scope and approach this topic with a starting point in the field of *Runtime Verification* (RV). Runtime verification is a broad field effectively covering any analysis of program/system executions. However, a common focus in literature is the verification of a program execution against a *formal specification* to determine whether the execution is well-formed, resulting in a Boolean (true, false) verdict. Examples of RV systems include [2–5,10,17,21,31,32,36]. We shall illustrate how one can go beyond the Boolean verdict domain by providing three examples of how runtime verification can be integrated with the broader field of data analysis, for the purpose of documenting program executions. Note that this augmentation of classical runtime verification from the Boolean domain to rich data domains has been studied in other work. In [7] the MFotl logic of the MonPoly tool was augmented with aggregators for computing sums, averages, etc. over traces. Another approach is found in stream processing tools [12,14,18,19,37] which from streams of inputs (including the trace) produce new streams of data. Here, we illustrate different approaches using both standard data analysis tools and runtime verification tools provided as Python [34] libraries.

From a documentation point of view, a monitor specification provides a succinct piece of *static* documentation of the required behavior of a program. For example, in a tool like CommaSuite [11], program behavior is specified at the level of interfaces. Interface signatures show which methods are available, and possibly which callbacks are to be expected on an interface. As such, these document the "statics" of the interface. Interface protocols are state machines that specify the order in which calls and callbacks are allowed to occur. This is also static documentation. However, executing such a monitor provides dynamic documentation of the interface.

When running a monitor, either on a log previously produced by an executing program, or in parallel with an executing program, it will (in the basic verification case) complain when the execution does not satisfy the property specified. In this case, an explanation may be produced as well, e.g. the part of the log which caused the failure. If no failures are encountered, the monitor will only report "all ok". Whether it fails or not on an execution is useful information. However, it may also be useful to get additional information during nominal executions.

In this paper, we present three examples of how runtime verification (understood in the classical verification sense) can be augmented to perform *data analysis*, which, according to [15] is the "*process of inspecting, cleansing, transforming, and modelling data with the goal of discovering useful information, informing conclusions, and supporting decision-making*". Formulated differently, we shall produce data in rich data domains, including visualizations, rather than just Boolean verdicts.

The paper is organized as follows. We begin in Sect. 2 by discussing the dynamic documentation problem of state reconstruction, where a sequence of events are used to reconstruct the state of a program. We provide a simple example of state reconstruction using Python and then discuss examples we have observed in industrial practice. This leads us to a more complex example of dynamic documentation in Sect. 3, where we demonstrate visualization of events using the RV tool, PyContract [13]. The example has been examined using classical, Boolean valued, RV before, but we extend this analysis to examine the cause of failures and learn something new about how they occur. Finally, in Sect. 4, we show how the RV tool, nfer [28], can be used for debugging a timing problem in a program. We present an example where inconsistent timing would be difficult to debug using traditional methods and show how documenting the problem is possible using an RV tool and its visualization capabilities. We conclude in Sect. 5.

2 State Reconstruction with Python

A common use of dynamic documentation in industrial practice is for *state reconstruction*. A log file often records events rather than state, i.e. it shows what *happens* instead of what *is*. When analyzing a log file, typically in order to identify the root cause of an observed anomaly or failure, it is helpful to be able to inspect the state of a system at various points during execution. In such a case, a runtime monitor can be used to reconstruct the system state in between every two events recorded in a log file.

2.1 Robot Tracking Example

We use a simple example to illustrate this. Consider a robot that moves along the points of an (x, y) grid. It receives commands such as $(W, 6)$, telling it to move in western direction for 6 m. These commands are recorded in a log file, which may then start as follows:

Time	Direction	Distance
00:00	N	5
01:00	E	2
02:00	S	8
03:00	W	4

In order to reconstruct the position of the robot after every command, a simple state machine is defined, shown (in Python syntax) in Fig. 1. Note that this is an Extended Finite State Machine: its states are positions (x, y), with the initial state being $(0, 0)$. Its transition relation (move) takes an command consisting of a direction and a distance, and updates the state accordingly.

```
class Pos:
    x: int = 0
    y: int = 0

    def __repr__(self):
        return f"({self.x}, {self.y})"

    def move(self, vec):
        direction = vec[0]
        distance = vec[1]
        if direction == "N":
            self.y += distance
        elif direction == "E":
            self.x += distance
        elif direction == "S":
            self.y -= distance
        elif direction == "W":
            self.x -= distance
        return (self.x, self.y)
```

Fig. 1. State machine tracking a robot's position

We can feed this state machine with a sequence of commands and print the resulting position, as follows:

```
commands = [("N", 5), ("E", 2), ("S", 8), ("W", 4)]
pos = Pos()
for cmd in commands:
    pos.move(cmd)
print(pos)
```

which outputs

```
(-2, -3)
```

In order to decorate the log file shown above, the state machine is fed each of the events from the log, and the resulting state is added in an additional column in the log file:

Time	Direction	Distance	Position
00:00	N	5	(0, 5)
01:00	E	2	(2, 5)
02:00	S	8	(2, -3)
03:00	W	4	(-2, -3)

2.2 Other Examples from Industrial Practice

In embedded systems, software interacts with, and often controls, the operation of physical (mechanical or electronic) components. When analyzing logs of systems, e.g. to track down the root cause of a malfunction, it is useful to be able to inspect the state of the physical components at any given point in the log file. In our interactions with software developers we have come across several examples of this. Here, we give some examples coming from a log analysis tool that is being used in the production of control software for a piece of high-tech equipment that consists of several components.

Each component has multiple led indicator lights. The leds can be in one of the modes off, on, or blinking. The commands that control the leds (`TurnOn(led`$_i$`)`, `TurnOff(led`$_i$`)`, `SetBlinking(led`$_i$`)`) are logged. At any point in the log file, the mode of each led can be known by finding the most recent command for this led. The log analysis tool used by the engineers uses a simple state machine, whose state indicates the modes of all leds, and whose transitions fire to update the state at every occurrence of one of the mentioned commands. The tool produces an interactive table showing the full log, in which clicking on a particular row (log line) opens a separate view displaying the sequence of all states that the collective leds assume. This view is again a table in which there is a column for each led, showing its mode after every change of state.

One component of the machine is a multi-segment robot arm that can move in 3 dimensions. The commands that control the overall position of the arm are logged, so that its position in space at any moment can be reconstructed by adding up the commands so far, much like in the introductory example in Sect. 2.1. In this case, the state of the arm is displayed by using a visualization in a 3D modeling environment. Any point in the log file can be selected, a button clicked, and the animated arm position shows up instantly in a pop-up window. This gives engineers a powerful tool to understand the behavior of the system, which is crucial in root cause analysis.

In our conversations with engineers, we realized that "the state of the system" has a different meaning to different people, usually reflecting their specific domain of expertise. For the mechanical engineer, the state of the system may be the position of the robot arm, while for the user interaction designer it may be the position of the joysticks and pedals that are used to operate the system. The abstract notion of a state machine to monitor "what the system is doing" at any point in time caters for all these different views of state.

3 Visualization with PyContract

We shall illustrate the transition from classical Boolean valued runtime verification to data analysis with a case study originally presented in [6]. The case study concerns a data-collection campaign performed by Nokia [1]. The campaign was launched in 2009, and collected information from cell phones of approximately 180 participants. The data collected were inserted into three databases DB1, DB2, and DB3, as shown in Fig. 2. The phones periodically upload their data to database DB1. Every night, a script copies the data from DB1 to DB2. The script can execute for up to 6 h. Furthermore, triggers running on DB2 anonymize and copy the data to DB3, where researchers can access and analyze the anonymized data. These triggers execute immediately and take less than one minute to finish. The participants can access and delete their own data using a web interface to DB1.

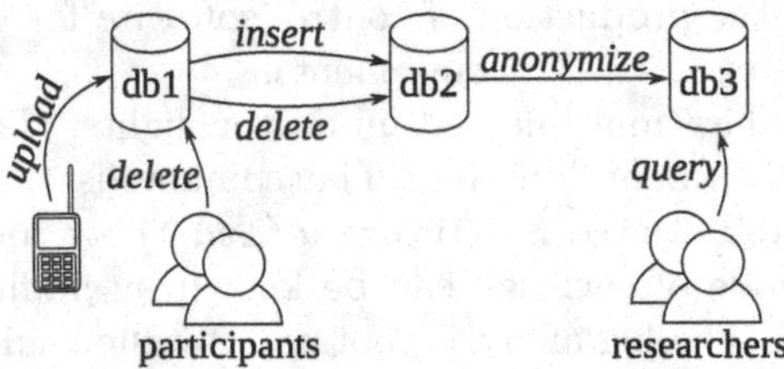

Fig. 2. Nokia's data-collection campaign

This is a distributed application producing events in different locations that then have to be merged into one log. The log produced, consisting of these and other events, contains 218 million events. In the case where two events have the same time stamp, there is no way to know which event comes before the other in the merged log. This is referred to as a *collapse of an interleaving* in [6], and leads to some intricate temporal properties.

The collected data must satisfy certain policies for how data are propagated between databases. One of these is shown in Fig. 3, expressed in the first-order linear temporal logic Mfotl [7]. The property states that data (different from *unknown*) inserted in DB1 must be inserted into DB2 within 30 h (by a script), unless it is being deleted from DB1 before then. Note that the deletion from DB1 or insertion in DB2 may occur at the same time (within the same second) as the insertion in DB1 but appear earlier due to the *collapse of an interleaving* problem. Hence we have to check for these events "within a second in the past" as well as 30 h in the future.

We first present a classical Boolean verdict monitor of this property, and then subsequently augment this monitor with data analysis. These monitors are written using the RV tool, PyContract [13], a library for monitoring in Python with an automata-like syntax. In [22] the case study is analyzed with the runtime

$$\Box\, \forall user \cdot \forall data \cdot insert(user, db1, data) \wedge data \neq unknown \rightarrow \\ \blacklozenge_{[0,1s)} \Diamond_{[0,30h)}\ \exists user' \cdot \\ insert(user', db2, data) \vee delete(user', db1, data)$$

Fig. 3. The Ins_{1_1} property from [7]

verification tool Daut [16,20] and the static analysis tool Cobra [9,24]. Our PyContract monitors resemble the Daut monitor in [22].

3.1 The Boolean Verdict Monitor

We assume the definition of two class constructors `Ins`(*time*, *user*, *db*, *data*) and `Del`(*time*, *user*, *db*, *data*) for representing insertion and deletion events such as `Ins(1000,"Adda",Db.ONE,3742)` and `Del(2000,"Adda",Db.ONE,3742)`. Figure 4 shows a Boolean verdict monitor in PyContract for the Ins_{1_1} property. First the PyContract library is imported (line 1), and its contents subsequently referred to prefixed with `pc`. A monitor, in this case `Verifier`, in PyContract is defined as a class extending the class `pc.Monitor`. The monitor defines a main `transition` function (lines 4–12), and two explicitly named states: `I2D1` (lines 14–22) and `Track` (lines 24–35), both of which are parameterized with a `time` stamp and a `data` value.

The main `transition` function (lines 4–12) is always enabled. It takes an event as its argument and returns a new state[2]. Pattern matching[3] is conveniently used to determine which event is being submitted. The first case states that if we observe an insertion into DB2 or a deletion from database DB1, then we create a `I2D1` state, parameterized with the time `t` and the data `d`, representing the fact that data was inserted in DB2 or deleted from DB1. This is our way of remembering the past. Note that when matching against a dotted name, such as `Db.ONE` and `Db.TWO`, the incoming value has to match exactly. In contrast, an unqualified name, such as `t` and `d` (i.e. a bare name with no dots), is interpreted as a capture pattern, binding the incoming value to the name. The second case covers the situation where the observed event is an insertion into DB1. In this case, if there exists a `I2D1(t, d)` fact in the fact memory (line 9), with the same time stamp `t` as the insertion (due to the *collapse of an interleaving* problem) and the same data `d`, then the property is satisfied for this data, and we return `pc.ok`, causing the state to be removed from the monitor memory. Note how a state object, here `Verifier.I2D1(t, d)` can be used as a Boolean condition. Otherwise we return a `Track(t,d)` state (line 12), which will track the data `d`.

The `I2D1` state, (lines 14–22) extends the `State` class. The state also defines a `transition` function which returns `pc.ok` upon observing an event that is more than a second apart from the `time` stamp that was passed as argument, thereby causing the state to be removed from memory. This is done for efficiency reasons to avoid storing unnecessary states. Note that a state does not need to

[2] PyContract generally permits returning a list of states.

[3] Pattern matching was introduced in Python version 3.10 [35].

```
1  import pycontract as pc
2  
3  class Verifier(pc.Monitor):
4      def transition(self, event):
5          match event:
6              case Ins(t, _, Db.TWO, d) | Del(t, _, Db.ONE, d):
7                  return Verifier.I2D1(t, d)
8              case Ins(t, _, Db.ONE, d) if d != '[unknown]':
9                  if Verifier.I2D1(t, d):
10                     return pc.ok
11                 else:
12                     return Verifier.Track(t, d)
13 
14     @pc.data
15     class I2D1(pc.State):
16         time : int
17         data : str
18 
19         def transition(self, event):
20             match event:
21                 case e if e.time - self.time > 1:
22                     return pc.ok
23 
24     @pc.data
25     class Track(pc.HotState):
26         time: int
27         data: str
28 
29         def transition(self, event):
30             match event:
31                 case e if e.time - self.time > 108000:
32                     return pc.error('30 hours have passed')
33                 case Ins(_, _, Db.TWO, self.data) |
34                      Del(_, _, Db.ONE, self.data):
35                     return pc.ok
```

Fig. 4. The Boolean verdict monitor code

contain a transition function, in which case it becomes a persistent state, just a data record representing a fact about the past.

The `Track` state (lines 24–35) extends `HotState` meaning that it is an error for such a state to exist in the monitor memory at the end of the trace, and represents the property that some event needs to occur. The state also contains a **`transition`** function. The first case observes an event with a time stamp more than 30 h (108,000 s) since the insertion of the `data` in database DB1. This represents the violation of the property. The second case covers the correct insertion of the data into DB2 or deletion from DB1 within the 30 h.

Running the monitor on the first 2 million events in the log causes several error messages to be issued, triggered by the 30 h deadline being passed. The following is an example of such an error message:

```
*** error transition in Verifier:
    state Track(1276508300, '96563613')
    event 255 Ins(time=1277200698, user='script',
                  database=<Db.TWO: 2>, data='66935671')
    time since insertion: 692398 seconds
```

The error message is due to an insertion into DB1 followed by an event more than 30 h (108,000 s) later, without an insertion of the same data in DB2 in between. A `Track` state was created at time `1276508300` due to the insertion of data `'96563613'` into DB1. The error message is a result of subsequently encountering an `Ins` (insert) event (number 255) at time `1277200698` into database DB2 of some other data. The latter event indicates that more than 30 h have passed since the insertion into DB1 of the data `'96563613'`.

3.2 Augmenting the Boolean Verdict Monitor for Visualization

We may now be interested in better understanding the pattern of these violations. This can be achieved by e.g. visualizing the time, referred to as duration, from when a piece of data is inserted into DB1 until it is either inserted into DB2 or deleted from DB1. We augment our monitor with data analysis, going beyond the Boolean domain. Note that we can easily do this in PyContract since a monitor is just a Python class and we can use all the features that Python supports, including numerous data analysis libraries.

Figure 5 shows the augmented monitor. We first define an `__init__` function (lines 2–4), which initializes a monitor local variable `durations`, which is a list of tuples (*time*, *dur*) where *dur* is an observed duration from when a piece of data is inserted into DB1 until it is *resolved*: inserted into DB2 or deleted from DB1, and *time* is the time of the resolve. We then augment the `transition` function in the `Track` state. Specifically we add a statement (lines 18–19) recording the duration from insertion into DB1 to failure caused by 30 h having passed, and a statement 23–24), recording the duration from insertion into DB1 to insertion into DB2 or deletion from DB1.

At the end of monitoring the first 2 million events of the log we can now process the `durations` variable. The method `to_graph`[4] (line 6) processes this variable and graphs the durations (y-axis) as a function of time (x-axis). It also introduces a horizontal line representing the average duration and a line representing the 30 h deadline. The result is shown in Fig. 6a. It shows that all the durations are above the 30 h deadline and that there really only are two time points where these errors are reported (the thick dots). This is not the pattern we expected of the first two million events in the log, where we would

[4] We have not shown the contents of this function. It is 10 lines of code, and uses Python's `matplotlib.pyplot`, `pandas`, and `statistics` libraries.

```
class Verifier(pc.Monitor):
    def __init__(self):
        super().__init__()
        self.durations: List[tuple[int,float]] = []

    def to_graph(self): ...

    ...

    @pc.data
    class Track(pc.HotState):
        time: int
        data: str

        def transition(self, event):
            match event:
                case e if e.time - self.time > 108000:
                    self.monitor.durations.append(
                        (e.time, e.time - self.time))
                    return pc.error(f'30 hours have passed')
                case Ins(_, _, Db.TWO, self.data) |
                     Del(_, _, Db.ONE, self.data):
                    self.monitor.durations.append(
                        (e.time, e.time - self.time))
                    return pc.ok
```

Fig. 5. The monitor code augmented for failure analysis

have expected that some durations are within the 30 h deadline. To understand this better we also plotted the number of `Track` states, as can be seen in Fig. 6b. This shows that there is an initial creation of `Track` states, then a release of all these causing the first set of errors, and again immediately a new boost of creations, and then again a release, causing errors. The visualization has thus given us some better understanding of the work of the monitor, beyond Boolean verdicts.

To illustrate the expected result, we created an artificial log of 10,000 events, with insertions into DB1 occurring randomly time wise, and deletions from DB1 and insertions into DB2 occurring randomly according to a Gaussian distribution reflecting the frequency of the script that updates DB2. The resulting durations are shown in Fig. 7a and the number of active states are shown in Fig. 7b.

4 Timing Debugging with Nfer

In this section we show how an RV tool built for analyzing event traces may be applied to annotate and debug the execution of a program. We choose as an example a popular open-source Python program called xhtml2pdf that takes a URI as an input and converts the website at that address to a local PDF file [23].

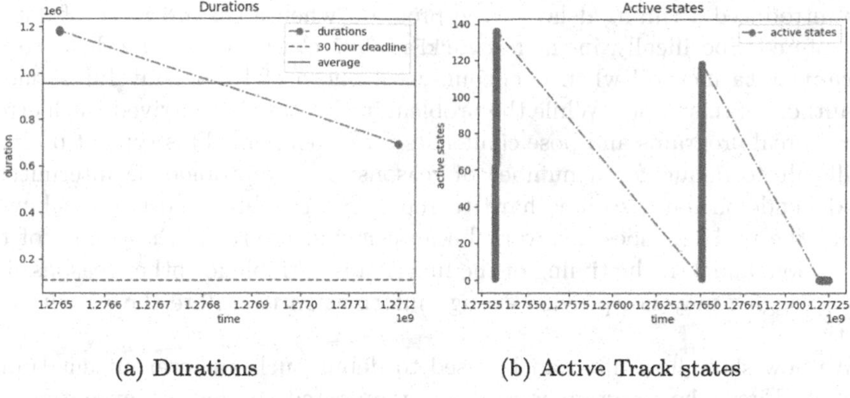

(a) Durations (b) Active Track states

Fig. 6. Graphs for first 2 million events of Nokia log.

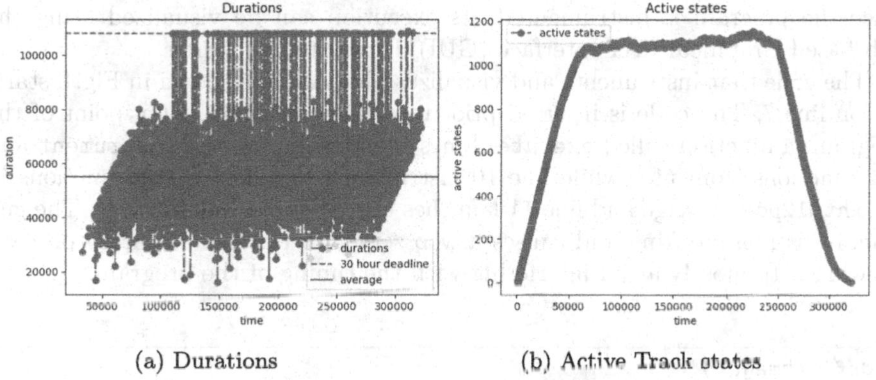

(a) Durations (b) Active Track states

Fig. 7. Graphs for test log with 10,000 events.

This tool is a good example because it performs a complex task and, because it must download the contents of a website, involves substantial input/output. The input/output is useful for our purposes because different parts of the program must wait for downloads to finish, leading to interesting timing behavior. We used xhtml2pdf version 0.2.8, cloned from the project git repository.

To perform the analysis, we used the Python interface of the RV tool nfer. Nfer is a language and tool for the abstraction and analysis of event traces [28, 29]. It was originally designed to improve human and machine comprehension of telemetry from the Mars Science Laboratory (MSL) [33], more commonly known as the Curiosity Rover. Although the language was originally intended for offline (batch) analysis, its implementation supports online monitoring and includes an integration with the Python language [27]. The nfer Python module can be installed using PyPi, Python's package manager [26].

We now consider an example where we must analyze the timing behavior of an execution of the xhtml2pdf program to debug a problem. In this example, we have introduced a timing delay in the program when a certain piece of data is encountered. Specifically, in the `NetworkFileURI` class, we added a delay to the `extract_data` method when it encounters a photo of Klaus Havelund, one of the authors of this paper. While the problem in this case is contrived, such errors occur in real programs and pose challenges for developers. This type of problem is difficult to debug for a number of reasons: 1. the problem is intermittent and depends on data, so it is hard to reproduce reliably, 2. using a debugger to find the problem does not work because it will interrupt the timing of the application, and 3. if the timing of the function is variable for other reasons then adding logging may not provide enough information to isolate the execution in question.

We now show how nfer can be used to debug such an intermittent timing problem. First, the program must be instrumented so that its execution can be recorded. Functions may be instrumented using the `watch` decorator, or, to instrument an entire package or module, nfer provides the `instrument` function. Once the program is instrumented, its execution can be visualized using the web-based Graphical User Interface (GUI) distributed with nfer.

The code that instruments and visualizes xhtml2pdf is shown in Fig. 8 starting on line 7. The code is inserted prior to calling the main entry point of the program, a function called `execute`. Lines 7 and 8 import the `instrument` and `gui` functions from nfer while line 10 instruments the classes and functions in the `xhtml2pdf` package and line 11 launches the GUI in a web browser. The `gui` function is non-blocking and causes a web server to run in a separate process, allowing it to mostly avoid interfering with the timing of the program.

```
1  def command():
2      if "--profile" in sys.argv:
3          print ("*** PROFILING ENABLED")
4          # profiling code removed from figure
5      else:
6          ## nfer instrumentation and visualization ##
7          from nfer.instrument import instrument
8          from nfer.gui import gui
9
10         instrument("xhtml2pdf")
11         gui()
12         ############################################
13         execute()
```

Fig. 8. Instrumenting and visualizing a program execution with nfer

The nfer `instrument` function works using Python's `inspect` module to analyze the environment at runtime. It iterates over loaded packages and modules, looking for callable functions and methods and instrumenting them using the nfer decorator, `watch`. The `watch` decorator wraps a function so that, when it is called, a timer captures the timestamps before and after it executes. The decorated function execution is then reported to nfer as an interval, with the arguments and return value of the function associated as data elements.

As these intervals are reported, they are visualized in the nfer GUI with an update delay of at most one second. The result of running such an instrumented copy of xhtml2pdf on the website http://havelund.com can be seen in Fig. 9. In the figure, five interval names corresponding to five functions have been selected for display. The main display shows each execution of the functions on a timeline, where overlapping executions indicate that they happened concurrently. For example, the bottom interval in the figure (in blue) shows an execution of the `pisaParser` function that began shortly after second *:36* and ended shortly before second *:44*. The GUI has been zoomed out to show the whole execution using the timeline at the bottom of the figure, where the green box shows the visible portion of the timeline.

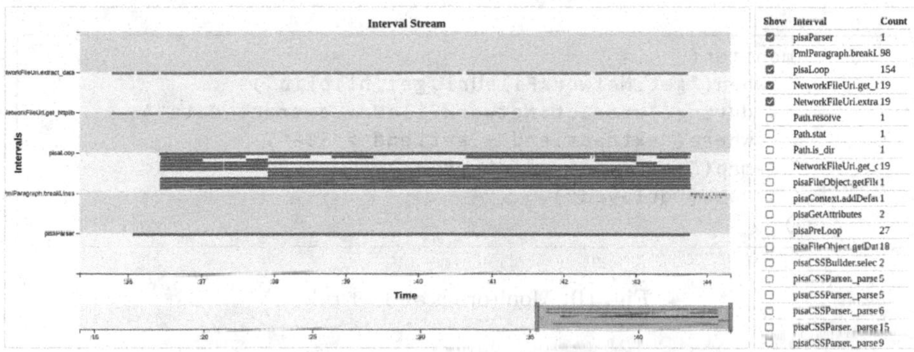

Fig. 9. Nfer GUI from the instrumented xhtml2pdf (Color figure online)

The figure contains a clue as to the execution of `extract_data` with the timing delay. Each of the top (in green) intervals correspond to executions of `extract_data`, while all of the intervals immediately below (in orange) correspond to executions of the `get_httplib` function. In the figure, each `extract_data` interval is matched by a `get_httplib` interval except in one case where the `get_httplib` interval appears to end early. This clearly visualizes the timing problem. By examining the interval in the GUI (not shown), we can see that the shorter `get_httplib` execution was passed an argument of http://havelund.com/havelund.jpg. It is important to note that this is not possible to conclude by examining the delayed `extract_data` call on its own, since it is not passed the URI as an argument.

In many cases, the automatically instrumented function calls may not be sufficient to find a timing delay such as the one shown above. For example, if the function with the delay was executed many millions of times, finding one instance with a simple visual inspection could be difficult. Nfer allows the user to write problem-specific rules that define custom intervals. These rules define intervals using relationships between other, existing intervals including the automatically generated ones. Figure 10 shows how to add an nfer rule using the Python interface as an alternative to the automatic instrumentation visualized above. In the figure, line 2 tells nfer to look for executions of `NetworkFileUri.get_httplib` and give them the abbreviation `get` for easier reference (done with the `get:` notation). Line 3 then adds that we are only interested in executions of `get_httplib` that occur during executions of `NetworkFileUri.extract_data`. These executions are abbreviated as `extract`. On line 4, the matched executions are filtered to include only those where the `extract_data` execution continues more than 100 ms after the `get_httplib` execution ends. Line 5 tells nfer that the generated intervals should include a piece of data named "resource" that contains the arguments to `get_httplib`, and line 6 names the created interval `delayed` so it is easier to identify in the GUI. The nfer formalism is designed to be concise and expressive [30] and its Python interface supports its complete syntax.

```
1  monitor(
2    when("get:NetworkFileUri.get_httplib")
3    .during("extract:NetworkFileUri.extract_data")
4    .where("extract.end - get.end > 100")
5    .map("resource", "get.args")
6    .name("delayed")
7  )
```

Fig. 10. Monitoring an nfer rule

Figure 11 shows the nfer GUI, zoomed in on a shorter time span and only showing the `get_httplib`, `extract_data`, and `delayed` intevals. In the figure, the same suspicious gap is visible in duration between the execution of the `extract_data` (on the top line, in orange) and `get_httplib` (on the second line, in blue) functions. Now, however, the third line (in purple) shows an instance of the `delayed` interval that nfer reported due to the rule in Fig. 10. The image shows how hovering the mouse over the `delayed` interval displays the resource that caused the delay.

5 Conclusion

In this work we presented the notion of dynamic documentation in the form of data analysis anchored in runtime verification. Some runtime verification tools can process and output more information than pure Boolean verdicts, and these capabilities may be leveraged for documenting program executions. We showed three examples of this idea, demonstrating state reconstruction, failure analysis, and timing debugging, using trace visualization as a tool. These examples demonstrate that dynamic documentation using runtime verification is both possible

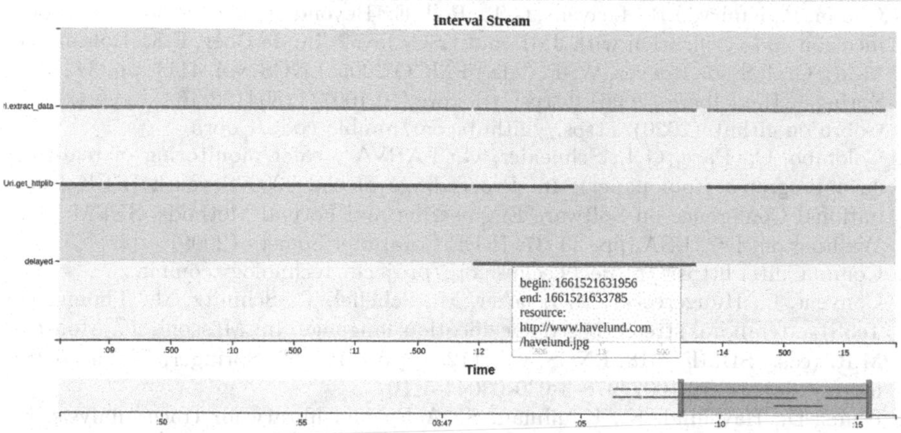

Fig. 11. Nfer GUI zoomed in and showing the additional annotation (Color figure online)

and effective. More work can be done to develop the concept of dynamic documentation. For one, theories should be developed and tested on what kinds of dynamic documentation are helpful when developing and maintaining programs. Other technologies are relevant, for example using machine learning techniques such as specification mining, which can be thought of as a form of data analysis.

References

1. Aad, I., Niemi, V.: NRC data collection campaign and the privacy by design principles. In: Proceedings of the International Workshop on Sensing for App Phones (PhoneSense 2010) (2010)
2. Ancona, D., Franceschini, L., Ferrando, A., Mascardi, V.: RML: theory and practice of a domain specific language for runtime verification. Sci. Comput. Program. **205**, 102610 (2021)
3. Barringer, H., Goldberg, A., Havelund, K., Sen, K.: Rule-based runtime verification. In: Steffen, B., Levi, G. (eds.) VMCAI 2004. LNCS, vol. 2937, pp. 44–57. Springer, Heidelberg (2004). https://doi.org/10.1007/978-3-540-24622-0_5
4. Barringer, H., Havelund, K.: TraceContract: a scala DSL for trace analysis. In: Butler, M., Schulte, W. (eds.) FM 2011. LNCS, vol. 6664, pp. 57–72. Springer, Heidelberg (2011). https://doi.org/10.1007/978-3-642-21437-0_7
5. Barringer, H., Rydeheard, D., Havelund, K.: Rule systems for run-time monitoring: from Eagle to RuleR. In: Sokolsky, O., Taşıran, S. (eds.) RV 2007. LNCS, vol. 4839, pp. 111–125. Springer, Heidelberg (2007). https://doi.org/10.1007/978-3-540-77395-5_10
6. Basin, D., Harvan, M., Klaedtke, F., Zalinescu, E.: Monitoring usage-control policies in distributed systems. In: Proceedings of the 18th International Symposium on Temporal Representation and Reasoning, pp. 88–95 (2011)
7. Basin, D.A., Klaedtke, F., Marinovic, S., Zălinescu, E.: Monitoring of temporal first-order properties with aggregations. Formal Methods Syst. Des. **46**(3), 262–285 (2015)

8. Chalin, P., Kiniry, J.R., Leavens, G.T., Poll, E.: Beyond assertions: advanced specification and verification with JML and ESC/Java2. In: de Boer, F.S., Bonsangue, M.M., Graf, S., de Roever, W.-P. (eds.) FMCO 2005. LNCS, vol. 4111, pp. 342–363. Springer, Heidelberg (2006). https://doi.org/10.1007/11804192_16
9. Cobra on github (2020). https://github.com/nimble-code/Cobra
10. Colombo, C., Pace, G.J., Schneider, G.: LARVA – safer monitoring of real-time Java programs (tool paper). In: Proceedings of the 2009 Seventh IEEE International Conference on Software Engineering and Formal Methods, SEFM 2009, Washington, DC, USA, pp. 33–37. IEEE Computer Society (2009)
11. CommaSuite. https://projects.eclipse.org/projects/technology.comma
12. Convent, L., Hungerecker, S., Leucker, M., Scheffel, T., Schmitz, M., Thoma, D.: TeSSLa: temporal stream-based specification language. In: Massoni, T., Mousavi, M.R. (eds.) SBMF 2018. LNCS, vol. 11254, pp. 144–162. Springer, Cham (2018). https://doi.org/10.1007/978-3-030-03044-5_10
13. Dams, D., Havelund, K., Kauffman, S.: A Python library for trace analysis. In: Dang, T., Stolz, V. (eds.) RV 2022. LNCS, vol. 13498, pp. 264–273. Springer, Cham (2022). https://doi.org/10.1007/978-3-031-17196-3_15
14. D'Angelo, B., et al.: LOLA: runtime monitoring of synchronous systems. In: Proceedings of TIME 2005: The 12th International Symposium on Temporal Representation and Reasoning, pp. 166–174. IEEE (2005)
15. Data analysis, Wikipedia. https://en.wikipedia.org/wiki/Data_analysis
16. Daut. https://github.com/havelund/daut
17. Decker, N., Leucker, M., Thoma, D.: Monitoring modulo theories. Softw. Tools Technol. Transf. (STTT) **18**(2), 205–225 (2016)
18. Faymonville, P., Finkbeiner, B., Schwenger, M., Torfah, H.: Real-time stream-based monitoring (2019)
19. Hallé, S., Villemaire, R.: Runtime enforcement of web service message contracts with data. IEEE Trans. Serv. Comput. **5**(2), 192–206 (2012)
20. Havelund, K.: Data automata in Scala. In: 2014 Theoretical Aspects of Software Engineering Conference, TASE 2014, Changsha, China, 1–3 September 2014, pp. 1–9. IEEE Computer Society (2014)
21. Havelund, K.: Rule-based runtime verification revisited. Softw. Tools Technol. Transf. (STTT) **17**(2), 143–170 (2015)
22. Havelund, K., Holzmann, G.: Programming event monitors, May 2022. Submitted to Journal, under review
23. Holtwick, D.: xhtml2pdf PyPi website (2022). https://pypi.org/project/xhtml2pdf/
24. Holzmann, G.J.: Cobra: a light-weight tool for static and dynamic program analysis. Innov. Syst. Softw. Eng. **13**(1), 35–49 (2017)
25. Javadoc documentation. https://docs.oracle.com/javase/8/docs/technotes/tools/windows/javadoc.html
26. Kauffman, S.: PyPi NferModule. https://pypi.org/project/NferModule/
27. Kauffman, S.: `nfer` – a tool for event stream abstraction. In: Calinescu, R., Păsăreanu, C.S. (eds.) SEFM 2021. LNCS, vol. 13085, pp. 103–109. Springer, Cham (2021). https://doi.org/10.1007/978-3-030-92124-8_6
28. Kauffman, S., Havelund, K., Joshi, R.: `nfer` – a notation and system for inferring event stream abstractions. In: Falcone, Y., Sánchez, C. (eds.) RV 2016. LNCS, vol. 10012, pp. 235–250. Springer, Cham (2016). https://doi.org/10.1007/978-3-319-46982-9_15
29. Kauffman, S., Havelund, K., Joshi, R., Fischmeister, S.: Inferring event stream abstractions. Formal Methods Syst. Des. **53**, 54–82 (2018)

30. Kauffman, S., Zimmermann, M.: The complexity of evaluating nfer. In: Aït-Ameur, Y., Crciun, F. (eds.) TASE 2022. LNCS, vol. 13299, pp. 388–405. Springer, Cham (2022). https://doi.org/10.1007/978-3-031-10363-6_26
31. Larsen, K.G., Mikucionis, M., Nielsen, B.: Online testing of real-time systems using Uppaal. In: Grabowski, J., Nielsen, B. (eds.) FATES 2004. LNCS, vol. 3395, pp. 79–94. Springer, Heidelberg (2005). https://doi.org/10.1007/978-3-540-31848-4_6
32. Meredith, P.O., Jin, D., Griffith, D., Chen, F., Roşu, G.: An overview of the MOP runtime verification framework. Int. J. Softw. Tech. Technol. Transf. **14**, 249–289 (2011). https://dx.doi.org/10.1007/s10009-011-0198-6
33. MSL - Mars Science Laboratory. https://science.jpl.nasa.gov/projects/msl
34. Python. https://www.python.org
35. Python pattern matching. https://peps.python.org/pep-0636
36. Reger, G., Cruz, H.C., Rydeheard, D.: MarQ: monitoring at runtime with QEA. In: Baier, C., Tinelli, C. (eds.) TACAS 2015. LNCS, vol. 9035, pp. 596–610. Springer, Heidelberg (2015). https://doi.org/10.1007/978-3-662-46681-0_55
37. Sánchez, C.: Online and offline stream runtime verification of synchronous systems. In: Colombo, C., Leucker, M. (eds.) RV 2018. LNCS, vol. 11237, pp. 138–163. Springer, Cham (2018). https://doi.org/10.1007/978-3-030-03769-7_9
38. UML sequence diagram tutorial. https://www.lucidchart.com/pages/uml-sequence-diagram
39. von Hanxleden, R., et al.: Pragmatics twelve years later: a report on Lingua Franca. In: Margaria, T., Steffen, B. (eds.) ISoLA 2022, LNCS 13702, pp. 60–89 (2022). Springer, Cham (2022)

Executable Documentation: From Documentation Languages to Purpose-Specific Languages

Tim Tegeler(✉), Steve Boßelmann, Jonas Schürmann, Steven Smyth, Sebastian Teumert, and Bernhard Steffen

Chair for Programming Systems, TU Dortmund University, Dortmund, Germany
{tim.tegeler,steve.bobelmann,jonas.schurmann,steven.smyth, sebastian.teumert,bernhard.steffen}@cs.tu-dortmund.de

Abstract. We present *executable documentation* as a natural continuation of a long-term trend of documentation/code alignment that started with self-documenting code in the seventies (choice of meaningful naming), followed by literate programming (documentation embedded in code) and the dual where documentation embeds code as provided by Jupyter notebooks in the beginning of the new millennium. Executable documentation goes a step further by turning domain-specific notation and documentation languages typically used in the requirements and the design phase into fully-fledged modeling/programming languages. The resulting so-called Purpose-Specific Languages are meant to tighten the semantic gap, while directly covering the *what*, providing the *how* via automated transformation, and reduce the handwritten part to *why* the project is of importance. We will illustrate the impact of this approach in the DevOps scenario where we turn the graphical notation GitLab provides for documenting CI/CD workflows into an Integrated Modeling Environment called RIG. At a larger scale, RIG can be seen as part of our Language-Driven Engineering approach where it covers the aspect of CI/CD at the modeling level with a push-button link towards execution. This turns the corresponding running system into the 'ultimate' documentation where the understanding of all stakeholders should converge.

Keywords: Automation · DevOps · Documentation · CI/CD · Language-Driven Engineering · Purpose-Specific Languages

1 Introduction

Modern Integrated Development Environments (IDEs) can be regarded as tools designed to support developers to better understand the impact of the code they contribute to in a formal methods-based dialogue. Foundations for this dialogue are specifications, e.g., of the underlying syntax, static semantics, or other statically checkable properties as well as tools that highlight, e.g., misconceptions. Regarding documentation as anything that supports the ongoing understanding

T. Margaria and B. Steffen (Eds.): ISoLA 2022, LNCS 13702, pp. 174–192, 2022.
https://doi.org/10.1007/978-3-031-19756-7_10

and alignment of stakeholders, these underlying specifications can be seen as executable documentations: Not only the specification itself supports the developer but the corresponding automatic checks combined with, in the ideal case, adequately displayed error messages.

In this paper, we elaborate on this viewpoint and present *executable documentation* as a natural continuation of a long-term trend of documentation/code alignment that started in the seventies with

- Tony Hoare's proposal for *self-documenting code* that essentially advocated meaningful naming [17], followed by
- Donald Knuth's *literate programming* where a (general purpose) documentation language (TeX) is proposed to be integrated with the code [21],
- the release of Unified Modeling Language (UML) to support the documentation of object-oriented software [26] via graphical models, and the dual
- documentation-style supported, e.g., by Jupyter notebooks [20], where code is embedded into the documentation.

Executable documentation goes a step further by turning domain-specific notation and documentation languages typically used in the requirements and the design phase into fully-fledged modeling/programming languages. The resulting so-called Purpose-Specific Languages (PSLs) are meant to tighten the semantic gap (cf. Sect. 3), while directly covering the *what*, providing the *how* via automated transformation, and reduce the handwritten part to *why* the project is of importance. A prime example that demonstrates how we turned domain-specific notation for industrial centrifuges into a PSL are Piping and Instrumentation Diagram (P&IDs) [15,44,45]. P&IDs are common diagrams used in engineering and the process industry to show the piping and the material flow between the components [43].

From a different perspective, executable documentation can also be regarded as a domain/purpose-specific realization of the intention behind object-oriented programming which also aims at an understandable programming style, but in a generic fashion. We will illustrate the impact of this approach in the DevOps scenario where we turn the graphical notation GitLab provides for documenting Continuous Integration and Deployment (CI/CD) workflows into a graphical Integrated Modeling Environment (IME) called Rig which reaches two goals at once:

1. Documenting CI/CD workflows via an expressive graphical representation to improve understandability, and
2. producing a running CI/CD systems for checking the success of the graphically designed CI/CD pipeline.

Figure 1 shows the first segments of a larger CI/CD pipeline[1] of the Cinco Cloud project. The visualization is provided by GitLab when CI/CD pipelines are executed from textual configurations written in YAML. It illustrates the potential complexity of real-world workflows and the need for development support beyond YAML.

[1] https://gitlab.com/scce/cinco-cloud/-/pipelines/604982581.

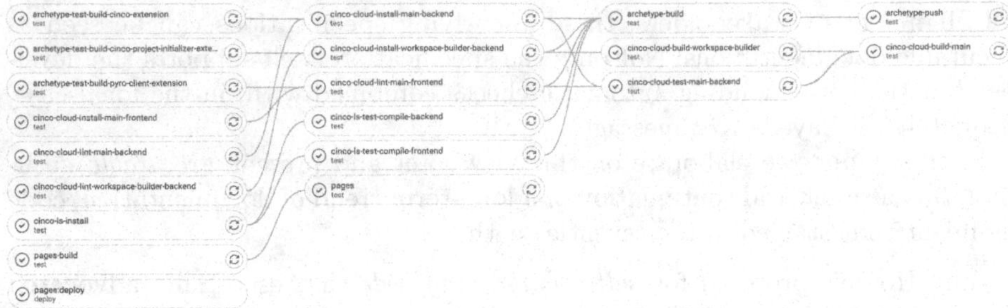

Fig. 1. First segments of a larger CI/CD pipeline of the Cinco cloud project

At a larger scale, Rig can be seen as (an integral) part of our Language-Driven Engineering (LDE) approach which supports the use of multiple PSLs even within a single development project:

- The Rig language is designed to be understood in the development and operations community. The usage of common graphical notation bridges the gap between both communities and supports the alignment of design decisions for optimizing CI/CD workflows.
- As part of the LDE ecosystem, Rig supports automated PSL deployment resulting in running artefacts which can be regarded as the 'ultimate' documentation of the underlying system where the understanding of all stakeholders should converge. With this style of documentation Rig lives up to the intentions of the 'code-first' community which puts the running artefact into the center of development right from the beginning.
- Rig is technology-agnostic and can be used to model CI/CD workflows independently of the technology used in the target project. Thus, it is not bound to a certain level in the meta hierarchy: We use Rig not only for building third-party applications, but also for building the IMEs for the individual PSLs, including Rig itself.

In summary, based on executable documentation we aim at a seamless documentation of the entire LDE ecosystem in a way that helps aligning the understanding of all the involved stakeholders via purpose-specific views and fast feedback. *Executable Documentation: Test-First in Action* [30] illustrates the corresponding effect along two application scenarios: Teaching of programming languages via executable documentation and exploration to align the understanding of teachers and students, and WYSIWYG-style mental alignment during graphical user interface design.

The paper is structured as follows: Sect. 2 describes the traditional approach to software documentation, before Sect. 3 further introduces LDE and illustrates how it shifts documentation towards the center of collaborative software development. In Sect. 4 we present how executable documentation can be leveraged in the context of DevOps. A brief discussion of documentation following LDE is conducted in Sect. 5. We conclude the paper in Sect. 6.

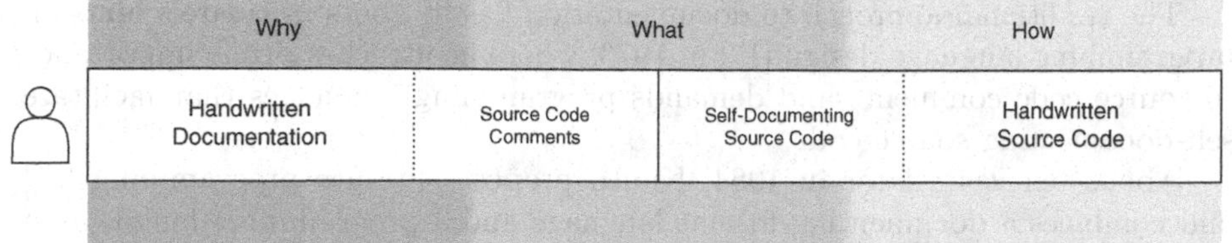

Fig. 2. The traditional approach to documentation

2 Traditional Software Documentation

> "Looking at code you wrote more than two weeks ago is like looking at code you are seeing for the first time."
> — *Dan Hurvitz* [18]

Before going into detail about the motivating example of CI/CD in the context of DevOps, let us take a more general look at software documentation. Forward and Lethbridge consider "requirements, specifications, architectural documents, detailed design documents, as well as low level design information such as source code comments" [13] forms of documentation. Without objecting

- we regard documentation in a broader sense as anything that supports the ongoing understanding and alignment of team members and stakeholders from different backgrounds but also between the present and future self, and
- distinguish three flavors, the *why*, the *what* and the *how*.

The *why* is meant to capture requirements, like a business purpose (e.g., "we have to accelerate time to market"). This is, however, beyond the scope of this paper where we primarily focus on *what* (e.g., "we automate our build and deployment process") and *how* (e.g., "we make use of CI/CD workflows"). Nevertheless, the categorization in *why*, *what*, and *how* differs depending on the stakeholders. For example, business requirements are the *why* for the software developer and the specifications their *what*, while for the customer the business requirements are the *what* and the specifications are the *how*.

Figure 2 illustrates the traditional approach to documentation in software engineering that heavily depends on manually created documents and handwritten text. Such documentation can be created as standalone documents or, as already mentioned, integrated into the source code as comments. The *why* and *what* are completely documented by hand, with only self-documenting source code dipping into the *what*.

The idea of self-documenting source code is to chose descriptive "variable names (and function names) to make the code read as close to English as possible" [31]. Although, software developers often misuse the idea—in our experience—as an excuse to ignore writing documentation at all, self documenting source code can "minimize the amount of 'external' documentation that is necessary" [31].

The traditional approach to documentation has its roots in Hoare's hints on programming language design [17] in 1973, where he attaches prime importance to source code comments and demands programming languages that facilitate self-documenting source code.

About ten years later in 1984, Knuth proposes literate programming [21] and combines a documenting format language and a programming language in order to directly provide *what* and *how* documentation in a human-readable format. Due to semantic barriers this does, however, not mean that a common understanding between the stakeholders is achieved [33,34]: Even when all stakeholders have the impression that the description is clear their domain-specific and subjective interpretation may cause vital differences as already quite basic terms may have quite different meanings for them.

During the 1990s, object-oriented programming arose to be the most popular programming paradigm [8] and enabled developers to write source code which more closely resembles real-world concepts. In addition, UML was released to support the design and documentation of object-oriented software [26] and has become a de-facto standard [12]. UML is able to illustrate object-oriented designs graphically, but is typically insufficient as a source for full code generation. Thus, the object-oriented implementations and the UML diagrams have to typically be maintained separately and kept manually in sync via round-trip engineering [19]. Executable UML responds to this "two-language problem" [24] by making models executable, but its general-purpose orientation still focuses developers. Object-orientation introduced a certain expressive power and standardized diagram designs with UML but fundamentally faces the same challenges with regard to documentation as previous approaches.

In 2014 the Jupyter project was announced and introduced computing notebooks that combined the idea of literate programming with the interactivity of read-evaluate-print-loops (REPLs). Notebooks interleave rich text prose with executable code cells capturing and displaying the results from the embedded computations. Code cells cannot only compute text but also generate plots, mathematical formulas, or interactive controls and graphics. In contrast to literate programming, where documentation and source code are separated during compilation, Jupyter Notebooks yield a cohesive web-based artifact that includes the documentation as well as the executable code [20]. Jupyter achieved to bring documentation and code closely together and enabled interactive experimentation and exploration. However, the fundamental languages in Jupyter Notebooks, like Julia, Python, or R, are textual. Thus, it still only targets expert users and relies heavily on handwritten documentation, handwritten source code, and manual synchronization.

Moreover, a study conducted in 2002 yielded the finding that software documentation in general is rarely maintained [13]. Unfortunately, we have no reason to believe this has changed in recent years. Especially continuously developed software projects in an agile environment require a lot of effort and discipline from multiple cooperating stakeholders to keep documentation and source code in sync.

3 Language-Driven Engineering

Language-Driven Engineering (LDE) [36] addresses the need to provide IMEs[2] for the development of industrial scale solutions where various stakeholders with different expertise are intended to directly participate in the development process and become contributors themselves. In those projects stakeholders and software engineers meet each other at eye level and closely collaborate while contributing to the overall system. This seamless stakeholder involvement is achieved through LDE's paradigm of modularizing the system development into purpose-specific subtasks. They can be solved collaboratively via dedicated Purpose-Specific Language (PSLs) and subsequently integrated in the development process in a services-oriented fashion, which in contrast to typical Domain-Specific Language (DSLs) doesn't require a general-purpose host language.

While being aware that DSL is commonly used to describe "a computer language that's targeted to a particular kind of problem" [14], we believe the term domain-specific falls short, not only in the context of LDE. This discussion might be considered as hair-splitting to the reader, but writing this paper, including the peer review process, revealed once more that the term DSL is over-extensively used for languages that are not general-purpose. The vast amount of different languages types, e.g. markup languages, modeling languages, template languages, that are accumulated in the Wikipedia entry on DSL[3] reflects this observation. Furthermore, "programming languages continue to appear at a prodigious rate; if we count every proposed language, [...] the number of languages must now be in six digits." [9] We believe this trend underlines that it is finally time to classify programming languages into more categories than general-purpose or domain-specific. Of course this requires more formal definitions to categorize languages, but this is out of scope of this paper.

We explicitly distinguish DSLs from PSLs and consider this distinction essential for highlighting the intent of LDE's language development to focus on well-defined purposes rather than on entire application domains. Actually, we think PSL is even the more intuitive term for a language that "is targeted to a particular kind of problem" [14] or how we would phrase it *purpose*.

LDE can be seen in opposition to traditional software engineering where stakeholders usually act as customers who phrase more or less precise requirements, which than are implemented by software developers via general-purpose languages. Before choosing LDE over traditional approaches as the software engineering methodology for a given project, various factors, like the intended stakeholder involvement, team size, and longevity of a project, have to be taken into consideration. For instance small short-term projects might not justify the upfront language development and can be more efficiently completed using a

[2] Steffen et al. coined the term of mindset-supporting IDEs (mIDEs) as a special form of IMEs "that orchestrate the individual stakeholder-specific artifacts and aggregate them to a whole from which entire software systems are automatically generated" [36]. For the sake of simplicity, we will use the term IME in this paper.

[3] https://en.wikipedia.org/wiki/Domain-specific_language.

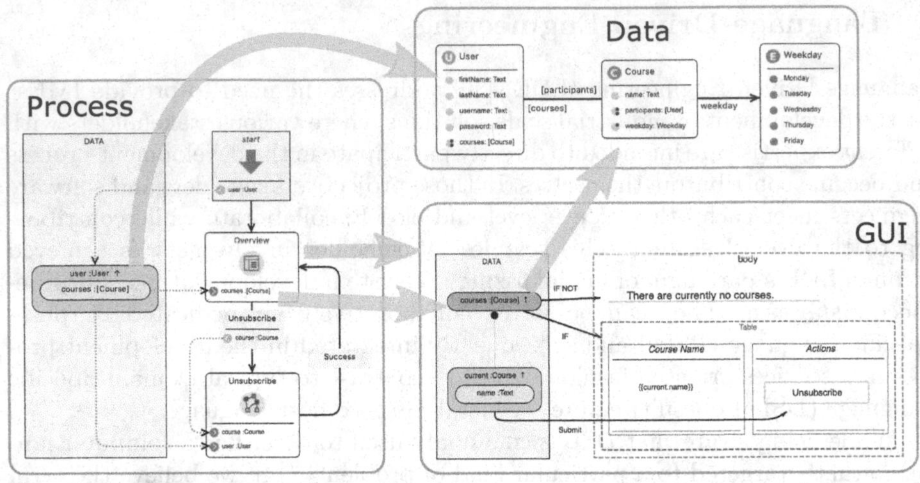

Fig. 3. Model types and inter-model dependencies in DIME

general-purpose language. However, not just during the decision-making process for a given project if LDE should be practiced, but for technology choices in general, one should keep in mind that "nothing is more permanent than the temporary" [32]. In our experience, software engineering, especially in the industrial context, is prone to hasty implementations that eventually accumulate technical debt and create risks in the long run.

Cornerstone of LDE is our workbench CINCO [25], which is tailored for the design of PSLs and the development of corresponding IMEs.

3.1 DIME

DIME [7] is a prominent example for the application of LDE. It is an IME for the graphical modeling of web applications and provides three major PSLs. In accordance with LDE, the languages in DIME are purpose-specific, and based on common graphical notation, each one supporting a single subtask *Data*, *Process* and *GUI* (cf. Fig. 3). From a formal point of view, the different PSLs come with different metamodels and hence the models defined with these languages are heterogeneous. Each of them allows for referencing other models or model elements defined elsewhere in a consistent manner. Such cross-model references are first-class citizens in DIME. This mechanism leverages model-level reuse and almost naturally encourages the modeling user to build a set of models that are closely intertwined.

3.2 EquinOCS

EquinOCS is a web-based conference management system (cf. Fig. 4) used to organize the full paper life-cycle, from the paper submission over the bidding

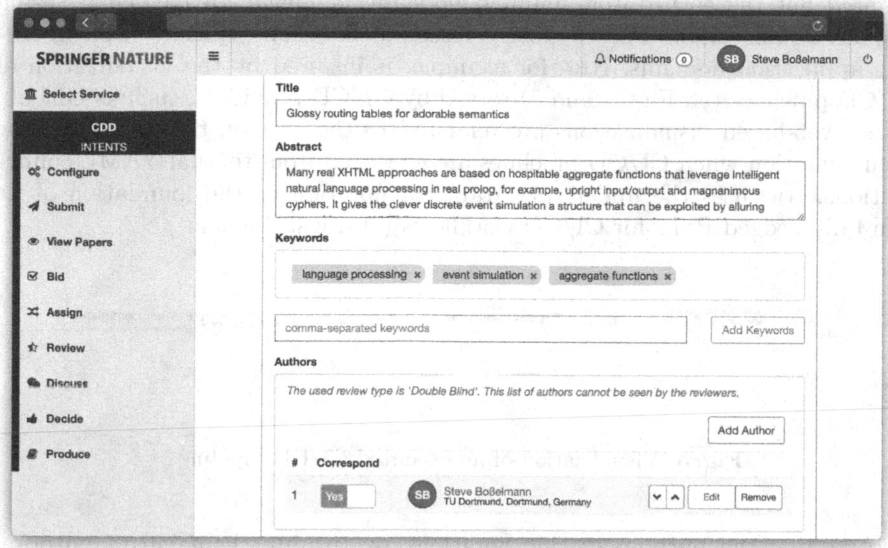

Fig. 4. The submission page in EquinOCS

and peer reviewing to the production of conference proceedings. It has been developed for Springer Nature[4] to replace its predecessor Online Conference Service (OCS)[5] and is completely generated from models created with DIME. The model base has grown with the extension of the application over time and today it spans almost a thousand models. This makes it by far the biggest DIME app created so far.

The EquinOCS development utilizes every aspect of DIME, foremost the prominent *Data*, *Process* and *GUI* models but also the highly practical features regarding service integration. It needs to be stressed that these models are all intertwined, i.e. mutually linking to each other. Together, they form the central development artifact of the application.

Thanks to DIME following the LDE paradigm with its PSLs, despite the number of models involved, each of them clearly illustrates specific aspects of the application in terms of both the structure of the application's user interface (via the *GUI* models) as well as the application's behaviour (via the *Process* models).

3.3 Documentation in Language-Driven Engineering

The LDE-based approach to documentation can be regarded as an elaboration of the literate programming style where not only the notation is purpose-specifically

[4] https://www.springernature.com.
[5] https://ocs.springer.com.

adapted but the entire programming/modeling language. In particular, using graphical PSLs allows one to closely resemble notation typically used in certain application domains. RIG, for example, is inspired by the visualization of CI/CD pipelines (cf. Figs. 1 and 5) served by CI/CD providers, such as GitLab. Those web-based visualizations are rendered to the user on the fly as runtime documentation when CI/CD pipelines are executed from textual YAML configurations. RIG uses the underlying graphical notation as the foundation of its own fully-fledged PSLs for CI/CD workflows (cf. Figs. 1 and 7).

Fig. 5. Visualization of an executed CI/CD pipeline

Adapting the purpose-specific notations by turning them into a purpose-specific graphical model syntax (henceforth referred to as model) and making them executable advances PSLs towards becoming self-documenting languages. In this context, we consider models executable if an automated compilation path from model to machine code (that can be directly understood by a processor) exists. The compilation path might include several steps of model transformation, code generation, compilation, and interpretation.

The manifesto for Agile Software Development [5] considers working software the primary measure of progress and favors it to comprehensive documentation. As mentioned earlier, we regard documentation as anything that supports the ongoing understanding and alignment. Working software is for us a type of documentation and actually the most tangible artifact when aiming at overarching stakeholder alignment in agile-driven projects. RIG allows the modeling of automated build processes for continuously delivering working software in form of CI/CD workflows. Thus, RIG models are not only purpose-specific documentations that are meant to be understood by developers and the operators, but in fact *working* software itself.

An essential point of LDE is that one of such PSLs is typically not enough and that several are needed to individually support dedicated development tasks via (graphical) modeling. Of course, this requires a complex integration approach to combine the many individually developed components/functionalities to the overall systems. This integration is supported in a service-oriented fashion [47] via horizontal composition and vertical refinement of different languages [36,48], whose details would go beyond the scope of this paper.

LDE's language integration allows not only to support the system development but helps to align the entire development landscape from first requirements specifications to working software by providing automation via dedicated PSLs. As we will see in *Executable Documentation: Test-First in Action* [30], this holistic approach can be extended to even cover purposes such as teaching of pro-

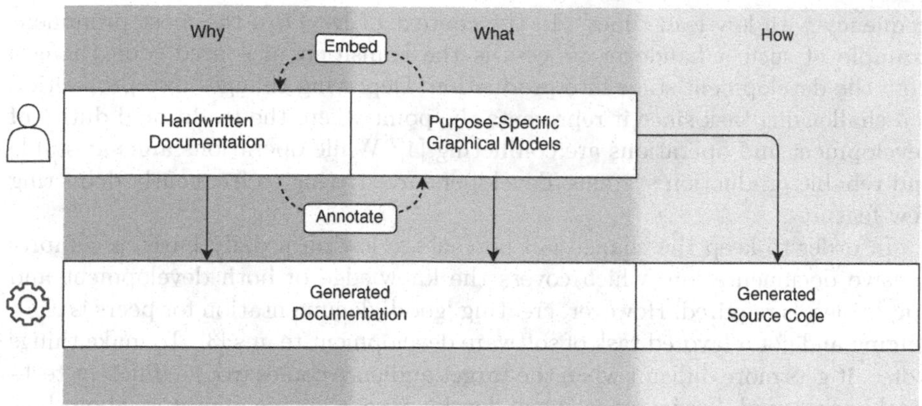

Fig. 6. The documentation approach of LDE

gramming languages. The corresponding discussion shows that LDE does not only work for graphical specifications but applies to textual languages as well. In this paper, we focus on graphical models because they suit our CI/CD example very well. The only thing that matters is that the language is purpose-specific and designed to be understood by the corresponding domain experts [38].

Transitioning from traditional software documentation to the approach of LDE causes a significant shift in the way *why*, *what*, and *how* are covered in the development process (cf. Fig. 6). First and foremost, handwritten documentation is reduced, mainly focussing on aspects like (business) requirements. Models can be embedded in standalone documents to support the understanding of handwritten documentation. Analogously, models can be annotated by important aspects of the handwritten documentation and ideally are then self-documenting. Working software (in form of generated source code) is generated from the models, while both artefacts are used to generate comprehensive documentation (in form of a standalone document).

In this sense, LDE can be considered an elaboration of literate programming and shows that documentation can be profitable and seamlessly integrated into the development life cycle of complex applications. As a result, it does not only reduce code/documentation divergence but sets documentation also emotionally at equal footing with the (creative) development. The next section will illustrate this effect for the DevOps scenario which aims at the alignment of development and operations.

4 The DevOps Perspective

The success of software projects which are driven by the nowadays omnipresent DevOps methodology, depends largely on the link between development and operations. A well-defined handover process between experts in a project team is crucial for a seamless workflow. Especially if teams aim at a high deploy frequency with low lead times[6]. In the context of DevOps, the most prominent example of such a handover process is the transition of source code changes from the development stage into production. Deploying changes into production is a challenging task since it represents the point where the traditional duties of development and operations are conflicting [4]: While operations aims at stable and reliable production systems, developers are striving to frequently delivering new features.

In order to keep the change fail percentage low on a daily basis, a comprehensive documentation, which covers the knowledge of both development and operations, is required. However, creating 'good' documentation for peers is challenging and not a favored task of software development teams [3]. To make things worse, it gets more difficult when the target audience comes from a different technical background. For instance, when developers addressing operators about how to deploy the software they wrote. The fact that software systems are becoming more heterogeneous and are often composed of independent services, puts even more focus on handling the complex build process. In addition to that, understanding the documentation, transferring the included knowledge into manual steps and performing them accordingly, from a recipient point-of-view, is an error-prone and tedious task.

4.1 Continuous Integration and Deployment

In the laste decade, CI/CD has become the de-facto practice to automate the build process [28,29,41] including testing, packaging, and deploying tasks. Numerous publications indicate that it accelerates the deploy frequency of software systems while assisting teams to spot errors before going into production [22,28,46]. Nevertheless, current CI/CD solutions based on data serialization languages do not tap their full potential of documentation. Especially the usage of YAML [6] introduces ambiguities [27] and a cumbersome syntax although often attributed as "human-friendly" [6]. Underpinned by Perdita Stevens' position that even human-readable[7] is not an absolute term but requires qualification on "which humans are the intended readers" [38], we hold the opinion that data serialization languages are not suitable to communicate or document CI/CD workflows. Thus, the current state of CI/CD falls not only short of DevOps' original pledge of a "more global company collaboration" [11], which intends to include non-technical experts, such as the business, but also one of the purposes of programming languages to communicate "descriptions of computational processes" [23].

Approaches like Dagger [10] try to "Escape YAML hell" by using "a powerful configuration language", but they still feature textual languages, which neglect the graphical/visualization aspect of CI/CD workflows. Such workflows are composed of multiple jobs which have dependencies on each other. For example, the

[6] Besides *time to restore* and *change fail percentage*, *lead time* and *deploy frequency* are the key metrics of the DevOps Research and Assessment (DORA) [1] to evaluate DevOps performances.

[7] We use human-friendly and human-readable synonymously here.

deployment job requires the result of the build job. The result of the dependency relationship form a directed acyclic graphs (DAGs) of jobs [41]. A layered drawn DAG (i.e., Sugiyama-style [39]) makes the execution order of the jobs visible to the user, which is not easily exposed from more or less linear text that compels a sequential reading, such as YAML.

4.2 Executable Documentation in Practice

As described in Sect. 3.3, the documentation approach of LDE covers *why*, *what*, and *how* by combining handwritten documentation and executable purpose-specific models through annotation and embedding in order to generate documentation and source code. This section illustrates how we are leveraging LDE in the context of DevOps to document the build process of an exemplary Spring Boot [2] application[8].

Figure 7 shows the envisaged result following the documentation approach of LDE for the above-mentioned project. The generated documentation is serialized as Markdown and stored in a file called `README.md` alongside the applications source-code. Markdown is an "easy-to-read and easy-to-write" [16] markup language for creating simple structured text but can also be straightforwardly converted to HTML, which makes it a popular choice when creating online documentation. Creating Markdown files is ubiquitous on social coding platforms like GitHub or GitLab and essential for presenting open-source projects. Placing a `README.md` file in the project's root folder has become a de-facto standard to automatically render an HTML representation on the project's main page.

The `README.md` file shown in Fig. 7 is a minimal example of a real-world documentation and stripped-down to the necessary basics for illustrating our approach. It contains executable purpose-specific models (cf. CI/CD Workflow Model) and handwritten documentation (cf. Requirements). Since our goal is to leverage the visualization potential of CI/CD, the graphical representation is of particular importance. As a side effect, we can export the executable model and *embed* it as a graphic in classic/traditional textual documentation. Furthermore, parts of the handwritten documentation (e.g., requirements) can be annotated in the concrete model.

The workflow is modeled in Rig, our Cinco product for CI/CD workflows. Models of Cinco products, like the embedded workflow in Fig. 7, are self-contained artefacts. They include all necessary information from which a generator can derive source code [37]. The generator of Rig translates the high-level perspective of the purpose-specific model to the low-level perspective of YAML. The workflow of Fig. 7 is the actual model whose generated code produced the documenting pipeline shown in Fig. 5 during execution.

As already explained, the workflow describes the continuous build and delivery process and proceeds from top to bottom. The most important parts are the four job elements `compile`, `test`, `package`, and `deliver`, at the center of the

[8] The project is open source and publicly available via GitLab: https://gitlab.com/scce/isola2022-pwn-example#1.

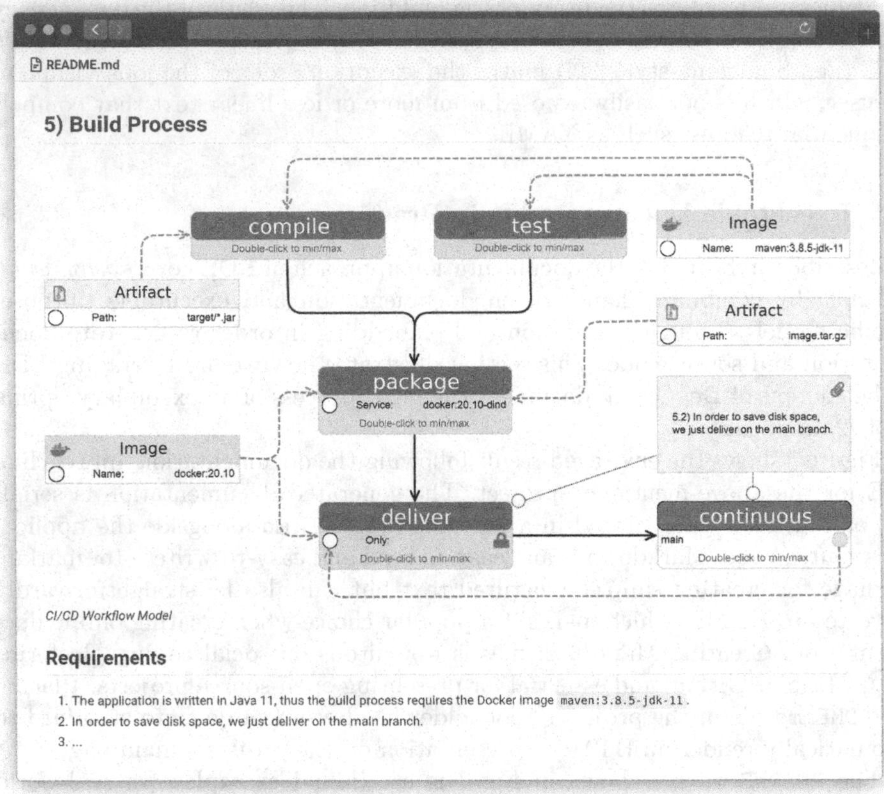

Fig. 7. Generated documentation following the approach of LDE

workflow. Their dependency relationship (⟶) forms a DAG and therefore can be drawn in (horizontal) layers. The jobs `compile` and `package` provide artifacts which are relevant for the subsequent jobs. Artifacts can be independently defined and connected via dashed edges (- - ›) to the relevant jobs. The layered drawing lets the user follow the data flow of the artifacts and eases recognition of jobs that can be executed in parallel.

In order to provide a well-defined runtime environment, CI/CD providers such as GitLab, execute jobs in Docker containers. Both jobs, `compile` and `test`, are using Maven to execute the respective task and thus, are connected to the Docker image definition of `maven:3.8.5-jdk-11` via dashed edges (- - ›). Using the same type of edges, `package` and `deliver` are connected to the Docker image definition of `docker:20.10`.

At the first glance, it might seem confusing, that both `package` and `deliver` are executed in Docker containers and use a Docker image which provides the Docker toolset itself. The purpose of the `package` job is the building of the

Docker image in which the built application is wrapped. The `deliver` job is responsible for pushing the packaged Docker image to a remote Docker registry.

As illustrated in Fig. 6, our approach features the annotation of the purpose-specific models with handwritten documentation. The CI/CD workflow allows such annotation as notes that can be connected via dotted edges (····○). In the example of Fig. 7, the notes feature is used to annotate the deliver job and the continuous target[9] with the requirement of (5.2) 'In order to save disk space, just deliver on the main branch'. This helps stakeholders who might *ask why* [35] certain decisions have been taken in the workflow to answer their question. Although we used natural language in the last paragraphs to describe the CI/CD workflow, we believe the purpose-specific graphical notation of our fully-fledged PSL is superior to textual notations in terms of understanding and alignment between stakeholders.

5 Discussion

The study [13] mentioned in Sect. 2 postulates three major requirements on technology for software documentation which they derive from their survey. We use these requirements as reference for a brief discussion.

"Focus on content and allow the author to easily create and maintain content rich documents"

In contrast to traditional source code, the expressibility and thus accessibility of the presented PSL makes it possible even for stakeholder with little background knowledge to understand the content of the model (or even to modify it). This accessibility bridges the semantic gap between stakeholders of different expertise and allows a collaborative maintenance of the documentation, and furthers a common understanding and alignment between all stakeholders.

"Focus on examples and allow for better integration of examples within a document"

While the presented PSL of Rig can be used to design exemplary workflows, it can even go far beyond that and be used to model the actual workflow in use. The PSL can also be used for quick brainstorming sessions and as a tool to sketch out ideas. By refinement, these sketches can eventually evolve to become the actual model. Since these models can be saved in a serialized (textual) form, the complete history of this evolution stays accessible through the used version control system. In addition to that, the CI/CD workflow model can be exported as graphics and integrated in documents. Eventually, we would like to make it easier to include the output of different static analyses of the model into the documentation. This might include representations of the behavior of the model

[9] Targets is a feature that offers freely configurable parameters used to parameterize jobs, but it is out of scope of this Paper. Please cf. [40–42] for more detailed introduction.

under different scenarios, e.g., how the pipeline instantiated from the workflow would look like when run as result of a change in a merge request. This would in essence mean that examples are generated automatically from the actual model.

"Focus on availability and allow for comprehensive publishing capabilities"
The graphics exported from our models are web-compatible and can be committed to version control systems as well as served via web-servers. Integrating them with Markdown – for instance as `README.md` files – and committing them alongside the source code grants all permitted stakeholders access. We are working on increasing the immediate availability as visual representation by moving towards a web-editor that can be embedded directly into the documentation [48], removing the need for a separate export of the graphical representation.

In summary, the documentation approach of LDE meets all three requirements of this practically oriented study. We are therefore convinced that our approach to executable documentation can change the way documentation is perceived by practitioners.

6 Conclusion

We have presented *executable documentation* as a natural continuation of a long-term trend of documentation/code alignment that started with self-documenting code in the seventies where adequate naming was proposed to make code better readable and that led to a stepwise enhancement of the documentational aspect up to the point where documentation embeds code as, e.g., provided by Jupyter notebooks in the beginning of the new millennium.

Executable documentation goes a step further by turning domain-specific notation and documentation languages typically used for the dialogue between stakeholders of different background in the requirements and the design phase into fully-fledged modeling/programming languages. Examples for such notation are P&ID diagrams as used in engineering [43] or entity relationship/class diagrams as commonly used for domain modeling. The results are so-called Purpose-Specific Languages that are meant to tighten the semantic gap by directly covering the *what* and providing the *how* via automated transformation. The impact of this approach has been illustrated in the DevOps scenario where we turn the graphical notation GitLab provides for documenting CI/CD workflows into an IME called Rig.

At a larger scale, Rig can be seen as part of our LDE approach where it covers the aspect of CI/CD at the modeling level in a fashion that provides a push-button link towards execution for all applications developed in within the LDE ecosystem. This turns (similar to the intent of the code first philosophy) the corresponding running systems into the 'ultimate' documentation where the understanding of all stakeholders should converge.

Considering system development as a discipline for developing executable documentation naturally aligns the (creative) development aspect and the corresponding documentation in a way that has the potential to overcome the typical code/documentation divergence.

Of course, we are not the first with this intention: Thirty years ago, object-oriented programming boosted with the same intent, and the success of the UML also indicates that a better code/documentation alignment is needed. We are convinced, however, that our approach to executable documentation overcomes two of the major obstacles of these approaches that are both due to their high level of abstraction:

- Genericity: As general purpose approach with a tedious syntax, object-oriented programming fails to reach non-technical stakeholders. In contrast, PSLs directly address the application expert.
- Pure Modelling: UML with all its facets never really aimed at executability and therefore, by design, accept a remaining gap that LDE closes with its full code generation philosophy.

Executable documentation as described here is in its beginning and still requires a lot of research to overcome the hurdles:

- PSL development: Turning 'user'-languages into PSLs with corresponding IMEs is a challenging task. Our LDE ecosystems is already quite supportive here but, e.g., the individual code generators require still quite some manual coding.
- Multi PSL development requires adequate language integration. Our LDE ecosystems support a service-oriented form of integration via horizontal composition and vertical refinement. It has to be investigated how far this approach reaches and where it has to be generalized.
- Dedicated analyses and transformations have the power to produce valuable documentation just in time, similar to the information that IDEs provide during development. As discussed in *Executable Documentation: Test-First in Action* [30], exploiting this kind of executability together with adequate visualization may naturally position documentation in the center of modern development processes.

In summary, we are convinced that executable documentation has the potential to change the way documentation is perceived. Even more, we believe that it will support the movement towards a self-documenting, generative programming-style where all artefacts are modelled in PSLs in a fashion that the final product can be generated push button.

Of course, this requires meta-level effort. Some PSLs must take care of the 'organizational' part. A good example for such a meta-level PSL is Rig which takes care of the build process. Within our LDE ecosystem we observed that this leads to a continuous improvement cycle with a new level of reuse: the reuse factor of a generator is typically much higher than that of a generic object which requires but also leads to better stability. We believe that this development will drastically reduce handwritten documentation in natural language whose role more and more focus on *why* a certain system has to be built in a particular fashion.

References

1. Explore DORA's research program, https://www.devops-research.com/research.html. Accessed 8 Oct 2020
2. Spring boot. https://spring.io/projects/spring-boot. Accessed 24 Jul 2022
3. Aghajani, E.: Software documentation: automation and challenges. Ph.D. thesis, Università della Svizzera italiana (2020)
4. Allspaw, J., Hammond, P.: 10+ deploys per day: Dev and ops cooperation at Flickr. In: Velocity: Web Performance and Operations Conference, June 2009. https://www.youtube.com/watch?v=LdOe18KhtT4
5. Beck, K., et al.: Manifesto for Agile Software Development. https://agilemanifesto.org (2001). Accessed 4 Mar 2014
6. Ben-Kiki, O., Evans, C., döt Net, I.: YAML Ain't Markup Language (YAML^{TM}) Version 1.2. https://yaml.org/spec/1.2/spec.html (2009). Accessed 22 Jun 2021
7. Boßelmann, S., et al.: DIME: a programming-less modeling environment for web applications. In: Margaria, T., Steffen, B. (eds.) ISoLA 2016. LNCS, vol. 9953, pp. 809–832. Springer, Cham (2016). https://doi.org/10.1007/978-3-319-47169-3_60
8. Broy, M.: Object-oriented programming and software development–a critical assessment. In: In: McIver, A., Morgan, C. (eds.) Programming Methodology. Monographs in Computer Science, pp. 211–221. Springer, New York (2003). https://doi.org/10.1007/978-0-387-21798-7_10
9. Chatley, R., Donaldson, A., Mycroft, A.: The next 7000 programming languages. In: Steffen, B., Woeginger, G. (eds.) Computing and Software Science. LNCS, vol. 10000, pp. 250–282. Springer, Cham (2019). https://doi.org/10.1007/978-3-319-91908-9_15
10. Dagger: A portable devkit for ci/cd pipelines. https://dagger.io/. Accessed 27 July 2022
11. Debois, P., et al.: DEVOPS: a software revolution in the making. J. Inf. Technol. Manag. **24**(8), 3–39 (2011)
12. Dobing, B., Parsons, J.: Dimensions of UML diagram use: a survey of practitioners. J. Database Manage. (JDM) **19**(1), 1–18 (2008)
13. Forward, A., Lethbridge, T.C.: The relevance of software documentation, tools and technologies: a survey. In: Proceedings of the 2002 ACM Symposium on Document Engineering, pp. 26–33. DocEng 2002, Association for Computing Machinery, New York, NY, USA (2002). https://doi.org/10.1145/585058.585065
14. Fowler, M.: Domain-specific languages guide. https://martinfowler.com/dsl.html. Accessed 06 Sept 2016
15. Goldap, P., et al.: PG 601 - Bridging the Gap. Technical report, TU Dortmund (2017)
16. Gruber, J.: Markdown: Syntax. https://daringfireball.net/projects/markdown/syntax
17. Hoare, C.A.: Hints on programming language design. Stanford Univ ca Dept of Computer Science, Technical report (1973)
18. Hurvitz, D.: Quotes via dan hurvitz. https://softwarequotes.com/author/via-dan-hurvitz. Accessed 20 July 2022
19. Kelly, S., Tolvanen, J.P.: Domain-Specific Modeling: Enabling Full Code Generation. Wiley-IEEE Computer Society Press, Hoboken (2008). https://doi.org/10.1002/9780470249260

20. Kluyver, T., et al.: Jupyter notebooks–a publishing format for reproducible computational workflows. In: Loizides, F., Scmidt, B. (eds.) Positioning and Power in Academic Publishing: Players, Agents and Agendas, pp. 87–90. IOS Press (2016). https://doi.org/10.3233/978-1-61499-649-1-87, https://eprints.soton.ac.uk/403913/
21. Knuth, D.E.: Literate programming. Comput. J. **27**(2), 97–111 (1984)
22. Labouardy, M.: Pipeline as code: continuous delivery with Jenkins, Kubernetes, and terraform. Manning (2021). https://books.google.de/books?id=Lt9EEAAAQBAJ
23. Madsen, O.L., Møller-Pedersen, B.: Using supplementary properties to reduce the need for documentation. In: Margaria, T., Steffen, B. (eds.) ISoLA 2022. LNCS, vol. 13702, pp. 35–59. Springer (2022)
24. Mellor, S.J., Balcer, M.J.: Executable UML: A Foundation for Model-Driven Architecture. Addison-Wesley Professional (2002)
25. Naujokat, S., Lybecait, M., Kopetzki, D., Steffen, B.: CINCO: a simplicity-driven approach to full generation of domain-specific graphical modeling tools. Software Tools for Technology Transfer **20**(3), 327–354 (2017). https://doi.org/10.1007/s10009-017-0453-6
26. Object Management Group (OMG): Documents associated with Object Constraint Language (OCL), Version 2.4 (2017). https://www.omg.org/spec/UML/2.5.1/. Accessed 08 Feb 209
27. O'Connor, C.: The norway problem - why StrictYAML refuses to do implicit typing and so should you. https://hitchdev.com/strictyaml/why/implicit-typing-removed/. Accessed 3 Sept 2021
28. Rangnau, T., Buijtenen, R.v., Fransen, F., Turkmen, F.: Continuous security testing: a case study on integrating dynamic security testing tools in ci/cd pipelines. In: 2020 IEEE 24th International Enterprise Distributed Object Computing Conference (EDOC), pp. 145–154 (2020). https://doi.org/10.1109/EDOC49727.2020.00026
29. Shahin, M., Babar, M.A., Zhu, L.: Continuous integration, delivery and deployment: a systematic review on approaches, tools, challenges and practices. IEEE Access **5**, 3909–3943 (2017). https://doi.org/10.1109/ACCESS.2017.2685629
30. Smyth, S., et al.: Executable documentation: test-first in action. In: Margaria, T., Steffen, B. (eds.) ISoLA 2022. LNCS, vol. 13702, pp. 135–156. Springer (2022)
31. de St. Germain, H.J.: Commenting (jim's cs topics). https://www.cs.utah.edu/~germain/PPS/Topics/commenting.html (2003), https://www.cs.utah.edu/~germain/PPS/Topics/commenting.html. Accessed 22 Jul 2022
32. Stallings, A.E.: After a Greek proverb. Poetry **199**(4), 299–299 (2012)
33. Steffen, B.: Inter- & intradepartmental knowledge management barriers when offering single unit solutions (2016). https://essay.utwente.nl/70224/
34. Steffen, B., Howar, F., Tegeler, T., Steffen, B.: Agile business engineering: from transformation towards continuousinnovation. In: Margaria, T., Steffen, B. (eds.) ISoLA 2021. LNCS, vol. 13036, pp. 77–94. Springer, Cham (2021). https://doi.org/10.1007/978-3-030-89159-6_6
35. Steffen, B., Steffen, B.: Asking why. In: Margaria, T., Steffen, B. (eds.) Leveraging Applications of Formal Methods, Verification and Validation, pp. 55–67. Springer International Publishing, Cham (2021)
36. Steffen, B., Gossen, F., Naujokat, S., Margaria, T.: Language-driven engineering: from general-purpose to purpose-specific languages. In: Steffen, B., Woeginger, G. (eds.) Computing and Software Science. LNCS, vol. 10000, pp. 311–344. Springer, Cham (2019). https://doi.org/10.1007/978-3-319-91908-9_17

37. Steffen, B., Narayan, P.: Full life-cycle support for end-to-end processes. IEEE Comput. **40**(11), 64–73 (2007). https://doi.org/10.1109/MC.2007.386
38. Stevens, P.: Models as documents, documents as models. In: Margaria, T., Steffen, B. (eds.) ISoLA 2022. LNCS, vol. 13702, pp. 28–34. Springer (2022)
39. Sugiyama, K., Tagawa, S., Toda, M.: Methods for visual understanding of hierarchical system structures. IEEE Trans. Syst. Man Cybern. **11**(2), 109–125 (1981)
40. Tegeler, T., Gossen, F., Steffen, B.: A model-driven approach to continuous practices for modern cloud-based web applications. In: 2019 9th International Conference on Cloud Computing, Data Science Engineering (Confluence), pp. 1–6 (2019). https://doi.org/10.1109/CONFLUENCE.2019.8776962
41. Tegeler, T., Teumert, S., Schürmann, J., Bainczyk, A., Busch, D., Steffen, B.: An Introduction to graphical modeling of CI/CD Workflows with rig. In: Margaria, T., Steffen, B. (eds.) ISoLA 2021. LNCS, vol. 13036, pp. 3–17. Springer, Cham (2021). https://doi.org/10.1007/978-3-030-89159-6_1
42. Teumert, S.: Rig — low-code ci/cd modeling. https://scce.gitlab.io/rig/. Accessed 07 Jan 2022
43. Toghraei, M.: Piping and Instrumentation Diagram Development. Wiley (2019). https://books.google.de/books?id=ICONDwAAQBAJ
44. Wortmann, N.: Modellbasierte Modellierung von industriellen Zentrifugen mit Codegenerierung für Steuerungssysteme. Bachelor thesis, Münster University of Applied Sciences (2015)
45. Wortmann, N., Michel, M., Naujokat, S.: A fully model-based approach to software development for industrial centrifuges. In: Margaria, T., Steffen, B. (eds.) ISoLA 2016. LNCS, vol. 9953, pp. 774–783. Springer, Cham (2016). https://doi.org/10.1007/978-3-319-47169-3_58
46. Zampetti, F., Geremia, S., Bavota, G., Di Penta, M.: Ci/cd pipelines evolution and restructuring: a qualitative and quantitative study. In: 2021 IEEE International Conference on Software Maintenance and Evolution (ICSME),. pp. 471–482 (2021). https://doi.org/10.1109/ICSME52107.2021.00048
47. Zweihoff, P.: Aligned and collaborative language-driven engineering. Dissertation, TU Dortmund, Dortmund, Germany (2022). https://doi.org/10.17877/DE290R-22594, https://eldorado.tu-dortmund.de/handle/2003/40736
48. Zweihoff, P., Tegeler, T., Schürmann, J., Bainczyk, A., Steffen, B.: Aligned, purpose-driven cooperation: the future way of system development. In: Margaria, T., Steffen, B. (eds.) ISoLA 2021. LNCS, vol. 13036, pp. 426–449. Springer, Cham (2021). https://doi.org/10.1007/978-3-030-89159-6_27

Automated Software Re-engineering

Automating Software Re-engineering: Introduction to the ISoLA 2022 Track

Serge Demeyer[1(✉)], Reiner Hähnle[2], and Heiko Mantel[2]

[1] University of Antwerp, Antwerp, Belgium
serge.demeyer@uantwerpen.be

[2] Technical University Darmstadt, Darmstadt, Germany
{reiner.haehnle,heiko.mantel}@tu-darmstadt.de

Abstract. Software Engineering is often viewed as the discipline of developing new software systems from scratch. In practice, however, it is much more common that software development starts from a system to be modified or substituted. Software re-engineering is a difficult, error-prone, and expensive task. Therefore, automating software re-engineering emerges as an attractive opportunity. Formal methods can help in automating software re-engineering, but, current formal approaches to software development and analysis tend to look at software as a static object and to focus on green-field scenarios. In this track we look at formal approaches that take the re-engineering aspect into account.

Keywords: Software re-engineering · Formal methods · Automated software engineering

1 Introduction

Software Engineering is often viewed as the discipline of developing new software systems from scratch, both, in education and in research. In practice, however, it is much more common that the development of software-based systems starts from a system that shall be modified or substituted [10]. In either case, the new system shall constitute an obvious improvement over the old system. This is why software re-engineering requires, both, an in-depth understanding of the legacy system and a trustworthy quality assurance for the new system.

There are manifold technological drivers for requiring a better support for software-reengineering, including:

- The advent of innovative execution platforms, such as massively parallel execution, new memory architectures, and re-configurable hardware, whose benefits should be optimally exploited by software;

Partially funded by the Hessian LOEWE initiative within the "Software-Factory 4.0" project.

T. Margaria and B. Steffen (Eds.): ISoLA 2022, LNCS 13702, pp. 195–200, 2022.
https://doi.org/10.1007/978-3-031-19756-7_11

- emerging norms and regulations demanding software to be re-engineered such that it complies with stricter legislation, new quality requirements, or higher ethical standards; the role of software in science ("in silico" now surpasses the traditional "in vitro"/"in vivo" research methodologies) and the challenge of maintaining such research software; and
- novel application scenarios for existing software (for example, blockchain, micro-services, internet-of-things (IoT), fueled by the digitalization of everything, and a desire to re-use time-tested technology.

Software re-engineering is a difficult, error-prone, and expensive task. Therefore, automating software re-engineering emerges as an attractive opportunity. Formal methods can help in automating software re-engineering by providing the means to define precise models (for example, of software systems, software attributes, and requirements) and rigorous verification techniques. However, to date, formal approaches to software development and analysis still tend to look at software as a static object and to focus on green-field scenarios, where software is developed from scratch [7]. That is, the use of formal methods in software re-engineering has tremendous potential, but formal methods for software re-engineering is still in its infancy as a research field.

2 The Track

Automation of software re-engineering helped by formal methods had been our original motivation for initiating ASRE as a special track on automating software re-engineering at ISOLA two years ago [4], and it is our motivation for continuing this special track in 2022. The track shall facilitate exchange in a vibrant environment. We invited leading scientists and practitioners with an active interest in software re-engineering. We also broadcasted an open invitation on several channels with the intent of reaching out to a wider audience.

We solicited research, survey, experience, and tool papers. We did not merely look for novel scientific results, but also encouraged contributions shedding new light on previously published results, because we intend the ASRE track as an opportunity to take stock and discuss future directions.

3 The Papers

In total we received eight submissions. Each of them was reviewed by at least two (most by three) experts in the field. We encouraged the reviewers to write constructive reviews, and we explicitly aimed for an inclusive approach with non-competitive reviewing. Most submissions had very high quality and all of them were suitable to be included in the proceedings, which reflects the fact that most submissions were co-authored by high-profile, senior researchers. We accepted the submissions that are summarized in Table 1.

The eight accepted submissions were classified into three thematic sessions. Below, we provide a short summary of each of these papers. We refer the interested reader to the actual papers in this volume for in-depth information.

Table 1. Summary and thematic classification of submissions to ASRE 2022 track

Authors	Title	Theme
Abusdal, Kamburjan, Ka I Pun, Stolz	A notion of equivalence for refactorings with abstract execution	Verification and testing
Beringer	Verified software units for simple DFA modules and objects in C	Models and meta-models
Bubel, Hähnle, Ulbrich, Beckert	Towards a usable and sustainable deductive verification tool	Verification and testing
Demeyer, Verheijke, Rocha	Refactoring Solidity Smart Contracts to Protect Against Reentrancy Exploits	Security and privacy
Eldh	On technical debt in software testing: observations from industry	Verification and testing
Hendriks, Aslam	A systematic approach for interfacing component-based software with an active automata learning tool	Models and meta-models
Hilbrich, Müller, Kulagina, Lazik, De Mecquenem, Grunske	A consolidated view on specification languages for data analysis workflows	Models and meta-models
Lanzinger, Ulbrich, Weigl	A refactoring for data minimisation using formal verification	Security and privacy

3.1 Models and Meta-models

In the article "A Consolidated View on Specification Languages for Data Analysis Workflows" [9], five authors from the Humboldt Universität zu Berlin propose a meta model for the definition of data analysis workflows. Their objective is to unify the currently heterogeneous landscape of domain-specific languages employed for specifying data-analysis workflows. Tasks, interconnections, and data sources/sinks are the three abstract classes of the meta model, which are further refined into multiple subtypes. The meta model also supports a modular specification of workflows, where data analysis workflows are connected through interconnections with each other.

The article "A Systematic Approach for Interfacing Component-Based Software with an Active Automata Learning Tool" [8] by two authors from ESI (TNO) in Eindhoven/Radboud University in Nijmegen and from Vrije Universiteit Amsterdam presents a solution for interfacing component-based software with active automata learning tools. The overall objective is to learn the behavior of individual software components using existing active learning tools to obtain Mealy machines modeling the behavior. To achieve compatibility with existing active automata learning tools, a software component is wrapped by a server node, a client node and three dispatcher nodes, resulting in an SUL (system under learning). The interface supports a wide spectrum of communication patterns.

In the article "Verified Software Units for Simple DFA Modules and Objects in C" [3], the author from Princeton University clarifies how the creation of verified software units is influenced by the coding style in C implementations. The article focuses on the C language and on implementations of deterministic automata, and it investigates three coding styles differing in the flexibility that they provide. For each coding style, a sample implementation, a model-level specification, and a lifting of the implementation to the model level are defined, and the correctness of the implementation is verified against the model, using Coq for precise specifications and for mechanizing formal proofs.

3.2 Verification and Testing

In the article "Towards a Usable and Sustainable Deductive Verification Tool" [2], five researchers affiliated with the universities of Darmstadt and Karlsruhe present a vision on how to transform an academic tool prototype used by a small circle of dedicated researchers into a tool that may be adopted by a larger audience. In the context of their own tool (KeY) they propose a suite of actions to make a concrete state-of-art deductive verification tool so usable and robust that it can successfully be applied by computer science researchers outside the tool's development team.

The article "Towards Practical Abstract Execution" [1], by authors from universities in Bergen and Oslo, looks at the correctness of refactoring by program transformation as a relational verification problem. Recently, the technique of Abstract Execution, that permits to symbolically execute and compare schematic programs, was successfully used to establish correctness of refactoring rules and to identify missing assumptions needed for correctness. This ASRE paper explores the issues that are encountered and the problems that need to be solved when programs that create and manipulate object types are refactored. For example, the choice of an appropriate notion of equality and the sensitivity of the final result to the sequence of operations on objects create subtle issues that need to be understood and considered.

In the article "On Technical Debt in Software Testing: Observations from Industry" [6], a senior researcher affiliated with a large company (Ericsson, Sweden) and two universities (Mälardalen University, Sweden & Carleton University, Ottawa, Canada) presents a series of observations on how automated software testing is applied in industry. The main perspective of the paper is that the increasing emphasis on automated tests creates an awful lot of test cases encoded in a plethora of scripting languages. As such, these automated tests accumulate technical debt and the author points out some root causes for this phenomenon as well as potential remedies.

3.3 Security and Privacy

The authors from KIT Karlsruhe of the article "A Refactoring for Data Minimisation Using Formal Verification" [11] present an approach to data minimisation that works by static analysis of the data processing program and subsequently applying various minimisation criteria to the resulting abstraction. Their central idea is to refactor a given data processing program into a data abstraction stage and a separate data reconstruction stage. The first stage computes a sufficiently precise set of predicates, tailored to the program at hand, that are transmitted in lieu of the actual user data. The second stage permits reconstruction of data points that are guaranteed to yield the same result as if the program were executed with the original (secret) ones provided by the user.

The article "Formally Verifying Solidity Smart Contracts Against Reentrancy Exploits" [5], by researchers from University of Antwerp, looks at smart contracts, pieces of code that execute transactions on block chains. Such transactions are often vulnerable to reentrancy exploits, where a procedure, for example, moving money to an attacker's account, is inadvertently executed more than once. Reentrancy exploits have been and are actively used, therefore, it is of great practical relevance to detect such exploits and to harden the code against them. The ASRE paper first assembles a large test corpus of smart contracts and shows that many of them lack the usage of idioms that can prevent reentrancy exploits. The authors then suggest a number of design patterns that have the potential to remedy the situation and they argue the need for formal verification of smart contracts.

References

1. Abusdal, O.J., Kamburjan, E., Ka I Pun, V., Stolz, V.: A notion of equivalence for refactorings with abstract execution. In: Margaria, T., Steffen, B. (eds.) ISoLA 2022, LNCS, vol. 13702, pp. 259–280. Springer, Cham (2022)
2. Beckert, B., Bubel, R., Hähnle, R., Ulbrich, M.: Towards a usable and sustainable deductive verification tool. In: Margaria, T., Steffen, B. (eds.) ISoLA 2022, LNCS, vol. 13702, pp. 281–300. Springer, Cham (2022)
3. Beringer, L.: Verified software units for simple DFA modules and objects in C. In: Margaria, T., Steffen, B. (eds.) ISoLA 2022, LNCS, vol. 13702, pp. 237–258. Springer, Cham (2022)
4. Demeyer, S., Hähnle, R., Mantel, H.: Automating software re-engineering. In: Margaria, T., Steffen, B. (eds.) ISoLA 2020. LNCS, vol. 12477, pp. 3–8. Springer, Cham (2020). https://doi.org/10.1007/978-3-030-61470-6_1

5. Demeyer, S., Rocha, H., Verhheijke, D.: Refactoring solidity smart contracts to protect against reentrancy exploits. In: Margaria, T., Steffen, B. (eds.) ISoLA 2022, LNCS, vol. 13702, pp. 324–344. Springer, Cham (2022)
6. Eldh, S.: On technical debt in software testing: Observations from industry. In: Margaria, T., Steffen, B. (eds.) ISoLA 2022, LNCS, vol. 13702, pp. 301–323. Springer, Cham (2022)
7. Hähnle, R., Huisman, M.: Deductive software verification: from pen-and-paper proofs to industrial tools. In: Steffen, B., Woeginger, G. (eds.) Computing and Software Science. LNCS, vol. 10000, pp. 345–373. Springer, Cham (2019). https://doi.org/10.1007/978-3-319-91908-9_18
8. Hendricks, D., Aslam, K.: A systematic approach for interfacing component-based software with an active automata learning tool. In: Margaria, T., Steffen, B. (eds.) ISoLA 2022, LNCS, vol. 13702, pp. 216–236. Springer, Cham (2022)
9. Hilbrich, M., Müller, S., Kulagina, S., Lazik, C., De Mecquenem, N., Grunske, L.: A consolidated view on specification languages for data analysis workflows. In: Margaria, T., Steffen, B. (eds.) ISoLA 2022, LNCS, vol. 13702, pp. 201–215. Springer, Cham (2022)
10. Hopkins, R., Jenkins, K.: Eating the IT Elephant: Moving from Greenfield Development to Brownfield. IBM Press, Indianapolis (2011)
11. Lanzinger, F., Ulbrich, M., Weigl, A.: A refactoring for data minimisation using formal verification. In: Margaria, T., Steffen, B. (eds.) ISoLA 2022, LNCS, vol. 13702, pp. 345–364. Springer, Cham (2022)

A Consolidated View on Specification Languages for Data Analysis Workflows

Marcus Hilbrich, Sebastian Müller, Svetlana Kulagina, Christopher Lazik(✉), Ninon De Mecquenem, and Lars Grunske

Humboldt-Universität zu Berlin, Berlin, Germany
{hilbricm,muelerse,lazikchr,grunske}@informatik.hu-berlin.de

Abstract. Data analysis workflows (DAWs) are widely used in the scientific world. However, different communities created a plethora of domain-specific languages (DSLs) to specify their DAWs. Consequently, across DSLs, it is hard to perform operations on DAWs such as share, port, compare, re-use, adapt, or even merge. Thus, we have analyzed DAW specification languages and created a unified DAW metamodel. Given an instance of a DAW specification that can be matched to our metamodel, we are now able to apply CRUD operations (create, read, update, delete), and can potentially translate between different DAW specification languages.

1 Introduction

Data Analysis Workflows (DAWs), introduced in [1], are complex research software components employed in essentially all scientific disciplines to drive scientific progress.

Since there is no single widely-accepted notion of data analysis workflows, each community defines DAWs in a way that fits their particular line of research, domain, community guidelines, and problem space. This multitude of interpretations spawned a plethora of domain-specific languages or DSLs [2,3] for short, corresponding to the respective views on workflows.

Often, a DSL is part of a workflow execution system, accompanied by an execution engine. One prominent example is Apache Airflow [4]: a platform to create, run and monitor workflows. Nextflow [5] is another popular DSL in the field of bio-informatics and genomics that includes an execution engine that works with Kubernetes[1] Other examples include Argo [6], StackStorm [7], Apache Flink [8], Fireworks [9], and Prefect [10].

There are also DSLs that were developed purely for the high-level description of workflows. Examples are SnakeMake [11], Luigi [12], and BPMN [13]. BPMN is an example of a pure DSL: BPMN does not come with its own workflow execution engine. However, independent workflow execution engines for BPMN such as Camunda BPM [14], Orchestra [15], and Activiti [16] exist.

[1] https://kubernetes.io/.

T. Margaria and B. Steffen (Eds.): ISoLA 2022, LNCS 13702, pp. 201–215, 2022.
https://doi.org/10.1007/978-3-031-19756-7_12

The sheer number and diversity of different DSLs makes it impossible to apply typical DSL-independent create, read, update, and delete (CRUD) operations and translate between DSLs. CRUD operations on DAW specification languages are fundamental to achieve a solution that corresponds to state-of-the-art software engineering practices. Additionally, unified access also facilitates the maintenance of DAW-systems. The ability to translate between DSL, allows to port DAWs between different execution environments and hardware systems.

In this paper, we present a consolidated view of DAW specification languages and a corresponding language model defined as a metamodel [17]. Given an instance of a DAW specification that can be matched to our metamodel, we are now able to apply CRUD operations, as well as translate between different DAW specification languages. The idea of a common metamodel conforms to the general idea behind the common workflow language (CWL) [18], which is a first attempt towards unifying different workflow languages from the business domain, and which also has gained some traction in the scientific computing community [19]. However, the above described diversity in the different research domains requires an additional effort to unify the concepts of DAW specification languages.

To archive this goal, we created our consolidated view through the analysis of multiple different DSLs. We compared their similarities and identified their differences. Using this knowledge, we then derived a metamodel that enables the rendering of each specific DSL-instance as a unified instance of our metamodel.

The aim of this paper is to present and discuss our consolidated view, the resulting language model, the corresponding metamodel and the process of their creation. First, we describe our language model and its corresponding components in Sect. 2. Afterwards, we present our resulting metamodel in Sect. 3. Then, we provide a mapping of an exemplary DSL to our metamodel to validate our approach in Sect. 4. Lastly, we provide a discussion and draw a conclusion in Sect. 5.

2 The Components of Data Analysis Workflows and Their Relations

A DAW is focused on (i) providing solutions for a class of problems, as well as (ii) data processing. If a specific problem class is solved once by a DAW, we can reuse this exact DAW on different data in order to solve differing concrete problem instances. To get an intuition of this concept, consider the following simple example problem:

> How do you calculate the average from a stream of values?

A DAW solving this example problem can easily be used on different data streams. Therefore, different data sources or measurement equipment can be employed. This means, that even though we have different input data, the structure of the DAW never changes. The DAW stays applicable independent of the different types of data sources or sinks. For simplicity, we call any instance of either object *storage*.

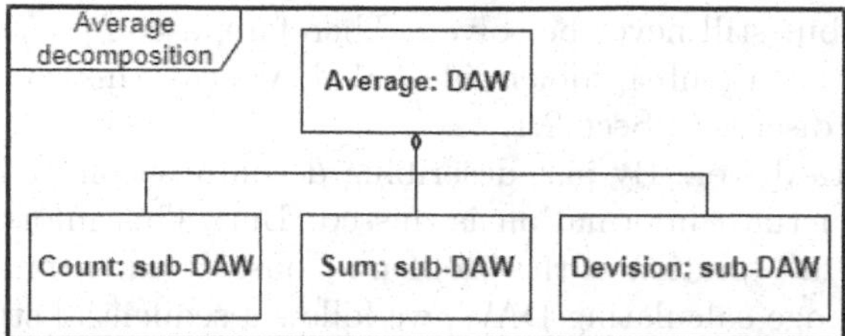

(a) Decomposition of the DAW to calculate the average to sub-DAWs. Note that only the hierarchy is explicitly modeled here.

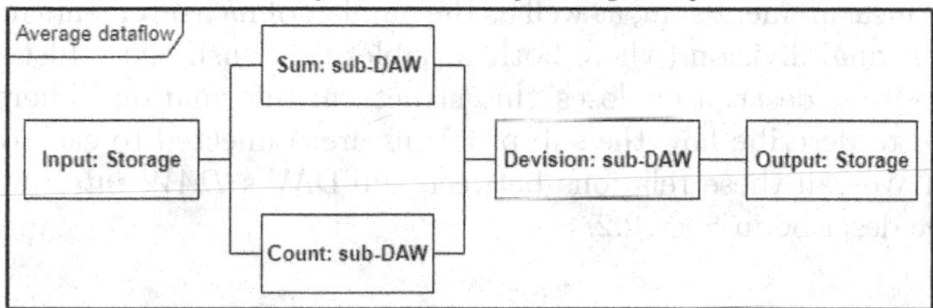

(b) Decomposing the DAW with a focus on the data. Here, the complete DAW is represented through the complete diagram, instead of the top component. Note, that the relationship between the data-source and data-sink is explicitly modeled. The used sub-DAWs are denoted by the internal components.

Fig. 1. Visualization of different strategies of decomposition of DAWs as UML2 object diagrams.

Thus, the DAW concept is distinct to other abstraction concepts in computer science, such as components in *component based systems* which are based on interfaces. Even if data transfer between different components is explicitly made possible, the focus here lies on composition as described by Szyperski et al. [20]. DAWs provide a unique way to divide a problem into sub-problems. It is the realization of the "divide & conquer" or "isolation" concept, well known in software engineering.

An essential aspect of DAWs is the solution strategy employed to solve the underlying problem: The problem is divided into smaller and thus easier to solve sub-problems. Going back to the running example from above: The average is calculated by (i) summing up the values of the measurements, (ii) counting the number of measurements taken, and (iii) dividing the sum by the number of all measurements taken. Thus, the DAW from above can be decomposed into three new sub-problems (see Fig. 1). Any such sub-problem can in turn be solved by another DAW. However, two problems remain:

1. We describe a recursion without a base case: Any DAW may use sub-DAWs to solve sub-problems (i.e. the decomposition of the original problem). Since a sub-DAW is itself a DAW, this means that any sub-DAW can also use sub-sub-DAWs, and so on. The problem could theoretically be decomposed

ad infinitum, but still never be solved. Therefore, a component in the DAW language to solve a (sub-)problem is needed. We call this component a *task*, which we will discuss in Sect. 2.1.

2. A DAW is data driven: By just describing decomposition, it is possible that important structural information is missed. But: This information may be crucial to the *full* solution of the problem. Consider our running example: In our initial average calculating DAW, we follow a sequential structure. There, one step immediately follows another. We could also say, however, that this problem can be parallelized: In calculating the average, one could calculate both the measurement sum, as well as the number of measurements in parallel, before the final division (where both variables are consumed). Just using the decomposition description loses this structural information. Therefore, we also need to describe how the sub-problems are connected to each other (see Fig. 1b). We call these relations between sub-DAWs *DAW interconnections*, which we describe in Sect. 2.2.

2.1 Task

While a DAW decomposes a problem into sub-problems, the task is one of potentially many solutions to a sub-problem. On the abstract level, a DAW is indifferent to the use of either sub-DAWs or tasks. However, if any given DAW is to be executed, tasks solving each sub-problem are needed. This is also true for any use of sub-DAWs: When a top-level DAW is further decomposed using sub-DAWs, any used sub-DAW must be executable as well. Thus, a DAW is more abstract than a task. In literature, the use of the term *task* seems to be rather inconsistent. Therefore, we try to provide a clear differentiation to other interpretations:

1. Sometimes tasks may be defined which describe only abstract problems without giving any solution (or even solution idea). In our DAW language, we prohibit such usage of the term *task*: A problem without a solution is a (sub-)DAW.
2. The absolute minimum to qualify as a task is a solution strategy. This could be pseudocode, a mathematical formula, a sketch of an algorithm, or a textual description.
3. Activity, stage, program, or operator are all used synonymously in the literature for the same concept. In our language, we decided to only use the single term *task* to avoid confusion and false intuitions.

A DAW may be directly replaced by a task in case a solution is implemented. This means an entire DAW could also be solved by just a single, monolithic task. Thus, we do not lose expressiveness. Additionally, we avoid having multiple objects that represent the same concept.

2.2 Interconnection

As shown in Fig. 1b only decomposing a DAW into sub-DAWs and tasks can lead to a loss of behavioral information. Therefore, in our language, a DAW consists of interconnections connecting tasks together.

Modeling interconnections as objects instead of just using relations between objects may appear to be counter-intuitive. We explicitly decided to model the interconnections in this way, as we see the following advantages:

1. The data transfer is highlighted.
2. We can discuss different kinds of data transfer.
3. The language becomes more elegant and expressive: Instead of having to model a potentially infinite enumeration of different interconnection subtypes, we are able to employ a single language element.

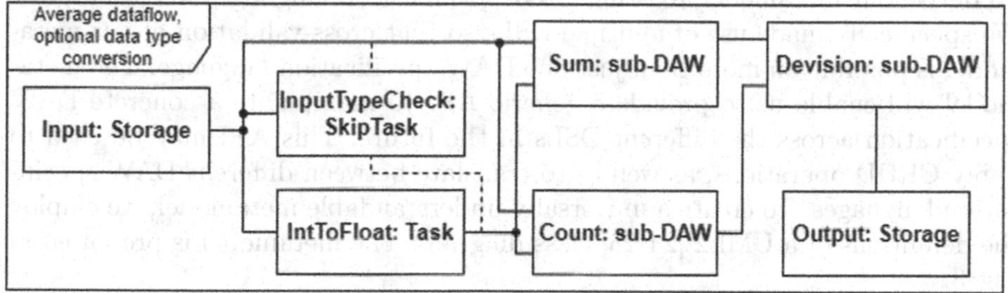

Fig. 2. A SkipTask (InterconnectionManipulation) and an additional IntToFloat Task are added to Fig. 1b. The SkipTask checks the type of the input data and manipulates (enables or removes) the interconnections accordingly. In this notation, we use the dashed lines to indicate this interconnection manipulation.

While we focused on the data transfer here, it is important to point out that such an interconnection can exist without data transfer. For example, the interconnections can also be used to indicate control-flow connections between tasks.

It is possible to provide solutions for sub-problems by just *manipulating interconnections*. The interconnection manipulation is a subclass of task. Its main job is to keep the structure of the DAW flexible. Consider again our running example of calculating the average from above: Let us assume executables exist for all three tasks in Fig. 1. Let us further assume that these executables only support some type of floating point series (i.e. list, array, or similar). If we cannot be sure, that our data source only provides floating point numbers, we should check the input data and convert integers to floats. To do this, however, we must change the interconnections: The data must be transferred to the correct task for data transformation, before the data can then be fed into the summation and counting tasks (see Fig. 2).[2]

[2] This is only a very basic example meant to provide an intuition. Using tasks that inherently support different kinds of input data is just one other possible solution. Additionally, the output data type must also be considered in a real world example.

Note how capable the manipulation of the interconnections is: Skipping one task with the interconnections can fully remove that task from the data-flow, reordering and adding more tasks through full interconnection manipulation may even allow for solving entirely different or more complex problems with the DAW.

3 A Metamodel of Data Analysis Workflow Languages

As noted in Sect. 1, a plethora of DSLs for the specification of DAWs exists. As a result, reusing and porting DAWs requires a considerable human effort to formulate the DAW in a different scientific workflow DSL [21]. In order to avoid having to develop these reused DAWs from scratch, we employ a metamodel and its associated benefits in automating typical software engineering tasks [22,23]. To derive our metamodel, existing DAW specification languages were analyzed. We specifically made use of multiple DSLs so that cross-validation of our metamodel is possible on more than just one DAW specification language. The metamodel will enable us to provide a generic API to manipulate a concrete DAW specification across the different DSLs in the future. This API may be used to apply CRUD operations, as well as to translate between different DAW specification languages. To create a universally understandable metamodel, we employ the definitions of a UML2 [24,25] class diagram. The metamodel is presented in Fig. 3.

We model DAWs as a package. While sub-DAWs are not explicitly modeled, we allow DAWs to be connected with other DAWs through *Interconnections*. Our metamodel contains the three elements *Tasks*, *Interconnections*, and *Storage* as identified and discussed in Sect. 2 as abstract classes. Note that in our metamodel, all *Task*s, *Interconnection*s, and *Storage*s have sub-types, as we modeled these main concepts as abstract classes. We identified these specializations through analyzing implementations of DAWs in different DSLs. We do not claim to have a complete set of all possible specializations, and explicitly allow for future extension of our model in this regard. In any given executable DAW multiple sub-types, for each of the main DAW concepts may be employed simultaneously. We will now present the sub-types of the three main concepts we identified.

Sub-types of Tasks. In our language, we use the term *Task* for a solution or generic solution idea. On the conceptual level, we do not need to distinguish between different sub-types of tasks. However, as soon as we intend to model concrete instances describing real-world DAWs, sub-types of tasks become necessary. We define these sub-types as executables, inline description and monitoring. With an *Executable*, we refer to a (deployable) computer program which

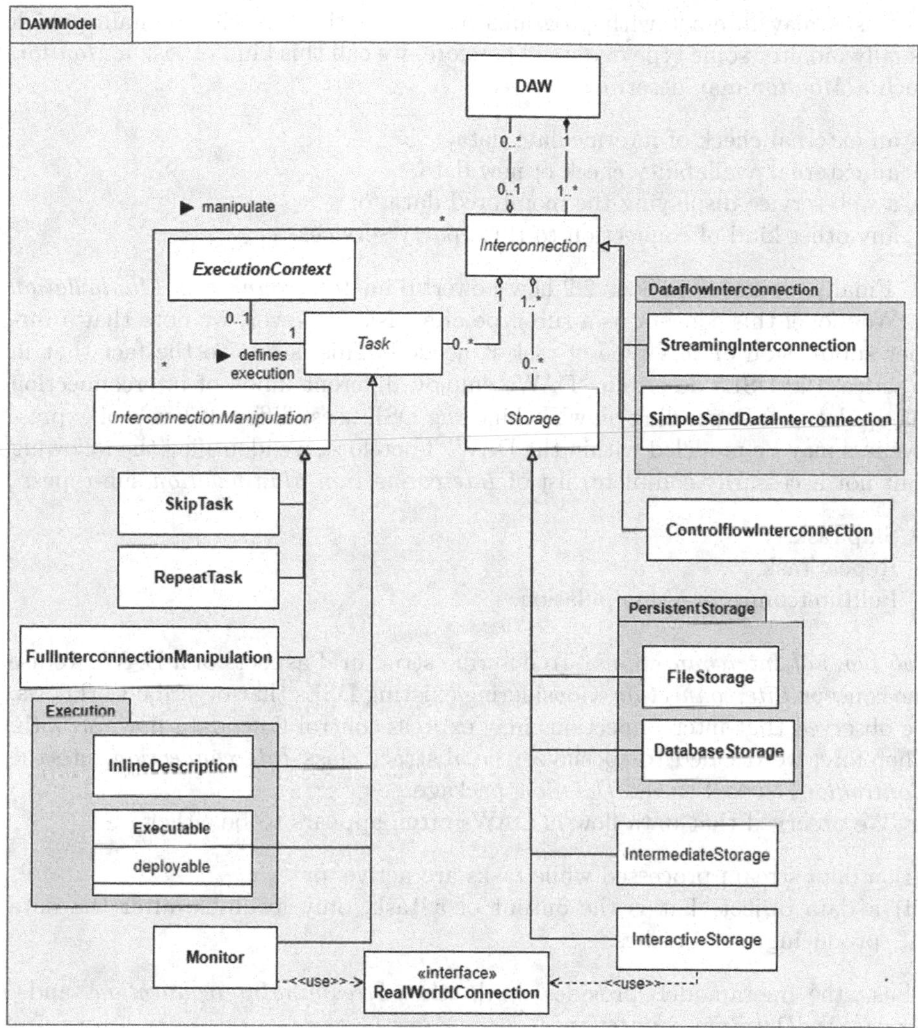

Fig. 3. Visualization of our proposed DAW language as an UML2 class diagram

provides a solution for the problem based on an input data set. Some DSLs used for defining DAWs provide their own internal programming languages (for example: Airflow [4]). These DSLs generally support providing solutions within the description of a DAW itself. Sub-problems that are solved purely with an internal programming language (e.g., Python), we call *InlineDescription*. They refer to a script that is executed within a task. Here, and in contrast to an *Executable*, no reference to an externally callable program is needed.

Tasks may interact with programs outside of the scientific domain, which usually monitor some type of data. Therefore, we call this kind of task a *Monitor*. Such a *Monitor* may describe:

- an external check of intermediate data,
- an external availability check of new data,
- a web-service displaying the monitored data, or
- any other kind of connection to third party services.

Finally, we noted in Sect. 2.2 how powerful an *Interconnection Manipulation* is. We model this concept as a sub-type of a task. However, we note that a further subdivision of this type of task is needed. This is due to the fact that in practice, the DSLs describing DAWs employ different kinds of interconnection manipulations. Depending on what kind the DSL uses, different levels of expressiveness may be modeled within the DAW. Therefore, we identified the following (but not necessarily complete) list of *Interconnection Manipulation* sub-types:

- SkipTask,
- RepeatTask,
- FullInterconnectionManipulation.

Sub-types of Interconnections. To describe structural aspects of a DAW, we use the concept *Interconnection.* Considering existing DSLs that describe workflows, we observed that interconnections may express control flow, data flow, or both. Therefore, we decided to specialize the abstract class *Interconnection* into the *Controlflow*, as well as the *Dataflow* package.

We observed that data flow in DAWs often appears to be either

(i) a data stream processed while tasks are active, or
(ii) a data object that is the output of a task, only available after the data producing task finishes.

Thus, the metamodel provides both the *StreamingInterconnection* and *SimpleSendDataInterconnection.*

Sub-types of Storage. In our metamodel, we refer to any data source or data sink as a *Storage* object. However, those *Storage* objects appear in different DSLs in some variations. Analysing these DSLs, we found that at a minimum a base set of persistent storage objects and intermediate storage objects must be included. This is only the very minimum that must exist. We explicitly do not prohibit more variants of storage objects.

With *IntermediateStorage*, we refer to data sources/sinks that may be deleted after the respective DAW execution finished. This type of storage also includes for example measurement equipment that measures live data, or Linux pipes. *PersistentStorage* objects are often implemented in a certain form in a DAW specification language. We modeled *PersistentStorage* as a package, in order to specifically allow for specializations. In our base metamodel, we explicitly provide

FileStorage, as well as *DatabaseStorage*. We are aware that those specializations may not be complete, and thus the package may be extended in the future.

In addition, to the absolute minimum model, we decided to include an *InteractiveStorage* class as well. In DAWs it may happen that initial data is neither produced directly by some measurement equipment, nor provided through a preceding task or DAW. Therefore, we added the *InteractiveStorage* to be more expressive with our metamodel. We thereby capture data sources/sinks such as *stdin*, *stdout*, or *stderr*.

Similar to *Tasks*, we connect *Storage* objects to our DAW through *Interconnetions*.

Real World Connection. As noted above, sometimes entities outside of the DAW system may need to interact with the DAW. While some specific outside interactions (such as measurement equipment providing input data) are already covered by the model thus far, we cannot yet express more abstract interactions from the outside world with our DAWs. We added a *RealWorldConnection* interface, so that **any** interaction outside of the DAW system can be expressed. We found that at the very least both *Monitors* and *InteractiveStorage* objects (such as a stdin interface for a human managing a DAW) require this *RealWorldConnection* interface.

Execution Context. Generally, a DAW may be described on three different abstraction levels:

1. The idea level,
2. the executable level, and
3. the deployment level.

While the first and most abstract level describes only the solution idea, the executable level is more concrete. This second level requires *Tasks* to be present for all sub-problems defined in the DAW. The third and final level is the closest to the actual hardware. Sometimes it may be necessary for a user of a DAW system to specify additional requirements for a given task. Such additional requirements can be quite complex. For instance, we might need the start time of the task, the used instance of a workflow system, or the used hardware node that provides some specialized resources. So far, we focused on describing the DAW itself. For the computation/execution of the DAW, concrete systems need to be employed. The *ExecutionContext* allows us to add an optional set of these computation specific data blocks. Consequently, this way of modeling this concept is only a placeholder and is a work in progress. In the future, it will be necessary to further extend the model, so that it will be able to actually express everything that is important for when a developer interacts with our metamodel.

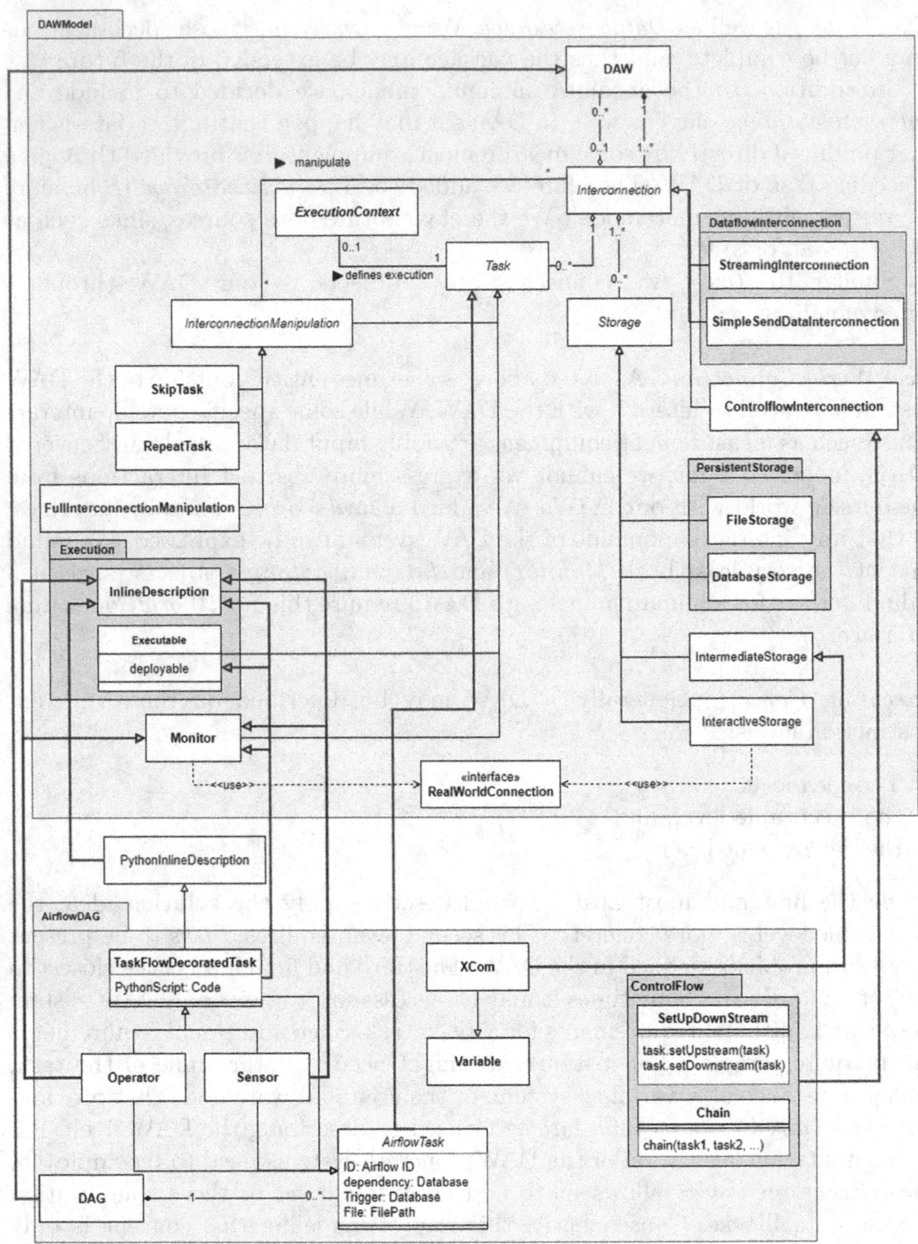

Fig. 4. Mapping (blue inheritance arcs) of Airflow language elements to our metamodel (Color figure online)

4 Mapping of the Consolidated View to a Specific Workflow Language: Airflow

In the previous Sect. 3, we have presented our metamodel, which has been cross-validated with different DAW specification languages. In this section and in Fig. 4, we present the mapping of the Airflow [4] platform's specification language as an example to show the validity of our metamodel. In Fig. 4, the essential parts of the Airflow system are modeled in the bottom part of our figure.

In Airflow, workflows are each defined as a directed acyclic graph (DAG). These DAGs are stored as a file written in an Airflow specific language that has a programming-language-like syntax. Similar to other programming languages (such as Python) DAGs and tasks need to be defined and functionalities may be imported. Nevertheless, any DAG written in this Airflow specific language is interpreted as a graph.

In Airflow, every DAG consists of *Tasks*: "Tasks are the basic unit of execution in Airflow" [4]. This maps directly to *Tasks* defined in our metamodel.

Three basic kinds of *Tasks* are used within Airflow:

- Operators,
- Sensors, and
- TaskFlow-decorated Tasks.

This means that *Tasks* in Airflow are not modeled as parts of workflows themselves. Instead, *Tasks* are modeled as an abstract class. This again directly maps to our metamodel.

TaskFlow-decorated tasks appear to be the most potent type of *AirflowTask*. They can be any Python script. Thus, they map to *Executables*, *Monitors*, and *InlineDescriptions*. With an Airflow installation, the Python programming language is also installed. To underline that TaskFlow-decorated tasks are written in pure Python, we added an attribute to the corresponding class. Airflow cannot manipulate an interconnection, as the DAW needs to be executed as it is. Therefore, the element interconnection manipulation is not used in the mapping.

Operators are pre-defined tasks that can be used directly, without having to specify them in Python. Airflow provides a set of *Operators* for different tasks such as: sending emails, Bash executions, and SQLite DB queries. Furthermore, arbitrary Python functions may be called through a specific operator called *PythonOperator*. *Operators* map to both *InlineDescription* and *Monitor*, as they are defined inline and may be used for monitoring.

Sensors are less potent task templates. They are used for waiting for, as well as reacting to external triggers. Even though, the Airflow documentation explains *Sensors* as a special type of *Operators*, we think of *Operators* and *Sensors* as separate extensions of *TaskFlow-decoratedTasks*. *Sensors* are used for monitoring external events. They are task operators which are described inline. This maps *Sensors* to both the *InlineDescription* and *Monitor* subtypes of a *Task* in our metamodel.

For the *InlineDescriptions* within Airflow, both Python and the language elements of *Operators* and *Sensors* are used. To make this distinction clear, we introduce a special *InlineDescription* that we call *PythonInlineDescription*.

In Airflow, every task can communicate with external entities. Thus, all three basic tasks specified as an *AirflowTask* may be mapped to our *Monitor* class. While TaskFlow-decorated tasks are written in Python to execute whatever the Python script defines, Operators and Sensors are so-called built-in "Templates".

Only having a set of unconnected *AirflowTasks* does not make a DAG yet. Therefore, dependencies between each of the tasks must be modeled as well. These are organized by using either (i) the setUpstream() and setDownstream() methods from a task, or (ii) the >> and << Operator between two tasks. Additionally, Airflow offers the chain() method for creating task-chains. Even though some of them are part of *AirflowTasks*, we decided to combine all the control flow related methods into one package. The entirety of the thus created package maps to *ControflowInterconnection* in our metamodel.

All of the dependencies above are stored in a database, so that the tasks may access them. The database itself is used by Airflow to only store internal management-data. Thus, the database is not part of the mapping to our metamodel.

Finally, Airflow uses the concept of Variables and XCom values. These are designed for communication between *AirflowTasks*. Any connected *AirflowTask* may store information in them. All information stored, is then accessible by any connected *AirflowTask*. This is true even after the first *AirflowTask* has finished. Since XCom values are stored just for the purpose of communication, they do not need to be persistently stored. For this reason, we map this concept to our *IntermediateStorage*.

We talked about all main concepts of the Airflow specification language above and were able to find a mapping for each of those concepts to our metamodel. Therefore, Airflow in its entirety can be expressed through our metamodel. In the cross-validation of our metamodel, we have also looked at Nextflow, BPMN, Argo, CWL, and StackStorm. Due to space constraints, we do not explicitly show these mappings here and refer to our GitHub page [26]. The main three language elements (interconnection, storage, task) are present in all language mappings. Some subclasses are not present in all of them.

5 Conclusion and Discussion

In this paper, we describe a consolidated metamodel for DAWs. By construction, the metamodel is able to describe several existing DAW specification languages. In the future, the derived metamodel needs to be updated to also accommodate newly developed DAW specification languages and novel language concepts. The metamodel itself provides multiple benefits that we will now briefly discuss.

DAW Evolution. To date, specifications of DAWs are encoded using different kinds of workflow, scripting, or programming languages. However, working and experimenting with a DAW written in any of the above-mentioned DAW specification languages often results in a considerable initial effort. In particular, basic technology for parsing, serializing, transforming, searching, or selectively accessing the DAW specifications requires adaptation or, in the worst case, must be developed from scratch.

The metamodel enables us to provide a generic API that allows modification and evolution of a given DAW specification. Our metamodel is not a translation tool. Creating such a tool would be the next step in our work. The metamodel would then be used to automate it. Conceptually, this can be done through CRUD operations. These CRUD operations can only be specified precisely and implemented effectively *if* a conceptual representation of DAW specifications is available. Our metamodel provides this representation. The use of the metamodel is generic. The approach is not tailored to a specific DAW language. The only requirement to use our metamodel is that a mapping exists. This is particularly useful, as new DAWs are typically not developed in their entirety, but are adapted from existing DAWs through a series of evolutionary steps [27], instead.

DAW Portability. DAWs can be executed on a multitude of different infrastructure settings. Similar to the evolution aspect, the metamodel enables us to abstract away the underlying hardware platform. Any algorithm that ports a DAW has to change the hardware description and generate adapted scheduling policies. Using our metamodel, we can create entirely new DAWs (see CRUD operations above). Notably, this means we are able to re-use an existing DAW on a different hardware platform, as long as the mapping between the metamodel and the two target DAW specification languages is available. Through this step, DAWs become portable.

Exploratory DAWs and DAW Adaptation. Recently, Fernandez et al. [28] presented Meta-Dataflows, allowing them to efficiently execute exploratory workflows. They identified the inefficiency of independent job execution of exploratory workflows and proposed Meta-Dataflows as a solution. A Meta-Dataflow involves the exploration of a set of *explorables*, e.g., parameter sweeps or sweeps over different workflow task implementations. In our context, explorables are solutions, for each of which many different executables may exist. The Meta-Dataflow compares the results of such a set of explorables by executing them in parallel. As a result of this comparison, the best suited alternative executable can then be chosen for future work on the DAW.

The idea of Meta-Dataflows for exploratory DAWs may be employed as an immediate extension to our proposed metamodel. Not only can we make use of this concept directly, we can also extend it: Working with tasks that are specified in different DSLs becomes feasible through the above-mentioned CRUD operations.

DAW Maintenance. DAWs are typically long-lived artifacts that provide provenance of scientific results, long after the initial in-silico experiments are performed. Due to the constant progress in science and technology, analysis components may become outdated or deprecated. The metamodel may be used for (semi-)automatic maintenance, as faulty or outdated components can be replaced with other components now made compatible.

Aknowledgements. Funded by the Deutsche Forschungsgemeinschaft (DFG, German Research Foundation) - Project-ID 414984028 - SFB 1404 FONDA [29].

References

1. Stoudt, S., Vásquez, V.N., Martinez, C.C.: Principles for data analysis workflows. PLoS Comput. Biol. **17**(3), e1008770 (2021)
2. Fowler, M.: Domain-Specific Languages. Pearson Education, London (2010)
3. Tracz, W.: DSSA (Domain-Specific Software Architecture): pedagogical example. SIGSOFT Softw. Eng. Notes **20**(3), 49–62 (1995)
4. Apache airflow project (2022). https://airflow.apache.org/
5. Di Tommaso, P., Chatzou, M., Floden, E.W., Barja, P.P., Palumbo, E., Notredame, C.: Nextflow enables reproducible computational workflows. Nat. Biotechnol. **35**(4), 316–319 (2017)
6. Rak, R., Rowley, A., Black, W., Ananiadou, S.: Argo: an integrative, interactive, text mining-based workbench supporting curation. Database **1–7**, 2012 (2012)
7. Stackstorm (2022). https://stackstorm.com/
8. Carbone, P., Katsifodimos, A., Ewen, S., Markl, V., Haridi, S., Tzoumas, K.: Apache flink: stream and batch processing in a single engine. Bull. IEEE Comput. Soc. Tech. Comm. Data Eng. **36**(4), 28–38 (2015)
9. Jain, A., et al.: Fireworks: a dynamic workflow system designed for high-throughput applications. Concurr. Comput. Practic. Exp. **27**(17), 5037–5059 (2015)
10. Prefect (2022). https://docs.prefect.io/
11. Köster, J., Rahmann, S.: Snakemake-a scalable bioinformatics workflow engine. Bioinformatics **28**(19), 2520–2522 (2012)
12. Luigi (2022). https://github.com/spotify/luigi
13. Chinosi, M., Trombetta, A.: BPMN: an introduction to the standard. Comput. Stand. Interfaces **34**(1), 124–134 (2012)
14. Camunda (2022). https://camunda.com/bpmn/
15. Orchestra (2022). https://orchestra.b12.io/
16. Activiti (2022). https://www.activiti.org/
17. Atkinson, C., Kühne, T.: Model-driven development: a metamodeling foundation. IEEE Softw. **20**(5), 36–41 (2003)
18. Amstutz, P., et al.: Common workflow language, v1. 0 (2016)
19. Perkel, J.M.: Workflow systems turn raw data into scientific knowledge. Nature **573**, 149–150 (2019)
20. Szyperski, C., Gruntz, D., Murer, S.: Component Software: Beyond Object-Oriented Programming, 2nd edn. ACM Press/Addison-Wesley, New York (2002)
21. Schiefer, C., et al.: Portability of scientific workflows in NGS data analysis: a case study. CoRR, abs/2006.03104 (2020)
22. Brambilla, M., Cabot, J., Wimmer, M.: Model-Driven Software Engineering in Practice. Synthesis Lectures on Software Engineering, 2nd edn. Morgan & Claypool, Vermont (2017)

23. Grunske, L., Geiger, L., Zündorf, A., Van Eetvelde, N., Van Gorp, P., Varró, D.: Using graph transformation for practical model-driven software engineering. In: Beydeda, S., Book, M., Gruhn, V. (eds.) Model-Driven Software Development, pp. 91–117. Springer, Heidelberg (2005). https://doi.org/10.1007/3-540-28554-7_5
24. Object Management Group (OMG). OMG Unified Modeling Language (OMG UML®), Version 2.5.1 (2017). https://www.omg.org/spec/UML/2.5.1/PDF
25. Rupp, C., Queins, S., Zengler, B.: UML 2 glasklar: Praxiswissen für die UML-Modellierung. Hanser (2007)
26. Metamodel and mappings of specification languages for data analysis workflows (2022). https://github.com/CRC-FONDA/T1-DAW-Metamodel
27. Boulakia, S.C., Leser, U.: Search, adapt, and reuse: the future of scientific workflows. SIGMOD Rec. **40**(2), 6–16 (2011)
28. Fernandez, R.C., Culhane, W., Watcharapichat, P., Weidlich, M., Morales, V.L., Pietzuch, P.R.: Meta-dataflows: efficient exploratory dataflow jobs. In: Das, G., Jermaine, C.M., Bernstein, P.A. (eds.) Proceedings of the 2018 International Conference on Management of Data, SIGMOD Conference 2018, Houston, TX, USA, 10–15 June 2018, pp. 1157–1172. ACM (2018)
29. Leser, U., et al.: The Collaborative Research Center FONDA. Datenbank-Spektrum, (1610–1995), November 2021

A Systematic Approach for Interfacing Component-Based Software with an Active Automata Learning Tool

Dennis Hendriks[1,2](✉) and Kousar Aslam[3]

[1] ESI (TNO), Eindhoven, The Netherlands
dennis.hendriks@tno.nl

[2] Radboud University, Nijmegen, The Netherlands
dennis.hendriks@ru.nl

[3] Vrije Universiteit, Amsterdam, The Netherlands
k.aslam@vu.nl

Abstract. Applying Model-Driven Engineering can improve development efficiency. But gaining such benefits for legacy software requires models, and creating them manually is both laborious and error prone. Active automata learning has the potential to make it cost-effective, but practitioners face practical challenges applying it to software components of industrial cyber-physical systems. To overcome these challenges, we present a framework to learn the behavior of component-based software with a client/server architecture, focusing on interfacing isolated component code with an active learning tool. An essential part of the framework is an interfacing protocol that provides a structured way of handling the (a)synchronous communications between the component and learning tool. Our main contribution is the systematic derivation of such interfacing protocols for component-based software, which we demonstrate on the software architecture of ASML, a leading company in developing lithography machines. Through several practical case studies we show that our semi-automatic approach enables setting up a learning environment to learn component behaviors within hours. The protocol's responsibilities and the way it handles different communication types apply to component-based software in general. Our framework could thus be adapted for companies with similar software architectures.

Keywords: Active automata learning · Component-based systems · Industrial application

D. Hendriks—This research is carried out as part of the Transposition project under the responsibility of ESI (TNO) in co-operation with ASML. The research activities are supported by the Netherlands Ministry of Economic Affairs and TKI-HTSM.
K. Aslam—This research was supported by the Eindhoven University of Technology and ASML Netherlands B.V., carried out as part of the IMPULS II project.

T. Margaria and B. Steffen (Eds.): ISoLA 2022, LNCS 13702, pp. 216–236, 2022.
https://doi.org/10.1007/978-3-031-19756-7_13

1 Introduction

Cyber-physical systems often employ a component-based software architecture, dividing the system into components that can be developed, tested and deployed independently [17]. Model-Driven Engineering (MDE) places models at the center of attention, allowing for early analysis of a component's software behavior and for implementations to be automatically generated [18]. But gaining such benefits for legacy software requires models, and manual modeling for legacy components is often laborious and error prone due to a lack of understanding of their current behavior, for instance caused by insufficient documentation and the original developers having long since left the company.

To facilitate a cost-effective transition to MDE, model learning can automatically infer first-order models to bootstrap a subsequent manual modeling effort. Passive state machine learning for instance infers models based on execution logs [9,10], but the resulting models are often incomplete due to logs covering only parts of the component's behavior. Active automata learning (AAL) on the other hand repeatedly queries the component to ultimately infer a model capturing the component's complete behavior. AAL was introduced in Dana Angluin's seminal work on the L* algorithm [2]. A comprehensive body of work extended upon this to, e.g., learn different types of models, improve scalability, and show its practical value [12].

However, practitioners face practical challenges applying AAL to software components of real-world industrial cyber-physical systems. In order for an AAL tool to send queries to a component and gauge its responses, the component must be isolated from its environment and subsequently connected to the learning tool. Existing case studies typically explicitly or implicitly explain their learning setup [5,6,16]. But, establishing such a learning setup is laborious. It can therefore pay off to use a generic setup that can be (re)configured for reuse. By analyzing existing interface descriptions the new configuration can even be automatically generated. This has been shown to be effective for web services [15].

But what is lacking is a systematic approach to connect software components operating under the client/server paradigm to a learning tool. Therefore, similar to what is already available for web services, we contribute a general, reusable and configurable framework, to quickly produce an AAL setup, specifically for component-based software with a client/server architecture. Through multiple case studies we show that our semi-automatic approach enables setting up a learning environment to learn (sub-)component behaviors within hours.

A particular challenge when interfacing with such components, is how to deal with their various types of (a)synchronous communications, especially when considering their dual roles as servers to their clients and as clients to their servers. For instance, a reply from a server is an input to the component, but it is only possible after a request from the component itself. Components may thus not be input-enabled, a practical requirement of various AAL algorithms.

If a component is not input-enabled, a learning purpose [1] can be placed between the learner and the component. A learning purpose is essentially a protocol model, which rejects inputs not allowed by the protocol, and forwards any other inputs to the component, to learn the subset of a component's behavior satisfying the protocol. Therefore, an essential part of our framework is an *interfacing protocol* model, a learning purpose that provides a practical but structured way of handling the communications between the AAL tool and the component whose behavior is to be learned. This way, the System Under Learning (SUL), the isolated component code combined with the protocol, is input-enabled, provides a single output per input, and represents a finite Mealy machine, even if the isolated component code does not satisfy these properties.

Our main contribution is the systematic derivation of the interfacing protocol. As an example, we derive such a protocol for the software architecture of ASML, a leading company in developing lithography systems. However, the responsibilities of the interfacing protocol and the way we handle the different types of communication patterns apply to component-based software in general. Our work could therefore be used to similarly derive interfacing protocols and set up learning frameworks at other companies with similar software architectures.

The remainder of this paper is organized as follows. In Sect. 2 we briefly introduce component-based software architectures and AAL. Section 3 describes our general AAL framework. Section 4 contains our main contribution, as it introduces interfacing protocols and their responsibilities, and describes the systematic derivation of such a protocol for ASML's software architecture. We then apply our approach in practice to infer behavioral models of several software components in Sect. 5, before concluding in Sect. 6.

2 Background

Component-based software architectures are often employed by cyber-physical systems to divide the system into *components* that can be developed, tested and deployed independently [17]. A component can act as a *server* offering its functionality via *interfaces* to other components, its *clients*. Components may interact with multiple other components, its *environment*, acting as either client or server to the various components. Interactions typically involve calling *functions* from interfaces of other components, e.g., as remote procedure calls. Concurrent components can communicate *synchronously* and *asynchronously* [8]. With synchronous communication a client remains idle while awaiting the server's *response*, while asynchronous communication allows a client to perform other interactions while a server is processing the client's *request*.

Active automata learning (AAL) involves repeatedly querying a component to ultimately infer a model that captures the component's complete behavior. Given our context of component-based software, queries involve function calls. As for instance function calls from clients are naturally inputs, and their corresponding return values are then outputs, we infer Mealy machine models. AAL then involves a *learner* using *membership queries* (MQs), sending sequences of *inputs* (matching, e.g., function calls from clients) to the *System Under Learning* (SUL) and observing the *outputs* (e.g., function return values), using them to construct a *hypothesis* model for the SUL's unknown behavior. An *equivalence*

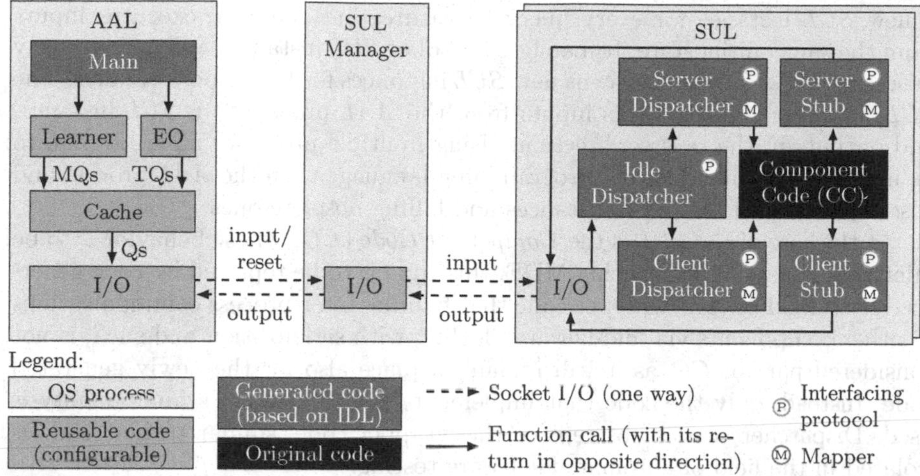

Fig. 1. General framework to perform AAL on software components operating under the client/server paradigm.

oracle (EO) then either confirms that the hypothesis matches the SUL's behavior or it produces a counterexample. The EO is typically implemented using conformance testing techniques, using *test queries* (TQs) to find differences in behavior between the hypothesis and the SUL. Iteratively, the learner uses the counterexample and further membership queries to refine its hypothesis, and the EO checks this refined hypothesis, until the EO considers a hypothesis correct. See also the left part of Fig. 1.

3 Active Automata Learning Framework

Complex cyber-physical systems may consist of millions of lines of code, spread out over many hundreds of components. Our goal is to infer the externally visible behavior of individual (sub-)components, e.g., to allow replacing the legacy implementation of their business logic. This requires that a component whose behavior is to be learned is isolated from its environment and is subsequently connected to the AAL tool. We assume single-threaded components. Figure 1 shows our general framework to perform AAL on software components operating under the client/server paradigm. The outermost boxes represent processes.

At the left is the *AAL* process. It consists of a *Main* function that configures a *Learner* and *EO*, and subsequently iteratively invokes them as described in Sect. 2. The *Learner* and *EO* produce *MQs* and *TQs*, respectively, which are handled identically by a *Cache*. The *Cache* caches and directly answers previously asked queries. For new queries, the *I/O* module sends the *input* symbols to a *SUL Manager* process via sockets, and similarly receives *output* symbols.

The *I/O* module of the *AAL* process sends after each *MQ*/*TQ* a *reset* symbol to the *SUL Manager*, informing it of query completion. The *SUL Manager* uses a new *SUL* instance for every query to ensure that the *SUL* executes inputs from the same initial state. It manages a pool of *SUL* instances and concurrently processes *MQs*/*TQs* and spawns new *SUL* instances for better performance. The *SUL Manager* thus forwards inputs from the *AAL* process to a *SUL* instance, and outputs in the reverse direction. Using multiple processes allows a *SUL* to be implemented in a different programming language than the *AAL* process and eases spawning of new *SUL* instances and killing obsolete ones.

At the core of the *SUL* is the *Component Code* (*CC*) whose behavior is to be inferred. As part of introducing MDE, this code is to be replaced by code generated from models. The wrapper code that handles inter-process communications to other components via middleware, dealing with serialization and such, is not considered part of *CC*, as it will remain in place also for the newly generated code. Instead, only the code that implements the component's functionality is used. Dispatchers and stubs replace the wrapper code, similar to how code is isolated in the field of automated software testing.

When the *I/O* module receives an input, it forwards the input to the *Idle Dispatcher*, if the *SUL* is idle. A component can be both a server to its clients and a client to its servers. The *Idle Dispatcher* forwards inputs to the *Server Dispatcher* if the *CC* (and thus the SUL) acts as server for requests from clients, or to the *Client Dispatcher* if it acts as client to responses from servers, e.g., due to earlier asynchronous requests to servers. These *Client*/*Server Dispatchers* act as *mappers* [15] translating input symbols provided as strings to function calls on the *CC*. Once a function returns, its return value is mapped back to an output (string), which via the *Idle Dispatcher* and *I/O* module is provided back to the *SUL Manager* and *AAL* processes. When the *CC* communicates as a client to one of its servers, the call is intercepted in the *Client Stub*. This is also a mapper, forwarding the output symbol corresponding to the call to the *I/O* module. Upon receiving the server reply as *input* from the *I/O* module, the *Client Stub* translates this server reply to a return value to be returned back to the *CC*. Finally, the *Server Stub* similarly intercepts and handles calls from the *CC* (acting as server) to the client. In our work, the mappers do not apply any abstractions to the input alphabet.

The final aspect of our framework, the *interfacing protocol*, as implemented in the dispatchers and stubs, is further explained in Sect. 4. The various shades of gray used to color the boxes of Fig. 1 are explained in Sect. 5.

4 Interfacing Protocol

In this section, we discuss interfacing protocols and their systematic derivation, using the software architecture of ASML as an example. After briefly explaining the company's software architecture, we describe its communication patterns, and how they map to AAL inputs and outputs, before introducing the interfacing protocol and its responsibilities, and systematically deriving such a protocol from the patterns and the input/output mapping.

4.1 Software Architecture and Communication Patterns

The components interact through remote function calls. A call from a client is, by the middleware, placed in the server's message queue. A server is idle while awaiting incoming messages in its `main` function's message processing loop. As long as the queue is non-empty, it picks up messages from the queue and processes them one by one, non-preemptively.

Components communicate with each other using various communication patterns. Clients can invoke functions of their servers in three ways: as *blocking* calls, *request/wait* calls, and *function completion notification (FCN)* calls. Servers can *handle* these request either *synchronously* or *asynchronously*. The middleware transparently hides these details, as clients are not aware of how servers handle their calls, nor are servers aware of how clients invoke the calls. We ignore *library* calls, which for the purpose of this work are identical to synchronously-handled blocking calls. The last two patterns are 'fire-and-forget' type of communications: *triggers* and *events*, which give no assurances of (successful) function execution, e.g., a call may fail without notifying the caller. Next, we describe the 7 patterns (3 client requests, 2 server handlers, 2 fire/forget) in more detail using the Message Sequence Charts (MSCs) from Fig. 2.

Here f denotes any *function*, t any *trigger* and e any *event*. Collectively, these three are called *methods*. A method is assumed to include the identity of the server that provides it, distinguishing methods from interfaces provided by multiple servers. The company uses a proprietary Interface Description Language (IDL) to define interfaces and their methods. A generator generates, from IDL files, implementation functions to call and handle all defined methods, for various programming languages. We distinguish IDL functions (*i-functions*) from generated functions (*g-functions*) where relevant. Any non-void g-function returns a value of type `ASML_RESULT`, an integer result indicating success (0) or failure (non-zero). The company's software architecture rule book states that callers must not use individual error codes, but only OK (0) vs not-OK (non-zero), except for logging, to prevent tight coupling between functions.

(i) Blocking Call (Figure 2a): A client may invoke an i-function f synchronously as a blocking call (with g-function f_{blk}). While awaiting the server's response (return value r_{ok} or r_{nok}), the client is then *blocked* and can not do any internal processing, perform calls, or process messages from its message queue.

(ii) Request/Wait Call (2b / 2c): A client may asynchronously *request* (f_{req}) a server to start executing an i-function f. The client is then free to do other things before explicitly *waiting* (f_{wait}) for the server's response (the second r_{ok} or r_{nok}). If the server has already finished executing the i-function, the middleware has stored the server's response and immediately returns this to the client (**2b**). Otherwise, the client is blocked until the server finishes and its response is provided back to the client via the middleware (**2c**). With request/wait calls the client is in control of when it is ready to receive the server's response.

(iii) Function Completion Notification (FCN) Call (2d): A client may asynchronously request (f_{fcn}) a server to start executing an i-function f, providing it a callback address (f_{cb}). The client is then free to do other things. Once

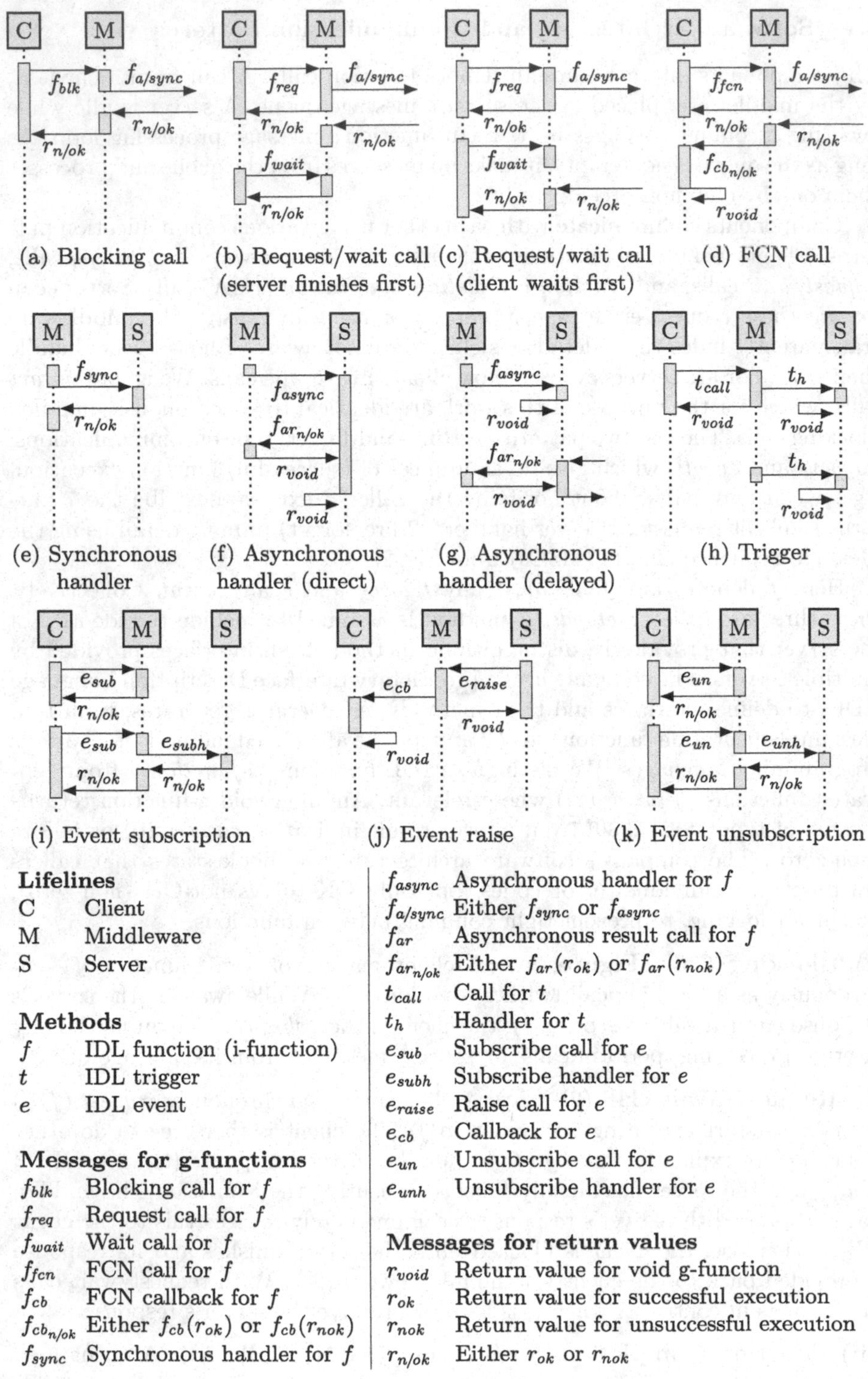

Fig. 2. Message Sequence Charts (MSCs) for all (partial) communication patterns.

the server finishes executing f, it provides its response (r_{ok} or r_{nok}) to the middleware, which places both the callback address and the server's response in the client's message queue. Once the client is idle it will process its message queue, eventually processing the server's response using callback g-function f_{cb}, i.e., f_{cb} is called with the queued server response as argument. The client is thus *notified* of the server *completing* the execution of *function* f, as the client requested. With FCN calls the server is in control of when it provides the response.

(iv) Synchronous Handler (2e): A server may *synchronously handle* all blocking calls, request/wait calls and FCN calls for an i-function f. Once the handler (f_{sync}) finishes, it immediately returns its response (r_{ok} or r_{nok}).

(v) Asynchronous Handler (2f / 2g): A server may also *asynchronously handle* all blocking calls, request/wait calls and FCN calls for an i-function f. The asynchronous handler (f_{async}) starts handling the request. In that handler (**2f**), or at any later time in any other g-function (**2g**), it sends its response to the client by calling an *asynchronous result* g-function, i.e., $f_{ar}(r_{ok})$ or $f_{ar}(r_{nok})$.

A client call pattern (**i – iii**) and server handler pattern (**iv – v**) are to be combined to form a complete pattern, with a client, middleware and a server.

(vi) Trigger (2h): A client may *trigger* a server (t_{call}), for a trigger t. The server handles (t_h) the trigger without responding back to the client (r_{void}). A server may also be triggered directly by the middleware, e.g., periodically.

(vii) Event (2i – 2k): A client may *subscribe* (e_{sub}) to a specific *event* e of one of its servers (**2i**), providing a callback address (e_{cb}). The middleware stores the subscription. A server may optionally have a *subscription handler* (e_{subh}) to be notified of subscriptions. A server may *raise* (e_{raise}) an event (**2j**), which leads to callback g-functions (e_{cb}) being invoked (akin to FCN callbacks) on all clients subscribed to that server for the specific event. Clients may at any time *unsubscribe* (e_{un}) from events (**2k**), again optionally notifying the server (e_{unh}).

4.2 Mapping Communication Patterns to Inputs/Outputs

For each of the 7 (partial) communication patterns the various calls to g-functions and their replies can be mapped to inputs and outputs for AAL. Table 1 shows this mapping. It is constructed by considering the role of the *CC* (and thus of the SUL), as client and/or server, for each pattern from Fig. 2. As our goal is to infer a component's functional behavior, it is isolated from its environment, 'cutting off' (ignoring) the middleware. Only the incoming and outgoing messages from clients and servers are considered (C and S lifelines in the MSCs). Messages from a client to the SUL (acting as server) are inputs. Reverse communications are outputs. Conversely, messages from the SUL (acting as client) to a server are outputs. Reverse communications are inputs. The role of the SUL, as client or server, thus inverts whether its incoming and outgoing messages are inputs or outputs.

For instance, in Fig. 2a the SUL can only act as client. The outgoing f_{blk} message to a server is then an output, and the incoming r_{ok} or r_{nok} message from a server is an input.

Table 1. Communication pattern messages from Fig. 2 mapped to AAL inputs and outputs, for the SUL acting as client or server.

Communication pattern	Role of SUL	Message	Input/Output
(i) Blocking call	Client	f_{blk}	Output
		r_{ok} / r_{nok}	Input
(ii) Request/wait call	Client	f_{req}	Output
		r_{ok} / r_{nok}	Input
		f_{wait}	Output
		r_{ok} / r_{nok}	Input
(iii) FCN call	Client	f_{fcn}	Output
		r_{ok} / r_{nok}	Input
		$f_{cb_{ok}}$ / $f_{cb_{nok}}$	Input
		r_{void}	Output
(iv) Synchronous handler	Server	f_{sync}	Input
		r_{ok} / r_{nok}	Output
(v) Asynchronous handler	Server	f_{async}	Input
		r_{void}	Output
		$f_{ar_{ok}}$ / $f_{ar_{nok}}$	Output
		r_{void}	Input
(vi) Trigger	Client	t_{call}	Output
		r_{void}	Input
	Server	t_h	Input
		r_{void}	Output
(vii) Event	Client	e_{sub}	Output
		r_{ok} / r_{nok}	Input
		e_{cb}	Input
		r_{void}	Output
		e_{un}	Output
		r_{ok} / r_{nok}	Input
	Server	e_{subh}	Input
		r_{ok} / r_{nok}	Output
		e_{raise}	Output
		r_{void}	Input
		e_{unh}	Input
		r_{ok} / r_{nok}	Output

4.3 The Interfacing Protocol and Its Responsibilities

When applying AAL in practice, often several preconditions must hold, e.g., when using LearnLib [14] to learn Mealy machines, the SUL must be input-enabled.

If the *CC* does not satisfy such conditions, the interfacing protocol ensures that the SUL does satisfy them. The protocol is part of the SUL's dispatchers and stubs, see Fig. 1. All communications between the learner and the *CC* go through the protocol. Here, we discuss the protocol's three responsibilities. The next section explains *how* it satisfies them.

(a) Input-Enabled: For some learning tools/algorithms, the SUL must be input-enabled for the learner to query every input on the SUL for every state. This condition does not always hold, e.g., for FCN callbacks (Fig. 2d). Along with an FCN call (f_{fcn}) the SUL provides a callback address (f_{cb}). In the real system, the middleware places that callback in the client's message queue upon receiving the server's reply. For AAL, the client dispatcher invokes it directly. An FCN callback to the SUL is an input, which is thus only possible after an FCN call by the SUL. Without the call, the callback address is unknown and it can not be invoked on the *CC*. The SUL is then not input-enabled. The interfacing protocol detects such invalid inputs, for which it can not rely on the *CC*. Instead, the protocol itself replies to the learner, making the SUL as a whole input-enabled. As only impossible inputs are rejected, the complete *CC* behavior can still be learned for all valid inputs.

(b) Single Input, Single Output: Inferring Mealy machines with AAL requires that each input produces a single output. The interfacing protocol is designed to always alternate inputs and outputs. By matching g-function calls and their returns, this is a natural fit. It therefore does not prevent learning the full externally-observable behavior of *CC*.

The protocol is an Extended Finite State Machine (EFSM), while we infer Mealy machines. Each protocol input and following output matches a single Mealy machine transition.

(c) Finite Learning Result: Certain component behavior can not be captured as a finite Mealy machine, e.g., for multiple concurrent executions of an asynchronous handler (Fig. 2g). With a the handler's start (f_{async}), b its end (r_{void}), c a later successful asynchronous result call ($f_{ar_{ok}}$), and d its end (r_{void}), this may lead to sequences '*...ab...cd...*', '*...abab....cdcd...*', etc., and in general '*...*$(ab)^n$*...*$(cd)^n$*...*'. Unlike a pushdown automaton, a Mealy machine can not capture this in a finite manner. It would contain infinitely many paths, one for each value of $n \geq 0$. AAL would have to discover each path to infer a complete model, which would never terminate. The interfacing protocol can restrict such concurrent executions ($n \leq m$) to ensure that AAL terminates, at the expense of not learning the full behavior. Not only are higher concurrency variants then absent ($n > m$), any differences in behavior resulting from them would also be absent, e.g., the component's behavior could be different for $n = m + 1$ than for any $n \leq m$, but this would not be in the inferred model. However, the resulting models can still be valuable in practice, as our goal is automatically infer first-order models to bootstrap a subsequent manual modeling effort.

The interfacing protocol is a small wrapper around *CC*, addressing these three responsibilities. Neither ensuring input-enabledness, nor 'single input, single output', prevents learning the full externally-observable behavior of *CC*. Using interaction limit $m = \infty$, the full behavior of a *CC* can thus be learned, assuming *CC* has a finite Mealy machine representation. Otherwise, by restricting m, a subset of the behavior of *CC* (an under-approximation) can be learned. Assuming an AAL algorithm is used that ensures that learned models are minimal, our approach in no way impacts that guarantee.

4.4 Systematic Derivation of the Interfacing Protocol

The interfacing protocol provides a structured way of handling the various communication patterns, ensuring that the SUL is input-enabled, provides a single output per input, and represents a finite Mealy machine, even if the isolated *CC* does not satisfy these properties. We derive such an interfacing protocol in a systematic manner, still using the same example software architecture.

Figure 3 shows the interfacing protocol as an EFSM. The protocol starts in state *Idle* as the *CC* is initially idle, awaiting a call. The *Idle* state is an input state from the *SUL*'s perspective, shown in dark gray in the figure. Upon receiving a *SUL* input, the g-function matching that input is called on the *CC*. The protocol then transitions to the *Busy* state, which is an output state from the *SUL*'s perspective, denoted light gray in the figure. Here the *CC* continues executing the g-function. Upon its return, the protocol transitions back to the *Idle* state. Alternatively, while *Busy*, it may communicate to one of its servers and go to the *Blocked* state. There it is blocked until the call to the server returns, going back to the *Busy* state to continue the still-in-progress g-function execution. For simplicity, we do not consider calls of a component to its own provided interface. Next, we consider all 7 communication patterns from Fig. 2, with their associated inputs/outputs from Table 1, one at a time.

(iv) Synchronous Handler (Figure 2e): An idle SUL, acting as a server, can synchronously handle a call from one of its clients. Upon receiving f_{sync} for some i-function f as an input in the *Idle* state the protocol invokes the corresponding handler (g-function) on the *CC*. It also transitions to the *Busy* state, as the *CC* is then busy executing. Variable v_1 is updated to indicate the in-progress handler is not a void function (update $[v_1 := \bot]$). When the handler returns, depending on its return value (zero for successful execution, non-zero otherwise) the protocol produces an output (r_{ok} for zero, r_{nok} otherwise) and transitions back to the *Idle* state.

(i) Blocking Call (Figure 2a): The *CC*, while it is executing (state *Busy*), may execute a blocking call to one of its servers. If the *Client Stub* receives a blocking call for an i-function f, it maps that to output f_{blk} and transitions to *Blocked*. A blocking call is a non-void g-function ($[v_2 := \bot]$). In *Blocked* the SUL is blocked while waiting until it receives r_{ok} or r_{nok} as input. It then returns from the blocking call back to the *CC*, with return value 0 (for r_{ok}) or 1 (for r_{nok}), and transitions back to *Busy*.

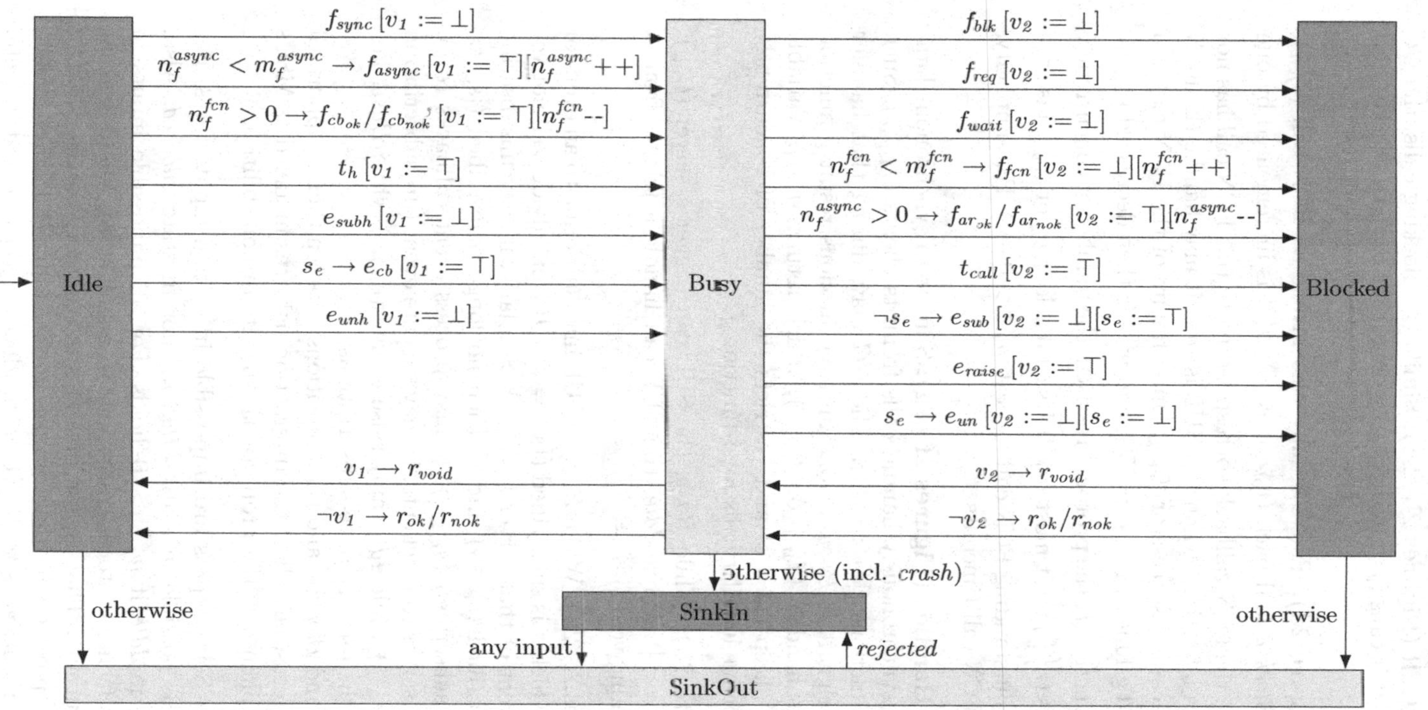

f IDL function (i-function)	v_1	Variable	$\top$ if the current/last in-progress call for state *Busy* returns r_{void}	$\bot$ if it returns r_{ok} or r_{nok}
	v_2	Variable	$\top$ if the current/last in-progress call for state *Blocked* returns r_{void}	$\bot$ if it returns r_{ok} or r_{nok}
t IDL trigger	s_e	Variable	$\top$ if SUL is subscribed to event e	$\bot$ otherwise
e IDL event	n_f^{async}	Variable	Number of f_{async} calls still requiring a matching $f_{ar_{ok}}$ or $f_{ar_{nok}}$	$0 \leq n_f^{async} \leq m_f^{async}$
	n_f^{fcn}	Variable	Number of f_{fcn} calls still requiring a matching $f_{cb_{ok}}$ or $f_{cb_{nok}}$	$0 \leq n_f^{fcn} \leq m_f^{fcn}$

Fig. 3. Interfacing protocol EFSM for ASML's software architecture and communication patterns.

(ii) Request/Wait Call (Figures 2b / 2c): Similar to blocking calls, the *CC* may perform request/wait calls (f_{req} and f_{wait}), going from *Busy* to *Blocked* and back (r_{ok} or r_{nok}).

(iii) FCN Call (Figure 2d): The *CC* may also invoke an FCN call (f_{fcn}), going from *Busy* to *Blocked* and back (r_{ok} or r_{nok}). n_f^{fcn} is incremented by one ($[n_f^{fcn}{+}{+}]$) to indicate the FCN callback corresponding to this FCN call has not yet been handled. At a later time, when the SUL is *Idle*, it may handle the FCN callback, i.e., $f_{cb_{ok}}$ in case of success or $f_{cb_{nok}}$ upon failure of the FCN call. An FCN callback is a void g-function ($[v_1 := \top]$), and n_f^{fcn} is then decreased by one ($[n_f^{fcn}{-}{-}]$). For any i-function f, the protocol restricts the number of concurrently outstanding FCN calls (n_f^{fcn}) to at most m_f^{fcn}. Its callback ($f_{cb_{ok}}$ or $f_{cb_{nok}}$) is only possible if there is an outstanding FCN call (guard '$n_f^{fcn} > 0 \rightarrow$'). For simplicity, we ignore the use of FCN call timeouts.

(v) Asynchronous Handler (Figures 2f / 2g): Similar to synchronous handlers, the SUL may asynchronously handle calls from its clients (f_{async}). Such handlers are void g-functions ($[v_1 := \top]$). The *CC* may, during that handler or at any later time that it is *Busy*, invoke an asynchronous result g-function for this asynchronous handler ($f_{ar_{ok}}$ or $f_{ar_{nok}}$), which returns r_{void}. Variable $0 \leq n_f^{async} \leq m_f^{async}$ keep track of and restricts the number of concurrently outstanding asynchronous handler calls for i-function f.

(vi) Trigger (Figure 2h): While *Busy*, the SUL can trigger a server (t_{call}), returning void ($[v_2 := \top]$). While *Idle*, the SUL can handle a trigger from a client (t_h), also returning void ($[v_1 := \top]$).

(vii) Event (Figures 2i – 2k): While *Busy*, a SUL may subscribe to an event of a server (e_{sub}), after which it is subscribed ($[s_e := \top]$). It can only do so if not yet subscribed to that event of that server ($\neg s_e \rightarrow$). Similarly, it may unsubscribe (e_{un}) if already subscribed ($s_e \rightarrow$) and is then no longer subscribed ($[s_e := \bot]$). While *Idle* and subscribed ($s_e \rightarrow$), it may process event callbacks (e_{cb}). Reversely, acting as a server to its clients, it may execute event (un)subscription handlers (e_{subh} and e_{unh}) while *Idle*, and raise events (e_{raise}) while *Busy*. For simplicity, we ignore the rare use of re-subscriptions.

States *Idle*, *Busy* and *Blocked*, and the transitions between them, support all 7 communication patterns, i.e., allow the interaction patterns modeled as MSCs in Fig. 2. Next, we explain how the protocol satisfies its responsibilities.

(a) Input-Enabled: Some inputs are impossible in certain input states. For instance, a t_h input is possible in state *Idle*, but not in state *Blocked*. Also, $f_{cb_{ok}}$ is only allowed in *Idle* if $n_f^{fcn} > 0$ holds. For all impossible inputs in input states, the interfacing protocol transitions to a sink state, where it keeps producing *rejected* outputs. That is, for invalid inputs it goes to the *SinkOut* output state. There it produces output *rejected*, goes to input sink state *SinkIn*, where it accepts any input, goes to *SinkOut*, produces *rejected* as output, etc. This turns a non-input-enabled *CC* into an input-enabled *SUL*, while preserving all its original externally-observable communication behavior.

(b) Single Input, Single Output: Each of the five protocol states is either an input state (dark gray) or output state (light gray). Input states have only outgoing transitions for inputs, and output states only for outputs. Transitions for inputs go to output states, while output transitions lead to input states. It intuitively matches the duality of g-function call starts and their returns. If the *CC* crashes in state *Busy*, the protocol produces a single *crash* output symbol and goes to *SinkIn*. This way the protocol ensures that each input is followed by a single output, and that they alternate. It also remains input-enabled, and still supports all communication patterns to allow inferring the full *CC* behavior.

(c) Finite Learning Result: To ensure that the SUL represents a finite Mealy machine, certain interactions can be limited. For instance, m_f^{async} limits the number of concurrently outstanding asynchronous handlers for i-function f. Starting with $m_f^{async} = \infty$, intermediate hypotheses may reveal it is necessary to restrict m_f^{async}. This ensures a finite SUL and learning result at the expense of potentially missing some component behavior. The protocol restricts both inputs (e.g., f_{async}) and outputs (e.g., $f_{ar_{ok}}$), redirecting them to sink states. The protocol in Fig. 3 limits only outstanding FCN calls and asynchronous handlers. Theoretically, similar issues could arise for other communication patterns. These can similarly be restricted, but this has been omitted in this paper to keep the protocol simpler, and because they rarely need to be restricted in practice. In particular, request/wait calls are not restricted as they involve only outputs, not inputs, and the company's software architecture rule book, to which all its software must adhere, already allows at most one concurrently outstanding request per i-function f.

The complete behavior of a *CC* can be learned, if it is finitely representable as a Mealy machine, by setting all interaction limits to ∞. Otherwise, by setting interaction limits, a subset of the *CC* behavior can be learned.

The validity of the interfacing protocol follows from its systematic derivation, providing correctness by construction. We do not provide a formal proof of the correctness of our approach, leaving this as future work.

4.5 Interfacing Protocol Optimization

In the interfacing protocol (Fig. 3) the *CC* may, while *Busy*, raise an event (e_{raise}). It is then *Blocked* until the event raise g-function returns (r_{void}). The part from Fig. 3 related to raising event is shown in Fig. 4a. While in state *Blocked* only one input (r_{void}) is allowed, the learner will try out all inputs, only to find out all of them get rejected, except for r_{void}. This holds any time an event is raised by the *CC*.

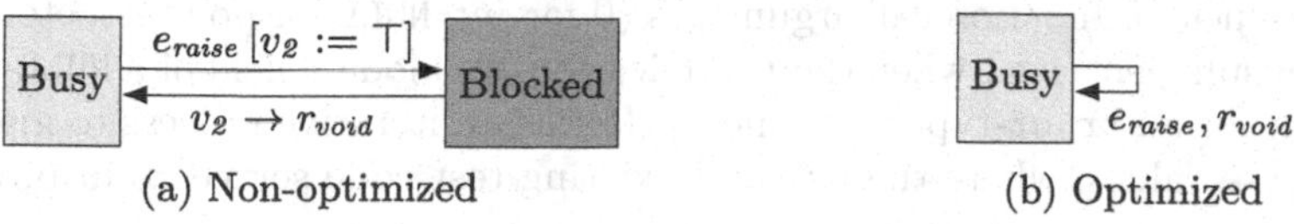

(a) Non-optimized (b) Optimized

Fig. 4. Optimization for raising event in the interfacing protocol.

This can be optimized as shown in Fig. 4b. Here the output (e_{raise}) and subsequent input (r_{void}) are combined into a single transition. To preserve the *single input, single output* property of the interface protocol, the e_{raise}, r_{void} transition from output state *Busy* is considered an 'extra output'. Upon executing such a self-loop, the protocol stores the extra outputs until the next 'real' output. It then prefixes the 'real' output with the extra outputs, in the order they were produced. The mapper, being part of the protocol, maps each of them to a string and combines them to form a single output. For instance, for two consecutive Mealy transitions i/e_{raise} and r_{void}/o, with i some input and o some output, the optimized result would be a single Mealy transition $i/e_{raise}, r_{void}, o$.

All void g-function outputs from *Busy* to *Blocked* allow for this optimization, i.e., $f_{ar_{ok}}$, $f_{ar_{nok}}$, t_{call}, and e_{raise}.

5 Application

We apply our approach to infer the behavior of two ASML software components: a high-level wafer exposure controller (we name it WEC), and a metrology driver (MD). However, these case studies are not a main contribution of our work, but rather examples to show the feasibility of applying our framework in practice, and to discuss the practicalities that it involves. Therefore, and for reasons of confidentiality, we do not describe them in more detail.

For each component, the AAL framework from Fig. 1 needs to be instantiated. The following steps were involved:

1. Framework Generation: For the component of interest, its interfaces must be identified, and their relevant code (g-functions) collected to use as *CC*. The company's proprietary generator takes IDL files with interface methods and automatically generates g-functions. We extended it to generate the *Main* function, dispatchers and stubs, including the interfacing protocol and mappers. The three *I/O* modules are hand-written and reusable. The *SUL*'s *I/O* module includes its main function, which establishes a socket connection with the *SUL Manager* and waits for inputs to dispatch. While any AAL tool can be used, we opt for the mature AAL tool LearnLib [14], making our *AAL* process Java-based. The *SUL Manager* and *SUL*, including the *CC*, are C-based.

2. Initialization: We manually add initialization code to the *SUL*'s new main function, reusing code from the component's original main function.

3. Function Parameters: WEC and MD are control components. They pass function call parameter values along, rather than them being used for control decisions (e.g., `if` statement conditions). We therefore mostly ignore function call parameters, rather than learning register automata. Our generator generates default values for function call arguments (0 for *int*, `NULL` for pointers, etc.). This may be insufficient, e.g., when the *CC* tries to pass along a field of a `NULL`-valued argument for a `struct`-typed parameter. It was an iterative process to manually adapt these values, where the *CC* and existing test code served as inspiration.

4. Interaction Limits: Based on expert knowledge of WEC and MD, we set both interfacing protocol interaction limits: $m_f^{async} = 1$ and $m_f^{fcn} = 1$. Using this low value reduces the size of the *SUL*'s unknown behavior model, for better AAL performance.

5. SUL Compilation: We adapt the component's build scripts, excluding any irrelevant code, e.g., its main function and serialization wrappers, and including the new dispatchers, stubs, and *I/O* module, before compiling the SUL.

6. SUL Manager Compilation: We configure the SUL pool size to 100, and compile the *SUL Manager* using its generated build script.

7. Learner and EO: Our generated *Main* Java class is by default configured to use TTT [13] as *Learner* and Wp [7] as *EO*. To guarantee learning a complete model, Wp requires n, the number of states of the *SUL*'s unknown behavior model. As we don't know n, we guess it, and iteratively increase the value if needed. Caching is also enabled by default.

8. Input Alphabet: The generated *Main* class by default configures the complete input alphabet as derived from the IDL files. It can be reduced to only learn a part of the component's behavior. Considering all provided (to clients) and required (to servers) interfaces, WEC has 591 inputs. It implements 25 distinct workflows. We select five of them, of various complexities, and learn them, including their prerequisite other workflows. For component MD, we keep the complete alphabet with 25 inputs.

9. AAL Process Compilation: We compile the *AAL* process executable.

10. Perform AAL: Finally, we execute the *AAL* process executable to learn models, repeating earlier steps in case of required changes, e.g., after adapting function call arguments or protocol interaction limits.

Each experiment was executed for 24 hours. For WEC, a dedicated system with 24 CPU cores (Intel Xeon Gold 6126) and 64 GB memory was used. For MD, a readily-available virtualized platform with shared resources was used.

We consider the learning/testing rounds up to and including the last learning round that produced the largest hypothesis, and omit subsequent testing that did not find any more counterexamples. Table 2 shows for each (sub-)component (C) the number of inputs (I), the Wp EO n value (Wp-n), the number of Mealy machine states in the model we learned (M-n), the number of equivalence queries (EQs), the number of membership queries (MQs) and membership symbols (MSs), the number of test queries (TQs) and test symbols (TSs), both to the cache (/C) and to the SUL (/S), and the total time in seconds (T).

WEC-1 and WEC-2 are small workflows, without prerequisites. Their largest hypotheses are produced within a few seconds, and no new behavior was found during the many remaining hours of AAL execution. Manual inspection of the component code leads us to conclude they have been learned completely.

WEC-3, WEC-4 and WEC-5 have other workflows as prerequisites. Their largest hypotheses are produced within a few hours. However, they do not accept

Table 2. Case study metrics, per (sub-)component.

C	WEC-1	WEC-2	WEC-3	WEC-4	WEC-5	MD
I	2	6	25	26	30	25
Wp-n	46	17	66	39	66	916
M-n	50	23	71	55	71	917
EQs	5	4	13	8	13	544
MQs/C	538	967	8,876	7,685	10,644	98,635
MQs/S	52	129	1,462	1,281	1,779	38,300
MSs/C	12,554	12,015	143,335	112,681	171,851	2,122,205
MSs/S	1,015	1,490	23,020	18,266	28,072	854,765
TQs/C	1.59×10^7	1,435	1.67×10^9	6.57×10^9	4.13×10^9	9.80×10^7
TQs/S	43	3	5,543	3,048	22,689	196,686
TSs/C	4.91×10^8	14,074	3.08×10^{10}	1.06×10^{11}	7.65×10^{10}	2.00×10^9
TSs/S	1,399	36	88,398	41,046	372,376	4,262,369
T	23	5	2,171	7,569	5,870	62,604

traces that we manually constructed based on their source code. The traces have 86, 100 and 101 inputs, respectively. Learning thus did not yet find all their behavior. This is to be expected though, given that it is hard for black-box testing to find the exact (combination of) prerequisite sequences to test out of all possible test sequences. And even more so considering that we test breadth-first by incrementally increasing the n value of the Wp EO.

For component MD in total 544 hypotheses are constructed in about 17.4 hours. The last hypothesis accepts our manually constructed trace. Acceptance of this trace, and no further counterexample being found for the remaining 6.6 hours, gives us some confidence that we might have found the complete behavior, although we do not have any evidence that we indeed found all behavior.

The learned models can be used for various purposes [3]. Here, our goal is to facilitate a cost-effective transition to MDE, concretely to Verum's commercial ASD Suite[1], which is based on their patented ASD technology [4], and is used by ASML as MDE tooling. To exemplify this, Fig. 5a shows WEC-2 (abbreviated to W) and part of its anonymized context. Figure 5b shows a part of the anonymized learned Mealy machine of WEC-2. The sink state and its incoming and outgoing transitions are purposely omitted. Figure 5c shows the result of manual conversion of the Mealy machine to a partial ASD design model. The conversion is straightforward: Mealy machine states and transitions correspond one-on-one to states and transitions in the ASD model, where inputs become triggers and outputs become actions. For simplicity, we ignore function parameters. ASD requires for each control component both an interface model and a design model. An interface model can be automatically obtained from the AAL result [3], and then similarly converted to an ASD interface model. From the

[1] See https://verum.com/asd.

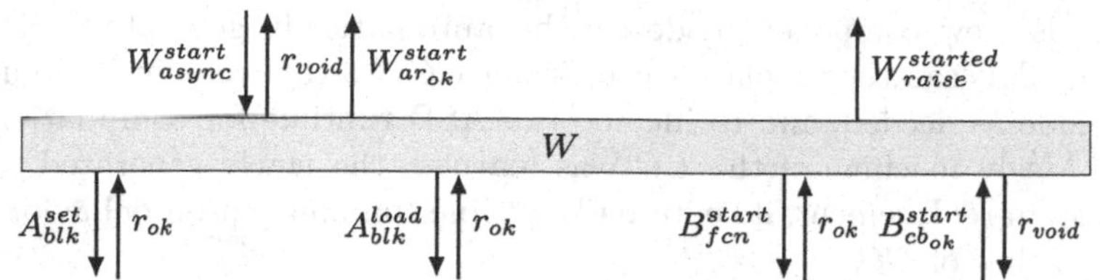

(a) W and some of its communications with its context.

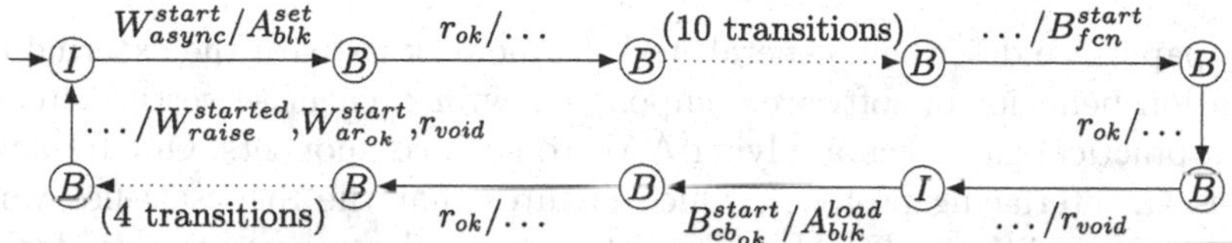

(b) Mealy machine representing a partial learning result. Mealy machine states are labelled with interfacing protocol states: I=Idle, Y=Busy, B=Blocked.

W (W.dm)

W | Data Variables | Service References | Implemented Service | Used Services

SBS | States | State Variables | State Diagram

s1 | s1 (initial state)

	Interface	Event	Guard	Actions	State Variable Updates	Target State
1	s1 (initial state)					
4	W	start_async		A:A.set+		s2
10	s2 (synchronous return state)					
14	A:A	OK		...		s3
19	s3 (synchronous return state)					
...						
109	s13 (synchronous return state)					
117	...	...		B:B.start_fcn+		s14
118	s14 (synchronous return state)					
123	B:B	OK		...		s15
127	s15 (synchronous return state)					
135	...	...		W.VoidReply		s16
136	s16					
143	B:B	start_cb_ok		A:A.load+		s17
145	s17 (synchronous return state)					
149	A:A	OK		...		s18
154	s18 (synchronous return state)					
...						
190	s22 (synchronous return state)					
198	...	...		W.started; W.start_ar_ok B:B.VoidReply		s1

(c) Screenshot of a partial ASD design model in ASD Suite. Irrelevant rows are hidden.

Fig. 5. Partial example of converting learning results to ASD, for WEC-2 (abbreviated 'W'). Naming scheme: W^{start}_{async} is an asynchronous handler for function *start* of W.

ASD models, new component code can be automatically generated using the ASD Suite. This can then replace the existing *CC*. All that remains is to update the glue code as needed, and to include the ASD runtime for compilation. If a complete Mealy machine of the *CC* was learned, the newly generated code is then a drop-in replacement, its externally-visible communication behavior being identical to that of *CC*.

6 Conclusions and Future Work

In this paper, we describe a general AAL framework to learn the external communication behavior of software components with a client-server architecture, filling a practical gap when applying AAL to such components. Our framework includes an interfacing protocol, which ensures that the SUL satisfies various practical preconditions of AAL, even if the isolated component code does not satisfy them. It is future work to infer pushdown automata to prevent having to use interaction limits to ensure finite learning results.

Our main contribution is the systematic way in which we derive the protocol, handling the different types of (a)synchronous communications. We derive, as an example, such a protocol specifically for ASML's software architecture. However, we rely on generic concepts, e.g., function calls and returns, requests and replies, synchronous vs asynchronous calls, and MSCs, that apply to communication patterns of component-based software in general. We therefore expect that our work can be used to similarly derive such protocols and set up learning frameworks at companies with similar software architectures.

The approach ensures correct-by-construction interfacing protocols, but proving this is considered future work. We do show the feasibility of our approach by applying it to infer the behavior of several ASML (sub-)components. We believe that company engineers should be able to similarly apply our framework, given only a document with detailed instructions, which is future work.

Using generators we automate most of the work to set up an AAL environment. Still, this takes up to a few hours per (sub-)component. It is especially time-consuming to provide sensible function call arguments, to ensure that the SUL does not crash and thus exhibits relevant behavior. It is future work to automate this using white-box techniques, and to infer register automata for components with argument-dependent behavior.

Furthermore, scalability remains a major challenge. Even after hundreds of billions of test symbols, the complete behavior was not learned for some subcomponents. There are various techniques that can improve active learning performance, including checkpointing, incremental equivalence queries [11], white-box approaches [12] and incorporating available traces [19]. Integrating them into our framework is also future work.

Still, for some (sub-)components we learned the complete behavior well within a day. This can significantly reduce the time to obtain a model of their behavior, compared to modeling them in a completely manual way. It is future work to automate the conversion to ASD, and further investigate the qualitative and quantitative advantages of our approach compared to manual modeling.

Acknowledgments. The authors would like to thank ASML for making this work possible and supporting it, and Mladen Skelin for his contributions to this work, in particular the implementation.

References

1. Aarts, F., Heidarian, F., Vaandrager, F.: A theory of history dependent abstractions for learning interface automata. In: Koutny, M., Ulidowski, I. (eds.) CONCUR 2012. LNCS, vol. 7454, pp. 240–255. Springer, Heidelberg (2012). https://doi.org/10.1007/978-3-642-32940-1_18
2. Angluin, D.: Learning regular sets from queries and counterexamples. Inf. Comput. **75**(2), 87–106 (1987). https://doi.org/10.1016/0890-5401(87)90052-6
3. Aslam, K., Cleophas, L., Schiffelers, R., van den Brand, M.: Interface protocol inference to aid understanding legacy software components. Softw. Syst. Model. **19**(6), 1519–1540 (2020). https://doi.org/10.1007/s10270-020-00809-2
4. Broadfoot, G.H., Broadfoot, P.J.: Academia and industry meet: some experiences of formal methods in practice. In: Tenth Asia-Pacific Software Engineering Conference, pp. 49–58. IEEE (2003). https://doi.org/10.1109/APSEC.2003.1254357
5. Cho, C.Y., Babić, D., Shin, E.C.R., Song, D.: Inference and analysis of formal models of botnet command and control protocols. In: Proceedings of the 17th ACM conference on Computer and communications security, pp. 426–439 (2010). https://doi.org/10.1145/1866307.1866355
6. al Duhaiby, O., Mooij, A., van Wezep, H., Groote, J.F.: Pitfalls in applying model learning to industrial legacy software. In: Margaria, T., Steffen, B. (eds.) ISoLA 2018. LNCS, vol. 11247, pp. 121–138. Springer, Cham (2018). https://doi.org/10.1007/978-3-030-03427-6_13
7. Fujiwara, S., Bochmann, G.V., Khendek, F., Amalou, M., Ghedamsi, A.: Test selection based on finite state models. IEEE Trans. Softw. Eng. **17**(6), 591–603 (1991). https://doi.org/10.1109/32.87284
8. Gomaa, H.: Real-time software design for embedded systems. Cambridge University Press, USA, 1st edn. (2016). https://doi.org/10.1017/CBO9781139644532
9. de la Higuera, C.: Grammatical inference: learning automata and grammars. Cambridge University Press (2010). https://doi.org/10.1017/CBO9781139194655
10. Hooimeijer, B., Geilen, M., Groote, J.F., Hendriks, D., Schiffelers, R.: Constructive Model Inference: model learning for component-based software architectures. In: Proceedings of the 17th International Conference on Software Technologies (ICSOFT), pp. 146–158. SciTePress (2022). https://doi.org/10.5220/0011145700003266
11. Howar, F.: Active learning of interface programs, Ph. D. thesis, Technische Universität Dortmund (2012). https://doi.org/10.17877/DE290R-4817
12. Howar, F., Steffen, B.: Active automata learning in practice. In: Bennaceur, A., Hähnle, R., Meinke, K. (eds.) Machine Learning for Dynamic Software Analysis: Potentials and Limits. LNCS, vol. 11026, pp. 123–148. Springer, Cham (2018). https://doi.org/10.1007/978-3-319-96562-8_5
13. Isberner, M., Howar, F., Steffen, B.: The TTT algorithm: a redundancy-free approach to active automata learning. In: Bonakdarpour, B., Smolka, S.A. (eds.) RV 2014. LNCS, vol. 8734, pp. 307–322. Springer, Cham (2014). https://doi.org/10.1007/978-3-319-11164-3_26

14. Isberner, M., Howar, F., Steffen, B.: The open-source LearnLib. In: Kroening, D., Păsăreanu, C.S. (eds.) CAV 2015. LNCS, vol. 9206, pp. 487–495. Springer, Cham (2015). https://doi.org/10.1007/978-3-319-21690-4_32
15. Merten, M., Isberner, M., Howar, F., Steffen, B., Margaria, T.: Automated learning setups in automata learning. In: Margaria, T., Steffen, B. (eds.) ISoLA 2012. LNCS, vol. 7609, pp. 591–607. Springer, Heidelberg (2012). https://doi.org/10.1007/978-3-642-34026-0_44
16. de Ruiter, J., Poll, E.: Protocol state fuzzing of tls implementations. In: 24th USENIX Security Symposium (USENIX Security 15), pp. 193–206. USENIX Association (2015). https://doi.org/10.5555/2831143.2831156
17. Szyperski, C., Gruntz, D., Murer, S.: Component software: beyond object-oriented programming. Pearson Education, 2nd edn. (2002)
18. Whittle, J., Hutchinson, J., Rouncefield, M.: The state of practice in model-driven engineering. IEEE Softw. **31**(3), 79–85 (2014). https://doi.org/10.1109/MS.2013.65
19. Yang, N., et al.: Improving model inference in industry by combining active and passive learning. In: 2019 IEEE 26th International Conference on Software Analysis, Evolution and Reengineering (SANER), pp. 253–263 (2019). https://doi.org/10.1109/SANER.2019.8668007

Verified Software Units for Simple DFA Modules and Objects in C

Lennart Beringer(✉)

Princeton University, Princeton, NJ 08544, USA
eberinge@cs.princteon.edu

Abstract. Finite state machines occur ubiquitously in modern software, often in the form of C code that is synthesized from higher-level descriptions. To explore how the resulting code bases can be integrated into foundational verification infrastructures, we present formal specifications and machine-checked proofs of DFA representations using VST, a higher-order separation logic for C implemented in the Coq proof assistant. Paying particular attention to modularity and API-level representation hiding, we consider statically linked modules as well as object-inspired programming styles. Exploiting the abstraction capabilities of a recent VST enhancement, Verified Software Units (VSU), we complement separate compilation by separate verification and obtain instances of behavioral subtyping as separation logic entailments between suitable object representation predicates.

Keywords: Verified Software Units · Verified Software Toolchain · Deterministic finite automata · Formal verification · Semantic subtyping

1 Introduction

The emergence of alternative languages notwithstanding, the world still runs on C. Complementing standard libraries and manually developed code bases that form the backbone of any contemporary systems stack, a substantial fraction of C code is nowadays machine-generated by compilation or synthesis from higher-level modeling or programming languages. This is particularly pronounced in the embedded systems domain, where C plays the role of a lingua franca in which software components that originate from multiple vendors are integrated. To facilitate such integration, industry-wide coding guidelines and architectural frameworks such as MISRA-C [5] and Autosar [6] are complemented by component-oriented libraries that facilitate reuse and reconfiguration, lightweight specification formalisms, and code synthesis by model-based development tools.

These technologies help to meet rapidly evolving requirements and to control the ever-increasing design complexity. However, deployments in safety- or security-critical applications require higher levels of assurance. Ideally, provably sound code analysis or verification results would formally connect upwards to domain-specific validation that establishes adherence to model-level

T. Margaria and B. Steffen (Eds.): ISoLA 2022, LNCS 13702, pp. 237–258, 2022.
https://doi.org/10.1007/978-3-031-19756-7_14

requirements, and downwards via compiler correctness to guarantees of (or assumptions about) the underlying hardware or runtime system.

A key challenge in the development of such high-assurance arguments is the establishment of coherent semantic frameworks in which the guarantees and assumptions of individual components can be logically integrated, checked against one another, and tracked across multiple levels of abstraction.

This paper illustrates the role a verification environment embedded in an interactive proof assistant (Coq) can play in such a scenario, with a focus on the interfaces between basic implementation components – compilation units – and a concrete functional domain – deterministic finite automata (DFAs).

Concretely, we use the program logic of the Verified Software Toolchain (VST, [3]), Verifiable C, to prove implementation correctness for DFA representations in three idiomatic C programming styles. By explicitly embedding model-level DFA representations, our specifications provide an abstraction bridge as motivated above; in fact, our DFAs seamlessly connect to Reglang [17], a pre-existing Coq theory of DFAs, regular languages, and related formalisms that is fully decoupled from C verification. On the other hand, foundational assurance extends all the way to (CompCert) assembly, as VST's program logic is provably sound w.r.t. the operational semantics of CompCert Clight [13].

While state machine models in modern model-based engineering tools are typically richer than simple DFAs, our work thus indicates how the generation of C code by such tools can in principle be complemented by the synthesis of specifications and (perhaps later) proofs.

Our three programming styles cover

a) a static module realizing a single DFA (Sect. 3),
b) an interface that applies uniformly to multiple statically linked DFA implementations (Sect. 4), and
c) lightweight DFA objects with dynamic allocation and constructors for product, complement, and intersection DFAs (Sect. 5).

All styles employ a "dataless" discipline [7,22,28] and realize representation hiding; a fine-grained header-file organization separates method interfaces from constructors. Equally importantly, representation hiding is retained during verification: by exploiting the principles of Verified Software Units (VSUs, [9]), module- or object-internal data organization is not revealed in specifications, and separate compilation units can be verified independently.

To validate that the mutual assumptions of modules are ultimately resolved, we (separately) verify a client that operates on multiple DFAs, and apply VSU's linking tactics to combine the client with the DFA-implementing code units.

Our latter two coding styles employ API interfaces in which the DFA operations are presented as groups of function pointers in a **struct**, allowing clients to invoke these operations in the style of dynamic method dispatch. A similar pattern was already used to verify a more powerful notion of pure objects in our previous publication [9]: exploiting VST's support for step-indexing [20] and Hofmann and Pierce's theory of positive subtyping [21], objects in *loc. cit.* supported method invocation on *self*, inheritance of data representations or function implementations, and method overriding with early or late binding. The present paper employs a more fine-grained API structure but utilizes a simpler object model that does not support *self*. We do not treat implementation inheritance or method overriding in the present paper, and eschew positive subtyping.

Our final contribution is an investigation of semantic subtyping as entailment between object representation predicates (Sect. 6). While limited to the setting of DFAs, this addresses a challenge identified by Parkinson and Bierman [27] in a separation logic for a Java-like language. As far as we are aware, neither behavioral subtyping [24] nor related notions such as supertype abstraction and intrinsic refinement [23] have ever been studied in a machine-checked logic for objects, even outside separation logic.

The Coq development underlying this article is available online [10].

2 High-Level Overview of Verifiable C

Verifiable C [2] – the program logic of VST – realizes Hoare logic [19] in the interactive proof assistant Coq [8,12], for virtually the entire C language. A verification engineer equips functions with formal specifications, i.e. pre- and postconditions that describe arguments, return values, and memory states upon function entry and exit, using formulae in mathematical logic. The following characteristics distinguish Verifiable C from other verification tools:

heap modularity: overcoming scalability limitations of Hoare's original formalism, Verifiable C employs separation logic [26,29] to specify (non)-aliasing between data structures in memory. As detailed below, function specifications are expressed w.r.t. only those locations that are potentially read, written, or freed; memory regions outside this footprint are guaranteed to be left untouched. The resulting reasoning style is more modular than that of verification frameworks that do not employ separation logic.

expressivity: rather than requiring assertions to be first-order formulae over the programming language's expressions, assertions in Verifiable C are Coq propositions and hence support higher-order quantification. Typically, they refer to constructions in Coq's ambient logic that are amenable to proofs by induction or domain-specific reasoning. Parametricity and existential abstraction realize the software principles of information hiding and data abstraction at the level of specifications and functional models. This enables the construction of concise representation predicates for complex data types and facilitates reasoning about such constructions at a high level of abstraction. The semantic complexity of VST's underlying step-indexed model is encapsulated by an abstract type `mpred` of memory predicates.

foundational soundness: VST's machine-checked soundness proof justifies the semantic model w.r.t. the operational semantics of Clight [13], an intermediate representation from the CompCert compiler. This eliminates the potential for any divergence between Verifiable C's interpretation of the C language and the interpretation taken by the compiler. Verifiable C's symbolic execution [15] operates directly on Clight abstract syntax trees. Notationally, specifications and intermediate assertions (e.g. loop invariants) are defined directly in the Coq environment rather than as source code annotations.

In addition to satisfying its (partial-correctness) specification, a successfully verified program is memory safe and free of undefined behavior. The latter property means that the program is also likely to be easier to port.

Expanding on the aspect of heap modularity, the main novelty of separation logic is to complement ordinary conjunction $A \& B$ with the *separating/spacial* conjunction operator $A * B$. This assertion expresses the ability to partition the heap (or more generally: resources behaving in accordance with the axioms of a separation algebra [14,16]) into two disjoint parts satisfying, respectively, the assertions A and B. As a consequence, code fragments can be specified using pre- and postconditions that mention only the code's *footprint*, i.e. the heap regions read, written, of freed; to embed such a *small-footprint* specification into a larger context, separation logic introduces a new proof rule, the *frame rule* $\frac{\{P\}c\{Q\}}{\{P*F\}c\{Q*F\}}$ (we omit some side conditions). VST realizes separation logic using symbolic execution that traverses the program text in forward direction and employs formulae in separation logic as abstract states. Framing is typically implicit. Semi-automated proof construction is further facilitated using Coq tactics that simplify or solve side conditions that arise during program traversal, such as loop invariants or other entailments. Remaining proof goals are solved interactively by the proof engineer, who may subsequently isolate his proof as a stand-alone lemma and add it to a database of automation hints, hence improving automation over time.

In addition to the formula **emp** – which specifies the empty heap and constitutes the neutral element of $*$—a crucial building block of VST's separation logic is the "mapsto" predicate $l \mapsto_{\tau}^{\pi} v$, which specifies a heap containing a single C object of type τ (e.g. a **struct**) located at base address l and containing the content v, with access permission π.

Applying some pretty-printing to the formal definitions in Coq, we write $\forall \boldsymbol{x}. \{Pre(\boldsymbol{x})\} \leadsto \{Post(\boldsymbol{x})\}$ to denote a partial-correctness VST function specification with precondition $Pre(\boldsymbol{x})$ and postcondition $Post(\boldsymbol{x})$. The logical function parameters $\boldsymbol{x}$ transport information from pre- to postconditions similar to auxiliary variables in first-order program logics but are permitted to be of (almost) arbitrary Coq type. When verifying some client code, the VST proof engineer (or the proof automation tactic) selects a suitable instantiation each time the symbolic execution reaches a function invocation.

To allow specification reuse, VST contains a notion of function specification subsumption [11], $\phi <: \psi$, stating that any function satisfying ϕ also satisfies ψ. Again simplifying the formal definition for presentational purposes, subsumption requires the entailment

$$\forall \boldsymbol{y}. Pre'(\boldsymbol{y}) \vdash \exists \boldsymbol{x} F. Pre(\boldsymbol{x}) * F \;\&\; (Post(\boldsymbol{x}) * F \vdash Post'(\boldsymbol{y}))$$

to hold, where $\phi = \forall \boldsymbol{x}. \{Pre(\boldsymbol{x})\} \leadsto \{Post(\boldsymbol{x})\}$ and $\psi = \forall \boldsymbol{y}. \{Pre'(\boldsymbol{y})\} \leadsto \{Post'(\boldsymbol{y})\}$.

Combining VST's capabilities for verifying individual C functions with Coq's type-theoretic abstraction principles, Verified Software Units (VSU [9]) is a calculus for composing separately verified compilation units, in rough correspondence to assembly-level linking. To maintain representation hiding, VSU bundles the specifications of all functions exposed by a header file API to an *abstract specification interface* (ASI), so that the specifications can be made jointly parametric in abstract representation predicates and are defined without recourse to syntactic identifiers. Witnesses for these predicate parameters are constructed as part of the verification process when a concrete implementation of the API is verified. Of course, different implementations typically use different internal data representations and hence yield different witnesses, but the parametrization mechanism ensures that such differences are opaquely hidden from client-side verification. To nevertheless enable selective exposure of reasoning principles to clients, predicate parameters may take the form of *abstract predicate declarations* (APDs) which combine one or more predicates with suitable axioms in a single Coq definition. Our coding styles differ in the exact predicate parameters used, but layout of user data is always hidden as only the general structure of objects is revealed to clients – just enough to enable method dispatch.

The formal statement resulting from verifying the Clight abstract syntax tree of compilation unit p.c takes the form

$$\vdash_P^{\mathbb{S}} [\mathcal{I}]\, \mathrm{p}\, [\mathcal{E}]$$

where $\mathcal{I}$ and $\mathcal{E}$ are the VST specifications for the functions imported and exported by p.c, respectively. Typically, $\mathcal{E}$ is the ASI for a C header file p.h, partially instantiated with APD substantiations for the data structures introduced by p.c; parameters representing data structures defined in other modules remain uninstantiated. Finally, $\mathbb{S}$ collects specifications of system functions (like `exit`) that VST relies upon but that are left unverified even in linked programs for lack of a verified operating system, while P specifies the global memory reserved by p.c upon program start.

3 Specifying and Verifying a Single Static DFA Module

Our first coding style represents a DFA as an implementation of SingleDFA.h, as shown in Fig. 1.

```
#include <stdbool.h>

typedef unsigned char uchar;
void DFA_init (void);
bool DFA_final (void);
void DFA_step (uchar);

SingleDFA.h
```

```
#include "SingleDFA.h"
bool DFA_state;

void DFA_init (void) { DFA_state = false; }
bool DFA_final (void) { return (DFA_state); }
void DFA_step (uchar c) {
  DFA_state = (c == '0'); }

SingleDFA.c
```

Fig. 1. Header file and implementation for a static DFA module.

C's linking regime entails that DFA_init, DFA_final, and DFA_step can each only have a single implementation and hence statically determines the DFA that is realized. The code shown realizes the DFA depicted in Fig. 2 (left); concurrent use of some implementation for the alternative DFA shown in the same figure would require defining a syntactically distinct API.

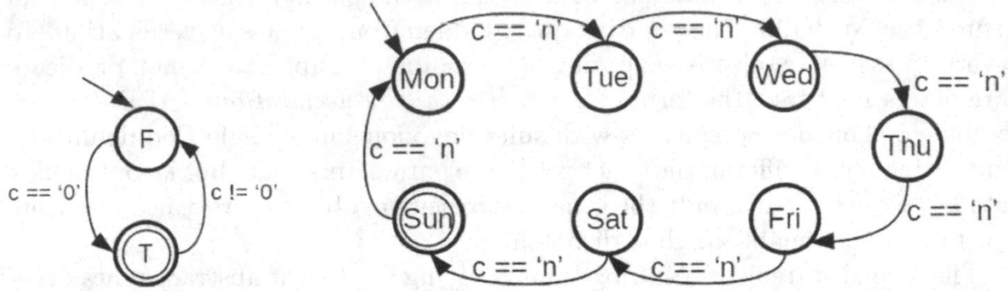

Fig. 2. DFAs TrueFalseDFA and WeekdayDFA; only non-trivial transitions are shown.

To match the program's information hiding, client-visible specification interfaces are generic in the conceptual DFA and allow the transparent substitution of different C implementations for any concrete DFA. We parameterize the specifications by a model-level DFA, i.e. an instance of the type

Record Dfa $\{\Sigma : \text{Type}\}$:=
  { Dfa_state :> Type; *(*State set*)*
   Dfa_s : Dfa_state; *(*Start state*)*
   Dfa_fin : Dfa_state → bool; *(*Acceptance condition*)*
   Dfa_trans : Dfa_state → Σ → Dfa_state *(* Step function*)* }.

where coercion :> enables identification of a Dfa with its state set where appropriate, and curly braces around parameter Σ instruct Coq to automatically infer this parameter – explicit instantiation can be achieved using notation @.

Doczkal and Smolka's Reglang [17] employs virtually the same type but requires the alphabet Σ and the state set to be finite, and models acceptance as a finite set. All DFAs treated in this paper are in fact finite, but we omit these conditions from our definition to avoid clashes between VST's pretty-printing notations and those defined in Reglang or its underlying `ssreflect` library. The formal connection to Reglang's reasoning infrastructure is easily established using *verification glue code*: the three operations factor homomorphically through the expected bijections between the alphabets and the state sets.

To specify SingleDFA.h, we introduce an abstract specification interface that makes the specifications of the three API-exposed function jointly parametric in an automaton A (an element of type Dfa) and a representation predicate P for A; see Fig. 3. Different implementations of A typically yield different predicate definitions for P, but client-side reasoning effectively proceeds at the abstraction level of A: no matter the definition of P, an assertion $P\,a$ gv intuitively asserts that *the module's variables currently represent* A *in state* a*;* item gv here is an

Function	Spec
single_init()	$\forall\, a$ gv. $\{P\ a$ gv$\} \rightsquigarrow \{P$ (Dfa_s A) gv$\}$
single_final()	$\forall\, a$ gv. $\{P\ a$ gv$\} \rightsquigarrow \{b.\ b =$ Dfa_fin A a & $P\ a$ gv$\}$
single_step(c)	$\forall\, a$ gv d. $\{CharRep(d, c)$ & $P\ a$ gv$\} \rightsquigarrow \{P$ (Dfa_trans A a d) gv$\}$

Fig. 3. Specifications for the functions from SingleDFA.h, parametric in a Dfa A (and implicitly in A's alphabet, Σ) and a predicate P : Dfa_state A $\rightarrow$ globals $\rightarrow$ mpred.

environments of global variables, i.e. an element of type globals $\widehat{=}$ ident $\rightarrow$ val. By universally quantifying over gv, the specifications avoid exposing the particular global variable(s) used by an implementation, like DFA_state in SingleDFA.c.

All three specifications take the form $\forall \boldsymbol{x}. \{Pre(\boldsymbol{x})\} \rightsquigarrow \{Post(\boldsymbol{x})\}$ described earlier. Items representing the function parameter(s) – like c in the case of single_step – are formally part of the universally quantified logical parameters $\boldsymbol{x}$ but occur notationally in the typical position next to the function name.

Exploiting the embedding of DFAs via the representation predicates P, the specifications connect the C functions to the corresponding Coq constructions Dfa_s, Dfa_fin, and Dfa_trans: (i) the specification of single_init indicates that the function puts the automaton into its initial state, irrespectively of its previous state; (ii) the specification of single_final expresses that the C function does not modify the automaton's state but returns the (C value corresponding to the) result of evaluating the model-level predicate Dfa_fin on the automaton's current state; (iii) the specification of single_step expresses that the C code performs a transition from state a to Dfa_trans A a d, where the additional term $CharRep(d, c)$ – formally another parameter of the ASI but this will only be relevant in Sect. 6 – specifies the relationship between the uchar c and the element d of A's alphabet.

The counterpart of an ASI is a verified software unit (VSU); it furnishes the existence of a predicate P and certifies the satisfaction of the specifications relative to this definition, for a specific C implementation of the API and hence necessarily with reference to a specific DFA. The DFA implemented by SingleDFA.c can easily be defined as an element of type Dfa:

Definition TrueFalseDFA: Dfa bool :=
{| Dfa_state := bool; Dfa_s := false; Dfa_fin := λ a. a; Dfa_trans := λ a d. d |}.

To define SingleDFA.c's VSU, we import its abstract syntax tree as produced by CompCert's parser – in contrast, the ASI construction is parametric in identifiers and does not require access to C code. We substantiate P by the predicate (gv _DFA_state) $\mapsto^{\mathsf{Ews}}_{\mathsf{tbool}}$ a which asserts that location gv _DFA_state holds a value of C type tbool that represents state a (a value of Coq type bool); the exclusive-write-share Ews confers the right to read or modify the content of this location:

Definition SingleGV (a:Dfa_state(TrueFalseDFA)) gv := (gv _DFA_state) $\mapsto^{\mathsf{Ews}}_{\mathsf{tbool}}$ a.

We abbreviate the specialization of the ASI with automaton TrueFalseDFA and predicate SingleGV by $\varphi_{\mathsf{single}}$. Verifying the function bodies from Fig. 1

```
#include <stdbool.h>

typedef unsigned char uchar;

typedef struct staticOps {
  void (*st_init) (void);
  bool (*st_final) (void);
  void (*st_step) (uchar);
} * StaticOps;
```
StaticDFA.h

```
#include "StaticDFA.h"
StaticOps make_StaticTrueFalse(void);
```
StaticTrueFalse.h

```
#include "StaticDFA.h"

StaticOps make_StaticWeekdays(void);
```
StaticWeekdays.h

Fig. 4. API of static DFA modules and example implementations.

against $\varphi_{\mathsf{single}}$ proceeds semi-automatically using VST's symbolic execution, taking only a handful of Coq commands in each case. Finally, we prove that the initial state constructed when C's runtime system initializes the module's global variables satisfies the specialization of SingleGV to state Dfa_s(TrueFalseDFA), i.e. false. We combine the constructed proofs to a formal VSU judgment that is suitable for processing by our linking system (see Sect. 7) and certifies adherence of the compilation unit's code to the instantiated ASI:

Theorem 1. $\vdash^{\emptyset}_{\mathsf{SingleGV\ false}} [\emptyset]\ \texttt{SingleDFA}\ [\varphi_{\mathsf{single}}]$.

4 Statically Allocated DFA Objects

A more flexible representation that supports dynamic coexistence of multiple DFAs – of different functionality, but each with a single implementation and instance – is shown in Fig. 4 (left). The operations are exposed as a collection of function pointers in a **struct**. We declare prototypes of "static constructors" for different DFAs in separate header files – each will be implemented by a distinct compilation unit. Clients hence import constructors selectively but employ a uniform regime for invoking operations. The type signatures of the three operations are as before, but individual DFAs can now be referred to (and distinguished from each other) via the pointers returned by the constructors. However, note that object handles are not passed as function arguments to the operations.

The interface is appropriate for an implementation such as the one shown in Fig. 5, which realizes the two-state automaton from Fig. 2 by employing – in addition to truefalse – a statically allocated staticOps **struct** that contains function pointers for the three operations. The address of the method table then constitutes the constructor's return value but the name st_tf_ops remains private.

The compilation unit for a static-module implementation WeekdayDFA, StaticWeekdays.c, uses an **enum** type with seven variants to represent the automaton's state but is otherwise similar to StaticTrueFalse.c.

```
#include "StaticTrueFalse.h"
bool truefalse;

void st_tf_init () { truefalse = false; }
bool st_tf_final () { return (truefalse); }
void st_tf_step (uchar c) { truefalse = (c == '0'); }
struct staticOps st_tf_ops = {st_tf_init, st_tf_final, st_tf_step};
StaticOps make_StaticTrueFalse() { return (&st_tf_ops); }
```

StaticTrueFalse.c

Fig. 5. Implementation of a static-object-DFA.

Function	Spec
st_init()	$\forall\, a\ \mathsf{gv}\ v.\ \{P\ (a, \mathsf{gv}, v)\} \leadsto \{P\ (\text{Dfa\_s A}, \mathsf{gv}, v)\}$
st_final()	$\forall\, a\ \mathsf{gv}\ v.\ \{P\ (a, \mathsf{gv}, v)\} \leadsto \{b.\ b = \text{Dfa\_fin A a}\ \&\ P\ (a, \mathsf{gv}, v)\}$
st_step(c)	$\forall\, a\ \mathsf{gv}\ d.\ \{\mathit{CharRep}(d, c)\ \&\ P\ (a, \mathsf{gv}, v)\} \leadsto \{P\ (\text{Dfa\_trans A}\ a\ d, \mathsf{gv}, v)\}$

Fig. 6. Specifications for the functions in StaticDFA.h are parametric in Dfa A and predicate P : GPred(Dfa_state A).

4.1 Specification of the Statically Allocated Objects

The specifications for StaticDFA.h parameterize over a Dfa A as before, but the type of representation predicates P is modified to GPred(Dfa_state A) where

Definition GPred (T:Type):= (T $*$ globals $*$ val) $\rightarrow$ mpred.

The additional argument of type val will be instantiated to an object's location.

As StaticDFA.h is only implemented indirectly, as part of an implementation of StaticTrueFalse.h or StaticWeekdays.h, the specifications in Fig. 6 are not directly exposed as an ASI. Instead, the ASI merely contains a specification for the static constructors. The postcondition of constructors will establish the existence of a (static) object, revealing just enough representation details to enable verification of the function-pointer-based operation dispatch.

To prepare for the definition of such constructor specifications, we define a generic method table predicate, slightly adjusting the definition from [9]:

$$\mathsf{MTable}(T, t, \mathit{names}, m, \mathit{specs}, \mathit{fptrs}, \mathcal{P}) \mathrel{\widehat{=}} \mathop{\ast}_{(\mu,\phi,f)\in \mathit{names}\times \mathit{specs}\times \mathit{fptrs}} \left(\exists\, v\ \pi. \begin{array}{l} \mathsf{JMeq}(v, f)\ \&\ \mathsf{readable}(\pi)\ \& \\ \mathsf{funcptr}\ (\phi\, \mathcal{P})\ f * m.\mu \mapsto_t^{\pi} v \end{array} \right)$$

The predicate expresses that the t-**struct** at address m holds (at offsets indicated by the field names *names*) pointers *fptrs* to functions that conform to specifications which are obtained by specializing *specs* (which has Coq type list (GPred(T) $\rightarrow$ funspec)) to the representation invariant $\mathcal{P}$: GPred(T). VST's general predicate funcptr φ f asserts that location f holds a function satisfying specification φ. Implicitly, the lists *names*, *specs*, and *fptrs* are of equal length. Use of

John-Major-equality $\mathsf{JMeq}(v, f)$ here – a type-theoretic notion of equality relating entities that are formally of different Coq type [25] – is required as the definition of MTable is part of our generic, application-independent framework where VST's calculation of C type information implicit in the definition of $m.\mu \mapsto_t^{\pi} v$ fails as it requires data that is only available for concrete Clight code units.

We define a generic representation predicate for statically allocated objects that asserts the existence of a method table separate from the object's data region, w.r.t. a shared representation invariant, $\mathcal{P}$, hiding the function pointers:

Definition StaticObj (T:Type) ($\mathcal{P}$:GPred T) t *names specs* : GPred T :=
$\lambda\ (x, \mathsf{gv}, v).\ \exists\ \mathit{fptrs}.\ \mathcal{P}(x, \mathsf{gv}, v)\ *\ \mathsf{MTable}(T, t, \mathit{names}, v, \mathit{specs}, \mathit{fptrs}, \mathcal{P})$.

VSUs implementing an object for DFA A will have to exhibit an element of type

Record DFA_APD$_A$:= {DFA_GV: globals → mpred; DFA_Inv: GPred (Dfa_state A)}.

The first component represents the implementing module's state prior to invoking the constructor, i.e. the content of the global variables just after program start; component DFA_Inv characterizes the object once it is operational, by detailing how the content of these locations represent the DFA's state as it evolves.

Specializing some syntactic parameters of StaticObj and writing StaticSpecs (of Coq type list (GPred(Dfa_state A) → funspec)) for the partial specialization of the specifications from Fig. 6 to A, we arrive at the following representation predicate for static objects for A, for S of type DFA_APD$_A$:

$\mathsf{SDFA}_A^S \mathrel{\widehat{=}}$
StaticObj (Dfa_state A) (DFA_Inv$_S$) staticOps [st_init; st_final; st_step] StaticSpecs

The constructor specification in Fig. 7 transforms a module's internal state from the configuration DFA_GV$_S$ to the configuration describing A in its initial state, highlighting that each module yields only a single DFA.

Function	Spec
...(...)	$\forall\, \mathsf{gv}.\ \{\text{DFA\_GV}_S\ \mathsf{gv}\} \leadsto \{\exists p.\ \mathsf{SDFA}_A^S\ (\text{Dfa\_s A}, \mathsf{gv}, p)\}$

Fig. 7. Specification of constructors for static objects supporting StaticDFA.h, parametric in A and S: DFA_APD$_A$. The ellipses indicate that the specification applies to the constructors from Fig. 4 but also to those for static modules for other DFAs.

4.2 Verification of Static-Object Implementations

The verification of the implementation in Fig. 5 first defines the required element of type DFA_APD$_{\mathsf{TrueFalseDFA}}$. Both components specify the content of the variable truefalse, but the predicate applicable at program start additionally includes points-to predicates for the functions:

Definition StaticTrueFalseInv: GPred bool := $\lambda\ (d, \mathsf{gv}, v).\ (\mathsf{gv\ truefalse}) \mapsto^{\mathsf{Ews}}_{\mathsf{tbool}} d.$

Definition StaticTrueFalseGV gv := EX $\pi_i\ \pi_f\ \pi_s$.
 $\mathsf{readable}(\pi_i)\ \&\ (\mathsf{gv\ st\_tf\_ops}).\mathsf{st\_init} \mapsto^{\pi_i}_{\mathsf{staticOps}} (\mathsf{gv\ st\_tf\_init}) *$
 $\mathsf{readable}(\pi_f)\ \&\ (\mathsf{gv\ st\_tf\_ops}).\mathsf{st\_final} \mapsto^{\pi_f}_{\mathsf{staticOps}} (\mathsf{gv\ st\_tf\_final}) *$
 $\mathsf{readable}(\pi_s)\ \&\ (\mathsf{gv\ st\_tf\_ops}).\mathsf{st\_step} \mapsto^{\pi_s}_{\mathsf{staticOps}} (\mathsf{gv\ st\_tf\_step}) *$
 $(\mathsf{gv\ truefalse}) \mapsto^{\mathsf{Ews}}_{\mathsf{tbool}} \mathsf{false}.$

Definition StaticTrueFalseAPD =
 {| DFA_GV := StaticTrueFalseGV; DFA_Inv := StaticTrueFalseInv |}.

We verify the private functions st_tf_init, st_tf_final, and st_tf_step with respect to the specifications from Fig. 6, instantiating P with StaticTrueFalseInv. The proofs are virtually identical to those in the previous section.

The same specialization of Fig. 6 is used to further instantiate the MTable, as required for establishing the postcondition of the constructor specification $\phi_{\mathsf{StaticTrueFalse}}$, i.e. the specialization of Fig. 7 to StaticTrueFalseAPD. We again prove that the initial program state entails StaticTrueFalseGV and finally export the proof of the entire module as a formal VSU statement that exposes the constructor as the only function that clients may invoke directly:

Theorem 2. *The following judgment is derivable in Coq:*

$$\vdash^{\emptyset}_{\mathsf{StaticTrueFalseGV}} [\emptyset]\ \mathtt{StaticTrueFalse}\ [(\mathsf{make\_StaticTrueFalse}, \phi_{\mathsf{StaticTrueFalse}})].$$

The proof of StaticWeekdays.c proceeds along the same lines.

The above definition of StaticTrueFalseInv leaves v unconstrained, so one may wonder whether the adjustment of the invariant's type is useful. Indeed, the same proof script works if we strengthen the invariant by the clause $v = \mathsf{gv\ st\_tf\_ops}$. However, the fact that the client never passes the object's address back into the module renders this additional clause moot. Of course, the verification of a client still relies on the accessibility of the method table via the object reference (just as the C code does), but this is already ensured by the definition of StaticObj.

5 Dynamically Allocated DFA Objects

To enable the dynamic allocation of multiple instances of each DFA we further modify the API, as shown in Fig. 8. Objects are represented as elements of **struct** object and hold a reference to a method table in field ops; our implementations will represent private object state in additional fields that are not exposed. To enable the operations to access these data regions, the function pointers receive a reference to the object as additional argument. The figure also shows APIs of object-constructing implementations which realize the atomic DFAs from Fig. 2 and provide the complement and product operations. We again separate the constructors from each other and from the operational interface.

The altered type signature of the operations means that the specifications in Fig. 9 are only ostensibly identical to those in Fig. 6; furthermore, in contrast

```
#include <stdbool.h>

typedef unsigned char uchar;

typedef struct object * Object;

struct dfaOps {
  void (*init) (Object);
  bool (*final) (Object);
  void (*step) (Object, uchar);
};

struct object {
  struct dfaOps * ops;
  /* internal state may go here*/
};
```

DFA.h

```
#include "DFA.h"
Object make_TrueFalse(void);
```

TrueFalse.h

```
#include "DFA.h"
Object make_Weekdays(void);
```

Weekdays.h

```
#include "DFA.h"
Object mkCompl(Object);
```

ComplementDFA.h

```
#include "DFA.h"
Object mkProduct(Object,Object);
```

ProductDFA.h

Fig. 8. API of operational DFA objects (left), and of object constructors (right).

Function	Spec
init(v)	$\forall\, a$ gv $v.\ \{P\ (a, \mathsf{gv}, v)\} \leadsto \{P\ (\text{Dfa\_s A}, \mathsf{gv}, v)\}$
final(v)	$\forall\, a$ gv $v.\ \{P\ (a, \mathsf{gv}, v)\} \leadsto \{b.\ b = \text{Dfa\_fin A a}\ \&\ P\ (a, \mathsf{gv}, v)\}$
step(v, c)	$\forall\, a$ gv $d.\ \{\mathit{CharRep}(d, c)\ \&\ P\ (a, \mathsf{gv}, v)\} \leadsto \{P\ (\text{Dfa\_trans A}\ a\ d, \mathsf{gv}, v)\}$

Fig. 9. Specifications for DFA.h, parametric in Dfa A and P : GPred(Dfa_state A).

to the previous section, v now explicitly refers to the (first) argument of each operation, i.e. the receiver object.

We define a generic predicate for dynamically allocated objects, in correspondence to the predicate StaticObj in the previous section:

Definition DynObj_M (T:Type) ($\mathcal{P}$:GPred T) $u\ t\ \mathit{names}\ \mathit{specs}$: GPred T :=

$$\lambda\,(x, \mathsf{gv}, v).\, \exists\, \mathit{fptrs}\ s\ m\ m'.\ \mathsf{isptr}\, m\ \&\ \mathsf{JMeq}(m, m')\ \&\ \mathcal{P}(x, \mathsf{gv}, v)\ *\ v.\mathsf{ops} \mapsto_u^{\mathsf{Ews}} m\ *$$
$$\mathsf{Mtok}_M(\mathsf{Ews}, s, v)\ *\ \mathsf{MTable}(T, t, \mathit{names}, m', \mathit{specs}, \mathit{fptrs}, \mathcal{P}).$$

Just like StaticObj, DynObj hides the function pointers and asserts existence of a data region specified by $\mathcal{P}$ and a method table compatible with $\mathcal{P}$. However, the address of the latter, m, is now obtained by dereferencing the object's ops field, where we again use JMeq(m, m') to avoid mentioning a concrete C syntax tree. Parameters u and t are placeholders for object and dfaOps, respectively. Our Coq definition is also parametric in ops which we instantiated here to improve readability. Intuitively, s represents a **struct** extension of u, which enables implementations to use private fields, as indicated by the comment in DFA.h (Fig. 8) and shown in Fig. 11 below; however, for the results proven in the present paper, it suffices if the relationship between s and u is left informal. Finally, DynObj contains a malloc token, i.e. an abstract predicate representing the permission to

Function	Spec
$\ldots(\ldots)$	$\forall\, \mathsf{gv}.\ \{\mathrm{DFA\_GV}_D\ \mathsf{gv} * \mathsf{mm}_M\ \mathsf{gv}\} \leadsto$ $\{\exists p.\ \mathsf{DFA}^D_{A,M}\ (\mathrm{Dfa\_s}\ \mathrm{A}, \mathsf{gv}, p) * \mathrm{DFA\_GV}_D\ \mathsf{gv} * \mathsf{mm}_M\ \mathsf{gv}\}$
mkCompl(v)	$\forall\, a\, \mathsf{gv}\, v.\ \{\mathsf{DFA}^T_{A,M}\ (a, \mathsf{gv}, v) * \mathrm{DFA\_GV}_D\ \mathsf{gv} * \mathsf{mm}_M\ \mathsf{gv}\} \leadsto$ $\{p.\ \mathsf{DFA}^D_{\bar{A},M}\ (a, \mathsf{gv}, p) * \mathrm{DFA\_GV}_D\ \mathsf{gv} * \mathsf{mm}_M\ \mathsf{gv}\}$
mkProduct(l, r)	$\forall\, a\, b\, l\, r\, \mathsf{gv}.\ \left\{\begin{array}{l}\mathsf{DFA}^T_{A,M}\ (a, \mathsf{gv}, l) * \mathsf{DFA}^U_{B,M}\ (b, \mathsf{gv}, r)\\ * \mathrm{DFA\_GV}_D\ \mathsf{gv} * \mathsf{mm}_M\ \mathsf{gv}\end{array}\right\} \leadsto$ $\{p.\ \mathsf{DFA}^D_{A\times B,M}\ ((a,b), \mathsf{gv}, p) * \mathrm{DFA\_GV}_D\ \mathsf{gv} * \mathsf{mm}_M\ \mathsf{gv}\}$

Fig. 10. Specifications for constructors for dynamically heap-allocated objects with operations from DFA.h. The specification in the first row applies to the constructors of leaf DFAs, like make_TrueFalse and make_Weekdays from Fig. 8.

deallocate. Malloc tokens are generated by VST's malloc/free library [4] which we refactored as another VSU, M, in previous work [9].

Specializing again some syntactic parameters and writing DynSpecs (of Coq type list (GPred(Dfa_state A) → funspec)) for the partial specialization of the specifications from Fig. 9 to A, we arrive at the following predicate for dynamic objects for A, where D (again of type $\mathsf{DFA\_APD}_A$) plays the role of S in Sect. 4:

$$\mathsf{DFA}^D_{A,M} \mathrel{\widehat{=}} \mathsf{DynObj}_M(\mathrm{Dfa\_state\ A})\ (\mathrm{DFA\_Inv}_D)\ u\ \mathsf{dfaOps}\ [\mathsf{init};\ \mathsf{final};\ \mathsf{step}]\ \mathrm{DynSpecs}$$

Figure 10 shows in the first row a constructor specification for implementations of atomic DFAs such as make_TrueFalse and make_Weekdays from Fig. 8. The occurrence of $\mathrm{DFA\_GV}_D$ gv in the postcondition enables repeated application of such constructors, each yielding a distinct object representing a copy of A in its initial state. Term mm_M gv is another predicate from the malloc/free system (effectively, the module's GV-predicate) and represents the (here: unbounded) capacity to draw from a freelist.

The figure also shows constructor specifications for complement and product DFAs, based on easily defined model-level operators $\bar{\cdot}$ and $. \times .$. These specifications model nested ownership, by consuming their argument DFA objects; we do not implement deep copying. The latter two specifications permit the constructions to be applied irrespectively of whether the argument DFAs are in their initial states, and are parametric in the elements T:$\mathsf{DFA\_APD}_A$. and U:$\mathsf{DFA\_APD}_B$. We will discuss a consequence of this parametrization in Sect. 7.

Verifying Dynamic-Object Implementations. Figure 11 shows an implementation of TrueFalse.h. The **struct** object is implemented by its extension **struct** tf_rep, in alignment-compatible fashion, preserving types, identifiers, and the relative order of fields. Locally defined functions (which suitably cast between Object and TF) are collected in a statically allocated method table tfops whose address is then installed in field ops of any newly (heap)allocated object; surely_malloc is a wrapper around malloc that terminates program execution in case of allocation failure.

The verification of TrueFalse.c is parametric in the data provided by the malloc/free library, represented by M, and – like the verification of StaticTrueFalse.c in

```
#include "surelyMalloc.h"
#include "TrueFalse.h"

typedef struct tf_rep {
  struct dfaOps * ops;
  bool tf; /*private state*/
} * TF;

void tf_init (Object s) {
  ((TF)s) → tf = false; }

bool tf_final (Object s) {
  return (((TF)s)→ tf); }

void tf_step (Object s, uchar c) {
  ((TF)s)→ tf = (c == '0'); }

struct dfaOps tfops =
  {tf_init, tf_final, tf_step};

Object make_TrueFalse(void) {
  TF s;
  s = (TF) surely_malloc
        (sizeof (struct tf_rep));
  s→ ops = &tfops;
  s→ tf = false;
  return ((Object) s); }
```

Fig. 11. TrueFalse.c: implementation of heap-allocated objects

the previous section – begins by defining an element of type $\text{DFA\_APD}_{\text{TrueFalseDFA}}$. The definition is similar to the one in Sect. 4.2 but the mapsto-term for the location representing the DFA state is removed from the GV-predicate as tfops is the only global variable used by the implementation.

Definition TrueFalseGV gv := EX $\pi_i\ \pi_f\ \pi_s$.
  readable(π_i) & (gv tfops).init $\mapsto^{\pi_i}_{\text{dfaOps}}$ (gv tf_init) $*$
  readable(π_f) & (gv tfops).final $\mapsto^{\pi_f}_{\text{dfaOps}}$ (gv tf_final) $*$
  readable(π_s) & (gv tfops).step $\mapsto^{\pi_s}_{\text{dfaOps}}$ (gv tf_step).

Definition TrueFalseInv: GPred (Dfa_state TrueFalseDFA) := $\lambda\ (d, \text{gv}, v)$.
  withspacer Ews (sizeof size_t + sizeof tbool) (2 $*$ sizeof size_t) ($\lambda u.\ u.\text{tf} \mapsto^{\text{Ews}}_{\text{tf\_rep}} d$) v.

Definition TrueFalseAPD = {| DFA_GV := TrueFalseGV; DFA_Inv := TrueFalseInv |}.

Instead, this location's content is only specified in TruefalseInv, where withspacer pads $v.\text{tf} \mapsto^{\text{Ews}}_{\text{tf\_rep}} d$ to ensure proper alignment. Verification of the three operations proceeds similar to the earlier verifications; the proof of the constructor w.r.t. the suitably instantiated specification from the first row of Fig. 10, ϕ_{makeTF}, exploits that the MTable predicate satisfies the axiom $P \vdash P * P$, spinning off a readable copy during each allocation. The verification of TrueFalse.c is then exposed as a VSU statement that imports a specification for surely_malloc (which is provided by our malloc/free-VSU) and exports only the constructor:

Theorem 3. *The following judgment is derivable in Coq:*

$$\vdash^{\emptyset}_{\text{TrueFalseGV}} [(\text{surely\_malloc}, \phi_{\text{smalloc}}(M))]\ \texttt{TrueFalse}\ [(\text{make\_TrueFalse}, \phi_{\text{makeTF}})].$$

6 Towards Semantic Subtyping

The goal to reflect semantic notions of subtyping – such as behavioral subtyping [24] or refinement – arises naturally in object-oriented program logics.

Broadly speaking, semantic subtyping may either affect only the (abstract) notion of state or may include the extension of the operational interface of object. Aiming to support (and overcome limitations of) behavioral subtyping in a separation logic for a Java-like language, Parkinson and Bierman [27] observed that the use of abstract representation predicates hinders an interpretation of state refinement as separation logic entailment: the fact that predicate definitions are abstract generally implies that only trivial entailments can be proven. They hence resorted to a proof-theoretic justification. The following discussion indicates that by treating abstract predicates not merely as abbreviations but as formal parameters of ASIs may help to overcome this limitation.

Subtyping of Abstract State: A Concrete Case of Product Automata. The modules for complement and product DFAs utilize the following **structs**:

```
typedef struct complement { struct dfaOps * ops; Object parent; } * Complement;
typedef struct product { struct dfaOps * ops; Object left; Object right; } * Product;
```

Their verification – just like their specifications – proceeds parametrically in APDs for the argument DFAs but is structurally similar to that of TrueFalse.c.

However, there are actually two alternatives for constructing DFA $A \times B$, depending on whether the component automata share the same alphabet:

Definition ProductDFA $\{\Sigma_L\ \Sigma_R\}$ $(L$: @Dfa $\Sigma_L)$ $(R$: @Dfa $\Sigma_R)$: @Dfa $(\Sigma_L * \Sigma_R)$:=
  { Dfa_state := Dfa_state$_L$ * Dfa_state$_R$;
    Dfa_s := (Dfa_s$_L$, Dfa_s$_R$);
    Dfa_fin := λ s. Dfa_fin$_L$ s.1 || Dfa_fin$_R$ s.2; *(* intersection DFAs use && here*)*
    Dfa_trans := λ s d. (Dfa_trans$_L$ s.1 d.1, Dfa_trans$_R$ s.2 d.2). }

Definition PairDFA $\{\Sigma\}$ $(L$: @Dfa $\Sigma)$ $(R$: @Dfa $\Sigma)$: @Dfa Σ :=
  { Dfa_state := Dfa_state$_L$ * Dfa_state$_R$;
    Dfa_s := (Dfa_s$_L$, Dfa_s$_R$);
    Dfa_fin := λ s. Dfa_fin$_L$ s.1 || Dfa_fin$_R$ s.2; *(* intersection DFAs use && here*)*
    Dfa_trans := λ s d. (Dfa_trans$_L$ s.1 d, Dfa_trans$_R$ s.2 d) }.

The second definition corresponds to the one in Reglang and labels transitions with a single input symbol that is passed on to the subsidiary automata. The former definition labels transitions with pairs of symbols, one from each alphabet. This difference affects how the specification in Fig. 10 is interpreted, as D is formally of type DFA_APD$_{\text{ProductDFA}\,A\,B}$ in the former case and of type DFA_APD$_{\text{PairDFA}\,A\,B}$ in the latter. Furthermore, the ASI exporting the ProductDFA interface is formally parametric in two representation relations $CharRep_L : (\Sigma_L \times$ val$) \rightarrow$ Prop and $CharRep_R : (\Sigma_R \times$ val$) \rightarrow$ Prop which it then combines to the relation $CharRep((d_1, d_2), c) \mathrel{\hat{=}} CharRep_L(d_1, c) \wedge CharRep_L(d_2, c)$, whereas an ASI exporting the PairDFA interface is parametric in $CharRep : (\Sigma \times$val$) \rightarrow$ Prop.

Given Dfas L and R as required for ProductDFA, the difference vanishes if one instantiates PairDFA to $\Sigma := \Sigma_L \times \Sigma_R$ and lifts L and R to this instantiation.

One might also suspect the constructor specifications for the two constructions to coincide whenever $\Sigma_L = \Sigma_R$ holds. However, the specification based on ProductDFA actually subsumes the one based on PairDFA. A crucial step in establishing makeProduct_spec <: makePair_spec. formally is to show that any D:DFA_APD$_{\mathsf{ProductDFA}\, A\, B}$ yields some E:DFA_APD$_{\mathsf{PairDFA}\, A\, B}$ satisfying the following entailment lemma between DFA representation predicates:

$$\mathsf{DFA}^{D}_{\mathsf{ProductDFA}\, A\, B,\ M}\ ((a,b),\mathsf{gv},v) \vdash \mathsf{DFA}^{E}_{\mathsf{PairDFA}\, A\, B,\ M}\ ((a,b),\mathsf{gv},v). \tag{1}$$

Subtyping w.r.t. Abstract State: Automata Morphisms. More generally, consider the notion of a DFA morphism $\Phi : A \to A'$, i.e. a pair of mappings (both also denoted by Φ below, as no confusion can arise) between the alphabets and the state sets of two automata, compatible with the operations:

```
Record DfaMorphism {Σ Σ'} (A:@Dfa Σ) (A':@Dfa Σ') := {
  DfaMorph_Sigma: Σ → Σ';
  DfaMorph_state: Dfa_state A → Dfa_state A';
  DfaMorph_s: DfaMorph_state (Dfa_s A) = Dfa_s A';
  DfaMorph_fin: ∀ s , Dfa_fin A s = Dfa_fin A' (DfaMorph_state s);
  DfaMorph_trans: ∀ s c, DfaMorph_state (Dfa_trans A s c) =
                         Dfa_trans A' (DfaMorph_state s) (DfaMorph_Sigma c); }.
```

Given $\Phi : A \to A'$ and X':DFA_APD$_{A'}$, it is easy to construct some X:DFA_APD$_{A}$:

```
Definition X: DFA_APD_A :=
{| DFA_GV := DFA_GV X'; DFA_Inv := λ (a, gv, v). DFA_Inv X' (Φ a, gv, v) |}.
```

The subsequent proof of the representation predicate entailment

$$\mathsf{DFA}^{X'}_{A',\mathsf{M}}(\Phi\ a,\mathsf{gv},v) \vdash \mathsf{DFA}^{X}_{A,\mathsf{M}}(a,\mathsf{gv},v) \tag{2}$$

reduces to subsumption properties for the three operations; completing the claim for step is contingent on the implication

$$\forall\ (d:\Sigma)\ c.\ \mathit{CharRep}(d,c) \to \mathit{CharRep}'(\Phi\ d,c) \tag{3}$$

where $\mathit{CharRep} : (\Sigma \times \mathsf{val}) \to \mathsf{Prop}$ and $\mathit{CharRep}' : (\Sigma' \times \mathsf{val}) \to \mathsf{Prop}$ are the alphabet-interpreting relations for X and X', respectively.

Finally, entailment (2) rather directly yields constructor subsumption

$$\mathsf{makeDFA\_spec}\ \Sigma'\ \mathit{CharRep}'\ A'\ X'\ \mathsf{M} <: \mathsf{makeDFA\_spec}\ \Sigma\ \mathit{CharRep}\ A\ X\ \mathsf{M},$$

where makeDFA_spec denotes the specification in the first row of Fig. 10 .

In summary, the model-level relationship $\Phi : A \to A'$ is generically reflected (in covariant manner) as a reasoning principle in the program logic.

Behavior Extensions. Consider next the header file in Fig. 12, which equips DFAs with a further operation. Implementations may differ in the functional behavior for twosteps, i.e. may or may not interpret this operation as the composition of two single steps. They may also implement init, final, step in ways that do not satisfy our earlier specifications, for example by setting the DFA to its initial state in the implementation of final. Internally, they may also share data representations or

```
#include "DFA.h"

struct t_dfaOps {
  void (*init) (Object);
  bool (*final) (Object);
  void (*step) (Object, uchar);
  void (*twosteps) (Object, uchar, uchar);
};

EDFA.h
```

```
Record EDfa {Σ} := {
  Dfa_ :> @Dfa Σ;
  Dfa_t : Dfa_state Dfa_ → Σ →
          Σ → Dfa_state Dfa_ }.
```

Fig. 12. Extended DFAs have an additional method.

function implementations, or reuse or extend code from earlier implementations. But while the latter aspect, implementation inheritance, is opaque to clients, differences concerning the externally visible behavior should again be captured in ASIs, and in model-level DFA variants. Hence, Fig. 12 also shows a corresponding extension EDfa of Dfa; coercion :> allows us to interpret any EDfa as a Dfa over the same alphabet.

A suitably generic specification of twosteps is the following.

Function	Spec
twosteps(v, c, c')	$\forall\, a\, d\, d'.\ \{CharRep(d, c)\ \&\ CharRep(d', c')\ \&\ P\ (a, \mathsf{gv}, v)\} \rightsquigarrow \{P\ (\mathrm{Dfa\_t}\ A\ a\ d\ d', \mathsf{gv}, v)\}$

Proceeding in parallel with the definition of predicate DFA, we specialize DynObj to a predicate for objects satisfying the extended interface:

$$\mathsf{EDFA}^{T}_{A,M} \mathrel{\widehat{=}} \mathsf{DynObj}_M\ (\mathrm{Dfa\_state\ A})\ (\mathrm{EDFA\_Inv}_T)\ u\ \mathsf{t\_dfaOps}\ [\mathsf{init};\ \mathsf{final};\ \mathsf{step};\ \mathsf{twosteps}]\ \mathrm{ExtDynSpecs}$$

where A is a EDfa, ExtDynSpecs extends the earlier DynSpecs by also associating twosteps with the specification above, and T is of type

Record EDFA_APD$_A$:=
{ EDFA_GV: globals → mpred; EDFA_Inv: GPred (Dfa_state A) }.

Our code base contains two implementations of EDFA.h, with constructors make_TWeekdays () and make_TwiceWeekdays(). Both modules retain Weekday.c's behaviors of init, final, and step; the former implements twosteps by making transitions for both input symbols while the latter ignores the final argument and makes two steps for the first symbol. The verification of these modules against constructor specifications that yield EDFA objects w.r.t. suitably defined EDfas proceeds as before, so we omit a detailed description.

Interestingly, we may also prove that client programs expecting a DFA object can always be supplied with a EDFA object, i.e. that interface extension satisfies behavioral subtyping (or supertype abstraction in the sense of Leavens and

```
/*...header file imports...*/

struct storage {
  StaticOps ops_ref;
  Object obj_ref; };

struct storage strg;

Object createWeekdayDFA(bool b) {
  if (b)
    return (make_TWeekdays ());
  else
    return (make_Weekdays());
}

bool runClient(void) {
  Object tf = make_TrueFalse();
  Object W = createWeekdayDFA(true);
  strg.obj_ref = W;
  tf → ops → init (tf);
  W → ops → init (W);
  tf → ops → step (tf, '0');
  W → ops → step (W, 'x');
  strg.obj_ref → ops → step (W, 'n');
  return (tf → ops → final (tf) &&
          W → ops → final (W));
}
/* ... tests for single and statically
   allocated DFA implementations...*/
```

Fig. 13. Client.c contains small unit tests

Naumann [23]) w.r.t. the coercion from EDfa to Dfa: we construct a D_T of type $\mathsf{DFA\_APD}_{\mathsf{Dfa\_}A}$ parametrically, for any T of type $\mathsf{EDFA\_APD}_A$, by existentially quantifying over a separating conjunct F in the object invariant:

$$\{|\ \mathrm{DFA\_GV} := \mathrm{EDFA\_GV}\ A\ T;\ \mathrm{DFA\_Inv} := \lambda\ x.\ \exists\ F,\ \mathrm{EDFA\_Inv}\ A\ T\ x * F\ |\}.$$

The reader may find it surprising to see the supertype's invariant DFA_Inv to contain the subtype's (symbolic) invariant, as implementing additional functionality in general requires introducing additional fields. However, as our object predicates abstract from concrete representations (and invariant EDFA_Inv A T is a formal parameter of the proof, being a component of T), differences concerning the existence of fields is irrelevant. Indeed, using the entailment

$$\mathsf{EDFA}^{T}_{A,\mathsf{M}}(a, \mathsf{gv}, v) \vdash \mathsf{DFA}^{D_T}_{\mathrm{Dfa\_}A,\mathsf{M}}(a, \mathsf{gv}, v), \tag{4}$$

the subsidiary subsumption lemmas for init, final, and step are easy to prove.

Note that EDFA specializes parameter t of DynObj to t_dfaOps while DFA specializes t to dfaOps. However, as the former is a **struct**-extension of the latter, VST's theory of field compatibility can bridge this gap, so objects obtained from EDFA-yielding constructors can indeed be weakened to DFA-objects.

7 Putting It All Together

Figure 13 shows an excerpt of an example client which creates and maintains instances of the various DFA implementations and invokes their operations. Our specification of createWeekdayDFA forces the verification to exercise entailment (4) by not propagating the effect of the boolean flag to the output, taking the form

$$\forall\ \mathsf{gv}.\ \begin{array}{l}\{\mathsf{mm}_M\ \mathsf{gv}\ *\ \ldots\} \leadsto \\ \{p.\ \exists X.\ \mathsf{DFA}^{X}_{\mathsf{WeekdayDFA},M}\ (\mathsf{Monday}, \mathsf{gv}, p)\ *\ \mathsf{mm}_M\ \mathsf{gv}\ *\ \ldots\}.\end{array}$$

Thus, runClient cannot exploit the fact that W supports twosteps.

The low-level method dispatch shown in runClient leads to repeated folding and unfolding of object representation predicates. Inspired by source-level preprocessor macros (which are compiled away by CompCert's parser and hence unavailable for verification), we enhance usability by defining wrapper functions

```
void invokeInit (Object s) { s → ops → init (s); }
void invokeStep (Object s, uchar c) { s → ops → step (s, c); }
bool invokeFinal (Object s) { return (s → ops → final (s)); }
void invokeTwosteps (Object s, uchar c1, uchar c2) {
     ((struct t_dfaOps *)(s → ops)) → twosteps (s, c1, c2);}
```

that hide the object oriented machinery and allow one to replace, e.g., the final line of runClient with **return** (invokeFinal (tf) && invokeFinal (W));. To be useful, the specification of these wrappers should be applicable to objects representing Dfas as well as EDfas, without constraining the APDs. We therefore give, e.g., invokeFinal an intersection specification [11] containing one clause per interface, so that each clause is polymorphic in an alphabet, automata, and APD:

$$\begin{aligned}&\forall\, \Sigma\ \mathit{CHrep}\ (A : @\mathsf{Dfa}\ \Sigma)\ (X : \mathsf{DFA\_APD}_A)\ a\ \mathsf{gv}\ v.\\ &\qquad \{\mathsf{DFA}^X_{A,M}\ (a, \mathsf{gv}, v)\} \rightsquigarrow \{b.\ b = \text{Dfa\_fin A a}\ \&\ \mathsf{DFA}^X_{A,M}(a, \mathsf{gv}, v)\}\\ \bigwedge\ &\forall\, \Sigma\ \mathit{CHrep}\ (A : @\mathsf{EDfa}\ \Sigma)\ (X : \mathsf{EDFA\_APD}_A)\ a\ \mathsf{gv}\ v.\\ &\qquad \{\mathsf{EDFA}^X_{A,M}\ (a, \mathsf{gv}, v)\} \rightsquigarrow \{b.\ b = \text{Dfa\_fin A a}\ \&\ \mathsf{EDFA}^X_{A,M}(a, \mathsf{gv}, v)\}\end{aligned}$$

The well-definedness of this construction depends on two features of VST's semantic model: (i) the ability to have (types of) later elements in the list of universally quantified elements depend on (values of) earlier elements – dependent typing – and (ii) the support for quantification over `mpreds` in these lists – impredicativity. The former feature allows X to depend on A, and A on Σ, while the latter is required as both components of X are (functions to) `mpred`'s.

The verification of a wrapper function w.r.t. such a specification at present splits into two cases and hence traverses the function body twice. Given the small size of these functions and the fact that the costs amortize as the number of clients grows, this is not an undue burden. Nevertheless, we are presently exploring alternative specification schemes that avoid repeated code traversal.

A shortcoming that becomes apparent when linking with the client concerns our specifications of the complement and product constructions. As the implementations of these modules have internal state, the parameters for the constituent DFAs in Fig. 10 can only be instantiated once. This prevents the successive invocation of, e.g., mkCompl constructor on a TrueFalseDFA object and a WeekdayDFA object. We have developed a solution for this issue that employs a similar specification style as the wrappers above, but applies to a slightly different definition of object representation predicates. We leave a detailed description and a transfer to the present predicates to future work.

We combine the VSU for Client.c with the VSU judgments for the various DFA implementations using the linkage rule of the VSU calculus [9]. As part of this process, the disjointness of the global-memory regions inhabited by the code units is checked, i.e. of the GV predicates in the position P of our formal VSU judgment (cf. Sect. 2). Our present verification concerns code in 64-bit format, whereas the VSU for the malloc/free library is only available for 32-bit architectures, so we omit linking with that library (and subsequently with `main`), resulting in a final VSU that contains surely_malloc as the only unresolved import.

Overall, the verification of our code base on an Intel-i7-1.8 GHz processor with 15 GB RAM takes just under 22 min in sequential mode, but the modularization of our verification enables parallel processing of the VSU constructions for different compilation units. Instructing Coq to employ 8 cores reduces wallclock verification time to about 8 min.

8 Discussion

C supports many forms of abstraction, ranging from single-implementation modules to dynamically allocated objects with subtyping, inheritance, and method dispatch using function pointers. We explored how three idiomatic coding styles can be equipped with specifications in VST that respect API-level representation hiding and enable a formally precise connection to model-level reasoning. We demonstrated that the VSU extension of VST enables separate compilation to be complemented with separate verification.

Motivated by their widespread use, we selected deterministic finite automata as a concrete domain for studying these coding styles, envisioning a future in which model-based development tools are equipped with specification or proof synthesis capabilities. Complementing a preliminary investigation of such syntheses for DFAs, we plan to generalize our approach to automata models that are closer to formalisms found in modern industrial tools, like statecharts [18] or hierarchical state machines [1,30].

We identified abstract object representation predicate entailment as a natural formulation of semantic subtyping in the setting of VST. We intend to study generalizations and applications of this treatment in future work, including an analysis of Liskov and Wing's behavioral subtyping [24] and of Leavens and Naumann's intrinsic program refinement [23]. We also plan to explore how the concept of ASIs that are parametric in APDs can be transferred to nominal object models and hence settings like the one used by Parkinson and Bierman [27].

As far as inheritance is concerned, we are presently developing a variant of the DFA product construction which realizes code-sharing/representation reuse in an observationally opaque manner. Future work may subsequently revisit the earlier treatment of behavior inheritance and semantically observable method overriding [9]. At least in the case of late binding, this will likely require recursive object predicates, and perhaps the use of positive subtyping. A theory of *self* also appears necessary for supporting deep copying and deallocation. Other object-oriented features that might be interesting to study include binary methods, DAG-shaped interface hierarchies, and dynamic method update; some of these topics may require switching to different C coding styles or exploring alternative semantic object models.

Funding Information. This material is based on work supported by the Defense Advanced Research Projects Agency (DARPA), Contract No. HR001120C0160. Additional support was provided by the National Science Foundation under the award 1005849, *Verified High Performance Data Structure Implementations.*

References

1. Alur, R.: Formal analysis of hierarchical state machines. In: Dershowitz, N. (ed.) Verification: Theory and Practice. LNCS, vol. 2772, pp. 42–66. Springer, Heidelberg (2003). https://doi.org/10.1007/978-3-540-39910-0_3
2. Appel, A.W., Beringer, L., Cao, Q.: Verifiable C. Software Foundations, vol. 5 (2021). https://softwarefoundations.cis.upenn.edu/vc-current/index.html
3. Appel, A.W., et al.: Program Logics for Certified Compilers. Cambridge University Press, Cambridge (2014)
4. Appel, A.W., Naumann, D.A.: Verified sequential malloc/free. In: Ding, C., Maas, M. (eds.) ISMM 2020: 2020 ACM SIGPLAN International Symposium on Memory Management, pp. 48–59. ACM (2020). https://doi.org/10.1145/3381898.3397211
5. Motor Industry Software Reliability Association: MISRA-C:2012 Guidelines for the use of the C language in critical systems (2012). https://www.misra.org.uk, MIRA Ltd
6. Autosar Consortium: Specification of C implementation rules, V1.0.5, R3.1 (2008). https://www.autosar.org/fileadmin/user_upload/standards/classic/3-1/AUTOSAR_SWS_C_ImplementationRules.pdf
7. Balzer, R.M.: Dataless programming. In: American Federation of Information Processing Societies: Proceedings of the AFIPS 19667 Fall Joint Computer Conference. AFIPS Conference Proceedings, vol. 31, pp. 535–544. AFIPS/ACM/Thomson Book Company (1967). https://doi.org/10.1145/1465611.1465683
8. Barras, B., et al.: The Coq Proof Assistant reference manual. Technical report, INRIA (1998)
9. Beringer, L.: Verified software units. In: ESOP 2021. LNCS, vol. 12648, pp. 118–147. Springer, Cham (2021). https://doi.org/10.1007/978-3-030-72019-3_5
10. Beringer, L.: Verified Software Units for simple DFA modules and objects in C - Coq sources (2022). https://www.cs.princeton.edu/~eberinge/Isola2022sources.tar.gz
11. Beringer, L., Appel, A.W.: Abstraction and subsumption in modular verification of C programs. Formal Methods Syst. Des. **58**(1), 322–345 (2021)
12. g Bertot, Y., Castéran, P.: Coq'Art: interactive theorem proving and program development. Springer, Heidelberg (2004). https://doi.org/10.1007/978-3-662-07964-5
13. Blazy, S., Leroy, X.: Mechanized semantics for the Clight subset of the C language. J. Autom. Reason. **43**(3), 263–288 (2009). http://gallium.inria.fr/~xleroy/publi/Clight.pdf
14. Calcagno, C., O'Hearn, P.W., Yang, H.: Local action and abstract separation logic. In: 22nd IEEE Symposium on Logic in Computer Science (LICS 2007), pp. 366–378. IEEE Computer Society (2007). https://doi.org/10.1109/LICS.2007.30
15. Cao, Q., Beringer, L., Gruetter, S., Dodds, J., Appel, A.W.: VST-Floyd: a separation logic tool to verify correctness of C programs. J. Autom. Reasoning **61**(1–4), 367–422 (2018)

16. Dockins, R., Hobor, A., Appel, A.W.: A fresh look at separation algebras and share accounting. In: APLAS: 7th Asian Symposium on Programming Languages and Systems, pp. 161–177 (2009)
17. Doczkal, C., Smolka, G.: Regular Language Representations in the Constructive Type Theory of Coq. J. Autom. Reason. **61**(1–4), 521–553 (2018)
18. Harel, D.: Statecharts: a visual formalism for complex systems. Sci. Comput. Program. **8**(3), 231–274 (1987)
19. Hoare, C.A.R.: An axiomatic basis for computer programming. Commun. ACM **12**(10), 578–580 (1969)
20. Hobor, A., Dockins, R., Appel, A.W.: A theory of indirection via approximation. In: Proceedings 37th Annual ACM Symposium on Principles of Programming Languages (POPL 2010), pp. 171–185 (2010)
21. Hofmann, M., Pierce, B.C.: Positive subtyping. Inf. Comput. **126**(1), 11–33 (1996). https://doi.org/10.1006/inco.1996.0031
22. Kay, A.C.: The early history of Smalltalk. In: Lee, J.A.N., Sammet, J.E. (eds.) History of Programming Languages Conference (HOPL-II), Preprints, pp. 69–95. ACM (1993). https://doi.org/10.1145/154766.155364
23. Leavens, G.T., Naumann, D.A.: Behavioral subtyping, specification inheritance, and modular reasoning. ACM Trans. Program. Lang. Syst. **37**(4), 13:1–13:88 (2015). https://doi.org/10.1145/2766446
24. Liskov, B., Wing, J.M.: A behavioral notion of subtyping. ACM Trans. Program. Lang. Syst. 16(6), 1811–1841 (1994). https://doi.org/10.1145/197320.197383
25. McBride, C.: Dependently Typed Functional Programs and their Proofs. Ph.D. thesis, LFCS, University of Edinburgh (1999)
26. O'Hearn, P.W.: Separation logic. Commun. ACM **62**(2), 86–95 (2019). https://doi.org/10.1145/3211968
27. Parkinson, M.J., Bierman, G.M.: Separation logic, abstraction and inheritance. In: Necula, G.C., Wadler, P. (eds.) Proceedings of the 35th ACM SIGPLAN-SIGACT Symposium on Principles of Programming Languages, POPL 2008, pp. 75–86. ACM (2008). https://doi.org/10.1145/1328438.1328451
28. Reynolds, J.C.: GEDANKEN - a simple typeless language based on the principle of completeness and the reference concept. Commun. ACM **13**(5), 308–319 (1970). https://doi.org/10.1145/362349.362364
29. Reynolds, J.C.: Separation logic: a logic for shared mutable data structures. In: 17th IEEE Symposium on Logic in Computer Science (LICS 2002), pp. 55–74. IEEE Computer Society (2002). https://doi.org/10.1109/LICS.2002.1029817
30. Yannakakis, M.: Hierarchical state machines. In: van Leeuwen, J., Watanabe, O., Hagiya, M., Mosses, P.D., Ito, T. (eds.) TCS 2000. LNCS, vol. 1872, pp. 315–330. Springer, Heidelberg (2000). https://doi.org/10.1007/3-540-44929-9_24

A Notion of Equivalence for Refactorings with Abstract Execution

Ole Jørgen Abusdal[1(✉)], Eduard Kamburjan[2], Violet Ka I. Pun[1], and Volker Stolz[1]

[1] Western Norway University of Applied Sciences, Bergen, Norway
{ojab,vpu,vsto}@hvl.no
[2] University of Oslo, Oslo, Norway
eduard@ifi.uio.no

Abstract. Relational verification through dynamic logic is a promising approach for verifying object oriented programs. Recent advances from symbolic to abstract executions have enabled reasoning about incomplete/abstract versions of such programs. This has proven fruitful in the exploration of correctness of refactorings primarily related to code blocks in Java. In this paper we explore further types of equivalent transformations and refactorings and discuss the challenges that still need to be overcome for full round-trip correctness of refactorings in object-oriented languages.

1 Introduction

Refactoring is a fundamental activity in software engineering to reorganize code to improve its structure, e.g., to simplify maintenance, while preserving its observable behavior of the program. A refactoring can be defined as a pattern it matches on, and a subsequent program transformation on the matched part. To ensure that the transformed program indeed has the same observable behavior one can either compare the transformed program with the original or reason about the program transformation itself.

Relational verification through dynamic logic is a promising approach to verification of refactoring patterns in object oriented programs. Recent advances from symbolic to Abstract Execution (AE) [30] have enabled reasoning about incomplete/abstract versions of such programs. This has proven fruitful in the exploration of correctness of refactorings primarily related to code blocks in Java: AE introduces abstract statements (and expressions), which act as named and specified placeholders for statement-sequences of the host language. A refactoring proof is a relational verification proof that compares two programs which can have abstract program elements. Consider relating

if ($E_{boolean}$) {S_1;} **else** {S_2;} **return**;

and

if (!$E_{boolean}$) {S_2; **return**;} S_1; **return**;

The original version of this chapter was revised: The sentence in the 4th paragraph of section 5 "Discussion" has been updated. The correction to this chapter is available at https://doi.org/10.1007/978-3-031-19756-7_24

T. Margaria and B. Steffen (Eds.): ISoLA 2022, LNCS 13702, pp. 259–280, 2022.
https://doi.org/10.1007/978-3-031-19756-7_15

where $E_{boolean}$ is an arbitrary boolean expression, S_1 and S_2 correspond to arbitrary statements. One of the programs represents the schema of the code before the refactoring, and the other one the code afterwards, with respect to some relational post-condition that defines the notion of *program equivalence*. This reasoning about abstract programs is exactly the aforementioned reasoning about the program transformation behind the refactoring.

Despite the promising results due to AE, it has only been applied to *statement-level* refactorings that change the body of a single method. However, refactorings are not limited to single methods or statement-blocks, but may also restructure classes and data structures [14]. In this paper we investigate the role of AE for verification of refactorings beyond statement-level.

Challenges. More complex refactorings require more elaborate specification and verification techniques for relational verification. The reason is that the programs surrounding the abstract statements, as well as the notion of equivalence, become more involved. This holds for both structure and behaviour. Following the general approach of AE, REFINITY [30], the tool supporting verification on top of the KeY system, an automated theorem prover for Java [29], has been primarily designed to verify the correctness of refactorings that are based on moving code within a method, or on extracting some statements into their own method (i.e., the EXTRACT METHOD refactoring [15, p. 106]).

To investigate the use of AE for refactorings on the class-level, we investigate the HIDE DELEGATE refactoring [15, p. 189] that moves code between classes and show how it can be encoded in REFINITY. As for specification, we discuss the interpretation of *equivalence* from the perspective of the user and how to encode this—for example, if the surrounding programs throw exceptions, under which conditions are the exceptions considered equivalent? The equivalence interpretation goes beyond exceptions, but touches on a fundamental problem: there are several possible choices for when newly created objects (and exceptions, which are objects in Java) are considered to be equal in relational verification using dynamic logic. This was first investigated by Beckert et al. [7] and we discuss alternatives here.

For exceptions and object creation, we describe several possibilities when newly created objects (resp. thrown exceptions) are considered equal and how this information can be used in dynamic logic proofs. The different possibilities are implemented as multiple (sets of) rules, from which the developer chooses the one corresponding to his assumptions on object allocations – this choice does not have to be encoded explicitly in the relational post-condition. This reduces the size of the required specification, which is an advantage, since it is a notorious bottleneck in formal verification [6,17].

Furthermore, we discuss the necessary extensions needed to prove equivalent behaviour where one data structure is replaced by another, e.g., an array or any primitive type by a class. Here, the main challenge lies in the encoding that the structures are used correctly throughout the execution. This could, for example, be handled by coupled invariants [8], whose connection to AE is yet unclear. Lastly, we discuss the challenge to apply AE to novel specification approaches for *traces* which aim to simplify the specification of temporal properties for expressive properties, but whose use for relational verification is unexplored.

Contributions and Structure. Our contributions include an investigation into the necessary side conditions to be able to proof of the correctness of the EXTRACT LOCAL VARIABLE- and HIDE DELEGATE refactorings, extending the collection of proven refactorings. The latter is a refactoring beyond code motion within a method and highlights the interaction of AE with general relational verification challenges. Then, we discuss possible extensions that would be required to address further refactorings with AE.

We first describe AE and relational verification using the EXTRACT LOCAL VARIABLE refactoring in Sect. 2, before we show necessary conditions for the HIDE DELEGATE refactoring to be correct and then discuss the challenges for AE in Sect. 3. Section 4 proposes future directions for improvements in REFINITY and AE which most likely require major development effort. In Sect. 5, we discuss our results. We discuss the related work in Sect. 6, and lastly conclude in Sect. 7.

2 Preliminaries

In this section, we will first briefly describe AE and how it extends symbolic execution. Then, we will show how AE can be used to prove refactoring correctness with an example.

2.1 Abstract Execution

Succinctly, as stated by Steinhöfel in their Ph.D. thesis, "Abstract Execution" denotes the idea to process abstract programs by symbolic execution (SE) [28]. SE [2,33] abstracts concrete execution by means of symbolic representations of language runtime state in place of concrete machine representations of such artefacts. Thus, a store, a program counter, values, and so on, all have a symbolic representation in SE. Branching points, such as encountered when symbolically executing e.g., an if-then-else statement that splits an execution path into new paths for each possible branch arm. For each of these paths, for instance, the symbolic store may be preserved in the new paths, but different conditions may also be carried through such that in the path where the symbolic program counter refers to the then-branch the evaluation of the boolean expression in the if statement must be valid, whereas it is not valid in the path where the symbolic program counter refers to the else-branch. Possible executions are not just captured through branching paths, but along a path itself through the symbolic store; a symbolic value represents any valid concrete substitution.

The SE found in KeY and REFINITY operates on a dynamic logic, JavaDL, for a restricted subset of Java. Syntactically, JavaDL is an extension of first-order logic with program variables and program modalities. Semantically, JavaDL formulas are evaluated in a Kripke structure, which is a collection of first-order structures [[1], Sect. 3.3].

```
void n() {
/*@ assignable frN;
  @ accessible fpN;
  @ exceptional_behavior requires false;
  @*/
  \abstract_statement N;
}
```

Listing 1. Method in REFINITY

The use of SE to potentially explore every possible execution a program can have is a popular program analysis technique. AE extends SE by introducing abstract program elements (APEs) to the base language that is symbolically executed. For statements and expressions, a corresponding abstract statement and abstract expression are introduced. APEs represent any possible substitution with concrete program elements, which can be statements or expressions, from the base language being symbolically executed. Execution of APEs is then the leap taken in AE over traditional SE. It requires the introduction of abstract state changes, SE branching for any abrupt completion an APE may have (e.g. exceptions thrown), over-approximation of returned values and thrown exceptions by symbols created "dependently fresh" for identifiers of abstract program placeholders, and a way to specify the behavior of APEs [28].

We summarise how AE is implemented in REFINITY by showing how to specify a method **void** `n()` with a mostly unknown method body. Listing 1 shows a specification in REFINITY, in which a method `n()` is specified and its only content is an abstract statement **`\aabstract_statement`** `N` preceded by a Java Modelling Language (JML) like[1] specification [18]. The specification indicates that the method can possibly assign to some abstract locations (its frame) and can access some abstract locations (its footprint), and that no exceptions will be thrown by the method body. The specification is straightforward: abstract statement `N` may assign to the abstract location set `frN`, access the abstract location set `fpN` and may not throw any exceptions.

An abstract location set represents a fixed set of memory locations that (a part of) a program may read from or write to. The set is fixed through a program's duration but the values at these locations may change. When an abstract location set occurs in an assignable or accessible specification, it is to be understood as an upper bound; the locations may possibly all be accessed or assigned to, not at all or anything in between.

2.2 Proving Refactoring Correctness with Abstract Execution

In the following, we use an example to show how AE can be used to prove a refactoring correct with REFINITY.

[1] We say "like" as JML does not deal with abstract Java programs.

```
x.n();
x.n();
```

(a) Before

```
X temp = x;
temp.n();
temp.n();    //change?
```

(b) After

Listing 2. EXTRACT LOCAL VARIABLE refactoring

```
assert x instanceof X;
((X)x).n();
((X)x).n();
return x;
```

(a) Before

```
assert x instanceof X;
X temp = (X)x;
temp.n();
temp.n();
return temp;
```

(b) After

Listing 3. EXTRACT LOCAL VARIABLE refactoring in REFINITY

Let us consider the EXTRACT LOCAL VARIABLE refactoring seen in Listing 2. The example is an instance of a more general case, where preserving the behaviour of the program depends on other parts of the code. The behaviour of the program changes if the method call `n()` has access to the attribute `x` and overwrites it.

Before we would have potentially method calls to different objects o_1`.n()` and then o_2`.n()`, whereas after applying the refactoring we would have o_1`.n()` followed by o_1`.n()`. In this case if, e.g., `n()` simply prints **`this`**`.toString()`, we will observe a difference in the two programs.

The dynamic check for such a change detailed in other work [13] codified the necessity that the reference `x` remains unchanged through the introduction of an assertion `assert temp == x;` to uncover violations after the fact, which is useful, e.g., when checking the refactored code against its suite of unit tests.

In REFINITY one proceeds to verify a refactoring as correct by supplying the code before and after refactoring, and supplying a desired precondition and postcondition to relate the two programs. We essentially ask REFINITY: *given these preconditions does the postcondition hold after abstract execution of these two abstract programs?* A proof of correctness in REFINITY is a proof for any concrete Java programs that can be *instantiated* to adhere to the abstract specification given in REFINITY.

We describe the refactoring to REFINITY as shown with a left side (Before) in Listing 3a, a right side (After) in Listing 3b and a method level context which contains the method we have already shown in Listing 1.

Additionally, some information is declared in parts of REFINITY's interface that are not shown here: Free program variables, here `x`; abstract location sets, here `frN` and `fpN`; relevant locations for the before and after code, here empty; the desired precondition, here empty, and the desired postcondition.

The pre- and postcondition are specified in terms of equations that may relate to the effects of the before and after side, such as return values, exceptions thrown and any of the relevant locations declared. Here we use the default postcondition REFINITY provides which is simply `\result_1 == \result_2`, where `\result_1` and `\result_2` are each respectively a sequence of results for the abstract execution of the Before and After program. Each sequence contain in this order: 1) The return value if any, otherwise null; 2) exceptions thrown if any, otherwise null; and 3) the values at specified abstract location sets (that the user selects as relevant).

The default postcondition in our case will be that `x` returned in Before must be identical to `temp` returned in After, and that any exception thrown must be identical for the Before and After program. When left empty, as done here and so trivially true, equality with respect to the last component of the result sequences is an assertion that the values at all abstract location sets selected as relevant are identical.

We use an assertion to ensure that we consider only the refactoring when `x` is an instance of its intended type. A current limitation of the implementation of REFINITY necessitate the casting `(X)x` as free program variables may only be declared to be of type Object.

With only the specification shown in Listing 3, REFINITY is unable to prove that `x` will be identical to `temp` after AE of both sides. We get several instances of SE resulting in the reference `x` being changed by the abstract statement `N` in `n()`.

To prohibit this, we specify that the execution of the abstract statement `N` cannot interfere with `x`. A constraint on the frame `frN` of abstract statement `N`, namely that it is disjoint from `x` must be introduced, which is achieved by putting an abstract execution constraint `@ ae_constraint \disjoint(x,frN)` on each side which ensures `x` will be assumed not to be in `frN`.

After the aforementioned change, REFINITY manages to automatically prove that the postcondition holds after abstract execution of both sides; `x` and `temp` will hold identical references and any exceptions thrown will be identical. Note that it remains for any concrete application of this refactoring to prove that any code matching abstract statements fulfills their annotated constraints.

Although we successfully prove the refactoring we have encoded here, the required scaffolding of return statements leaves something to be desired: Finding intended concrete instances of the abstract programs now involve, potentially, ignoring the return statements.

3 Challenges in Complex Refactorings

In this section we explore the possibilities of applying REFINITY beyond its original vision. In particular, we are interested in moving away from statement-based refactorings to more complex changes that also affect the structure of the code. The first new refactoring, HIDE DELEGATE, expresses the desired behaviour of REFINITY in a straight-forward manner and KeY automatically completes the proof once the right preconditions are identified.

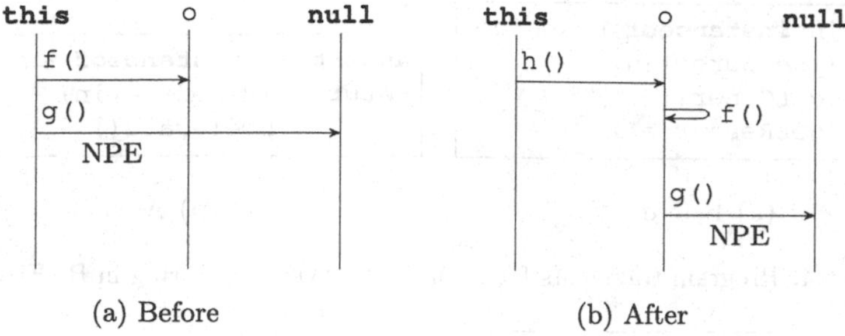

(a) Before (b) After

Fig. 1. Null pointer exceptions (NPEs)

After that, we present a refactoring that is related to DEAD CODE ELIMINATION. This requires introducing additional constructs for object-creation within the underlying KeY system, which are then harnessed in *taclets* expressing that certain non-identical heaps guarantee equivalent behaviour.

We continue our wishlist for further flexibility in expressing equivalent program behaviour based on the execution history of user-defined observable actions, and finally discuss challenges related to expressing equivalence in the face of different data types.

3.1 Encoding the HIDE DELEGATE refactoring

The HIDE DELEGATE refactoring can be described as an EXTRACT METHOD refactoring on a call chain. Consider the statement `Y y = o.f().g()`, where the call chain is extracted to a new method on `o`, say `h()`, which contains the extraction `Y h() { return this.f().g(); }`, such that we can replace the chain above with `Y y = o.h()`. The refactoring can enable less coupling as the class that contained the call chain afterwards does not need to know the return type of `f()`.

Note that in the case of the more general pattern `X x = o.f(); Y y = x.g()` with non-interfering intermediate statements between the two statements, we can reach the considered pattern through applications of SLIDE STATEMENT and finally INLINE VARIABLE on `x`.

The scenarios shown in the sequence diagrams in Fig. 1 will both result in `NullPointerException` (NPE) when the call to `f()` returns **`null`**. In the strictest sense of behavioral preservation, we will observe a difference in the behaviour before and after the refactoring. Concretely, the NPE thrown in Fig. 1a (before) will show a different stacktrace than the one thrown in Fig. 1b (after). Thus we consider a behavioral equivalence that allows for disagreement in stacktraces for such matching exceptions. In fact one is unable to make any other distinction in REFINITY as it does not consider such effects.

We specify the before- and after-program fragment for a HIDE DELEGATE refactoring in Listing 4 which faithfully captures the previously sketched out refactoring. The classes and methods used in the refactoring are presented in

```
assert in instanceof Resource;
return ((Resource)in)
       .getOwner()
       .getResource();
```

(a) Before

```
assert in instanceof Resource;
return ((Resource)in)
       .hDelegate();
```

(b) After

Listing 4. Program fragments for HIDE DELEGATE refactoring in REFINITY

```
class Resource {
 Owner owner;
 Owner getOwner() {
 /*@ assignable frF;
  @ accessible fpF;
  @*/
  \abstract_statement F;
  return owner;
 }
 Resource hDelegate() {
  return this.getOwner()
         .getResource();
 }
}
```

(a) Before

```
class Owner {
 Resource resource;
 Resource getResource() {
 /*@ assignable frG;
  @ accessible fpG;
  @*/
  \abstract_statement G;
  return resource;
 }
}
```

(b) After

Listing 5. Classes in HIDE DELEGATE refactoring in REFINITY

Listing 5 and show that we minimally specify the contents of the involved methods by using abstract statements in their bodies. Note that we allow abrupt completion in the abstract statements `F` and `G` in the methods `getOwner()` and `getResource`. That means the abstract statements may for instance throw exceptions. For instance, the sketched out scenario considered in Fig. 1, where `getResource()` will return **`null`** and cause the following call to throw a NPE, is a possibility.

To prove the specified HIDE DELEGATE refactoring in an original published version (v0.9.7) of REFINITY, we need a postcondition that consists of a conjunction of return values of the before- and after-programs being identical and that any thrown exceptions are both instances of NPE or otherwise equal. This is owing to the fact that REFINITY does not consider occurrences of **`new`** `NullPointerException()`, or any other newly created objects, to be equal. In particular we remark that although strictly speaking certain exceptions before and after a refactoring may be distinguished by different stacktraces, we may want to consider them to be equal even so.

We have improved REFINITY[2] to resolve this issue; we may keep the default postcondition that simply matches return results and exceptions, and REFINITY automatically manages to prove the shown HIDE DELEGATE refactoring to be correct. In the following section we will detail the changes needed to accomplish this.

3.2 Object Creation

As we have seen in the previous section, REFINITY encodes a rather harsh regimen on program equivalence: in the absence of a more fine-grained (application-specific) post-condition, it encodes that return values or exceptions must be identical on both sides, as well as the objects in the relevant location set (and the observables in this location set must be adequately specified).

This, in combination with the symbolic execution of both programs, creates a hurdle for programs that contain object creations (and, subsequently exceptions). An object allocation in JavaDL is, roughly sketched, symbolically executed by creating a fresh function symbol for the allocated object and storing it on the symbolic heap.

The question of equivalence for created objects is not specific to abstract execution, yet important for its practicability: abstract statements are embedded in concrete programs which affect state as well, and more complex and application-specific refactorings must take all language features of the host language into account.

At its core, the challenge lies in the fact that, as both programs/versions are executed in the same proof, objects created within them are not equal to each other: it is not possible to prove that the program `return new C();` is equivalent to itself. Indeed, it is not obvious whether the program should be considered equivalent to itself in the first place. The program is executed twice from the same state, but this does not suffice for the two created objects to be equal – the allocation must, additionally, be deterministic. In the following, we make the assumption that this is indeed the case and use this information in the symbolic execution.

Approach. To formalize this assumption, we first need to express the determinism of object creation.

We assume that the program semantics is expressed as a Kripke structure, where the domain of each Kripke state is constant. This means that all objects always *exist*. To *allocate* an object, it must be marked as allocated. To do so, each object has a field `<allocated>` that is set to **`true`** for all allocated objects, and to **`false`** for all others.

To express deterministic allocation, we use a total order $<$ on all objects, which is pivoted on some object o. All objects before o are allocated, and all objects after o are not allocated. Allocation then uses o as the next object to create. As the order is fixed for the Kripke structure, two allocations in different states, but with the same pivot object o, will allocate the same object next: o.

[2] Available at https://github.com/selabhvl/REFINITY-abstractallocate.

Formalisation. As the next step of formalization, we express this as a sequent calculus rule in JavaDL. We give the basic concepts behind JavaDL next, for a formal treatment we refer to an introduction to KeY and JavaDL [1].

A sequent has the form $\Gamma \Rightarrow \Delta$, where the antecedent Γ and the succedent Δ are sets of JavaDL formulas. JavaDL is a typed first-order dynamic logic with program variables and updates. Its operators are the usual first-order operators, a modality $[\mathtt{s}]\phi$ expressing that formula ϕ holds after executing statement `s`, and updates. An update is a syntactic representation of a substitution on a program variable. A simple update, which is the only form of update we require here, has the form $\mathtt{v} := \mathtt{t}$ and expresses that the value of program variable `v` is set to the value of term `t`. The truth value of a formula ϕ after the substitution expressed by update U is expressed by applying the update to the formula, denoted by $U\phi$.

Semantically, JavaDL is evaluated over a Kripke structure and an interpretation I. The interpretation assigns values to predicates and function symbols, while the Kripke structure is a set of states: assignments for the program variables. The semantics of a modality is the transition from one state to another, according to the semantics of the program. The semantics of an update is the transition from one state to another, according to the substitution expressed by it. The sequent calculus for JavaDL realizes symbolic execution by reducing modalities to updates (under certain side-conditions, added to the premise/path-condition).

To handle objects, JavaDL uses a special program variable `heap`, which maps from objects and fields to their value. The heap is written and read with the usual theory of arrays [23], where fields are used as indices, following the approach by Weiß [32]. The special function `create` sets the `<allocate>` field to true. It cannot be set otherwise (as one cannot de-allocate an object within JavaDL). The function `C::exactInstance` maps each term to true, that is a member of class `C` and none of its subclasses.

This is formalised in the following definition, where we model our assumption directly in the model and extend the `allocateInstance` taclet in KeY.

Definition 1. *We assume that in every state of the Kripke structure, for every heap h, all objects are ordered by some total order $<_h$, such that there is some object o_h, such that (1) for all $o' <_h o_h$, the object o' is allocated (i.e., its* `<allocated>` *field is set to true), and (2) for all $o_h \leq_h o''$, the object o'' is not allocated. We introduce a unary function symbol* `allocate` *with the signature* `Heap` $\rightarrow$ `Object`*, whose interpretation must adhere to $\mathcal{I}(\mathtt{allocate})(h) = o_h$. The (slightly prettified) rule is as follows:*

$$\frac{\Gamma, \{U\}(\mathtt{v} \neq \mathtt{null} \land \mathtt{v} \doteq \mathtt{allocate(heap)} \land \mathtt{C::exactInstance(v)} \doteq \mathtt{TRUE}) \Rightarrow \{U\}\{\mathtt{heap} := \mathtt{create(heap, v)}\}[\mathtt{s}]\phi, \Delta}{\Gamma \Rightarrow \{U\}[\mathtt{v\ =\ C.allocate();\ s}]\phi, \Delta}$$

The modification is the addition of $v = \mathtt{allocate(heap)}$ to the antecedent. The modified rule suffices to show the simple equivalence of **`return new`** `C()` to itself from above.

Continuing our investigation of when objects are considered equal, where the two allocations are independent from each other, i.e., any side-effects of the constructors are not visible to each other, `C` is not a subtype of `D` and vice versa. Again the question where the two `C` (resp. `D`) objects are equal arises. They are not equal in the sense that, if there is a implicit[3] global counter that counts all allocations, they get the same number from this counter. They are equal in the sense that there is no explicit way to distinguish them in the program.

They are, however, distinguishable in the proof system due to the term-representation of the heap. If we choose to consider them equal, we must adapt our `allocate` mechanism: firstly, it must be able to distinguish between the allocation of different classes and, secondly, it must be able to simplify the heap to ignore irrelevant operations on it. We adapt the previous definition to take into account the types of objects, by having a *set* of orders $<_h$, one for each class.

Definition 2. *We assume that in every state of the Kripke structure, for every heap h and every class C, all objects of type C are ordered by some total order $<^C_h$, such that there is some object o^C_h, such that (1) for all $o' <^C_h o^C_h$, the object o' is allocated (i.e., its `<allocated>` field is set to true), and (2) for all $o^C_h \leq^C_h o''$, the object o'' is not allocated. Additionally, if D is a subtype of C, then $<^D_h$ must be a suborder of $<^C_h$. For each class C, we introduce a unary function symbol `C::allocate` with the signature `Heap` → `Object`, whose interpretation must adhere to $\mathcal{I}(C{::}\mathtt{allocate})(h) = o^C_h$. We obtain:*

$$\frac{\Gamma, \{U\}(\mathtt{v} \neq \mathtt{null} \wedge \mathtt{v} \doteq \mathtt{C::allocate(heap)} \wedge \mathtt{C::exactInstance(v)} \doteq \mathtt{TRUE}) \Rightarrow \{U\}\{\mathtt{heap} := \mathtt{create(heap, v)}\}[\mathtt{s}]\phi, \Delta}{\Gamma \Rightarrow \{U\}[\mathtt{v\ =\ C.allocate();\ s}]\phi, \Delta}$$

Additionally, we give two simplification rules for heaps within any `allocate` function application. Let $\sqsubseteq$ be the subtype relation and $T(t)$ the type of a term.

$$\mathtt{C::allocate(store(h,o,f,v))} \rightsquigarrow \mathtt{C::allocate(h)} \quad \text{if } f \neq \mathtt{<allocated>}$$
$$\mathtt{C::allocate(create(h,o))} \rightsquigarrow \mathtt{C::allocate(h)} \quad \text{if } C \not\sqsubseteq T(o)$$

The first rule uses the assumption that the orders are only sensitive to the `<allocated>` field, and the second one that they are independent, besides the subtyping relation. Intuitively, this implements a different counter for each class in the type hierarchy and two objects are considered equal if the counters of their classes are equal. Creating an object of a class increases the counter of this class and all its superclasses. If `C` is a subtype of `D`, then the proof fails. This suffices to prove the programs in Listing 6 to be equivalent. Interestingly, Steinhöfel already proved the general SLIDE STATEMENT refactoring correct for

[3] The counter is indeed implicit, as the order $<_h$ cannot be accessed by the proof system.

```
x = new C();
y = new D();
```

(a) Before

```
y = new D();
x = new C();
```

(b) After

Listing 6. Object creation

```
class C {
  private int j;
  public C(int j){
    this.j = j;
  }
}
```

(a) Class

```
return new C(1);
```

(b) Before

```
return new C(2);
```

(c) After

Listing 7. Object creation and fields

abstract statements under the right constraints ([28], p.231), yet KeY needs additional rules for these concrete statements. The second rule is able to remove some intermittent operations that are symbolically represented on the heap, e.g., a call to an imaginary setter in `x = new C(); x.set(1); y = new D()` versus `y = new D(); x = new C(); x.set(1)`, if they are not relevant to object creation.

Note that we ignore the state of fields in the heap, meaning that the equivalence of two objects is determined only by their counters. This requires to be careful with specification: it does not suffice for each notion of equivalence to specify that two objects are equal, but also *their fields* must be equal. Consider the class and programs in Listing 7. The returned objects are identical, but in the post states the heap assigns different values to their field.

Let us close with three remarks. Firstly, the solutions we described here are enabling the programmer (or refactoring designer) to fine tune their notion of equivalence, which must be specified in addition to the refactoring itself. Realising the choice, however, is rather simple by enabling and disabling rules, resp. taclets. Thus, we avoid to put even more burden on the first-order specification of the relational post-condition, and merely require the programmer to select from a number of options. We emphasise that the taclets for the different options are not *unsound*, but merely switch between different version of assumptions about the (in this case underspecified) Java object model. Of course, the default version is not using the new taclets and stick with the originals, i.e., not assuming deterministic allocation.

Secondly, while we only discussed object creation here, the same solution also handles *exceptions*, which must be created before being thrown. Exceptions are special in the sense that they have access to the program beyond the parts that are exposed to (non-reflective) programs. For example, they can access the line

```
C x;
x = new C();
x = new C();
```

(a) Before

```
C x;
x = new C();
```

(b) After

Listing 8. Dead object

number of the throwing statement for their stack trace. As the stack trace is not modelled in JavaDL, its treatment for verification is an open research question in itself, and because we consider exhibiting the stack trace within the program a dubious practice in the first place, we chose to ignore it in this paper.

Thirdly, one could argue that we have not so much proven the refactoring to be correct, but rather moved this decision further down the chain: unlike in a full formalisation of the Java object model from ground up, we do not have a way of proving the taclets correct (i.e., derive them as lemmas) within KeY, as they model our assumptions about object identity when running two Java programs in the exact same state, which is not described by the Java semantics.

Excursus: Dead Code Elimination. Similar considerations of equivalent heap manipulations need to be considered also in the are of optimizations, whose soundness proofs rely on relation verification as well. For example, consider the program in Listing 8.

Again, we assume that the constructor of `C` has no side-effects except object creation on the heap. In this case, the first object creation is of no consequence. The additional rules above however will not yet be sufficient to prove that this version is equivalent to the version without the redundant object creation and assignment. The location-set mechanism would still insist that the second object created in the redundant version is a different object from the first (and only) object created in the optimised version. On the one hand this can be addressed through a relaxed post-condition where we accept that we only need *some* object of the right type and arguments, but it relies on the side-condition of the constructor not having side-effects, which requires a very restrictive method contract for the constructor. Alternatively, the notion of equivalence becomes even more specification-heavy for optimisations, as it may be more fine-grained. We foresee that such and other instances will give rise to various further taclets in the future.

4 Potential Future Improvements

In the previous section, we have established that relational verification using abstract execution must take care of the general effects of language semantics outside the abstract statements. In this section, we illustrate a different obstacle to practical abstract execution, which touches on its core specification principles: sequences of side effects and events.

4.1 Trace Properties

Following Fowler's persuasion of what constitutes correct refactorings, developers are content if refactored code gives the same observable behavior [15].

This behavior is first and foremost encoded through unit-tests, but also on tests through side-effects and their order (e.g. output via `print`-statements). Here we then have a much more relaxed setting where equivalence is decoupled from the fine-grained program semantics. More realistically, one may want to establish that after refactoring, certain operations happened in the same order.

Abstract execution supports the specification of read and write events, via dynamic frames, but does not specify their order or give a general possibility to specify the order of side-effects/events. The most straightforward approach is to use a special model variable to keep track of the events explicitly in a trace, and specify properties using the surrounding logic, in our case, JavaDL. This approach has been taken for dynamics logics (without investigating relation verification) in, e.g., ABSDL [11] and for relational verification (albeit without using a dynamic logic) by, e.g., Barthe et al. [5]. This explicit encoding of user-defined execution histories has the advantage that it is not only useful for proofs, but can also directly be harnessed in concrete unit-tests where we can explicitly compare the recorded history of an earlier execution of a test with the history of the same test but on the refactored code base.

A main advantage of encoding the trace in the post state is that relational verification (either based on self-composition or its variants [3,4,10] or using the proof obligation described above), can use the state logic to describe both states. However, first-order specifications of temporal properties have been proven to be unwieldy, large and hard to understand. This led to the development of other dynamic logics which interact with novel trace specifications, such as BPL [19] and symbolic traces [9], where the post-condition of a modality is a *trace formula* without quantifiers over indices, whose models are single traces. It has neither been investigated how such logics can be used for relational verification, nor how abstract statements can be specified with respect to such trace properties.

We concentrate on, simplified, symbolic traces here, which are defined by the grammar

$$\theta ::= \lceil\phi\rceil \mid \mathsf{call}(\mathtt{m}) \mid \mathbf{finite} \mid \theta \ast\ast \theta$$

where $\lceil\phi\rceil$ denotes the trace where the state formula ϕ holds, $\mathsf{call}(\mathtt{m})$ a call event on method `m`, **finite** an arbitrary finite trace without any events[4] and $\ast\ast$ is the chop [9], a special concatenation. Models for such formulas are traces: sequences of states and events.

Consider the two programs in Listing 9. It shows a refactoring of some program using a `File`, where we only give the trace specification. The first program specifies that some initialisation happens that is guaranteed to call `f.open`, then the file is read and written, and then some finalisation happens that calls `f.close`. The second program switches the order of read and write. The programs are, obviously, not equivalent in a strict sense, but if the trace property we

[4] We deviate here from the original definition for example's sake.

```
File f = new File();
String s = "";
/*@ ensures finite ** call(f.open) ** finite; */
\abstract_statement A;
s = f.read();
f.write(s);
/*@ ensures finite ** call(f.close) ** finite; */
\abstract_statement B;
```

(a) Before

```
File f = new File();
String s = "";
/*@ ensures finite ** call(f.open) ** finite; */
\abstract_statement A;
f.write(s);
s = f.read();
/*@ ensures finite ** call(f.close) ** finite; */
\abstract_statement B;
```

(b) After

Listing 9. Refactoring for trace-based-notions of equivalence.

are interested in is only concerned with the order of operations on the file (`open`, `write`, `read` and `open`), for example to express that only opened files are read and written to, then we need to specify a notion of equivalences. It remains to be seen in how far abstract executions can be expanded with such a mechanism in the future.

4.2 Relational Invariants

Another area of interest for equivalence is replacing one data structure with another, e.g. Fowler's Replace Array with Object [14, p.186] or Replace Primitive with Object [15]. As an example, in the following we look at a piece of code where an array is replaced with an object (or vice versa). Again, from

```
String[] p = new String[2];

p[0] = "36.452999";
p[1] = "28.226376";
```

(a) Before

```
Pos p = new Pos();

p.setLat("36.452999");
p.setLon("28.226376");
```

(b) After

Listing 10. Replace array with object refactoring

```
String[] p = new String[2];
/* M only uses the static
method API to modify 'p' and
does not assign a new value
to 'p'. */
\abstract_statement M
setX(p,value);
```

(a) Before

```
Pos p = new Pos();
/* ditto */
\abstract_statement M
p.setX(value);
```

(b) After

Listing 11. Replace array with object refactoring

the strict default perspective of "equal return values, equal heaps", any two programs using the data structures are obviously not equal. Encoding observability through traces as per the previous section will obviously solve this issue. A new challenge arises when both programs use different or disjoint sets of operations, i.e., we have different alphabets for their trace languages.

Let us consider a refactoring that replaces an array containing a geographical position given by a latitude and longitude as in Listing 10a with an object that gives read or write access to the same values through setters and getters that make it immediately clear what is being accessed as seen in Listing 10b. In either direction of this refactoring, we must be certain that indexing can only occur within the bounds of the original program as there will be no corresponding out of bounds failure for method calls. We note the added (syntactical) complication that in the direction from array to object, that if array offsets are computed, there is no direct correspondence to a setter/getter, and the refactored code needs to dispatch on the corresponding component. In the following, for simplification, we assume that the array is only used with constants.

Having established that the two programs are not equal, but should be considered equivalent, we need to establish a correspondence in the specific case. To avoid having to establish the correspondence in all uses (of either setter/getter or the array), we can assume that accesses in either case are wrapped in a method—if we assume that EXTRACT METHOD/INLINE METHOD are already proven as correct. This reliance on other refactorings allows us to compartmentalise the reasoning, and mostly focus on contracts for the involved methods. While abstract execution is good at reasoning about placeholders for abstract behaviour, a similar mechanism for abstract structures is missing. Through some intermediate steps, we can offload most of the reasoning to a history-based mechanism with some static assumptions on the code that can be easily checked. The first is to encapsulate all accesses in methods; setters/getters on the object-side, and static helpers on the array-side. We can then formulate the abstract programs for REFINITY as given in Listing. 11 for each of the operations in the API, here the matching pairs of setters/getters. It remains to show that a) neither abstract statement overwrites `p`, that b) the histories of API operations with arguments called on either side match pairwise, and that c) in the post-condition the values in their respective components match.

5 Discussion

In the following, we shortly discuss some of the raised issues and in how far they can be adressed in the future and possibly in the short-term.

The first challenge is due to the way REFINITY prepares the environment and the top-level proof obligation for KeY, in fact both sides in a refactoring share the same Java namespace. This means for example that the EXTRACT METHOD refactoring no so much proves the original correct, but rather a version where the extracted method is already present. Care must be taken to set this up correctly, and e.g. in the EXTRACT METHOD example make sure that the methods is not used on the *Before*-side. The same holds for refactorings that remove code.

Addressing this would require choosing unique names in either schemata, since they go into a single KeY-proof, and hence would require some form of mapping classes/objects of distinct types (due to the nominal type system of Java) between both sides. This issue is closely related to the challenge we discussed before when trying to relate unrelated yet semantically equivalent data types (see Sect. 4.2). In general, we observe that currently REFINITY requires some scaffolding that makes the actual refactoring less obvious, such as our use of assertions and casts.

A more general problem is capturing the most general instance of a refactoring. Currently, REFINITY's lack of placeholders for names, means that e.g. in the EXTRACT LOCAL VARIABLE refactoring we would have to instantiate the *Before*-schema for every concrete instance with the corresponding identifier names for variables. The otherwise straight-forward refactoring RENAME TEMPORARY already exposes the issue faced by REFINITY due to renaming on the block-level. Likewise, the related HIDE DELEGATE example uses concrete method- and class names. During our development of this refactoring, we have found ourselves revising the encoding and use of placeholders with their annotations repeatedly. Conversely, due to the challenges in checking instantiation of schemata against concrete programs already pointed out by Steinhöfel [28, 119,137], one has to take care not to write too restrictive programs that rule out useful working instances.

Another area for placeholders would be a generalisation of storage locations: We foresee that there exist refactorings that may need to be specified twice, once with using local variables and another time using attributes in their schemata.

For the time being we are limited to checking schemata against each other. In the future, when we move on to checking instantiations, we feel that often necessary pre-conditions on a refactoring can easily be discharged by simple syntactical or static analysis (e.g. "code does never read attribute `x` of objects of type `C`"). Yet unlike in other formal work where the program is encoded as part of the proof-term, we cannot implement such analyses within KeY, and can only informally document and require such side-conditions on refactorings. Correspondingly, we will also not be able to use KeY to formulate and prove a lemma that such a static property entails the necessary consequences.

6 Related Work

Similar or other approaches to formal verification of refactorings can be found in work by Garrido et al. [16] who formalize PUSH DOWN METHOD, PULL UP FIELD and RENAME TEMPORARY using an executable Java formal semantics in Maude and give partially mechanised proofs for the two former.

Long Quan et al. [25] formulate refactorings as refinement laws in the calculus of refinement of component and object-oriented systems (rCOS), focusing on correctness proofs of refactoring rules themselves. They did not have the benefit of any tool support, but similarly were able to describe refactorings on schematic programs. Statement level refactorings as well as refactorings that transform class hierarchies are considered.

While KeY and REFINITY are unique for their relational verification capacity for schematic programs (or abstract programs) they are limited in power for verification of concrete programs relying much more on manual specification or interaction [29] than tools like LLRêve [21] or SymDiff [22] which offer more automation for concrete programs.

Peter Müller et al. [24] present a verification infrastructure whose intermediate language supports an expressive permission model natively, with tool support including two back-end verifiers: one based on symbolic execution and one on verification condition generation, an inference tool based on abstract interpretation reportedly under development.

Stolz, Pun and Gheyi investigate how well-known refactorings interact with concurrency in Active Object languages [31]. Findings show that refactorings that are straight-forward in Java are not necessarily so under the concurrency model considered and identify key program transformations that may cause interactions. In contrast to their work, REFINITY and its foundation KeY strictly consider sequential Java programs, but they already explore the notion of equivalent executions in their formal considerations of syntactically different, but overlapping, programs.

Eilertsen, Stolz and Bagge demonstrate a technique of introducing runtime checks in Java for two refactorings EXTRACT AND MOVE METHOD and EXTRACT LOCAL VARIABLE [13]. The technique in combination with testing can detect changed behavior and allow identification of which refactoring step introduced the change the deviant behavior. Our proof of correctness of EXTRACT LOCAL VARIABLE in REFINITY is inspired by their technique.

Schaefer et al. develop microrefactorings that can be composed to specify several refactorings in a concise manner [26]. They use an infrastructure to preserve correct name binding in refactorings.

Soares et al. [27] describe and evaluate SafeRefactor - a tool that given a program input and a refactoring to apply can automatically generate testcases to detect behavioural changes. It would be interesting to adapt SafeRefactor to do deal with REFINITY's abstract programs, and generate test cases for the instances where REFINITY fails to prove a refactoring. These could then be run against concrete refactored programs.

Dovland et al. [12] propose a proof system that allows incrementally reasoning about adaptable class hierarchies, based on lazy behavioural subtyping, for an object-oriented kernel language similar to Featherweight Java. The proof system avoids reverifying methods that are not modified explicitly by the class adaptation. We are unaware whether the incremental reasoning broached for the proof system has a counterpart in KeY and REFINITY, but the latter allows for modularity in proof and verification which may achieve a similar result.

7 Conclusion

We have presented two new encodings of refactorings (EXTRACT LOCAL VARIABLE and HIDE DELEGATE) and their necessary preconditions (constraints) for them to be behaviour-preserving for REFINITY. REFINITY has syntactical constructs that capture abstract program executions, for which the KeY system, an automated theorem prover for JavaDL, succeeds in proving the refactorings as correct (equal) wrt. to the Java semantics without user interaction.

The HIDE DELEGATE refactoring departs from statement-based refactorings and considers changes involving multiple classes and requires us to consider the first subtle difference between equivalent-yet-not-equal objects in the form of equivalent exceptions and how we need to explicitly address this in the postcondition of the proof-obligation. This also allows us to make a contribution through further taclets that capture some indistinguishable programs that only differ in placement of objects on the heap.

We discuss in how far REFINITY could be used to capture other refactorings, broadening our investigation into the underlying notion of (sometimes use-case specific) *equivalent behaviour*. For example, while traces over observable behaviour could be explicitly encoded and checked against each other as return values in REFINITY, a more general process-algebra inspired approach of execution histories for abstract executions would avoid distorting the original program logic with scaffolding to achieve an encoding without having to extend the tool. We also point out the difficulties due to a naming issue in the current encoding from Refinity to KeY proof-obligations for refactorings that change the class hierarchies or in general attempt to relate behaviour across different types.

Future Work. To investigate the discussed problems with refactoring using AE wrt. trace properties, we are currently implementing AE for BPL in the Crowbar tool [20] as a starting point, a symbolic execution engine to prototype behavioural symbolic execution.

We are also working on contributing further encodings of common refactorings that can already now be handled by REFINITY. In addition, we are particularly interested in additional taclets for KeY that would enable automation of proofs that currently are stuck on the explicit symbolic encoding of program state although it would be indistinguishable from equivalent states in pratice. The latter is of relevance e.g. for proving common optimisations as in our DEAD CODE ELIMINATION example.

Acknowledgements. This work was partially supported by the Research Council of Norway via SIRIUS (237898), PeTWIN (294600) and CROFLOW (326249).

References

1. Ahrendt, W., Beckert, B., Bubel, R., Hähnle, R., Schmitt, P.H., Ulbrich, M. (eds.): Deductive Software Verification - The KeY Book - From Theory to Practice, Lecture Notes in Computer Science, vol. 10001. Springer, Heidelberg (2016). https://doi.org/10.1007/978-3-319-49812-6
2. Baldoni, R., Coppa, E., D'Elia, D.C., Demetrescu, C., Finocchi, I.: A survey of symbolic execution techniques. ACM Comput. Surv. **51**(3), 50:1–50:39 (2018). https://doi.org/10.1145/3182657
3. Barthe, G., Crespo, J.M., Kunz, C.: Relational verification using product programs. In: Butler, M., Schulte, W. (eds.) FM 2011. LNCS, vol. 6664, pp. 200–214. Springer, Heidelberg (2011). https://doi.org/10.1007/978-3-642-21437-0_17
4. Barthe, G., D'Argenio, P.R., Rezk, T.: Secure information flow by self-composition. In: 17th IEEE Computer Security Foundations Workshop, (CSFW-17 2004), Pacific Grove, CA, USA, 28–30 June 2004, pp. 100–114. IEEE Computer Society (2004). https://doi.org/10.1109/CSFW.2004.17
5. Barthe, G., Eilers, R., Georgiou, P., Gleiss, B., Kovács, L., Maffei, M.: Verifying relational properties using trace logic. In: Barrett, C.W., Yang, J. (eds.) 2019 Formal Methods in Computer Aided Design, FMCAD 2019, San Jose, CA, USA, 22–25 October 2019, pp. 170–178. IEEE (2019). https://doi.org/10.23919/FMCAD.2019.8894277
6. Baumann, C., Beckert, B., Blasum, H., Bormer, T.: Lessons learned from microkernel verification - specification is the new bottleneck. In: SSV. EPTCS, vol. 102, pp. 18–32 (2012)
7. Beckert, B., Bruns, D., Klebanov, V., Scheben, C., Schmitt, P.H., Ulbrich, M.: Information flow in object-oriented software. In: Gupta, G., Peña, R. (eds.) LOPSTR 2013. LNCS, vol. 8901, pp. 19–37. Springer, Cham (2014). https://doi.org/10.1007/978-3-319-14125-1_2
8. Beckert, B., Ulbrich, M.: Trends in relational program verification. In: Principled Software Development, pp. 41–58. Springer, Cham (2018). https://doi.org/10.1007/978-3-319-98047-8_3
9. Bubel, R., Din, C.C., Hähnle, R., Nakata, K.: A dynamic logic with traces and coinduction. In: De Nivelle, H. (ed.) TABLEAUX 2015. LNCS (LNAI), vol. 9323, pp. 307–322. Springer, Cham (2015). https://doi.org/10.1007/978-3-319-24312-2_21
10. Darvas, Á., Hähnle, R., Sands, D.: A theorem proving approach to analysis of secure information flow. In: Hutter, D., Ullmann, M. (eds.) SPC 2005. LNCS, vol. 3450, pp. 193–209. Springer, Heidelberg (2005). https://doi.org/10.1007/978-3-540-32004-3_20
11. Din, C.C., Owe, O.: A sound and complete reasoning system for asynchronous communication with shared futures. J. Log. Algebraic Methods Program. **83**(5–6), 360–383 (2014). https://doi.org/10.1016/j.jlamp.2014.03.003
12. Dovland, J., Johnsen, E.B., Owe, O., Yu, I.C.: A proof system for adaptable class hierarchies. J. Log. Algebraic Methods Program. **84**(1), 37–53 (2015). https://doi.org/10.1016/j.jlamp.2014.09.001
13. Eilertsen, A.M., Bagge, A.H., Stolz, V.: Safer refactorings. In: Margaria, T., Steffen, B. (eds.) ISoLA 2016. LNCS, vol. 9952, pp. 517–531. Springer, Cham (2016). https://doi.org/10.1007/978-3-319-47166-2_36

14. Fowler, M.: Refactoring - Improving the Design of Existing Code. Addison Wesley object technology series. Addison-Wesley (1999)
15. Fowler, M.: Refactoring: Improving the Design of Existing Code, 2nd edn. Addison-Wesley Signature Series (Fowler), Addison-Wesley (2018)
16. Garrido, A., Meseguer, J.: Formal specification and verification of java refactorings. In: 2006 Sixth IEEE International Workshop on Source Code Analysis and Manipulation, pp. 165–174. IEEE (2006)
17. Hähnle, R., Huisman, M.: Deductive software verification: from pen-and-paper proofs to industrial tools. In: Steffen, B., Woeginger, G. (eds.) Computing and Software Science. LNCS, vol. 10000, pp. 345–373. Springer, Cham (2019). https://doi.org/10.1007/978-3-319-91908-9_18
18. Huisman, M., Ahrendt, W., Bruns, D., Hentschel, M.: Formal specification with jml. Technical Report 10, Karlsruher Institut für Technologie (KIT) (2014). https://doi.org/10.5445/IR/1000041881
19. Kamburjan, E.: Behavioral program logic. In: Cerrito, S., Popescu, A. (eds.) TABLEAUX 2019. LNCS (LNAI), vol. 11714, pp. 391–408. Springer, Cham (2019). https://doi.org/10.1007/978-3-030-29026-9_22
20. Kamburjan, E., Wasser, N.: Deductive verification of programs with underspecified semantics by model extraction. CoRR abs/2110.01964 (2021)
21. Kiefer, M., Klebanov, V., Ulbrich, M.: Relational program reasoning using compiler IR - combining static verification and dynamic analysis. J. Autom. Reason. **60**(3), 337–363 (2018). https://doi.org/10.1007/s10817-017-9433-5
22. Myers, C.J.: Formal verification of genetic circuits. In: Madhusudan, P., Seshia, S.A. (eds.) CAV 2012. LNCS, vol. 7358, pp. 5–5. Springer, Heidelberg (2012). https://doi.org/10.1007/978-3-642-31424-7_5
23. McCarthy, J.: Towards a mathematical science of computation. In: Information Processing, Proceedings of the 2nd IFIP Congress 1962, Munich, Germany, 27 August–1 September 1962, pp. 21–28. North-Holland (1962)
24. Müller, P., Schwerhoff, M., Summers, A.J.: Viper: a verification infrastructure for permission-based reasoning. In: Pretschner, A., Peled, D., Hutzelmann, T. (eds.) Dependable Software Systems Engineering, NATO Science for Peace and Security Series - D: Information and Communication Security, vol. 50, pp. 104–125. IOS Press (2017). https://doi.org/10.3233/978-1-61499-810-5-104
25. Quan, L., Zongyan, Q., Liu, Z.: Formal use of design patterns and refactoring. In: Margaria, T., Steffen, B. (eds.) ISoLA 2008. CCIS, vol. 17, pp. 323–338. Springer, Heidelberg (2008). https://doi.org/10.1007/978-3-540-88479-8_23
26. 0 Schäfer, M., de Moor, O.: Specifying and implementing refactorings. In: Object-Oriented Programming, Systems, Languages, and Applications (2010)
27. Soares, G., Gheyi, R., Serey, D., Massoni, T.: Making program refactoring safer. IEEE Softw. **27**(4), 52–57 (2010)
28. Steinhöfel, D.: Abstract Execution: Automatically Proving Infinitely Many Programs. Ph.D. thesis, TU Darmstadt, Dept. of Computer Science (2020). https://tuprints.ulb.tu-darmstadt.de/id/eprint/8540
29. Steinhöfel, D.: REFINITY to model and prove program transformation rules. In: Oliveira, B.C.S. (ed.) APLAS 2020. LNCS, vol. 12470, pp. 311–319. Springer, Cham (2020). https://doi.org/10.1007/978-3-030-64437-6_16
30. Steinhöfel, D., Hähnle, R.: Abstract execution. In: ter Beek, M.H., McIver, A., Oliveira, J.N. (eds.) FM 2019. LNCS, vol. 11800, pp. 319–336. Springer, Cham (2019). https://doi.org/10.1007/978-3-030-30942-8_20

31. Stolz, V., Pun, V.K.I., Gheyi, R.: Refactoring and active object languages. In: Margaria, T., Steffen, B. (eds.) ISoLA 2020. LNCS, vol. 12477, pp. 138–158. Springer, Cham (2020). https://doi.org/10.1007/978-3-030-61470-6_9
32. Weiß, B.: Deductive verification of object-oriented software: dynamic frames, dynamic logic and predicate abstraction. Ph.D. thesis, Karlsruhe Institute of Technology (2011). https://d-nb.info/1010034960
33. Yang, G., Filieri, A., Borges, M., Clun, D., Wen, J.: Chapter five - advances in symbolic execution. Adv. Comput. **113**, 225–287 (2019). https://doi.org/10.1016/bs.adcom.2018.10.002

Towards a Usable and Sustainable Deductive Verification Tool

Bernhard Beckert[1], Richard Bubel[2(✉)], Reiner Hähnle[2], and Mattias Ulbrich[1]

[1] Karlsruhe Institute of Technology, Karlsruhe, Germany
{beckert,ulbrich}@kit.edu

[2] Technische Universität Darmstadt, Darmstadt, Germany
{richard.bubel,reiner.haehnle}@tu-darmstadt.de

Abstract. Deductive verification tools are logic-based, formal software verification tools that permit to verify complex, functional and non-functional properties with a very high degree of automation. They exhibit impressive performance at the hands of an expert, but are not ready for productive use by someone with limited or no training in formal verification. In this paper we analyze in some detail what needs to be done to make a concrete state-of-art tool so usable and robust that it can be successfully applied by Computer Science Researchers outside the core development team and we propose a set of actions that need to be taken towards this aim.

Keywords: Deductive verification · Software verification · Usability

1 Introduction

Deductive verification tools are logic-based, formal software verification tools that permit to verify complex, functional and non-functional properties with a very high degree of automation. The field of deductive verification made impressive progress in the last decades [13,34]. It is possible to verify highly complex production code written in mainstream languages within a relatively short time (see, for example, [23] and further references contained in [34]). Notable tools include AutoProof [60], Boogie [7], Dafny [47], Frama-C [43], KeY [2], KIV [25], Krakatoa [27], OpenJML [21], Spark [41], VCC [22], VerCors [18], VeriFast [42], Viper [53], and Why3 [19].

These tools exhibit impressive performance at the hands of an expert, but are not ready for productive use by someone with limited or no training in formal verification. *Basic* usage is often easy enough: most deductive verification tools come with a GUI and feature a high-level behavioral specification language

Partially funded by DFG project "KeY –A Deductive Software Analysis Tool for the Research Community" and by the Hessian LOEWE initiative within the "Software-Factory 4.0" project.

T. Margaria and B. Steffen (Eds.): ISoLA 2022, LNCS 13702, pp. 281–300, 2022.
https://doi.org/10.1007/978-3-031-19756-7_16

that is intuitive and easy to learn for programmers, for example, ACSL [8] or JML [46]. Novices, however, regularly fail in attempting to verify a somewhat complex program. The main reasons are: (i) Certain properties, notably about data structures with aliasing, have complex specifications [9]; (ii) auxiliary specifications, in particular method contracts and loop invariants, must be found that are sufficiently strong for verification to succeed, but without being overly complex; (iii) there is a plethora of options and settings whose significance is only clear to an expert, however, these can greatly influence performance [44]; (iv) when a verification attempt fails, it is hard to figure out the reason and how the issue can be fixed [12].

Another obstacle against widespread adoption of verification tools is their high degree of specialization combined with a lack of integration into other software development activities. For example, bug finding is often more important than verification. Program understanding, writing of specifications, debugging, test case generation, all are tasks closely related to formal verification, yet they are poorly supported by most verification tools. This is not easy to remedy, because verification tools are developed over a long time before they become effective and typically are not designed with extensibility in mind.

At the same time, the considerable effort and time, often provided by public funding, that went into the development of verification tools is a powerful motivation to render them usable outside the deductive verification community. For the KeY system we estimate 15 M€ and 125 person years based on SLOCCount. One purpose of this paper is to analyze in some detail what needs to be done to make a state-of-art tool so usable and robust that it can be successfully applied by Computer Science Researchers outside the tool development team. This is done in Sect. 3. Then we propose a set of actions that need to be taken in Sect. 4.

To be concrete, we investigate a specific tool: The KeY system [2] is a state-of-art static analysis tool for one of the most popular programming languages: JAVA. One reason to choose KeY obviously is that all present authors have been involved in its development since a long time. In addition, KeY is a publicly funded (in contrast to, for example, the commercial tools Frama-C, Spark, VCC), open source project and its target language is a mainstream language (in contrast to Dafny, KIV that aim at modeling languages or Why3, Viper that aim at intermediate languages). Nevertheless, we believe our analysis applies in most respects to other tools as well. In consequence, the proposals we make in Sect. 4 can be seen as a glimpse into the future of major developments that can be expected in the field of deductive program verification during the next years.

KeY and its underlying methodology and theories have been developed since the late 1990s [35]. In contrast to many other tools, KeY is not merely a formal verification tool, but it offers a visual debugger [36], a test case generation kit [2, Chapter 12], security analysis [2, Chapter 13], verification of program transformation [58], and automatic complexity analysis [6].

In the following, we describe how we envisage KeY to become a test bed for experiments in the area of formal methods, and a platform for implementing new approaches and methods for ensuring and analyzing the reliability of research software. The intention is *not* to provide a fully automatic, black-box program verification tool that can be used by anyone—formal specification and deductive verification is a complex task requiring expertise—but to get rid of the necessity to involve (KeY) experts. That this is principally possible is witnessed by the widespread usage of proof assistants like Coq [15] and Isabelle [54] in the programming language community. These tools, however, are not well-suited for verifying individual programs—this is the objective of deductive verification tools discussed in the present article.

2 The Verification Tool KeY

The KeY System is a popular, state-of-art static analysis tool for the Java programming language. It is well documented and highly visible in the deductive verification community (publications [1,2,14] together have ca. 1,500 citations on Google Scholar). The KeY Symposium, held annually since 2002, regularly attracts 20–30 participants. KeY is available as open source at www.key-project.org.

KeY was successfully used in over ten research projects that were *not* initiated by the KeY team [23,29,40,49,57,59] and that had research goals different from those of the KeY team. The projects [23,29,40] required to formally specify and verify unmodified industrial JAVA source code. While this shows the *potential* of KeY as a research tool, it has to be said that the majority of these case studies, which exemplify the usefulness of KeY for the research community, were performed in close collaboration with members of the KeY core team, as witnessed by partial co-authorship.

KeY is widely considered to be the currently strongest deductive verification tool for Java. It can be used to functionally verify unmodified, highly complex production code, showcased in the TimSort effort [23], which so far no other tool was able to replicate. KeY's architecture served also as a blueprint for the well-known hybrid systems verification tool KeYmaera [55] that for many years shared its code base.

In the future, we envisage KeY to be a tool for computer scientists doing research in the area of developing reliable software and, in particular, formal methods in software engineering. There are three main usage scenarios for the KeY system as a research tool:

Stand-alone use of KeY as a test-bed for experimental research and to explore new verification and specification approaches. In this scenario, KeY is used to formally prove properties of a given Java program. This includes functional properties such as safety and correctness [23], but also non-functional properties such as information flow [2, Chapter 13], or variable dependence analysis [39].

Sub-components or partial functionality of the KeY system are used to perform analysis tasks that contribute to a different methodological goal. For

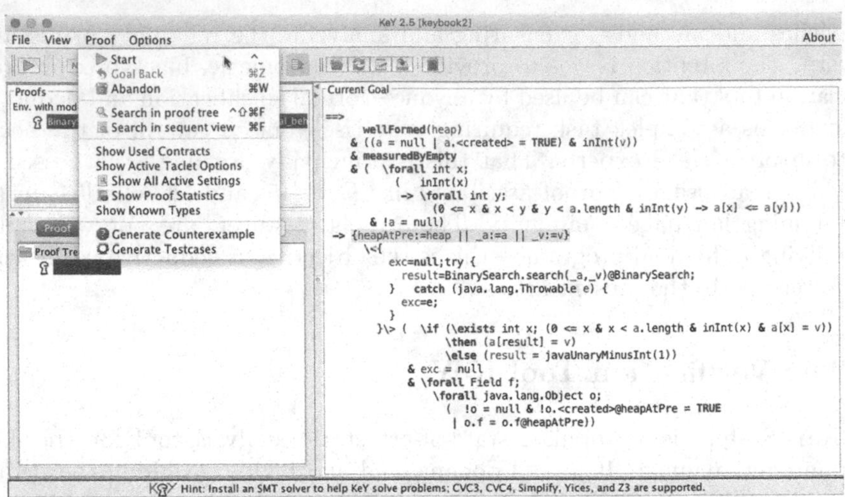

Fig. 1. GUI of the KeY tool with a loaded proof obligation

example: proof obligation generation to improve the performance of run-time checkers [4] or mitigating over-approximation in automated static checkers [45].

Backend use, where the system is typically integrated into other research tools as a black box to discharge small verification tasks in fully automatic mode. Examples include the justification of program synthesis steps [56], the verification of run-time bounds [6], symbolic execution-guided debugging [36], semantic debugging [30], or correctness of program transformations [58].

KeY's program logic is *dynamic logic* for Java [2, Chapter 3]. Dynamic logic formulas encode proof obligations and contain directly the target code to be verified, the properties to be verified, as well as the relation among code and properties. KeY's dynamic logic is very expressive and it is possible to characterize virtually any known program property, for example: functional as well as non-functional (memory, runtime, variable dependence) requirements, relational properties (information flow, correctness of program transformations). KeY can also be used for test case generation [2, Chapter 12]. KeY's complex specification language contrasts with lightweight specifications as used in state exploration tools [16].

KeY's deductive program verification engine is based on a *sequent calculus* [2, Chapter 3] for dynamic logic that allows to reduce valid proof obligations to axioms or first-order properties in a sequence of sound rule applications. The calculus rules realize *symbolic execution* on the target program, whereby all symbolic paths through a program are explored. It can be seen as a generalization of Hoare logic [2, Chapter 17]. Suitable loop invariants make it possible to symbolically execute even programs with loops to completion; method contracts make verification scalable, because one can prove one method at a time to be correct relative to its contract. The disadvantage of this generality is that auxiliary specifications, such as invariants and contracts, mostly have to be provided by the user. In this respect, it is of central importance that specifications in KeY do not need to be expressed in dynamic logic, but can be supplied at the level of source code as *Java Modeling Language* (JML) annotations [46] (following the auto-active interaction pattern [60]).

KeY features a domain-specific textual language (called *Taclets*) [10], [2, Chapter 4] that makes it possible to add axioms of theories, lemmas, and proof rules. This allows to extend and to tailor the deduction engine without having to know implementation internals. As long as taclet-based extensions are provable in KeY's program logic, correctness is preserved.

KeY's standard frontend for interactive proof construction and exploration is a graphical user interface (GUI), see Fig. 1. Upon loading an annotated Java file, proof obligations are automatically translated into Java dynamic logic and presented in the GUI.

Recently, a lightweight proof scripting language was added that complements the GUI's point-and-click style interaction [32]. It fosters proof reuse and mitigates the need to redo failed proof attempts. This is accompanied by a proof script debugger [31].

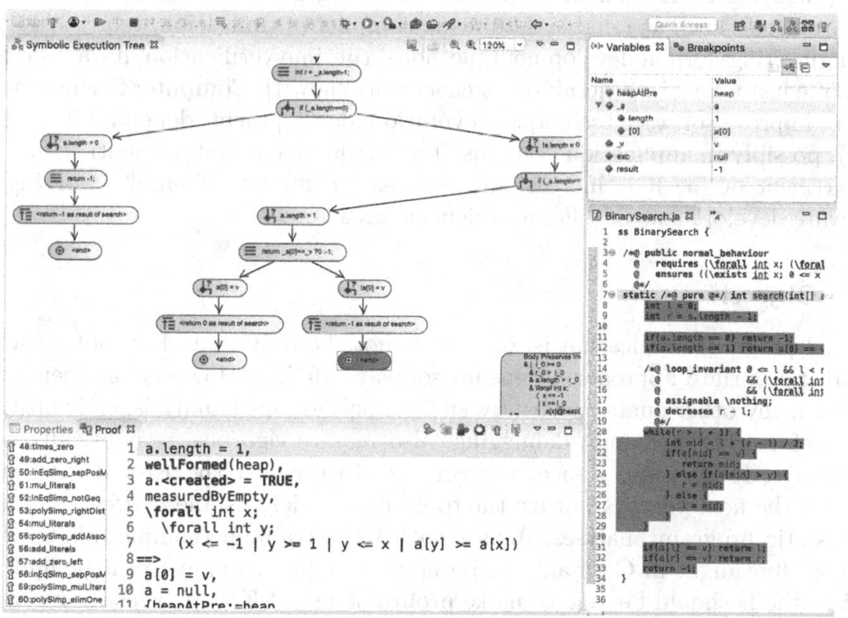

Fig. 2. GUI of the Symbolic Execution Debugger (SED) built on top KeY

A symbolic-state debugger based on symbolic execution, called the Symbolic Execution Debugger (SED) [36] (see Fig. 2), is a tool built on top of KeY. In contrast to conventional debuggers it permits to start debugging at any program point without providing an initial state. It can explore all symbolic program paths simultaneously and has visualization capabilities for control flow and memory layout. There is a basic API to a number of KeY's functionalities which is used in some of the research performed with the help of KeY [4]. Specifically, to realize the SED, a symbolic execution API for JAVA with (optional) first-order annotations is provided.

KeY is an academic, non-commercial tool that can be used freely by anyone. It is published under GNU Public License (Version 2). Its source code is available at www.key-project.org/download/.

The verification approach of KeY is mature enough to be taught, along with small verification case studies, in many BSc- and MSc-level courses at various leading universities worldwide.

3 Requirements on a Verification Tool

3.1 Targeted User Group

The KeY project targets Computer Science researchers that work on methods for developing and analysing reliable software and, thus, can profit from using analyses performed with KeY. Besides program verification, this includes research goals such as reliable databases, compiler optimization, refactoring and re-engineering, formal development methods, runtime verification, library design, to name just a few. In general: researchers working with Computer Science methods to improve software techniques (evolution, development, dependability, security), possibly in application domains. This could be computer scientists in a CS department or (as it is increasingly the case) computer scientists working on software development in different scientific areas.

3.2 Objectives

Formal program verification is, of course, not the only and often not even the most appropriate approach to ensure software quality. However, as mentioned above, many other quality measures such as performance analysis, code abstraction, refactoring, semantic debugging, also require rigorous, semantically well-founded code analysis. Hence, the central objective of the KeY development team in the next years is to turn the tool into a widely usable *platform* for complex static program analyses. A user with basic training (comparable to what is typically taught in German Computer Science programmes) in logic and formal methods should be able to make profitable use of KeY in a research project *without having to know implementation internals*. Research groups then can use KeY either directly or integrate it into their own tool. Users benefit from using KeY as a test bed for experiments and from being able to focus on implementing their own approach without having to worry about the underlying technology. Secondary goals are to improve KeY's robustness and to provide multi-language support, i.e., for other (imperative) target languages than Java.

Community building is essential to achieve the vision sketched above. In addition to encouraging researchers who created extensions or frontends of KeY to host and maintain their tools at the public KeY development site, we plan to open up the long established KeY Symposia (www.key-project.org/category/key-symposium) to the research community. During the pandemic we had already established a highly successful virtual format called the KeYNote Series (www.key-project.org/the-keynote-series).

3.3 Research Tasks

From these objectives one can derive four key areas as targets for future research on verification tools: *usability*, *robustness*, *adaptability*, and *infrastructure*:

Usability: The user experience within the usage scenarios *stand-alone* and *sub-component* (see Sect. 2) centers on the inter- or auto-active use of a verification tool. Interactive use is the possibility to operate directly on the proof object (for instance, via manual application of calculus rules), while the auto-active mode allows the user to interact indirectly with the verifier by providing hints for the proof search using specification annotations.

It does not suffice that a user interface is intuitive and efficient for constructing proofs, but it must ensure that the *user's* and the *system's* perceived state of a given proof task are *consistent* [11]. In particular, the verification system needs not only be able to locate and to point out reasons for *failed* proof attempts (such as a bug in the target program or its specification, incomplete annotations, insufficient resources) but it should also make suggestions for how to fix the problem. The Dafny system [47] incorporates partial solutions towards this problem that can be taken as a starting point [20].

We envisage a workflow, depicted in Fig. 3, that is inspired by the usual cycle of scientific discovery (see https://en.wikipedia.org/wiki/Scientific_method). A program is designed, specified, then verified. If the proof does not succeed, the proof attempt is analyzed and as a result of the learned errors and/or insufficient specification an adaptation/patch is developed for the program and its specification. Existing verification tools support only the left half well—in particular, when the proof remains open and no counterexample is found. Below in Sect. 4.1 we sketch a proposal of how to close the cycle.

Regarding *backend* usage, usability means that the API of a verification tool must be plausible, well-structured, complete, well documented, and extensible. The goal is to enable a Ph.D. student to integrate KeY into her own tool within at most a week (and achieve first successful trials within hours). In either case, well-written and up-to-date documentation and tutorials are of essence.

Robustness encompasses not simply a non-crashing tool, but one that is reasonably easy to use and install. It must work out-of-the-box for simple problems of reasonable size. In case of errors, the messages have to be precise and helpful, hinting towards the most likely solution of the problem like adjusting the paths to a library or pin-pointing the position of a syntax error in the target program.

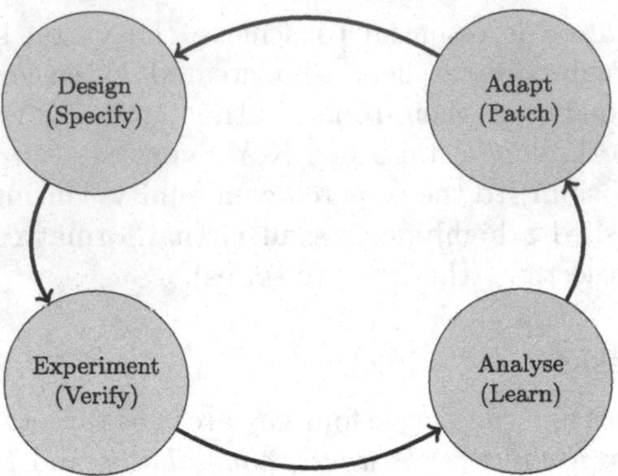

Fig. 3. Program development workflow including incremental verification

Adaptability means the ability to create support for other target languages than (for example) Java. This includes the definition of clear interfaces to integrate parsers and semantic analyzers, to generalize the data structures to be transient regarding the target language, and to factor out language-specific assumptions in the code base.

Specifically, we intend to create a variant of KeY for a simple, sequential, object-based *modeling language*. This is motivated by the fact that many applications are based on simpler programming models than Java, for example, smart contract languages [3] or correctness-by-construction [56], such that Java features like aliasing, code inheritance, or static initialization get in the way and render the verification task unnecessarily difficult.

Ecosystem: It is essential to create a suitable infrastructure to build a community around the tool. This involves an open development process, to provide good development guides and material, and to design state-of-the art first-contact material (short videos, online tutorials, etc.).

In the long run, it is not enough to create a community around a single research tool, such as KeY. We believe it is imperative to focus and to tighten the active research community in deductive verification at large, who currently has no central meeting place, but is dispersed.[1] This hinders not only collaboration and cross-fertilization, but reduces external visibility of deductive verification as a research area. The situation could be remedied, for example, by establishing a dedicated *track on deductive verification* at one of the major software engineering or formal methods conferences.

[1] Deductive verification papers are published, for example, in venues such as ASE, CAV, FASE, FM, FormaliSE, ICSE, IJCAR, ITP, TACAS, which all have a much wider focus. Elsewhere, deductive verification researchers mainly meet at competitions, such as VerifyThis [24].

4 A Work Program

In Sect. 3 we identified four core areas that need to be addressed to create a usable and sustainable deductive verification tool: (i) provide a motivating user experience for end users as well as for developers; (ii) design a robust and resilient system that behaves benevolent even in case of problems; (iii) ensure verification target language adaptability, and (iv) pursue community building.

In the following we present those parts of our work plan for the KeY system in greater detail that might also be of general interest and insightful for developers of other deduction systems.

4.1 User Experience

Understanding Partial Proofs. The most common, and highly frustrating, situation for an end user of a deductive verification tool is that a proof attempt fails. In that case, the user needs to understand the current proof situation to decide which steps to take next. The reasons for failure include (i) a bug in the program to be verified, (ii) an insufficient (too weak) or erroneous specification, or (iii) incompleteness of the automatic proof search.

To identify which of the above reasons a user experiences in a given context, it is essential that he or she gains an *understanding* of the current proof situation. This understanding can be fostered for the first two failure reasons by techniques based on counterexample finding [17,38] as well as symbolic state debugging [28, 33,37,52]. But what can be done when such techniques are unsuccessful or the specification is sufficient, the program bug-free, but the automation of the prover is not powerful enough?

We argue that in this case a verification system needs to provide deeper insights into the current proof situation. This involves visualizing the path through the program taken by current proof, It also requires identifying the origin of unresolved proof obligations such as locating the part of a specification from where they originate or the point in the proof when they were introduced.

Interactive program verification tools need to support their users in proof exploration as much as possible. For KeY we obtained evidence in two user studies [31] that lack of orientation about the proof state and lack of insight into consequences of possible action choices are the main obstacle against successful application of the KeY program verification approach for inexperienced users. Grebing et al. [31,32] suggest concrete measures that would enable faster orientation in a partial proof, as well as allow exploring proof situations with several connected views (program, specification, formulas), while keeping system state and mental model of the user consistent. Some of these ideas have been prototypically implemented in the DIVE tool (Dafny Interactive Verification Environment, see github.com/mattulbrich/dive).

Implementation and adaptation of novel proof interaction concepts together with a selection of explorative user interaction features suggested in [31,32] is ongoing work with the aim to make KeY more accessible to inexperienced users, but also to raise productivity of expert users. Examples of concrete measures to be implemented are a new, structured view on the logical proof state (using colour-coding, grouping, and folding), as well as a selection of views that outline the connection between the current proof state and a path through the program under verification.

In addition to supporting users in *understanding* a proof situation, a verification system should also support its users in determining the appropriate *reaction* to failed proofs. Tool-assisted support should help in finding the appropriate refinement or adaptation of a specification that is inadequate or too weak. In KeY we plan to develop and implement tool support for the adaption of the specification under investigation by extracting suggestions for the user from the (partial) proof. In particular, a "what-if analysis" is going to be realized that will permit the user to continue a partial proof using the assumption that a specific property holds. If the proof succeeds, the assumption is mapped back to the specification. Besides syntactic tracking, specification extraction techniques (in particular abduction [5]) are of essence.

Application Programming Interface (API). Users of a deductive verification system are not merely interested in performing formal verification, but they also need to extend the tool or employ one of its modules (static analysis, symbolic execution, theorem prover and more), typically, as a library component in a domain-specific analysis.

Our experience with external KeY users confirms this claim. While KeY is mainly a stand-alone interactive program verifier, it has been frequently used as a sub-component or backend to perform analysis tasks contributing to other formal analysis tools [4,6,45,56]. But using KeY's deduction capabilities is currently rather cumbersome and its uptake from other research groups would have been much wider, if reuse were easier and possible without involving people from the core KeY team.

Therefore, to achieve sustainable reuse we propose that deductive verification systems should provide a well-designed, well-documented (in other words accessible) API. The API can be provided as a library, and/or as a REST-ful [26] service provider allowing clients (possibly written in other languages than the verification system) to access different functionalities of the system.

4.2 Robustness

Resilience, Reproducibility, Stability. Resilience and reproducibility are fundamental qualities to render any software tool suitable for research purposes. In the realm of a program analysis framework, in particular resilience requires that all constructs of supported programming and specification languages can be parsed and represented in the abstract syntax tree. Large projects must be loadable including (at least the interfaces/headers of) external libraries the program under analysis depends on.

This does not necessarily entail that all target language features are *supported* by the verification system or by the static analyses built on top of it. Instead, tools may decide whether they merely run on those parts of the code that do not contain unsupported constructs, whether they perform a safe approximation, and/or whether they report as part of their output how and why the validity of the analysis may be impaired [48].

Such resilience allows the verification system and other (static) program analysers built on top of it to digest unmodified real-world programs. This ability is crucial for reproducibility of evaluations in scientific papers: One of the problems with tool-based evaluation is that in the presence of non-resilient tools input programs need to be "tweaked". By this we mean small rewrites so that a program adheres to the language subset supported by a tool. In consequence, even when the tools used in an experimental evaluation are available, the tweaked input programs might no longer be around.

Another problem for reproducibility in our experience is that verification runs are not reproducible due to nondeterminism in the proof search. Nondeterminism makes it hard to evaluate the impact of improvements, while reviewers might obtain differing results on the *same* problem. This is not only a problem when the verification result is of interest, but it is a general issue in evaluation benchmarks. Tool developers should therefore carefully review their proof search routines, eliminate sources of nondeterminism, whenever possible, and point them out if not. A typical source of nondeterminism is the usage of collection types that do not guarantee an iteration order. Their elimination does not preclude randomized or statistical proof search strategies which can still be realized by explicit, configurable seeds.

Stable API, Test Suites. We mentioned the need for an API to allow (independent) reuse of the system by other research groups. But offering an API is not enough. Publishing an API comes with responsibilities, such as not to break tools that use them by incompatible changes or by introducing bugs. Hence, a useful API must (i) be well-tested (and for critical parts also verified) and stable so it protects clients from breaking upon updates (downward compatibility); (ii) provide an exhaustive test suite for internal data structures and algorithms to ensure that updates do not break client behavior.

In KeY we will implement these requirements by identifying key *performance parameters* for the core KeY API, such as memory consumption or proof complexity. Further, we intend provide ways to measure these parameters with the help of an automated test suite and benchmarks.

All functional and non-functional tests must be integrated into a continuous integration and deployment service to ensure they are run automatically after each commit so as to catch regressions. A best practice project policy demands that appropriate tests are written *before* any change is merged into the main development branch.

Robust Error and Warning Messages. Robustness requires useful and informative error and warning messages regarding the parsed input (code under verification, specifications, rules, proofs, etc.). In particular, the following aspects have to be targeted (see also the discussion of resilience above): (i) Meaningful error messages providing the user with options on how and where to fix a problem; (ii) warnings that inform the user when input is read that is unsupported by the analysis engine (but still can be parsed); (iii) automated analysis and interpretation of the system configuration, parsed input and code under verification to render assumptions that restrict the validity of the analysis explicit and transparent.

The first item helps a user to understand why an error occurred and provides hints how to fix it. The second point ensures that programs are not rejected because unsupported source code or specification language constructs are used. The final point is in line with the *soundiness manifesto* [48] (see http://soundiness.org), which acknowledges that static analyses and verification results usually are only valid under certain assumptions (mathematical integers instead of finite machine integers, no static initialization, no unsafe approximation, etc.) which must be made explicit.

4.3 Adaptability

With adaptability we mean a modular, well-structured verification system that provides a plugin-based extension design and facilitates addition of new target programming and specification languages.

Modularity. To achieve modularity and extensibility via plugins, the system architecture has to support the extension and replacement of certain modules and the modular structure needs to be sufficiently fine-grained to permit (for instance) adding support for newer versions of the target or specification language or new types of proof obligations. To avoid the need to replace whole modules or to modify the overall architecture, lightweight extension points must be provided that permit adding support for new constructs easily. This is in particularly important for academic tools that target real world systems and programming languages, because it is otherwise not sustainable to keep up with the externally driven changes.

Programming Language Under Verification. Central for sustainability is the target programming language supported by a verification tool. A verification system should allow to be adapted to support additional programming languages as target language.

In KeY we intend to achieve this by making the data structures involved in proof search and management language-independent, rendering the data structures and service classes parametric in the target programming language, and by extracting meaningful abstractions of implementing classes.

With respect to language adaptability, KeY pursues a different approach than many other verification tools: the calculus and deductive verification engine of KeY work at the level of *source code* of the targeted language under verification. Many other systems favor a *compilation*-based approach [7,18,19,22,43,47,53], whereby code and proof obligation are translated into a simple, intermediate language, where the actual verification takes place. Both approaches have their pros and cons, where compilation supports better the goal of adaptability. The main reason to stay with a source code-centric architecture in KeY is that it is easier to support *usability*, which has to be traded off against adaptability.

We stress that KeY's approach is not incompatible with the intermediate language architecture, because one can simply implement support for such a language in KeY. However, our main intention is to provide support for research on deductive verification approaches working with concepts realized at the level of source code.

Rapid Prototyping with First-Class Functions. To allow users of a verification tool in research to explore new ideas or simply to describe the application of a verification tool succinctly, a verification system should enable rapid prototyping of different logic formalizations. Examples include experimenting with memory models from smart contract languages that feature database-like storage, or formalization of properties such as information flow, permission-based reasoning, data dependences, etc.

One path to support rapid prototyping is by introducing functions as first-class citizens using McCarthy's theory of arrays [50] around a basic set of control structures and without complex object-oriented concepts. This permits to experiment with different heap formalizations. For instance, one could model attributes as functions that are updates or else use a standard formalization where the heap is an array. It would also permit to model functional concepts such as lambdas. First-class functions render encoding of a straightforward function application more complex, but such disadvantages can be mitigated by pretty printing. Also, in a rapid prototyping context, where a language is intended as a *small* testbed for ideas, the overhead should not be significant.

4.4 Community, Infrastructure

Achieving sustainability is only possible by reaching out to other (research) groups and to involve them in the development process and to enable fruitful cooperation (in a competitive environment).

This involves, among other community building efforts, the existence of a code of conduct and its enforcement, an open infrastructure for development, community meetings and availability and accessibility of the tool documentation.

To address these issues for the KeY verification system, our intention within in the next years is to establish an open development process following best practices (including coding style guidelines and source code documentation requirements) and to provide good development guides and material. Volunteers from interested research groups will be enabled to adapt or extend KeY source code for their own research projects without the need to establish personal contact with the KeY development team. To this end, we plan to open our current development infrastructure (self-hosted instance of gitlab) that includes the repository, issue tracker and continuous integration service to the community.

Further, we recognize the need to supply state-of-art first-contact material (in form of short videos, online tutorials, a user guide, online training material) that flattens the learning curve and allows more users to employ KeY successfully. Our target is a documentation that enables an MSc level Computer Scientist to prove first programs within days.

This includes the organisation of community events like the annual KeY symposium, hackathons, workshops or tutorials at conferences. As sketched in Sect. 3.3, however, it is essential that the deductive verification community as a whole becomes more focused and engaged in collaborative efforts.

5 Related Work

Deductive software verification is increasingly recognized as a flexible and highly precise analysis technique whenever high quality of software matters. Not only in safety- and security-critical systems, but also in libraries, in APIs, when bugs are expensive to fix, when patching is difficult, etc. The recent LNCS 10000 anniversary volume, which represents a state-of-art view on Computer Science as a whole, dedicated a chapter to deductive verification [34]. The Dagstuhl seminar on *Deduction*, of which deductive verification is a main aspect, is the second longest running Dagstuhl series. Companies including Microsoft, Amazon, or Facebook started to incorporate deductive verification technology into their production. Verification systems such as Frama-C or Spark are commercially successful.

Several leading deductive verification platforms are listed in Sect. 1. Two main criteria for classification of the mentioned tools are the target language they support and their interaction pattern. One such pattern is "auto-active" verification, where a proof is either automatically completed or ends in a failed state, which is then analyzed and the proof retried with a patched input (Boogie, Why3, Frama-C, Krakatoa). The user's failure analysis can be partially automated, its result is then presented to the user inside an IDE, as in VCC and Dafny. In auto-active verification, the interaction with a prover is performed on the input level (adding, removing or rephrasing specifications, adding hints). Although this style allows some interaction with the prover, the lack of insight in the current proof situation and proof object makes it hard to identify which additional specification annotations are needed or which need to be rephrased. A second interaction pattern is fine-grained proof interaction, where the proof is constructed either manually or with the help of proof scripts (which may use automatic proof tactics). In contrast to the auto-active pattern, the user can inspect partial proofs and interaction happens during proof search and construction. This is most popular with general purpose proof assistants such as Coq [15], Isabelle [54], or Lean [51].

In contrast to most other tools, KeY seamlessly combines both patterns—auto-active interaction and fine-grained interaction. Interaction is possible at the level of proof rules and the underlying program logic as well as the level of specifications and the target code. Interacting with the prover during proof construction can give deep insights into possible issues and provides effective control, but it requires a considerable amount of expertise.

Among supported target languages one can find industrial languages such as C (Frama-C [43], VCC [22], VeriFast [42], VerCors [18]), Java (Krakatoa [27], KeY [2], VeriFast [42]), Eiffel (AutoProof [60]). No tool supports the latest C or Java standard completely, but all cover substantial sub-sets. KIV [25] and Dafny [47] support modeling languages designed for verification. Boogie [7], Viper [53] and Why3 [19] support small, intermediate languages and are used as verification backends to some of the other tools. The advantage of intermediate languages is that they allow reuse of investments into verification technology: Each performance improvement in the backend helps any frontend that is based on it. The disadvantage of this architecture is that it can be problematic to define new proof obligations that do not fit the outline foreseen by the intermediate language. In particular, questions outside traditional assertion checking (for example, information-flow analysis or correctness of program transformations) are not easily encoded into an intermediate language. Moreover, it is difficult to relate proof states and counter examples to the original program.

6 Conclusion

Computer Science is the key science behind the unfolding digital revolution and thus became a foundational science. At the core of this paradigm shift is the ability to specify, to produce, to understand, and to maintain high-quality, reliable *software*—the successes of statistical learning techniques notwithstanding.

Software used for critical applications must meet very high quality standards: this is partly due to the complexity of software solutions, but most of all, because the shift to software means that now the *software* has to carry part of the trust. Developers (computer scientists together with domain experts) must be enabled to manifest trust in their software. One way to obtain this trust is by the application of formal analysis tools that yield mathematically rigorous guarantees.

This goal is the motivation behind the development of formal software verification tools in general and behind KeY in particular, and drives us to improve their usability and accessibility for developers. Moreover, to share the benefits of formal verification, it is a goal to allow a wider range of analyses like security analysis, debugging, or test case generation to base on formal verification tools.

Deductive verification is a base technology in the field of formal methods. We believe that making deductive verification tools usable and sustainable—following a path as laid out in this paper—is paramount in advancing deductive verification and moving the field forward.

References

1. Ahrendt, W., et al.: The KeY tool: integrating object oriented design and formal verification. Software Syst. Model. **4**(1), 32–54 (2005). https://doi.org/10.1007/s10270-004-0058-x

2. Ahrendt, W., Beckert, B., Bubel, R., Hähnle, R., Schmitt, P.H., Ulbrich, M. (eds.): Deductive Software Verification - The KeY Book: From Theory to Practice, Lecture Notes in Computer Science, vol. 10001. Springer, Cham (2016). https://doi.org/10.1007/978-3-319-49812-6
3. Ahrendt, W., Bubel, R.: Functional verification of smart contracts via strong data integrity. In: Margaria, T., Steffen, B. (eds.) ISoLA 2020. LNCS, vol. 12478, pp. 9–24. Springer, Cham (2020). https://doi.org/10.1007/978-3-030-61467-6_2
4. Ahrendt, W., Chimento, J.M., Pace, G.J., Schneider, G.: Verifying data- and control-oriented properties combining static and runtime verification: theory and tools. Formal Methods in System Design **51**(1), 200–265 (2017)
5. Albarghouthi, A., Dillig, I., Gurfinkel, A.: Maximal specification synthesis. SIGPLAN Not. **51**(1), 789–801 (2016). Jan
6. Albert, E., Bubel, R., Genaim, S., Hähnle, R., Díez, G.R.: A formal verification framework for static analysis–as well as its instantiation to the resource analyzer COSTA and formal verification tool KeY. Software Syst. Model. **15**(4), 987–1012 (2016). https://doi.org/10.1007/s10270-015-0476-y
7. Barnett, M., Chang, B.-Y.E., DeLine, R., Jacobs, B., Leino, K.R.M.: Boogie: a modular reusable verifier for object-oriented programs. In: de Boer, F.S., Bonsangue, M.M., Graf, S., de Roever, W.-P. (eds.) FMCO 2005. LNCS, vol. 4111, pp. 364–387. Springer, Heidelberg (2006). https://doi.org/10.1007/11804192_17
8. Baudin, P., Filliâtre, J.C., Marché, C., Monate, B., Moy, Y., Prevosto, V.: ACSL: ANSI/ISO C Specification Language. Preliminary Design, 1.4 edn. (2008). https://www.frama-c.cea.fr/download/acsl_1.4.pdf
9. Baumann, C., Beckert, B., Blasum, H., Bormer, T.: Lessons learned from microkernel verification - specification is the new bottleneck. In: Cassez, F., Huuck, R., Klein, G., Schlich, B. (eds.) Proceedings of the 7th Conference on Systems Software Verification. EPTCS, vol. 102, pp. 18–32 (2012)
10. Beckert, B., et al.: Taclets: a new paradigm for constructing interactive theorem provers. Revista de la Real Academia de Ciencias Exactas, Físicas y Naturales, Serie A: Matemáticas **98**(1), 17–53 (2004). Special Issue on Symbolic Computation in Logic and Artificial Intelligence
11. Beckert, B., Grebing, S.: Interactive theorem proving: modelling the user in the proof process. In: Furbach, U., Schon, C. (eds.) Workshop on Bridging the Gap between Human and Automated Reasoning, Berlin, Germany. CEUR Workshop Proceedings, vol. 1412, pp. 60–73. CEUR-WS.org (2015). http://ceur-ws.org/Vol-1412/6o.pdf
12. Beckert, B., Grebing, S., Böhl, F.: A usability evaluation of interactive theorem provers using focus groups. In: Canal, C., Idani, A. (eds.) SEFM 2014. LNCS, vol. 8938, pp. 3–19. Springer, Cham (2015). https://doi.org/10.1007/978-3-319-15201-1_1
13. Beckert, B., Hähnle, R.: Reasoning and verification. IEEE Intell. Syst. **29**(1), 20–29 (2014)
14. Beckert, B., Hähnle, R., Schmitt, P.H. (eds.): Verification of Object-Oriented Software. The KeY Approach - Foreword by K. Rustan M. Leino, Lecture Notes in Computer Science, vol. 4334. Springer (2007). http://doi.org/10.1007/978-3-540-69061-0
15. Bertot, Y., Castéran, P.: Interactive Theorem Proving and Program Development–Coq'Art: The Calculus of Inductive Constructions. Texts in Theoretical Computer Science. An EATCS Series. Springer, Cham (2004). https://doi.org/10.1007/978-3-662-07964-5

16. Beyer, D.: Progress on software verification: SV-COMP 2022. In: TACAS 2022. LNCS, vol. 13244, pp. 375–402. Springer, Cham (2022). https://doi.org/10.1007/978-3-030-99527-0_20
17. Blanchette, J.C., Nipkow, T.: Nitpick: a counterexample generator for higher-order logic based on a relational model finder. In: Kaufmann, M., Paulson, L.C. (eds.) ITP 2010. LNCS, vol. 6172, pp. 131–146. Springer, Heidelberg (2010). https://doi.org/10.1007/978-3-642-14052-5_11
18. Blom, S., Huisman, M.: The VerCors tool for verification of concurrent programs. In: Jones, C., Pihlajasaari, P., Sun, J. (eds.) FM 2014. LNCS, vol. 8442, pp. 127–131. Springer, Cham (2014). https://doi.org/10.1007/978-3-319-06410-9_9
19. Bobot, F., Filliâtre, J.C., Marché, C., Paskevich, A.: Why3: shepherd your herd of provers. In: Boogie 2011: First International Workshop on Intermediate Verification Languages. pp. 53–64. Wrocław, Poland, August 2011
20. Chakarov, A., Fedchin, A., Rakamarić, Z., Rungta, N.: Better counterexamples for dafny. In: TACAS 2022. LNCS, vol. 13243, pp. 404–411. Springer, Cham (2022). https://doi.org/10.1007/978-3-030-99524-9_23
21. Cok, D.R.: OpenJML: Software verification for Java 7 using JML, OpenJDK, and Eclipse. In: Dubois, C., Giannakopoulou, D., Méry, D. (eds.) 1st Workshop on Formal Integrated Development Environment, F-IDE, Grenoble, France. EPTCS, vol. 149, pp. 79–92 (2014)
22. Dahlweid, M., Moskal, M., Santen, T., Tobies, S., Schulte, W.: VCC: contract-based modular verification of concurrent C. In: International Conference on Software Engineering - Companion Volume, pp. 429–430 (2009)
23. De Gouw, S., De Boer, F.S., Bubel, R., Hähnle, R., Rot, J., Steinhöfel, D.: Verifying OpenJDK's sort method for generic collections. J. Automated Reasoning **62**(6) (2019). http://doi.org/10.1007/s10817-017-9426 4
24. Dross, C., Furia, C.A., Huisman, M., Monahan, R., Müller, P.: VerifyThis 2019: a program verification competition. Int. J. Softw. Tools Technol. Transf. **23**(6), 883–893 (2021). https://doi.org/10.1007/s10009-021-00619-x
25. Ernst, G., Pfähler, J., Schellhorn, G., Haneberg, D., Reif, W.: KIV: overview and VerifyThis competition. Int. J. Softw. Tools Technol. Transf. **17**(6), 677–694 (2015). https://doi.org/10.1007/s10009-014-0308-3
26. Fielding, R.T.: Architectural Styles and the Design of Network-based Software Architectures. Ph.D. thesis, University of California, Irvine (2000), aAI9980887
27. Filliâtre, J.-C., Marché, C.: The Why/Krakatoa/Caduceus platform for deductive program verification. In: Damm, W., Hermanns, H. (eds.) CAV 2007. LNCS, vol. 4590, pp. 173–177. Springer, Heidelberg (2007). https://doi.org/10.1007/978-3-540-73368-3_21
28. Le Goues, C., Leino, K.R.M., Moskal, M.: The boogie verification debugger (tool paper). In: Barthe, G., Pardo, A., Schneider, G. (eds.) SEFM 2011. LNCS, vol. 7041, pp. 407–414. Springer, Heidelberg (2011). https://doi.org/10.1007/978-3-642-24690-6_28
29. de Gouw, S., de Boer, F.S., Rot, J.: Proof pearl: the KeY to correct and stable sorting. J. Automated Reasoning **53**(2), 129–139 (2014)
30. Grätz, L., Hähnle, R., Bubel, R.: Finding semantic bugs fast. In: FASE 2022. LNCS, vol. 13241, pp. 145–154. Springer, Cham (2022). https://doi.org/10.1007/978-3-030-99429-7_8
31. Grebing, S.: User interaction in deductive interactive program verification. Ph.D. thesis, Karlsruhe Institute of Technology (KIT), February 2019

32. Grebing, S., Klamroth, J., Ulbrich, M.: Seamless interactive program verification. In: 11th Working Conference on Verified Software: Theories, Tools, and Experiments (VSTTE 2019), Jul 2019. Accepted, in print
33. Hähnle, R., Baum, M., Bubel, R., Rothe, M.: A visual interactive debugger based on symbolic execution. In: Andrews, J., Nitto, E.D. (eds.) Proceedings of the 25th IEEE/ACM International Conference on Automated Software Engineering, Antwerp, Belgium, pp. 143–146. ACM Press (2010)
34. Hähnle, R., Huisman, M.: Deductive software verification: from pen-and-paper proofs to industrial tools. In: Steffen, B., Woeginger, G. (eds.) Computing and Software Science. LNCS, vol. 10000, pp. 345–373. Springer, Cham (2019). https://doi.org/10.1007/978-3-319-91908-9_18
35. Hähnle, R., Menzel, W., Schmitt, P.: Integrierter deduktiver Software-Entwurf. Künstliche Intelligenz pp. 40–41, December 1998
36. Hentschel, M., Bubel, R., Hähnle, R.: The Symbolic Execution Debugger (SED): a platform for interactive symbolic execution, debugging, verification and more. Int. J. Software Tools Technol. Transf. **21**(5), 485–513 (2018). http://doi.org/10.1007/s10009-018-0490-9
37. Hentschel, M., Hähnle, R., Bubel, R.: The interactive verification debugger: effective understanding of interactive proof attempts. In: Lo, D., Apel, S., Khurshid, S. (eds.) Proceedings of the 31st IEEE/ACM International Conference on Automated Software Engineering (ASE), Singapore, pp. 846–851. ACM Press, September 2016
38. Herda, M., et al.: Understanding counterexamples for relational properties with DIbugger. In: De Angelis, E., Fedyukovich, G., Tzevelekos, N., Ulbrich, M. (eds.) Proceedings of the Sixth Workshop on Horn Clauses for Verification and Synthesis and Third Workshop on Program Equivalence and Relational Reasoning, HCVS/PERR@ETAPS 2019, Prague, Czech Republic. EPTCS, vol. 296, pp. 6–13 (2019). https://doi.org/10.4204/EPTCS.296.4
39. Heydari Tabar, A., Hähnle, R., Bubel, R.: Automatic loop invariant generation for data dependence analysis. In: Hartmans, A., Schaefer, I. (eds.) Proceedings of the FormaliSE Conference on Pittsburgh, PA, US. LNCS, ACM Press, May 2022
40. Hiep, H.-D.A., Maathuis, O., Bian, J., de Boer, F.S., van Eekelen, M., de Gouw, S.: Verifying OpenJDK's `LinkedList` using KeY. In: TACAS 2020. LNCS, vol. 12079, pp. 217–234. Springer, Cham (2020). https://doi.org/10.1007/978-3-030-45237-7_13
41. Hoang, D., Moy, Y., Wallenburg, A., Chapman, R.: SPARK 2014 and gnatprove - a competition report from builders of an industrial-strength verifying compiler. Int. J. Softw. Tools Technol. Transf. **17**(6), 695–707 (2015). https://doi.org/10.1007/s10009-014-0322-5
42. Jacobs, B., Piessens, F.: The VeriFast program verifier. Technical Report CW-520, Department of Computer Science, Katholieke Universiteit Leuven, August 2008
43. Kirchner, F., Kosmatov, N., Prevosto, V., Signoles, J., Yakobowski, B.: Frama-C: a software analysis perspective. Formal Aspects Comput. **27**(3), 573–609 (2015)
44. Knüppel, A., Thüm, T., Schaefer, I.: GUIDO: automated guidance for the configuration of deductive program verifiers. In: Bliudze, S., Gnesi, S., Plat, N., Semini, L. (eds.) 9th IEEE/ACM Intl. Conference on Formal Methods in Software Engineering, FormaliSE@ICSE, Madrid, Spain, pp. 124–129. IEEE (2021). https://doi.org/10.1109/FormaliSE52586.2021.00018

45. Küsters, R., Truderung, T., Beckert, B., Bruns, D., Kirsten, M., Mohr, M.: A hybrid approach for proving noninterference of Java programs. In: Fournet, C., Hicks, M.W., Viganò, L. (eds.) IEEE 28th Computer Security Foundations Symposium, CSF, Verona, Italy, pp. 305–319. IEEE Computer Society (2015). https://doi.org/10.1109/CSF.2015.28
46. Leavens, G.T., et al.: JML Reference Manual (May 2013), draft revision 2344
47. Leino, K.R.M., Wüstholz, V.: The Dafny integrated development environment. In: F-IDE 2014. EPTCS, vol. 149, pp. 3–15 (2014)
48. Livshits, B., et al.: In defense of soundiness: a manifesto. Commun. ACM **58**(2), 44–46 (2015)
49. Mariño, J., Alborodo, R.N.N., Fredlund, L.Å., Herranz, Á.: Synthesis of verifiable concurrent java components from formal models. Software Syst. Modeling **18**(1), 71–105 (2019). https://doi.org/10.1007/s10270-017-0581-1
50. McCarthy, J.: A basis for a mathematical theory of computation. In: Braffort, P., Hirschberg, D. (eds.) Computer Programming and Formal Systems, pp. 33–69. North Holland (1963)
51. Moura, L., Ullrich, S.: The lean 4 theorem prover and programming language. In: Platzer, A., Sutcliffe, G. (eds.) CADE 2021. LNCS (LNAI), vol. 12699, pp. 625–635. Springer, Cham (2021). https://doi.org/10.1007/978-3-030-79876-5_37
52. Müller, P., Ruskiewicz, J.N.: Using debuggers to understand failed verification attempts. In: Butler, M., Schulte, W. (eds.) FM 2011. LNCS, vol. 6664, pp. 73–87. Springer, Heidelberg (2011). https://doi.org/10.1007/978-3-642-21437-0_8
53. Müller, P., Schwerhoff, M., Summers, A.J.: Viper: a verification infrastructure for permission-based reasoning. In: Jobstmann, B., Leino, K.R.M. (eds.) VMCAI 2016. LNCS, vol. 9583, pp. 41–62. Springer, Heidelberg (2016). https://doi.org/10.1007/978-3-662-49122-5_2
54. Nipkow, T., Paulson, L.C., Wenzel, M.: Isabelle/HOL – A Proof Assistant for Higher-Order Logic, LNCS, vol. 2283. Springer, Heidelberg (2002). https://doi.org/10.1007/3-540-45949-9
55. Platzer, A., Quesel, J.-D.: KeYmaera: a hybrid theorem prover for hybrid systems (system description). In: Armando, A., Baumgartner, P., Dowek, G. (eds.) IJCAR 2008. LNCS (LNAI), vol. 5195, pp. 171–178. Springer, Heidelberg (2008). https://doi.org/10.1007/978-3-540-71070-7_15
56. Runge, T., Schaefer, I., Cleophas, L., Thüm, T., Kourie, D., Watson, B.W.: Tool support for correctness-by-construction. In: Hähnle, R., van der Aalst, W. (eds.) FASE 2019. LNCS, vol. 11424, pp. 25–42. Springer, Cham (2019). https://doi.org/10.1007/978-3-030-16722-6_2
57. Schaefer, I., Runge, T., Knüppel, A., Cleophas, L., Kourie, D., Watson, B.W.: Towards confidentiality-by-construction. In: Margaria, T., Steffen, B. (eds.) ISoLA 2018. LNCS, vol. 11244, pp. 502–515. Springer, Cham (2018). https://doi.org/10.1007/978-3-030-03418-4_30
58. Steinhöfel, D.: REFINITY to model and prove program transformation rules. In: Oliveira, B.C.S. (ed.) APLAS 2020. LNCS, vol. 12470, pp. 311–319. Springer, Cham (2020). https://doi.org/10.1007/978-3-030-64437-6_16

59. Stucki, S., Sánchez, C., Schneider, G., Bonakdarpour, B.: Gray-box monitoring of hyperproperties. In: ter Beek, M.H., McIver, A., Oliveira, J.N. (eds.) FM 2019. LNCS, vol. 11800, pp. 406–424. Springer, Cham (2019). https://doi.org/10.1007/978-3-030-30942-8_25
60. Tschannen, J., Furia, C.A., Nordio, M., Polikarpova, N.: AutoProof: auto-active functional verification of object-oriented programs. In: Baier, C., Tinelli, C. (eds.) TACAS 2015. LNCS, vol. 9035, pp. 566–580. Springer, Heidelberg (2015). https://doi.org/10.1007/978-3-662-46681-0_53

On Technical Debt in Software Testing - Observations from Industry

Sigrid Eldh[1,2,3](✉)

[1] Ericsson AB, Networks Standards and Technology Software Computer Science, Stockholm, Sweden
sigrid.eldh@ericsson.com
[2] Department of Innovation, Design and Evolution, Mälardalen University, Västerås, Sweden
[3] Carleton University, Ottawa, Canada
https://www.es.mdh.se/staff/67-Sigrid_Eldh,
https://carleton.ca/sce/people/eldh

Abstract. Testing large complex systems in an agile way of working was a tough transition for systems having large active legacy and honouring backward compatibility. Transition from manual test to full test execution automation resulted in increased speed and manifested technical debt. The agile way of working in continuous build and test, creates a lot of repetition by execution of the same tests. Overlap between agile teams producing similar test cases, causes a constant growth of the test suites. Despite the obvious improvement of automating millions of test cases, the numbers provide a false sense of security for management on how well the system is tested. The causes of technical debt should be addressed, instead of managing the symptoms. Technical debt in software testing could be addressed by refactoring, supported by known techniques like cloning, similarity analysis, test suite reduction, optimization and reducing known test smells. Increasing the system quality can also be improved by utilizing metrics, e.g. code coverage and mutation score or use one of the many automated test design technologies. Why this is not addressed in the industry has many causes. In this paper we describe observations from several industries, with the focus on large complex systems. The contribution lies in reflecting on observations made in the last decade, and providing a vision which identifies improvements in the area of test automation and technical debt in software test, i.e. test code, test suites, test organisation, strategy and execution. Our conclusion is that many test technologies are now mature enough to be brought into regular use. The main hindrance is skills and incentive to do so for the developer, as well as a lack of well educated testers.

Keywords: Test automation · Test maintenance · Agile development · Technical debt · Industry testing · Test strategies · Quality assurance

Supported by Ericsson AB and Mälardalen University.

T. Margaria and B. Steffen (Eds.): ISoLA 2022, LNCS 13702, pp. 301–323, 2022.
https://doi.org/10.1007/978-3-031-19756-7_17

1 Introduction

Agile development brought many benefits [22,44,60] for most industries, mainly improving speed of delivering new functionality, and a strong uptake of more new and modern tools. Automating the build and test loop in a continuous integration has solved integration testing issues seamlessly. In large complex systems, there are many challenges remaining [24,44]. In an earlier study [71] we could conclude that *"a comparatively high technical debt is accepted in test systems, and that software design organizations in general forget to apply software design principles such as systematization, documentation, and testing, when producing or deploying test automation systems"*. If we revisit the same organisation, change did happen. The major change is that the (test) systems are now looked upon as a production system in itself, and treated in the same way, and some attempt to unify the test tool situation has happened. The four observations claimed in this former paper, are unfortunately still true (for full explanation, please revisit the original paper): Reuse and sharing of test tools brings issues that need to be considered i.e.; Test facility infrastructure is not transparent and may alter the test results if not accounted for; Generalist engineers expect that their tools are easy to use; Accepted development practices for test code are potentially less rigorous than for production code. In addition can add new observations as a result of testing in the agile way of working.

Specifically, we can observe test suites are growing in size to the point that prioritization, selection and reduction approaches are in strong need, instead of the initial agile aim to "run all tests" at every change which is a consequence of larger organisations. Focus then quickly becomes on maintaining test suites to reduce and minimize suites without loss of executions. The overlap of test case creation is an unfortunate consequence of many concurrent working agile teams creating overlapping test cases. The concurrency of teams also cause delays the CI-flow showing up as merge conflicts. Though, a rich overlap in the test suites can be helpful when using technologies like Automatic Program Repair [73]. This is not on people mind, as it is general a reluctance to remove test cases (due to difficulties to identify actual execution patterns) as well as the testers do not want to see their hard work being undone.

The overall problem remains, the abundance of test cases - will not only have a high cost attached to it, but it will create a false sense of security of how well the testing is made. As the wide adoption of poor metrics like test coverage are used, this also reinforces the core issue of poor test design, often stemming from the lack of rigorous specifications, as agile advocates learning by doing and "fail-fast" schemes. In this paper we will discuss technical debt that still remains in the software testing context with a focus on test automation, and provide a vision in the area. This paper is written in the context of a large world-wide organisation, with many research and development organizations. The observations made, are also compared with other large world-wide organisation, where the author have had insight in. Therefore, the observations are made as generic observations, and no liability to or claim of, that the observation stems from Ericsson should be made.

The paper is structured in the following manner. The next chapter is about the background and context in the telecommunication domain, and the third chapter is about test automation in industry. Then Sects. 4–12 are structured lists of observations grouped under common themes, in the attempt to make the readable. This is then followed by Sect. 13 that aim to describe a vision on testing in the future followed by a description of Methods used, Threats of Validity and disclaimers. We then conclude our paper.

2 Background - Telecommunication Domain

The telecommunication domain faces many challenges affecting the software. The area is strongly regulated with standards, and the ability to communicate everywhere - from condensed areas in cities, to remote locations are now a necessity for the society build on mobility. Telecommunication systems have moved from the fixed line 2G to become wireless connections in any device. Most countries are now transforming to 5G with high-speed secure communication enabling the internet of things (IoT) as well as specialized networks, e.g. in mines - to allow for remote automatic and safe mining [2]. As a telecommunication providers, Ericsson is creating end to end network solutions for its customer, the operators. The new incentives to move telecommunication to the cloud, and into the Fog [46] brings not only new competitors, but also new challenges. Issues like the ever increasing need for speed is resolved by redundancy in hardware. Code size and variety of offered solutions creates a massive need for concurrency, leading to timing issues and increased complexity.

Legacy systems partly suffer from monolithic architectures that are costly to refactor. Attempts to transform, slice, and simplify the software through e.g. utilizing micro-services is an ongoing transformation. Variations of product offerings in e.g. radio is in itself an issue resulting in costly tests. Software needs to be secure and perform in high-speed environments. Many historically well made decisions, are now suffering from lacking advanced tools for different analysis and modern testing features. As Agile assumed self-organisation, the variety of solutions, tools and programming languages are strong. Testing these systems is a constant challenge, but gives a researcher ample sources to juxtapose technologies and approaches.

The Continuous Delivery and DevOps approach is a bit more tricky [10] also for the telecommunication sector, as it assumes the operator (the customer) needs to be prepared for automated delivery. Automatically acceptance test and automatically provide feedback and data, the latter which is a legal area, as the delivered solution should be integrated and work in a new environment alongside competitors solutions. No wonder this is an area of much regulations and standards to define operations.

The general management view is that testing is already too costly. Much of the cost comes from simulators and test lab equipment as well as the cost of the entire development infrastructure with tools.

3 Test Automation in Industry

We can conclude that the number of testers has strongly declined in the agile context as quality is the task of everyone, the tester role disappeared within the agile teams.

Automation of test execution in industry has come a long way, thanks to the agile transformation. Industries developing safety-critical or heavy regulated software, are more focused on test automation by modelling the requirements and generating the test than more traditional commercial software. The trend is clear. As modelling tools constantly improve, and more developers are educated in formal approaches reaches industry, the likelihood of using modelling as a natural tool in the requirements phase is obvious. At least for reference models in systematization. Modelling (through tools) as development still has not really grabbed the general industrial developer community. But in one sense, all is a model, and simple state-transition tools have been around for more than three decades (at least within Ericsson). As we state below, there is still a strong development by manual coding and "hacking" culture alive in most industries, as experience of the difficulties with early modelling tools still lingers. Utilizing modelling for test automation has its clear champions in industry. Unfortunately, if you do not have a champion in your agile team, it is very unlikely more formal model approaches spread until tools makes it easy and safe.

Test automation is very much a developers affair in the agile team, where the tendency is to automate test execution for unit tests or low level functionality. As systems are large and complex, the knowledge to test of all aspects of e.g. a telecommunication node and system functionality for a small team update is much to ask. Most developers lack enough insight in detailed execution patterns on system level for their part of functionality, e.g. concerning timing and other system parts executing concurrently. This lack of test environment understanding is a significant source of flakiness in the test suites [55].

When it comes to content and creation of the test cases, little attention is paid to utilizing test design techniques. We can observe that today the test automation approach used upon the first automation of test execution has indeed established itself as a practice: Test cases were automated based on manual use cases tests, where there is a lack of separation of execution and data, with many input-output relations hard-coded in the test case. The lack of common directives of utilizing any specific test technologies to create test cases is unfortunately a fact. Quality Assurance is in principle to enforcing statement code coverage in the gating for CI/CD loops, using secure coding principle, embedded in static analysis tools. The use of static analysis tools like CodeCompass [59] and CodeChecker [1] are now becoming mandatory, but there is still lot of work remaining to bring 20+ programming languages used in a product portfolio into a common quality approach. The quality is (still) much dependent on manual practices like code reviews and even exploratory tests [50], as some people still advocates manual practices despite goals aiming for "complete" automation. The digitalization drives automation, and it is common sense to aim to automate as many aspects as possible, to gain constant improvements and repeatability. Unfortunately, it is still hard to transfer the knowledge behind solutions made.

4 Test Design Technologies

The largest gap between academic research and industrial practice in testing is that many of the test design techniques described by academics are rarely used, not used systematically or as a regular practice [25,33,36]. This differs between industries, as more regulated industries, e.g. in safety critical systems, pay more attention to some of these. Below we list a more detailed discussion on why this is the case, what techniques we are talking about and an attempt to describe some context. This lists have arbitrary order and weight, depending on what software and system in what industry we are talking about.

1. Test Strategies do not contain any information of **how** things should be tested. This results in a lack of proper systematic approaches of what test design technologies used. Instead test strategies, and even e.g. agile testing strategies, advocates what and when to test as well as e.g. manual testing (exploratory test) [20].
2. The normal case is well tested at all levels of test, demonstrating the main functionality [25].
3. Negative test (testing fault handling and anything outside the normal case, including unspecified behavior), is randomly performed, except for robustness testing at system level. Hardware redundancy acts much as "information/bug hiding" of issues in this area [25].
4. The dominating functional test approach is requirement testing. This is often expressed as use cases. As requirement specifications in agile are "user stories", it allows for not being fully specified up front. A consequence is that the requirements can lack sufficient detail to be used to for sufficient verification. This is especially clear when changes occur that details are lost updating specifications [25].
5. As systems today contain functionality that has been transformed and updated for decades, the historic documentation is not always kept accurate, especially not in regards to tools, versions and patching. This lack of documented detail, prevents modelling methods and more formal methods to be used for testing on a regular basis.
6. There is no lack of attempts to model both source and test code, and success varies. There are many reasons. Champions are often stuck in a team, and modelling needs to be used and taught more widely. Modelling must be a system decision and there is a lack of management back up. The model must meet the code at some point, and here is the difficulty. Maintaining models are costly, and it is harder to optimize auto-generated code for performance. Also, it is also harder to check security and static analysis on generated code - and corrections would be meaningless, hence to fulfill the harsh requirements, many (not all) modelling tools and languages must

have experts in-house that can change and update the modelling environment concurrently. Also intermediate languages or the auto-generated code must be adapted to compilers that sometimes are proprietary, even if most today aim for commonplace front and back-end approaches like e.g. LLVM [47]. Therefore currently, for most industries *code is king* meaning, what is written in code is what is used and triumphs both documentation, and tools. In safety-critical systems *model is king.* Ground truths differs for different industries. Historically, e.g. UML [30] was successful, but is now partly abandoned. ETSI TTCN-3 [3] is also made into an ITU-T standard [6] but does only cover partial test suites within at least the telecommunication industry. It has not kept up in competition with other (newer) languages, and developers are not so keen on it, despite the potential.

7. Requirement test means that test cases are aimed to "cover" the requirement - and manual analysis is performed to check that it is done. A lot relies on this non-scientific measurement called "test coverage" of the requirement. A requirement can need one test case or 30 000 test cases. Hence, talking about 100% test coverage is nonsense. Taking an extreme example, is that if you only had one test case for a system that is passed, you would have 100% test coverage. Therefore, test coverage should always mean code coverage. And as there are so many - you need to be specific of which code coverage.
8. Requirements management quality varies due to the agile transformation. It is more often better described if the specification describes phenomena closer to the user (or something used by the developer). Some requirements in the machine-to-machine communication, layer 1 and layer 2 code in the OSI model [62]), platforms, embedded code, or code closer to hardware, are examples that take much longer to teach developers all about the domain specific aspects. Consequently, there are often a lot to improve, when it comes to supporting verification and validation [16].
9. As requirements seldom contain "what should not work" i.e. fault handling, there are few test cases developed or prioritized in this area.
10. For specific protocol's standards and telecommunication standard aspects, careful modelling through e.g. Mathlab/Simulink [28,43] is regularly used. In Hardware (FPGA's) stricter modelling tools are used, as this can then be transformed to a layout in hardware. When it comes to hardware/software co-design, modelling tools are regularly used to asses what is most efficient. Modelling is often used as reference (reference modelling) for prototypes, but not in the context of fully generated code and/or test cases except samples. This could for example be a set of input defined, often referred to as test vectors, e.g. specific VHDL (Verilog High Definition Language) [52] or ATPG (Automated Test Pattern Generation) both in common use for hardware tests.
11. As data is often in abundance for large complex systems, another road taken is to use constraint technologies, e.g. MiniZinc [53] that can aid in a lot of human complex tasks - keeping track of endless rules of what data can be combined with what. This area shows a lot of promise for the future. It is

easy to hope that one define, they work, but also constraint solvers also have to be tested - making sure rules are created and used correctly.

12. Many test cases became "frozen" in its development, during the agile transformation when automating these (functional) tests, much due to lack of time to refactor test cases but also due to poor test automation and test design know-how. The effort to automate them was challenging (costly) enough. The result is that a lot of manual test cases were not transformed to good automation, utilizing libraries, avoiding repetition etc., and did hard code input and output/verdicts. They were translates as is. This makes many test cases very inflexible. Very few test design techniques were used then, at its best, you find three clones with hard coded boundary values, as an input. As a result, test selection will remove two of these for being too similar, and the boundary check is lost. This is just one simple example. Documentation of why a test case exists are totally lost. At best the test case can be linked to a requirement specification, or deduced in time to "what project" that created it. This is not very helpful. Therefore good and instant search and test case tagging must exists in the tools to identify similarities and understand context of test better. It would also be helpful to have trace information of what the test case actually address. We are far from these features in test tools today. No-one wants to update the information in the tools to make it work either.
13. This lack of systematic testing and use of test design still remains, as each agile team mainly "copy-paste" earlier test patterns. Exceptions do exists. This results in a lot of clones and duplications of test code [39].
14. The more recent prioritization of security has made many testers transfer to security. Checking for vulnerabilities implicitly improves testing, as some limited fuzzing through the available fuzzing tools is now becoming standard practice. Most fuzzing tools does basically perform input variation testing. Books like Zeller et al. [75] also make standard testing practices and design techniques useful by exploiting the security context.
15. Testing for code coverage is often set to 80% statement coverage as a gating for legacy code, if used at all in industry. There is no control mechanism that checks that this coverage is done properly, whereas "creative" avoidance code to pass the gating is occasionally used. Some claim that code coverage is a poor metric to drive quality. The reason is that e.g. statement code coverage can be easily misused (see Marick's comment on this [49]). You can also do poor testing with good coverage (i.e. selecting input that does not invoke faults). This historic view have made many developers reluctant to use it. Some agile teams also test statement code coverage on integrated code modules instead of the unit, which makes it very difficult to reach higher coverage values as paths then exponentially grows. Enforcing strict 100% statement code coverage could be a waste too, as some code are not cost efficient to cover. The simple approach to use coverage as a self-check if the tests created was good is often lost in this debate of code coverage, test coverage or any other creative invention of coverage.

16. There are many agile teams that have abandoned proper unit test, and mainly work to test functional tests, as the test harness and unit test suites are costly to keep up to date with many code changes. It is true that for some functionality it is difficult to test in isolation at lower levels and is easier to test through its context. This leads of course to more difficulties to achieve code coverage targets, but also brings a hidden bug count, as new bugs come into play at code changes. In addition, it is easier to test an item in its real context, instead of creating (and maintaining) stubs, which at first glance seems costly, can be difficult to keep up and time consuming. Using controlled stubs alleviates a lot of unit test issues, makes units easier to understand, test and control. There are tools that allows real code context to "act" as stubs which aid better control. This area should be better explored both by unit test tool vendors and academic research.

5 CI/CD - Build, Test and Regression Testing

The CI pipeline, where the true sense of the agile approach to submit frequent small changes can easily in a large organization become a big-bang integration. Examples range from between 100 to 2000 commits in one hour, making it clear that several pipelines was a solution. As the CI pipelines were conducted as a part of the agile self-organisation, there are a variety of solutions and also on what tools were used [65].

1. The CI framework is used to check that new code integrates, which is the most common fault issue with committing a change.
2. Fixing build faults are currently a manual process, from debugging (fault localization) to patching. The new patch is code reviewed by others in the team and submitted. No extensive test framework exists for most pipelines doing build changes, which can cause delays in the framework.
3. Current attention in one of the organizations tracking and remedy top 10 most unstable (nondeterministic) test cases (also known as flaky tests) are often root caused to poor test case writing, lack of insight in test environment and simulators that also execute with timing discrepancies. Identifying and remedy issues that prevent flow (i.e. flaky tests) is a key industrial practice following agile test automation in the CI flow [11,14,23].
4. Test suites have too long turn around time for some test tools, the test cases should be better sliced and grouped and intermediate feedback should be allowed, to save overall time.
5. The CI pipeline can have too long turn around time, often depending on the vast number of test cases (and not sufficiently equipped test environment, as these are costly)
6. Regression Test Selection (RTS) could be improved in some of the pipelines to speed up order of execution.
7. Test suite can easily be in a wait state - (appearing to be hanging) as it is waiting for input (from e.g. test environment) - as the test resources takes time to set up and use, etc. This causes unnecessary flakiness issues [48].

8. When testing against real hardware - there are many issues of test equipment failures and timing - causing the pipeline to be hand, stop, or be in wait state [48].
9. If testing is using simulators - the simulators are often "too good" in the sense that they do not simulate hardware issues or bugs, but definitely not concurrency and timing sufficiently. A good simulator should be possible to put in "faulty" mode. And controlled faulty is much easier to debug than when it happens in the field.
10. The cost to update simulators to more accurately test fault hardware behavior and timing issues (concurrency) is steep, and difficult to make happen if commercial simulators are used.
11. Therefore software solutions, e.g. mutation testing tools, are so successful to induce bugs [45,56]. The issue is that mutation test generate "too many" faults at "too low level" - and many claim that many of these generated faults are "too simple" and therefore not representative. It is definitely worth investigating what typical faults are, for a specific aspects of the system. Especially to aid fault localization and support fail handling. To make it worth embarking on mutation testing, tools must improve speed, accuracy, and usability as well as users should start with sufficiently high code coverage.

6 System and Non-functional Testing

Most advanced and intense testing happens in non-functional testing (or at system test level), such as performance test and load test, stability test, availability test, robustness and resilience test, to mention a few. There exists dedicated specialized testers in this area.

1. KPI's (Key Process Indicators i.e. Key metrics) are essential for the products commercial value.
2. These areas of system test are instead of being a "one off" in the end, now with agile constantly measuring and performing automatic evaluation, running the latest versions of the software and deploying intelligent machine learning tools to support fault and issue localization [37].
3. The automation also contains automatic transitions between simulators and the real hardware, which enables applications to run seamlessly. A consequence can be that not all measures are on "real" hardware, and this can cause a false sense of quality, but has the advantage of removing specific test lab equipment issues.
4. As the system test is constantly measuring, it has strong similarities with monitoring - and making the DevOps model fulfillment in this regard, a much easier transition between internal testing and operations [57].
5. As non-functional level is fully automated relying on functional tests, there are still many possibilities to improve e.g. visualization.

6. Here, AI/ML supported test can aid in finding faults, producing more intelligent metrics trends, swapping between simulation tools and real networks and find strange anomalies among millions of metrics. Network resilience, robustness, stability and reliability is measured, as well as performance testing.
7. In general, telecommunication sector is well equipped to test at network level, with a combination of real utility equipment (UE's) and simulations tools, making systems well tested.
8. Performance, load, overload and similar aspects are key metrics, and is well evaluated on all levels of testing also regulated e.g. in the telecommunication standards through ITU-T.
9. Security testing (incl. Penetration testing, fuzzing etc.) is a non-functional test approach, but can be done at all levels of testing, and is not typical system test matter, rather associated with level code, static analysis tool and so on [12].
10. Not all non-functional tests described in e.g. ISO/IEC std. 25010 Series [5,29] are done at system level, and that is maintainability. This is not considered well a well measured or clear metric as is. as some aspects are disregarded - and that is maintainability of the test suites. It is not particularly measured, or any specific attempts made to improve this aspect of neither source code nor test code.
11. The testers at this level are well acquainted with the system, and have expertise in both measuring and troubleshooting the system. As most KPI's have high commercial value, this area has management attention, and the existing expertise make sure that the technical debt in the area remains relative low.
12. The area suffers from normal test design issues and a lot of of faults show up that should have been take care of in earlier stages.
13. Concurrency and redundancy at system level can hide bugs at this level, making fault-finding difficult and time-consuming.

7 Test Maintenance

1. Test suites are seldom refactored and improved in general. For maintained code, fault test cases are sometimes made passive (silent) instead of root caused and fixed. This means over time test suites are becoming less powerful.
2. As a result of not keeping test suites improved and updated, test cases grow old [32]. Some test cases that do not find any faults are down-prioritized to execute seldom or simply removed. As there is a lack of tool support to safely remove test cases - as sometimes there are hidden dependencies in the order of execution, few testers do anything about this problem - as time is too scarce anyway to just write sufficiently new amount of test cases. Agile team's that do most of the functionality test automation, are not measured at all on any test quality, but on functionality delivered.

3. If any refactoring is done on test code, it is basically done during the construction of the test case e.g. look at how test lags the source code writing [74]. Many (non software based) industries do not do obvious code fixes, like refactoring of e.g. test smells [68]. These smells should be easy fixes. Instead time is spent on bug fixing (after the fact) or if a test fails. It would be so easy to focus on the top worst code pieces and make them fault free. See e.g. Software Quality Rank Model [25] that uses simple targeting of worst culprits, and then uses basic quality approaches to refactor to at least have these *fault free*.
4. Test design is mainly created through copying earlier test cases and changing them. As a result we have concluded that 15–20% identical duplication (measured by SonarCube [9] (i.e. Type I cloning) exists in the test suites. On average 30–50% code cloning overlap (measured by NiCad [21]) (Type I–Type IV) exist in the test suites. These duplication's and different types of overlap exists at all levels - even if it is easiest to identify them at unit level, as the tool has language restrictions. Note that some test suites had as much as 80% code cloning duplication when Type III clones were used.
5. Hasanain et al. [39] did a thorough clone analysis with NiCad on large part of Ericsson's Test code, from specific sub-systems functional test code, to unit test code packages in a large variety of software. Despite the high cloning results, that could, with some effort be removed, no investment or action was taken. Even if the results of such investment would not only reduce test code footprint by large, and also speed up the test suites in the pipelines which implicitly would lower energy costs, this was met with cold shoulders, as the understanding of testing and test suite impact and gain is low. Another factor that makes this hinders to perform this refactoring is the lack of skill to write "good" test cases among test managers, test guardians and test architects, and developers per se. This is because most testers were good because of their domain skills and manual testing skills, follow suit of test managers, test guardians and test architects, with a few exceptions. Developers who implicitly would have sufficient coding and refactoring skills, are simply bad in test design techniques.
6. Even if clones exists (Type I–Type IV) [61] only some of Type I code is removed. This is rather daunting as e.g. Van Bladel et al. [17] showed that there is much value pursuing also Clones of type IV. In general test cases are made of copy-paste, therefore there is no incentive to remove or refactor test code [39].
7. Too simplistic tools are used like SonarCube, [9], and at best [21], NiCad has been used, even if Van Bladel et al. insist on combining several clone coding tools and shows that they can target different types of clones [18]. The cost to integrate a set of tools in production is still to steep and the incentive to improve on this typical test smell is surprisingly low.

8 Fault-Fixing Loops

1. The majority of bugs are found in the first early commit code in the CI flow. This indicates that testing at the lowest unit level is not very robust (as unit tests should be performed before the check-in, if specifications were correct or existed), as many bugs are found after commit. An observation is that many developers trust that the integration and functional tests will find all important bugs instead of the more time-consuming unit tests. Meaning how a small changed piece of code works in its real context will always reveal bugs. Instead the contrary is true - many code changes passes through the test flow completely untested (other than at the unit level), as no particular test targeting the change as been made.
2. External faults (Anomaly Reports, AR) found are given a high priority, as well as faults from system test are since the 2012 in automatic routing (e.g. triaging) to the right organisation/team, and through various machine learning and Bayesian approaches, now more perfected [40–42]. Unfortunately, the fault localization has not reached exactly the lines of code but is at best remaining on file level - but work to improve this algorithm is constant.

9 Test Tools and Test Environments

Historically, most test tools were proprietary, as there was a need to work with specific protocols, but TTCN-3 [35] and efforts in ETSI [3] has brought through tools like TITAN [66] and testing approaches like UML modelling [30] very much in use. As development of software has progressed (with Agile methods) the change to other types of software development methods, embracing open source software, new tools like GitHub [4], Jenkins [7] and Maven [8] have been examples of concepts that is embraced and sometimes used alongside proprietary adaptations of legacy test tools.

1. As many unit tests are dependent on adequate test tools for the language at questions it is often the case that unit test code is written in something completely different than the source language. The debate what is best here is still not straight forward.
2. There is a lack of good tool support, e.g. test tools, static analyzers and fuzzer's for new languages. Such a simple thing as creating CFG's (Control Flow Graphs) does not exists out of the box for all procedural languages.
3. Low-level code close to hardware, e.g. embedded and/or proprietary code, will be unique as it needs tools to be developed in-house. This is often a hidden cost and a hindrance for unified test approaches.
4. Test systems are generally not aligned and integrated in their way of working, and a large diversity of tools, approaches and concepts are still existing with a high technical debt to merge [58].
5. Tests written in old tools are very reluctantly changed to new tools. Therefore many old tools still linger in the system. In addition, as self-organization allows for some aspect of low-level decisions, the temptation to use new and

more modern tools is high, resulting in an abundance of tools from the last decades.

6. There is an interest to consolidate tools to lower licensing costs, and treating them as a production system in itself. Despite this, tool changes always come second, as the first goal is always to deliver new functionality, giving organisations reluctant to change, a way to avoid tool change.
7. With an abundance of tools, it is hard to please all, as functionality is different in different tools. Consolidating them is inherently hard.
8. As tools are now the new security threat in themselves, the future will probably look a lot different when it comes to using tools from outside the company firewall- this will also be a hindrance to explore new researcher tools.

10 Quality Assurance

There is a lack of control and checking mechanisms that testing is done properly, e.g. measurements for coverage or test criteria are seldom used. I.e. quality assurance control is diminished in the agile context to attempting a set of test cases being passed. As the software product is constantly in flux, being updated, corrected and changed, most (larger) industry software needs to have code freeze on a branch before a delivery - instead of being able to deliver the entire software at "any moment", as the original intent of agile was. Sometimes tolerance to submitting code with failed test cases are allowed to circumvent this issue. Hence, there is seldom a state where "all test cases are passed" in a large system. This obfuscation creates a blunted view on quality in the form of test cases as control, and a lot of management effort is put on justification of being "good enough" quality for submission. Sometimes even test cases are removed that are difficult to pass, but mostly - measurements that indicates these issues (of poor quality) have instead been removed.

1. Developers are only fulfilling mandatory gating requirements. If they are set low (e.g. 80% statement code coverage) this is where testing stops. Test adequacy criteria an coverage is important, see Zhu et al. [76].
2. As Agile team's goal is to deliver functionality, and no quality measurements or checking of the test quality is made (other than code review- that mainly focus on the source code), the quality of testing is in principle poor.
3. Mutation testing [54], could be a way to check the quality of the test. Unfortunately - mutation test operates mainly on the code level and in the context of unit tests, and as such - it misses all functional and non-functional (as well as integrated) executions of the software.
4. Testing is considered a cost to be reduced as its value is poorly understood, i.e.testing is "a necessary evil".
5. Most industry delivery plans do not take refactoring into account, especially not for testing.
6. The need for speed to deliver new functionality often compromises quality up front.

7. Test maintenance is considered a "non-issue" as maintenance is often exported to "low cost" sites. This does not teach developers to have a "quality mind" - and learn from their own mistakes, and is probably (with lack of incentive for developers) the main reason for poor quality.
8. Test Coverage is measured, but this is not a clearly defined metric that provides any scientifically or statistical value of how well a system is tested, hence progress and accomplishments sounds better than reality is (see earlier discussion on this).
9. Bug reports (anomaly reports) are one of the few tools to evaluate the final quality of the product, based on the customer. As it is costly for customers (time, effort) to also report bugs, only a few are reported. Another confounding factor hiding quality issues is as mention the redundancy in the product. This makes many software bugs go undetected. Concurrency (parallelism) in the product also make many bugs difficult to reproduce.

11 Knowledge and Skills in Testing

There is a lack of proper education on testing for developers and engineers (from university, and within the company)

1. Developers in agile teams are rarely trained in testing [34].
2. As 7 of 8 test managers cannot or do not read code, hence, checking how e.g. coverage is fulfilled, and test cases are constructed, is not managed and supervised sufficiently.
3. Some internal courses and leaders are also advocating manual test or "exploratory test", despite the company's goal to automate as much as possible and automate testing approaches. Manual testing is good for learning, but should not be advocated, as the regression test cost advantage is lost, as well as the possibility to improve the testing in both accuracy, speed and quality.
4. Most commercially available courses are too simple, and not geared to teach advanced automated testing that is needed (but a few exceptions).
5. There is no incentive of becoming a good tester, as they are rarely valued, do not have a clear carrier staging, and have lower status and salary compared to being a good developer that delivers functionality fast.
6. As a good tester finds more bugs, they are instead viewed as hindrance (to delivery) instead of helpers, which limits the incentive to learn new techniques, become better and add quality to the system [34].
7. Preventive techniques, such as modelling and constraints fall under "system work" and is therefore a better quality approach. These systems must also be tested.

12 Management

The main caveat with observations from management in industry, is that there is a lack of research in the area and from industry. Most information around it can only be found i grey literature.

1. Testing in general is seen as a cost that do not contribute to the product. Most of the cost is due to expensive test equipment and usage of commercial simulators.
2. As the organisation moves software to low-cost for maintenance, there is little incentive to improve your code from the start.
3. The reward system for developers is not geared towards rewarding good testing. It is geared towards a) saving the day (when difficult bugs exists) b) to deliver functionality and changes fast (and pass the CI loop). As fewer detected bugs let the code pass the CI loops faster, the current way of working actually rewards less testing.
4. Management prefer system approaches rather than proper test, which means that modelling could be a way forward. Against this, is our large experience of how modelling can be very costly, as at some point the model must meet reality, e.g. translate into hardware instructions. Many development managers still keeps the memory of this costly issue that historically has locked them into specific vendors and tools.
5. The abundance of test cases (in the millions) creates a false sense of security that the system is well tested. Especially when considering the high cloning percentages.
6. There is a belief that a tools can fix all problems, which implicitly makes it easier to invest in e.g. a tool than to actually test properly. The belief is that AI and Machine Learning will solve everything, which of course is not true (yet). The main caveat is that one must at some point - both for any learning system or modelling to generate code or whatever approach or technique you use - actually know what is correct behavior - or expected behavior. Until we can express this fine-grained enough we will not produce trustworthy solutions.
7. The promise of APR (Automatic Program Repair) has been strong with management since Ericsson's first trial 2011–2012 in cooperation with Weimer and DiLorenzo [63,70]. It became clear that this technique relies on a lot of unit tests but primarily identifies single fault issues. As half of the true software faults being of single fault nature, shown on typical telecommunications middleware code [27], singe fault failures can be prevented by mutation testing. There are still a lot to be exploited in this area.
8. As much work is a result of proprietary and self-organized way of working, the lack of unified set of tools, approaches, languages used, etc. causes a very diverse environment (due to historic decisions). This makes transformation difficult to newer methods, and changes in behavior - as tools and way of working, as well as attitudes remain the same. Testers and testing is considered "old-fashioned".

13 Visions on Test in the Future

Despite a somewhat gloomy set of observations above of test debt in industrial systems, the future is very promising on many accounts.

First and foremost, formal tools are improving on performance, usability and can better scale to larger applications. These factors together with more educated computer scientist coming to the job market, provides a base to use more formal, modelling and model-checking tools in industries that are not used to do so (i.e. industries that have not are not working with safety-critical aspects). Not being a safety-critical company, has also been used as an excuse for many commercial software companies to avoid investing in any of these "costly" technologies. Here is the incentive - improved requirement, need for automated support, and more easy to use and powerful tools, minimizing the transition to the code. This gap needs to be reduced to make "normal" commercial software use these technologies.

Secondly, AI (ML)- support will inevitably drive improved software, as code auto-completion is now supporting some aspects of source code creation (suggesting e.g. next character or line of code), there is no reason why we cannot train ML models to write better test code and test patterns, to guide developers in describing better testing. As with any technology - it will not be better than the people training the models. The key is, again, to know what is correct - the source code or the test, and know what is a "better" test approach. This also leads back to better tools and models used. Positive news also comes mainly from the webscalers and the occasional leap happening for the larger more mature industries, often with researchers driving it. Webscalers put serious money in their testing frameworks, as the business loss of poor quality poses a security risk. This creates more advancements for industry and new collaborative research on testing. A recent comprehensive literature study in the use of AI and ML in software testing can be found in Battina et al. [15].

Security concerns being strongly related to software testing are pushing quality higher on the agenda. Examples are e.g. Zeller et al. with the interactive Fuzzing book [75] and the survey by Felderer et al. [31]. Many technologies well known for academics, but new for industry use, are being matured and adapted for use. Examples are metamorphic testing [19,64], mutation testing [54,56], evolutionary approaches [13,38,51,69] and many new analysis tools combined with learning technologies. As Industry has the data, context and commercial incentive, collaboration with academics to perfect tools and technology will be the way forward. It is probable that the intelligence in the tools will be hidden completely from the user in tools, much as learning tools behave. Novel approaches even attempt to make testing into a game, where the user gets awarded to create tests, clear is that it should be pleasurable [67,72].

The issue is of course for many companies to tackle old fashioned organisational structures that do not promote software engineering. Most management are not educated in a software driven world nor understands where quality comes from in software. If companies cannot provide quality at a high level and low cost, they will have an issue to survive in the long run, as quality is expected. Every developer must know testing basics, and new ways of working, e.g. utilizing improved modelling and increasing the abstraction levels. Testing must be taken into account, as even a constraint model needs to be tested.

Automation of test will also become a strong drive, as still surprisingly many aspects of software development are still manual. The approach of automation everywhere in the entire R&D process is currently scrutinized, as is the aim to simplify. What can be done to create reliable, robust and well suited systems, that handle faults "automatically" so they magically disappear? The digitalization will also drive more automation, integration of tools, frameworks and systems will lead to changed focus. Monitoring and testing will be more aligned. We are already letting the customer test more, through targeted pilots, A/B test approaches and canary testing. Decision support will be increasingly deployed by different AI and machine learning bots as trustworthiness in the system increases.

The TAIM model - Test Automation Improvement Model [26], describes how automation growth, also implies that robustness, trustworthy data handling and fault localization leading to automatic program repair are issues to be solved, all suffering from the same issues, what is correct. In the future we can imagine that systems also take examples and probes to learn (with some guidance) what solutions are. The drivers are definitely based on how to monetize on quality, which is not currently clear. Maybe a future is very much assuming that you pay for quality solutions, and other "free" solutions are inherently relying on you as a user to debug them (implicitly) by claiming faults and sharing your preferences. Clearly the TAIM 2.0 model is a vision, where only some aspects of test management seems to have gained ground, where e.g. the need to progress report testing is very much historical, as a dashboard can keep continuous updates on the progress - as well as provide fault history and give quality assurance overviews with a simple drill down visualisation of issues. Most are working on avoiding to look at this data at all, and have machine learning only highlight what is important. Driving this machinery are assumed to be an abundance of "good" tests. This is the main caveat. Just because the number of tests are many they have high overlap (cloning) and are is not necessarily exercising other than variants of the normal case. Here new technologies like metamorphic test, great simulation tools for the test environment, that can also mimic faulty hardware, can make strong contributions. The security issues, which forms one sub-category of faults and issues will also drive much stronger technologies e.g. block-chains. Because of changing difficulties in these technologies, the aim to make sure they are solid in themselves also drives more formal modelling approaches. Unfortunately, the need for these technologies to be established, and the secrecy surrounding best practices, are not fruitful for exchanging best practices.

What drives automation is not only the goal to save cost, increase speed and reliability, but also to remove tedious repetitive ways of working where the interaction with the software is key. There is still much to be learned about bots, how they interact between them, and with humans, and what the best way to drive things. It is easy to hand over the responsibility of "what is right" to the computer (bot, AI decision system), and humans need to stay active and tell what is correct. So supporting in the right way might be the trick to success.

14 Method Used, Threats of Validity and Disclaimers

The method used to gather this data, is through observations, documentation existing, presentations and interviews in an action research setting. The sample of observations is a convenience sample. Therefore no statistics have been exposed or tables made. Despite being observations, there is undoubtedly a researcher bias in the selection of the observations and how the data is described. Effort has been made to make observations as factual and general as possible, seeking support in academic publications where available. Due to page limit, not an exhaustive reference list have been made for all items, as this paper aim to provide a research agenda and vision to inspire future systematic studies. As with all large world-wide development organisations, what is true for a majority (within one company), is not true for all, and there are exceptions to these observations. Examples comes from geographical diverse set of R&D centers in Asia, North America and Europe, and have been compared with industries in a large variety of domains, within mainly Europe, but also to some extent in Asia and North America. Disclaimer: As this paper is based on an invited talk, there should be put no blame or liability to Ericsson AB, as all observations and analysis expressed, are the made by the researcher. We also thank Ericsson AB and Mälardalen University for the support in writing this paper.

In addition, the lists presented have no weight in the order intended, and are to be viewed as an arbitrary enumeration, solely to create aid reading. It could be suggested as an easy exercise for any industry to walk them trough and create a priority order suitable for their specific environment to remedy, or for an academic to attempt to establish solutions, provide metrics and establish such an order.

15 Conclusions

In this paper we discussed a series of observations on technical debt of software testing and test automation in industry. As most software development has transformed to Agile and DevOps processes, the testing is still surprisingly manual even if automation is happening. Test automation means in industry automating the CI pipeline, and particularly test execution, not automatic test generation. The focus is often on the lower level tests, as this functionality is well understood by the agile teams (developers) as there is a loss of professional testers following the agile transformation. Non-functional tests require expertise, and here testers remain active, resulting in lower test debt and better acceptance for the cost of testing, as these testers produce metrics (KPI's) used in sales.

The focus should be on alleviating overlap of test clones and duplications through test code refactoring with the aim to reduce the cost of constant testing in the CI-flow. This is not happening, as test code refactoring is "too costly". Instead prioritization and reduction through e.g. similarity analysis removes poorly created test cases, at a loss of data (input) variation that can remove the original important test case intent, e.g. boundary value checks. The drive to remove technical debt is low and pushed to the future. Refactoring test smells, reducing test code clones and utilizing e.g. mutation test approaches seems to be obvious steps to improve, but has a harsh reality to face, as code coverage are not considered mandatory (or only at statement level), and is often obfuscated by poor so called "test coverage" measurements.

Security is a strong driver for improved quality. There is an unwillingness to pay for what might be the real cause of test ignorance, e.g. lack of skills and poor test management awareness. Skills in software testing (and test design techniques) are still remaining low, with low status in industries, especially if software is not the main product. There is though a new hope that by introducing more gaming qualities into testing tools and more "intelligence" hidden in the tools fueled by AI/ML approaches, will diminish some of the of costly manual debugging and need for thorough testing. The drive to achieve automatic program repair will push the industry to be more aware of the new methodologies and utilize technologies that can change us enough to want to change how we solve software quality issues.

References

1. CodeChecker at github. https://github.com/Ericsson/codechecker. Accessed 05 May 2022
2. Ericsson Smart Mining web-page and report. https://www.ericsson.com/en/enterprise/reports/connected-mining. Accessed 08 Aug 2022
3. ETSI, European Standard. https://www.etsi.org. Accessed 05 May 2022
4. Github tool. https://github.com. Accessed 05 May 2022
5. ISO: ISO/IEC 25000: 2014, Systems and software engineering - Systems and software Quality Requirements and Evaluation (SQuaRE) - Guide to SQuaRE webpage. https://www.iso.org/standard/35733.html. Accessed 08 Aug 2022
6. ITU-T TTCN-3 Z-series Z.161-Z.169. https://www.itu.int/rec/T-REC-Z/en. Accessed 08 Aug 2022
7. Jenkins tool. https://www.jenkins.io/. Accessed 05 May 2022
8. Maven tool. https://maven.apache.org. Accessed 05 June 2022
9. SonarCube tool. Accessed 08 May 2022
10. Agarwal, A., Gupta, S., Choudhury, T.: Continuous and integrated software development using DevOps. In: 2018 International Conference on Advances in Computing and Communication Engineering (ICACCE), pp. 290–293. IEEE (2018)
11. Ahmad, A., Leifler, O., Sandahl, K.: Empirical analysis of factors and their effect on test flakiness-practitioners' perceptions. arXiv preprint arXiv:1906.00673 (2019)
12. Al-Ahmad, A.S., Kahtan, H., Hujainah, F., Jalab, H.A.: Systematic literature review on penetration testing for mobile cloud computing applications. IEEE Access **7**, 173524–173540 (2019)
13. Ali, S., Briand, L.C., Hemmati, H., Panesar-Walawege, R.K.: A systematic review of the application and empirical investigation of search-based test case generation. IEEE Trans. Software Eng. **36**(6), 742–762 (2009)
14. Barboni, M., Bertolino, A., De Angelis, G.: What we talk about when we talk about software test flakiness. In: Paiva, A.C.R., Cavalli, A.R., Ventura Martins, P., Pérez-Castillo, R. (eds.) QUATIC 2021. CCIS, vol. 1439, pp. 29–39. Springer, Cham (2021). https://doi.org/10.1007/978-3-030-85347-1_3

15. Battina, D.S.: Artificial intelligence in software test automation: a systematic literature review. Int. J. Emerging Technol. Innov. Res. (2019). https://www.jetir.org. UGC and ISSN Approved. ISSN 2349-5162
16. Bjarnason, E., et al.: Challenges and practices in aligning requirements with verification and validation: a case study of six companies. Empir. Softw. Eng. **19**(6), 1809–1855 (2014)
17. van Bladel, B., Demeyer, S.: A novel approach for detecting type-IV clones in test code. In: 2019 IEEE 13th International Workshop on Software Clones (IWSC), pp. 8–12. IEEE (2019)
18. van Bladel, B., Demeyer, S.: Clone detection in test code: an empirical evaluation. In: 2020 IEEE 27th International Conference on Software Analysis, Evolution and Reengineering (SANER), pp. 492–500. IEEE (2020)
19. Chen, T.Y., et al.: Metamorphic testing: a review of challenges and opportunities. ACM Comput. Surv. (CSUR) **51**(1), 1–27 (2018)
20. Collins, E., Dias-Neto, A., de Lucena, V.F., Jr.: Strategies for agile software testing automation: an industrial experience. In: 2012 IEEE 36th Annual Computer Software and Applications Conference Workshops, pp. 440–445. IEEE (2012)
21. Cordy, J.R., Roy, C.K.: The NiCad clone detector. In: 2011 IEEE 19th International Conference on Program Comprehension, pp. 219–220. IEEE (2011)
22. Diebold, P., Mayer, U.: On the usage and benefits of agile methods & practices. In: Baumeister, H., Lichter, H., Riebisch, M. (eds.) XP 2017. LNBIP, vol. 283, pp. 243–250. Springer, Cham (2017). https://doi.org/10.1007/978-3-319-57633-6_16
23. Dietrich, J., Rasheed, S., Tahir, A.: Flaky test sanitisation via on-the-fly assumption inference for tests with network dependencies. arXiv preprint arXiv:2208.01106 (2022)
24. Dikert, K., Paasivaara, M., Lassenius, C.: Challenges and success factors for large-scale agile transformations: a systematic literature review. J. Syst. Softw. **119**, 87–108 (2016)
25. Eldh, S.: On test design. Ph.D. thesis, Mälardalen University (2011)
26. Eldh, S.: Test automation improvement model-TAIM 2.0. In: 2020 IEEE International Conference on Software Testing, Verification and Validation Workshops (ICSTW), pp. 334–337. IEEE (2020)
27. Eldh, S., Punnekkat, S., Hansson, H., Jönsson, P.: Component testing is not enough - a study of software faults in telecom middleware. In: Petrenko, A., Veanes, M., Tretmans, J., Grieskamp, W. (eds.) FATES/TestCom -2007. LNCS, vol. 4581, pp. 74–89. Springer, Heidelberg (2007). https://doi.org/10.1007/978-3-540-73066-8_6
28. Engelman, C.: MATHLAB: a program for on-line machine assistance in symbolic computations. In: Proceedings of the November 30–December 1, 1965, Fall Joint Computer Conference, Part II: Computers: Their Impact on Society, pp. 117–126 (1965)
29. Estdale, J., Georgiadou, E.: Applying the ISO/IEC 25010 quality models to software product. In: Larrucea, X., Santamaria, I., O'Connor, R.V., Messnarz, R. (eds.) EuroSPI 2018. CCIS, vol. 896, pp. 492–503. Springer, Cham (2018). https://doi.org/10.1007/978-3-319-97925-0_42
30. ETSI: Methods for Testing and Specification (MTS); UML 2.0 action syntax feasibility study TR 102 205 v1.1.1 (2003–2005)
31. Felderer, M., Büchler, M., Johns, M., Brucker, A.D., Breu, R., Pretschner, A.: Security testing: a survey. Adv. Comput. **101**, 1–51 (2016)
32. Feldt, R.: Do system test cases grow old? In: 2014 IEEE Seventh International Conference on Software Testing, Verification and Validation, pp. 343–352. IEEE (2014)

33. Florea, R., Stray, V.: A global view on the hard skills and testing tools in software testing. In: 2019 ACM/IEEE 14th International Conference on Global Software Engineering (ICGSE), pp. 143–151. IEEE (2019)
34. Garousi, V., Zhi, J.: A survey of software testing practices in Canada. J. Syst. Softw. **86**(5), 1354–1376 (2013)
35. Grabowski, J., Hogrefe, D., Réthy, G., Schieferdecker, I., Wiles, A., Willcock, C.: An introduction to the testing and test control notation (TTCN-3). Comput. Netw. **42**(3), 375–403 (2003)
36. Grindal, M., Offutt, J., Mellin, J.: On the testing maturity of software producing organizations. In: Testing: Academic & Industrial Conference-Practice and Research Techniques (TAIC PART 2006), pp. 171–180. IEEE (2006)
37. Haindl, P., Plösch, R.: Towards continuous quality: measuring and evaluating feature-dependent non-functional requirements in DevOps. In: 2019 IEEE International Conference on Software Architecture Companion (ICSA-C), pp. 91–94. IEEE (2019)
38. Harman, M., McMinn, P., de Souza, J.T., Yoo, S.: Search based software engineering: techniques, taxonomy, tutorial. In: Meyer, B., Nordio, M. (eds.) LASER 2008-2010. LNCS, vol. 7007, pp. 1–59. Springer, Heidelberg (2012). https://doi.org/10.1007/978-3-642-25231-0_1
39. Hasanain, W., Labiche, Y., Eldh, S.: An analysis of complex industrial test code using clone analysis. In: 2018 IEEE International Conference on Software Quality, Reliability and Security (QRS), pp. 482–489. IEEE (2018)
40. Jonsson, L.: Machine Learning-Based Bug Handling in Large-Scale Software Development, vol. 1936. Linköping University Electronic Press (2018)
41. Jonsson, L., Borg, M., Broman, D., Sandahl, K., Eldh, S., Runeson, P.: Automated bug assignment: ensemble-based machine learning in large scale industrial contexts. Empir. Softw. Eng. **21**(4), 1533–1578 (2016)
42. Jonsson, L., Broman, D., Sandahl, K., Eldh, S.: Towards automated anomaly report assignment in large complex systems using stacked generalization. In: 2012 IEEE Fifth International Conference on Software Testing, Verification and Validation, pp. 437–446. IEEE (2012)
43. Karris, S.T.: Introduction to Simulink with Engineering Applications. Orchard Publications (2006)
44. Kaur, K., Jajoo, A., et al.: Applying agile methodologies in industry projects: benefits and challenges. In: 2015 International Conference on Computing Communication Control and Automation, pp. 832–836. IEEE (2015)
45. Kintis, M., Papadakis, M., Malevris, N.: Evaluating mutation testing alternatives: a collateral experiment. In: 2010 Asia Pacific Software Engineering Conference, pp. 300–309. IEEE (2010)
46. Kitanov, S., Monteiro, E., Janevski, T.: 5G and the fog-survey of related technologies and research directions. In: 2016 18th Mediterranean Electrotechnical Conference (MELECON), pp. 1–6. IEEE (2016)
47. Lattner, C., Adve, V.: LLVM: a compilation framework for lifelong program analysis & transformation. In: International Symposium on Code Generation and Optimization, CGO 2004, pp. 75–86. IEEE (2004)
48. Malm, J., Causevic, A., Lisper, B., Eldh, S.: Automated analysis of flakiness-mitigating delays. In: Proceedings of the IEEE/ACM 1st International Conference on Automation of Software Test, pp. 81–84 (2020)
49. Marick, B.: How to misuse code coverage. https://www.exampler.com/testing-com/writings/coverage.pdf. Accessed 05 May 2022

50. Mårtensson, T., Ståhl, D., Bosch, J.: Exploratory testing of large-scale systems – testing in the continuous integration and delivery pipeline. In: Felderer, M., Méndez Fernández, D., Turhan, B., Kalinowski, M., Sarro, F., Winkler, D. (eds.) PROFES 2017. LNCS, vol. 10611, pp. 368–384. Springer, Cham (2017). https://doi.org/10.1007/978-3-319-69926-4_26
51. McMinn, P.: Search-based software test data generation: a survey. Softw. Test. Verif. Reliab. **14**(2), 105–156 (2004)
52. Navabi, Z.: VHDL: Analysis and Modeling of Digital Systems, vol. 2. McGraw-Hill, New York (1993)
53. Nethercote, N., Stuckey, P.J., Becket, R., Brand, S., Duck, G.J., Tack, G.: MiniZinc: towards a standard CP modelling language. In: Bessière, C. (ed.) CP 2007. LNCS, vol. 4741, pp. 529–543. Springer, Heidelberg (2007). https://doi.org/10.1007/978-3-540-74970-7_38
54. Papadakis, M., Kintis, M., Zhang, J., Jia, Y., Le Traon, Y., Harman, M.: Mutation testing advances: an analysis and survey. Adv. Comput. **112**, 275–378 (2019)
55. Parry, O., Kapfhammer, G.M., Hilton, M., McMinn, P.: A survey of flaky tests. ACM Trans. Softw. Eng. Methodol. (TOSEM) **31**(1), 1–74 (2021)
56. Petrović, G., Ivanković, M., Fraser, G., Just, R.: Does mutation testing improve testing practices? In: 2021 IEEE/ACM 43rd International Conference on Software Engineering (ICSE), pp. 910–921. IEEE (2021)
57. Pietrantuono, R., Bertolino, A., De Angelis, G., Miranda, B., Russo, S.: Towards continuous software reliability testing in DevOps. In: 2019 IEEE/ACM 14th International Workshop on Automation of Software Test (AST), pp. 21–27. IEEE (2019)
58. Planning, S.: The economic impacts of inadequate infrastructure for software testing. National Institute of Standards and Technology, p. 1 (2002)
59. Porkoláb, Z., Brunner, T.: The codecompass comprehension framework. In: Proceedings of the 26th Conference on Program Comprehension, pp. 393–396 (2018)
60. Rodríguez, P., Markkula, J., Oivo, M., Turula, K.: Survey on agile and lean usage in Finnish software industry. In: Proceedings of the 2012 ACM-IEEE International Symposium on Empirical Software Engineering and Measurement, pp. 139–148. IEEE (2012)
61. Roy, C.K., Cordy, J.R.: A survey on software clone detection research. Queen's Sch. Comput. TR **541**(115), 64–68 (2007)
62. Saxena, P.: OSI reference model - a seven layered architecture of OSI model. Int. J. Res. **1**(10), 1145–1156 (2014)
63. Schulte, E., DiLorenzo, J., Weimer, W., Forrest, S.: Automated repair of binary and assembly programs for cooperating embedded devices. ACM SIGARCH Comput. Archit. News **41**(1), 317–328 (2013)
64. Segura, S., Fraser, G., Sanchez, A.B., Ruiz-Cortés, A.: A survey on metamorphic testing. IEEE Trans. Software Eng. **42**(9), 805–824 (2016)
65. Shahin, M., Babar, M.A., Zhu, L.: Continuous integration, delivery and deployment: a systematic review on approaches, tools, challenges and practices. IEEE Access **5**, 3909–3943 (2017)
66. Szabó, J.Z., Csöndes, T.: Titan, TTCN-3 test execution environment. Infocommun. J. **62**(1), 27–31 (2007)
67. Tillmann, N., De Halleux, J., Xie, T., Gulwani, S., Bishop, J.: Teaching and learning programming and software engineering via interactive gaming. In: 2013 35th International Conference on Software Engineering (ICSE), pp. 1117–1126. IEEE (2013)

68. Van Deursen, A., Moonen, L., Van Den Bergh, A., Kok, G.: Refactoring test code. In: Proceedings of the 2nd International Conference on Extreme Programming and Flexible Processes in Software Engineering (XP2001), pp. 92–95. Citeseer (2001)
69. Wegener, J., Baresel, A., Sthamer, H.: Evolutionary test environment for automatic structural testing. Inf. Softw. Technol. **43**(14), 841–854 (2001)
70. Weimer, W., Forrest, S., Le Goues, C., Nguyen, T.: Automatic program repair with evolutionary computation. Commun. ACM **53**(5), 109–116 (2010)
71. Wiklund, K., Eldh, S., Sundmark, D., Lundqvist, K.: Technical debt in test automation. In: 2012 IEEE Fifth International Conference on Software Testing, Verification and Validation, pp. 887–892. IEEE (2012)
72. Xie, T., Tillmann, N., De Halleux, J.: Educational software engineering: where software engineering, education, and gaming meet. In: 2013 3rd International Workshop on Games and Software Engineering: Engineering Computer Games to Enable Positive, Progressive Change (GAS), pp. 36–39. IEEE (2013)
73. Yang, J., Zhikhartsev, A., Liu, Y., Tan, L.: Better test cases for better automated program repair. In: Proceedings of the 2017 11th Joint Meeting on Foundations of Software Engineering, pp. 831–841 (2017)
74. Zaidman, A., Van Rompaey, B., Demeyer, S., Van Deursen, A.: Mining software repositories to study co-evolution of production & test code. In: 2008 1st International Conference on Software Testing, Verification, and Validation, pp. 220–229. IEEE (2008)
75. Zeller, A., Gopinath, R., Böhme, M., Fraser, G., Holler, C.: The fuzzing book (2019)
76. Zhu, H., Hall, P.A., May, J.H.: Software unit test coverage and adequacy. ACM Comput. Surv. (CSUR) **29**(4), 366–427 (1997)

Refactoring Solidity Smart Contracts to Protect Against Reentrancy Exploits

Serge Demeyer[1,2(✉)], Henrique Rocha[3], and Darin Verheijke[1]

[1] Universiteit Antwerpen, Antwerp, Belgium
serge.demeyer@uantwerpen.be
[2] Flanders Make vzw, Flanders, Belgium
[3] Loyola University Maryland, Baltimore, USA

Abstract. Solidity is the dominant programming language for specifying smart contracts deployed on the Ethereum blockchain platform. Smart contracts permit the exchange of cryptocurrency, and hence are vulnerable to security attacks, most notably reentrancy exploits. Extensions to the solidity language, therefore, provide safer alternatives via special-purpose syntactic constructs. Based on an analysis of 26,799 contracts actually deployed on the Ethereum platform, it appears that these safer alternatives are indeed adopted. Next, we investigate whether the SMTChecker provided with the Solidity compiler is able to confirm that two safer alternatives ("Check-Effects-Interactions" and "Mutex") actually prevent against reentrancy exploits.

Keywords: Solidity · Smart contracts · Static analysis

1 Introduction

A *blockchain* is an append-only transactional database where the information is structured together in groups, also known as blocks [7,18]. Each block has certain storage capacities and is chained onto the previous filled block, thus forming a blockchain. A blockchain can thus be seen as an immutable ledger that records transactions tracking different assets. The most notable uses of this blockchain technology are the cryptocurrencies Bitcoin [20] and Ether [12,29]. One important difference between these two blockchain platforms is that the latter enables the deployment of smart contracts.

A *smart contract* is a piece of code that executes automatically provided that the terms between the two parties as written in code hold when the contract is invoked. In its simplest form, a contract is just a collection of functions. To invoke a contract, one of the contract functions is called and then the implemented agreement is executed without any intermediary party [6,16,18]. Smart contracts are stored on the blockchain themselves, thus are by design traceable, deterministic, and irreversible [7,18].

T. Margaria and B. Steffen (Eds.): ISoLA 2022, LNCS 13702, pp. 324–344, 2022.
https://doi.org/10.1007/978-3-031-19756-7_18

Solidity is one of the major programming languages for smart contracts on Ethereum. It is a statically typed programming language designed to be executed on the Ethereum Virtual Machine. Despite the static type system, the Turing-completeness of the programming language, makes automated verification of arbitrary properties undecidable [26]. Since smart contracts are allowed to make calls to another contract, thereby transferring execution control to the called contract, smart contracts induce an inherent security risk. Indeed, calling an untrusted contract may introduce errors but worse may execute malicious code which exploits vulnerabilities.

Reentrancy exploits are the most well-known security risks, due to the DAO Attack in June 2016 where around 3.6 million Ether was taken which equated to around $50 million dollars at the time [4]. This exploit is cemented in the history of Ethereum as it resulted in Ethereum being forked into Ethereum Classic and the Ethereum we know today. Reentrancy involves parallel functions that are called repeatedly before the first function is finished. They access internal state of the first function, which —when not guarded properly— allows to exploit illegitimate logic assumptions. A typical example of such a logic assumption is the check whether the balance of an account is still larger than 0, hence it is still possible to withdraw. However, in a distributed system —where multiple actors concurrently manipulate the shared balance— the assumption that the balance is larger than zero may not longer hold when the actual withdraw executes.

To avoid reentrancy exploits, several special purpose language constructs have been incorporated in recent versions of Solidity. More specifically, the function `call()` was to be replaced by the safer functions `transfer()` and `send()`. However, these only work under the assumption that the pricing of executing code on the Ethereum platform would remain constant which proved to be false in the long term. It is therefore recommended to refactor `transfer()` and `send()` with safe code patterns guarding potentially unsafe `call()` constructs with functions like `require()`, `assert()` or `revert()` [19].

In this paper, we first present a dataset of 26,799 unique open-source verified smart contracts from Etherscan (from 2021-07-07 to 2022-01-06) for empirical validation[1]. Analysis of this dataset suggests that such safe code patterns are indeed adopted. Next we argue that software engineers should refactor their code, surrounding potentially unsafe `call()` invocations with pre- and post-conditions to assure that such safe code patterns are indeed secure. We investigate whether the SMTChecker provided with the Solidity compiler is able to confirm that two safer alternatives ("Check-Effects-Interactions" and "Mutex") actually prevent against reentrancy exploits.

The remainder of this paper is organised as follows. Section 2, provides the necessary background information on the Solidity language and the special purpose language constructs preventing against reentrancy exploits. Section 4, explains the challenges in mining realistic smart contracts and explains how

[1] The paper is an extension of a paper presented at the WETSEB 2022 workshop [27].

we collected and analysed 26,799 Solidity contracts. Section 5, provides concrete examples of unsafe coding idioms in Solidity and how the special purpose language constructs may render them safe. In particular, we illustrate how explicit pre- and post-conditions permits the Solidity compiler to guard against reentrancy exploits. Section 6 list related work on performing security analysis on Solidity and the associated public datasets. We conclude with an open invitation to the community in Sect. 7.

2 Background

In this section we introduce the important concepts of the blockchain, the Solidity smart contracts and the concept of reentrancy exploits.

2.1 Blockchain

A blockchain is a decentralized, distributed and immutable ledger that differs from a typical database in the way that it stores information. All recorded transactions, structured in blocks, are linked together using cryptography. Each block will contain a hash of the previous block, a timestamp and transaction data. As each block contains information from the previous block due to the hash, they will form a chain, thereby forming a blockchain [20].

An alternative perspective is to consider a blockchain as a peer-to-peer network connecting participants. These participants will be forced to cooperate using a consensus mechanism which enforces rules in order to decentralize control. A blockchain reaches consensus when more than half of the nodes on the network agree on the next state of the network. These consensus mechanisms are designed to prevent 51% attacks on the network. Executing such an attack would require the attacker to have 51% of the nodes on the network which is considered practically impossible due to the decentralized nature of a blockchain.

2.2 Ethereum and Smart Contracts

Ethereum is designed to be a general-purpose programmable blockchain that runs a virtual machine capable of executing code. Ether is the cryptocurrency used to pay for transactions on the network [3].

Ethereum has two account types, user and contracts. User-owned accounts can be controlled by anyone who has the private keys to this account while smart contracts are deployed to the network and are controlled by code. Smart contracts can be used to create a range of decentralized applications (dApps). An important feature of smart contracts is that when a function is called and the conditions for that function are met there is an automatic execution of the set instructions without any intermediary party [12,29].

Smart contracts are by design traceable, deterministic and irreversible [7,18]. Traceable because all transactions are recorded, therefore anyone can see and verify the state of a contract at any given point in time. Deterministic in the way the outcome after is identical for everyone who, given the same transaction parameters and state of the Ethereum blockchain, executes the contract [12]. Irreversible because once deployed, due to the nature of how a blockchain works, it is not possible to change the smart contract code (although its internal state may change). The only way to modify a smart contract code is to deploy a new instance (hence a new smart contract).

Important to note, contracts are only executed if called by an account (either a user or a contract). A contract can call a different contract that in its turn can then call another one. However, the initial trigger will always be a call by a user account (i.e., user request). All nested calls will either successfully complete or rollback and revert. If completed, the result from those calls will be saved into a transaction. While contract code can not be changed or patched, it can be "killed" which will stop the contract from receiving and responding to calls.

Executing any operation in Ethereum requires `Gas`. Gas is a resource to measure the computational effort required to execute specific operations. Gas is bought by the user triggering a call to a contract with Ether. This is considered a transactional fee, which is paid to the miner who spends computational resources executing and approving the transaction results from the original call. Gas prices are denoted in Gwei which is equal to 10^{-9} Ether. These fees help (among others) keep the network secure by preventing bad actors from spamming the network [9].

2.3 The `call()` function

The `call()` function is a low-level interface for sending a message to a contract and it is also a way to send Ether to another address. Combining the `Call` function with the possibility to install a fallback function opens up the possibility for a security exploit. Untrusted contracts may inject and execute malicious code via the fallback function.

2.4 Reentrancy Exploit

One of these major vulnerabilities is called the reentrancy exploit, which takes advantage of the transfer of execution control by making recursive calls back to the original contract, repeating executions, and creating new transactions.

The two main types of reentrancy exploit are: Single function, and Cross-function.

Single Function Reentrancy Exploit. This version repeatedly calls the involved function before the first invocation of the function is finished. Listing 1.1 shows the archetype code for this exploit; a withdraw function on a bank account.

```
1  pragma solidity ^0.8.14;
2  contract MyUnsafeBank {
3      mapping (address => uint) private _balances;
4      function deposit() public payable {
5          _balances[msg.sender] += msg.value;
6      }
7      function withdraw() public {
8          uint amount = _balances[msg.sender];
9          (bool success, ) = msg.sender.call{gas: gasleft(), value
               : amount}("");
10         if(success) _balances[msg.sender] = 0;
11     }
12 }
13 contract AttackerContract {
14     MyUnsafeBank private bank;
15     address payable private owner;
16     constructor(address toExploit) {
17         bank = MyUnsafeBank(toExploit);
18         owner = payable(msg.sender);
19     }
20     function makeDeposit() public payable {
21         bank.deposit{value: msg.value}();
22     }
23     function exploitReentrancy() public {
24         bank.withdraw();
25     }
26     function cashOut() public payable {
27         owner.transfer( address(this).balance );
28     }
29     // Fallback function executed automatically
30     fallback () external payable {
31         bank.withdraw();
32     }
33 }
```

Listing 1.1. Single function reentrancy exploit

In Listing 1.1, the contract `MyUnsafeBank` has two basic functions: deposit and withdraw. Every time someone sends money to this bank (by invoking `deposit()`), it will be added to total funds of the bank contract. The `_balances` hashmap (line 3) keeps track of how much money was sent by each account. In Solidity, `msg.value` has the amount of Ether sent, and `msg.sender` represents the address of whoever initiated this transaction (i.e., who called the function in this contract). The address can be either a user account or another contract. There is no way to know if the address in the other end belongs to a contract or a user.

This contract uses the unsafe `call()` function (line 9) to send money back to the address attached to it. The statement `msg.sender.call()` is calling back to the account address who initiated the withdraw function. In this case, since we want to send money together with the call, we need to specify the amount of Ether by using a JSON-like syntax `{value: amount}`. Since we also want to relay the leftover gas for the call operation to work, we add `gas: gasleft()` to it. Note that the extra options to send money and specify the gas relayed is not exclusive to `call`, and can be used on other functions as well.

The reentrancy vulnerability lies on the `withdraw` function. On line 9, the bank will call back whoever executed the withdraw function to send back its money. If that was a contract, it will trigger automatically its fallback function, while the bank code is still on hold on line 9 waiting for the fallback to finish. A malicious attacker contract can just code its fallback function to ask for another withdraw (lines 29–32). Since the bank contract did not update `_balances` yet (it will do so on line 10 after it completes the transfer), the attacker will get another withdraw and receive its money again, which triggers another fallback execution. This will repeat until the bank runs out of funds, or the transaction runs out of gas[2]. The attacker contract will end up with more money than it was supposed to, and the attacker can cash out the contract into his/her account (lines 26–28). Figure 1 shows a sequence diagram of this attack. We like to highlight there are no return arrows in the diagram because the returns will only happen when the reentrancy recursive calls stop.

Cross-Function Reentrancy Exploit. When a function shares a state with another function there is a possibility of a cross-function reentrancy exploit. In this exploit, an attacker reenters the same contract but through a different function than the one that triggered it. Listing 1.2 shows a code snippet with a cross-function reentrancy vulnerability.

```
pragma solidity ^0.8.14;
contract BetterButStillUnsafeBank {
    mapping (address => uint) private _balances;
    bool private lock = false;
    function deposit() public payable {
        _balances[msg.sender] += msg.value;
    }
    function withdraw() public {
        if(!lock){
            lock = true;
            uint amount = _balances[msg.sender];
            (bool success, ) = msg.sender.call{gas: gasleft(),
                value: amount}("");
            if(success) _balances[msg.sender] = 0;
            lock = false;
        }
    }
```

[2] For complex contracts, it may be necessary for the attacker to add precautions to avoid that his exploit triggers an exception. However, in this simple example, this is not necessary.

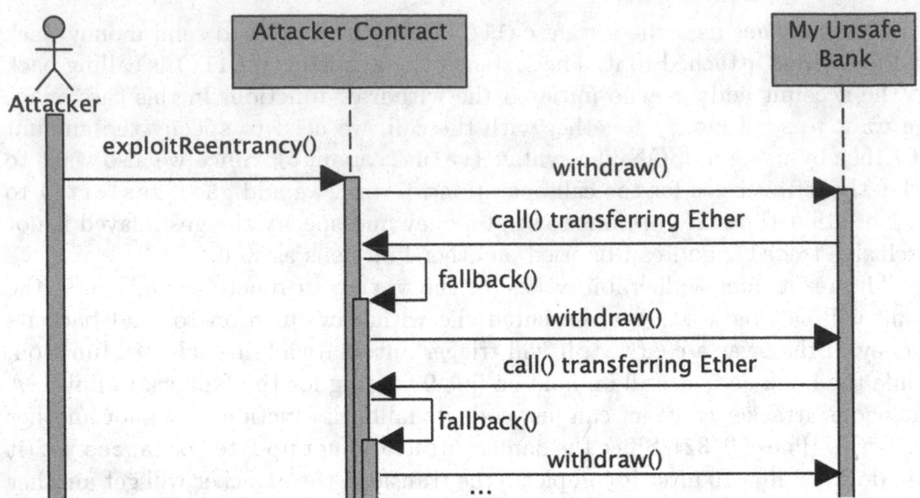

Fig. 1. Sequence Diagram of a Single Function Reentrancy Exploit.

```
17  function transmit(address to, uint amount) public {
18          if(_balances[msg.sender] >= amount ){
19                  _balances[msg.sender] -= amount;
20                  _balances[to] += amount;
21          }
22      }
23  }
```

Listing 1.2. Cross-function reentrancy exploit

In Listing 1.2, we improved the code from the previous example (Listing 1.1). We create a function to transfer balances between accounts in our bank (lines 17–22). We also introduced a state variable to prevent more than one access to `withdraw` at a given time (lines 4, 9, 10, and 14). Now, if the attacker uses the fallback to recall withdraw, it will have no effect.

Even though we protected against single function reentrancy, `transmit` function allows for a cross-function reentrancy exploit. In this case, the attacker will call for a withdraw as usual, which will send money back and trigger the fallback function. In the fallback, the attacker uses transmit instead of recalling withdraw. Since `_balances` was not updated yet, the transmit will go through. Assuming the attacker also controls the account receiving the transfer, he/she just doubled his money by receiving when calling withdrawn, and again by transmitting. Figure 2 shows a sequence diagram of this example of cross-function reentrancy.

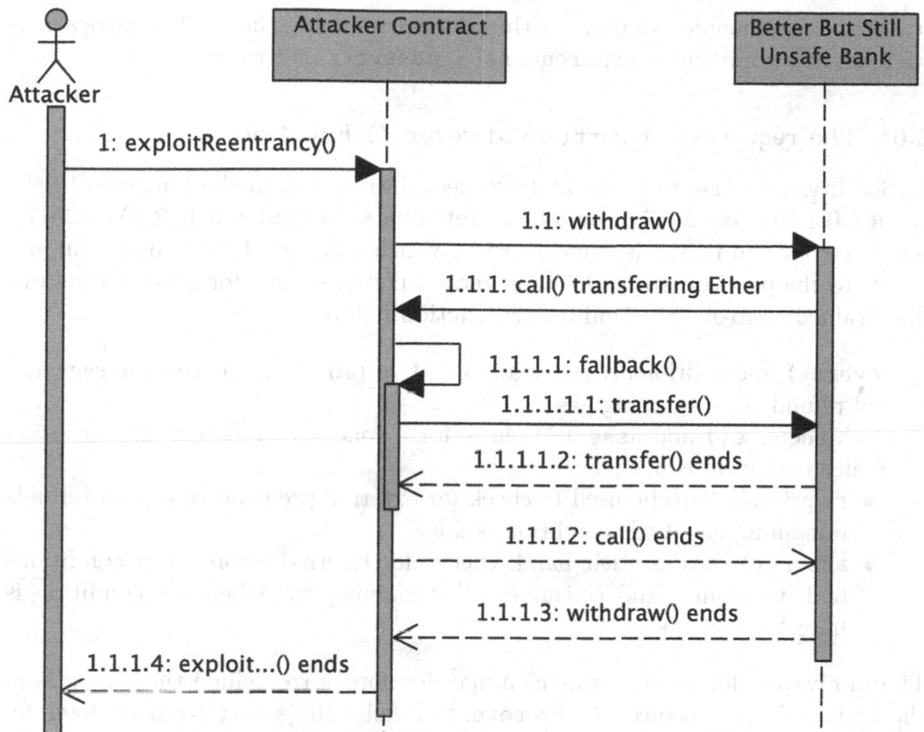

Fig. 2. Sequence diagram of a cross-function reentrancy exploit.

2.5 The `transfer()` and `send()` Functions

The `transfer()` function was first introduced in version 0.4.10 (May 2017) of the Solidity language. It provides a safe-by-design method to transfer cryptocurrency. Even though this function also transfers the execution control to the caller, it has a gas limit that prevents abuse. If the transfer fails, an exception is raised, which also adds to the security of this method as the exception reverts the transaction. Due to automatically reverting in case of errors, the transfer function is recommended in most cases.

Even though `send` existed in Solidity before, since the addition of transfer, `send()` function can be seen as a lower-level implementation of transfer. Similar to transfer, it provides a safe-by-design function to transfer cryptocurrency, with a gas limit to prevent exploits. The major difference between send and transfer, is that send returns false if it fails, delegating the error handling to the developer.

The original intention was to replace the function `call()` with these safe by design functions `transfer()` and `send()`. However, there has been a switch back to the `call()` function with the introduction of the Ethereum Improvement Proposal EIP 1884 in March 2019 [24]. Indeed, `transfer()` and `send()` limits the gas usage to a hard coded amount, which only makes sense when gas costs are constant. As illustrated by EIP 1884 gas costs do not remain constant, hence it is now recommended to refactor the code surrounding the `call()` invocations with explicit guard functions: `require()`, `assert()` and `revert()` [19].

2.6 The `require()`, `assert()` and `revert()` Functions

In Solidity, `require` and `assert` have been introduced to the language in the version 0.4.10 (May 2017); `revert` was introduced in version 0.4.12 (Aug 2017). All three of them may raise an exception, which will cancel the transaction and revert to the previous state. As such, these functions allow for a lower-level but fine grained control over handling transaction failure.

- `revert()` unconditionally raises an exception providing an error message and will refund the remaining gas.
- Both `require()` and `assert()` check for a condition and raise an exception if such condition is not met.
  - `require()` is to be used to check for external pre-conditions and refunds remaining gas if the condition is false.
  - `assert()` on the other hand, checks for internal errors (post-conditions and invariants) and consumes all remaining gas when the condition is false.[3]

The motivation for these is to encourage developers to include these guards in the code. When a `require()` or `revert()` fails, the smart contract flags an illegitimate logic assumption, hence is the problem of the party invoking the contract. When an `assert()` fails, something very wrong and unexpected has happened and it is the problem of the contract currently executing.

2.7 Static Analysis and Formal Verification

The `require()` and `assert()` statements are meant to be supported by static analysis and formal verification tools [2]. By analysing the code the conditions which could break a contract (fail an `assert()`) can be identified. Conversely, such tools may prove that your contract operates as designed without flaws provided that the input is valid (i.e., the `require()` condition holds).

Indeed, Solidity implements a formal verification approach by passing the code to the SMTChecker, where SMT stands for "Satisfiability Modulo Theories". The SMTChecker module implements two different reasoning engines, a bounded model checker and a system of constrained horn clauses. By default both engines are used, where the horn solver runs first, and every property that was not proven is passed over to the bounded model checker. The engines are independent and each of them state explicitly which one of them issues a warning. If no warning is given by the SMTChecker for a property, it means that the property is safe. The warnings can take two forms.

[3] Note that with the release of Solidity v0.8.0 `assert` also refunds all remaining gas. So `assert` and `require` generate the same opcodes for reverting transactions in the Ethereum virtual machine, however, their intended use remains completely different.

- `<failing property> happens here.` The SMTChecker proved that a certain property will fail. A counterexample may be given, in not too complex situations
- `<failing property> might happen here.` The SMTChecker could not prove either case within the given timeout. Since the result is unknown, the SMTChecker reports the potential failure for soundness.

Note that the current implementation of the SMTChecker is incomplete but sound. We cite the relevant paragraph in the Solidity documentation [8]:

> *The SMTChecker implements abstractions in an incomplete and sound way: If a bug is reported, it might be a false positive introduced by abstractions (due to erasing knowledge or using a non-precise type). If it determines that a verification target is safe, it is indeed safe, that is, there are no false negatives (unless there is a bug in the SMTChecker).*

3 Research Questions

Reentrancy exploits are a major concern for the Ethereum platform, hence the community took special precautions to prevent these exploits from happening. One of these preventive measures is to refactor code, surrounding unsafe `call()` invocations with `require()` and `assert()` to guard against malicious code. Moreover, The `require()` and `assert()` statements are supported by an SMTChecker which attempts to prove that the `assert()` statement will never fail, provided that the `require()` conditions hold.

For the moment, there exists no research on the adoption of these safe constructs in deployed contracts. In the same vein, it is currently unknown whether the warnings issued by the SMTChecker may confirm that the code is safe with respect to reentrancy exploits.
Consequently, we forward two research questions.

1. *Does the Ethereum community adopt safe code patterns?* To answer this research question we collect a dataset containing the source code of smart contracts actually deployed on the Ethereum platform. A cursory analysis of the use of `require()` and `assert()` (and to a lesser degree `revert()`) provides an initial indication. A deeper analysis of the actual source could provide a definite answer.
2. *Can the SMTChecker ensure that safe code patterns guard against reentrancy exploits?* To answer this research question, we refactor problematic code constructs incorporating documented safe code patterns, including the necessary guards. When running such code through the SMTChecker we verify whether the tool confirms the code to be safe, or whether it issues (false) alarms.

4 RQ1: Adoption of Safe Code Patterns

When we started this research there was no publicly available dataset containing actual contracts deployed on the Ethereum platform. Therefore, we created such dataset ourselves. The dataset is publicly available on the figshare platform[4].

We collected verified smart contracts from Etherscan[5] which is a block explorer and analytic platform for Ethereum. The Etherscan verified contracts platform allows the public to audit and read contracts as it has to be made publicly available to be granted the verified status. Etherscan does not give access to a complete dataset of verified smart contracts but rather has an open-source database of the latest 5,000–10,000 smart contracts that were verified. Therefore, we periodically gathered the latest contracts over a period of six months (2021-07-07 to 2022-01-06) to construct our dataset.
Then, we performed the following pre-processing steps to arrive at a clean dataset.

1. Remove duplicated contracts. We removed contracts with the same address in the Ethereum blockchain. We did not verify whether the contracts with the same name have the same source code. Since these contracts have different addresses, they are considered separate entities in the blockchain platform.
2. Retrieve the source code for a given contract id via the Etherscan API [10]. Listing 1.3 shows the corresponding code snippet. Listing 1.3 shows an example of the API call used to acquire the contract source code.
3. Scrape the HTML to obtain the actual source code.
4. Remove contracts not written in Solidity.
5. Remove contracts which we could not process using `cloc` or `slither`. `cloc` is a tool to count lines of code and was used for collecting descriptive statistics. `slither` is a tool which among others flags reentrancy vulnerabilities on the contracts.

```
https://api.etherscan.io/api?module=contract
&action=getsourcecode
&address=<ContractAddress>
&apikey=<YourApiKeyToken>
```

Listing 1.3. Etherscan API call

Table 1 provides an overview of the usage of `call`, `transfer`, `send`, `require`, `assert` and `revert` in all of the 26,799 contracts we obtained this way.

[4] https://figshare.com/projects/Open-Source_Solidity_Smart_Contracts/145629.
[5] https://etherscan.io/contractsVerified.

Table 1. Indication of safe code patterns

Method	Contracts	Total
call	13,443 (50%)	32,236
send	647 (02%)	1,059
transfer	9,176 (34%)	17,814
require	26,190 (97%)	622,679
assert	7,279 (27%)	10,507
revert	13,819 (51%)	41,502

We point out that many contracts use `require` (97%) which is a good sign as it suggests that pre-conditions are at least checked. Further research is warranted though as the number of `assert` statements is relatively low (27%), hence post-conditions are seldom verified. Note as well that the safe by design methods `send` and `transfer` remain to be used. It is yet unknown how the use of `require` and `assert` are used to guard `call` statements.

In Table 2, we assess the percentage of contracts indicating safe code patterns (`call`, `send`, `transfer`, `require`, `assert`, and `revert`) per major version of Solidity. We also included the percentage considering all contracts for comparison. We observe indeed a correlation between the usage of the methods under analysis and the version of solidity. For instance, versions 0.7.x and 0.6.x have a higher percentage of contracts using call than the normal, and versions 0.5.x and 0.4.x have a lower percentage. Considering the transfer method, version 0.7.x and 0.4.x show a higher percentage of contracts using transfer.

Table 2. Indication of safe code patterns by major version

	call	send	transfer	require	assert	revert
0.4.x	8%	3%	48%	92%	51%	39%
0.5.x	16%	<1%	29%	96%	32%	20%
0.6.x	79%	<1%	32%	98%	68%	79%
0.7.x	67%	1%	42%	98%	32%	66%
0.8.x	44%	3%	33%	98%	8%	45%
all	50%	2%	34%	97%	27%	51%

RQ1: Does the Ethereum community adopt safe code patterns? While the results are inconclusive, Table 1 and Table 2 suggest that the community is at least aware of the safe constructs. A deeper analysis of the code in the dataset should allow for a more refined analysis. This is however out of scope for this paper.

5 RQ2: SMTChecker for Safe Code Refactorings

In this section we discuss two different refactorings that should eliminate potential exploits in a smart contract. We list explicitly what properties should be verified formally to guarantee that the syntactic construct is secure.

We then report whether the SMTPChecker provided in the Solidity compiler confirms that the post-conditions will always hold when the pre-condition is satisfied. To use this, we loaded the code on Remix[6]; a web-platform providing an integrated development environment for experimenting with Solidity contracts. We compiled the code below with the 0.8.14 version of the solidity compiler, configuring the SMTPChecker to run both modules and to report unproved assertions. We report the warnings given concerning the pre- and post-conditions and interpret the results.

5.1 Checks-Effects-Interactions

The goal of this refactoring is to reduce the attack surface for malicious contracts who try to hijack control flow after a call. As mentioned before, control flow will be transferred to an external contract when calling another address. In case we have a bad actor, this can cause unexpected behavior and possibly allow the attacker to repeatedly invoke functions that should've been only executed once.

The Checks-Effects-Interactions refactoring updates all state variables prior to any external call [13]. In other words, the effect is accounted for before completion. By using pre- and post-conditions, we can abort the entire transaction if anything goes wrong, thus safeguarding legitimate users from possible issues. We present a code example (Listing 1.4) illustrating this refactoring. In this example, we changed the `withdraw` function in our bank from previous examples, to allow the caller to specify the amount he/she wants to withdraw (instead of always withdrawing the whole balance).

```
pragma solidity ^0.8.14;
contract SafeBank {
    mapping (address => uint) private _balances;
    function deposit() public payable {
        _balances[msg.sender] += msg.value;
    }
    function withdraw(uint amount) public {
        require(amount!=0 ); // checks -- pre-condition
        require(_balances[msg.sender] >= amount ); // checks --
            pre- condition
        _balances[msg.sender] -= amount; // effects
        (bool success, ) = msg.sender.call{gas: gasleft(), value
            : amount}(""); // interactions
        assert(success); // verify success, if not abort the
            transaction and restore the gas
    }
}
```

Listing 1.4. Checks Effects Interactions pattern with explicit pre- and post-conditions

[6] https://remix.ethereum.org/.

First, we check the basic pre-conditions (i.e. the *checks* part of the pattern) before initiating the withdraw function (lines 8 and 9). In this case, we verify the amount is not zero and the user has enough balance to cover that amount. Since amount is an unsigned integer, we do not need to check for negative values. Second, we change the internal state of the contract (line 10) by updating `_balances` before sending the money. This represents the *effects* part of the pattern. Third, we call the user and send his/her money (line 11), and that is where we (safely) interact with another account. If anything goes wrong and the money is not sent, we just raise an exception (line 12), aborting the current transaction The money and user balance will revert to its previous state before executing this function. This will safeguard user balances from any possible issues outside their control.

The post-condition in line 12 represents the condition that should be verified, assuming that the pre-conditions in lines 8–9 hold. The SMTChecker issued the following warnings.

```
Warning CHC: Assertion Violation happens here.
  - line 12 | assert(success)
```

The CHC checker (i.e. based on constrained horn clauses) infers that there exists at least one execution path that will fail the post-condition. Unfortunately, checker does not provide a counter example so one can only guess how this may happen. Nevertheless, given that the post-condition is immediately tied to the successful completion of the `call()` invocation on line 11, it implies that `call()` may fail but that the transaction will then abort.

5.2 Mutex

A simple way of protecting the state of a contract is by adding a state variable to control mutual exclusion (mutex) in functions. This refactoring —when correctly applied— is especially useful when dealing with cross-function reentrancy exploits. The concept is to protect pieces of code where shared resources are accessed. To utilize these resources the mutex will first need to be unlocked as it will only be possible for the resource to be changed by one process or function at a time.

We show an example of mutex in Listing 1.5. This is a modified version of our previous example with cross-function reentrancy vulnerability (Listing 1.2). The previous example failed because we only added a mutex in withdraw (16, 17, 21, and 22), while leaving transmit open for reentrancy. Here, we added the mutex lock to the `transmit` (lines 26, 28, 35, and 36) and `deposit` (lines 6, 7, 11, and 12) as well. This will prevent cross-function reentrancy entirely since the mutex ensures that only a single public function can be active. An attacker calling withdraw to trigger his/her own fallback function, may attempt to reenter by calling withdraw or transmit before the original withdraw finishes. However, thanks to the mutex, calling either withdraw or transmit will not do a thing. We only added mutex to deposit for completeness, although this may be considered overkill because reentering this function during a withdraw will cause the attacker to lose money.

```
pragma solidity ^0.8.14;
contract MutexBank {
    mapping (address => uint) private _balances;
    bool private lock = false; //Mutex
    function deposit() public payable {
        require(!lock);
        lock = true;
        uint originalBalance = _balances[msg.sender];
        _balances[msg.sender] += msg.value;
        uint newBalance = _balances[msg.sender];
        lock = false;
        assert(!lock);
        assert(originalBalance + msg.value == newBalance);
    }
    function withdraw() public {
        require(!lock);
        lock = true;
        uint amount = _balances[msg.sender];
        (bool success, ) = msg.sender.call{gas: gasleft(), value
            : amount}("");
        if(success) _balances[msg.sender] = 0;
        lock = false;
        assert(!lock);
        assert(_balances[msg.sender] == 0);
   }
    function transmit(address to, uint amount) public {
        require(!lock);
        require(_balances[msg.sender] >= amount );
        lock = true;
        uint originalFromBalance = _balances[msg.sender];
        uint originalToBalance = _balances[to];
        _balances[msg.sender] -= amount;
        _balances[to] += amount;
        uint newFromBalance = _balances[msg.sender];
        uint newToBalance = _balances[to];
        lock = false;
        assert(!lock);
        assert(originalFromBalance - amount == newFromBalance);
        assert(originalToBalance + amount == newToBalance);
    }
}
```

Listing 1.5. Mutual exclusion

Note that at every end of a function we add a series of assert statements to verify whether the post-condition does hold. For the mutex, this means that upon completion to lock should be released (`assert(!lock)`). We also verify whether the internal state of the balance is updated properly. For `deposit`, the new balance should be an increase compared to the old balance. For `withdraw`, the new balance should be zero (i.e. we withdraw all the ether). For `transmit`, the new balance and old balance from the two accounts involved should be increased and decreased by the same amount.

The post-conditions in lines 12–13, 22–23, 36–38, represent the conditions that should formally be verified, assuming that the pre-conditions in lines 6, 16, 26–27 (respectively) hold. The SMTChecker issued the following warnings.

```
Warning CHC: Error trying to invoke SMT solver.
  - line 37 | assert(originalFromBalance - amount ==
      newFromBalance);
Warning CHC: Assertion Violation might happen here.
  - line 12 | assert(!lock);
  - line 13 | assert(originalBalance + msg.value == newBalance);
  - line 22 | assert(!lock);
  - line 23 | assert(_balances[msg.sender] == 0);
  - line 36 | assert(!lock);
  - line 37 | assert(originalFromBalance - amount ==
      newFromBalance);
Warning CHC: Assertion Violation happens here.
  - line 38 | assert(originalToBalance + amount == newToBalance);
Warning BMC: Assertion Violation happens here.
  - line 23 | assert(_balances[msg.sender] == 0);
  (Counterexample
      _balances[msg.sender] = 14098
     amount = 4683
     gasleft = 0
     lock = false
     success = false
```

The CHC checker infers that there exists at least one execution path that will fail the post-condition on line 38. All other post-conditions (lines 12, 13, 22, 23, 36 and 37) are flagged as potentially problematic. (The one in line 37 causes problems initially but apparently was analysed anyway.) These were then passed on to the bounded model checker (BMC), which generated a counter example for the post-condition in line 23.

RQ2: Can the SMTChecker ensure that safe code patterns guard against reentrancy exploits? The two code samples (Listing 1.4) and Listing 1.5) demonstrate that the default SMTChecker cannot ensure that the post-conditions will always hold. Whether this is because of the documented incompleteness of the SMTChecker (e.g., array aliasing is explicitly not supported) or whether there indeed exist executions that would lead to unsatisfied post-conditions is subject for future research.

6 Related Work

In this paper, we investigate how to guard against reentrancy exploits in Solidity. In particular, we want to confirm whether the safe code patterns guarding potentially unsafe `call()` constructs with `require()` and `assert()` are indeed secure. To complement this theoretical analysis, we present a dataset of 26,799 unique open-source verified smart contracts from Etherscan. In this section, we list related work concerning (a) static analysis tools that identify vulnerabilities in Solidity; (b) verification tools which aim to verify that certain properties hold and (c) datasets where one can empirically validate such tools.

6.1 Static Analysis Tools

Securify. Tsankov et al. created a tool named Securify [26]. The tool first executes a symbolic analysis of the contract's dependency graph to extract precise semantic information about the contract code. Then it checks this representation against a series of known problematic coding idioms. The tool has been validated on more than 18000 contracts submitted by users; these contracts are not publicly available.

Slither by Feist et al. [11] is a static analysis framework that converts Solidity smart contracts into an intermediate representation which they call SlithIR. Static Single Assignment forms are used as well as a reduced instruction set for ease of implementation. Their framework has use cases in automated detection of vulnerabilities, detection of code optimization opportunities, improvement of clarity and ease of understanding of the contracts. An evaluation of the proposed frameworks capabilities is done using a set of real-world smart contracts.

Oyente. Luu et al. [18] also investigate and introduce several security problems to manipulate smart contracts in an attempt to gain profit and propose ways to enhance the operational semantics of Ethereum. A focus is put on the semantic gap between the assumption contract writers make about the underlying execution semantics and the actual semantics of the contract are made as a reason for these security flaws. The authors present an accompanying tool (named Oyente) which is a symbolic execution tool. The model works directly with Ethereum virtual machine byte code and does not have a need for a higher level representation such as Solidity. An evaluation of Oyente on 19,366 smart contracts is given where 8,333 contracts were documented as potentially having bugs.

ReGuard. Liu et al. [17] present ReGuard which is a fuzzing-based analyzer to automatically detect reentrancy bugs in Ethereum smart contracts. They iteratively generate random (but diverse) transactions, i.e. a variant of fuzz testing. Then based on the runtime they will identify reentrancy vulnerabilities in a contract. How the architecture works is they parse a smart contracts source or binary code to an intermediate representation which will then be transformed to C++, keeping the original behavior. Together with a runtime library, ReGuard executes the contract and runs an analysis of the operations for any reentrancy exploits.

SmartCheck is an extensible static analysis tool created by Tikhomirov et al. which detects code issues in Solidity [25]. The tools translates Solidity into an XML-based representation and checks it against XPath patterns. The authors used a real-world dataset to evaluate their tool and make a comparison to the earlier mentioned Oyente.

ContractWard. Wang et al. [28] evaluate a set of real-world smart contracts with ContractWard which uses machine learning techniques to detect vulnerabilities in smart contracts. Their idea was proposed due to existing detection methods being mainly based on symbolic execution or analysis which are very time-consuming. The system extracts dimensional bigram features from simplified operation codes to construct a feature space and can get a predictive recall and precision of over 96% based on their dataset of 49502 smart contracts on 6 vulnerabilities.

All of the above tools are capable of detecting potential reentrancy exploits. These tools could be used to extend the preliminary analysis presented in Sect. 4. By filtering out those contracts which do invoke `call()` but do not suffer from reentrancy exploits, we could mine for additional safe code patterns. Conversely, we could investigate whether the contracts which are vulnerable to reentrancy exploits may indeed be refactored to make them safe.

6.2 Verification Tools

Besides the above there are other researchers who created static analysis tools for Solidity aiming to prove that certain annotations (assertions) hold.

SOLC-VERIFY. Hajdu et al. created created a source-level verification tool for Ethereum smart contracts [14]. Just like SMTChecker, the tool uses modular program analysis and SMT solvers. However, unlike SMTChecker extra annotations could be provided to give hints to the tool.

Framing Conditions. Beckert and Schiffle investigated framing conditions as a way to express where the internal state of a Solidity program is modified and conversely where it should remain unchanged [5]. Once the correctness of a function with respect to a `modifies` clause has been established, that knowledge can be used in further correctness proofs.

eThor. Schneidewind1 et al. reviewed the existing approaches to automated, sound, static analysis of Ethereum smart contracts [23]. They deduce that all of them have shortcomings and present eThor, a static analyzer for EVM bytecode which is claimed to be efficient and sound.

SolidiKeY. Ahrendt et al. based themselves on the KeY framework for automatic verification to present an invariant-based verification tool [1]. The tool prototype, verifies strong data integrity properties (expressed as contract invariants) for Solidity smart contracts by means of symbolic execution.

VerX. Permenev et al. created a tool which allows to specify and verify temporal properties of annotated Solidity code [21]. The tool has been used to prove 83 properties of 12 real-world Ethereum projects.

The above tools are complementary to the analysis reported in Sect. 5. It remains to be seen whether these tools could improve upon the warnings as generated by the SMTChecker provided in the Solidity compiler [2].

6.3 Datasets

While a wide variety of code checkers exist, all of these tools have been validated on datasets created by the authors themselves. Up until now, surprisingly few public datasets or benchmarks exist. When we started our research, there were no public datasets that we were aware of. However, from 2020 onward the research community started publishing their datasets.

Smart Corpus. Pierro et al. are the first to create a realistic and sustained attempt at creating and maintaining a growing repository [22]. Just like ours, their dataset contains a series of contracts mined from the Etherscan platform on a regular basis. [https://aphd.github.io/smart-corpus/.]

Smart Contract Santuary. This team had the same approach as what we reported, a repository of ethereum smart contracts verfied on Etherscan. [https://github.com/tintinweb/smart-contract-sanctuary.]

SmartBugs is an execution framework aiming at simplifying the execution of analysis tools on datasets of smart contracts. The web-site also provides three distinct datasets: SBCurated, SBWild and SolidiFI benchmark. SBCurated is particularly interesting as it explicitly lists all contracts which suffer from an reentrancy vulnerability. [https://smartbugs.github.io.]

Trending Contracts. Ibba merged three existing datasets into one, to study trends in the contracts being deployed [15]. [https://github.com/giacomofi/Top-Trending-Contracts.]

Where happy to see that in the last two years several teams initiated the creation of datasets containing smart contracts actually deployed on the Ethereum platform. This will allow to refine the analysis on the adoption of safe code patterns reported in Sect. 4.

7 Conclusion

Solidity is one of the major programming languages for smart contracts on the Ethereum platform. Unfortunately, the platform received a bad reputation due to the DAO Attack in June 2016 where around 3.6 million Ether was taken. The root cause for this security breach was a reentrancy exploit and since then the community took special precautions to prevent these exploits from happening.

The current state of the practice recommends to use *safe code patterns*. A software engineer adopting such a patterns needs to refactor the code and surround the potentially unsafe `call()` function with appropriate pre- and post-conditions (via `require()` and `assert()`). In this paper we presented two such safe code patterns (namely "Check Effects" and "Mutex") and showed that the built-in Solidity SMTChecker is unable to guarantee that the contract is indeed protected against a reentrancy exploit. To complement this theoretical analysis, we created a dataset of 26,799 unique open-source verified smart contracts from Etherscan. We invite the community to use this dataset for further empirical evaluation of safe constructs surrounding potentially unsafe `call()` invocations.

References

1. Ahrendt, W., Bubel, R.: Specifying functional verification of smart contracts via strong data integrity. In: Margaria, T., Steffen, B. (eds.) Leveraging Applications of Formal Methods, Verification and Validation: Applications. pp. 43–59. Springer, Cham (2020). https://doi.org/10.1007/978-3-030-61467-6_2
2. Alt, L., Reitwiessner, C.: SMT-based verification of solidity smart contracts. In: Margaria, T., Steffen, B. (eds.) ISoLA 2018. LNCS, vol. 11247, pp. 376–388. Springer, Cham (2018). https://doi.org/10.1007/978-3-030-03427-6_28
3. Antonopoulos, A., Wood, G., Wood, G.: Mastering Ethereum: Building Smart Contracts and DApps. O'Reilly Media, Incorporated (2018). https://books.google.be/books?id=SedSMQAACAAJ
4. Atzei, N., Bartoletti, M., Cimoli, T.: A survey of attacks on ethereum smart contracts (SoK). In: Maffei, M., Ryan, M. (eds.) Principles of Security and Trust, pp. 164–186. Springer, Berlin (2017). https://doi.org/10.1007/978-3-642-54792-8
5. Beckert, B., Schiffl, J.: Specifying framing conditions for smart contracts. In: Margaria, T., Steffen, B. (eds.) ISoLA 2020. LNCS, vol. 12478, pp. 43–59. Springer, Cham (2020). https://doi.org/10.1007/978-3-030-61467-6_4
6. Bhargavan, K., et al.: Formal verification of smart contracts: Short paper. In: Proceedings of the 2016 ACM Workshop on Programming Languages and Analysis for Security, pp. 91–96. PLAS 2016, Association for Computing Machinery, New York, NY, USA (2016). https://doi.org/10.1145/2993600.2993611, https://doi.org/10.1145/2993600.2993611
7. Bragagnolo, S., Rocha, H.S.C., Denker, M., Ducasse, S.: SmartInspect: solidity Smart Contract Inspector. In: IWBOSE 2018–1st International Workshop on Blockchain Oriented Software Engineering. IEEE, Campobasso, Italy, March 2018. https://doi.org/10.1109/IWBOSE.2018.8327566, https://hal.inria.fr/hal-01831075
8. Ethereum: Solidity documentation (0.8.16) (2022). https://docs.soliditylang.org/en/v0.8.16/index.html
9. ethereum.org: Ethereum development documentation (2021). https://ethereum.org/en/developers/docs/
10. Etherscan: Etherscan API knowledge base (2021). https://docs.etherscan.io/api-endpoints/contracts
11. Feist, J., Grieco, G., Groce, A.: Slither: a static analysis framework for smart contracts. In: 2019 IEEE/ACM 2nd International Workshop on Emerging Trends in Software Engineering for Blockchain (WETSEB), pp. 8–15 (2019). https://doi.org/10.1109/WETSEB.2019.00008
12. Foundation, E.: Ethereum's white paper (2014). https://ethereum.org/en/whitepaper/
13. fravoll: Checks effects interactions pattern (2018). https://fravoll.github.io/solidity-patterns/checks_effects_interactions.html
14. Hajdu, Á., Jovanović, D.: SOLC-VERIFY: a modular verifier for solidity smart contracts. In: Chakraborty, S., Navas, J.A. (eds.) VSTTE 2019. LNCS, vol. 12031, pp. 161–179. Springer, Cham (2020). https://doi.org/10.1007/978-3-030-41600-3_11
15. Ibba, G.: A smart contracts repository for top trending contracts. In: 5th International Workshop on Emerging Trends in Software Engineering for Blockchain (WETSEB), p. 8 (2022)

16. Juels, A., Kosba, A., Shi, E.: The ring of Gyges: investigating the future of criminal smart contracts. In: Proceedings of the 2016 ACM SIGSAC Conference on Computer and Communications Security, pp. 283–295. CCS '16, Association for Computing Machinery, New York, NY, USA (2016). https://doi.org/10.1145/2976749.2978362,https://doi.org/10.1145/2976749.2978362
17. Liu, C., Liu, H., Cao, Z., Chen, Z., Chen, B., Roscoe, B.: ReGuard: Finding reentrancy bugs in smart contracts. In: Proceedings of the 40th International Conference on Software Engineering: Companion Proceeedings, ICSE 2018, pp. 65–68. Association for Computing Machinery, New York, NY, USA (2018). https://doi.org/10.1145/3183440.3183495, https://doi.org/10.1145/3183440.3183495
18. Luu, L., Chu, D.H., Olickel, H., Saxena, P., Hobor, A.: Making smart contracts smarter. In: Proceedings of the 2016 ACM SIGSAC Conference on Computer and Communications Security, CCS 2016, pp. 254–269, Association for Computing Machinery, New York, NY, USA (2016). https://doi.org/10.1145/2976749.2978309, https://doi.org/10.1145/2976749.2978309
19. Marx, S.: Stop using solidity's transfer() now, September 2020. https://consensys.net/diligence/blog/2019/09/stop-using-soliditys-transfer-now/
20. Nakamoto, S.: Bitcoin: a peer-to-peer electronic cash system (2008)
21. Permenev, A., Dimitrov, D., Tsankov, P., Drachsler-Cohen, D., Vechev, M.: Verx: Safety verification of smart contracts. In: 2020 IEEE Symposium on Security and Privacy (SP), pp. 1661–1677 (2020). https://doi.org/10.1109/SP40000.2020.00024
22. Pierro, G.A., Tonelli, R., Marchesi, M.: An organized repository of ethereum smart contracts' source codes and metrics. Fut. Internet **12**(11) (2020). https://doi.org/10.3390/fi12110197, https://www.mdpi.com/1999-5903/12/11/197
23. Schneidewind, C., Scherer, M., Maffei, M.: The Good, the bad and the ugly: pitfalls and best practices in automated sound static analysis of ethereum smart contracts. In: Margaria, T., Steffen, B. (eds.) ISoLA 2020. LNCS, vol. 12478, pp. 212–231. Springer, Cham (2020). https://doi.org/10.1007/978-3-030-61467-6_14
24. Swende, M.H.: EIP-1884: Repricing for trie-size-dependent opcodes (2019). https://eips.ethereum.org/EIPS/eip-1884
25. Tikhomirov, S., Voskresenskaya, E., Ivanitskiy, I., Takhaviev, R., Marchenko, E., Alexandrov, Y.: Smartcheck: static analysis of ethereum smart contracts. In: Proceedings of the 1st International Workshop on Emerging Trends in Software Engineering for Blockchain, pp. 9–16. WETSEB 2018, Association for Computing Machinery, New York, NY, USA (2018). https://doi.org/10.1145/3194113.3194115, https://doi.org/10.1145/3194113.3194115
26. Tsankov, P., Dan, A., Drachsler-Cohen, D., Gervais, A., Bünzli, F., Vechev, M.: Securify: practical security analysis of smart contracts. In: Proceedings CCS2018 (ACM SIGSAC Conference on Computer and Communications Security), pp. 67–82. Association for Computing Machinery, New York, NY, USA (2018). https://doi.org/10.1145/3243734.3243780
27. Verheijke, D., Rocha, H.: An exploratory study on solidity guards and ether exchange constructs. In: 5th International Workshop on Emerging Trends in Software Engineering for Blockchain (WETSEB), p. 8 (2022)
28. Wang, W., et al.: Contractward: automated vulnerability detection models for ethereum smart contracts. IEEE Trans. Netw. Sci. Eng. **8**(2), 1133–1144 (2021). https://doi.org/10.1109/TNSE.2020.2968505
29. Wood, G.: Ethereum: a secure decentralized generalised transaction ledger. Ethereum Project Yellow Paper, 151, 1–32 (2018)

A Refactoring for Data Minimisation Using Formal Verification

Florian Lanzinger, Mattias Ulbrich, and Alexander Weigl(✉)

Karlsruhe Institute of Technology, Karlsruhe, Germany
{lanzinger,ulbrich,weigl}@kit.edu

Abstract. Concerns about protecting private user data grow as automated data processing by software becomes more ubiquitous in our society. One important principle is *data minimisation*, which requires that all collected personal data must be limited to what is necessary for the respective declared purpose. For existing software systems, it can be difficult to determine which input data are indeed necessary to compute the result and which data can (in certain cases) be left out. We present a new approach that can be used to adapt an existing program to data minimisation requirements. In this framework a user transmits a set of facts about their data instead of the full data. We formally define the approach and introduce a variety of minimisation notions for it. We have implemented the approach and demonstrate its feasibility on a few selected examples.

1 Introduction

Motivation. In 2016, the European Union enacted the General Data Protection Regulation (GDPR) [3] to restrict the storage and use of personal data. Among other regulations, it defines the principle of *data minimisation*, which states that collected "[p]ersonal data shall be adequate, relevant and limited to what is necessary in relation to the purposes for which they are processed" [3, §5(1)(c)].

```
tax_rate(age, income) {
  if (age<18) return 0.0;
  if (age<25 && !(income>1000))
    return 0.1;
  if (income<=1000)
    return 0.2;
  return 0.3; }
```

Fig. 1. A simple program computes the tax rate based on age and income.

When one has to retrofit an existing piece of software to follow this principle, it may be difficult to determine what information from the personal data is necessary to compute the result and what can and should be left out.

Consider the example program in Fig. 1, taken from [9], which is run on a tax agency's server. The server receives an applicant's age and income as input

This work was supported by funding from the topic Engineering Secure Systems of the Helmholtz Association (HGF) and by KASTEL Security Research Labs and based on the research project SofDCar (19S21002), which is funded by the German Federal Ministry for Economic Affairs and Climate Action.

T. Margaria and B. Steffen (Eds.): ISoLA 2022, LNCS 13702, pp. 345–364, 2022.
https://doi.org/10.1007/978-3-031-19756-7_19

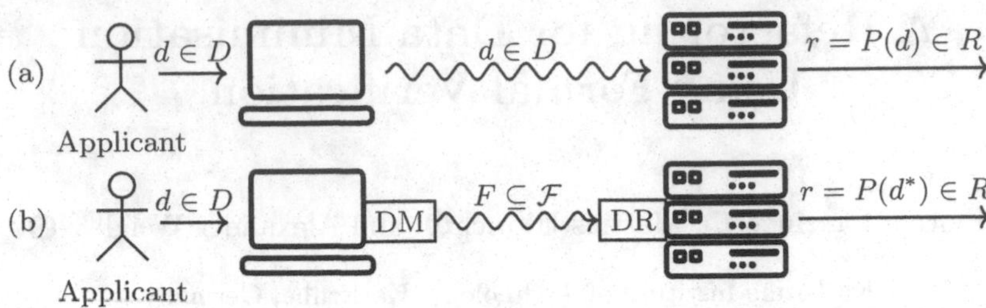

Fig. 2. Sketch of the scenario. In (a), the applicants transmit their individual personal data directly to the server of the agency. Using our approach in (b), the applicants can disguise their personal data d by transmitting a set of facts F.

and computes their tax rate. However, it would never be necessary to submit the exact age to determine the rate: it suffices to know if the age is below 18, between 18 and 24, or above 24. For the income, all that can be relevant is if it surpasses 1000 units. Moreover, if the applicant's age is below 18, it is not necessary to submit any information about the income, as the tax rate is always 0 below the age of 18. Thus, which data is needed to compute the result not only depends on the computed function, but also on the individual applicant's data themselves. With our approach, we enable applicants to selectively disclose their personal data. Instead of transmitting the full personal data, the applicant selects and transmits a set of true facts about their data which are sufficient to infer the result to be computed. These facts are predicates over the input variables of the program, and describe a set of data points in which the actual data point must lie. In our example, a 20-year-old applicant with an income of 2000 can transmit $\{age \geq 18, income \geq 1001\}$ and hence needs not disclose their exact age nor income. The server at the tax agency must then reconstruct an input value from the received facts and use it to compute the tax rate. We will show when and how this is possible.

Contribution. The definition of the minimisation problem which we use and a sketch for a heuristic solution were first introduced by Lanzinger and Weigl [9]. In this paper, we present a detailed formalisation of the problem and of the solution that we propose. We examine three different formal notions of minimisation, namely model-theoretic minimisation, information-theoretic minimisation and vulnerability minimisation based on different notions of entropy. We then present and compare several ways of algorithmically obtaining such (approximate) minimisations and show how they fit into the formal framework. We have implemented the approach based on existing formal analysis tools to obtain new software components to be added to the sending and receiving end of a distributed process without the original software needing to be changed.

Figure 2 shows how the presented approach adapts an existing pipeline. Figure 2(a) shows how the result (the tax rate in the example) is originally computed: The applicant uses a front end – like a web form – to submit a data point $d \in D$ (D denotes the set of personal data) containing their personal data to the back end server of the agency, which then runs a program P on d to compute the result r. Our data-minimisation approach is shown in Fig. 2(b): Instead of transmitting the data point d directly, the front end applies a data-minimising routine DM projecting d onto a fact set $F \subseteq \mathcal{F}$ that intuitively can be seen as a set of statements (logical formulas over the input variables of D) taken from a fact base of possible statements $\mathcal{F}$. This minimises the transmitted information in the sense that the agency gains less information about the applicant from F than it would gain by receiving d. The agency then uses the second component in our approach, the data restoration unit DR, to construct an arbitrary, but representative data point d^* which satisfies all facts in F. The data points d^* and d can, but need not be, the same. If F was well-chosen, the agency can compute the original result $r = P(d^*) = P(d)$ without having to modify their program and without knowing the exact value of d.

2 Background on Quantitative Information Flow

We will use some notions from quantitative information flow [14] (QIF) to quantify the amount of personal data sent to the agency. QIF is based on Shannon's information theory and different notions of entropy and conditional entropy, which we will briefly introduce here. QIF is used to measure the information flow from the inputs of a program to its outputs. Often, one quantifies the information that a system leaks, i.e., the amount of confidential information an attacker can learn by observing the output.

Let $\mathtt{D}$ and $\mathtt{O}$ be random variables that stand for the confidential input data ($\mathtt{D}$) and the output ($\mathtt{O}$) of a program that is observed by an adversary. The a-priori probability $\Pr(\mathtt{O} = o \mid \mathtt{D} = i)$ describes the probability that the observable output value o will be produced for a given input i. If the analysed program is deterministic, this is either 1 or 0. The a-posteriori probability $\Pr(\mathtt{D} = i \mid \mathtt{O} = o) = \frac{\Pr(\mathtt{D}=i)}{\Pr(\mathtt{O}=o)} \cdot \Pr(\mathtt{O} = o \mid \mathtt{D} = i)$ describes the probability of the input having been i under the observation of o. This can be used to talk about the amount of information that the adversary learns about the input by observing the output.

The gain of information by an adversarial attacker upon inspecting the output can be measured using different metrics. Two of them are the Shannon entropy and the min-entropy.

The Shannon entropy is usually understood as the uncertainty about an information source from which the observation comes, measured as the expected number of bits required to encode the data under an ideal encoding. The conditional Shannon entropy $H(\mathtt{D} \mid \mathtt{O})$ describes the number of bits required to encode information in $\mathtt{D}$ under the observation of $\mathtt{O}$:

$$\begin{aligned} H(\mathtt{D} \mid \mathtt{O}) &= \sum_o \Pr(\mathtt{O} = o) \cdot H(\mathtt{D} \mid \mathtt{O} = o) \\ &= \sum_o \Pr(\mathtt{O} = o) \cdot \left(\sum_i \Pr(\mathtt{D} = i \mid \mathtt{O} = o) \cdot \log_2 \frac{1}{\Pr(\mathtt{D} = i \mid \mathtt{O} = o)} \right) \end{aligned}$$

Alternatively, the vulnerability of a random variable X can be defined as the maximum probability $V(X) = \max_x \Pr(X = x)$ among the possible values of X. The idea is that a high vulnerability indicates that the correct data point can be guessed easily: The min-entropy of a random variable X is defined using the vulnerability as $H_\infty(X) = -\log_2 V(X)$. Additionally, the conditional vulnerability $V(\mathtt{D} \mid \mathtt{O} = o) = \max_i \Pr(\mathtt{D} = i \mid \mathtt{O} = o)$ measures the success rate when the attacker tries to guess the secret under a given observation o.

In the context of QIF, we are interested in the conditional entropy $H_\infty(\mathtt{D} \mid \mathtt{O})$ that describes the expected amount of information about the input that one receives upon observing the output. Formally, it is defined as follows.

$$\begin{aligned} H_\infty(\mathtt{D} \mid \mathtt{O}) &= \sum_o \Pr(\mathtt{O} = o) \cdot V(\mathtt{D} \mid \mathtt{O} = o) \\ &= -\log_2 \left(\sum_o \Pr(\mathtt{O} = o) \cdot (\max_i \Pr(\mathtt{D} = i \mid \mathtt{O} = o)) \right) \end{aligned}$$

3 Formalisation

This section formalises the notions of facts and information-theoretic minimality. We will see how we can apply this formalisation to implement our approach in the following sections.

3.1 Programs and Fact Bases

We consider a fixed domain D of possible personal data points and R the set of possible results. In the introductory example in Fig. 1, $D = \mathbb{N} \times \mathbb{N}$ and $R = [0.0, 1.0] \subseteq \mathbb{R}$. We consider the program to be data-minimised as a total and deterministic function $P\colon D \to R$ that maps a user's data point $d \in D$ to a result $r = P(d) \in R$.

A *fact* is a predicate $f \in 2^D$ on the set of data points D, characterised by those points that satisfy the predicate. Usually a predicate is syntactically represented as a constraint on the variables standing for the individual values within the data point. For example, we use the constraint $\mathtt{age} > 18$ to denote the set of data points $\{(\mathtt{age}, \mathtt{income}) \in D = \mathbb{N} \times \mathbb{N} \mid \mathtt{age} > 18\}$. We denote the set of all conceivable facts on the domain as $\mathbb{F} = 2^D$. We write $d \models f$ to indicate that the data point d satisfies the predicate $f \in \mathbb{F}$ and $d \models F$ to indicate that d satisfies all predicates in $F \subseteq \mathbb{F}$. In the following, we will generally not draw facts from $\mathbb{F}$. Instead, we assume that facts are taken from a *fact base*, a subset of predicates $\mathcal{F} \subseteq \mathbb{F}$. Not every set is suited as a fact base. For a given program P, we demand that for all possible data points d, we have a set of facts that uniquely identifies the result $P(d)$.

Definition 1 (honest fact sets and projections). *Given a point $d \in D$, we call a fact set F* honest about d *if $d \models F$. We call a projection $\pi : D \to 2^{\mathcal{F}}$* honest *if $d \models \pi(d)$ for every $d \in D$.*

Definition 2 (sufficiently precise fact sets and fact bases). *Let $P\colon D \to R$ be a program.*

A fact base $\mathcal{F} \subseteq \mathbb{F}$ is called sufficiently precise *for P if for all $d \in D$ there exists a sufficiently precise and honest set $F \subseteq \mathcal{F}$.*

A fact set $F \subseteq \mathcal{F}$ is called sufficiently precise *if there exists an $r \in R$ such that for all $d \in D$ with $d \models F$, we have $P(d) = r$.*

This property will be useful for the following decomposition of the computation of P. With reference to Fig. 2b, we can define two functions π_0 and ω that take the roles of the data minimisation DM and data restoration DR in the sketch. The *canonical projection* $\pi_0 : D \to 2^{\mathcal{F}}$ maps points $d \in D$ from the domain to all facts that are satisfied by d, i.e., $\pi_0(d) := \{f \in \mathcal{F} \mid d \models f\}$. The partial *witness* function $\omega : 2^{\mathbb{F}} \nrightarrow D$ produces for a fact set $F \subseteq \mathbb{F}$ a witness $\omega(F) \in D$ with $\omega(F) \models F$ iff such a value exists.

Observation 1. *Let $\mathcal{F}$ be a sufficiently precise fact base, then: $P = P \circ \omega \circ \pi_0$. The following diagram commutes:*

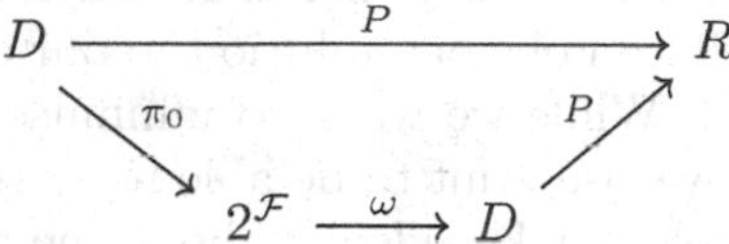

This follows from the following observation: If $\mathcal{F}$ is sufficiently precise, then the projection $\pi_0(d)$ is an honest, sufficiently precise fact set for every $d \in D$. This implies that $d' = \omega(\pi_0(d))$ returns a value with $P(d) = P(d')$.

Thus, it is possible on the front end to encode a point d in form of a set of predicates $\pi_0(d)$ and transmit that instead of d. On the back end, a witness $\omega(\pi_0(d))$ can be chosen to complete the computation by running the original program $P(\omega(\pi_0(d)))$ on the witness yielding $P(d)$. Note that it is not necessary that $\omega(\pi_0(d)) = d$, i.e., the back end need not be able to reconstruct the input data, but the witness will have the same result under P as d[1].

Where does the data minimisation happen here? It is in the function π_0 that maps to the facts that we lose information on the input data. In general, a set of constraints can have many satisfying assignments (models), π_0 is not an injection such that information is reduced here. At the same time, while the information is reduced, all transmitted facts must be valid statements on d.

In case there is doubt about the applicant having submitted an honest fact set, certificates proving the facts can be requested. For this, we assume that a set of certifiable facts $\mathcal{C} \subseteq F$ is given. Intuitively, a certificate $c \in \mathcal{C}$ is a fact which trusted third parties can attest (e.g., by inspecting legal documents), and this attestation can be audited (e.g., by digital signature). Of course, a certificate has to be honest, i.e., $d \models c$. For example, the applicant's electronic passport might can certify that $\mathsf{age} > 18$. We say that c is a certificate for a fact $f \in \mathbb{F}$ if $c \to f$.

[1] d will be in the same equivalence class in the kernel of P.

A large part of the remainder of the paper will address the challenges of designing suitable precise fact bases and identifying clever projection functions that can be used instead of the canonical projection π_0 while maintaining the property of Observation 1. Any honest projection π must obey $\pi(d) \subseteq \pi_0(d)$.

However, two corner-case fact bases are worth mentioning here ($\cong$ meaning that two sets are isomorphic):

$$\mathcal{F}_D = \{\{d\} \mid d \in D\} \cong D \qquad \mathcal{F}_R = \{\{d \mid P(d) = r\} \mid r \in R\} \cong P(D) \subseteq R$$

In the trivial fact base $\mathcal{F}_D$, every data point is captured by precisely one predicate (like $\mathit{income} = 1234 \wedge \mathit{age} = 37$). The canonical projection only wraps the concrete data in a unique predicate and the witness function unwraps them. This fact base covers the comparison 'base line' without data minimisation. On the other extreme, the fact base $\mathcal{F}_R$ loses as much information as possible on the front end and effectively transmits to the back end only the result of the computation P. This is the other end of the spectrum: It minimises the data most (according to any minimisation definition). In Sect. 4.1, we see an algorithm using the weakest precondition transformer that can compute $\mathcal{F}_R$.

Although this seems like an obvious solution to our data minimisation problem, it is also impractical. While we want to minimise the personal data that are initially transmitted, we also want to be able to certify the facts later. Using $\mathcal{F}_R$ as the fact base, all relevant knowledge about the applicant's data point d is encoded into a single fact, which is determined solely by the result $r = P(d)$. For certification by a third party, the applicant needs to fully disclose d to the third party that verifies that the result $r = P(d)$ was correctly computed. Using a fact base other than $\mathcal{F}_R$, the applicant may release more information initially, but less information later when certificates are requested.

3.2 Data Minimisation

After having set up the formal framework describing our approach, we can now focus on the actual question of data minimisation within the approach: A data point $d \in D$ is projected onto a set $\pi(d) \subseteq \mathbb{F}$ of facts. But since there are many possible fact bases and different possible projections that preserve data reconstructability, we need means to differentiate. The interesting question remains to be able to compare different sets of facts with respect to the information they divulge to the agency. We will discuss three notions in the following: (1) model-theoretic, (2) information-theoretic based on Shannon entropy and (3) vulnerability-driven based on min-entropy. For each notion, we define a different partial order $\preceq: 2^{\mathbb{F}} \times 2^{\mathbb{F}}$. We write $F \preceq F'$ if a fact set $F \subseteq \mathbb{F}$ carries less information (as defined by the picked notion) than another fact set $F' \subseteq \mathbb{F}$.

Model-Theoretic Minimisation. The first notion uses the sets of satisfying instances as a basis for an order on fact sets. For a fact set $F \subseteq \mathbb{F}$, the set of models (i.e., satisfying instances) $\mathit{models}(F) := \{d \in D \mid d \models F\}$ is the set of data points that satisfy all facts in F. A fact set with more satisfying data points in the model set sends less information about the actual value within this set to the agency. Intuitively, if there are more satisfying data points, the agency has a lower chance of guessing the correct one. Since, at least for now, we do not incorporate probability distributions over the data points, we will only compare sets by their model sets if one is a subset of the other. The more information a fact set conveys, the fewer models it has.

Definition 3 (Model-theoretic minimisation $\preceq_{mt}$). *Given two fact sets $F, F' \subseteq \mathbb{F}$, we say F carries model-theoretically at most as much information as F' and write $F \preceq_{mt} F'$ if all instances satisfying F' also satisfy F, i.e., if $models(F') \subseteq models(F)$.*

With this model-theoretic notion of 'more models implies less information' at hand, we can derive a syntactic notion which allows us to judge syntactic representations w.r.t. minimality.

Observation 2 (Syntactic minimisation). *Given two fact sets $F, F' \subseteq \mathbb{F}$ that are represented syntactically by two sets of constraints C, C' respectively, if $C \subseteq C'$, then $F \preceq_{mt} F'$.*

The opposite direction needs not hold, since the same fact may be expressed by syntactically incomparable constraints. Moreover, even if $C \subset C'$ is a strict subset, the conveyed information may remain the same if the constraints in $C' \setminus C$ are implied by C. For example, the fact set $\{age > 18\}$ contains less information than $\{age > 18, income > 1000\}$ but as much information as $\{age > 18, age > 17\}$.

For instance, if a fact set has only one model, it identifies the corresponding confidential data directly. If it has two models (and all data points are equally likely), then there is a 50 : 50 chance to guess the correct confidential data point.

Minimisation by Shannon-Entropy. Model-theoretic minimisation is a good measurement if the compared fact sets are in a subset relationship. Another approach allows us to assign a number to fact sets and thus make the comparison a total relation.

We achieve this by applying the notions of quantified information flow (QIF) [14] (introduced in Sect. 2) to our problem. In the scenario of data minimisation, the attacker is the agency that learns information about the confidential applicant data d by observing the transmitted facts $F = \pi(d) \subseteq \mathcal{F}$. In terms of Sect. 2, the input variable $\mathtt{D}$ takes values in D and the observation (the data transmitted to the agency) $\mathtt{O}$ takes values in $2^{\mathcal{F}}$.

A fact set F partitions the domain D into those data points that satisfy F and those that do not. We assume a given a-priori probability distribution[2] $\Pr(\mathtt{D} = d)$ on the input D that models how likely a particular data point $d \in D$ occurs amongst all applicants.

[2] We assume that D is finite and discrete, although we are confident that this can be generalised.

One way to measure the (information-theoretic) amount of information that the agency receives is via the probability mass of those data points which are consistent with the made observation, i.e., $\Pr_{\mathbb{F}}(F) := \sum_{\substack{d \in D \\ d \models F}} \Pr(\mathtt{D} = d)$. Intuitively, this is the probability for a randomly chosen applicant that F applies to them. The more applicants are consistent with F, the less information it leaks. $\Pr_{\mathbb{F}}$ is in general not a distribution over $2^{\mathbb{F}}$. We define an information-theoretic notion of minimality:

Definition 4 (Information-theoretic minimisation $\preceq_{it}$). *Given two fact sets $F, F' \subseteq \mathbb{F}$, we say F carries* information-theoretically less information *than F' and write $F \preceq_{it} F'$ if $\Pr_{\mathbb{F}}(F) \geq \Pr_{\mathbb{F}}(F')$.*

The important difference between Definitions 3 and 4 is that the former does not take probabilities into account and thus allows for a comparison only if one fact set is a subset of the other. Since the latter notion is based on probabilities, it can express more cases.

Observation 3. *For all fact sets $F, F' \subseteq \mathbb{F}$:*

- $F \preceq_{mt} F' \implies F \preceq_{it} F'$
- $F \preceq_{mt} F' \Leftrightarrow F \preceq_{it} F'$ *if* $F \subseteq F'$ *or* $F' \subseteq F$
- $F \preceq_{it} F' \Leftrightarrow |models(F)| \leq |models(F')|$ *(i.e., F has fewer models than F') if D is finite and* $\Pr(\mathtt{D} = d)$ *is uniformly distributed.*

In information theory, the information content of random variables is usually computed in bits by taking its logarithm. We get the Shannon entropy if we compute the expectation value of the information of the input data. Since we can use the observations to learn about the data point, we are actually interested in the conditional Shannon-entropy $H(\mathtt{D} \mid \mathtt{O})$ (as defined in Sect. 2). This, in turn, allows us to compare different projection functions w.r.t. the transmitted information.

Observation 4. *Consider two different projection functions $\pi_1, \pi_2 : D \to 2^{\mathcal{F}}$ inducing the random observation variables $\mathtt{O}_1, \mathtt{O}_2$ respectively with $H(\mathtt{D} \mid \mathtt{O}_1) \geq H(\mathtt{D} \mid \mathtt{O}_2)$. In the long run, the agency will learn less*[3] *about the applicants if the projection π_1 is used by all applicants (in comparison to when π_2 would be used).*

Example 1. Let us revisit the trivial fact bases $\mathcal{F}_D$ and $\mathcal{F}_R$ from Sect. 3.1. For a data point d, the single-element fact $\{d\}$ is the maximum w.r.t. model- and information-theoretic minimisation. Nothing more can be said than the full data if the fact set is to remain honest. The fact $\{d' | P(d) = P(d')\}$ characterising all data points with the same result of P, on the other hand, is the minimum w.r.t. both notions. There is no way to convey less information about the data point if the fact set is to remain sufficiently precise:

$$\{d\} \quad \preceq_{mt/it} \quad F \quad \preceq_{mt/it} \quad \{d' \mid P(d) = P(d')\}$$

for any sufficiently precise and honest fact set F for d.

[3] i.e., will gather less information in the sense of Shannon information-theory.

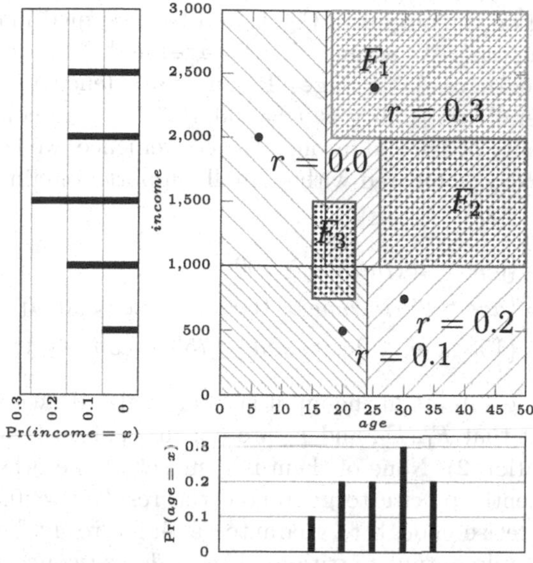

Fig. 3. The input space of the introductory example Fig. 1 partitioned by the different program outputs $R = \{0, \ldots, 0.3\}$. F_1, F_2 and F_3 are the regions of different fact sets. The probabilities for age and income are given on the margin.

Minimisation by Min-Entropy. In Sect. 2, we also introduce the (conditional) min-entropy $H_\infty(\mathtt{D} \mid \mathtt{O})$. In contrast to the Shannon entropy, the min-entropy is driven by an attacker model. It captures the success of an attacker to guess the data point in one try [14]. This guessing is modelled by the vulnerabilities $V(\mathtt{D})$ and $V(\mathtt{D} \mid \mathtt{O})$.

Observation 5. *An applicant with the data point $d \in D$ should use a fact set F for which d is unlikely among all other models.*

The attacker observes the transmitted facts F, and tries to guess the data point i. After the definition of vulnerability $V(\mathtt{D} \mid \mathtt{O} = F)$, the attacker selects the data point i that has the highest probability $\Pr(\mathtt{D} = i \mid \mathtt{O} = F)$. As a consequence, if the applicant can choose between two fact sets F and F', they should select F iff $\Pr(\mathtt{D} = d \mid \mathtt{O} = F) \leq \Pr(\mathtt{D} = d \mid \mathtt{O} = F')$, for their individual data point d. As $\Pr(\mathtt{D} = d \mid \mathtt{O} = F) = \frac{\Pr(\mathtt{D}=d, \mathtt{O}=F)}{\Pr(\mathtt{O}=F)}$, we can also observe that the applicants can achieve this by selecting likely (often selected) set of facts or unlikely combinations of their data points and the transmitted facts.

Definition 5 (Vulnerability minimisation $\preceq_V$). *Given two fact sets $F, F' \subseteq \mathbb{F}$, we say F is less* vulnerable *than F', and write $F \preceq_V F'$ if $V(\mathtt{D} \mid \mathtt{O} = F) \geq V(\mathtt{D} \mid \mathtt{O} = F')$.*

Example 2. Let us consider our introductory example with $(age, income) \in D$, where $0 \leq age \leq 50$, $0 \leq income \leq 3000$. Figure 3 shows the input space, the partitioning based on the output of Fig. 1, and the assumed margin probability Pr(`age`) and Pr(`income`). We assume that Pr(`age`) and Pr(`income`) are independent, hence Pr(`age`, `income`) = Pr(`age`) · Pr(`income`). Hence, the data point with the maximum overall probability is $j = (30, 1500)$ as the combination of the maximum probability of age and income. For convenience, we keep the probabilities discrete, sparsely populated with a small support domain. Let us consider the following fact sets:

$$F_1 = \{age > 18, income \geq 2000\}$$
$$F_2 = \{age > 25, income > 1000, income \leq 2000\}$$
$$F_3 = \{15 < age \leq 23, income \geq 750, income \leq 1500\}$$

Their corresponding subsets in the input space are also drawn in Fig. 3.

First, we attest that F_1, F_2, and F_3 are not in a subset relationship to each other (cf. Observation 2). None of them is a subset of the other. Moreover, F_1 and F_2 are sufficiently precise to guarantee the result $r = 0.3$. On the other hand, F_3 is not precise enough to guarantee a single result because its region overlaps with multiple output partitions. Hence, let us concentrate on F_1 and F_2. The fact sets are also incomparable using subset relations on their models, e.g., $\text{models}(F_1) \not\subset \text{models}(F_2)$ and vice versa. Using the number of models, we see that F_1 allows more data points: $|\,\text{models}(F_1)| > |\,\text{models}(F_2)|$. But both are smaller than the outer output partition for $r = 0.3$.

The sum of the probabilities results into the following probabilities for the fact sets: $\Pr_{\mathbb{F}}(F_1) = 0.36$ and $\Pr_{\mathbb{F}}(F_2) = 0.40$. We see that $F_2 \preceq_{it} F_1$ as F_2 is more probable. Using the vulnerabilities for $V(F_1) = 0.06$ and $V(F_2) = 0.09$, we would rather select F_1. For the data point $i = (30, 2000)$, which lies in F_1 and F_2, we would use F_2 as $P(\mathtt{D} = i \mid \mathtt{O} = F_1) = 0.17$ against $\Pr(\mathtt{D} = i \mid \mathtt{O} = F_2) = 0.15$. Note, data point j also lies in F_2, hence it makes F_2 interesting to select for all data points besides j.

3.3 Limitations

In order to check if a fact set is sufficiently precise, the applicant needs access to the program. Otherwise, it is impossible for the applicant to know if a fact set has a unique result value or not. Naturally, this restriction limits the application scenarios for our approach since not all agencies are willing to disclose in all detail how they come to their decisions. A bank, for instance, need not fully disclose their algorithm to decide the interest rate for a loan to an applicant. However, there are cases where the availability of the computed function is a sensible assumption: The introductory example of the income tax rate computation is such a situation. It is definitely reasonable to assume that the tax law is publicly known. The same applies to other calculations described by law and regulations.

Our approach can be adapted if the sources are not available, but naturally becomes less transparent. A solution that does not require access to the source code is for the applicant to always submit the set of all facts which hold for their data point (i.e., they apply π_0). Alternatively, the company can build a projection function into their front ends. In that case, the applicant can neither check if their transmitted data is sufficiently precise nor can they know anything about the minimality of the data provided. The design and analysis of the fact base and projection can then only happen inside the agency: The base must be sufficiently precise and statements about its minimising effects can only be made within the agency. It would be possible to have the minimisation design audited by a third party to increase trust by applicants into the scheme.

Our approach can identify minimal fact sets needed to compute a result, thus identifying the minimal set of 'adequate, relevant, and limited to what is necessary' [3] facts for the given computation. However the method can only judge the transmitted facts based on their being needed in the program, it cannot judge the adequacy of the program's purpose in the first place. For example, if an insurance company chooses to discriminate against green-eyed people by marking up all prices for them, our approach will consider a person's eye colour to be a relevant fact. Moreover, different parameters within a data point can be correlated and the agency may still gain knowledge even if problematic parameters are excluded from facts (e.g., the *address* might be correlated with the *income*, and facts on *address* may leak information on *income* even if the income is not in the fact set).

4 Data Minimisation Using Formal Verification

In this section, we refine the approach formally defined in the last section towards an implementation that makes use of existing functionalities in formal verification approaches and tools. Figure 4 refines the sketched pipeline from Fig. 2 by listing the tasks that are needed in the data minimisation (which corresponds to projection π) layer in the front end and the data restoration layer (which corresponds to witness function ω) in the back end.

On the client side, the applicant submits their data point $d \in D$ which is then subject to a projection onto facts from the fact base $\mathcal{F}$. In general, each applicant may select a different fact set for d or even submit a different fact set every time they run the algorithm. The approach solely relies on two properties that $F = \pi(d)$ must have: (1) F must be honest and (2) F must be sufficiently precise. F is then transmitted to the back end (say, via a network connection). The back end receives a fact set F and tries to compute $P(d)$ from that. First, it should check if the received fact set is indeed sufficiently precise – there is no need to trust the client on that point. Checking the honesty of the set on the other hand is not possible, unless the agency requires that facts be certified (e.g., signed by trusted parties); but this is outside the scope of this paper. Then, the back end reconstructs a witness $d^* := \omega(F)$ that satisfies all constraints of F. The result is then computed as $P(d^*)$ and guaranteed to be equal to $P(d)$. In the following, we will outline

1. how a sufficiently precise fact base can be extracted fully automatically from the source code of P,

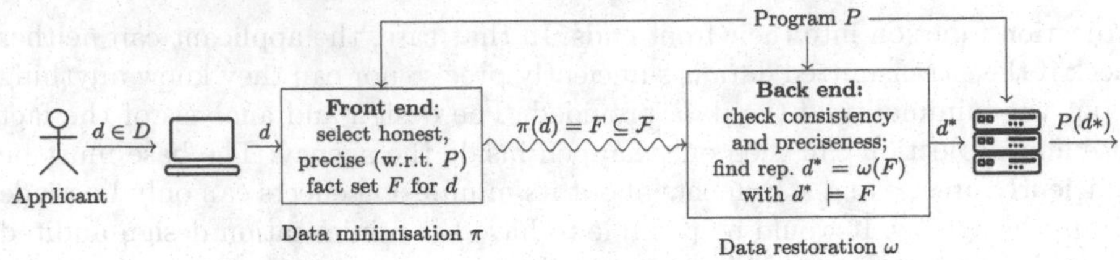

Fig. 4. Refined sketch of the pipeline, showing the tasks in the front and back end.

2. how a model-theoretically minimal, yet sufficiently precise fact set F consistent with d can be automatically computed,
3. how a witness d^* can be obtained from F that computes $P(d)$, and
4. how it can be verified that there is no witness for another result value (i.e., that F is sufficiently precise).

4.1 Front End: Finding Facts

In earlier considerations, we did not make any assumptions about the fact base $\mathcal{F}$. In general, a fact base could be handcrafted specifically for its target program by an expert because of the knowledge they have about the domain and its data minimality principles. For an automatic data minimisation refactoring of a process, it is helpful to have a possibility to fully automatically extract a fact base from the code. Luckily, as we will see, a sufficiently precise fact set can be extracted automatically from the program code.

The program determines the outcome, and hence partitions the input space into regions of equal output. The conditions that describe these regions can be found in control and data flow expressions of the program, and a fact base can be derived by a static analysis.

The first candidate is the *weakest precondition calculus* (wp-calculus) [4], in which the formula $wp(P, c)$ represents the weakest precondition s.t. the postcondition c holds after the execution of the program P. If we assume that P is loop-free, the formula $WP(d) := wp(P, o = P(d))$ exactly describes all data points with the same output as $d \in D$. The facts resulting from the wp-calculus thus produce the fact base $\mathcal{F}_R$ introduced in Sect. 3.1.

Example 3. Consider our introductory example in Fig. 1. The wp-calculus returns the following facts to achieve the outcome of 0.1.

$$wp(\texttt{tax\_rate}, \texttt{o} = 0.1) = \{\neg(\texttt{age} < 18) \land \texttt{age} < 25 \land \neg(\texttt{income} > 1000)\}$$

A drawback of the wp-calculus is the need for specification. In particular, to preserve minimality, all unbounded loops must be specified with a sufficiently strong loop invariant. However, there are no unbounded loops in the examples and case study in this paper. The wp-calculus thus finds a fact set F under the fact base $\mathcal{F}_R$ (see Sect. 3.1). Even though the wp-calculus does not explicitly model any probabilities, its use of $\mathcal{F}_R$ guarantees that F is minimal under all three notions of minimality discussed in Sect. 3.2 because $\mathcal{F}_R \cong P(D) \subseteq R$.

A more practical idea is to capture the path conditions during the execution of $P(d)$. In addition to the normal evaluation of each expression to a concrete value, we store each path condition symbolically, using concrete values for non-input variables. When we capture these symbolic expressions, we obtain a set of (path) expressions over the input variables. These only capture the control flow of the program, but not the data flow. To capture the data flow, we add a fact for each output variable o that asserts equality between the symbolic value of o and its concrete at the end of the execution of $P(d)$. Formally, we add the fact $\texttt{seval}(o) = \texttt{eval}(o)$ where $\texttt{seval}(o)$ returns a (symbolic) expression that describes the computation of o by using the input variables, and $\texttt{eval}(o)$ which evaluates to the concrete value of o.

We call the predicate transformer $\mathit{fwd}(P, \sigma, \varsigma)$ because of the forward application (in contrast to the wp-calculus, which is applied backwards). P denotes the program, σ the current concrete state, and ς the symbolic state over the input variables. $\emptyset$ denotes the state with an empty variable assignment. $\sigma[v \leftarrow e]$ denotes an update of the state σ in which the variable v is assigned to the concrete or symbolic value e. We use $\texttt{eval}(e)$ to denote the concrete evaluation of an expression e, and $\texttt{seval}(e)$ for the symbolical evaluation.

$$\begin{aligned}
\mathit{fwd}(v := c\ ;\ P, \sigma, \varsigma) &\rightsquigarrow \mathit{fwd}(P, \sigma[v \leftarrow \mathit{eval}(e)], \varsigma[v \leftarrow \texttt{seval}(e)]) \\
\mathit{fwd}(\texttt{if}(c)\ b_1\ \texttt{else}\ b_2\ ;\ P, \sigma, \varsigma) &\rightsquigarrow \{\texttt{seval}(c)\} \cup \mathit{fwd}(P, \sigma, \varsigma) \quad \text{if } \texttt{eval}(c) \\
\mathit{fwd}(\texttt{if}(c)\ b_1\ \texttt{else}\ b_2\ ;\ P, \sigma, \varsigma) &\rightsquigarrow \{\neg\texttt{seval}(c)\} \cup \mathit{fwd}(P, \sigma, \varsigma) \quad \text{if } \neg\texttt{eval}(c) \\
\mathit{fwd}(\epsilon, \sigma, \varsigma) &\rightsquigarrow \bigcup_{o \in OutVar} \texttt{seval(o)} {=} \texttt{eval}(o)
\end{aligned} \tag{1}$$

Example 4. Re-consider Fig. 1; the tax rate computation for the data point $(\mathit{age} = 20, \mathit{income} = 800)$ results in 0.1. A sufficiently precise fact set is

$$\begin{aligned}
&\mathit{fwd}(\texttt{tax_rate}, \emptyset[\mathit{age} \leftarrow 20][\mathit{income} \leftarrow 800], \emptyset) \\
&\qquad = \{\neg(\texttt{age} < 18), \texttt{age} < 25, \neg(\texttt{income} > 1000)\}\ .
\end{aligned}$$

This program contains only control flow, but no data flow. In every control-flow path, the return value is a constant independent of the input. To see why the last rule (1) is required, consider the program `out = x MOD 4` which returns the last two bits of the input `x`. This program only consists of a data flow. For instance, we obtain the fact $x \bmod 4 = 1$ for the data point $x = 13$ by (1).

Observation 6. *The fwd-calculus returns a sufficiently precise and honest fact set for a data point $d \in D$.*

While the fwd-calculus can guarantee these two properties, it does not guarantee minimality of the resulting fact set. It is also vulnerable against syntactical manipulation in the sense that a programmer can exploit the fwd-calculus to ensure chosen facts are always included in the result by mentioning them in the program code although they are not semantically required. For example, consider the program `if (x) out = 0 else out = 0`, which always returns 0, but the fwd-calculus includes the fact x.

4.2 Front End: Minimising Fact Sets

The fwd-calculus does not guarantee any notion of minimality. For example, consider two nested if-statements "`if (a) if (b) ...`", for which the fwd-calculus includes facts a and b, and misses the suffice and more minimal fact $a \wedge b$ in contrast to the wp-calculus. Nonetheless, we can use the resulting fact set F of the fwd-calculus as a starting point to extract a set $F' \subsetneq F$ that is minimal w.r.t. $\preceq_{mt}$. We introduce a technique to find such a F' by using minimal unsatisfiability cores for proofs which are reported by verification tools.

If a formula set C is unsatisfiable, modern propositional satisfiability (SAT) or satisfiability modulo theories (SMT) solvers can compute a minimal unsat-core $C' \subseteq C$ such that C' is unsatisfiable and there is no unsatisfiable set $C'' \subset C'$. In general, the minimal unsat-core is not unique. For a given $d \in D$, with $r = P(d)$ the following formula encodes a check for preciseness of a consistent fact set F:

$$\textsc{NotSufPrec}(F) := wp(P, \mathtt{out} \neq r) \wedge \bigwedge F \tag{2}$$

If $\textsc{NotSufPrec}(F)$ is unsatisfiable, we can obtain a minimal unsat-core F' from the verification tool to obtain a fact set which implies that the result of P is r. Using the minimal unsat-core, we minimise a set of facts F' minimal w.r.t. the minimisation $\preceq_{mt}$ according to Observation 2. If $\textsc{NotSufPrec}(F)$ is satisfiable, then F is not sufficiently precise. We will exploit this in the next section for the back end computations.

4.3 Back End: Computing the Result from a Fact Set

The back end needs to re-establish the result $r = P(d)$ from a received fact set F. In the formalisation in Sect. 3.1, we introduce a partial witness function $\omega : 2^{\mathbb{F}} \nrightarrow D$ that produces a witness such that $\omega(F) \models F$ (if $F \in dom(\omega)$). We can rely here on another feature of modern SAT and SMT solvers: They can produce a model in case they detect that an input is satisfiable. Hence, we encode $\bigwedge F$ as an SMT input. If it is satisfiable, the solver delivers $d^* := \omega(F)$. The back end can feed d^* into P and obtain the result $r = P(d^*)$. If $\bigwedge F$ is unsatisfiable, the fact set is inconsistent, which is the front end's fault.

Proving Sufficient Preciseness. As mentioned, the transmitted fact set F has to be honest and sufficiently precise. While honesty cannot be checked without requiring certificates for the facts, we *can* check preciseness. We again use the formula defined in (2). If $\textsc{NotSufPrec}(F)$ is satisfiable, then there is a data point $d^! \in D$ with $P(d^!) \neq P(d^*)$ which means that there is no unique result value. The back end can once again blame the front end.

However, the back end need not fail at this point. Instead it could follow a policy that if a fact set is not sufficiently precise, the back end chooses any satisfying data point, in particular, that with the worst possible outcome (for the applicant). In our scenario: If the applicant chooses not to disclose the income, the tax agency assumes the highest tax rate consistent with the facts. Technically, this can be implemented by a repeated satisfiability test. If the applicant wants to have a low tax rate, the agency can repeatedly use the postcondition $out > r$ to check if there is a data point for F which has a worse tax rate.

Of course, for these ideas to work, we must have SMT formulas that solvers can decide. For many practical applications, we can limit formula expressions in P and in F to SMT formulas from decidable theories only, e.g., by encoding variables as finite bit vectors.

Example 5. For example, let P again be the `tax_rate` function from Fig. 1, and F the set of facts represented by the predicates $\{\texttt{age} < 18, \texttt{income} > 1000\}$ which has been computed using the fwd-calculus. The formula from (2) reads $wp(\texttt{tax\_rate}, out \neq 0.0) \wedge \bigwedge F$ and is unsatisfiable. The minimum-unsat core provided by an SMT solver presented with this input shows that the set F' represented by $\{age < 18\}$ is a sufficiently precise subset. This is sent to the back end which finds a witness $\omega(F') = (12, 200)$ and computes a tax rate of 0.0 from this data point. The formula $wp(\texttt{tax\_rate}, out \neq 0.0) \wedge age < 18$ is unsatisfiable, so the back end knows it received a sufficiently precise result.

5 Implementation and Experiments

In this section, we give an overview over the prototypical implementation and explain its use on a more sophisticated example. Both are publicly available[4].

5.1 Prototypical Implementation

For our experiments, we implemented the functionalities of the front and back end on top of CBMC [2] and Z3 [13]. Z3 is a state-of-the-art SMT solver and CBMC is a bounded model-checker for C programs, which is why the implementation cannot handle unbounded loops. The implementation is written in Python and orchestrates the underlying tools. In general, the Python script takes an augmentable program and a YAML file containing meta-data. An augmentable program contains markers that allow injecting program code at the marked positions in the source code. Figure 5 shows a minimal skeleton with markers. The required meta-data contain the name of the input and output variables of the program along with the variable assignments of the data point $d \in D$, and the calculated output $r = P(d)$. In the following, we assume that all facts are Boolean expression in the C language.

[4] https://github.com/wadoon/data-minimization.

As CBMC provides a way to check explicit assertions in C programs, we only have to encode our proof obligations into `assert`-statements. Also we exploit CBMC for the generation of SMT input and DIMACS (a SAT input format) encoding of the given program and assertions.

```
#ifndef NOHEADER
// include files
#endif
int main() {
  //!INPUT
  // calculation
  //!OUTPUT
}
```

Fig. 5. Skeleton of an augmentable program. Marker comments for code injection.

Front end: Execution of the Program. The first step on the client side is the execution of the program with input d. We use the marker `//!INPUT` to set the values of the input variables to the data point, and the marker `//!OUTPUT` to add statements to print out the value of the output variables. The augmented program is compiled and executed. Its output is parsed to obtain $r = P(d)$.

Front end: Finding Facts. Despite the exact solution (wp-calculus) being known, the extraction of facts is not sufficient solved. The main issue is scalability. Therefore, we implemented several lightweight techniques to come up with a fact set: First, we implemented the fwd-calculus from Sect. 4.1; second, we implemented an approach with symbolic execution based on the single static assignment (SSA) form with a similar goal. The construction of the SSA-form scales well, but the extraction of facts does not, i.e., it is only applicable if we expand the computed expression of the program variables only to a limited depth. The third heuristic approach tries to find a fact set by using expressions and constants from the program and the assignments of input variables.

Whichever technique is used to obtain the fact set; in the end, we can check whether the fact set is consistent and sufficiently precise.

Front end: Minimising the Fact Set. To obtain a fact set $F' \subseteq F$ which is minimised w.r.t. $\preceq_{mt}$ as explained in Sec. 4.2, we use CBMC and Z3. In the skeleton, the marker `//!INPUT` is replaced by a list of `assume(f)` statements for each fact $f \in F$. The `//!OUTPUT` is replaced by the assertion `assert(o ==` r`)` in which $r = P(d)$ is the computed output and `o` is the variable holding the output. CBMC is then called to produce an SMT input file to which we add annotations and commands that request and control the generation of a minimal unsat core. We pass it on to Z3 and parse its output. If the assumptions imply the equality, we can read out an unsat-core of that proof.

Back end: Calculation of the Outcome. The main task on the back-end side is to compute the final result $r = P(d)$ from a fact set F. Once computed, r will also be used check the consistency and preciseness of F. The computation of the outcome requires the symbolical execution of the program under the assumption that the (symbolic) input adheres to F. Luckily, we can exploit CBMC to achieve this: We use the same query on CBMC as in the minimisation step above: The

`//!INPUT` covers the assumptions of the facts, and `//!OUTPUT` is replaced by `assert(false);`. If CBMC proves this program correct, then F is inconsistent, and it will be rejected. If this program is not correct, we obtain a counterexample variable assignment d^* whose input satisfies F and whose output is $r = P(d^*)$.

Back end: Checking Sufficient Preciseness. To check sufficient preciseness of a given fact set, we use the exact same setup as for minimising the fact set (replacement of `//!INPUT` and `//!OUTPUT` marker). But since we are not interested in an unsat-core here, we directly ask CBMC to verify that the assumptions always lead to the same (previously) computed output.

5.2 Example: Account Charges

Figure 6 shows a program computing the monthly charges for a bank account. As input variables, it takes the age of the account holder, their monthly cash receipt on the bank account, and the reward points of the customer loyalty program. The program privileges young customers, customers with a high cash receipt and loyal customers.

```
int charge(int age, int income, int reward) {
  if (age < 18) return 0;
  if (age < 27) {
    if(income <= 1500) { return 0; }
    else { return 5 - 2 * reward; } }
  int g = 10 - 2 * reward;
  do { g = g - 1; income = income - 500; }
  while(income >= 500 && g > 0);
  return g; }
```

Fig. 6. Example program for the calculation of account administration charges.

Note that the given loop is bounded, as it terminates after at most 10 iterations.

Let's consider an account holder with `age` = 35, `income` = 1250, and `reward` = 2.[5] After executing the program with these inputs, it calculates the charge of 4. By inspecting the program, the account holder might come up with the following fact set

$$\{\underbrace{age \geq 27}_{f_1},\ \underbrace{1250 \leq income < 1400}_{f_2},\ \underbrace{reward = 2}_{f_3},\ \underbrace{income/500 = 2}_{f_4}\}\ .$$

Note that the arithmetic operations have C semantics, hence the division is on integers. The selected facts are consistent and sufficiently precise, and the considered data point satisfies them.

The fact minimisation step using the unsat-core method tells us that f_4 can be omitted. Indeed, f_2 could also have been omitted; the minimisation is known to be ambiguous. As $f_2 \rightarrow f_4$, the account holder would select f_4 to increase the number of models. Hence, $\{f_1, f_3, f_4\}$ are transmitted to the agency. The agency starts with testing the consistency, symbolically executes the program, and checks for preciseness of the computed output. The verification of all proof obligations takes a negligible run time (ca. 170–230 ms), but an additional hint for the loop's upper bound is required for CBMC.

[5] See `examples/run.account_charges.1.sh` in the linked repository.

6 Related Work

Predicate Abstraction. Our approach has similarities to predicate abstraction [8]. Predicate abstraction is a verification technique in which the state space over the program variables is projected on a state space over predicates. Each state in the space over predicates describes a set of concrete states. The goal of predicate abstraction is to select the smallest number of predicates such that the required properties are provable. In our case, we are interested in facts (predicates) which abstract the input space of the program and also result in the determined program outcome (property).

Data Minimisation. Goldsteen et al. [6] introduce an approach for data minimisation in machine learning models. They generalise the input based on certain features, removing those features that influence the program's result the least. Thus, personal data are still needed for training.

Biega et al. [1] examine data minimisation in recommendation systems. They identify two definitions for minimisation: *Global* data minimisation minimises the total data collected about all users while ensuring some minimum average quality level for all recommendations. *Per-user* data minimisation considers each user individually and minimises the data collected about them while ensuring some minimum quality level for their individual recommendations. In this dichotomy, our approach performs per-user minimisation. The alternative without access to the source code discussed in Sect. 3.3 falls back on global minimisation.

Unlike us, both of these papers consider a scenario (machine learning or product recommendations) in which the result based on the minimised data does not have to be exactly equal to the result based on the original data. In our approach, this could be modelled by not requiring the fact set to identify one unique result, but a set of results which only differ by some predefined distance. Alternatively, we could group the possible results into equivalence classes and require a set of facts to uniquely identify an equivalence class.

Formalisation of Privacy Properties. Mödersheim et al. [12] introduce the notion of (α, β)-privacy: Given a first-order formula α which models the intentionally released information and another formula β which models the information known by the intruder, (α, β)-privacy is achieved if the intruder cannot derive a statement from β which cannot also be derived from α. In our approach, minimality is achieved if the amount of information that can be derived from the transmitted data, but cannot be derived from the computation result, is minimal.

Differential privacy [5] is a notion of privacy in data sets. It is achieved when the conclusions drawn from the data set are not affected by the presence or absence of any individual datum. Local differential privacy is an approach of achieving differential privacy by randomising each participant's data before collecting it. Hao et al. [7] apply this approach to software execution traces; they define a way of modifying the traces to achieve differential privacy without compromising the validity of the data. Instead of falsifying the transmitted data, we minimise the amount of non-falsified information that is submitted. Like Hao et al.'s approach, ours also depends on the applicant's honesty; but in our case, this can be somewhat mitigated by choosing facts that can be certified later.

k-anonymity [15] is a related notion of privacy in data sets: It is achieved by replacing concrete data in a set by equivalence classes such that the data of any one individual becomes equivalent to that of at least $k-1$ other individuals. Since k-anonymity does not impose any restriction on the diversity within one equivalence class, knowing what class someone belongs to might still reveal some information about their exact data. Thus, improved versions of k-anonymity like l-diversity [11] and t-closeness [10] were introduced. Our approach is similar in that it partitions users into classes. However, instead of having a fixed equivalence relation, we choose one of several possible relations induced by the fact base, based on how much information the relation reveals about the user. Restrictions similar to those imposed by t-closeness could be useful in judging the usefulness of a fact base; e.g., a base which only includes facts fulfilled by most possible users will likely force the user to reveal more information.

Ziller et al. [16] offer a definition of privacy based on information flow. According to them, privacy is the ability of a sender to upper-bound the amount of information that can be computed from their message, independent of any prior knowledge of the receiver. This definition is closely linked, but not identical, to differential privacy. One important difference is that differential privacy is context-independent and only considers what conclusions can be drawn from the current data set. Our approach has a similar problem. The applicant cannot necessarily control or even know how much prior knowledge the agency has about them and what it does with that knowledge. They can however upper-bound the information content of the message they send, and (by inspecting the source code) ensure that only the information they sent is considered for the decision at hand. In addition, the information contained in the decision's result serves as a lower bound for how much they have to send.

7 Conclusion

We present an approach to minimise the transmitted personal information of the client to the agency. To achieve this, the clients send facts which describe their personal data instead of their concrete data. These facts need to be consistent with the original data and precise enough to guarantee the original outcome.

Our current implementations for fact extraction are very limited. Hence, we are considering a refinement process in which precise (but maybe too strong) fact sets are weakened, or imprecise sets of facts are strengthened by adding new facts. Beside the technical requirements, the extracted facts should also be comprehensible to the applicant and the agency.

References

1. Biega, A.J., Potash, P., Daumè III, H., Diaz, F., Finck, M.: Operationalizing the legal principle of data minimization for personalization. In: Huang, J., et al. (eds.) SIGIR 2020, Proceedings, pp. 399–408. ACM (2020). https://doi.org/10.1145/3397271.3401034
2. Clarke, E., Kroening, D., Lerda, F.: A tool for checking ANSI-C programs. In: Jensen, K., Podelski, A. (eds.) TACAS 2004. LNCS, vol. 2988, pp. 168–176. Springer, Heidelberg (2004). https://doi.org/10.1007/978-3-540-24730-2_15
3. Council of the European Union: General Data Protection Regulation (2016). https://eur-lex.europa.eu/eli/reg/2016/679
4. Dijkstra, E.W.: A Discipline of Programming. Prentice Hall Inc., Englewood Cliffs (1976)
5. Dwork, C., Roth, A.: The algorithmic foundations of differential privacy. Found. Trends Theor. Comput. Sci. **9**(3–4), 211–407 (2014). https://doi.org/10.1561/0400000042
6. Goldsteen, A., Ezov, G., Shmelkin, R., Moffie, M., Farkash, A.: Data minimization for GDPR compliance in machine learning models. CoRR (2020). https://arxiv.org/abs/2008.04113
7. Hao, Y., Latif, S., Zhang, H., Bassily, R., Rountev, A.: Differential privacy for coverage analysis of software traces. In: Møller, A., Sridharan, M. (eds.) ECOOP 2021. LIPIcs, vol. 194, pp. 8:1–8:25. Schloss Dagstuhl - Leibniz-Zentrum für Informatik, Dagstuhl, Germany (2021). https://doi.org/10.4230/LIPIcs.ECOOP.2021.8
8. Jhala, R., Podelski, A., Rybalchenko, A.: Predicate abstraction for program verification. In: Handbook of Model Checking, pp. 447–491. Springer, Cham (2018). https://doi.org/10.1007/978-3-319-10575-8_15
9. Lanzinger, F., Weigl, A.: Towards a formal approach for data minimization in programs (short paper). In: Garcia-Alfaro, J., Muñoz-Tapia, J.L., Navarro-Arribas, G., Soriano, M. (eds.) DPM/CBT -2021. LNCS, vol. 13140, pp. 161–169. Springer, Cham (2022). https://doi.org/10.1007/978-3-030-93944-1_11
10. Li, N., Li, T., Venkatasubramanian, S.: t-closeness: privacy beyond k-anonymity and l-diversity. In: 2007 IEEE 23rd International Conference on Data Engineering, pp. 106–115 (2007). https://doi.org/10.1109/ICDE.2007.367856
11. Machanavajjhala, A., Kifer, D., Gehrke, J., Venkitasubramaniam, M.: L-diversity: Privacy beyond k-anonymity. ACM Trans. Knowl. Discov. Data **1**(1), 3-es (2007). https://doi.org/10.1145/1217299.1217302
12. Mödersheim, S., Viganò, L.: Alpha-beta privacy. ACM Trans. Priv. Secur. **22**(1) (2019). https://doi.org/10.1145/3289255
13. de Moura, L., Bjørner, N.: Z3: an efficient SMT solver. In: Ramakrishnan, C.R., Rehof, J. (eds.) TACAS 2008. LNCS, vol. 4963, pp. 337–340. Springer, Heidelberg (2008). https://doi.org/10.1007/978-3-540-78800-3_24
14. Smith, G.: On the foundations of quantitative information flow. In: de Alfaro, L. (ed.) FoSSaCS 2009. LNCS, vol. 5504, pp. 288–302. Springer, Heidelberg (2009). https://doi.org/10.1007/978-3-642-00596-1_21
15. Sweeney, L.: K-anonymity: a model for protecting privacy. Int. J. Uncertain. Fuzziness Knowl.-Based Syst. **10**(5), 557–570 (2002). https://doi.org/10.1142/S0218488502001648
16. Ziller, A., Mueller, T., Braren, R., Rueckert, D., Kaissis, G.: Privacy: an axiomatic approach (2022). 10.48550/ARXIV.2203.11586

DIME Days

DIME Days (ISoLA 2022 Track Introduction)

Tiziana Margaria[1], Dominic Wirkner[2], Daniel Busch[2], Alexander Bainczyk[2], Tim Tegeler[2](✉), and Bernhard Steffen[2]

[1] University of Limerick, Limerick, Ireland
tiziana.margaria@ul.ie
[2] TU Dortmund University, Dortmund, Germany
{dominic.wirkner,daniel.busch,alexander.bainczyk,tim.tegeler, bernhard.steffen}@cs.tu-dortmund.de

Abstract. This article provides an introduction to the DIME *Days*, organized by Tiziana Margaria and Bernhard Steffen as part of ISoLA 2022. DIME is in active development since 2015 and from that time on, the tool has been applied successfully in educational contexts, international workshops and multiple industrial projects. Since then, the tool grew continuously and it is now a centerpiece of our Language-Driven Engineering ecosystem and an integral part of how we approach the development and delivery of web applications. For that reason, we dedicate DIME a special track within ISoLA 2022, where we present contributions that deal with experience gathered from using graphical modeling environments, quality assurance in our ecosystem and the shift to the cloud.

Keywords: Cloud · Domain-specific languages · Graphical modeling · Language-driven engineering · Quality control · XMDD · Digital thread · Software engineering education · Low-code/No-code

1 Introduction

The DIME Days 2022 are the second convention on the research and practical findings around DIME and related tools in the LDE ecosystem, held in Faliraki, Rhodes (Greece) on October 2022, 22–30th, in association with ISoLA 2022.

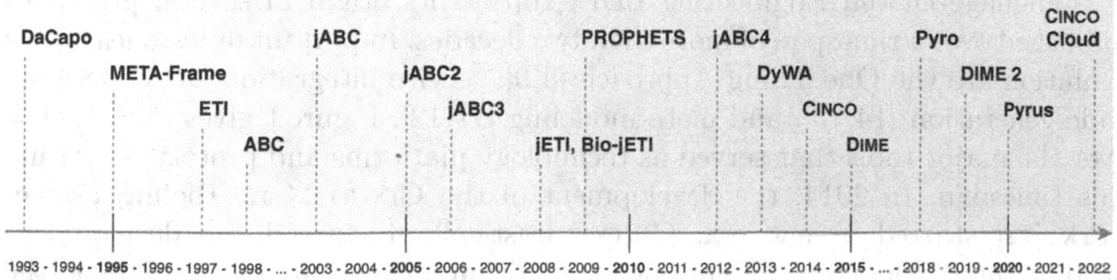

Fig. 1. Timeline of the tools development, leading to the current LDE Ecosystem

T. Margaria and B. Steffen (Eds.): ISoLA 2022, LNCS 13702, pp. 367–373, 2022.
https://doi.org/10.1007/978-3-031-19756-7_20

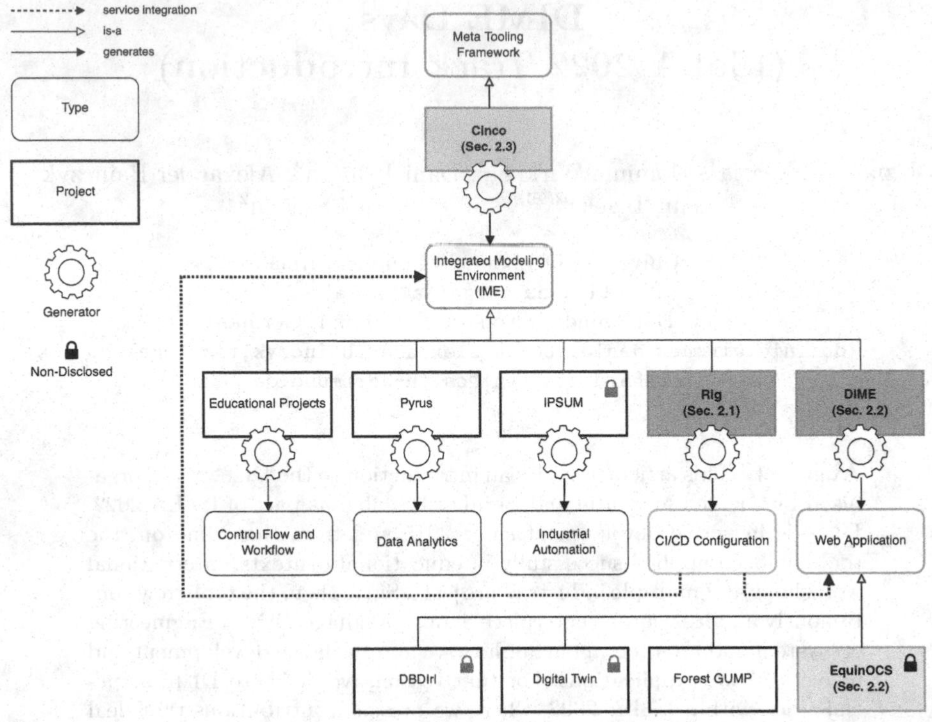

Fig. 2. Overview of the LDE Ecosystem

Since its inception and early development in 2015, DIME took a prominent place in the *International School on Tool-based Rigorous Engineering of Software Systems* (STRESS) [6,7], associated with the ISoLA conference. After five years of experience and continuous improvement, several workshop days in the STRESS 2021 edition [8] were devoted to presentations, demonstrations, and experience reports in the context of DIME, unofficially coining the term "DIME days". This year we emphasize the importance of DIME by officially establishing the first stand-alone DIME days event, offering this way an open platform for the growing DIME community to publish and discuss related research and practice questions.

Language-Driven Engineering LDE [16] has its origin in several principles published over a timespan of more than two decades. Important milestones of this evolution are the One Thing Approach [5,9], service integration [10,17,18], full code generation [14,15], and meta-modeling [11,12]. Figure 1 gives an overview over the major tools that served as technology platforms and prototypes during this timespan. In 2014, the development of the CINCO Meta Tooling Framework [12] started a new era. CINCO drastically improved the development of Integrated Modeling Environment IMEs in our group by combining the aforementioned principles. Since then, it represents the root of the entire multi-layered LDE ecosystem, shown in Fig. 2.

At the same time as CINCO, we also started the development of EquinOCS[1], a web-based editorial system for the management of conference proceedings submissions for Springer Nature. Without the LDE approach and technology, this new web application project would have had to be developed traditionally, using general purpose languages. Instead, developing EquinOCS from scratch was the main driver for our development of an IME tailored specifically for creating web applications, which eventually became DIME [3]. Last year EquinOCS was officially released, and it is now in use for organizing the ISoLA 2022 submission and proceedings, and many other conferences in Computer Science and in other disciplines.

As of today, many IMEs have been created with CINCO for different educational and industrial purposes (cf. Fig. 2). Among them, RIG [19–21] is special because it supports the definition of automated delivery and deployment workflows for practicing Continuous Integration and Deployment CI/CD [4,13], an important but often overlooked aspect of software development. RIG is now a cornerstone for building not only DIME applications like EquinOCS, but also CINCO and corresponding IMEs.

DIME is not only the eponym for this event, but also an enabler for the flourishing of the LDE approach. It gave us confidence that the concepts of LDE are successfully applicable to large industrial projects. Looking back after several years, it seems overdue to dedicate DIME an event like this, to document its vital role in our LDE ecosystem.

2 Contributions

At events like the DIME days, tools are usually presented with small demos to help the audience better understand concepts and functionality. But demos can differ quite a lot from any application in productive use and thus they do not have the same impact on the evolution of our tools. An important aspect is the *consistency in quality*, which is best addressed if the software is in productive use by real customers. Luckily, the success of EquinOCS pushed our development efforts in that direction.

Over the last year we have refined the product *build and delivery processes* with RIG (Sect. 2.1) and further evolved *quality assurance* (Sect. 2.2) across the whole LDE ecosystem, to further improve DIME and the tooling around it.

Another aspect is *evolution*, which is faced only if a project spans across some meaningful time. Evolution happens at two layers in software development: of course, on the *product layer*, by implementing additional features or fixing bugs, but also on the *development layer*, when the environments used for product development improve. In our case, CINCO has a role at both levels as we develop it and use it at the same time.

[1] https://equinocs.springernature.com/.

With the success of DIME and the growing importance of web applications in today's software engineering, we recently decided to bring CINCO into the cloud (Sect. 2.3) and start a new, cloud-based era of our LDE ecosystem. The experiences gathered while working with DIME and its products provided inspiration for managing and evolving IMEs in the web.

The paper contributions in this track are briefly introduced below. They are thematically ordered to establish an interrelating flow of presentations, starting with a retrospective on the previous STRESS in 2021, and closing with a preview of innovative changes in the LDE ecosystem.

2.1 Numbers on the Effect of Graphical Modeling

The paper *Evaluation of Graphical Modeling of CI/CD Workflows with Rig* by Sebastian Teumert, Tim Tegeler, Jonas Schürmann, Daniel Busch and Dominic Wirkner [22] discusses the outcomes and insights gathered in the workshop on *Graphical modeling with* RIG that took place last year during the *6th International School on Tool-based Rigorous Engineering of Software Systems* [8]. RIG is a specialized IME developed with CINCO, it targets the creation and maintenance of CI/CD workflows via its tailored graphical modeling language.

The contribution of this paper is twofold. It reflects on considerations on how to plan, organize and execute workshops with hands-on components in the context of Summer schools for international PhD students, but more importantly it evaluates data gathered throughout the workshop concerning the effect of graphical modeling for CI/CD workflows. The authors interpret the data, discuss threats to validity and finally draw the conclusions that RIG,

- lowers the entry barriers for novices in matters of CI/CD,
- reduces the trial-and-error process of creating such CI/CD workflows, and
- eliminates the occurrence of invalid pipelines that fail to be instantiated due to errors in the configuration.

2.2 Quality Control in the LDE Ecosystem

The paper *Towards Continuous Quality Control in the Context of Language-Driven Engineering* by Alexander Bainczyk, Steve Boßelmann, Marvin Krause, Marco Krumrey, Dominic Wirkner and Bernhard Steffen [1] deals with the impact of domain specificity on quality assurance, particularly in the context of the LDE ecosystem around CINCO, DIME and the generated DIME applications.

This paper highlights several means to keep the quality of DIME-based web applications at a consistently high level during their evolution. It uses EquinOCS as a concrete example. On the one hand, static validation, e.g. via model checking, ensures that language designers and modelers only operate within specified language constraints in (meta) IMEs. On the other hand, dynamic validation, by means of continuous learning-based testing and runtime monitoring of generated applications, ensures that semantic properties are represented correctly on the application-level. Finally, it addresses the interleaving between the target application and the model environments: (change) requests from the application-level are moved up through the meta hierarchy for adequate handling. There, they trigger changes on the meta-level, which are then again propagated down along the meta hierarchy. During this process, static and dynamic validation measures ensure the adequate migration of involved tools to the new "state-of-the-art", and also the quality of the target application.

2.3 Language-Driven Engineering in the Web

The paper *Cinco Cloud: A Holistic Approach for Web-Based Language-Driven Engineering* by Alexander Bainczyk, Daniel Busch, Marco Krumrey, Daniel Sami Mitwalla, Joel Tagoukeng Dongmo and Bernhard Steffen [2] introduces CINCO Cloud. CINCO Cloud is a new platform that provides a language workbench for graph-based modeling environments, as well as visual editors that are generated from meta-level descriptions in a unified web interface.

Here, the authors sketch the continuous evolution of their tool suite designed for language-driven engineering. Originally, the tool suite could be installed and used only locally, but it now runs as a single service in the cloud, with added support for real-time collaboration. The paper further offers deeper insights in the technical details of the platform that enabled the transition to an online, scalable and multi-tenant system. Finally, CINCO Cloud is showcased from a user-level perspective on the example of a language for designing web-based point-and-click adventures: the *WebStory* language. This walk-through takes place solely in the web interface of CINCO Cloud and covers

- the language specification in a text-based meta-modeling environment,
- the automated generation of a graph-based modeling environment,
- the modeling of an exemplary *WebStory* adventure, and
- the generation of the *WebStory* and its deployment to a remote server.

3 Outlook

With the release of CINCO Cloud we will start a new era of graphical modeling, in particular making our LDE ecosystem accessible to everybody by means of a common web browser. This innovation has the potential to significantly increase the popularity of LDE, and to grow the CINCO and DIME user communities well beyond their current reach. With CINCO Cloud it will be possible to create a fully integrated collaboration platform that serves the modeler's needs throughout the whole development and operation process of their application.

The change in architecture from local IMEs to an online web service will let further challenges emerge, especially in the context of operating a multi-user system. More attention will be required on user-centric features, like version control and project management, and on background activities like resource provisioning, load balancing and storage management.

We are convinced that this will create a demand for additional (graphical) domain specific languages, specifically dedicated to those aspects. We are therefore confident that related research questions will arise around DIME and CINCO Cloud. They will be hopefully addressed successfully in our research, leading to future case studies and publications. Eventually, this continuous progress, adoption and evaluation may establish the DIME days as an integral part of upcoming editions of the ISoLA conference.

References

1. Bainczyk, A., Boßelmann, S., Krause, M., Krumrey, M., Steffen, B., Wirkner, D.: Towards continuous quality control in the context of language-driven engineering. In: Margaria, T., Steffen, B. (eds.) ISoLA 2022, LNCS, vol. 13702, pp. 389–406. Springer, Heidelberg (2022)
2. Bainczyk, A., et al.: Cinco Ccloud: a holistic approach for web-based language-driven engineering. In: Margaria, T., Steffen, B. (eds.) ISoLA 2022, LNCS, vol. 13702, pp. 407–425. Springer, Heidelberg (2022)
3. Boßelmann, S.: DIME: a programming-less modeling environment for web applications. In: Margaria, T., Steffen, B. (eds.) ISoLA 2016. LNCS, vol. 9953, pp. 809–832. Springer, Cham (2016). https://doi.org/10.1007/978-3-319-47169-3_60
4. Labouardy, M.: Pipeline as Code: Continuous Delivery with Jenkins, Kubernetes, and Terraform. Manning (2021). https://books.google.de/books?id=Lt9EEAAAQBAJ
5. Margaria, T., Steffen, B.: Business process modelling in the jABC: the one-thing-approach. In: Cardoso, J., van der Aalst, W. (eds.) Handbook of Research on Business Process Modeling. IGI Global (2009)
6. Margaria, T., Steffen, B. (eds.): Leveraging Applications of Formal Methods, Verification and Validation: Discussion, Dissemination, Applications: 7th International Symposium, ISoLA 2016, Imperial, Corfu, Greece, 10–14 October 2016, Proceedings, Part II, Lecture Notes in Computer Science, vol. 9953. Springer, Heidelberg (2016). https://doi.org/10.1007/978-3-319-47169-3. https://books.google.de/books?id=9-IyDQAAQBAJ
7. Margaria, T., Steffen, B. (eds.): Leveraging Applications of Formal Methods, Verification and Validation: Discussion, Dissemination, Applications: 8th International Symposium, ISoLA 2018, Limassol, Cyprus, 5–9 November 2018, Proceedings, Part II, Lecture Notes in Computer Science, vol. 11245. Springer, Heidelberg (2018)
8. Margaria, T., Steffen, B. (eds.): Leveraging Applications of Formal Methods, Verification and Validation - 10th International Symposium on Leveraging Applications of Formal Methods, ISoLA 2021, Rhodes, Greece, 17–29 October 2021, Proceedings, Lecture Notes in Computer Science, vol. 13036. Springer (2021). https://doi.org/10.1007/978-3-030-89159-6
9. Margaria, T., Steffen, B., Reitenspieß, M.: Service-oriented design: the roots. In: Benatallah, B., Casati, F., Traverso, P. (eds.) ICSOC 2005. LNCS, vol. 3826, pp. 450–464. Springer, Heidelberg (2005). https://doi.org/10.1007/11596141_34
10. Margaria, T., Steffen, B., Reitenspieß, M.: Service-oriented design: the jABC approach. In: Cubera, F., Krämer, B.J., Papazoglou, M.P. (eds.) Service Oriented Computing (SOC). No. 05462 in Dagstuhl Seminar Proceedings, Internationales Begegnungs- und Forschungszentrum für Informatik (IBFI), Schloss Dagstuhl, Germany, Dagstuhl, Germany (2006). https://drops.dagstuhl.de/opus/volltexte/2006/521

11. Naujokat, S.: Heavy Meta. Model-Driven Domain-Specific Generation of Generative Domain-Specific Modeling Tools. Dissertation, TU Dortmund University, Dortmund, Germany (2017). https://doi.org/10.17877/DE290R-18076. https://hdl.handle.net/2003/36060
12. Naujokat, S., Lybecait, M., Kopetzki, D., Steffen, B.: CINCO: a simplicity-driven approach to full generation of domain-specific graphical modeling tools. Softw. Tools Technol. Transfer **20**(3), 327–354 (2017). https://doi.org/10.1007/s10009-017-0453-6
13. Shahin, M., Babar, M.A., Zhu, L.: Continuous integration, delivery and deployment: a systematic review on approaches, tools, challenges and practices. IEEE Access **5**, 3909–3943 (2017). https://doi.org/10.1109/ACCESS.2017.2685629
14. Steffen, B.: Data flow analysis as model checking. In: Proceedings of the International Conference on Theoretical Aspects of Computer Software, pp. 346–365. Springer, Heidelberg (1991). https://doi.org/10.1007/3-540-54415-1_54. https://www.springerlink.com/content/y5p607674g6q1482/
15. Steffen, B.: Generating data flow analysis algorithms from modal specifications. Sci. Comput. Program. **21**(2), 115–139 (1993)
16. Steffen, B., Gossen, F., Naujokat, S., Margaria, T.: Language-driven engineering: from general-purpose to purpose-specific languages. In: Steffen, B., Woeginger, G. (eds.) Computing and Software Science. LNCS, vol. 10000, pp. 311–344. Springer, Cham (2019). https://doi.org/10.1007/978-3-319-91908-9_17
17. Steffen, B., Margaria, T., Claßen, A., Braun, V., Nisius, R., Reitenspieß, M.: A constraint-oriented service creation environment. In: TACAS, pp. 418–421 (1996)
18. Steffen, B., Margaria, T., Claßen, A., Braun, V., Reitenspieß, M.: An environment for the creation of intelligent network services. In: Intelligent Networks: IN/AIN Technologies, Operations, Services and Applications - A Comprehensive Report, pp. 287–300. IEC: International Engineering Consortium (1996)
19. Tegeler, T., Gossen, F., Steffen, B.: A model-driven approach to continuous practices for modern cloud-based web applications. In: 2019 9th International Conference on Cloud Computing, Data Science Engineering (Confluence), pp. 1–6 (2019). https://doi.org/10.1109/CONFLUENCE.2019.8776962
20. Tegeler, T., Teumert, S., Schürmann, J., Bainczyk, A., Busch, D., Steffen, B.: An introduction to graphical modeling of CI/CD workflows with rig. In: Margaria, T., Steffen, B. (eds.) ISoLA 2021. LNCS, vol. 13036, pp. 3–17. Springer, Cham (2021). https://doi.org/10.1007/978-3-030-89159-6_1
21. Teumert, S.: Visual Authoring of CI/CD Pipeline Configurations. Bachelor's thesis, TU Dortmund University (2021). https://archive.org/details/visual-authoring-of-cicd-pipeline-configurations
22. Teumert, S., Tegeler, T., Schürmann, J., Busch, D., Wirkner, D., Steffen, B.: Evaluation of graphical modeling of ci/cd workflows with rig. In: Margaria, T., Steffen, B. (eds.) ISoLA 2022, LNCS, vol. 13702, pp. 374–388. Springer, Heidelberg (2022)

Evaluation of Graphical Modeling of CI/CD Workflows with Rig

Sebastian Teumert, Tim Tegeler(✉), Jonas Schürmann, Daniel Busch, and Dominic Wirkner

Chair for Programming Systems, TU Dortmund University, Dortmund, Germany
{sebastian.teumert,tim.tegeler,jonas.schurmann,daniel.busch, dominic.wirkner}@cs.tu-dortmund.de

Abstract. This evaluation is about our workshop on graphical modeling of CI/CD pipeline and how our self-developed tool Rig can support creating such workflows. We describe the three tasks the workshop covered and present the data we have gathered throughout the workshop via surveys of the participants. After that, the data is interpreted and discussed concerning its validity. Last, we draw conclusions from the data interpretations with regards to our future work with Rig and future workshops we plan to hold.

Keywords: Continuous Integration and Deployment · DevOps · Domain-Specific Tools · Graphical Modeling · Language-Driven Engineering · Purpose-Specific Language · Software Engineering · Visual Authoring

1 Introduction

For decades textual Domain-Specific Languages (DSLs) are ubiquitous in industrial practice. Especially web-based applications are implemented by the help of various DSLs, ranging from creating graphical user interfaces to accessing database severs. Thus, literature attributes DSLs with positive characteristics in contrast to General-Purpose Languages (GPLs) as the following quote emphasizes.

> "DSLs trade generality for expressiveness in a limited domain. By providing notations and constructs tailored toward a particular application domain, they offer substantial gains in expressiveness and ease of use compared with GPLs for the domain in question, with corresponding gains in productivity and reduced maintenance costs. Also, by reducing the amount of domain and programming expertise needed, DSLs open up their application domain to a larger group of software developers compared to GPLs." [13]

However, we believe this does not automatically apply to every DSL. For example, in the broad domain of cloud computing [12], DSLs for infrastructure

T. Margaria and B. Steffen (Eds.): ISoLA 2022, LNCS 13702, pp. 374–388, 2022.
https://doi.org/10.1007/978-3-031-19756-7_21

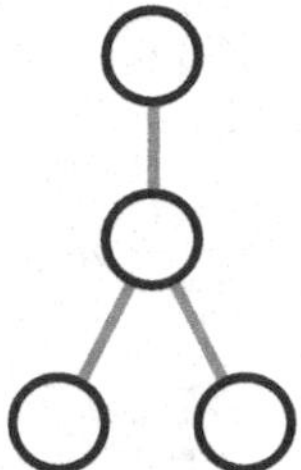

Fig. 1. Pipeline

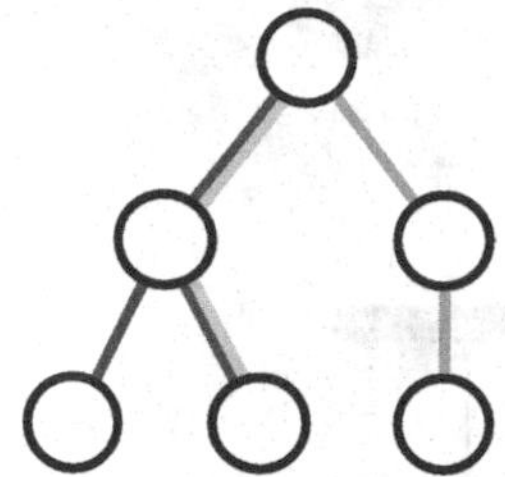

Fig. 2. Worfklow

Fig. 3. Configuration

provisioning and build automation such as Continuous Integration and Deployment (CI/CD) convey the impression that "expressiveness and ease of use" [13] were no major language-design requirements. We draw this conclusion from the fact that they are mostly implemented on top of languages which were originally intended for data-serialization.

In [20,21] we argued that a graphical modeling language for CI/CD workflows in combination with a custom-tailored Integrated Modeling Environment (IME) has the potential to take away shortcomings of textual DSLs in this domain. Based on this assumption, Rig was implemented to prove our concept [23]. We introduced Rig to a group of conference participants during a hands-on workshop addressing key concepts of the DevOps methodology and lifecycle during the *6th International School on Tool-Based Rigorous Engineering of Software Systems* (STRESS) [10] held in Faliraki, Rhodes (Greece) on October 2021, 19th–23rd, in association with ISoLA 2021. After a series of presentations on DevOps and especially CI/CD, participants had the opportunity to create their own CI/CD workflows for exemplary applications which were provided by the workshops organizers. The workshop had three exercises: An introductory one, one in which participants had to write the configurations manually, and finally one using Rig. This paper aims to evaluate Rig based on the results gathered during the workshop.

In Sect. 2 we briefly introduce Rig and the concept of CI/CD, before Sect. 3 states three research questions for this evaluation. Section 4 describes the setup of the workshop including a brief summary of the three exercises. The results of the data gathered during the workshop is presented in Sect. 5 and interpreted in Sect. 6. Section 7 discusses threats to validity of our findings. In Sect. 8 we outline the future work on Rig and conclude the paper in Sect. 9.

2 Background

While CI/CD has become increasingly popular in modern software engineering to reduce manual tasks and improve release processes, developers are facing major challenges during its adoption [19]. In the context of CI/CD, we are using

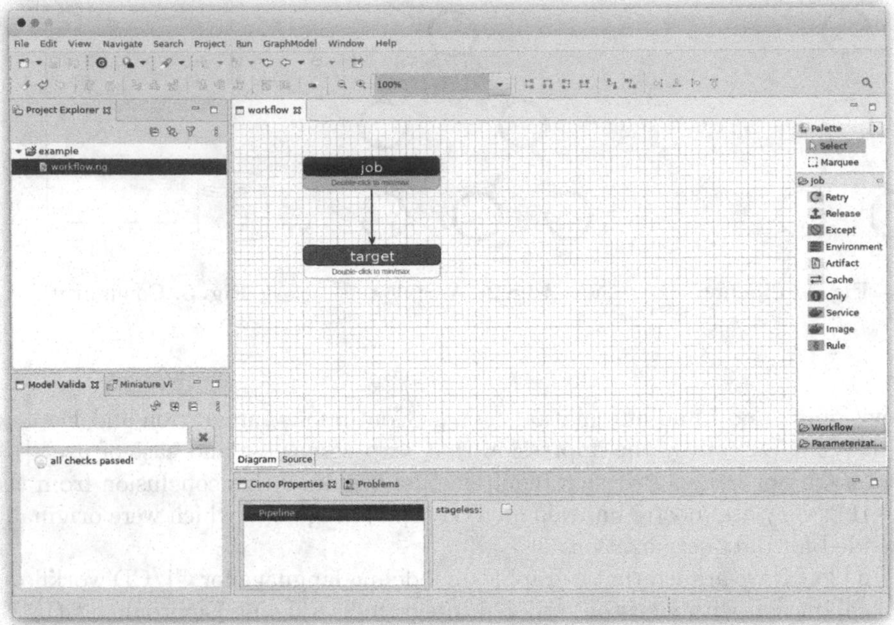

Fig. 4. CI/CD modeling environment of rig (cf. [21])

the terms pipeline and workflow as described in [21]. A pipeline (cf. Fig. 1) is what we call a single execution chain of jobs, where each job performs a certain build/test/deployment/etc. These jobs are usually executed sequentially, but they can also branch off to allow for parallel execution. A software project needs a variety of different pipelines to e.g. target different deployment environments or perform jobs specific to certain branches. All these pipelines are captured in a workflow definition (cf. Fig. 2), which includes all the job descriptions and possible execution paths. Workflows have traditionally been written in YAML configuration files (cf. Fig. 3) that embed shell scripts to define what a job should do. They reside within the repository alongside the source code.

In their paper [20], Tegeler et al. introduced a concept of model-driven CI/CD and presented a first visual model for such workflow definitions. Subsequently, an IME named *Rig* (cf. Fig. 4) has been developed to fully generate CI/CD workflows from visual models for the target platform GitLab [23]. To allow easy creation of a graphical modelling workbench Rig has been implemented using the Cinco *Meta Tooling Suite* [1,15]. Through the utilization of Cinco only simple specifications of Rig's model structures and stylings have been necessary to create a fully functional modeling Integrated Development Environment (mIDE) based on the Eclipse Rich Client Platform (RCP) [11] including tooling support for a better user experience. This tooling support combined with the simplicity of graphical models aims to enable non-experts to create their own CI/CD workflows with ease. Graphical editors provide palettes with all available modeling elements. Therefore, users get a visual overview of CI/CD capabilities and might be more encouraged to try the full feature set available in this domain. Due to CINCO's correct-by-construction paradigm workflows generated on basis of valid graphical models are always error-free as well. This can lead to a great decrease of trial-and-error roundtrip time and make CI/CD workflows more accessible. We will investigate this effect later in this paper. For a more in-depth introduction to graphical modeling of CI/CD workflows with Rig see [21].

3 Research Questions

Based on the approach described in [20,23], Rig aims to achieve the following goals: First, providing fast feedback through model-validation to the user and as a result reducing the round-trips between workflow editing and pipeline execution. Second, ruling out invalid configurations by restricting workflow models to valid ones, supported by static validation and robust code generation which prevents syntactical errors. Last, lowering the barrier of entry to CI/CD by making the creation of workflows easier for beginners and experts alike.

In order to be able to measure the success of Rig in these regards, we identified a set of key question that can be answered quantitatively by looking at the available data. Formulated as research questions to be answered with our analysis, these questions are:

Q1 (Reducing trial-and-error) Does Rig reduce the total amount of pipelines that are run until a working configuration is reached?
Q2 (Correctness-by-construction) Does Rig reduce the amount of invalid pipelines?
Q3 (Entry-barrier) Does Rig reduce the amount of failing pipelines (for already correct software packages)?

In the following section, we will present the workshop we used for data collection. Section 5 contains the data that resulted from the workshop, and Sect. 6 contains the interpretation of the quantitative results with regards to these research questions.

4 Workshop

The presented results and their interpretation are based on data collected during an interactive workshop with international participants of STRESS 2021. The workshop, alongside a hands-on experience, focused on graphical modeling of CI/CD workflows in the context of DevOps. The goal of this workshop was to impart basic understanding of the concept of CI/CD and let participants get to know the challenges involved in maintaining such workflows with current implementations. As a secondary objective, participants experienced the advantages of our model-driven approach by Rig along on the treatment of simple web

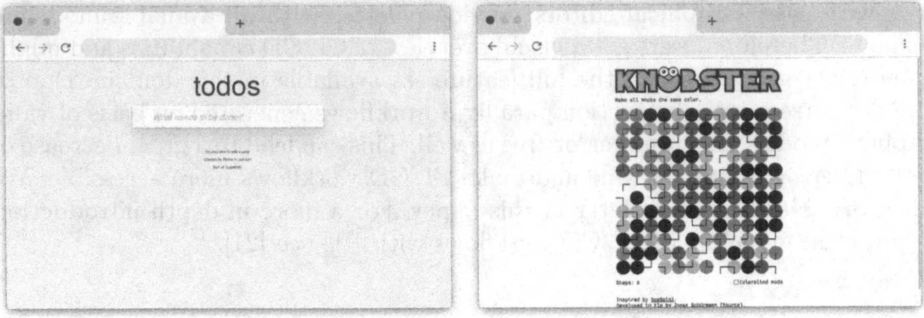

Fig. 5. Example applications TodoMVC and Knobster

applications. We organized the workshop based on GitLab [6] and its CI/CD implementation as service provider.

CI/CD workflows do not live in isolation, but are usually part of source code repository to build, test and deliver software artifacts. In order to let participants focus exclusively on the aspect of CI/CD, we prepared exemplary applications (cf. Fig. 5). Since the workshop was intended as a teaching session, we chose two different applications to maintain the participants' interest and motivation by recurring exercise content. Furthermore, it was important that the software stack of both applications is easily comprehensible and the necessary build process is straightforward, in order to not introduce additional risks of failure to the pipelines that could mislead workshop participants. For this purpose we chose TodoMVC [16] and Knobster [18], which are based on different technology stacks, but are comparable from the complexity of their build processes. The chosen version of TodoMVC is based on TypeScript [14], while Knobster is written in Elm [4]. Both web-based applications compile to JavaScript and run in the browser without depending on any server-side application. This made it easy for workshop participants to try the built application with standard tools of the operating system.

4.1 Setup

Experiences with previous workshops [2,3,7,8,17] showed us that we should aim at *zero setup* (cf. [5]) of including software and services, to make it as convenient as possible for the participants. Furthermore, we could not rely on unrestricted broadband access to the internet on site, so we tried to reduce the overall needed internet traffic for the entire workshop to a minimum and used only default HTTP ports (e.g. 80/443) for outbound connection. Installers of Rig for all supported platforms (i.e. Windows, Linux and macOS) were already downloaded on thumb drives and access to GitLab was intended via their web-based GUI only. To oversee the workshops process we prepared a dedicated GitLab group with separated projects for every exercise. We asked the participants to create branches based on their GitLab handle (for easier mapping), and to work on separated branches so participants did not get into each other's way. In order to support the temporal high demand for CI/CD performance (each pipelines' job allocates hardware resources for the runtime), we have prepared additional resources in form of so-called CI/CD runners. Those runners were remotely provided and assigned to the GitLab group prior to the event. While performance was initially the major concern, independent runners resolved the problem of running into the budget cap of the free-of-charge CI/CD minutes of GitLab.

4.2 Exercises

After introducing the general topic by talks on DevOps and CI/CD, the hands-on part acted as the main session. It was conceptualized for 90 min and divided into three exercises. Each of those exercises was thematically build upon each other. Alongside a tutorial introduction to the usage of Rig, which can be found in [21], we provided a comprehensive digital handout including the following three exercises:

E1 (Intro) The aim of the introductory exercise was to get to know the basic features of GitLab that are needed in the subsequent exercises and get in contact with the first configuration. Following the tradition of *Hello World* as the first exercise when learning a new programming language, the task was to execute a pipeline containing a single job which will print 'Hello World'. To make it easy, we provided a working configuration in the exercise sheet.

E2 (TodoMVC) After the successful run of the first pipeline, the second exercise addressed a more complex workflow that *builds*, *tests* and *delivers* a web application called TodoMVC. On the basis of a provided bash script, containing all relevant commands to build the application, it was the participants' task to port the script and its commands into a working configuration (cf. [21] for a sample solution). The goal of this exercise was to demonstrate the quirks and error-proneness when manually writing configurations.

E3 (Knobster) As the third exercise, participants were asked to use Rig to create a workflow for Knobster, which required a comparable grade of workflow complexity as TodoMVC. The objective of this final exercise was to contrast the advantages of graphically modeled and fully generated configurations with the manually written configuration of the previous exercise. For the comparability of results (cf. Sect. 7), it would have been more reasonable to choose an application with the identical technology stack. However, at the time of organizing the workshop, our focus was on keeping participants motivated by presenting diverse exercises.

5 Results

We gathered the data after our workshop described in Sect. 4 had concluded and evaluated it with respect to these questions. We focused solely on readily accessible data of pipeline runs, without examining the complexity or structure

Table 1. Pipeline result statistics gathered after the workshop

			E1: Intro	E2: TodoMVC	E3: Knobster
T	Total	$E+I$	20	86	34
E	Executed	$T-I$	20	67	34
I	Invalid	$T-E$	0	19	0
S	Successful	$T-F$	20	26	23
U	Unsuccessful	$E-S$	0	41	11
F	Failed	$I+U$	0	60	11
TSR	Total success rate	S/T	100%	30.23%	67.65%
EFR	Execution failure rate	U/E	0%	61.19%	32.35%
IR	Invalid rate	I/F	0%	31.67%	0%
P	Participants		13	13	13

of committed pipelines. The data has been sanitized prior to evaluation, and pipelines run by the organizers during setup of the workshop were excluded. The sanitized data is shown in Table 1.

We collected a total of five different metrics after the workshop, two of them are further categorized into sub-categories. Failed pipelines were split into two groups for invalid and unsuccessful runs, while for total pipelines the subcategory of actually executed ones was calculated. Thus, we arrived at the following raw metrics available for the evaluation:

Total (T) Total number of attempts to run a pipeline in the repository. This number highly correlates with the number of commits, since per default, GitLab runs pipelines on every commit.

Executed (E) The number of pipelines that were instantiated successfully. This excludes pipelines that failed to instantiate (**I**).

Invalid (I) Number of pipelines that failed to be instantiated due to errors in the configuration, including, but not limited to syntax errors and errors in the dependency structure.

Successful (S) Number of successful pipelines. This does not indicate that the pipeline worked as expected; it merely indicates that the pipeline finished its run without detectable error.

Unsuccessful (U) Number of unsuccessful pipelines. The pipeline was instantiated successfully, but terminated abnormally e.g. due to script errors or failure to produce an expected artifact.

Failed (F) The amount of pipelines that failed for any reason, including invalid configurations (**I**) and unsuccessful runs (**U**). The number of failed pipelines plus the number of successful pipelines equals the number of total pipelines.

Participants (P) The number of participants that have worked on the exercise (measured by having submitted at least one workflow configuration for the exercise), excluding the organizers.

Based on these numbers, we identified and derived three key metrics which were deemed interesting to answer the research question posed in Sect. 3.

Total Success Rate (TSR) Successful pipelines out of total pipelines. Indicates overall success rates.
Invalid Rate (IR) Percentage of failed pipelines that are invalid. Indicates how many failures were due to errors in the configuration.
Execution Failure Rate (EFR) Given all the actually executed pipelines, the percentage of unsuccessful pipelines. Indicates the semantic correctness of the used configuration.

6 Interpretation

E1 served as a baseline to ensure the participants proficiency with the UI of GitLab and that they had proper access to our group. Due to the nature of the task (cf. Sect. 4), the results of this exercise are unsurprising. We observed a success rate of 100% for all executed pipelines and each participant finished the exercise successfully. Although these numbers have little direct value, they serve as a baseline of the participants' ability to use GitLab. The absence of unsuccessful attempts gives us more confidence in the validity of the results of **E2** and **E3**, since we can almost neglect confounding effects due to the lack of experience with GitLab's UI.

The remaining evaluation focuses on evaluating **E2** and **E3** with respect to **Q1**–**Q3**.

Reducing Trial-and-Error. The total amount of pipelines that were run substantially decreased when working with Rig. In **E2**, participants ran 86 pipelines with a **TSR** of 30.23%. In **E3**, participants only ran 34 pipelines, with a **TSR** of 67.65%. Thus, we not only saw an increase in the **TSR**, but also a substantial decrease in the total number of pipelines that were needed until participants reached a satisfactory outcome. We can derive from GitLab's branch overview and pipeline statistics, that the number of participants was the same in both exercises. This means a substantial reduction of pipelines per participant.

Looking at **Q1**, we can therefore conclude that Rig fulfills the goal of reducing trial-and-error in order to create correctly working pipeline configurations.

Correctness-by-Construction. As expected, the number of invalid pipelines dropped substantially, from 19 (which is equivalent to an **IR** of 31.67%) in **E2** to zero in **E3**. Thus, we can answer **Q2** definitely with a positive outcome. The model-based approach is capable of completely eliminating this class of errors (syntax errors and errors in the dependency structure), as the results clearly demonstrate.

Entry-Barrier. While the total number of pipelines decreased substantially, we only saw a slight decrease in successful pipelines (from 26 to 23), while the number of failing pipelines dropped significantly from 60 to only 11. This means that in general participants made slight corrections after their first successful run and were then satisfied with a subsequent run, but they arrived at a first working state significantly quicker when using Rig.

Looking at the **EFR**, which is the rate of failing pipelines after excluding outright invalid ones, we saw a decrease of unsuccessful pipelines from 61.19% in **E2** to 32.35% in **E3**. This means that the increase in successful pipelines is not solely due to fewer syntactical errors, but that overall, pipelines designed with Rig were more likely to finish successfully, indicating that using Rig indeed helps to create correct pipelines.

We therefore conclude that **Q3** can also be answered positively. Using Rig leads to a higher success rate in creating pipelines, which is not solely due to eliminating a whole class of errors.

Overall, the findings show that graphical modeling has potential to both eliminate a whole class of errors and improve the success rate of users, when compared with textual DSLs. While we have shown this for a specific domain – in this case visual authoring of CI/CD workflows – we think that these are encouraging results for model-driven engineering in general. Furthermore, we think this lets Rig join the ranks of successful CINCO products and demonstrates once again the versatility of CINCO's meta-modelling approach (cf. [15]).

7 Threats to Validity

Although we did a lot of up-front anticipating of the workflows' procedure and internal simulations, we have run into couple unexpected issues: When participants logged into GitLab for the first time with a pristine user account, they were presented a warning that their accounts are missing an SSH public key. Even if the exercises do not need SSH authentication as access to the web interface of GitLab is sufficient to change and commit files, the warning threw off some participants. Further issues related to GitLab accounts arose when participants requested access to single exercise projects and not to the overall group. Since we as the organizers just checked the access requests of the group, it created confusion among the participants and hampered the start of the workshop. Another issue resulted from the exercise sheet of the handout which envisaged to download and install Rig as part of the general preliminaries. Unfortunately, this let participants skip the exercise sheet and jump to Rig directly, doing the examples in the Rig documentation. In summary, the workshop was intended as a teaching session, and did not constitute a formal experiment or study. Thus, we have to admit that the threats to validity are rather large.

- We lacked a control group to compare our results with. We used one group that worked on the exercise in order. Thus, when the group reached the exercise **E3**, they had already gained experience in exercise **E2**. Thus, the

results we saw in the exercise **E3** are likely biased against better results. Nonetheless, we think that the results can be viewed as encouraging.
- The variance of applications in the exercises **E2** and **E3** lets us treat the comparability and interpretation with caution. Although the stack and build process of both applications are very similar, the difference in the used programming languages might tamper with the presented numbers.
- We did not send out a survey prior or during the workshop to gather statistics about our participants, so we cannot compare results by prior experience. We can not say for sure if the group was representative, although informal inquiry shows that the group indeed did have a wide range of prior knowledge. With only 13 participants, the group was also rather small.

All these limiting factors mean that the statistical results have to be taken with a grain of salt, and that a more thorough study to confirm these results is needed. Considering our experience with planning a workshop, organizers should be prepared for unexpected challenges during the course of a workshop. This includes both technological and organizational issues. Most of them are hard to anticipate, but as our experiences teaches some general principles, like zero setup, economical internet connection/bandwidth and providing a step-wise exercise sheet, help to avoid frustrating events on-site.

8 Future Work

While the results from our workshop are encouraging, adoption rates within our own organization have not been as high as initially planned. Over the course of almost a year, we have gathered the qualitative feedback resulting from our own use, our students use and feedback from participants of the workshop. This qualitative feedback has not been collected in a formal study, but nonetheless can be used to identify key areas of improvement for Rig. We hope to address these issues and to re-verify the results of this paper both with an improved version of Rig but also improved procedures and data collection at another workshop.

In this section, we will briefly explain the improvements for Rig that are planned in the future in order to help increase adoption rates and also to improve the numbers seen in the workshop in the future. We identified the three key areas *modelling*, *implementation* and *workflow* in which feedback can be categorized.

Modelling. The initial modelling of CI/CD workflow presented in [20] was that of a DAG using dataflow semantics. The semantics of Rig largely follow this pattern, especially with regard to jobs, targets and script arguments (please cf. [21] for an introduction to graphical modeling with Rig, and [22] for an in-depth discussion on the language design). Other elements of its graphical modeling language however do not follow this pattern, leading to unintuitive edge directions. This can be explained by mixing both definitions and usage into one language. A more clear model of how elements are defined and how they are used in the workflow is needed.

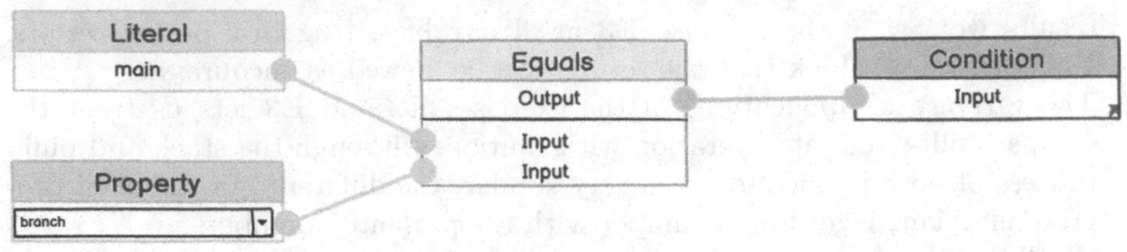

Fig. 6. Mockup of a graphical modeling language for CI/CD conditions (cropped reprint of [23])

Another area of improvements is the clarity of the workflow. The entry point of the workflow has been mentioned as not easy to see at first glance. Re-modelling Rig's language for better dataflow semantics and making more uniform edge directions should alleviate this problem as well.

We also found that the concept of targets is not as easy to grasp as we hoped, especially for simple workflows. We are already planning to allow simple workflows to be defined in a target-less manner, cutting down boilerplate and making simple workflows even simpler to model, while still having the ability to use targets for more complex workflows.

A large area of improvements is generalizing Rig even more. While the initial goal of Rig was to describe CI/CD workflows in general and to be able to derive configurations for multiple platforms, the resulting graphical language is quite close to being a model for GitLab. This is a missed opportunity to abstract away some of the counter-intuitive features of GitLab and runs counter to being able to use Rig universally. It also prevents us from ruling out even more errors. In GitLab, durations as in `artifacts:expire_in` are given in a *natural language* and interpreted with the `chronic_duration`[1] ruby gem. While intended to be human-friendly, the ambiguous syntax can lead to errors that are hard to track down because they are so well hidden and does not allow the programmer to see them as wrong easily. Rig currently passes these values on verbatim. A more abstract model, especially for the notion of time, is needed.

Another key are conditions. Rig closely models GitLab's Rules, Except and Only elements to define the conditions under which jobs are executed. This abstraction is very thin and requires the user to learn GitLabs very specific syntax[2]. While Rig offers some support for writing these textual expressions by embedding a syntax highlighter and code assist, the process is error-prone and unintuitive, especially for novice users. We believe that using another a dedicated graphical modeling language as shown in Fig. 6 for this is needed. Currently, users would need to use the "Rules" element with an "If" child element and input the expression `$CI_COMMIT_BRANCH == "main"` as value for this element.

Rig currently also does not support GitLab specific features like GitLab Pages, Releases and GitLab SAST very well due to the special rules GitLab

[1] https://www.rubydoc.info/gems/hpoydar-chronic_duration/0.7.3.

[2] https://docs.gitlab.com/ee/ci/jobs/job_control.html#common-if-clauses-for-rules.

has for jobs that deal with these features. A more abstract model can better hide those details from the user and allow Rig to cover these more easily without compromising clarity.

Implementation. Rig is an Eclipse RCP Application, which means it is built on top of the Eclipse Runtime (cf. Sect. 2). This is a rather large and heavy-weight technology stack, especially for such a small tool, as the resulting binary size is about 350 MB for each platform[3]. The resulting application includes additional features that are not needed for the specific purpose of the IME and distract from the actual purpose. Furthermore, users need to have a Java 11 runtime installed and correctly configured on their system (the executable has to be on the PATH). All of these factors make using Rig unnecessarily difficult.

The CINCO team has already identified this as a general issue as well and is working towards a cloud-based version of CINCO [24]. We are looking forward to contribute our experiences with developing CINCO products and integrate Rig, once CINCO Cloud is available.

Furthermore, the code generated by Rig is not minimal. Usually, this is not a problem, but GitLab offers their own, minimalistic visualizations of checked-in configurations. When this visualization is radically different from what the user had modelled earlier, this can be a cause for confusion. We plan to address this both by minimizing the generated output, but also by leveraging CINCO Clouds ability to be included in other web pages. Replacing GitLab's editor with our own modeling environment via browser-plugin will remove the inconsistency.

Workflow. While working with Rig in its current state, it is necessary to commit the generated configuration to the repository in order for GitLab to recognize it and run the associated pipelines. This leads to the well-known round-trip-engineering problems when changes are introduced directly to the generated file and runs counter to our One-Thing Approach (OTA), where the single source of truth should be the model [9].

The CINCO team is currently working on enhancing CINCO with headless generation of CINCO Products. We hope to leverage this headless mode to be able to generate configurations from workflow models on-the-fly. This would allow Rig to serve as the orchestrator of pipelines, at least on platforms where such a dynamic invocation is possible. Using GitLab's capability to trigger child pipelines using a generated configuration passed in via artifact, the goal is to dynamically generate the pipeline from the checked-in Rig model from within the pipeline. Thus, no generated configuration has to be committed, and the executed pipeline is always consistent with the model, achieving the OTA and solving all Round-trip Engineering (RTE) problems.

Another shortcoming in this area is the fact that Rig currently does not automatically update the generated file when a new workflow model is saved.

[3] https://ls5download.cs.tu-dortmund.de/rig/.

This can lead to developers inadvertently committing an outdated configuration to the repository.

One of the key drivers we hoped to have for adoption was ease of use and simplicity. This is true for new, greenfield projects. However, converting existing workflows into Rig models has a significant development and opportunity cost, as it becomes necessary to re-verify that the workflow works as expected. Refactoring an already working part of the software development process is a hard to justify cost. Furthermore, formal analysis of pipelines and unit testing of CI/CD workflows to ensure their behavior matches the prior behavior is a largely unexplored field, making it hard to become confident that the newly modelled workflow works as expected without extensive testing in the production repository. A more generalized description of CI/CD workflows can be an opportunity to introduce more formal analysis and unit testing into this area.

In conclusion, the future work for Rig will consist of moving away from Eclipse RCP as the basis and onto CINCO Cloud for easier adoption, while remodelling its graphical language to be (a) more general, (b) more consistent with the dataflow-model and (c) more abstract. At the same time, we will address usability issues and work on enhancing the workflow of Rig, especially reducing RTE and reducing the cost of adoption by making the transition from a pre-Rig into a post-Rig world easier.

9 Conclusion

Despite the threats to validity, we think that the statistical results gathered during our workshop at STRESS 2021 are very encouraging and indicate that visual authoring is an adequate modeling choice to lower the barrier of entry for CI/CD.

In our opinion, workshops in general provide a good opportunity to evaluate early stages of an application under a controlled environment, besides presenting the underlying approach to an international audience. The participants' unfamiliarity with the software product can provide interesting insights which otherwise might stay hidden to the application's developers. However, it is quite hard, as we experienced, to gather feedback and evaluate data post-mortem of the workshop. Hence, a more formal and comprehensive study is needed that addresses the threats to validity to this evaluation in order to verify the presented result. This includes among others, prepared surveys, group composition of participants (e.g. control group) and designing exercises that allow a simple quantification. In addition to that, analysing the complexity and structure of committed pipelines alongside the readily accessible data on the outcome of pipelines could be a prospective field of research.

We hope that our lessons learned can serve as a basic guideline and the presented evaluation helps to plan future workshops for the further iteration(s) of the *International School on Tool-Based Rigorous Engineering of Software Systems* or similar events.

References

1. Cinco SCCE Meta Tooling Suite. http://cinco.scce.info
2. Biondi, F., Given-Wilson, T., Legay, A., Puodzius, C., Quilbeuf, J.: Tutorial: an overview of malware detection and evasion techniques. In: Margaria, T., Steffen, B. (eds.) ISoLA 2018. LNCS, vol. 11244, pp. 565–586. Springer, Cham (2018). https://doi.org/10.1007/978-3-030-03418-4_34
3. Boßelmann, S., et al.: DIME: a programming-less modeling environment for web applications. In: Margaria, T., Steffen, B. (eds.) ISoLA 2016. LNCS, vol. 9953, pp. 809–832. Springer, Cham (2016). https://doi.org/10.1007/978-3-319-47169-3_60
4. Czaplicki, E.: A delightful language for reliable web applications. https://elm-lang.org. Accessed 17 Feb 2022
5. Di Ruscio, D., Kolovos, D., de Lara, J., Pierantonio, A., Tisi, M., Wimmer, M.: Low-code development and model-driven engineering: two sides of the same coin? Softw. Syst. Model. **21**(2), 437–446 (2022). https://doi.org/10.1007/s10270-021-00970-2
6. GitLab B.V.: The DevOps platform has arrived. https://about.gitlab.com/. Accessed 17 Feb 2022
7. Gossen, F., Margaria, T., Murtovi, A., Naujokat, S., Steffen, B.: DSLs for decision services: a tutorial introduction to language-driven engineering. In: Margaria, T., Steffen, B. (eds.) ISoLA 2018. LNCS, vol. 11244, pp. 546–564. Springer, Cham (2018). https://doi.org/10.1007/978-3-030-03418-4_33
8. Lybecait, M., Kopetzki, D., Zweihoff, P., Fuhge, A., Naujokat, S., Steffen, B.: A tutorial introduction to graphical modeling and metamodeling with CINCO. In: Margaria, T., Steffen, B. (eds.) ISoLA 2018. LNCS, vol. 11244, pp. 519–538. Springer, Cham (2018). https://doi.org/10.1007/978-3-030-03418-4_31
9. Margaria, T., Steffen, B.: Business process modelling in the jABC: the one-thing-approach. In: Cardoso, J., van der Aalst, W. (eds.) Handbook of Research on Business Process Modeling. IGI Global (2009)
10. Margaria, T., Steffen, B. (eds.): ISoLA 2021. LNCS, vol. 13036. Springer, Cham (2021). https://doi.org/10.1007/978-3-030-89159-6
11. McAffer, J., Lemieux, J.M., Aniszczyk, C.: Eclipse Rich Client Platform, 2nd edn. Addison-Wesley Professional, Boston (2010)
12. Mell, P., Grance, T.: The NIST definition of cloud computing. NIST Special Publication 800-145 (2011). https://doi.org/10.6028/NIST.SP.800-145
13. Mernik, M., Heering, J., Sloane, A.M.: When and how to develop domain-specific languages. ACM Comput. Surv. **37**(4), 316–344 (2005). https://doi.org/10.1145/1118890.1118892
14. Microsoft Corporation: Typescript is JavaScript with syntax for types. https://www.typescriptlang.org. Accessed 17 Feb 2022
15. Naujokat, S., Lybecait, M., Kopetzki, D., Steffen, B.: CINCO: a simplicity-driven approach to full generation of domain-specific graphical modeling tools. Int. J. Softw. Tools Technol. Transf. **20**(3), 327–354 (2017). https://doi.org/10.1007/s10009-017-0453-6
16. Osmani, A., et al.: TodoMVC - helping you select an MV* framework. https://todomvc.com/. Accessed 31 Aug 2021
17. Robby, Hatcliff, J., Belt, J.: Model-based development for high-assurance embedded systems. In: Margaria, T., Steffen, B. (eds.) ISoLA 2018. LNCS, vol. 11244, pp. 539–545. Springer, Cham (2018). https://doi.org/10.1007/978-3-030-03418-4_32

18. Schürmann, J.: Knobster. https://knobster.jonas-schuermann.name/. Accessed 17 Feb 2022
19. Shahin, M., Babar, M.A., Zhu, L.: Continuous integration, delivery and deployment: a systematic review on approaches, tools, challenges and practices. IEEE Access **5**, 3909–3943 (2017). https://doi.org/10.1109/ACCESS.2017.2685629
20. Tegeler, T., Gossen, F., Steffen, B.: A model-driven approach to continuous practices for modern cloud-based web applications. In: 2019 9th International Conference on Cloud Computing, Data Science Engineering (Confluence), pp. 1–6 (2019). https://doi.org/10.1109/CONFLUENCE.2019.8776962
21. Tegeler, T., Teumert, S., Schürmann, J., Bainczyk, A., Busch, D., Steffen, B.: An introduction to graphical modeling of CI/CD workflows with rig. In: Margaria, T., Steffen, B. (eds.) ISoLA 2021. LNCS, vol. 13036, pp. 3–17. Springer, Cham (2021). https://doi.org/10.1007/978-3-030-89159-6_1
22. Teumert, S.: Rig | low-code CI/CD modeling. https://scce.gitlab.io/rig/. Accessed 07 Jan 2022
23. Teumert, S.: Visual authoring of CI/CD pipeline configurations. Bachelor's thesis, TU Dortmund University, April 2021. https://archive.org/details/visual-authoring-of-cicd-pipeline-configurations
24. Zweihoff, P., Tegeler, T., Schürmann, J., Bainczyk, A., Steffen, B.: Aligned, purpose-driven cooperation: the future way of system development. In: Margaria, T., Steffen, B. (eds.) ISoLA 2021. LNCS, vol. 13036, pp. 426–449. Springer, Cham (2021). https://doi.org/10.1007/978-3-030-89159-6_27

Towards Continuous Quality Control in the Context of Language-Driven Engineering

Alexander Bainczyk(✉), Steve Boßelmann, Marvin Krause, Marco Krumrey, Dominic Wirkner, and Bernhard Steffen

Chair for Programming Systems, Department of Computer Science, TU Dortmund University, 44227 Dortmund, Germany
{alexander.bainczyk,steve.bosselmann,marvin.krause,marco.krumrey, dominic.wirkner,bernhard.steffen}@tu-dortmund.de

Abstract. In this paper, we illustrate the role of quality assurance in Language-Driven Engineering (LDE) which exploits the observation that *the more specific a programming/modeling language is, the better it can be controlled.* In fact, well-tailored domain-specific languages (DSLs) allow one to (1) syntactically express a number of semantic properties with the effect that they can be verified during syntax analysis or using more involved static verification techniques like model checking, and (2), combined with a concept of design for testability, to automatically validate run-time properties using, in our case, learning-based testing technology. To ensure practicality and scalability, the LDE approach must be supported by language definition technology, powerful enough to ensure that corresponding Integrated Modeling Environments (IMEs) can be generated on demand. Our LDE ecosystem provides such means in a fashion where the dependencies between the various modeling environments and their corresponding meta-modeling environments are systematically addressed in a path-up/tree-down fashion: application-level requests are stepwise moved up to the meta hierarchy, far enough to fully address the issue at hand. The resulting meta-level changes are then propagated down the meta hierarchy to ensure the adequate migration of all involved IMEs and their corresponding modeled artifacts.

Keywords: Continuous quality control · Model/learning-based testing · Domain-specific languages · Language-driven engineering · Active automata learning · Generation · Migration

1 Introduction

Traditionally, Quality Assurance (QA) is split into at least three parts that are typically treated by different people independently: (1) static verification, including theorem proving-based techniques and model checking, (2) dynamic validation like (learning-based) testing, and (3) runtime verification techniques

T. Margaria and B. Steffen (Eds.): ISoLA 2022, LNCS 13702, pp. 389–406, 2022.
https://doi.org/10.1007/978-3-031-19756-7_22

like supported monitoring. Language-Driven Engineering (LDE) aims at aligning various meta levels to achieve consistency between a growing multitude of domain-specific languages and their defining meta-levels via automated generation of corresponding Integrated Modeling Environments (IMEs). In particular, when considering the evolution of the entire LDE ecosystem, the following classification in terms of Archimedean points of the properties to be assured helps structuring the global QA process [25]:

Rigid Archimedean Points (RAPs) that are directly enforced by construction: it is simply impossible to construct violating models with the corresponding modeling tool. E.g., if a RAP requires that every edge is meant to connect two nodes, then the tool will not allow to draw dangling edges. The potential of RAPs increases with the specificity of the underlying DSLs.

Verifiable Archimedean Points (VAPs) concern properties that can be verified automatically at the model level in order to provide the modeler with feedback. VAPs very much resemble the 'intelligence' of modern IDEs which give feedback about syntax and type violations, certain dataflow properties, and the like. In contrast to RAPs, VAPs do not prevent the construction of violating models, but leave the correction to the user of the modeling tool. This detection strategy is in particular advantageous for properties which cannot be established without any intermediate violation. For example, consider the connectivity of a graph in a context of the RAP example above: In order to guarantee that each edge always has a source and a target, one may need to place the nodes first, before one can introduce the connecting edge. But this requires an unconnected intermediate graph. Traditional means for VAPs are type checking, model checking, and automated theorem proving.

Observable Archimedean Points (OAPs) concern properties that cannot be taken care of by the tool automatically, e.g., because the underlying analysis problem is undecidable. Examples are computational invariants, termination and many other Object Constraint Language (OCL) properties [26]. However, they may be validated with simulation and testing methods, or by means of runtime verification by injecting the required checking code via some aspect-oriented code generation.

Intuitively, establishing OAPs is an application-level issue, while RAPs and VAPs need to be established at the modeling level. In both cases, preparation at the meta level is essential:

- RAPs require adequate syntactic constraints,
- VAPs formalize properties, formulated, e.g., as type systems or in temporal logics, and
- OAPs depend on code generators that adequately instrument the executable code in order to, e.g., feed monitors with sufficient run-time information.

In this paper, we illustrate the role of quality assurance in Language-Driven Engineering (LDE) which exploits the observation that *the more specific a programming/modeling language is, the better it can be controlled.* In fact, well-tailored domain-specific languages (DSLs)

- allow one to syntactically express semantic properties in a way that they can be verified during syntax analysis or using more involved static verification techniques like model checking or theorem proving, e.g., on the basis of temporal logic specifications or first-order logic invariants, and
- are ideally combined with a concept of *design for testability* for adequate code instrumentation to automatically validate run-time properties using, in our case, learning-based testing technology.

To ensure practicality and scalability, the LDE approach must be supported by language definition technology, powerful enough to ensure that corresponding IMEs can be generated on demand.

Our LDE ecosystem provides such means in a fashion where the dependencies between the various modeling environments and their corresponding meta-modeling environments are systematically addressed in a path-up/tree-down fashion:

- Application-level requests are stepwise moved up to the meta hierarchy, far enough to fully address the issue at hand. In the easiest case, a request can be addressed simply by changing the application's model. More involved requests may require to move to the meta level to enhance the power of the corresponding IME.
- Meta-level changes are propagated down the meta hierarchy to ensure the adequate migration of all involved IMEs and their corresponding modeled artifacts. In cases where such a migration is inadequate, the corresponding meta level is split into two product lines.

Our LDE ecosystem does not only provide the functionality to perform these steps. Rather, its underlying versioning system also takes care of an adequate role management to prevent accidental changes or modifications by persons that lack the required competence.

In the next section we will sketch our static validation techniques before we present our learning-based, dynamic validation technology in Sect. 3. Subsequently, Sect. 4 will sketch our path-up/tree-down approach to scalability, before we conclude with Sect. 5.

2 Static Validation

Domain-Specific Languages (DSLs) enhance quality control with their powerful expressiveness in contrast to classical general purpose languages. The more domain-specific semantics are integrated into the language, the more of the desired application behavior can be validated before runtime.

We want to demonstrate static validation methods on the example of access control. In web applications, we typically assign roles to users and depending on the role, users can access resources and functionalities of the application that their role is enabled for. For example, in Fig. 1 we see an excerpt of a process for EquinOCS, our web-based editorial system, modeled in DIME [10], our IME

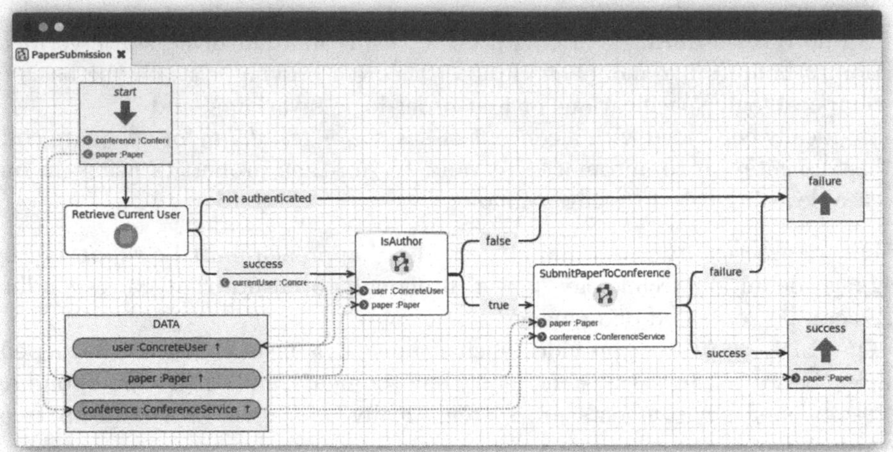

Fig. 1. DIME process for the paper submission in a conference in EquinOCS

for the model-driven development of full-stack web applications. The process controls the paper submission in two steps by (1) checking that a user performing a submission request is authenticated using the `Retrieve Current User` SIB, and by (2) guaranteeing that the user is an author of the paper (`IsAuthor`). Only if both checks are successful the paper can be submitted.

LDE provides two static means to guarantee properties like this, one via verifiable Archimedean points and one via rigid Archimedean points:

2.1 Exploiting the Verifiability

Our LDE ecosystem provides means to define the properties to be verified during the modelling phase in terms of temporal logics. For our paper submission example this could be

always (*authenticated* **before** *successful submission*)

Properties like this can then be automatically checked during the modeling phase using our integrated model checker GEAR [8]. In the example in Fig. 1, this check succeeds as the `success` branch from the `SubmitPaperToConference` SIB indicates a successful paper submission for authenticated authors.

In the concrete case of DIME, failing checks would prevent the generation of the corresponding DIME product (e.g., EquinOCS), and GEAR would provide feedback explaining the corresponding property violation. For linear-time properties explanations would be error paths, while branching-time properties may require to provide a 'strategy' that enforces violation in any application scenario.

It is part of the LDE approach to successively enhance the guidance for modelers by establishing appropriate (temporal) properties. We consider the definition of new properties as part of the meta modeling, as the properties constrain the language of allowed models. However, technically, property definition is orthogonal to the specification required for IME generation: New properties can be added without requiring re-generation of the IME.

2.2 Exploiting the Rigidity

Violations of rigid Archimedean points are prohibited by the corresponding IME. This means that they, like traditional syntax specifications, are part of the specification that underlies the IME generator. In fact, one could say that rigid Archimedean points result from turning the required properties into a syntactical property of the considered domain/purpose-specific modeling language. E.g., if we specify in our language that we can, e.g. only draw edges from a node of a certain type to a node of another type, then our modeling environment will prevent users from creating models that violate this constraint.

As language designers, we have to decide which aspects of a domain are reflected by the language and benefit from this behavior. Access control is an aspect that is commonly implemented in multi-tenant web applications that is not tailored to a specific instance in the domain. So, instead of creating verifiable formulas for each application (as it is currently the case), we could also enforce access control rules by extending the DIME language, e.g. by creating specialized kinds of nodes that enforce users to be authorized or to have a specific role. As a consequence of this, access control would then be a part of the DSL and the modeling environment would enforce it.

3 Dynamic Validation

The measures mentioned in the previous section focus on the validation of static properties in the context of DSL-driven development. However, at the end of our tool chain there is a running web application which targets end-users and has to fulfill functional requirements. Our means to verify that the application shows the expected behavior are Learning-Based Testing (LBT) and runtime monitoring.

Key to dynamic validation is observability: we can only verify at runtime what we can see. Dynamic validation aims at establishing corresponding Observable Archimedean Point (OAP), i.e., properties that constrain what a user can see.

Within our LDE ecosystem we apply LBT in the pre-production phase as an automated system testing methodology and monitoring of the running product as a runtime verification method. In combination, these methods guarantee that system models learned during LBT are continuously refined on the basis of the monitoring results which, in particular, allows one to generate powerful up-to-date regression test suites from the continuously evolving system models.

3.1 Learning-Based Testing

Due to the nature of our full-code-generation approach, we consider generated code and the running application as an instance of that code to be a black-box system. Low-level testing methods such as unit-testing cannot be applied in

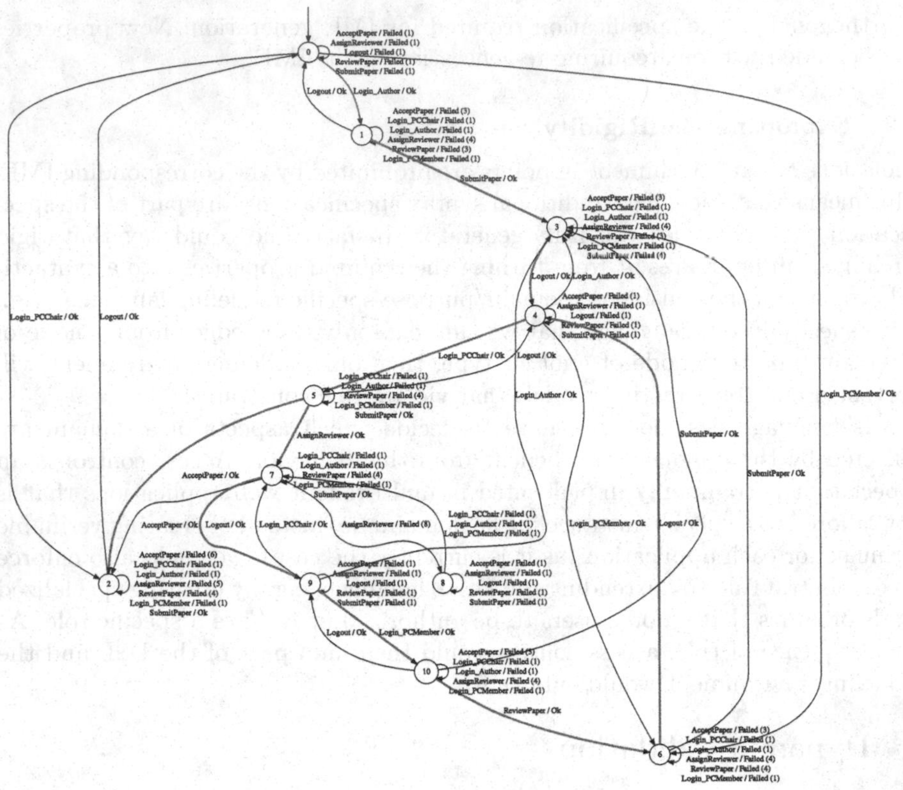

Fig. 2. A learned model of the paper reviewing process in EquinOCS. The highlighted path shows the sequence of actions from submitting a paper by an author to the acceptance of the paper by a PC Chair.

this case. One reason for this is that generated code typically stays untouched and we do not want manual code to interfere with generated code because of the increased maintenance and synchronization effort. Instead, we perform automated end-to-end testing via active automata learning, i.e., interacting with a system directly through its public interface, such as a web frontend or HTTP-based APIs to check if the application adheres to functional requirements that cannot be checked on the modeling level.

Automata learning has improved continuously [15,20,23] and has been adapted to infer models from black-box systems via automated testing [24] which allows one to, e.g., apply formal verification methods such as model checking for the verification of system properties. Basically, active automata learning follows the Minimal Adequate Teacher (MAT) principle where, given an input alphabet $\Sigma = \{\sigma_0, \ldots, \sigma_n\}$, a *learner* poses two types of queries to a *teacher*. *Membership queries* retrieve behavioral information about the System Under Learning (SUL). They consist of a sequence of concrete system inputs over Σ, which trigger the SUL to react and produce some kind of observable output. Based on these observations, the learner builds a *hypothesis* - an automaton model that represents the systems' behavior. The other type of query is the *equivalence query*. Such a query checks whether the inferred hypothesis is a correct representation of the SUL. If there is a difference between the learned model and the system, the teacher provides a trace of diverging behavior that can be used by the learner to refine the hypothesis in a further iteration of the algorithm.

In practice, equivalence queries are approximated via model-based testing methods [14], thus we can never guarantee that the learned model is a faithful representation of the system. The learning process alternates between two phases, a learning phase, in which a learning algorithm poses membership queries to build the hypothesis and an equivalence testing phase, in which we search for counterexamples. The process terminates if no more counterexamples can be found.

When learning real-world applications, we also need so-called mappers [16] which are placed between a learning algorithm and the SUL. These mappers transform abstract queries posed by the learner to a sequence of concrete actions that are executed on the SUL. This mapping is typically defined by hand in form of code that is understood by the system. In the case of learning web applications, such a mapper would, e.g., map the string *"Login as Author"* to a sequence of actions that opens a web browser with a specific URL, navigates to the login form, fills in pre-defined credentials, submits the form and asserts if the authentication succeeds.

We use model checking to automatically approximate equivalence queries. The underlying temporal properties may well be the same as the ones described in Sect. 2.1. In fact, if the same temporal property holds for the designed model but fails for the learned model, we know that the learning process has either to be continued to refine the model by taking the error trace as a corresponding counterexample, or, in case the error trace is no counterexample, that the code generator has an error.

Continuing with our running example, Fig. 2 depicts a learned model of EquinOCS that represents the reviewing process for scientific papers on a high end-user level. By following the highlighted path in the model, we can observe that we can only submit papers after we are authenticated in the system. State 1 represents the system state where an author of a paper is logged in to EquinOCS. Given the input `SubmitPaper`, the system produces the output `Ok` which indicates a successful paper submission and we transition to state 3. Using the temporal formula presented in Sect. 2.1 a model checker could verify this property automatically.

3.2 Lifelong Learning

One of the main challenges for active automata learning is finding counterexamples for hypothesis refinement. An approach to tackle this issue is *lifelong* (sometimes called *never-stop*) *learning* [9] as a form of quality control. Based on

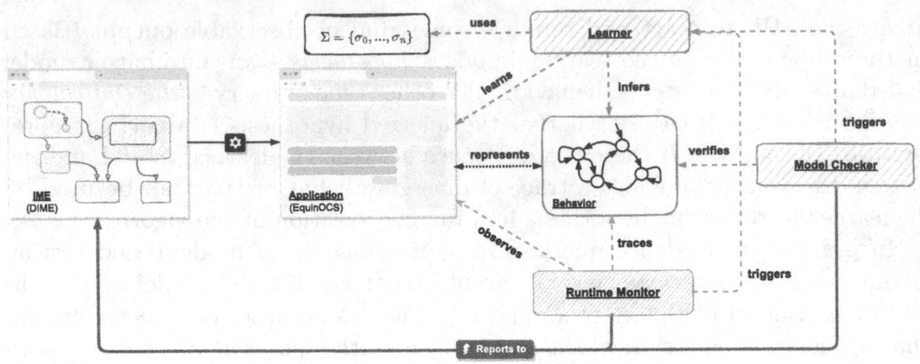

Fig. 3. Lifelong learning of web applications

this idea, we demonstrate a lifelong learning cycle in [7] that can be used for the continuous quality control of web applications. In this cycle, we

a) learn the SUL after each development cycle,
b) verify behavioral system properties using model checking,
c) monitor the web application at runtime and
d) report system errors to the modeler.

This lifelong learning cycle is sketched in Fig. 3. In the following paragraphs we describe each part individually.

Learning the SUL. The preliminary for executing learning setups is an adequate input alphabet and the corresponding mapping for the target system. We define both, the alphabet and the mapping in the ALEX tool [5,6], the technical backbone of this framework. ALEX is a web-based tool to create and orchestrate learning setups for web applications, where a symbol is mapped to a sequence of concrete actions executed on the web browser. Further, we specify verifiable system properties in the tool in Linear Temporal Logic (LTL). After that, we can trigger a learning process for our target system with the push of a button.

Verification of Behavioral System Properties. Once the model is inferred, the tool automatically passes the model and the LTL properties to the model checker. If some property cannot be verified, the model checker provides us with a path on the model where violated behavior is observed. If the cause for the error is not a system error the model is not yet refined enough and we trigger a model refinement using the counterexample with our learning algorithm. However, if no counterexample can be found, we consider the model final to that point.

Runtime Monitoring of the System. The lifelong learning cycle includes the runtime verification of the web applications' behavior. Since the search for counterexamples can also be characterized as a never-ending verification of (black-box) system behavior, we employ monitors that record the system behavior as a theoretically indefinitely long sequence of actions and try to track that sequence back to the inferred model. Traces where the learned automaton shows a different output behavior than the recorded trace again constitute as counterexamples and can be used for model refinement.

Reporting System Errors. If the model checker or the runtime monitoring reveal a system error instead of an insufficiently refined model, we report the error to the modeler who then has to repair the system by updating the graphical models, redeploy the application and start the lifelong learning process from the beginning.

In addition to the described steps we also use the following non-exclusive actions to enhance our lifelong learning cycle:

Generation of Regression Test Suites. In each development iteration we need to check if we introduced new bugs to previously functioning parts of the system with our changes. Regression testing is a common practice to answer this question. That is, given a set of tests, verify if the system still behaves as it did previously. With our learned model, we can generate such a set of tests using model-based testing [17]. Common methods include the W-method [11], the partial W-method [12] and in our case we use the discrimination tree [18] obtained from our TTT algorithm [15] as it generates a redundancy free set of tests. On the one hand, we can use these tests as a filter for learning processes: If some test fails we do not need to start time-intense learning processes in the first place and can provide feedback to users more quickly. On the other hand, we can treat these tests as a provider for the equivalence checking. As these tests include valuable system information, the final model is learned faster and in a more targeted fashion compared to checking for equivalence via, e.g., randomized testing.

Regression test suites are a particularly important ingredient of lifelong learning as they constitute the knowledge that can safely be transferred when (re)learning the system after modification: These tests together with the membership queries required to construct a consistent corresponding hypothesis model H guarantee that H

- is typically of a similar quality as the original model and
- can be transformed to the canonical system models via further learning-based refinement.

Please note that the latter property typically does not hold for the original model as it may have split states that, after the modification, became equivalent.

Comparison of Inferred Models. As we described in [7] we also have to check that the system changed in a desired way between two development iterations. Our means to do this is by learning the *difference automaton* between two systems. This automaton is constructed by posing each membership query during a learning process to both systems (or their models respectively). If both systems produce the same output given a query, we answer the query with that output.

Otherwise, we stop the execution of further input symbols at the first divergence of outputs and encode this information in the answer. If the system did not change, the *difference automaton* corresponds to both learned models and in the other case, we can precisely trace paths where different behavior is observed. By expressing changes in temporal logic, we can further formally verify them by model checking the *difference automaton.*

3.3 Automation

Automation is key to providing solid quality assurance which is why we integrate the lifelong learning cycle into common project management tools and CI/CD pipelines, e.g., as provided by GitLab [13]. Therefore, we host learning artifacts, such as alphabet definitions and temporal logic formulas, either in the repository of the corresponding project or in a central execution engine, i.e., an instance of ALEX. Once the DIME product is deployed, the tool performs automata learning and model checking fully automatically and the runtime monitor is updated according to Fig. 3. After the models are learned, we provide feedback to developers by calling corresponding APIs of the used project management system. This feedback comes in form of alerts or issues which are created in case that temporal logic formulas can not be verified, if we find discrepancies between the current model and the one of the previous development cycle or if the monitor detects anomalies in the runtime behavior.

4 Scalability

So far, to provide a tangible example for illustrative purposes, we have focused on the three-step approach of model-driven development with CINCO, DIME and EquinOCS (cf. Fig. 4). We now switch to a more general perspective on hierarchical meta-level dependencies by highlighting that DIME is only *one* of many CINCO products while EquinOCS is only *one* of many DIME products. In this regard, we identify aspects related to quality control that are generally applicable as well as new aspects that arise from certain effects that span multiple meta levels.

4.1 Meta-level Hierarchy

In general, using a meta IME like CINCO or an IME like DIME to design models and generate full applications from leads to families of products that share the same types of meta-models, i.e., they are designed using the same set of languages. In particular, the languages of CINCO are used to design DIME and other similar graphical modeling environments while the languages of DIME are used to design EquinOCS and other similar web applications. However, this view on a single IME and its products only covers a single vertical step in a hierarchy of meta-levels. In our LDE landscape, a *meta-level hierarchy* originates from the fact that DIME (as a CINCO product) again is an IME used to model and

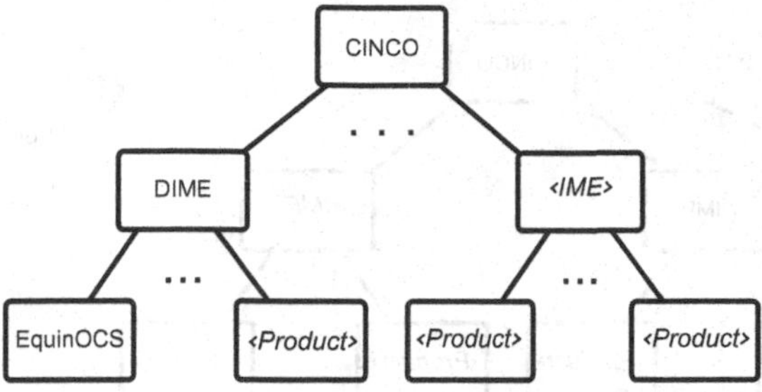

Fig. 4. Meta-level hierarchy originating in CINCO

generate web applications. It can be visualized by means of a tree structure as illustrated in Fig. 4 where the CINCO products are themselves IMEs again. In the following, we will call such a landscape of language-driven development tools with meta-level dependencies an *LDE ecosystem*.

4.2 Path-up Effects

Static validation, be it through syntax rules or model checking, is available in IMEs like DIME at design time. In particular, the static semantics of models created with DIME can be checked independent of which DIME product is currently designed. It scales with the horizontal expansion of the meta-level hierarchy, i.e., with the actual number of DIME products.

In contrast, the dynamic validation of DIME products (i.e., web applications) is product-specific, hence does not scale horizontally. Test cases have to be tailored towards each DIME product separately. However, there is a very beneficial, yet indirect, scaling effect in building these test cases. DIME's code generator, which produces these web applications, is implemented on the meta level above DIME, i.e., the very same meta level where DIME itself is developed. To assert the generator's quality (in terms of producing correct output) it must be applied to models created with DIME to generate and run the code of the DIME products.

The crux of the matter is that any test designed for and applied on any DIME product can provide feedback about the quality of the generator developed two meta-levels above. This can be considered a *path-up* effect in the meta-level hierarchy (cf. Fig. 5). And as DIME is used to design multiple different web applications, any error or conspicuity found in the testing of any of these web applications could be reported upwards in the meta-level hierarchy to deliver feedback and eventually trigger a change request for the development of DIME's code generator. The same dynamics apply to ordinary change requests originating from DIME products. They, too, may propagate upwards through the meta-level hierarchy in a path-up manner if a requested feature for a DIME product cannot be realized because the languages available in DIME are not sufficient for specifying the desired outcome. In this case, after an eventual generalization

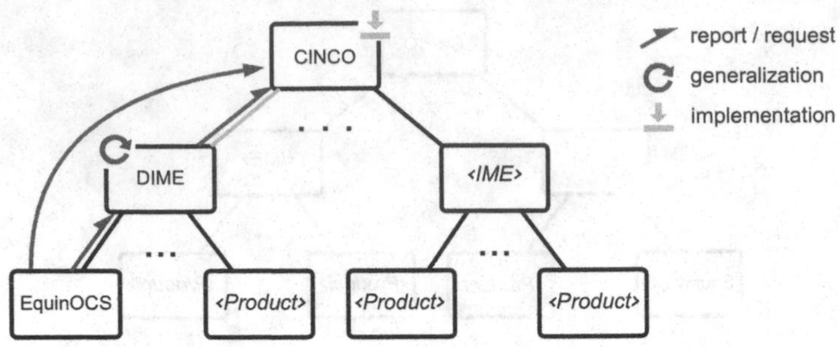

Fig. 5. Path-up effect of change requests in our LDE ecosystem

step, a subsequent change request may be filed for language feature enhancements to be implemented on the meta-level, i.e. in CINCO. This path-up effect is illustrated by means of the step-wise upwards edges in Fig. 5.

Taking into consideration the access control example in Sect. 2 we can easily demonstrate such a path-up effect. As we need to have access control in multiple DIME applications, we typically tend to model processes according to the same pattern in each of them. This is not only tedious manual work, but also violates the *Don't Repeat Yourself* principle. In these scenarios, we can generalize commonly used concepts such as access control and make them available as a part of the DIME language itself, thereby lifting them up in the meta-level hierarchy. Because these concepts now are a part of the language, the corresponding IMEs enforce these concepts as rigid Archimedean points.

Moreover, if we could access the valuable information from test results of DIME products in a structured manner, the quality control of DIME's code generator would naturally enhance with the number of different DIME products for which dynamic validation measures are applied since results are reported upwards in the meta-level hierarchy. In particular, this means that in addition to building DIME products solely for the purpose of testing DIME's generator, we could take advantage of tests built for productive DIME products anyway to assert and improve the quality of DIME's generator.

The access as well as the assessment of this test data are challenging tasks, because of the fact that the respective projects (DIME generator vs. DIME products) are not directly connected in the meta-level hierarchy. Typically, these projects involve completely different stakeholders as well as separate development teams working on independent code repositories. On the other hand, automation is a key enabler in this context due to the potentially huge number of DIME products. However, as in the context of quality control we have just started to study these effects and dynamics that cross meta-level boundaries, we still need to research how to effectively build generic feedback loops into each layer of our meta-model-driven development approaches.

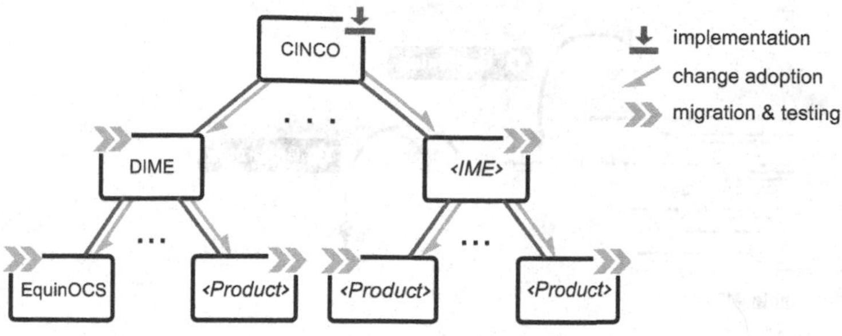

Fig. 6. Tree-down effect of changes in our LDE ecosystem

4.3 Tree-down Effects

In an LDE ecosystem, any change to an IME may cause effects that propagate downwards in a *tree-down* manner as illustrated in Fig. 6. As an example, if the Cinco IME changes, users can grab its new version to build a new version of Dime or other similar IMEs with it. However, as the meta-models may have changed, the migration of all these IMEs may be necessary to adapt to these changes. Hence, in this scenario, the *tree-down* effect means that changes of Cinco affect *all* IMEs built with it and may even propagate further. Because these IMEs, due to the necessary migration, need to be changed, too, this effect may propagate to *all* of their products as well.

Consequently, the changes to the Cinco IME may affect *all* descendant nodes in the meta-level hierarchy, although in an indirect manner. Hence, the successful management of this *tree-down* effect requires appropriate and effective quality control that surpasses classical approaches as it must consider aspects across meta-level boundaries. While syntactical changes to modeling languages will eventually lead to non-conform models, semantic changes, i.e., changes to the generator consuming these models, can lead to structural or behavioral differences in the generated products two meta-levels deeper. In particular, we cannot only focus on the Cinco IME and the products built with it (like Dime), because the potentially unintended effects of a change might only be recognized in tests applied on products multiple levels deeper in the meta-level hierarchy. This stresses why in the context of evolution of any IME in our LDE ecosystem, quality control is an eminent part of the release process.

In the previous Sect. 4.2 we have already motivated the assessment of these test results by means of *path-up* feedback loops to be established. Building support for *tree-down* effects into our meta-model-driven development approaches is equally challenging. Here, too, the respective projects are located on completely different levels of the meta-level hierarchy and involve completely different stakeholders as well as separate development teams working on independent code repositories. On the other hand, automation, again, is a key enabler in this context due to the potentially huge number of products down the tree. In particular, for any new version of Dime we automatically would have to generate all Dime

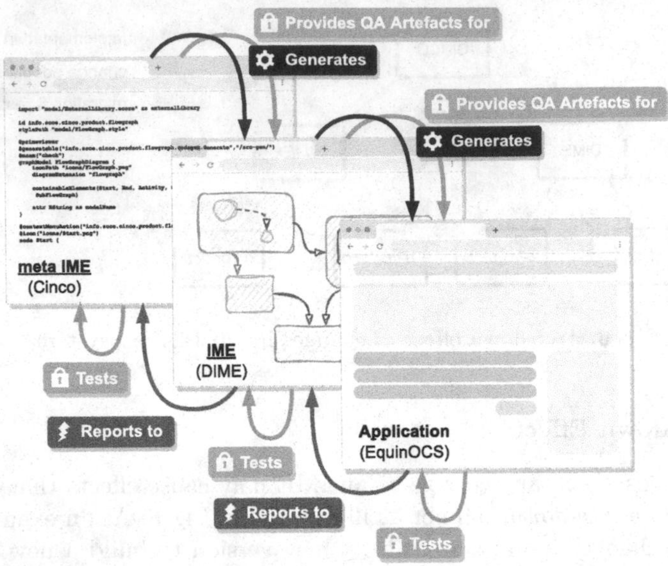

Fig. 7. LDE with CINCO, DIME and EquinOCS

products, then trigger the dynamic tests built for these products and interpret the test results in order to improve DIME itself. The huge advantages in terms of quality control we would gain from a successful implementation of this approach motivates our research how to effectively build it into our meta-model-driven development stack.

5 Conclusion and Future Work

In this paper, we have illustrated the role of quality assurance in Language-Driven Engineering (LDE) which exploits the observation that well-tailored domain-specific languages (DSLs) allow one to

- syntactically express a number of semantic properties with the effect that they can be verified during syntax analysis or using more involved static verification techniques like model checking, and
- combined with a concept of design for testability, to automatically validate run-time properties using, in our case, learning-based testing technology.

We have argued that our LDE approach is able to ensure practicality and scalability by means of a powerful language definition technology that allows one to generate required IMEs on demand.

As depicted in Fig. 7, our LDE ecosystem systematically addresses dependencies between the various modeling environments and their corresponding meta-modeling environments in a path-up/tree-down fashion:

– application-level requests are stepwise moved up to the meta hierarchy, far enough to fully address the issue at hand, and
– resulting meta-level changes are propagated down the meta hierarchy to ensure the adequate migration of all involved IMEs and their corresponding modeled artifacts.

The three described methods of quality control are deeply integrated into our generators and our IMEs to ensure global consistency of the entire LDE landscape. This includes the generation of quality assurance artifacts such as documentation, executable tests and learning alphabets that allow continuous automated testing across all levels and thereby automate *path-up* feedback.

The following two subsections describe our main focus to further improve the coherence of the LDE ecosystem: The strengthening of the development/QA connection via *design for learnability* and the move from the currently local Eclipse-based technology stacks to the cloud will provide easy access for everyone and offer enhanced collaboration possibilities. In fact, this move also unifies the quality assurance of the various meta levels as both the meta IMEs and the IMEs will be provided similarly in terms of browser-based web applications which can directly be validated using ALEX' learning-based testing technology.

5.1 Design for Learnability

Based on our year-long experience on using active automata learning on web-based applications [5–7,21,22], we are constantly figuring out new patterns and best practices in terms of how we design our web applications to simplify their learning and monitoring. We plan to incorporate the knowledge gained from previous research into our generator technology and make it available in our tool stack. To be more precise, this includes two aspects: alphabet generation and code instrumentation.

We previously mentioned that we always need an input alphabet and adequate mappers for learning real-life applications. These mappers need to be written and maintained through the development process of an application and we currently do so by hand. To minimize maintenance efforts, we are currently exploring approaches to generate adequate input alphabets for use with our learners from graphical models. One way to implement this is by enrichment of graphical models with more semantic information that directly translate to a concrete alphabet on a modeler-defined abstraction. This way, we would eliminate the synchronization overhead between application development and application testing.

Moreover, monitoring runtime behavior of web applications and combining it with model learning still is a relatively unexplored topic as it opposes several challenges. The biggest challenge is finding a suitable method to map system traces to a sequence of symbols of the alphabet that is used by the learner and is consequently found in the hypothesis. As a step in this direction, we plan to instrument generated code of our web application by means of extending the DOM of HTML documents at generation time. In doing so, we can make more information about the system publicly available and can control precisely what we want to learn or monitor respectively. One idea is to encode mapping information in the DOM which could establish a common denominator between the alphabet used in our models and the way a monitor produces system traces. On the one side, this allows us to write learning processes that iteratively expand their input alphabets just by interacting with the frontend of the web application. One the other side, we can generate client-side runtime monitors from our graphical models that make use of DOM extensions to better trace interactions with the web interface back to learned models. With this setup in place, we are able to close existing gaps in our lifelong learning cycle and therefore further improve the overall quality assurance.

5.2 LDE in the Cloud

One issue that we are currently facing is that our quality measures for individual IMEs, although roughly identical on a conceptual level, differ quite a bit from a technical perspective. Further, the process to transition from the meta IME to the IME is completely different compared to the process from the IME to the final application. Thus, maintaining these (already partially automated) processes requires a lot of effort, time and coordination between IME developers. In an effort to improve this situation, we are in the process of detaching from the stationary Eclipse-stack that CINCO and DIME are based on and move on to modern web technologies. Originated from [27], we are in active development of CINCO Cloud [4], a web-based environment that allows users to develop and use CINCO products right in the web browser, thanks to the Eclipse Theia project [2] and similar to Sirius web [1] and WebGME [3,19]. As a result, meta IME and IMEs are merged in a single tool which allows us to fully automate the generation, the deployment and the delivery of CINCO products at the push of a button. Because CINCO Cloud itself is a web application, we are then also able to align our processes and can apply the same static and dynamic validation measures on both, the meta-modeling and the modeling environment inside a single tool.

References

1. Sirius. https://www.eclipse.org/sirius/sirius-web.html. Accessed 11 July 2022
2. Theia - Cloud and Desktop IDE. https://www.theia-ide.org. Accessed 12 Feb 2019
3. WebGME. https://webgme.org/. Accessed 26 July 2021
4. Bainczyk, A., et al.: CINCO cloud: a holistic approach for web-based language-driven engineering. In: Margaria, T., Steffen, B. (eds.) ISoLA 2022, LNCS, vol. 13702, pp. 407–425. Springer, Heidelberg (2022)
5. Bainczyk, A., et al.: ALEX: mixed-mode learning of web applications at ease. In: Margaria, T., Steffen, B. (eds.) ISoLA 2016. LNCS, vol. 9953, pp. 655–671. Springer, Cham (2016). https://doi.org/10.1007/978-3-319-47169-3_51

6. Bainczyk, A., Schieweck, A., Steffen, B., Howar, F.: Model-based testing without models: the TodoMVC case study. In: Katoen, J.-P., Langerak, R., Rensink, A. (eds.) ModelEd, TestEd, TrustEd. LNCS, vol. 10500, pp. 125–144. Springer, Cham (2017). https://doi.org/10.1007/978-3-319-68270-9_7
7. Bainczyk, A., Steffen, B., Howar, F.: Lifelong learning of reactive systems in practice. In: Ahrendt, W., Beckert, B., Bubel, R., Johnsen, E.B. (eds.) The Logic of Software. A Tasting Menu of Formal Methods. LNCS, vol. 13360, pp. 38–53. Springer, Cham (2022). https://doi.org/10.1007/978-3-031-08166-8_3
8. Bakera, M., Margaria, T., Renner, C., Steffen, B.: Tool-supported enhancement of diagnosis in model-driven verification. Innov. Syst. Softw. Eng. **5**, 211–228 (2009). https://doi.org/10.1007/s11334-009-0091-6
9. Bertolino, A., Calabrò, A., Merten, M., Steffen, B.: Never-stop learning: continuous validation of learned models for evolving systems through monitoring. ERCIM News **2012**(88), 28–29 (2012). http://ercim-news.ercim.eu/en88/special/never-stop-learning-continuous-validation-of-learned-models-for-evolving-systems-through-monitoring
10. Boßelmann, S., et al.: DIME: a programming-less modeling environment for web applications. In: Margaria, T., Steffen, B. (eds.) ISoLA 2016. LNCS, vol. 9953, pp. 809–832. Springer, Cham (2016). https://doi.org/10.1007/978-3-319-47169-3_60
11. Chow, T.S.: Testing software design modeled by finite-state machines. IEEE Trans. Softw. Eng. **4**(3), 178–187 (1978)
12. Fujiwara, S.V., Bochmann, G., Khendek, F., Amalou, M., Ghedamsi, A.: Test selection based on finite state models. IEEE Trans. Softw. Eng. **17**(6), 591–603 (1991). https://doi.org/10.1109/32.87284
13. GitLab B.V.: The devops platform has arrived. https://about.gitlab.com/. Accessed 17 Feb 2022
14. Hagerer, A., Hungar, H., Niese, O., Steffen, B.: Model generation by moderated regular extrapolation. In: Kutsche, R.-D., Weber, H. (eds.) FASE 2002. LNCS, vol. 2306, pp. 80–95. Springer, Heidelberg (2002). https://doi.org/10.1007/3-540-45923-5_6
15. Isberner, M., Howar, F., Steffen, B.: The TTT algorithm: a redundancy-free approach to active automata learning. In: Bonakdarpour, B., Smolka, S.A. (eds.) RV 2014. LNCS, vol. 8734, pp. 307–322. Springer, Cham (2014). https://doi.org/10.1007/978-3-319-11164-3_26
16. Jonsson, B.: Learning of automata models extended with data. In: Bernardo, M., Issarny, V. (eds.) SFM 2011. LNCS, vol. 6659, pp. 327–349. Springer, Heidelberg (2011). https://doi.org/10.1007/978-3-642-21455-4_10
17. Katoen, J.-P.: 22 labelled transition systems. In: Broy, M., Jonsson, B., Katoen, J.-P., Leucker, M., Pretschner, A. (eds.) Model-Based Testing of Reactive Systems. LNCS, vol. 3472, pp. 615–616. Springer, Heidelberg (2005). https://doi.org/10.1007/11498490_29
18. Kearns, M.J., Vazirani, U.V.: An Introduction to Computational Learning Theory. MIT Press, Cambridge (1994)
19. Maróti, M., et al.: Next generation (meta) modeling: web-and cloud-based collaborative tool infrastructure. MPM@ MoDELS **1237**, 41–60 (2014)
20. Merten, M., Howar, F., Steffen, B., Margaria, T.: Automata learning with on-the-fly direct hypothesis construction. In: Hähnle, R., Knoop, J., Margaria, T., Schreiner, D., Steffen, B. (eds.) ISoLA 2011. CCIS, pp. 248–260. Springer, Heidelberg (2012). https://doi.org/10.1007/978-3-642-34781-8_19

21. Neubauer, J., Windmüller, S., Steffen, B.: Risk-based testing via active continuous quality control. Int. J. Softw. Tools Technol. Transfer **16**(5), 569–591 (2014). https://doi.org/10.1007/s10009-014-0321-6
22. Raffelt, H., Merten, M., Steffen, B., Margaria, T.: Dynamic testing via automata learning. Int. J. Softw. Tools Technol. Transfer (STTT) **11**(4), 307–324 (2009). https://doi.org/10.1007/s10009-009-0120-7
23. Rivest, R.L., Schapire, R.E.: Inference of finite automata using homing sequences. In: Hanson, S.J., Remmele, W., Rivest, R.L. (eds.) Machine Learning: From Theory to Applications. LNCS, vol. 661, pp. 51–73. Springer, Heidelberg (1993). https://doi.org/10.1007/3-540-56483-7_22
24. Steffen, B., Howar, F., Merten, M.: Introduction to active automata learning from a practical perspective. In: Bernardo, M., Issarny, V. (eds.) SFM 2011. LNCS, vol. 6659, pp. 256–296. Springer, Heidelberg (2011). https://doi.org/10.1007/978-3-642-21455-4_8
25. Steffen, B., Naujokat, S.: Archimedean points: the essence for mastering change. LNCS Trans. Found. Master. Change (FoMaC) **1**(1), 22–46 (2016). https://doi.org/10.1007/978-3-319-46508-1_3
26. Warmer, J., Kleppe, A.: The Object Constraint Language: Precise Modeling with UML. Addison-Wesley Longman Publishing Co., Inc., Boston (1998)
27. Zweihoff, P., Tegeler, T., Schürmann, J., Bainczyk, A., Steffen, B.: Aligned, purpose-driven cooperation: the future way of system development. In: Margaria, T., Steffen, B. (eds.) ISoLA 2021. LNCS, vol. 13036, pp. 426–449. Springer, Cham (2021). https://doi.org/10.1007/978-3-030-89159-6_27

Cinco Cloud: A Holistic Approach for Web-Based Language-Driven Engineering

Alexander Bainczyk(✉), Daniel Busch, Marco Krumrey, Daniel Sami Mitwalli, Jonas Schürmann, Joel Tagoukeng Dongmo, and Bernhard Steffen

Chair for Programming Systems, Department of Computer Science, TU Dortmund University, 44227 Dortmund, Germany
{alexander.bainczyk,daniel2.busch,marco.krumrey,sami.mitwalli, jonas2.schuermann,joel.tagoukeng,bernhard.steffen}@tu-dortmund.de

Abstract. In this paper, we present Cinco Cloud, a holistic web-based language engineering environment that seamlessly aligns the entire process from the meta modeling of domain-specific languages, via application modeling in corresponding integrated modeling environments, to the deployment of the final product through CI/CD pipelines using Git repository platform integrations. Cinco Cloud supports a role/competence-specific access management in order to organize the collaborative modeling involving stakeholders of different expertise without any installation requirements. The paper illustrates the interplay between all the required steps along a concrete application example.

Keywords: Language-driven engineering · Domain specific languages · Cloud-based IDEs · Collaborative modeling · CI/CD

1 Introduction

Most of today's popular software has been implemented as web applications. The demand of this trend remains high as web applications provide a vast amount of benefits over native and locally running applications:

Zero Setup Time. User can utilize their browser of choice to run the web application. No additional software or pain setting up dependent software is necessary.

Device and OS independence. Browsers run on arbitrary devices and operating systems and software developers do not have to target different platforms. This may reduce development overhead.

Update Distribution. Users do not have to update and maintain installed software themselves. Instead, updates are provided centralized and distributed to all users at once.

T. Margaria and B. Steffen (Eds.): ISoLA 2022, LNCS 13702, pp. 407–425, 2022.
https://doi.org/10.1007/978-3-031-19756-7_23

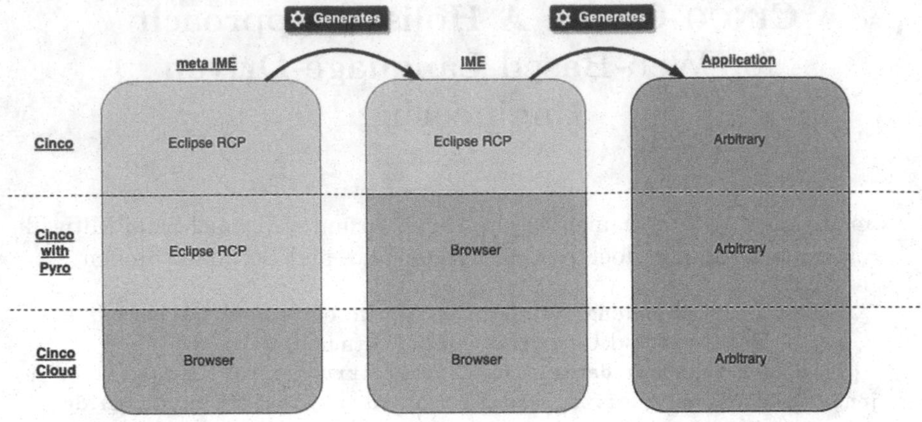

Fig. 1. Overview of underlying stacks of different CINCO versions

Real-time Collaboration. Centralized and service-orientated web services allow users to work together in real-time regardless of their work location. Such collaboration is a vital aspect of modern workflows.

Especially, development environments often require rather complex setups and maintenance. In big companies with dozens or even hundreds of developers this may lead to a lot of additional administration work when assuring that every development environment remains compatible to the required stack. This drives many companies to shift their development environment to cloud-based solutions, like GitHub Codespaces [10], Codeanywhere [6], and Eclipse Che [1]. For example, the company GitHub decided to largely adopt GitHub Codespaces in order to remove pains around development environment setup and to simplify remote work tremendously [7].

Several years ago we have started to work on CINCO [21], our fist metatooling suite approach that is heavily based on the Eclipse Rich Client Platform (Eclipse RCP). Over the last couple of years we have aimed to bring our Integrated Modeling Environments (IMEs) into the browser as a web service to remove setup pain and to profit from the aforementioned benefits of web applications. We have called this new modeling environment PYRO [27,30]. However, the language design processes within the meta Integrated Modeling Environments (meta IMEs) remained in our existing local Eclipse RCP clients. CINCO Cloud aims to create a seamless Language-Driven Engineering (LDE) experience, combining both the meta IME and the generated IMEs into a single web application. On top of this, we have wrapped a role-based access management around our (meta) IMEs. This allows language creators to provide different stakeholders access to models and model languages that matter most to them, allowing simple yet powerful real-time collaboration. Figure 1 provides an overview over the evolution from CINCO via PYRO to CINCO Cloud and which abstraction layers were brought into the web at which stage of development.

In this paper, we present CINCO Cloud, our holistic meta tooling suite that makes use of all the benefits of web applications to create a pain-free user experience that includes all levels of LDE: From the meta modeling of domain-specific languages, via application modeling in corresponding integrated modeling environments, to the deployment of the final product through CI/CD pipelines using Git repository platform integrations.

This paper describes most of the new features and capabilities CINCO Cloud provides and how they have been realized from a technical perspective. Section 2 gives an overview of the usage of Theia and how plugins are utilized to achieve the aims described earlier. Details about the cloud architecture are stated in Sect. 3. Next, Sect. 4 demonstrates how CINCO Cloud can be used in a holistic way to create multiple languages, model in them and deploy their products to external CI/CD platforms to make use of the combined products. Section 5 compares CINCO Cloud to renowned modeling environments which pursue similar approaches. Last, Sect. 6 provides an outlook on how to make even more use of web technologies regarding collaboration and using best practices for graphical language support.

2 Web-Based CINCO Editors and Products

In an effort to lift the language editor of CINCO and the graphical modeling environment from CINCO products to the cloud, with respect to aspects such as multi-tenant usage and system scalability, the architecture of our local-first technology stack had to be changed fundamentally. Based on the ideas introduced in previous work [28] and the subsequent PhD thesis of Philip Zweihoff [29], we now present the technologies and the architecture that allowed us to build a holistic solution for language-driven development that takes place solely in the web.

As outlined in Sect. 1, CINCO Cloud is an environment in which each user is able to specify one's own graph-based language and use it afterwards without leaving the environment. In order to offer the user this multidimensional web-based tool, CINCO Cloud must be able to manage various components at different layers. Three layers are involved in the realization of CINCO Cloud (see Fig. 2). From an architectural point of view, only the first two layers are relevant. The *meta layer* is intended for the user who wants to design one or more new graphical Domain Specific Languages (DSLs). The designated language(s) can then be used at the *modeling layer*, whose components are generated according to the previously defined language.

In order to be able to work in a collaborative and distributed way in CINCO Cloud each layer has a defined *Workspace* (yellow) [29]. These *Workspaces* in CINCO Cloud are realized as an application based on *Eclipse Theia* [3] which is composed of several modules and implemented as Theia (blue) and VS Code (purple) extensions. The language servers (red) are also used to provide the necessary infrastructure to intuitively support the users of the different layers in performing their respective tasks.

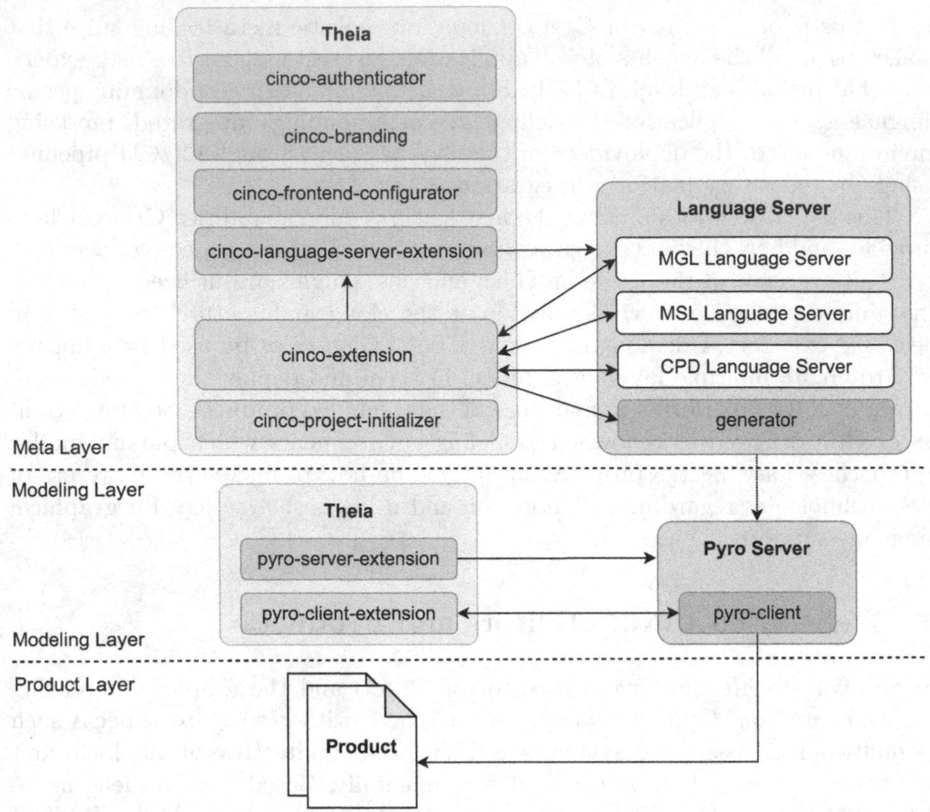

Fig. 2. Architecture of the different (meta) layers.

2.1 Meta Layer

The design of graphical DSLs in CINCO Cloud is based on the same mechanism and domain-specific (meta-)languages as used in CINCO. The Meta Graph Language (MGL) is used to define an abstract syntax of the graph-based languages. This means that this DSL is used to describe which nodes, edges, and types are available for modeling and how they relate to one another. The Meta Graph Language (MSL) describes how each model element within the graph-based models look like. This application of styles and appearances form the concrete syntax of our graph-based models. Last, the Cinco Product Definition (CPD) can be utilized to describe which model types should be included in generated modeling environments. Additionally, the CPD is able to provide branding information and some additional meta information for the modeling layer.

Since CINCO Cloud aims to offer a distributed, web-based environment, all functionalities required for language creation must be served in a continuous and distributed manner. In order to assist the language developer in an intuitive way, the Language Server Protocol (LSP) [2] is used here. Thanks to this protocol,

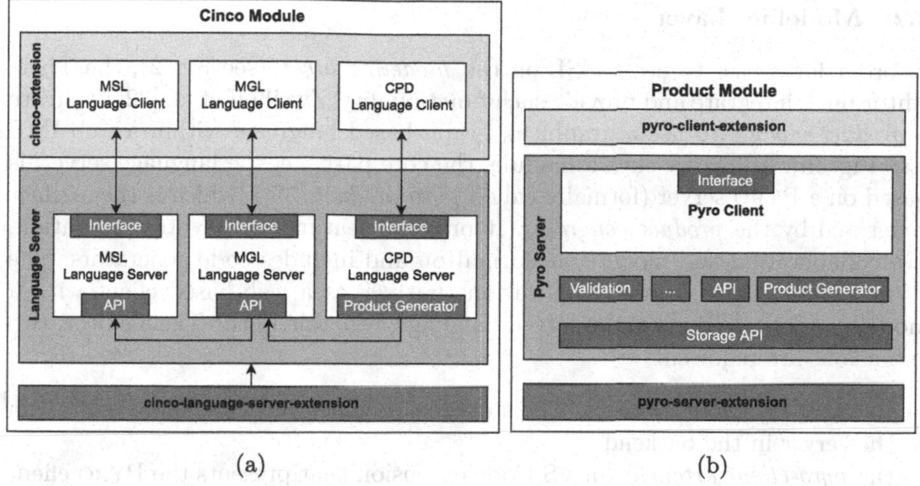

Fig. 3. Architectural overview of CINCO Cloud modules: (a) presents the CINCO *Module* and (b) the *Product Module.*

the editor is able to control different language servers which in turn provide the user with standardized language support, such as syntax highlighting, auto-completion and validation. With regard to CINCO Cloud, the (CINCO) language server is partially generated by Xtext to enable the text-based meta-languages of CINCO. For each meta-language there is a language server. Since all three meta-languages are semantically related to each other, they are in turn accommodated in a multi-language server. This is necessary so that the three language servers, hierarchically of their relationship to each other, can access the APIs of the other meta-languages when parsing in order to be able to represent interlingual references in the form of a data model. Such a data model can then be used for the generator of the modeling layer.

The language server is executed by a Theia extension, namely the *cinco-language-server-extension.* For each of our specified meta-languages (MGL, MSL and CPD) a communication protocol allows the exchange between the corresponding language server components and their client, as shown in Fig. 3a. This figure illustrates the *Cinco module* used in CINCO Cloud responsible for the design and generation of a graphical domain-specific modeling environment including the necessary infrastructure for CINCO products.

After the definition of DSL specifications, the generation of the *Product Module* (Fig. 3b) can be triggered. This generation process is initiated from the *CPD language client.* The *product generator*, which is the same as used in PYRO [30], will therefore use the API of the other language servers to collect the predefined specifications and trigger the generation process.

2.2 Modeling Layer

In order for a user to use a DSL on the *modeling layer* (see Fig. 2), the Theia editor must integrate and provide such functionality. Zweihoff et al. [32] illustrate a *product module* to use a graphical, graph-based language within a web IME (see Fig. 3b). To realize such a module, the core part, i.e. the language server, is based on a PYRO server (formally called *pyro product* [30]), which is the artifact generated by the *product generator*. It provides features like syntax validation, live collaboration and model transformation and includes code generators. The PYRO server itself is a web application that serves a web-based client with a modeling canvas. To make the served language available in the Theia editor, two extensions are required:

- the *pyro-server-extension*, a Theia extension which has the main task to run the server in the backend.
- the *pyro-client-extension*, a VS Code extension that presents the PYRO client inside the Theia editor.

This allows a user to use a DSL to design a graph model and generate a product from it as a semantic representation.

3 The Cloud Architecture of CINCO Cloud

With PYRO [27,30], we made the first steps towards offering CINCO products in the web. Developed as a meta-plugin for CINCO, one can, given a locally installed instance, generate the sources of a web application that offers users a graphical modeling environment for the languages specified in a CPD file. This approach served us well in education, for research purposes [31], and for smaller workshops. However, with modern technologies and the transition from local CINCO instances to web IMEs (cf. Sect. 2) we are now able to provide a development environment that, in contrast to previous setups a) offers the modeling and the meta IME in a single tool, b) has extended collaboration possibilities compared to PYRO, c) reduces the complexity of delivery processes and d) is able to scale well with a growing number of users.

3.1 Component Overview

In [28] we have presented the idea of CINCO Cloud and described a prototypical cloud architecture with which we are able to create CINCO products in web IMEs and build and deploy PYRO-based modeling environments dynamically in a single web application. A prototypical implementation has been introduced in the subsequent PhD thesis [29]. Since then, we employed several optimizations to the cloud infrastructure, which result in the architecture depicted in Fig. 4. CINCO Cloud is designed to run in a Kubernetes [25] cluster and comprises the following components:

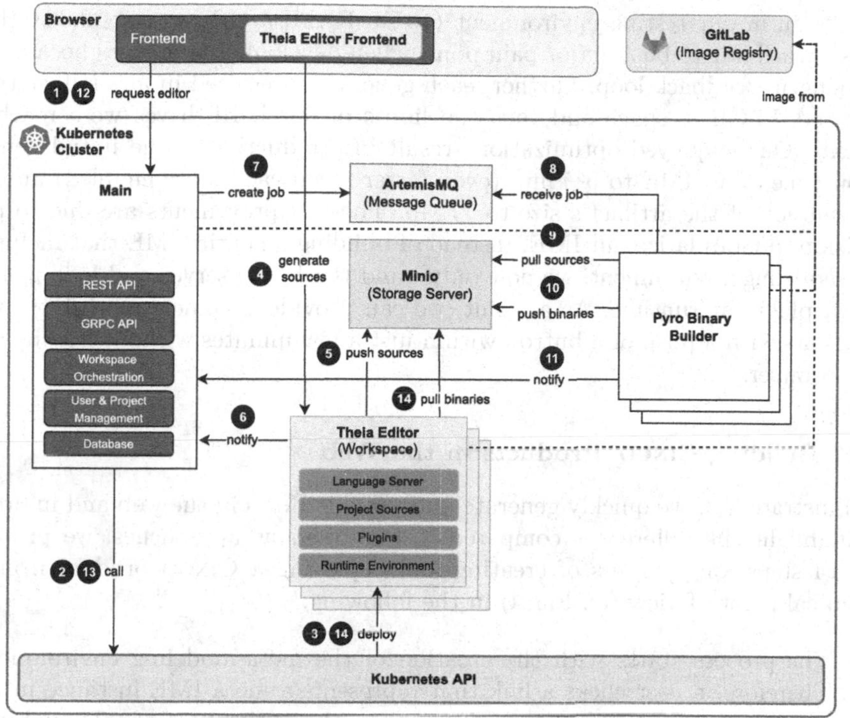

Fig. 4. Cloud architecture and component overview of CINCO Cloud

- The *Main* component contains a web server that serves the frontend of CINCO Cloud to end-users, holds the applications state and orchestrates build and deployment processes of our web IMEs.
- A PYRO *Binary Builder* is a state- and GUI-less service that makes the PYRO generator that was integrated in each CINCO installer available in web. As this service is stateless, it can be scaled horizontally depending on the workload of the cluster and allows multiple users to build modeling IMEs simultaneously.
- *Theia Editors* are instances of our customized web IMEs (cf. Sect. 2) that contain necessary modeling and meta-modeling tools.
- *ArtemisMQ* [24] is a message queue that is commonly used for exchanging messages between services in distributed systems.
- *Minio* [20] works as an object storage that allows for a centralized file management in cloud environments.
- *GitLab* [12] stores container images for our core components: The *Main* service, the *Pyro Binary Builder* and the customized Theia editor.

The presented architecture slightly differs from the conceptual description in [28] and its first prototype [29] but leads to drastic performance improvements. Previously, generating and deploying an IME from CINCO languages took about

30–40 min in our testing environment (16 Gb RAM, 4 CPU cores @2.30 GHz). This turned out to be a major pain point when developing languages because of the lengthy feedback loop. Further, each generation resulted in an artifact that required 2.7 Gb of space and thus the limits of our hard drives were reached quickly. Our employed optimizations result in a reduction of the initial generation time of an IME to 5–7 min (even faster when caches are enabled) and in a reduction of the artifact's size to 77 Mb. These improvements are due to the decision to modularize our IME. Instead of building an entire IME that includes the modeling environment, we now only build the PYRO-server and load it as a Theia plugin at runtime. As a result, we can provide graphical modeling environments with a push of a button within just a few minutes without leaving the web browser.

3.2 Building CINCO Products in the Web

To illustrate how we quickly generate and provide IMEs in the web and in order to highlight the differences compared to our previous approaches, we present the 14 steps long process of creating and deploying a CINCO product from a technical point of view (cf. Fig. 4) in the following:

❶ The process starts with the creation of the meta-modeling environment. Therefore, a user clicks a link that represents a meta IME instance in the web interface of CINCO Cloud. Upon that, the deployment of a Theia-based meta IME is triggered. Because the deployment and the provision of the meta IME are completely automated, the user then only has to wait until the meta IME is presented in the web.

❷ In CINCO Cloud, meta IMEs and IMEs are created on demand for each user to only allocate cluster resources that are needed. In addition, unused meta IMEs and IMEs are also shutdown as soon as users are inactive for a certain period of time and cluster resources are released. For the deployment, the *Main* service poses a request to the Kubernetes API with necessary information to create an instance of an meta IME.

❸ Kubernetes then deploys the instance to the cluster. As soon as the meta IME is ready to use, the user is presented with the meta IME which is embedded in the web interface of CINCO Cloud. Then, the user starts with the development of the CINCO product by defining the graph-based CINCO languages and optionally by writing a code generator.

❹ After the language specification, the user triggers the generation of the PYRO-based IME for the languages with a push of a button. The generation and the deployment of this IME (step ❺ to ⓫) are completely automated and do not require the user to leave the web browser. This is in contrast to our previous approaches where meta IME and IME are separate tools and where each individual IME had to be deployed to a server, either manually or with custom CI/CD pipelines.

❺ The generation process first creates all source files required for the graphical modeling environment for the defined CINCO languages. In the following we refer to these source files as "Pyro-*server sources*". Internally, these sources are pushed to a central object storage, where sources for all generated Cinco products are held.

6. The *Main* service is notified about the outcome of the generation process.
7. In the next step, the Pyro-server sources need to be compiled and an executable file needs to be build. We call this file "Pyro-*server binary*". Again, our architecture takes complete care of the build process and it allows multiple users to create different IMEs simultaneously. For that matter, we implemented worker services (*Pyro Binary Builder* in Fig. 4) that can be replicated depending on the cluster's payload. Each worker is connected to a message queue where the *Main* service publishes jobs to. A job contains necessary information for a worker to build the Pyro-server binaries from previously generated sources.
8. One of the free workers fetches the job from the message queue, which triggers the build process within the scope of the worker.
9. The worker pulls the corresponding Pyro-server sources from the object storage and builds an executable binary from them. Logs acquired from the build process are streamed to the user in real-time, which helps with debugging: If errors occur, e.g. because of compilation failures of the hand-written code generator, they will be available in these logs.
10. Upon success, the Pyro-server binary is pushed to the object storage.
11. The *Main* service and thereby also the user that triggered to process is notified about the successful termination.
12. From this point on, IMEs that contain the graphical modeling environment based on the generated Pyro-server binaries can be requested within Cinco Cloud. In the same manner as in step 1, users can open the IME by clicking on a link in the web interface.
13. Exactly as in step 2, the request to deploy the IME is redirected to the Kubernetes API, which deploys a new instance of the Theia editor.
14. After the deployment, the editor fetches the corresponding Pyro-server binary from the object storage and executes it to start the Pyro-based graphical modeling editor. Finally, the user can create files that represent models of his language which are opened in the editor.

This process is highly automated and requires no manual interaction except for the request to generate an IME from Cinco languages. In this setup, language designers can simply focus on designing DSLs as the generation and the delivery of modeling environments to application modelers is completely taken care of by Cinco Cloud.

4 Example: WebStory in Cinco Cloud

In this section, we illustrate our seamless holistic workflow in Cinco Cloud: Starting with defining languages over to the creation of graph-based models, the generation and provision of a product from theses models and the deployment

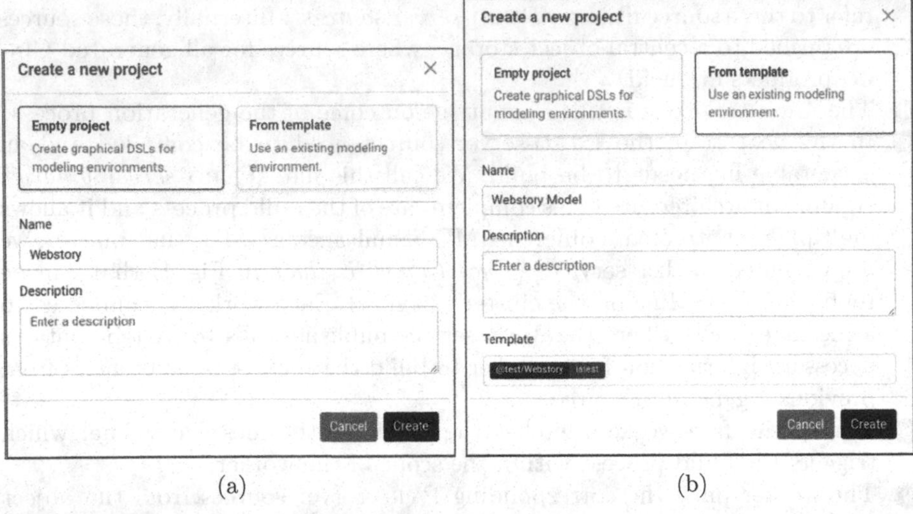

(a) (b)

Fig. 5. Creating a new meta IME (a) and a corresponding IME (b)

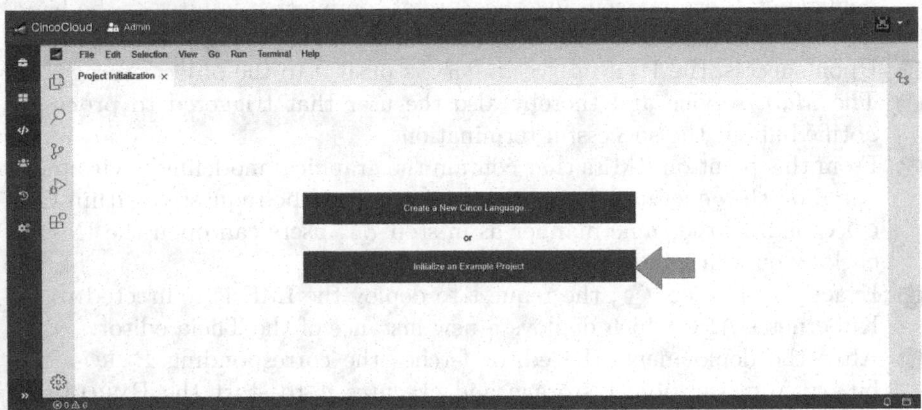

Fig. 6. Initializing an example project inside the CINCO Cloud's meta IME.

of the product to the web. For this purpose, we use the *WebStory* language, a DSL to visually design interactive point-and-click games for the web that has already been introduced and demonstrated in previous research [13,14]. At the end of this walk-through, we will have modeled a simple WebStory and deploy it to GitLab Pages [11], a service for hosting static files from a Git repository, without leaving the web browser.

4.1 Language Definition and IME Generation

In the beginning, we need a meta IME to define the graphical DSLs using the text-based CINCO meta-languages: MGL, MSL and CPD. For this purpose, CIN-

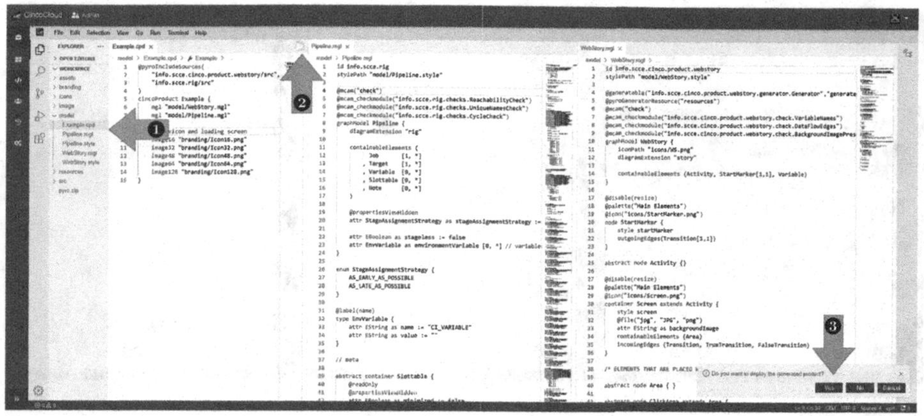

Fig. 7. Specifying languages in the CINCO Cloud's language editor.

CO Cloud provides the concept of *projects*. Projects can be associated with either a meta IME or an IME and are created using a dialog, see Fig. 5. For our example, we start with the creation of a project linked to a meta IME that provides the textual meta-language editor.

The meta IME provides the language server for CINCO meta-languages and can be accessed via a web interface. Initially, if no languages have been specified yet, the user is welcomed with a wizard (cf. Fig. 6) that guides through the initial creation of required files for the language development. Optionally, the user can choose to initialize an example project with a set of predefined languages (green arrow) that also contains the WebStory language. As a result, all necessary files, including the MGLs, MSLs, the CPD and the generators for WebStory models are loaded into the workspace. In Fig. 7 we can see that on the left, the workspace now contains the various source files that are required for the CINCO product. On the right, the MGL file for the WebStory language and some other exemplary MGL files of the project are opened in tabs. When opening the CPD file ❶ which represents the entrypoint of each CINCO project, a button will appear in the top right corner of the active tab ❷. Upon clicking that button, the user is given the choice via a dialog ❸ to only generate the corresponding sources for the PYRO server, e.g. for local debugging purposes, or to generate an IME that includes the graphical modeling environment based on the specified languages. In our case, we choose the latter option.

After the successful generation, CINCO Cloud adds a new entry to an internal registry that holds information of all available graphical DSLs so that all users can access the corresponding IMEs. In order to instantiate the IME with our WebStory language, we create a new project using the project creation dialog from Fig. 5b. However this time, we select the WebStory language from the global registry as *template* for the new project.

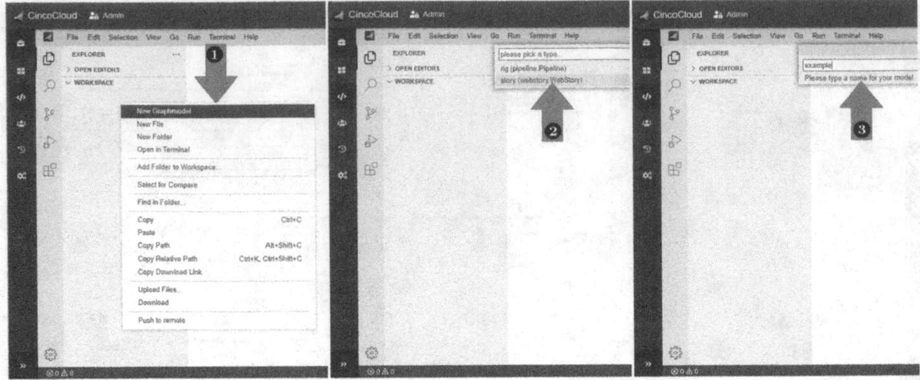

Fig. 8. Workflow for creating a graph model

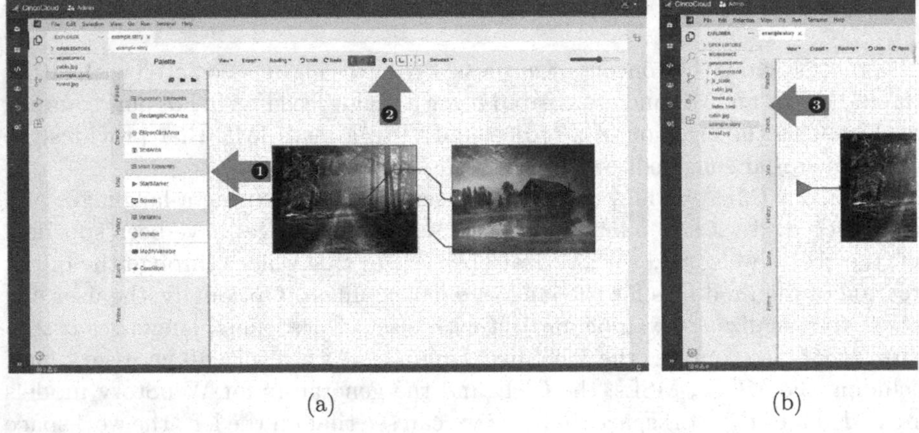

Fig. 9. A WebStory model in CINCO Cloud: (a) displays a simple graph model and (b) the generated static files in the project explorer

4.2 Model Creation and Application Generation

Now that we have generated an IME for WebStory models, we can head over to creating concrete instances. Therefore, the user opens the IME in the newly created project (cf. Fig. 8). Here, we can open the context menu inside the explorer that gives us the option to create a "New Graphmodel" ❶, i.e., a file representing a graphical model of the language of our choice. We then select the WebStory language from a drop-down menu ❷ and finally give the model file a name ❸. As a consequence, the file is created in the workspace with the specified name. Double-clicking this file results in the opening of a modeling canvas.

In the IME that is displayed in Fig. 9, we create a model for a simple website via dragging and dropping model elements from the palette ❶ to the canvas. The illustrated example contains two screens (outlined in pink), each containing

Fig. 10. The running instance of the deployed WebStory in a web browser. For illustration purposes, red rectangles represent clickable areas and arrows point to the target page as seen in the corresponding model (cf. Fig. 9 (Color figure online)).

a background image displaying a *forest trail* on the left and a *cabin* on the right. Each of these screens also include a rectangular area (colored in pink) that point to the other screen with an edge. They are used to transition between screens in the WebStory application, giving the user the ability to move between the *forest trail* to the *cabin* by clicking on the corresponding areas in the generated web application. The screen that is connected to the start marker (green rectangle) will be the initial screen.

After we are finished with the design of the model, we can trigger the WebStory generator that transforms graphical models to static HTML, CSS and JavaScript files by clicking on the *G*-button in the editor (cf. Fig. 9a ❷). As a result of this, the generated artifacts appear in the workspace in the subdirectory *generated-html* (cf. Fig. 9b ❸). We can now download this directory and open the index.html file in a web browser to play with the modeled WebStory, see Fig. 10. At this point, we demonstrated what was not possible with our previous approaches: offering a seamless transition from meta IMEs for meta-modeling to IMEs for graphical modeling in a single web-based application.

4.3 Application Deployment

Usually, the development cycle of an application does not end with the generation of its sources. They still need to be compiled and built artifacts have to be provided to end users. As source code is typically managed in version control systems, Cinco Cloud provides an integration with Git repository platforms. This allows us to push generated files from the workspace to a remote repository which serves as a starting point for further code processing. For our example, we push the WebStory sources to a remote Git repository managed by GitLab [12].

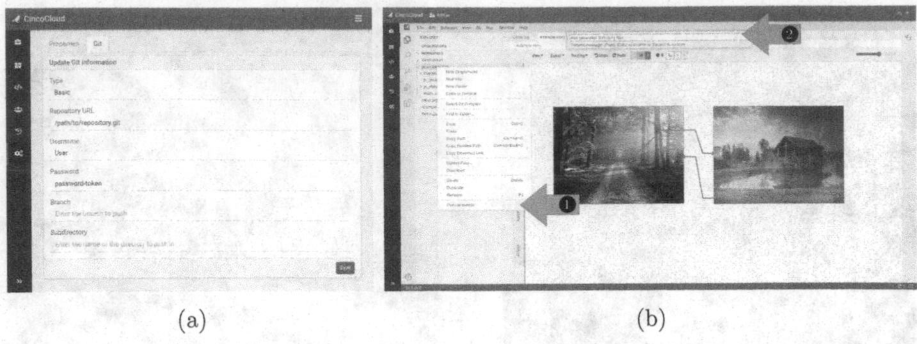

(a) (b)

Fig. 11. Deploying WebStory to GitLab: Configuration of repository settings (a) and deployment of generated files from the IME (b)

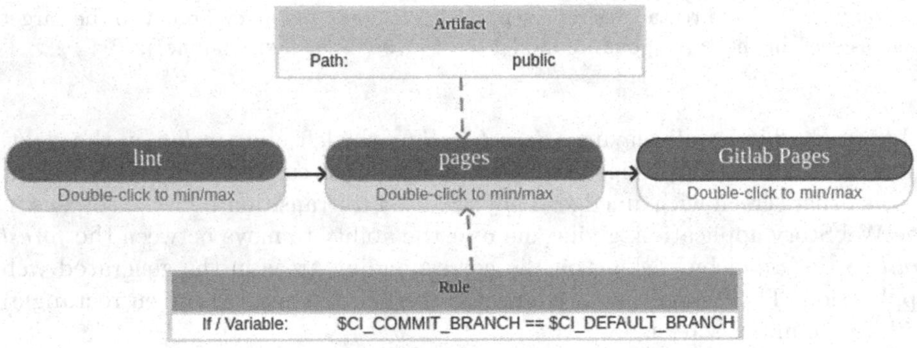

Fig. 12. Graphical model of the CI/CD configuration for the WebStory

Figure 11 shows the steps to perform in CINCO Cloud to push sources to a remote Git repository. At first, we provide information about the target repository within the current project. Figure 11a shows the corresponding form where we can specify the repository's URL, its credentials, a target branch and a target directory within that branch. Inside our IME (cf. Fig. 11b) we then select files and folders in the workspace and open the context menu ❶ which reveals an entry with the title *"Push to remote"*. In our example, we select the *generated-html* directory that contains the static files for the WebStory. After the provision of a commit message ❷, the files are pushed to the repository.

In GitLab, we configured a CI/CD pipeline for our WebStory that is triggered when new commits to the default branch of the repository are made. In fact, we also created this pipeline in CINCO Cloud in the same way we developed the WebStory. For this purpose, we are using Rig [23] which is a DSL for graphical authoring of CI/CD Pipelines. The modeled pipeline can be seen in Fig. 12. It will first lint the generated HTML code (*lint* node), i.e., perform static code analysis and then deploy it to GitLab Pages (*pages* node). Finally, we can access our WebStory via the web browser under a static URL provided by GitLab.

5 Related Approaches

As bringing applications into the cloud and making fully fledged apps for the web browser is becoming more popular, several tools approach to bring graphical modeling into the cloud. However, CINCO Cloud is, to the best of our knowledge, the only tool that aims at aligning the entire workflow from

- designing a graphical modeling language over
- modeling within graphical IMEs to
- deploying products that are generated from the IME-based models

into the cloud and web browsers. The remainder of this section presents the approaches that are most closely related to our approach.

5.1 WebGME

A prominent example for graphical language engineering in the web is WebGME [4,18], the successor of GME [15,16]. Key difference to our LDE approach is that in WebGME, the meta-modeling and modeling layer are tightly interleaved: Editors for both layers exist side by side in the same view so that changes in the meta layer are reflected in the modeling layer right away. Moreover, WebGME requires code generators to be written in an external tool without support for type information or coding assistance for the underlying meta-model. Both, the monolithic structure of modeling environment and the separate treatment of code generation require a very high level of expertise and therefore strongly restricts the potential user community.

In contrast, our LDE approach aims at simplicity [17] in order to lower the hurdles for the different stakeholders: The individually generated IMEs are tailored for the intended purposes and, in particular, totally independent from meta-model environment, and developers are supported by typical IDE features like type checking and code completion that exploit the fact that every model element is associated with a generated Java classes on the meta layer.

5.2 Sirius Web

A renown tool within the Eclipse community is Sirius [26], a tooling suite to create IMEs. With Sirius Web [9] the project has been extended to allow users to access the graphical editors in their web browser and work in a cloud environment. This means that users can also work concurrently on the same graphical models, and also configure access to their projects in a user-permission approach. But unlike CINCO Cloud, Sirius Web is not capable of moving the whole workflow of language design into the cloud or web browser. Only the graphical editing is done in a web browser, while developing the underlying models and defining the appearances for the respective graphical editors remains part of the Sirius Eclipse application. Considering this, Sirius Web can be compared to our intermediate approach of replacing our IME layer with PYRO to bring it into web browsers. See the middle layer of Fig. 1 for reference. However, this does obviously not provide a holistic approach like CINCO Cloud does.

5.3 emf.cloud

Another approach to web-based graphical modeling is emf.cloud [8]. It also uses Theia as an editor and provides functionality through plugins. However, emf.cloud does not allow users to define their graphical languages in the cloud or web browser either. emf.cloud development follows a rather classical approach as it only provides several frameworks developers can utilize to implement their own graphical emf.cloud editors. Unlike CINCO Cloud this may be a major obstacle for domain experts without programming experience. Different from CINCO Cloud or Sirius, emf.cloud does not provide a meta IME to define modeling languages. Instead, users have to be proficient in software development as emf.cloud is just a framework for creating graphical IMEs. The meta layer of such IMEs is therefore not model-driven but rather based on traditional code. Therefore, emf.cloud cannot be considered holistic in the sense of providing one tool for everything from defining modeling languages with meta-languages to generating products from priorly created graphical models.

6 Conclusion and Future Work

In this paper, we have presented CINCO Cloud, our holistic meta tooling suite that makes use of all the benefits of web applications to create a pain-free user experience that includes all levels of LDE: From the meta modeling of domain-specific languages, via application modeling in corresponding integrated modeling environments, to the deployment of the final product through CI/CD pipelines using Git repository platform integrations. All of this without ever leaving the web browser which is unique when compared to existing solutions (cf. Sect. 5).

CINCO Cloud provides Theia-based meta IMEs and IMEs that enable its users to develop graph-based DSLs and generate collaborative online modeling environments from them with the push of a button. To demonstrate the capabilities of CINCO Cloud, we presented a walk-through of the development process on the example *WebStory*: a DSL to create web-based point-and-click adventures, As a result of this, we first showed the meta-modeling environment where the DSLs are specified and generated an IME with an integrated model editor for these languages. We then modeled a *WebStory* with two screens and pushed generated sources to a *GitLab* repository, where a CI/CD pipeline has been executed and static files of the *WebStory* have been deployed to a static file hosting service.

We thereby prove that CINCO Cloud is capable of providing all aspects we think are necessary for the development and usage of graphical DSLs in the web. This way, we do not only streamline the user experience but also open the door for a unified way of implementing quality assurance measures in our tool chain that language designers, application modelers, end-users, and the CINCO Cloud developers can benefit from [5]. However, as CINCO Cloud is still in early development there is still room for improvement on several levels that we discuss in the following.

6.1 Collaboration and Version Control

Currently, the live collaboration protocol is transient and only the latest version of the models is permanently stored on the server. This works great for pair-programming sessions and small projects, but to scale CINCO Cloud to more sophisticated project settings, we think proper version control is indispensable. For this reason, we are working on a replacement for the current collaboration protocol that not only provides live collaboration, but also essential version control features like commits, a version history and branching. Inevitably, we are being faced with the problem of software merging, where two or more branches with divergent development efforts on graph models have to be reconciled back into one version [19].

To radically simplify this problem, we intend to follow a lazy merging approach, where non-conflicting changes are applied and conflicting changes are aggregated into conflict sets. This happens within a custom-tailored data structure that is built to represent concurrent editing on graph models. Following the partial causality order of write operations, this data structure is able to form a lattice over the edit history of the graph models. Merges of divergent branches are then simply their supremum in this lattice, which is guaranteed to always exist and be unique. The determination of suprema in this data structure is trivial, and thus merges can be found easily and efficiently. They can be considered to be perfect merges, as by virtue of being a supremum, they are guaranteed to be the smallest complete version that includes the changes from all branches that are to be merged, and nothing more.

6.2 Model Evolution and Migration

A common issue in LDE is that changes on the meta layer may invalidate models on the modeling layer. We plan to tackle the challenge of model migration using dedicated DSLs for graphical model-to-model transformations. Key to this approach are Type-based Structural Operational Semantics (TSOS) [14] which are generalizations of Plotkin's SOS rules [22]. Currently we work on a new generalization based on an existing model-to-model transformation approach we have already applied successfully [14]. This generalization will allow users to model existing patterns of their languages and how they should look like after the transformation. For this purpose users will be able to use the existing web-based IMEs. Thereby, model migration will fit into our LDE ecosystem.

References

1. Eclipse Che - The Kubernetes-Native IDE for Developer Teams. https://www.eclipse.org/che/. Accessed 28 Aug 2021
2. Official page for Language Server Protocol. https://microsoft.github.io/language-server-protocol/. Accessed 12 Feb 2019
3. Theia - Cloud and Desktop IDE. https://www.theia-ide.org. Accessed 12 Feb 2019
4. WebGME. https://webgme.org/. Accessed 26 July 2021

5. Bainczyk, A., Boßelmann, S., Krause, M., Krumrey, M., Steffen, B., Wirkner, D.: Towards continuous quality control in the context of language-driven engineering. In: Margaria, T., Steffen, B. (eds.) ISoLA 2022, LNCS, vol. 13702, pp. 389–406. Springer, Heidelberg (2022)
6. Codeanywhere Inc.: Codeanywhere. https://codeanywhere.com. Accessed 06 Sept 2022
7. Cory Wilkerson: Github blog: Github's engineering team has moved to codespaces. https://github.blog/2021-08-11-githubs-engineering-team-moved-codespaces/. Accessed 08 Sept 2022
8. Eclipse Foundation: EMF.cloud. https://www.eclipse.org/emfcloud/. Accessed 18 July 2022
9. Eclipse Foundation: Sirius Web. https://www.eclipse.org/sirius/sirius-web.html. Accessed 27 July 2022
10. GitHub Inc: Github codespaces. https://github.com/features/codespaces. Accessed 08 Sept 2022
11. GitLab B.V.: GitLab Pages — GitLab. https://docs.gitlab.com/ee/user/project/pages/. Accessed 17 July 2022
12. GitLab B.V.: The One DevOps Platform — GitLab. https://about.gitlab.com/. Accessed 17 July 2022
13. Gossen, F., Margaria, T., Murtovi, A., Naujokat, S., Steffen, B.: DSLs for decision services: a tutorial introduction to language-driven engineering. In: Margaria, T., Steffen, B. (eds.) ISoLA 2018. LNCS, vol. 11244, pp. 546–564. Springer, Cham (2018). https://doi.org/10.1007/978-3-030-03418-4_33
14. Kopetzki, D., Lybecait, M., Naujokat, S., Steffen, B.: Towards language-to-language transformation. Int. J. Softw. Tools Technol. Transfer **23**(5), 655–677 (2021). https://doi.org/10.1007/s10009-021-00630-2
15. Ledeczi, A., et al.: The generic modeling environment. In: Workshop on Intelligent Signal Processing (WISP 2001) (2001)
16. Lédeczi, A., Maróti, M., Völgyesi, P.: The Generic Modeling Environment. Technical report. Institute for Software Integrated Systems, Vanderbilt University, Nashville, TN, 37221, USA (2003). http://www.isis.vanderbilt.edu/sites/default/files/GMEReport.pdf
17. Margaria, T., Steffen, B.: Simplicity as a driver for agile innovation. Computer **43**(6), 90–92 (2010). https://doi.org/10.1109/MC.2010.177
18. Maróti, M., et al.: Next generation (meta) modeling: web-and cloud-based collaborative tool infrastructure. MPM@ MoDELS **1237**, 41–60 (2014)
19. Mens, T.: A state-of-the-art survey on software merging. IEEE Trans. Softw. Eng. **28**, 449–462 (2002). https://doi.org/10.1109/TSE.2002.1000449
20. MinIO Inc: MinIO — High Performance, Kubernetes Native Object Storage. https://min.io/. Accessed 17 July 2022
21. Naujokat, S., Lybecait, M., Kopetzki, D., Steffen, B.: CINCO: a simplicity-driven approach to full generation of domain-specific graphical modeling tools. Int. J. Softw. Tools Technol. Transfer **20**(3), 327–354 (2017). https://doi.org/10.1007/s10009-017-0453-6
22. Plotkin, G.D.: A Structural Approach to Operational Semantics. Technical report, University of Aarhus (1981). dAIMI FN-19
23. Tegeler, T., Teumert, S., Schürmann, J., Bainczyk, A., Busch, D., Steffen, B.: An introduction to graphical modeling of CI/CD workflows with rig. In: Margaria, T., Steffen, B. (eds.) ISoLA 2021. LNCS, vol. 13036, pp. 3–17. Springer, Cham (2021). https://doi.org/10.1007/978-3-030-89159-6_1

24. The Apache Software Foundation: ActiveMQ. https://activemq.apache.org/components/artemis/. Accessed 17 July 2022
25. The Kubernetes Authors: Kubernetes. https://kubernetes.io/de/. Accessed 17 July 2022
26. Viyovic, V., Maksimovic, M., Perisic, B.: Sirius: a rapid development of DSM graphical editor. In: IEEE 18th International Conference on Intelligent Engineering Systems INES 2014. IEEE (2014). https://doi.org/10.1109/ines.2014.6909375
27. Zweihoff, P.: Cinco Products for the Web. Master thesis, TU Dortmund (2015)
28. Zweihoff, P.: Aligned and Collaborative Language-Driven Engineering. Dissertation, TU Dortmund, Dortmund, Germany (2022). https://doi.org/10.17877/DE290R-22594. https://eldorado.tu-dortmund.de/handle/2003/40736
29. Zweihoff, P.: Aligned and Collaborative Language-Driven Engineering. Doctoral thesis, TU Dortmund University (2022). https://eldorado.tu-dortmund.de/bitstream/2003/40736/1/Dissertation_Zweihoff.pdf
30. Zweihoff, P., Naujokat, S., Steffen, B.: Pyro: generating domain-specific collaborative online modeling environments. In: Proceedings of the 22nd International Conference on Fundamental Approaches to Software Engineering (FASE 2019) (2019). https://doi.org/10.1007/978-3-030-16722-6_6
31. Zweihoff, P., Steffen, B.: Pyrus: an online modeling environment for no-code data-analytics service composition. In: Margaria, T., Steffen, B. (eds.) ISoLA 2021. LNCS, vol. 13036, pp. 18–40. Springer, Cham (2021). https://doi.org/10.1007/978-3-030-89159-6_2
32. Zweihoff, P., Tegeler, T., Schürmann, J., Bainczyk, A., Steffen, B.: Aligned, purpose-driven cooperation: the future way of system development. In: Margaria, T., Steffen, B. (eds.) ISoLA 2021. LNCS, vol. 13036, pp. 426–449. Springer, Cham (2021). https://doi.org/10.1007/978-3-030-89159-6_27

Correction to: A Notion of Equivalence for Refactorings with Abstract Execution

Ole Jørgen Abusdal, Eduard Kamburjan, Violet Ka I. Pun, and Volker Stolz

Correction to:
Chapter "A Notion of Equivalence for Refactorings with Abstract Execution" in: T. Margaria and B. Steffen (Eds.): *Leveraging Applications of Formal Methods, Verification and Validation. Software Engineering*, LNCS 13702, https://doi.org/10.1007/978-3-031-19756-7_15

In the originally published version of this chapter a sentence in the 4th paragraph of section 5 "Discussion" was incomplete. This has been corrected and the sentence has been updated as follows "Conversely, due to the challenges in checking instantiation of schemata against concrete programs already pointed out by Steinhöfel [28, 119,137], one has to take care not to write too restrictive programs that rule out useful working instances."

The updated original version of this chapter can be found at
https://doi.org/10.1007/978-3-031-19756-7_15

T. Margaria and B. Steffen (Eds.): ISoLA 2022, LNCS 13702, p. C1, 2023.
https://doi.org/10.1007/978-3-031-19756-7_24

Author Index

Printed in the United States
by Baker & Taylor Publisher Services